T0300875

CAMBRIDGE LIBRARY COLLECTION

Books of enduring scholarly value

British and Irish History, Nineteenth Century

This series comprises contemporary or near-contemporary accounts of the political, economic and social history of the British Isles during the nineteenth century. It includes material on international diplomacy and trade, labour relations and the women's movement, developments in education and social welfare, religious emancipation, the justice system, and special events including the Great Exhibition of 1851.

The Illustrated Record of the International Exhibition ... of All Nations, in 1862

An American inventor and entrepreneur, Taliaferro Preston Shaffner (1818–81) collaborated with the Rev. W. Owen on this 'guided tour' of London's 1862 International Exhibition, showcasing Victorian achievements in technology and the arts. Described here are exhibits, originating from Britain, her empire and beyond, which include early washing machines and lawnmowers, as well as grand ideas for metropolitan drainage systems and a Channel Tunnel. The arts are also well covered, with descriptions of the latest fabrics, wallpapers, musical instruments, ceramics and photography. The authors also give background details of how the International Exhibition built upon the success of the Great Exhibition of 1851. Illustrated with sixty full-page steel engravings, this is a highly detailed guide to a very modern event. Also relating to the exhibition, Edward McDermott's *Popular Guide* and both the official and illustrated catalogues of the industrial department have been reissued in this series.

Cambridge University Press has long been a pioneer in the reissuing of out-of-print titles from its own backlist, producing digital reprints of books that are still sought after by scholars and students but could not be reprinted economically using traditional technology. The Cambridge Library Collection extends this activity to a wider range of books which are still of importance to researchers and professionals, either for the source material they contain, or as landmarks in the history of their academic discipline.

Drawing from the world-renowned collections in the Cambridge University Library and other partner libraries, and guided by the advice of experts in each subject area, Cambridge University Press is using state-of-the-art scanning machines in its own Printing House to capture the content of each book selected for inclusion. The files are processed to give a consistently clear, crisp image, and the books finished to the high quality standard for which the Press is recognised around the world. The latest print-on-demand technology ensures that the books will remain available indefinitely, and that orders for single or multiple copies can quickly be supplied.

The Cambridge Library Collection brings back to life books of enduring scholarly value (including out-of-copyright works originally issued by other publishers) across a wide range of disciplines in the humanities and social sciences and in science and technology.

The Illustrated Record of the International Exhibition ... of All Nations, in 1862

Taliaferro Preston Shaffner
Rev. W. Owen

CAMBRIDGE
UNIVERSITY PRESS

CAMBRIDGE
UNIVERSITY PRESS

University Printing House, Cambridge, CB2 8BS, United Kingdom

Published in the United States of America by Cambridge University Press, New York

Cambridge University Press is part of the University of Cambridge.
It furthers the University's mission by disseminating knowledge in the pursuit of
education, learning and research at the highest international levels of excellence.

www.cambridge.org
Information on this title: www.cambridge.org/9781108068611

© in this compilation Cambridge University Press 2014

This edition first published 1862
This digitally printed version 2014

ISBN 978-1-108-06861-1 Paperback

THE INTERNATIONAL EXHIBITION

THE

ILLUSTRATED RECORD

OF THE

INTERNATIONAL EXHIBITION

OF THE

INDUSTRIAL ARTS AND MANUFACTURES, AND THE FINE ARTS,

OF ALL NATIONS, IN 1862:

IN A SERIES OF TINTED STEEL ENGRAVINGS, COMPRISING VIEWS OF THE BUILDING, AND OF THE
PRINCIPAL OBJECTS EXHIBITED ;

ALSO, SEVERAL VIEWS OF THE EXHIBITION OF 1851, FROM DAGUERREOTYPES TAKEN AT THE TIME.

FORMING A COMMEMORATIVE WORK OF THE TWO GREAT EXHIBITIONS OF THE WORLD'S INDUSTRY IN 1851 AND 1862.

WITH HISTORICAL AND DESCRIPTIVE LETTERPRESS.

BY COLONEL TAL. P. SHAFFNER, F.R.S.A., F.R.G.S, F.R.A.S. ;
AND THE REV. W. OWEN.

LONDON:
WARD AND LOCK, 158, FLEET STREET.

PREFACE.

THE Great International Exhibition of 1862, was designed to show the progress which the world has made in material prosperity, as evidenced by specimens of its Arts and Manufactures, the Fine Arts, Raw Produce, and articles of Commerce, in the last eleven years. The promoters of the Exhibition of 1851, were aware that, to render such great displays of industrial products of any practical value, they must be held periodically. It was, therefore, no matter of surprise to those who had paid attention to the subject, when, in 1858, the Society of Arts proposed to repeat the important and interesting experiment of 1851; and, after contending with various obstacles, it was at last finally settled that the second great International Exhibition should be held in London, in 1862.

In the arrangements for the holding of the Exhibition of 1862, a very marked improvement was made in the determination to admit in its programme paintings, drawings, and engravings, which were excluded in 1851; and, for the first time in this country, the painting and sculpture of all Europe were brought, by selected examples, into juxtaposition with those of England, in the vast galleries which skirted three of the four sides of the great building at Kensington.

On the 1st of May, 1862, amid the flourish of trumpets, the roar of artillery, and the applause of thousands, the Exhibition of the Industry of all Nations was declared to be opened; and after a most successful career, it was closed on the 1st of November. During the six months of its existence it afforded an interesting spectacle to hundreds of thousands, who, from all quarters of the earth, thronged to view the wonders which it contained. To aid in carrying out the great objects contemplated by the Commissioners, thirty-six foreign countries, thirty-one British Colonies, and every city and town in the United Kingdom, sent in articles to be exhibited, in order that they might take their place in this great industrial competition. In fact, "from each of the great divisions of the globe; from countries where civilisation may hardly be said to exist; from empires, states, territories, kingdoms, and republics; from cities towns, and districts famous for arts and handicrafts, for intelligence, for industry, and for skill; from swarming abodes of industry, where hammers rattle and the loom is busy; from the gloomy spots where tall chimneys pour forth their ceaseless tribute to the murky air; from the dark mine where, amid noisome gases and foul air, the miner extracts the mineral treasures; from the quiet and lonely haunts where, in the field and in the wood, labour pursues its course, there were sent forth contributions to the second World's Festival of Art and Industry."

The hastiest survey of the treasures thus brought together in this great World's Display, convinced every one of the immense step in human progress which it recorded. In quantity, the number of objects greatly surpassed those in the former

Exhibition. The mind was overwhelmed by the extraordinary abundance and richness of the objects exhibited; and it required a considerable time to recover sufficiently from this overwhelming impression, to concentrate the attention on details. The improvement in quality, was, however, far more important, and far more remarkable than the vast increase in quantity; and no one can calculate what advantages may still be derived from thus gathering together, on one spot, and at one time, all that can win the eye, or gratify the ear.

But in order that this advantage should be fully enjoyed and rendered valuable, it becomes necessary that a full and careful record should be made of all the points of advancement and shortcoming which have shown themselves in this great Exhibition; that those things which are felt to be wanting may be supplied, and those improvements which have been made, may be carried to a still higher degree of excellence. To aid this purpose is the object of the present Work; and while its Pictorial Illustrations will give exact representations of the objects exhibited, its Letterpress Descriptions will be written with a view to making this great International Display what it ought to be—a School of Instruction on those subjects on which the greatness of this country depends—its MANUFACTURING INDUSTRY.

In order to accomplish the objects which we aim at, we shall take frequent opportunities of comparing the articles shown in the Exhibitions of the World's Industries in 1851 and 1862. It was originally proposed by the Royal Commissioners, that, in this later Exhibition, the works selected should be "arranged according to classes, and not countries." This, no doubt, would have afforded a very ready and valuable mode of reference; but, unhappily, it was not found practicable to carry it out, except to a limited extent, each nation being anxious to have "a local habitation and a name," instead of permitting its individuality to be lost, by mixing the various articles of its produce with those of other countries; and to this wish, in which our own nation participated, the Royal Commissioners felt themselves compelled to defer. The writer of a pamphlet on this subject, so well expressed, in a few terse sentences, the advantages which would have accrued from a classified, and not a geographical arrangement of the objects exhibited, that we are tempted to make an extract from his *brochure*. He says:—

"It should be a Classified Exhibition; how entirely distinct must it be, then, from the Exhibition of 1851. Who that had occasion to collect the information contained in that Exhibition, as every member of the press who wrote for the guidance and instruction of the public had, but felt the want of classification? To have been able to have compared the porcelain of Sèvres, Belgium, Austria, Dresden, Berlin, and Prussia, with that of Staffordshire, Worcestershire, and other parts of the United Kingdom, what an incomparable advantage would it have been! How important to our Yorkshire woollen trade, had our manufacturers been able, side by side, to have contrasted the productions of France, Belgium, Vienna, Saxony, Aix-la-Chapelle, and Prussia, with the cloth and mixed goods produced at Leeds, Bradford, Stroud, and Dublin. What labour and fatigue would have been saved, had we been able to view the metal-work and jewellery of France, Belgium, Holland, and Spain, with that of England in a court by itself. How will those attending the next Exhibition divide themselves into groups under such an arrangement? There will be the Swiss side by side with the man of Coventry and Clerkenwell, discussing each the merits of his competitor for the trade in watches; the silk manufacturers of Lyons, Spitalfields, and Manchester, comparing their silks; and chemists and dyers, the effects resulting from the discovery of new sources of supply of colour, and new methods of applying those already known. How interesting will it be to juxtapose the wood-carvings of Switzerland and Italy with the productions of Rogers in England, or the results of the application of machinery in that direction; the inlaid wood of Austria with that of other countries. A court of the cabinet marqueterie and buhl work of the world, how instructive may it be made; and the same principle, if applied to the paper-hangings of France, London, and Manchester, the agricultural machines of America and England, the steel of Germany, Sweden, America, and Sheffield, will tend to render the Exhibition of 1862, not merely a monster bazaar, but a book, well digested and arranged for ready reference, affording at once the information so frequently sought for, and oft-times in vain, in its predecessor."

In the arrangement of the present Work, the geographical classification will not be strictly adhered to, and thus the reader will be afforded greater facilities for comparing the products of all countries, and the skilled industry of the various exhibitors who have claimed favourable awards, than he could even obtain in the courts of the Exhibition itself.

Considering the vast extent of the Exhibition, and the number as well as variety of the articles exhibited, it will obviously be necessary, in our illustrations and descriptions, to select those objects which are most attractive to the general reader, and of the greatest importance to persons interested in the various branches of the Arts, Manufactures, and Commerce. In performing this part of our task, we shall do equal justice to every nation which has entered into friendly competition with our own, and, as far as practicable, allow the whole globe to revolve under the eye of the spectator; showing the peoples of every land applying their skill to the varied produce of each country, and ministering to the wants and wishes, the comfort and refinement of the universal family. It will be gratifying to notice the vast amount of skill and labour, which, during the last eleven years, has been applied to the necessities and comfort of the great mass of the people; furnishing proofs that the World's Industry has been moving in a healthy direction, effecting the progress of true civilisation among all classes, rather than providing for the luxury of the few.

It will be our object to place the reader in the position of the traveller at home, who, without fatigue, retraces his pilgrimage through many lands, and his voyages to distant shores. We shall bring to his recollection many of the scenes he has visited, and, in some instances, tell him of what he might have seen, had his leisure been greater, or his observant faculties more active. We shall be in attendance in his home-travels through Great Britain and Ireland, and assist to imprint on his memory what he may have learned as to the products of their workshops and manufactories.

As thirty-one British Colonies, and our great Oriental Dependency, have, at much labour and expense, sought to uphold the greatness of the British Empire, in this World's Display, it will be our pleasing duty to claim attention to the valuable products and the skilful manufactures which they exhibited.

In the progress of our review of the objects exposed by Exhibitors, we shall have the gratification of noticing the arts and manufactures which have sprung into existence since 1851; and others which were beginning their career at that period, and have since been fully developed; besides the many improvements shown in the methods of production, and the greater cheapness of various products with which the world has long been familiar.

Electric Telegraphy, which in 1851 was still in its infancy, has progressed so rapidly throughout the world, that the whole globe may be said to be encircled by its wires; and the new inventions and contrivances for the more rapid transmission of intelligence by this means, form one of the most interesting courts in the Exhibition. But to give the reader some idea of the rapid strides which have been made within the last ten years, in all that relates to material improvement, we cannot do better than quote the following from the Report of Mr. Hawes, the Registrar-General:—

"Most important discoveries have been made in the preparation of colours for printing and dyeing, producing what are called the 'Aniline' series; great economy has been effected in the manufacture of glass; and a process has just been made perfect for transferring photographs to that material. The manufacture of agricultural implements, and especially the application of steam power to them, has been so improved and extended, that it is now a highly important branch of trade.

"Photography, hardly known in 1851, has become an important branch of art and industry, used alike by the artist, the engineer, the architect, and the manufacturer.

"Marine telegraphy, only just accomplished in 1851—the public communication with Dublin having been opened in June, and that with Paris in November, 1852—has now become almost universal, linking together distant countries. The electric telegraph has become universal; and, in every direction, facilities for communication have been increased. We have repealed the duties on soap and paper, the only manufactures the prosperity of which was then thwarted by Excise restrictions.

"We have abolished all taxes on the dissemination of knowledge, and have given increased facilities for the circulation of knowledge by post. We have repealed the Import duties, or very nearly so, on raw materials, the produce of foreign countries.

"We have admitted free of duty, confident in our strength, the manufactures of foreign countries to compete with our own. Old industries have been stimulated and improved. New industries have arisen.

"In fine art, painting, and sculpture, it is hardly possible, except in very extraordinary periods, that a marked change can be observed in a single ten years; but this country certainly holds its own as compared with the productions of other countries.

"In the manufacture of iron, improvements have also been made; new bands of ore have been discovered; and day by day we are economising its production; and a metal between iron and steel is now produced at one process, which heretofore required two or more processes alike expensive and difficult.

"In steam power, especially that applied to railroads and to ocean steam navigation, economical appliances have advanced rapidly. The use of coal for locomotives in place of coke, and super-heating steam and surface condensing in ocean steamers, tend to increase the power and economise the cost of these powerful engines of civilisation.

"In ship-building, the past ten years have produced great changes. Our navy and mercantile marine have alike advanced in scientific construction and in mechanical arrangements. The ocean steamers which were then employed in the postal service included but one of two thousand tons; now there are many of nearly double that tonnage, with corresponding power and speed—increasing the facilities, and decreasing the risk of communication with our colonies and foreign countries.

"In printing, great advances have been made. By the perfection of chromatic printing, views of distant countries, copies of celebrated pictures, most beautifully coloured, have been brought within the reach of almost every class, displacing works which neither improved the taste nor gave useful information; and by the application of most expensive and most beautiful machinery to the printing of our daily journals, we have been enabled profitably to meet the increased demand caused by the cheapness of our newspapers. Invention and mechanical contrivance have thus kept pace with the requirements of intellect and the daily increasing love of knowledge."

To do full justice to the subjects indicated in the above extract, would form no uninteresting work; but, in addition to the notice which will be taken of these novelties, our readers will be put in possession of ample details of all improvements, discoveries, and inventions which have had their representative specimens displayed in the great Exhibition of 1862.

INTRODUCTION.

GREAT EXHIBITIONS FROM 1851 TO 1862.

THE Palace of Industry, in Hyde Park, closed to the public on Saturday, the 11th of October, 1851. The great financial and general success of the experiment naturally induced other cities, in this kingdom and abroad, to imitate the example we had set, and to reproduce, though in smaller proportions, similar attractions, which would prove of great local and national interest.

The city of Cork was the first to follow the example of London; and in 1852 opened its Exhibition, which, assuming an international character, awakened an intense interest in the south of Ireland, and served to stimulate the industries of that important part of the empire, and to educate the public taste. The favour with which it was regarded is evident from the fact, that the gross number of daily admissions reached 74,095; while the admissions by season tickets were 54,936. The rich products and the numerous industries which were exhibited, were described as calculated to give an exalted idea of the natural wealth of the country, and the great skill of its people. Among them were to be found specimens of raw materials and manufactured goods: of the latter, the linens, diapers, cambrics, poplins, tabinets, velvets, and laces, maintained the reputation of former days; whilst some excellent samples of preserved provisions, butter, whisky, fancy biscuits, and confectionery, were also shown. In the Fine Arts Court, the citizens of Cork had great pride in exhibiting several of the works of their distinguished townsman, Hogan, the sculptor; among which were his colossal " Head of Minerva," "Dead Christ," portions of the " Hibernia," and other works.

In 1853, an Exhibition was held in Dublin, which conferred the greatest honour on the Irish metropolis. The favour with which this Exhibition was regarded, is shown by the number of visits paid by the Dublin population as compared with that of London, the proportion being two-and-a-half visits for each person in London, and four for each person in Dublin. In the latter city, the gross number of daily visitors, during the period the Exhibition was open, was 634,523, of which number the season-ticket holders were 366,745.

A most advantageous site for the erection of the building was found in the lawn of the Royal Dublin Society, extending from that noble edifice to Merrion Square. In accordance with its title, the great Industrial Exhibition consisted principally of raw materials, machinery and manufactures; but, as every one who visited that attractive scene well remembers, the Fine Arts also were duly represented.

In the Industrial departments were found a plentiful display of mining and mineral products; animal substances; manufactures from minerals; from flax and hemp; woollen, worsted, silk and mixed fabrics; cotton; furs, leathers, saddlery, harness; printing, book-binding, paper and stationery; printed and dyed fabrics; iron and general hardware; cutlery, china, glass, furniture, chemical and pharmaceutical processes; and other important classes. The relics of ancient art included a general collection of ancient weapons, implements, and ornaments found in different parts of Ireland. Among the machinery exhibited, were machines for utilising the water-power so abundant in Ireland; steam-engines; "electric apparatus; voltaic batteries of various forms, in which chemical action involves electricity; magno-electric machines, in which magnetism was combined with mechanical power; and induction coils, which, by the intermittence of a feeble current of electricity, produces one of considerable intensity." The electro-magnetic, the electro-metallurgic, and the photographic apparatus, had their place in this important class.

The Fine Arts Court presented valuable examples of the Lombardic, Venetian, Raphaelite, Bolognese, and ancient Flemish schools; and of the schools of France, Belgium, Germany, and Great Britain. There were also good illustrations of Greek and Roman sculpture during the post-Phidian era; as well as those of our own age and kingdom. There was a Mediæval Court, enriched with sculpture, painting, monumental brasses, coronæ lucis, and windows of stained and painted glass; and an Archæological Court, with a valuable collection of objects of ancient art, principally Irish; illustrating the art and industry of Ireland during several centuries.

In New York, also, an Exhibition was held in 1853. As a commercial enterprise, it is to be regretted that the experiment proved unsuccessful; but the objects exhibited were of great value, and peculiarly adapted to a country of vast extent with a comparatively thin population. The principal achievements of American inventors were in the department of machinery, more especially in those by which automatic action supplied the more abundant hand-labour of older manufacturing countries.

The Munich Exhibition, held in 1854, was not designed to be international. It was not, however, limited to Bavaria, but thrown open to the whole of Germany. The building was in the form of a cross, and was constructed of iron, glass, and wood. The cost of this structure, which approached 800 feet in length, and 280 feet in the transept, was about £88,000 sterling. About one-third of the whole space was occupied by Bavaria, and the contributions of Austria were considerable; but the produce of Prussia and the Northern States was very inadequately represented. The industries of Vienna, Moravia, and Bohemia were prominent; but there were no adequate specimens of the rich materials of Gallicia, Hungary, Transylvania, and the Lombárdo-Venetian territory. The Exhibition may, therefore, be considered as a display of the industrial powers of Southern Germany, rather than of those of the entire country.

In 1855, Paris opened its first French International Exhibition, in the permanent structure in the Champs Elysées, which was a decided success. It is not proposed, in this brief reference to the Paris Exhibition, to give even a summary of the important artistic and industrial phenomena it presented. The official reports form a most valuable record, not simply of those natural products and specimens of skill and industry which were exhibited, but of the judgment of the most competent authorities who were sent from this country, to report on the various departments on whose merits they were most fitted to pronounce. In those reports we have a permanent record of the World's Industry in 1855; the subjects they embrace being the manufactures of linen, cotton, woollen and worsted, and silk; machinery, and iron manufactures; general produce; coachmakers' work, harness, &c.; prepared and preserved alimentary substances; Birmingham manufactures; furniture and decoration; printing and printing machines; military arts; colonial woods; mining and metallurgic products; general metal work; optical and other instruments; warming and ventilating; naval constructions; ceramic manufactures; glass; vegetable products; Indian and colonial products; civil construction; and the present state of design as applied to manufactures. When it is mentioned that, among the authors of these reports, we find such names as those of Sir W. Hooker, Dr. Arnott, Mr. Digby Wyatt, Professor Owen, and Sir David Brewster, it will be readily perceived that these documents bear a stamp of the highest value, and that they have greatly augmented the value of the Exposition they are intended to commemorate.

The Exhibition of Art Treasures of the United Kingdom, held in Manchester, in 1857, fully realised the conception of Mr. J. C. Deane, that the Art wealth of England would supply examples of equal interest, and an aggregate of greater value than any other country in the world, and that the application for the loan of those treasures, for an object of public utility, would be met with promptness and liberality by their owners. The collection embraced 1,178 ancient, and 689 modern pictures, many of them of the highest value; 386 portraits, 969 water-colour drawings, 10,000 objects of art in the General Museum, 260 sketches and original drawings, 1,475 engravings, 500 miniatures, 597 photographs, 63 architectural drawings, and 160 pieces of sculpture. The favour with which this noble project was received, was shown in the readiness of all ranks, from the Sovereign downwards, to entrust their rich treasures to the executive committee; in the numbers by whom the building was thronged from day to day; and in the satisfactory fact that the undertaking was successful in a financial aspect. The spirited conductors of this noble work were justified in the hope that their labours have promoted the love of the beautiful in Art, and produced the conviction in the popular mind, "that it is not incompatible with the honest performance of the daily duties and hard labours of life, to brighten its course, by the cultivation of the imagination and other more delicate faculties of the mind, by encouraging a love of the Fine Arts."

Florence, in 1861, presented to the world the first fruits of Italian unity and freedom in its Italian National Exhibition. Previous to this memorable year, several of the Italian States had held their Exhibitions, which, whatever their excellence, had never brought under one roof the productions of all Italy, so as to afford the opportunity of comparison and instruction. Italians and their visitors could now, for the first time, form a correct estimate of the products, the industries, and the Fine Arts, as they were found in every portion of the country, extending from the plains of Lombardy to the most distant parts of Calabria.

The building occupied by the Exhibition had been a railway terminus; but, from the admirable taste with which it was decorated, proved quite suitable to this new purpose. For the first week, the visitors had an opportunity of viewing the cattle of Italy, which were shown in a building near the Exhibition, the various breeds exciting much admiration. The agricultural implements presented a remarkable variety, extending, as they did, from a plough, as rude as any used in the time of the ancient Romans, to the most perfect imitations of our own improvements. A very great attraction was the house of a Tuscan peasant, with its living occupants, all the implements of his craft, and his live stock. The horticulture and agriculture of the country were well represented in most beautiful specimens. Among the minerals was the iron of Elba, the copper of Tuscany, the marble of Carrara, and the sulphur of Sicily. The hemp of Italy, which exceeds that of every other country, was shown in the greatest perfection; as was also the rich silk, both in its raw state and its various manufactures. The straw-plait of Italy was found to maintain its former high character, and woollen cloths were shown of very great excellence. Among the productions of iron, were the wrought iron gates, sent over to our own Exhibition; and the excellent surgical instruments of Pistoia displayed the skill of the artist in steel.

The Victorian Exhibition, which was opened on the 1st of October, 1861, although confined to the colony after which it was named, deserves a place in our record, on account of its relation to the International Exhibition, for which it was prepared. The building for the Victorian Exhibition had been previously erected for the purpose of receiving the contributions sent to Paris in 1855, and was, after some enlargements, found sufficient for this second great display.

Among the prominent features of the Victorian Exhibition, was the collection of indigenous timber, containing eighty varieties, from different localities. There was a set of models of the principal autumnal fruits and vegetables of the colony, made of gypsum, and coloured so as to represent the natural hue and bloom of the plant; there were, also, specimens of the essential oils distilled from indigenous trees and plants. Wine was exhibited among the new products of the colony; and from the growths then shown, to which additions were made before sending to London, there is reason to hope that, at no distant period, this produce will be of excellent quality, and large in quantity. "Oil from the olive, with the fruit itself, were seen, for the first time, grown, and made almost within the precincts of the town." Gold, of course, was the principal attraction of the Exhibition; and, in reference to this precious element, the governor observed at the inauguration, that, "so far from showing symptoms of exhaustion, upwards of a hundred million's worth had been extracted from the alluvial flats and intersecting quartz reefs. It is unnecessary here to refer to the specimens of zoology, and other branches of natural history, or to the display of arts and manufactures (among which a new method of stereotype-printing deserves mention), as the whole Exhibition was afterwards transported to London, and will come under notice in its proper place.

INDEX.

LIST OF ILLUSTRATIONS.

ILLUSTRATED RECORD

INTERNATIONAL EXHIBITION

OF ALL NATIONS, IN 1862.

CHAPTER I.

THE ORIGIN OF THE INTERNATIONAL EXHIBITION IN 1862.

As mentioned in a previous page, the world is indebted to the Society of Arts for originating the International Exhibition of 1862, as well as for carrying out the great work by which it was preceded in 1851. In the earlier undertaking, this venerable Society proceeded under the high patronage and most able conduct of the Prince Consort; and, in the latter work, it was enabled to persevere, notwithstanding the discouragement and privation produced by his much-lamented death. The initiative of the 1851 undertaking was taken by the Society submitting to the Prince a plan for a National Exhibition, on a more enlarged scale than any which had previously been held in this country. His Royal Highness expanded the idea, by recommending that the Exhibition should comprehend the four divisions of Raw Materials, Machinery and Mechanical Inventions, Manufactures, Sculpture, and Plastic Art; and the patronage of her majesty's government was obtained in consequence of an address being directed by the Illustrious President of the Society of Arts to the then Home Secretary of State.

But as funds were required to set the machinery in motion, and the ordinary resources of the Society were not available for such a purpose, it became necessary to provide for an estimated outlay in building, and preliminary expenses, of £70,000. In this position they were compelled, at the commencement of their proceedings, to make an arrangement with a firm willing to advance the sum likely to be required, in consideration of a share in the contingent profits.

The next step taken by the Society of Arts, was to send Mr. Henry Cole and Mr. Francis Fuller to visit the principal towns in England, Ireland, and Scotland, to collect the opinions of agriculturists and manufacturers as to the proposed Exhibition of 1851: it also, through its commissioners, sought to ascertain what the people of France would do to promote such an undertaking. At a dinner given by the Lord Mayor of London, Prince Albert pronounced his judgment that the proposed Exhibition would give a true test, and a living picture, of the point of development at which the whole of mankind had arrived in this great task, and a new and starting-point from which all nations would be able to direct their future exertions. After this, and much more preparatory work had been accomplished, the Royal Commission was issued, providing that "a full and diligent inquiry should be made into the best mode by which the productions of English colonies and foreign countries might be introduced into the kingdom; as to the site for, and the general conduct of, the proposed Exhibition; and as to the best mode of determining the nature of the prizes, and of securing the most impartial distribution of them."

In the Exhibition of 1862, the Society of Arts also took the initiative; and as early as 1858, framed important resolutions, with a view to holding a second Exhibition; and, at the close of that year, made its appeal to the Royal Commissioners of 1851. The Commissioners not having funds to meet the expenses of the proposed Exhibition, the Society responded to the wish that it should furnish information as to the probable success of the undertaking, and offered to establish a guarantee fund of a quarter of a million sterling. The disturbed state of the continent in 1859, rendered it necessary to postpone the Exhibition for a time; but the close of the Italian war, and the restoration of European tranquillity, rendered it practicable to hold it in 1862.

The Society of Arts, during the inquiries made as to the progress of European and American society since the Exhibition of 1851, and in support of its repetition, collected a number of interesting facts, to which it gave publicity. By the assistance of Mr. William Hawes, the Registrar-General, Mr. C. M. Willich, Colonel Owen, and Sir Cusack P. Roney, it was ascertained that "the population of Great Britain, which was 25,180,555 in 1851, would be about 29,000,000 in 1862, and that London then would contain half a million more people than it did at the period of the first Exhibition. They showed that one-half of this population would consist of persons between the ages of fifteen and fifty, and that one-fourth would consist of persons who were too young to benefit by the Exhibition of 1851. They showed that the length of railways in England alone, would be nearly 11,000 miles in 1862, compared with 6,755 in 1851, and that the general system of railway management would be much improved. The continental managers had learned to appreciate through-booking, return-tickets, and excursion traffic at reduced rates, which they would not look at a few years previously. Many continental lines had been opened since the year of the Great Exhibition, all more or less converging towards this country, and several others of great importance in shortening existing routes, and putting us in communication with new districts. The steam passages between America and Europe had been more than quadrupled, and the fares lowered at least thirty per cent. The chain of railways joining New York, Boston, Portland, and Quebec, had been tripled since 1851; the distance between London and India had been decreased twenty-five per cent., and between England and Australia fifty per cent.; the time taken for passages to and from our West Indian Colonies had been diminished one-third; and there was a well-organised steam communication with South America and Africa, which did not exist in 1851."

Facts of an interesting kind, relative to the progress of Art, were collected, and presented in such an attractive form, as to produce a popular conviction, that the time for a second International Exhibition in London had arrived. The Marquis of Chandos, Earl Granville, Mr. C. W. Dilke, Mr. Thomas Baring, and Mr. Fairbairn, were invited to become trustees for the new Exhibition, and the Commissioners of 1851 were asked to grant a site on the South Kensington estate, on which the trustees might erect a building suitable for the Exhibition, on the condition that at least one-third of the sum expended by them should be applied to buildings of a permanent character, suitable for decennial Exhibitions, as well as for other purposes tending to the encouragement of arts, manufactures, and commerce. In case of a deficiency, it was agreed that the buildings should be sold; and if, after their sale, a deficiency still remained, the guarantors were to subscribe *pro ratâ* for its supply.

The Commissioners of 1851 accordingly granted, rent free, until the end of 1862, the whole land on the main square of their estate—about sixteen acres—on the condition that all the buildings to be erected should be subject to their approval, and that all the temporary buildings should be removed within six months after the close of the Exhibition, if so required by the Commissioners; and the trustees also were left at liberty to remove the permanent building, if they found the Exhibition a pecuniary failure. In favour of the Society of Arts, the Commissioners also expressed their willingness, as an acknowledgment of long-continued services, in advancing the interests of the arts and manufactures, and for promoting the Exhibition of 1851, to grant a lease for ninety-nine years, at a moderate ground-rent, of the permanent buildings, on condition that not less than £50,000 should be expended on them by the trustees, and that they should not cover more than an acre of ground.

Thus was a basis made for the new Exhibition; and those arrangements were carried out by the trustees, though with some important modifications. The sum to be expended on that portion of the buildings to be leased to the Society, was reduced to £20,000 instead of £50,000, on condition that, if the necessary surplus should exist at the close of the Exhibition, the trustees should lay out as much money in improving the architectural character of the permanent portion of the building, as was at first proposed—viz., £50,000.

The new trustees having applied for the loan of an unoccupied portion of land between the western arcades of the Horticultural Gardens and Prince Albert's-road, and also for the loan of the south arcades as refreshment rooms, both these requests were granted by the Commissioners, as was also a subsequent application for ground on which to erect another annexe. All these important preliminaries arranged, the Society of Arts had completed its share of the work, and the management passed into the hands of the Commissioners for the Exhibition of 1862, who were created by a royal charter, sealed on the 14th of February, 1861. A point of great practical importance was the co-operation of the Bank of England, whose Directors were willing, on the execution of the deed of guarantee, to advance the necessary funds on liberal terms.

During the negotiations already described, the Commissioners instituted inquiries as to the best method of fulfilling the important trust committed to them. " The most pressing point was the building required for the Exhibition. In 1850, notwithstanding the possession of considerable funds, and the assistance of the most eminent architects and and engineers, seven months elapsed before a design was adopted.'' To avoid delay, and increased expense, the Commissioners for 1862 directed their attention to the character of the proposed building, which they considered should be more substantial than that of 1851, as it was to include pictures, a branch of art not shown on the previous occasion.

It was then ascertained that Captain Fowke, R.E., the engineer and architect to the government department of science and art, and who had been secretary to the British department of the Paris Exhibition, was able to furnish the design required without delay. He had, while superintending the southern arcades of the Royal Horticultural Society's gardens, formed the plan of a building on the Kensington Gore estate, which should fill up the open side of the gardens, and serve the purpose of future Industrial and Fine Art Exhibitions.

Immediately after their appointment, the Commissioners were, therefore, in a condition to speak of the plan which had been submitted to them by this gentleman, as "intended to meet the practical defects which experience had shown to exist both in the buildings in Hyde Park and in the Champs Elysées. It appeared well adapted for the required purposes; and its principal features were of a striking character, and likely to form an attractive part of the Exhibition." The Commissioners "submitted the design to the competition of ten eminent contractors, four of whom took out the quantities. Three tenders (one a joint one from two of the contractors invited) were sent in on the day named in the invitation; but all were greatly in excess of the amount which the Commissioners could prudently spend, with a due regard to the interest of the guarantors." The Commissioners, therefore, had to direct considerable modifications of this plan, which would reduce its cost without destroying its merits.

Before entering on a description of the enormous erection in South Kensington, we propose to revive the public recollection of the Crystal Palace in Hyde Park, for the purpose of comparing the merits of the two structures; and further to assist the reader, we shall give several pictorial representations, taken originally by the Daguerreotype, and now produced by the new process of chromatic printing.

It must be remembered that the palace of crystal was the result of a happy conception of Sir Joseph Paxton, after great constructive ingenuity had been expended on the first 233 designs of the building, and the arrangements for its erection had actually been made. The idea of laying aside the use of bricks and mortar first occurred to the famous superintendent of the gardens of the Duke of Devonshire, at Chatsworth and Chiswick. Sir Joseph Paxton, like many other distinguished inventors, was indebted for his discovery to the study of the manner in which the Divine Architect produces the great effects which man has to accomplish in his humble works. The type of the celebrated "Paxton roof" was furnished by the *Victoria Regia*, the enormous water-lily, brought from South Africa to the gardens, under his superintendence, at Chatsworth. In that large umbrella-shaped leaf, he saw the pattern of those longitudinal and transverse girders and supporters, which were to give to the crystal structure in Hyde Park its principal characteristic.

This careful study of the natural method of producing effects, has often led to the most successful results. The bony structure of the duck gave a model to

THE OPENING OF THE GREAT EXHIBITION

BY HER MOST GRACIOUS MAJESTY QUEEN VICTORIA MAY 1 1851

CLOSING OF THE GREAT EXHIBITION.

Drawn & Engraved by H.Bibby

SOUTH TRANSEPT, GREAT EXHIBITION

Engraved by R Tuloy from a Daguerreotype by Mayall

ship-builders; the egg furnishes the form of greatest strength for the construction of the tunnel; the triplet achromatic eye-piece of Dollond was produced by studying the structure of the eye; the shield employed successfully in forming the Thames Tunnel, was produced by observing the manner in which the *Teredo* protects itself from accident while carrying forward its boring operations. By this careful study and imitation of nature, man may hope to make fresh discoveries, and add to the number of his noblest inventions.

The Commissioners of 1851, although furnished with no less than 233 plans, could find among them none that would afford the conveniences necessary to their purpose, and had even added another of their own, when it occurred to Sir Joseph Paxton that he could release them from their perplexity. The thought, which afterwards became a reality, was first hinted during a conversation between that gentleman and another member of the House of Commons; when Sir Joseph Paxton expressed his apprehension that a great blunder would be perpetrated in the proposed building, at the same time intimating that he had an idea in his mind which he was prepared to work out if not too late. The nine days asked for having been granted, Sir Joseph Paxton, in the midst of other important avocations, completed his plans, which immediately commanded the approval of all concerned, and for which the estimates were completed with astonishing rapidity.

The description of this marvellous structure was furnished by its author during its progress, and will enable us to employ his own words in recalling its leading peculiarities.

" One great feature in the present building is, that no stone, brick, or mortar need be used; but the whole is composed of dry material, ready at once for the articles to be exhibited. By combination of no other materials but iron, wood, and glass, could this important point be effected; which, when we consider the limited period allowed for the erection of so stupendous a structure, may almost be deemed the most important object. The absence of any moist material in the construction, together with the provision made for the vapours which must arise and be condensed against the glass, enables the exhibitor at once to place his manufactures in their respective situations, without the probability of articles, even of polished ware, being tarnished by their exposure.

" I may state that it is unnecessary to cut down any of the large timber-trees, provision being made, by means of a curvilinear roof over the transept, for their reception within the building; and, by a proper diffusion of air, they will not suffer by the enclosure.

" The dimensions of the building are 1,851 feet in length, and 456 feet in breadth in the widest part. It covers altogether more than 18 acres; and the whole is supported on cast-iron pillars, united by bolts and nuts, fixed to flanges turned perfectly true, and resting on concrete foundations. The total cubic contents are 33,000,000 feet.

" The six longitudinal galleries, 24 feet in width, running the whole length of the building, and the four transverse ones of the same dimensions, afford 25 per cent. additional exhibiting surface to that provided on the ground-floor. This extra space is suited for the display of light manufactured goods; and from it a complete view of the whole of the articles exhibited, together with an extensive view of the interior of the building, will be obtained.

" The roof is built on the ridge-and-furrow principle, and glazed with British sheet-glass, as previously described; the sheets being 49 inches long—i. e., an inch longer than those of the Great Conservatory at Chatsworth. The rafters are continued in uninterrupted lines the whole length of the building. The transept portion, although covered by a semicircular roof, is also on the angular principle.

" All the roof and upright sashes being made by machinery, are put together and glazed with great rapidity; for, being fitted and finished before they are brought to the ground, little more is required on the spot than to fix them.

" The length of sash-bar requisite is 205 miles. The quantity of glass required is about 900,000 feet, weighing upwards of 400 tons. All round the lower tier of the building, however, will be boarded, with fillets planted on in a perpendicular line with the sash-bars above.

" The gutters are arranged longitudinally and transversely : the rain-water passes from the longitudinal gutter into a transverse gutter over the girders, and is thus conveyed to the hollow columns, and thence to the drains below. As these transverse gutters are placed at every 24 feet apart, and as there is a fall in the longitudinal gutters both ways, the water has only to run a distance of 12 feet before it descends into the transverse gutters, which carry it off to the hollow columns, or down-pipes. The grooves for carrying off the moisture which condenses on the inside of the glass, are cut out of the solid ; in fact, the whole gutter is formed by machinery at one cut. The gutter is cambered up by tension-rods, having screws fixed at the ends, so as to adjust it to the greatest nicety, as is the case with the wrought-iron girders which span the Victoria Lily House.

"Floors.—I have tried many experiments in order to find out the most suitable floors for the pathways of horticultural structures. Stone was objectionable, chiefly on account of the moisture and damp which it retained. The difficulty of getting rid of the waste from the watering of plants was also an objection ; but perhaps the greatest is the amount of dust from sweeping. I likewise found that close boarding for pathways was open to many of the same objections as stone ; for although damp and moisture were in part got rid of, yet still there were no means of immediately getting rid of dust. These various objections led me to the adoption of trellised wooden pathways, with spaces between each board, through which, on sweeping, the dust at once disappears, and falls into the vacuity below.

"Whilst the accomplishment of this point was most important in plant-houses, it is doubly so with the Industrial Building, where there will be such an accumulation of various articles of delicate texture and workmanship. Before sweeping the floors, the whole will be sprinkled with water from a movable hand-engine, which will be immediately followed by a sweeping-machine, consisting of many brooms fixed to an apparatus on light wheels, and drawn by a shaft. Thus a large portion of ground will be passed over very quickly.

"The boards for the floor will be 9 inches broad and 1½ inch thick, laid half an inch apart, on sleeper-joists 9 inches deep and 3 inches thick, placed four feet apart.

"This method of flooring, then, possesses the following advantages :—It is very economical; dry, clean, pleasant to walk upon ; admits of the dust falling through the spaces ; and even when it requires to be thoroughly washed, the water at once disappears betwixt the openings, and the boards become almost immediately fit for visitors."

In this simple matter-of-fact style, we learn how the inventor produced the marvellous "temple made of glass," which realised the dream of Chaucer, who had a pre-vision of its "many a pillar of metal," its "images of gold," its "jewels," its "curious portraitures," and its

> "Right great company withal,
> And that of sundry regions,
> Of all kinds of conditions,
> That dwell on earth, beneath the moon,
> Poor and rich."

Our views of the Building in its whole extent—of the Main Avenue from three stand-points, of the Transept looking north and south, and of the Opening (all drawn by the unerring pencil of light)—will recall the charming vision to the eyes of those who once were privileged to gaze upon it ; while, from their unerring fidelity, they will impart a faithful representation to those who have never beheld it in its original position, or before the alterations were made which it has undergone at Sydenham.

While the Crystal Palace was admirably adapted to the great purposes for which it was designed, there were sufficient reasons why it should not be regarded as the type of its successor. As the new Exhibition was to contain a valuable collection of pictures, sent from other countries as well as our own, it was considered necessary to give it a more substantial character for their safe preservation ; and important modifications in the arrangement were required for their effective display.

In comparing these two structures, it is necessary that reference should be made to the conditions they were to fulfil, and also to the sites they were to occupy ; and, if justice be done to the Commissioners and their ingenious architects, it will be admitted that there was an equally wise adaptation in each case. The secondary purposes to which the buildings were destined should also be remembered.

Engraved by H Bibby from a Daguerreotype by Mayall

THE TRANSEPT OF THE GREAT EXHIBITION.

LOOKING SOUTH

HELD IN LONDON IN 1851

Engraved by T Hollis, from a Daguerreotype by Mayall.

THE TRANSEPT OF THE GREAT EXHIBITION.

LOOKING NORTH

NORTH TRANSEPT, GREAT EXHIBITION.

Drawn & Engraved by H.Bibby

GREAT EXHIBITION, MAIN AVENUE.

LOOKING EAST

Engraved by T Hollis from a Daguerreotype by Mayall

THE INTERNATIONAL EXHIBITION – THE TRANSEPT LOOKING SOUTH

When Sir Joseph Paxton described his palace of glass, he said—" After the Exhibition is over, I would convert the building into a permanent winter-garden, and would then make carriage-drives and equestrian promenades through it. There would be about two miles of galleries, and two miles of walks upon the ground floor, and sufficient room would be left for plants. The whole intermediate spaces between the walks and drives, would be planted with shrubs and climbers from temperate climates. In summer, the upright glass might be removed, so as to give the appearance of continuous park and garden." Captain Fowke, on the other hand, in designing his building, had to adapt it to future International Exhibitions, and, consequently, to impart to it a more permanent character. In an excellent description of the more recent building, Captain Phillpots says—" It differs, therefore, from its predecessor in many essential particulars. It is more commodious, more imposing in its interior, more varied and more suitable for Exhibition purposes; while, from without, its aspect is of impressive magnitude and character."

The above extract is taken from a paper read by Captain Phillpots to the Society of Arts, on the Building for the International Exhibition of 1862, which furnishes a very accurate and detailed description of the whole building, and the principles on which it was constructed.

The Site on which the main building stands is about sixteen acres in extent. Nearly rectangular in shape, it measures about 1,200 feet from east to west, by 560 feet from north to south, and lies immediately south of the Royal Horticultural Society's gardens, the southern arcade of which was lent to the Exhibition for refreshment rooms. The whole of this area is covered by permanent buildings; and two long strips of land have been added for the eastern and western annexes, covering about seven acres, and making the whole extent of the Exhibition twenty-four acres and a-half. The Cromwell-road forms its southern boundary; on the east it adjoins the Exhibition-road; and Prince Albert's-road is on the west. It is important to notice that the general level of the ground is from four to six feet below the adjoining roads, as we shall see that this circumstance has been turned to a valuable account in planning the interior of the building.

The total covered area in Hyde Park, occupied 799,000 square feet; that in Brompton is considerably larger, being 988,000 square feet, and contains 35,000 feet more than the area roofed in by the Paris Exhibition.

The myriads who had admired the fairy-like palace in Hyde Park, had some feeling of disappointment when, instead of looking on a transparent structure of glass and iron, they saw a huge pile of brickwork, which, but for its enormous glass domes, presented a very utilitarian pile of solid masonry, with less pretension to architectural effect than some of the edifices we have erected for our pauper and criminal population. We must not, however, tax our imagination to add to the exterior an ideal beauty, and conceal the dull reality it is our duty to record. Let us, therefore, take a walk round these unadorned walls, and look first at—

The South Front, which is chiefly of plain brickwork, and truly described as having "no more ornament than that work admits of." This frontage is 1,150 feet long, and 55 feet high in brickwork, with two projecting towers at each end, rising sixteen feet above the general outline, with a large tower in the centre, forming the principal entrance into the picture gallery. The main entrance on this side is through three arches, fifty feet high, in this central tower, and decorated with terra-cotta columns. Above these arches is the cornice and frieze, surmounted by an ornamental clock-dial. Comparing this length of south frontage with that of the building in 1851, it will be readily perceived why we cannot have the grand perspective effect obtained in the former structure. It is easy to remember the 1,851 feet that measured the length of the Crystal Palace, whose date is recorded by the same number; but the nave of the second building is not more than 800 feet long, 85 feet wide, and 100 feet high to the ridge of the roof. Semicircular-headed panels, separated by pilasters, are built at intervals of twenty-five feet throughout the whole length; and between the arches are circular niches, at present vacant, but admitting of future decoration. In the lower portion of each panel is a window, to admit light and air to the ground floor, and for ventilation to the picture gallery.

To do justice to the south front, and, indeed, to all the frontage of this vast building of brick, it should be observed that the panels are plastered in cement; and that it is intended to raise a sufficient fund to furnish these spaces with English mosaics, representing the arts and manufactures of this kingdom.

THE EAST AND WEST FRONTS are similar in their general effects, and are especially distinguished by the great domes of glass which form the principal features of the whole building. Each of these domes rises 200 feet in height, and is surmounted by a handsome finial 55 feet high. Severe critics, wanting in gratitude for the pains taken to please the public eye, have failed to notice that, to the observer below, the form of each dome appears that of a semicircle—an effect which has been obtained by making the height of the dome eleven feet more than half its diameter, and so compensating for the apparent loss occasioned by the perpendicular perspective.

Without following the technical details of those much-admired and much-abused structures, we may observe, that by a plan for which the merit of novelty as well as great ingenuity is claimed, the dome of twelve sides appears to stand on an octagonal base—an arrangement by which an uninterrupted vista is obtained of the nave and transept, at the intersections of which they are placed. Each of the heavy-groined ribs of the dome rests its weight on two columns outside the octagon; so that the whole structure rests on sixteen points, its pressure on the angles of the octagon being nearly five times as much as on the columns of the nave and transepts. The iron in each dome weighs 120 tons. These domes are larger than those of St. Paul's, in London, and St. Peter's, at Rome. St. Paul's is 112 feet in external diameter, and St. Peter's 157½ feet; while each of the Exhibition domes has an external diameter of 160 feet. The domes of Brompton, however, receive less admiration than those of St. Peter and St. Paul, from the circumstance that they rise from a lower base than those solid structures. It was the boast of Buonarotti that he would raise the Pantheon to the summit of the Colliseum; and the cross of St Peter's is 430 feet above the pavement, and that of St. Paul's Cathedral 340 feet; while those at Brompton, measured inside from the daïs, are not more than 200 feet.

These East and West fronts are distinguished further by the large arched recesses,

THE GREAT EXHIBITION, MAIN AVENUE,

LOOKING WEST

Engraved by H Bibby, from a Daguerreotype by Mayall

THE INTERNATIONAL EXHIBITION - THE TRANSEPT LOOKING NORTH.

containing the main entrances to the Industrial Courts, above which are the richly decorated rose windows, each visible from end to end of the building.

THE NORTH FRONT, visible only from the gardens of the Royal Horticultural Society, presents a pleasing variety of architectural features. Its ground floor consists of the Southern Arcade of the gardens, composed of twisted columns of terra-cotta of very great beauty, over which is another floor; and the whole treated so as to harmonise with the adjoining arcades. This very pleasing façade presents five divisions, the central portion seventy feet high, and containing the arcade of the gardens, a low floor, called by the Italians *a mezzanine*, and an upper storey. On each side of this centre are ornamented brick arches, on terra-cotta columns, separated by pilasters; and the same arrangement applies to the upper lights. This front of the building is by far the most beautiful, combining, as it does, an agreeable blending of general uniformity with much diversity. The whole of the upper and lower floors of this handsome exterior, making an area of 26,800 square feet, were, during the Exhibition, occupied with the gastronomic industry of all nations, of which, it must be confessed, they furnished the most satisfactory proofs.

Having travelled round the building, we will now pass within its walls, and carefully perambulate

THE INTERIOR.—It has been already observed, that the ground covered by the Exhibition is about five feet below the adjoining roads; and it is due to the architect to admire the ingenuity with which this circumstance has been improved. To raise the ground to a level with the roads would have occasioned a vast expense; and to have descended at once to the original level, would have greatly marred the effect which the first glance at the interior ought to produce. By the arrangement of Captain Fowke, the visitor, on entering from the east or west front, ascends two steps, when he finds himself standing beneath the dome, on a daïs six feet above the floor of the building, into which he may descend by three flights of steps, eighty feet wide.

Our spectator is now standing under the eastern dome, whence he may take a glance at the principal features of the building, and look forward and backward on the right hand and the left, above and below. He seeks in vain for the long perspective, and those ethereal and atmospheric effects of colour which imparted a peculiar charm to the roof of the Crystal Palace; and, instead, he gazes on a nave and transept resembling a magnificent Gothic cathedral, whose pointed roofs are enriched with a gorgeous display of polychromatic colouring. The light, instead of coming through the roof and the walls, as in the Crystal Palace, is admitted through the clerestory windows, preserving the ideal of the Gothic cathedral; which, however, ceases as the eye of the observer falls on the light-looking iron columns by which the galleries and the roofs are supported.

The mass of rich colouring which now greets the eye; the elaborate rose window that terminates the perspective of the nave; the portions of the eastern transept that run off to the right and left—all decorated in the same rich style as the nave—produce an effect which has not failed to excite the admiration of all except the most fastidious pretender to taste.

The dome, under which our spectator stands, bears the appropriate inscription, in English—

"O LORD, BOTH RICHES AND HONOUR COME OF THEE, AND THOU REIGNEST OVER ALL; AND IN THINE HAND IS POWER AND MIGHT; AND IN THINE HAND IT IS TO MAKE GREAT."

While that of the western dome, in the further end of the nave, is in Latin:—

"TUA EST DOMINE MAGNIFICENTIA, ET POTENTIA, ET GLORIA, ATQUE VICTORIA: ET TIBI LAUS: CUNCTA ENIM QUÆ IN CŒLO SUNT, ET IN TERRA TUA SUNT, TUUM DOMINE REGNUM."

At the west end of the nave is—

"GLORIA IN EXCELSIS DEO, ET IN TERRA PAX."

And at the east end—

"THE WISE AND THEIR WORKS ARE IN THE HAND OF GOD."

Appropriate legends adorn other parts of the edifice.

To preserve a correct record of the whole structure, we must again quote from the paper of Captain Phillpots—a very safe guide to follow—and which has often been followed, but without due acknowledgment.

"The supports on either side consist of square and round cast-iron columns, coupled together; the former carry the gallery floor, and the latter, advancing into the nave, receive the principals of the roof. These columns are 50 feet high, in two lengths of 25 feet high; and from their capitals spring the roof-frames, which consist of three thicknesses of plank, from 18 inches to 2 feet 6 inches deep, firmly nailed and bolted together, and so arranged that their ends break joint. The centre plank is four inches thick, and each of the outer ones is three inches; the lower edges are tangents to an imaginary semicircle, round which they form half a nearly regular polygon. From the springing rise the posts of the clerestory windows, 25 feet high. The principal rafters of the roof-frames rise from the top of these posts, and are carried up, after passing a tangent, to the extrados of the arch to meet at the ridge, in a point 25 feet above the top of the clerestory. The angles over the haunches and crown of the arch are firmly braced together, so as to reduce the thrust as much as possible.

"The rib is repeated thirty times in the length of the nave; and, from its graceful curve and lightness, it produces a fine effect. Between every roof principal is a clerestory light, 25 feet high, consisting of three arches, springing from the intermediate mullions. The roof is covered with felt and zinc, on one-and-a-half inch plank, which is laid diagonally, so as to brace the whole together. The nave is, therefore, entirely dependent on the clerestory windows; but this arrangement is found to be entirely satisfactory, and a substantial water-tight covering is thus insured, having the advantage of obviating all chances of that unpleasant glare which the experience of 1851 proved to be unavoidable with a glass covering. The rain-water from the roof is conducted, by means of gutters, down the columns supporting the ribs, to drains laid under the ground-floor, which carry it off to the drains under the adjoining roads."

A transept runs at right angles with each end of the nave, for a length of 600 feet, being of the same width and height as the nave, and having the ribs of its roof of the same construction.

Our spectator must now leave his first post of observation, and traverse various parts of the building, which are not sufficiently seen from beneath the domes.

There are three open courts on each side the nave, having glass-covered roofs, on the ridge and valley plan. These roofs are carried on square iron columns, fifty feet apart, carrying on their summits, fifty feet above the ground, wrought-iron trellis girders, parallel to the length of the building. These columns and girders support the principals of the roof, which are all of iron, on the trussed rafter plan, and eight feet apart. These roofs are drained by channels in the valleys, conducting the water down the hollow iron columns. The courts, from their abundance of light, remind the visitor of the Crystal Palace of 1851; and from their admission of the rain, towards the close of the Exhibition, have fully justified the requirement of a more substantial kind of building in 1862. To complete our view of the ground floor of the main building, we must notice the aisles, fifty feet wide, which run on both sides the nave, and the inner sides of the transepts; and another aisle twenty-five feet wide, carried along the outer sides of the transepts, and along the back wall of the south front.

On this ground floor, also, we have to notice the two temporary buildings known as the Eastern and Western Annexes. The western annexe was 975 feet long; of which, for 720 feet, it was 200 feet wide, the remaining length being only 150 feet in width. It was covered by a ridge and valley roof, and supported on light wooden ribs, placed at intervals of fifteen feet. Its superficial extent was about four-and-a-half acres, or 184,000 square feet. It deserved great praise for its simplicity, ingenuity, and economy; displaying the most skilful mechanical contrivances of the age. It required no bolting or framing; and any person of ordinary intelligence, who could drive a nail, could have constructed the ribs, which had nothing in them but nails and sawn planks. The eastern annexe was similar to the western in construction, but somewhat smaller in the area covered in, as it inclosed a large open court of 350 by 100 feet.

The vast galleries, twenty-five feet above the ground floor, were commensurate with the whole building, except the glass courts, and occupied a space of 203,000 square feet. These extensive floors were supported on cast-iron girders fixed to the columns, and over them were laid two strong suspended trusses to carry the joists and boarding. The utmost care was taken to impart strength and security to these important portions of the structure. The description already quoted, which is the authority for these statements, says—"Supposing a floor to be loaded with 140 lbs. to the square foot—which, being more than the weight of a dense crowd of people, is heavier than any weight it can have to bear—the greatest load that can be placed on a girder is thirty-four tons. The breaking weight of the girders used is eighty-eight tons, and every one of them is proved in a hydraulic press, specially constructed for the purpose, to a load of thirty-eight tons, to avoid all risks from imperfect castings being used. Over each gallery is a flat roof covered with felt, supported like the floor, but of much lighter construction."

Those who are experienced in the construction of large buildings, and know the importance of providing against the effect of excessive thrust and pressure, will be prepared to estimate the following description of the method employed to counteract the thrust of the roof of these galleries. To Mr. Ordish is ascribed the merit of the particular form of bracing in these galleries, which formed an abutment to the nave and transept roof. From the outward thrust of the roof, tending to throw the columns out of the perpendicular, it was found necessary that strong iron braces should be anchored to the foundation of the inner column, and carried up to the top of the opposite outer column. Another bracing was anchored to the footing of the outer column, and carried up to the top of the inner column, to secure it against being acted on by the force of the wind. By this arrangement, which occurred at every hundred feet, or every fourth bay, the valuable effect of a horizontal girder was secured to resist the thrust of the three intervening ribs. This arrangement is regarded as "very

D

clever, and an admirable example of the perfect control which the simplest mechanical means, properly applied, give us of dealing with enormous masses." No observant person could fail to notice, also, that "the bracing is all adjusted by connecting screw-links, on a plan very similar to the method of joining railway carriages;" an arrangement by which the bracing could be "adjusted at pleasure, and the position of the columns corrected to the minutest fragment of an inch."

The galleries we have thus noticed were appropriated to the industrial portion of the Exhibition. We have now to traverse those specially prepared for the display of the Fine Arts, and which occupied the east, south, and west sides of the whole structure. Perhaps no portion of the building has afforded more satisfaction than these picture galleries; certainly none has been more free from unfavourable criticism. By a very skilful arrangement they escape a disadvantage which is experienced in many of the finest picture galleries of this country and the continent, and have enabled the visitors really to see the pictures, instead of being annoyed by the *glitter* produced by the reflection of light. Every one who has attempted to examine pictures in rooms lighted in the ordinary manner, has found great difficulty in placing himself in such a position as to escape from the "glitter" thus produced; and in consequence of which many of our best pictures are never seen to perfection.

The roofs of these galleries have been so constructed as to secure the requisite degree of light, and to diffuse it over the pictures in such a manner as to afford the greatest facilities for their examination. The arrangement for securing this valuable result is thus described:—The light is admitted "at a particular angle from the roof, by means of a skylight extending along its entire length; and which, in the present case, measures 31 feet in width; that is, 15 feet 6 inches from the ridge on either side. The entire width of the opening, measured on a horizontal plane, is 29 feet 2 inches. Each room is 50 feet wide; and at a height of 32 feet 9 inches, a cove, springing from a cornice on either side, reaches to the height of the tie-bar of the principals (42 feet 10 inches above the floor), 12 feet 4 inches from the wall; thus leaving a space 25 feet 4 inches between the coves. In this space, a transparent calico ceiling (hereafter to be replaced by ground glass) is introduced, which, however, is raised 2 feet 4 inches above the highest point of the cove, or 45 feet 7 inches from the floor." These picture galleries furnish 4,600 feet of hanging space, from 17 to 30 feet in height, being equal to 9,500 square yards, or two acres; the extent for the visitor to travel being half a mile all but thirty yards.

One practical result of this department of the Exhibition, will be the improvement in the construction of picture galleries at home and abroad, since the admirable method, which, during the last few years, was successfully adopted in the museum at South Kensington, has now commanded the unqualified approval of visitors from all parts of the civilised world.

THE DECORATION of the entire building having been entrusted to Mr. Crace, was executed with remarkable expedition, admirable taste, and great regard to economy. It is related, that Mr. Crace was asked, on a Saturday, if his designs for the eastern picture gallery were ready; that he decided on his colours on the Monday following; and that at mid-day the work was commenced, and completed on the succeeding

Saturday. All the picture galleries are painted sage-green, which forms a suitable background for the pictures; the cove is tinted, to correspond; the cornices and soffits being of vellum colour, relieved with maroon lines and ornaments.

By means of stencilling and distemper, a very rich colorific effect is produced in the nave and transepts, where the roofs have a warm grey colour, with upright scroll ornaments in maroon-red, rising from the sides to the apex. The main arches have a warm brown colour, with panellings of blue and red, relieved with light lines and ornaments, and separated by medallions in black, on which are stars of gold. In harmony with the design of the building, the artist has inscribed, on the crowns of these arches, the names of the countries by whose contributions the treasures of the Exhibition were supplied. The iron columns supporting the roof of the nave and transepts, are coloured to resemble pale bronze, relieved with light-coloured vertical lines; the capitals are red and blue alternately; and the raised ornaments richly gilded. The gallery railings are painted to resemble bronze, and are also richly gilded. The two domes are decorated in a style in keeping with the nave and transepts; the twelve main ribs being painted red and gold, bordered with black and white, and relieved with stars of gold on lozenges of blue.

Some portions of the machinery employed in putting this vast structure together, deserve honourable mention, partly from their novelty, and principally from their enormous bulk, and the ingenuity displayed in their construction.

The dome scaffolds, as Captain Phillpots correctly states, were " on a greater scale than anything of the kind ever constructed: they are literally forests of timber, occupying nearly the whole interior space of the domes—cross-braced and bolted together in every possible way, so as to give them sufficient strength." There were eight stages in each scaffold; between which were placed horizontal beams, the central portion being a square of 24 feet, and rising to a height of 200 feet. From the centre a scaffold radiated into each triangle of the dome, to which it was conformed in shape, and nearly in size. These radiating scaffolds had independent vertical bracing; while at each stage they were cross-braced horizontally. This *chef-d'œuvre* of scaffolding was so skilfully constructed, that very little of the timber was spoiled by cutting; every portion of it, amounting to 40,627 cubic feet in each scaffold, being afterwards as available for any other work as if it had just come from the builder's yard.

The travelling scaffolding, for raising the principals to the roof of the nave, also showed great skill in the design. Although the scaffolding for the nave contained 4,740 cubic feet of timber, and weighed 87 tons, it was moved along the rails by four men working crowbars under the wheels. By the aid of this apparatus, and the steam hoist, one-half of a rib was first hoisted to its place: when in position, the other half was raised; and as soon as both were fixed true, they were joined together by completing the arch, and bracing it over the crown. One rib being thus secured in its place, the purlins and boarding were fixed; the movable scaffold was pushed on to the next bay, and another rib completed in the same manner. A standing scaffold was employed for the transepts, in which 30,336 cubic feet of timber were used.

The steam hoist—an ingenious winch invented by Mr. Ashton—performed great service among this array of unconscious workers. This machine was described, by Captain Phillpots, as having " two grooved cast-iron barrels, which are made to revolve by means of a system of toothed wheels, connected with a portable steam-engine. On the fall being manned, and the barrels set in motion, the coils of the rope were gathered up, and a great hoisting power obtained. By means of snatch-blocks and pulleys, ropes were led to all parts of the building, and the heaviest materials, such as girders, columns, scaffold beams, &c., were hoisted to their position with the greatest ease and rapidity. As an instance," he states, "that the heavy floor girders, weighing about $1\frac{1}{4}$ tons, were raised in two minutes; columns in about the same time; and the ponderous ribs of the nave, weighing $6\frac{1}{2}$ tons, required only from ten to twenty minutes to raise them to their full height."

According to the terms of the contract, the building was delivered by the contractor, into the hands of Her Majesty's Commissioners, on the 12th of February, 1862, although part of the western dome, many of the minor details, and much of the decoration were incomplete. Two days previously, the strength of the galleries and other floors had been put to a severe test; which is thus described, with its satisfactory results, by Messrs. Fairbairn and Baker:—" They first caused a large body of men, about 400 in number, to be closely packed upon a space, twenty-five feet by twenty-five feet, on one lay of flooring." Their report says—" We then moved them in step, and afterwards made them run over the different galleries and down each staircase; at the same time, we caused the deflections of the girders carrying the floors to be carefully noted at several places, and had the satisfaction of finding that, in each case, the deflections were very nearly the same, thus exhibiting a remarkable uniformity in the construction. The cast-iron girders, with twenty-five bearings, deflected only one-eighth of an inch at the centre; and the timber-trussed beams of the same bearing, placed between these girders, deflected half an inch at the centre. In every instance, the girders and trusses recovered their original position immediately on the removal of the load." The report also stated that, when the two large domes were deprived of their temporary support, no observable settlement took place.

To perfect the description of this enormous edifice, we must add the statistics which have been furnished as to the quantities of materials employed in its construction. There were 7,000,000 of bricks supplied by Messrs. Smeed, of Sittingbourne; and upwards of 4,000 tons of iron from the Stavely iron-works, in Derbyshire The iron columns were 82,025, equal to four miles in length; and the 1,266 girders, if placed end to end, would measure six miles. To these quantities we have to add the iron for the domes, the groined ribs for the fifty-feet roofs, and the iron trellis-girders which support them, amounting to 1,200 tons. The timber-work was executed partly at the works of Messrs. Lucas, at Lowestoft, and partly at Mr. Kelk's works at Pimlico. The former prepared all the window-sashes, &c., by machinery; and the latter constructed the heavy ribs of the nave and transepts. The flooring extended over 1,300,000 superficial feet. The roofs were covered with 486,000 feet of felt, equal to eleven acres; and the glass required was 247 tons, making 553,000 superficial feet, or twelve acres and three-quarters. The work of construction gave employment to about 30,000 mechanics, and 50,000 labourers.

THE STATE OPENING of the International Exhibition of 1862 took place on Thursday, the 1st of May. The Queen's Commissioners assembled at Buckingham Palace, and, with his Royal Highness the Crown Prince of Prussia, and his Royal Highness the Prince Oscar of Sweden, escorted by the Life Guards, proceeded through Hyde Park, and arrived about one o'clock at the entrance to the Picture Galleries in Cromwell-road, where a guard of honour of the Grenadier Guards was stationed. The line of road was kept by the Life and Horse Guards.

Her Majesty's ministers, the foreign Commissioners, and others who took part in the procession, assembled in the south central court at half-past twelve; and on the arrival of the Queen's Commissioners, which was announced by a flourish of trumpets, the procession was formed. It started from the south centre of the nave, and proceeded by the south side of the nave to the western dome, where there was a throne and chairs of state. One verse of the National Anthem was sung.

When his Royal Highness the Duke of Cambridge, and the other Commissioners, had taken their seats, Earl Granville said:—

"In the name of the Commissioners of the International Exhibition of 1862, I have the honour to present to your Royal Highness, your Lordships, and Mr. Speaker, our humble address to her Majesty. In it we respectfully offer our condolences on the irreparable loss which her Majesty and the nation have sustained, and we express our gratitude to her Majesty for having appointed your Royal Highness and your colleagues as her Majesty's representatives, and we thank the Crown Prince of Prussia and Prince Oscar of Sweden for their presence on this occasion. In it we describe the rise and progress of the Exhibition, and the manner in which we propose to reward merit. We express our thanks to the Foreign and British Commissioners who have aided us in the work, and we express a humble hope that this undertaking may not be unworthy to take its place among the periodically recurring exhibitions of the world."

Earl Granville then handed to the Duke of Cambridge the address, of which his speech was a brief summary.

His Royal Highness read the following reply:—

"We cannot perform the duty which the Queen has done us the honour to commit to us as her Majesty's representatives on this occasion, without expressing our heart-felt regret that this inaugural ceremony is deprived of her Majesty's presence by the sad bereavement which has overwhelmed the nation with universal sorrow. We share most sincerely your feelings of deep sympathy with her Majesty in the grievous affliction with which the Almighty has seen fit to visit her Majesty and the whole people of this realm. It is impossible to contemplate the spectacle this day presented to our view without being painfully reminded how great a loss we have all sustained in the illustrious Prince with whose name the first Great International Exhibition was so intimately connected, and whose enlarged views and enlightened judgment were conspicuous in his appreciation of the benefits which such undertakings are calculated to confer upon the country. We are commanded by the Queen to assure you of the warm interest which her Majesty cannot fail to take in this Exhibition, and of her Majesty's earnest wishes that its success may amply fulfil the intentions and expectations with which it was projected, and may richly reward the zeal and energy, aided by the cordial co-operation of distinguished men of various countries, by which it has been carried into execution. We heartily join in the prayer that the International Exhibition of 1862, beyond largely conducing to present enjoyment and instruction, will be hereafter recorded as an important link in the chain of International Exhibitions, by which the nations of the world may be drawn together in the noblest rivalry, and from which they may derive the greatest advantages."

The procession then passed along the north side of the nave to the eastern dome, where the special musical performances took place. The music, specially composed for this occasion, consisted of a grand overture by Meyerbeer; a chorale by Dr. Sterndale Bennett (to words by the Poet Laureate); and a grand march by Auber. The orchestra, consisting of 2,000 voices and 400 instrumentalists, was presided over by Mr. Costa, except during the performance of Dr. Sterndale Bennett's music, which was conducted by M. Sainton.

At the conclusion of the special music, a prayer was offered up by the Bishop of London. The Hallelujah Chorus and the National Anthem were then sung; after which, his Royal Highness the Duke of Cambridge said, "By command of the Queen, I declare the Exhibition open."

This declaration having been made, it was announced to the public by a flourish of trumpets, and the firing of a salute on the site of the Exhibition of 1851. The procession then proceeded to the Picture Galleries, and the barriers were removed.

The military bands were those of the Grenadier, the Coldstream, and the Scots Fusilier Guards, conducted by Mr. Godfrey, and were stationed in the centre of the western dome.

About 25,000 persons were present.

This portion of our record will be incomplete without the Ode prepared for the occasion by our Poet Laureate, and sung by 2,000 voices, to the music of Dr. Sterndale Bennett :—

Uplift a thousand voices full and sweet,
In this wide hall with earth's invention stored,
And praise th' invisible universal Lord,
Who lets once more in peace the nations meet,
Where Science, Art, and Labour, have outpour'd
Their myriad horns of plenty at our feet.

O silent father of our Kings to be,
Mourn'd in this golden hour of jubilee,
For this, for all, we weep our thanks to thee !

The world-compelling plan was thine ;
And lo ! the long laborious miles
Of palace ! Lo ! the giant aisles,
Rich in model and design ;
Harvest-tool and husbandry,
Loom, and wheel, and engin'ry,
Secrets of the sullen mine,
Steel and gold, and corn and wine,
Fabric rough, or fairy fine,
Sunny tokens of the Line ;
Polar marvels and a feast
Of wonder, out of West and East,

And shapes and hues of art divine !
All of beauty, all of use,
That one fair planet can produce ;
Brought from under every star,
Blown from over every main,
And mix'd, as life is mix'd with pain,
The works of peace, with works of war.

And is the goal so far away ?
Far, how far, no man can say;
Let us have our dream to-day.

O ye, the wise who think, the wise who sigh,
From growing commerce loose her latest chain,
And let the fair white-winged peace-maker fly
To happy havens under all the sky,
And mix the seasons, and the golden hours,
Till each may find his own in all men's good.
And all men work in noble brotherhood,
Breaking their mailed fleets and armed towers,
And ruling by obeying nature's powers,
And gathering all the fruits of peace, and crown'd with
    all her flowers.

CHAPTER II.

A WALK THROUGH THE NAVE.

THE barriers being removed, and the whole Exhibition thrown open to her Majesty's lieges and the good people of all nations, we invite our friends to a promenade from dome to dome, that we may examine the varied and attractive treasures of the nave, noticing, by the way, the more prominent objects in the transepts and the middle avenue.

Before commencing their little tour, our friends may take the time from the *monstre* clock, whose face forms the circular stained-glass window at the eastern end of

INTERNATIONAL EXHIBITION.—THE NAVE, LOOKING EAST.

the building. The diameter of this dial is 38 feet 5 inches; the length of the hour figures, 1 foot 10 inches; the minute-hand is 21 feet 7 inches long, and the hour-hand, 18 feet 10 inches; in both cases including the counterpoises. The great wheel is 3 feet 8 inches in diameter; and the pendulum, which has a minute and a-half seconds' beat, weighs about three hundredweight. This would have been the largest clock-face in the world, but for that in Malines, the diameter of which is 40 feet. This enormous production has done the greatest honour to Messrs. Dent, by whom it was constructed, as, notwithstanding its vast dimensions, its gaining time, since it was fairly set, did not exceed six seconds—a circumstance the more noteworthy, considering the position of the works which were immediately under the clock-face, and close to the eastern entrance, where considerable disturbing forces were in operation throughout the day.

The Victoria Gold Trophy, the first claimant of our attention on this daïs, was an obelisk nearly seventy feet in height, an excellent contrivance for representing the enormous quantity of gold sent from our colony of Victoria to this country since the 1st of October, 1851. The amount thus represented was 26,162,432 ounces troy, equal to 1,793,995 lbs. avoirdupois; or 800 tons, 17 cwt., 3 qrs., 7 lbs.; a bulk of 1,492½ cubic feet; and a value of £104,649,728. The obelisk, large as it was, will no longer suffice to represent the gold obtained from Victoria, as we learn from a tablet on one of its sides, that, " Since the construction of this pyramid, the quantity of gold shipped from Victoria from Oct. 1st, 1861, to July 17th, 1862, amounts to 1,608,234 ounces, or 49 tons, 4 cwt., 2 qrs., 115 lbs. Value, £6,432,936. Eight such obelisks, composed of the material thus represented, it has been correctly observed, would pay our national debt in full. We had in this attractive object, one of the most skilful applications of simple materials for the production of a very satisfactory result; those materials being only wooden poles, canvas, and gold leaf; while the effect produced was that of an enormous mass of bullion.

The St. George's Fountain, in the centre of the daïs, furnished a greater attraction than the golden obelisk. It is said, that the late Mr. Thomas, the eminent sculptor, by whom it was designed, sacrificed health and life in his endeavours to secure the completion of this work in time for the opening of the Exhibition. His designs were admirably executed in *terra-cotta* by Messrs. Minton, who, under the skilful direction of the lamented artist, have removed from our country the reproach of being unable to prepare a fountain worthy of admiration. Apart from the large basin of perfumed water, occasionally supplied in abundance for public use, the fountain, in its elegant design and beautiful details, proved a great attraction. " St. George for Merrie England and Victory," the motto on the frieze, gives what may be termed the theme of this very poetical and thoroughly English work. Surmounting the whole structure we have our champion, valorously contending with the fabulous, but much-dreaded dragon; the champion being seven feet high, and the dragon great in proportion. In the four niches in the tall circular shaft, are winged caryatides, crowned with laurel, emblematic of victory, and bearing wreaths of laurel in their outstretched hands. Opposite each of the four niches is a graceful vase, standing on a tripod formed of winged griffins; and between the vases, but at a lower level, and at the angles of the base, are lions, supporting shields on which the cross of St. George is emblazoned.

Very tasteful are the trusses projecting from these angles; and at the end of each truss we have the richest gems in this diadem of British art—the famous bird fountains, in which the stork performs important service, and where nymphs appear amidst the shell basins, on which are flowing plenteously the waters falling from above. We look with the greater interest on these bird fountains, as we remember that they originated under the superintendence of the Prince Consort, to adorn the Queen's dairy at Windsor. As outliers of this great majolica formation, we have to notice, on the large basin which encloses the whole, the eight exquisite tazzæ, standing on pedestals; nor may we fail to register the beautiful wreath of oak-leaves, in their vivid green, and roses in full bloom, by which the edge of the basin is decorated. The admirable structure is thirty-six feet in height, and the diameter of its basin, nearly forty feet, for whose supply 7,000 gallons of water were required every hour.

The eastern daïs presented several noble specimens of sculpture: the famous " Milo Attacked by a Wolf," of Lough, in bronze; " Wedgwood," by E. Davis, also in bronze; some fine marbles and casts; among which a place was assigned to " Oliver Cromwell," as well as to " Roger Ascham," " Crompton," " Hallam," " Babbington," and other of our great men, who, like Sheldon, have been " the glory of England."

This may be the best time in which to refer to the statuary which adorned the nave, as well as the daïs at either end, that our attention may not be diverted from the trophies we shall presently have to notice. The south side of the nave presented a beautiful figure of " Rebecca," by E. Davis. " Armed Science" stood frowning near the class of military engineering, speaking but too faithfully of the sad uses to which so much of the practical science of our age is applied. But next we have " Dr. Isaac Barrow;" then that " Earl of Pembroke," so distinguished at Runnymede. " Marius in the Ruins of Carthage," by E. Baily, and " Samson Strangling the Lion," by T. Milnes, two noble works, adjoined the centre. In order, follow the " Orphan Flower Girl," by Crittenden; a bust of " Sir Francis Burdett," from a cast of the face, taken after death; a " Nymph," by Baily. Busts of " Viscount Palmerston," " Lord Brougham," the " Earls of Clarendon and Carlisle," by J. E. Jones; " Eva;" " Vice Tempting Virtue;" " Vanity of the Toilet;" " Garibaldi;" the " Venus" of Canova; " La Maddalena;" " A Shepherd;" and Power's " Greek Slave," reproduced in fictile marble, were among the beautiful sculptured works that extended to the western dome.

On and near the western daïs, besides the fine busts of the " Queen," and the late " Prince Consort," there were some of the most elaborate productions of the age— " Achilles Plucking the Arrow from his Foot," and a " Victor in the Olympic Games thanking the Gods," both by Karl Cauer. Fine groups are " Jason having overcome the Dragon," by Kaehsmann; and " Mars and Venus," with Amor, that busy little deity, known best in these parts by the name of " Cupid," officiously carrying the sword of Mars: the group by L. Kissling.

Returning along the north side of the nave, were the " Discobolus," in a sitting posture, by Kessel; the " Angel of Evil," by Geefs; the " Naïs of Frison," and " The Youthful Fawn." Then came—

The " Mercury" of Thorwaldsen; and next, "Thorwaldsen" himself, holding his hammer and chisel. " La Desalazione" is an exquisite work, by Filippo Spaventi. " General Sir Charles Napier," and " Sir W. C. Ross, R.A.,"

Engraved from a Photograph taken by the London Stereoscopic Company

THE INTERNATIONAL EXHIBITION.—THE NAVE LOOKING WEST.

were distinguishable among the recently produced busts. The "Moses" of Michael Angelo (perhaps his greatest work) was shown in a cast taken by the new method—the plaster backed with cloth. A Georgian "Lady of the Harem," enclosed in a glass case : on the figure a rich light fell from the roof of yellow glass. Next came "California," by Hiram Power; "L'Allegra," by Earle; the "Duchess of Wellington;" the late "Catherine Hayes;" the "Ariel" of Westmacott; the "Clio" of J. Lawlor; a bust of the "Duke of Newcastle;" and the interesting group of "British Youths exhibited as Slaves in the Roman Market"—"*Non Angli sed Angeli*"—reminding us of the happy contrast of our age with that in which Gregory the Great uttered these complimentary words.

And now that we have returned to the eastern daïs, our first attentions are due to the trophy case of Messrs. Hunt and Roskell, who, at the suggestion of the Commissioners, removed it to this point, from the position it had occupied in the over-crowded nave. Here was a necklace of pearls, each averaging thirty-nine grains—the whole worth £8,000—being the largest pearl necklace on sale; a very extraordinary row of black pearls, for which a rage exists just now among the *cognoscenti ;* the Nassuck and Arcot diamonds, the property of the Marquis of Westminster; a head ornament, containing a remarkably fine *pierre d'échantillon*, set with rubies and diamonds. Here, too, were some of the richest specimens of testimonial plate; the Lawrence plate, intended to have been presented by "his friends of the Punjaub," but which, alas ! he never lived to see; and the table-plate of the Goldsmiths Company, including the grand candelabrum, illustrating the granting of the royal charter to the company by Richard II. Special mention must be made of the vase of oxydised silver, representing the combat of the Centaurs and the Lipithæ, the pedestal of which is enriched by the introduction of cornelian and lapis lazuli; and another vase of oxydised silver, presenting a marine composition, in which are bassi-relievi, representing Venus and Adonis, and Thetis presenting to Achilles the armour forged by Vulcan. All these, the works of Antoine Vechte, have a melancholy interest, as they are the property of her Majesty, and were produced at the command of the late Prince Consort.

Anxious to descend, and begin our walk through the nave, we must yet linger, and admire the trophies of Mechi and Bazin, Leuchin and Asprey, devoted to dressing-cases, and other articles of the toilet—suitable for kings and queens; and if for subjects, only the richest and most luxurious. Well has it been said by a writer on these expensive productions—"We can easily figure to ourselves the blank amazement which would fill the soul of a woad-dyed ancient Briton, if he could be brought back to the land where, in his day, a dye-pot and brush constituted the entire wardrobe and dressing-case of a dandy; and informed him that he must now operate upon himself with all these queer-looking little tools, before he could be considered fit to mingle in polite society." We are not to charge upon this year of grace, 1862, all the luxuriousness which these things indicate; for among them, in the Large Trophy, was placed the dressing-case made for George IV.—perhaps the most magnificent ever seen, and which cost 2,000 guineas. It must be confessed that the toilets of our day are sufficiently rich and rare; for Mr. Asprey, of Bond-street, showed us a dressing-case, a *chef-d'œuvre* of the manufacturing art, the price of which is £1,500. The gold work of the interior is most elaborately chased, and set with the finest carbuncles and pearls—in all, nearly 900 stones. In Mr. Asprey's trophy, we saw, also, a dressing-case made for the Viscountess Lismore, in the Moorish style, after the rich pattern on the walls of the Alhambra; and another, made for Lady Harriet Ashley, in gold and turquoise.

Descending now into the British nave, we find it difficult, but quite necessary, to select from among the trophies with which it was unduly crowded.

The Cheesewring Granite Obelisk, twenty-seven feet high, is a fine specimen of this beautiful stone, which is obtained about six miles from Liskeard in Cornwall, whose Duke, the Prince of Wales, is its proprietor. It was the wish of the late Prince Consort that a monolith of this granite should form a memorial of the Exhibition in Hyde Park. It is perfect in its classical form and proportions, especially in the gradual swelling of the shaft, and would have formed an excellent model, if the design of such a memorial of his late Royal Highness could have been realised. No such commendation can be given to the granite obelisk from Glasgow, in which a meretricious taste has been employed, to improve on a form which is perfect in its primitive simplicity.

As the result of a not very successful attempt to balance the trophies in the nave, there stood, on the corresponding side, the colossal Drinking Fountain of Mr. Earp, enriched with coloured marbles and sculptured groups, but certainly not a model for that most useful class of objects which are gradually supplying a great want in our metropolis and other great towns and cities.

Considering the great excellence in Leather displayed in the foreign department, it was patriotic in Messrs. Bevington to erect their magnificent trophy in the British nave. They displayed not only every class of leather manufactured in England, but the implements, the materials, and processes of the leather trade; adorning their trophy with the heads of the animals subjected to the skill of the tanner. They gave also eight large photographs of men at work in the manufacture of leather; while the sixteen compartments of their elaborate structure presented the moroccos, roans, and skivers used by cabinet-makers, coach-builders, and book-binders; the heavy ox-hide for soles and machinery; the curried leather used by the shoemaker and saddler; and numerous other varieties; among which were samples of chamois, or oil-leather, exhibited as an important and distinct branch of this art. On the table was a machine for testing the strength of the manufactured article; and there was, open to the visitors, a book containing specimens of skins in the various stages of manufacture.

A sort of companion trophy was presented in the collection of woollen cloths from Yorkshire; the staple of whose industry is happily unaffected by the causes which have thrown our Lancashire operatives into the extremes of distress. These fine productions will, hereafter, claim our particular consideration, under the head of Textile Fabrics.

The Armstrong gun, and many terrible engines of war, we hold in reserve until it becomes necessary to enter into the vexed question of their relative merits. A passing notice, however, must be given to the Birmingham Trophy of Small Arms, the guns and bayonets, rifles and revolvers, which, from the tasteful designs into which they were formed, gave little indication of the destructive work for which they are intended. Nor may we pass, without notice, the model of the *Warrior*, the iron-plated frigate, which may be regarded as the type to which our navy is gradually being conformed,

MAGNI'S CELEBRATED STATUE OF THE READING GIRL.

IN THE POSSESSION OF G S NOTTAGE ESQ^R

and by which the wooden walls of the old England of our forefathers are to be superseded. The graceful lines of this terrific vessel, her rigging and equipments, have elicited universal admiration; while an excellent transverse section has made us pretty well acquainted with the interior arrangements.

More gratifying is the task of commemorating the peaceful triumphs gained by the fur-trapper, whose rich spoils adorned the well-filled cases of Messrs. Poland, Bevington, Jeffs, and Morris. The trophy furnished by the combined efforts of these gentlemen, rich as it was in sables and ermines, the fur of the seal, the arctic fox, and other rare products of the north, conferred the highest credit on their taste and enterprise. Messrs. Nicholay and Son maintained the pre-eminence they enjoyed in the last Exhibition, not only for the novelties by which their trophy was adorned, but for their illustrations of the natural history of the animals laid under contribution for their rich patrons. They seem to have aimed at imparting amusement and instruction to the young, while showing the people of all countries how the grey lamb, the grebe, or Swiss duck, from the Lake of Geneva, the silver fox, the leopard, the tiger, the lion and bear, are compelled to minister to the taste and comfort of our *genus homo*.

In our last stroll through the nave, it was our good fortune to find there that great popular favourite, the "Reading Girl" of Pietro Magni, which had been removed from the Italian court. Such has been the admiration of this simple and beautiful creation, that, by the second week after the close of the Exhibition, the Stereoscopic Company is said to have realised £3,000 by the sale of its photographs. The success of the sculptor has excited the genius of the poet, who has happily expressed the feelings awakened in many a spectator; surpassing them all, however, by a happy conceit of the writer, S. C. S., in the closing verse—

Who art thou ? Hast thou not a look,
   Which thou canst give away,
For ever poring o'er thy book,
   Throughout the livelong day ?

Hast thou just stolen from thy nest,
   As morning gilds the skies ;
Or wilt thou shortly seek thy rest,
   And close thy weary eyes ?

What is the page that chains thee down,
   And rivets thought and sight ?
Art seeking an immortal crown,
   By Scripture's heavenly light ?

Or does some tale, by mortal writ,
   Bewitch thee with its charm,
Of two fond hearts together knit,
   Whom malice sought to harm ?

May be, thou drinkest in the stream
   Of poetry divine,
Where fancy's rainbow-tinted beam
   Illuminates each line :

Some patriotic strain, inspired
   By sense of wrong sustained,
Yet, with prophetic visions fired,
   Of future glories gained :

A requiem o'er the mighty dead,
   Slain in their country's cause ;
Yielding her sons—whose blood was shed—
   Their country's just applause.

Read on ! read on ! I will not try
   To rouse thee from thy theme :
Thy rush-made chair, thy robe thrown by,
   Too real for sculpture seem !

I take thee for some living maid,
   Enthralled by magic art,
And hither, o'er the sea, conveyed,
   To play a cunning part.

Ambitious of a prize, beyond
   All other wonders shown,
The Necromancer waved his wand,
   And turned thee into *stone*.
             S. C. S.

Anticipating, by a few paces, our further progress through the nave, we may now refer to another highly popular photograph, " The Sleep of Sorrow, and the Dream of

Joy," in which Monti has happily given solidity and permanent shape to the well-known vicissitudes of diurnal experience. There lies the exhausted sufferer, so sunk and depressed, as to excite our own sorrow, until we look up, and see the gloomy countenance now radiant with delight, and the crouching form, instinct with ethereal life, as it floats along in its joyous course, keeping its holiday of dreams, and speaking to us of the relief which a kind Providence affords the suffering amidst their woes.

If art has been compelled, during the last ten years, to minister to the cause of defensive war, she has also proved the handmaid of science. We are now amidst telescopes and other philosophical instruments, exhibited by Dalmeyer and others, on account of important improvements in their lenses and adjustments. Mr. Dalmeyer exhibited an equatorially-mounted telescope of between six and seven feet focal length, the aperture of the object-glass about five inches diameter, which had a magnifying power of 500. This instrument deserves notice from the novel method of its mounting, which consists of the base or pedestal, the steadiest that could well be devised for the weight of metal employed; its transverse section resembles the letter Y, and affords a convenient descent for the clock-weight, which is brought near the centre of gravity. The upper, or equatorial portion, which carries the telescope, is constructed entirely separate from the pedestal, to admit of its being separated or put together without sending a workman for the purpose. The driving apparatus consists of a powerful clock, and has a self-acting maintaining power, invented by the Astronomer Royal. The hour-circle is loose on the polar axis; and by means of two verniers, one fixed to the gnomon, and the other to the axis, the rate of the clock is checked by one, and the right ascension is determined by the other. When the hour-circle has been once adjusted, the driving apparatus having been regulated, it continues to move on, so that objects can be formed without readjustment or computation. The tangent-screw of the hour-circle is mounted on a rectangular slide, and, by means of an eccentric, can be thrown in or out of gear at pleasure. There is also a "fetching-up screw," which enables the observer to correct the inequalities of clock-rate, or the eccentricity of eye-pieces, without deranging the previous adjustment of verniers. The declinator axis is made accessible, for the purpose of applying a level direct on its bearings. The telescope and declination circle, with its tangent screw, as fixed to the opposite ends of the axis, nearly counterbalance each other.

The instruments employed at the Kew Observatory consisted of the most delicate thermometers, barometers, and magnetographs. In this interesting collection were shown the first photographs taken of the sun, and depicting the spots on its face. Here was the Self-registering Anemometer of Dr. Robinson, of Armagh, with an ingenious improvement of Mr. Beckley, for packing the whole in a much smaller compass than when that important apparatus was first invented. Some years ago, it was deemed a great triumph of practical science to register, by a self-recording instrument, from hour to hour, through the day and night, the direction of the wind, and the strength of its pressure on the square foot: much more remarkable is the apparatus now at work at Kew and Greenwich, for recording the variations of the magnet at all periods of the day and night. This apparatus, the Magnetograph, is one of the most admirable applications of photography ever imagined. A roll of sensitive paper, set in motion by clock-work, is acted upon by a ray of light reflected from a little semicircular mirror, which mirror is suspended from a horizontal magnet, so as to record all the variations the magnet undergoes. The mirror receives the ray from a small lamp; and, the angle of reflection being equal to the angle of incidence, the means of a perfect registration are secured. Other instruments are for eye observation, and for the vertical magnet; and the whole are employed to assist our acquaintance with the subject of magnetism, which, in former years, we were supposed to understand, and are only now learning.

The Norwich Gates, designed by Mr. Thomas Jekyll, and executed by Barnard & Co., deserve our notice and admiration for their exquisite beauty; for they are rich in heraldic figures, in scroll-work and foliage, oak and holly, the vine, the hawthorn, convolvulus, briony, periwinkle, ivy, and double rose. They are the more admired for the manner in which they have been executed, by combining cast and wrought iron, so as to secure solidity by the former, and beauty by the latter process. Well may Mr. Hunt say—" These gates are a fine example of the blacksmith's craft." But his admiration seems, like that of every Englishman who has examined them, to be all the greater from the fact, that " they are made entirely with the hand, with hammer, and pincers, as they would have been 500 years ago."

The elegant little structure, designed by Owen Jones, for the display of the *monstre* glass gems of Messrs. Osler, was almost lost amidst the attractions by which it was surrounded. In a more isolated position, its tall pillars and rich moresque dome would have called forth much admiration, as would also the large masses of lapidary-cut glass, in whose honour the pretty fabric was created. In this temple we have, perhaps, the triumph of glass-cutting. Certain it is, that no such work could have been performed until a machine was constructed by Mr. Osler for the purpose. Here are gems of the purest white flint glass, quite as large as the hand can well hold, and, to the unpractised eye, as brilliant as the Koh-i-Noor, and large enough for the crown of a Brobdignagian emperor. The facets are cut with mathematical accuracy; and, according to the sizes of the gems, their numbers increase. The smallest gem, " the small oval," has 282 facets; the next has 440: then we have the " round-ended," 544 facets; the " half-round," 740; and the greatest gem, the " round." in the centre of the temple, has no less than 1,360 facets.

The nave presented few objects more deserving attention than those relating to the preservation of vessels at sea from wreck, by the improvement in Light-ships and Lighthouses. The Floating Light-Lantern of Messrs. Wilkins, if not a very sightly and attractive object, was certainly one of the greatest utility. Their machinery for producing the revolution of the light, is secured under the deck of the vessel, instead of being placed on the mast with the light. By means of three silver-plated parabola reflectors, their light shows red, green, and white colours in succession, as the revolutions are performed. The same exhibitors showed a Holophotal Lens Apparatus, constructed of the St. Gobain glass, which is greatly approved for its high powers of refraction, and of producing a flashing light. They exhibited also, as a Direction Light, a lens on the Holophotal principle, for a railway light; and a silver-plated

Parabolic Reflector for lighthouses, affording very powerful lights by means of an Argand burner.

In close proximity, but a little further west, Messrs. Chance, of Birmingham, displayed the Dioptric Revolving Light, with its Lantern and accessories. The reader, perhaps, needs not to be reminded, that a dioptrical light is that in which the light shines through the glass, as distinguished from a catoptric light, in which the rays are reflected from a polished surface. The distinction is that of the lens and the mirror. Until recently, the highest importance was attached to parabolic reflectors for lighthouses; but, of late years, lenses and prisms, through which the light passes, have grown into higher esteem. Hence we hear now so much of dioptric lights in connexion with lighthouses; and as it is of the utmost importance to save all the light that can be obtained, we have the most ingenious contrivances for that purpose. As we have a new thing in the *Whole Light* Distributor, so we have a new word, *holophotal*, to express it.

The iron structure, surmounted by a large octagonal lantern, and placed near the Turkish department, was a DIOPTRIC REVOLVING APPARATUS OF THE FIRST ORDER. It is formed, according to the description of the exhibitors, of an eight-sided frame, in the centre of which the flame is placed. Each side comprises a compound lens, and a series of totally reflecting prisms, both above and below the lens; all these prisms, as well as the rings of the compound lens, being concentric round a horizontal axis, passing through the centre of the lens. By this arrangement, the light proceeding from the central flame is condensed into eight beams of parallel rays, without the aid of unnecessary reflections or refractions, so as to produce the maximum effect at sea. The light-room, made of cast iron, is seven feet high, being cylindrical within, and having, externally, sixteen sides, alternately large and small, to suit the lantern which it supports. It is provided, outside, just beneath the lantern, with a gallery or balcony, on which the keepers can stand to clean the lantern panes; and also with an inside gallery, for the service of the apparatus. The lantern is formed of sixteen standards, alternately inclosed to the right and left; made of wrought iron, covered with gun-metal facings; by which combination, the greatest strength, and the least interception of light are obtained together, with the usual protection from the sea air. It has a double copper dome, supported on iron rafters; and the whole is surmounted by a revolving copper ball, carrying a wind-vane. The rotatory motion of the lantern is secured by means of clock-work, so constructed as to maintain a uniform speed of rotation, without any check during the winding up. The light is obtained from an oil pressure-lamp, which consists of a metal cylinder, in which the piston that forces the oil into the burner is worked by a weight placed outside the cylinder, instead of inside, as formerly; and each of the four concentric wicks of the burner is supplied with oil by two independent feed-tubes, communicating with the main pipe. One of these Holophotal revolving lights was placed on Lundy Island, in the British Channel, in 1857; and the following official report affords sufficient proof of its excellence :—" July, 1859.—Saw the light soon after sunset, distant about fifteen miles. It is intended to be seen at thirty; and one of the mariners has seen it at forty-five, the greatest distance at which any light, at home or abroad, has been seen by any one of 814 witnesses." As Messrs. Chance have, within a few years, supplied nearly ninety complete lights for lighthouses, we have given, thus early, a notice of the kind of apparatus which is now employed extensively for the protection of the world's commerce, and for the safety of human life.

Toys for children, and food for all ages, had their trophies in this portion of the nave, affording no small delight to the little folks, and reminding man of the great industry employed to minister to the support and enjoyment of his material nature. A very ingenious means of calling attention to the principal article of human food, was employed by Mr. Hallett, of Brighton, who, in letters formed by the large ears of wheat, bespoke the favourable consideration of his method of improving the quality of grain. The "pedigree wheat" will claim our notice hereafter, in the class of substances used as food, to which all the contents of this trophy properly belong—cigars only excepted.

Though out of position in the British nave—for it is a foreign subject, and the work of a foreign artist—we must make a place for the well-executed model of the Milan Cathedral. Had the Exhibition not oppressed us with the *embarras de richesse*, so that we could have bestowed an hour on any object worthy of it, the Milan Cathedral would have well repaid a pilgrimage to West Brompton. How faithful are all the details, within and without; the sculpture; the richly-coloured windows; the side chapels; the elegant architectural details; and the spire, over which the artist has thrown a veil of Mechlin lace. No less than £1,200 was the price set on this exquisite work, during the days of sale at the close of the Exhibition.

We have now to work our way through the Garrard Straits, to take our time at Elkington's, and Harry Emmanuel's; for here, and in this immediate neighbourhood, we have the greatest wealth in the Exhibition. We have also to admire the porcelain of Alderman Copeland, of Goode & Sons, of Kerr & Co., and the furniture trophies of Jackson & Graham, and other exhibitors.

Garrard & Co. claim precedence here as the exhibitors of the Koh-i-Noor, as well as other treasures belonging to her Majesty. The millions who had seen the Mountain of Light in 1851, were gratified in again recognising an old friend with a new face, or rather with many new faces. An excellent opportunity of comparing the former with its present aspect, was afforded by placing, in juxta-position with the diamond, a glass model, to show the appearance the diamond presented in 1851. The admiring crowd, to whom this richest of gems appeared larger than when they last saw it, will be surprised to find that it now weighs only 106 carats, instead of 186½, in its former unshapely state. The work of recutting was regarded by many as a most dangerous experiment, the failure of which was predicted by a very eminent authority. Messrs. Garrard, however, encountered the great risk, assigning to the Iron Duke the honour of cutting the first facet, and carrying the great work to completion in their establishment in London. The case of these exhibitors was enriched by ornaments of the most costly kind, in which were pearls, emeralds, turquoises, and rubies, the richest and rarest on which mortal eyes ever gazed. Among them, a foremost place was assigned to the three large and fine rubies from the treasury at Lahore, mounted as a necklace, in gold and enamel, in the Indian style, with large diamonds pendant. There, also, was the centre table ornament, representing a covered fountain, designed in the style of the palace of the Alhambra, executed in silver, silver-gilt, and enamel; having, round the base, a group of horses, portraits of favourite animals of her Majesty, to whom all the treasures belong.

The trophy of Mr. Harry Emmanuel, so worthy of its rich contents, well deserved its prominent position in the nave. It was composed of ebonised wood, ornamented with bronze enrichments, and inlaid with marble. Square in form, it had projecting angles, the plinths of which supported four bronze caryatides, representing the Seasons. Above the carved cornice was a dome, of light and elegant proportions, on which was placed a magnificent bronze copy of the celebrated "Mercury" of John of Bologna. On the summit of the projecting angles, were placed four oxidised silver vases, each three feet in height, copied from the Museo Borbonico.

To the praise of Mr. Harry Emmanuel, it should be recorded, that every article in his trophy was made expressly for the Exhibition, two years having been occupied in the work of preparation. Here we had an astonishing display of wealth—for the jewels were estimated at £350,000 in value—and a most gratifying proof of the progress of the jeweller's art since 1851. This exquisite display has fully realised the object of the exhibitor; which, according to his own statement, was to prove, "that correct drawing, beauty of finish, and general harmony of design, can be obtained, at no greater outlay than has hitherto been required for articles of wretched drawing and shape, and with inharmonious combinations of colour." The exhibitor has laboured successfully to impress the public with the truth, that "a good model costs no more than a bad one; and that the object of a silversmith or jeweller, should not be to cram as many ounces of silver, or carats of diamonds, into a work, as possible, but to make even the commonest and most ordinary articles, of a beautiful form, and no heavier than the strength requires." The contents of this rich trophy, as well as the displays of other exhibitors, have furnished the most gratifying proof that, since the Exhibition of 1851, the taste, both of the producer and consumer, has been improving, and that we have now the prospect of becoming as successful in works of taste, as in those of a mere utilitarian character. We select a few of the attractive objects which constituted the wealth of this rich collection.

The PERSEUS and ANDROMEDA CUP, a brown topaz or cairngorm, carved in the form of a cup, and mounted into a gold vase. Andromeda is chained to the rocks which form the base of the cup; whilst the dragon has climbed up to attack Perseus, who, armed with the sword of Vulcan, and the shield of Minerva, is mounted on Pegasus. The gold work is *repoussé* throughout, and partly enamelled. The subject is treated in the style of Cellini, with whose works it bears a favourable comparison.

The UNDINE EWER is entirely covered with the most delicate chasings, portraying the history of Undine; while the body is divided into compartments, representing the leading facts of the romance of Lamotte Fouqué. This vase, which is twenty-seven inches high, is also a fine specimen of *repoussé*, and therefore remarkable for the comparative smallness of its weight, as, by this method of treatment, the interior of the vessel is the counterpart of the exterior.

The LAPIZ LAZULI FOUNTAIN, formed of the material from which it takes its name, was unsurpassed, for beauty and execution, by anything in the building. On the square base are children holding urns, from which jets of water gush forth into crystal shells; while, from beneath a dome supported by lapiz lazuli and silver columns, a fountain sends a stream aloft. On this dome is seated a Venus supporting a vase of flowers.

One of the finest beams of ivory procurable has been carved into the figure of a slave-girl, which stands two feet high. Though a captive herself, she is giving freedom to a bird; and the artist represents her in the act of cutting the thread by which the little captive is secured. The lines on which Mr. Chesneau has based his work, tell a pretty tale—

"In gilded cage, like me you pine,
    And long for home and playmates dear,
I cut the chain that makes thee mine:
    Go, thou art free; I must stay here!"

Among the jewels in this collection, there were five diamonds mounted as stars, and valued at £20,000; and three very large black diamonds, also mounted as stars, as a head ornament. The black diamond, in chemical composition, is the same as the brilliant, but gives out none of its prismatic hues, having no greater lustre than polished steel. It is valued for its rarity, and not for its beauty. There was also a brooch, which had for its centre the splendid emerald which once sparkled on the turban of the Lion of the Punjaub, and, for its pendant, a pearl as large as a plover's egg, and worth £10,000; £9,000 was the price of a suite of opals and diamonds.

Electro-metallurgy, one of our most recent arts, has been diligently cultivated during the last eleven years, and was well represented in the magnificent trophy of Messrs. Elkington. The fine British subject, the bronze group of " Boadicea threatening to avenge the insult offered to her daughters by the Romans," formed the appropriate summit of the Elkington trophy; and, although seven years since in Paris, is but little known in this country. On one side of the trophy was an electrotype copy of a suit of armour, from one belonging to the Tower of London. Here was also an electrotype statue of " General Murray," and another of " Prince Blucher," both belonging to Wellington College, to which the latter was presented by the late Prince Consort. On the same side was an electrotype bronze of " Canmore," son of Duncan I.; and, at the base, were the " Young Naturalist," " A Daughter of Eve," and " A Slave," all in bronze, deposited by electrotype. On the other side of the famous trophy were several of the barons of Magna Charta, models of part of the series of eighteen, prepared also by Messrs. Elkington: among them, "Langton, Archbishop of Canterbury;" the " Earl of Norfolk;" and " Almeric."

A very exquisite work was the table surmounted by a mirror, executed after a model of the Alhambra, and giving, with admirable faithfulness, the rich details of the original. On this table stood the celebrated silver statue of the " Lady Godiva riding through Coventry," by Thomas.

We must not pass unnoticed the work on which M. Morel Ladul, a pupil of Vichte, has spent more than three years. We speak of a poem in silver, in which the artist has embodied his pleasant ideas in that precious metal. Although passing under the name of a silver table, what a marked contrast it presents to an article of that name,

G

which was deemed a rare production in the days of George III., in whose castle of Windsor it was an object of special admiration. The artist appears to have dreamed, and then to have given the solidity of metal to his dreams. The labourer, the warrior, and the troubadour, are reclining in sleep at the foot of the stem by which this table is supported; and their state of slumber is sufficiently described by the aid of the poppy, and other narcotics. The labourer dreams of corn and wine, of fruit and flowers, of peace and plenty; the minstrel, of love and fortune, and all the poetries that fill up this dreamer's heaven. The soldier is following in his victorious career, and enjoying honour and fame; and taking a place in history, on whose pages the muse is inscribing his name. All these things are told in the three portions into which the upper part of this exquisite work is divided.

If we do not now linger over the ceramic trophies of Alderman Copeland, Messrs. Burns and Kerr, of Worcester, Messrs. Goode and Sons, Sir James Duke, and Wedgwood, it is not for want of admiration of the treasures of porcelain and china, of which those trophies are composed, but because they will more particularly claim our attention when viewed in comparison with similar products in the class to which they belong. A porcelain dessert service, of the finest *pâte tendre*, rich with turquoise and gold, and painted with exquisite art, was exhibited by Messrs. Goode; and some magnificent specimens of the service lately executed for her Majesty, by Burns and Kerr, of Worcester. A part only of this service had been prepared previous to the Exhibition; but it consisted of eighty plates, each of different design; as were, also, the grape-baskets, wine-coolers, and compotees. A peculiarity of this fine set, is the method of turning over the edges, by which the rich ornaments of the dishes were seen, although filled with the contents, by which usually the most expensive parts of decorations are concealed.

Special admiration was excited by the English porcelain, the modern Palissy ware, the Limoges ware, the Majolica, the Parian statuary, which filled the cases of Wedgwood and Sir J. Duke; in all of which, the progress of this important branch of art-manufacture, since 1851, has done the highest honour to our countrymen, and demonstrated, in the most satisfactory manner, the great value of our Schools of Design, and to which they have afforded the highest encouragement. Nor may we omit to notice the new material employed by Mr. Battam, in the "Daphne," and the bust of "Her Majesty," and which promises successfully to compete with Parian, if not to supersede it in works of this character, in consequence of its small degree of contraction, producing a finer definition of its lines.

The Art Union exhibited, in this part of the nave, in its own trophy, proofs of the value of the stimulus it has afforded to art-design in connection with ceramic manufactures; of which the most beautiful products were presented in Armstead's "Satan Dismayed," Foley's "Youth at a Stream," and "Caractacus;" Chantry's bust of "Her Majesty," Marshall's "Dancing-Girl Reposing," Lawlor's "Solicitude," Flaxman's "Michael and Satan," and Wyon's "Stepping Stones."

The sideboard of Jackson and Graham, composed of pollard oak, and enriched by carvings in brown English oak, well deserved its prominent place in the British nave. How skilfully has the artist designed all the materials, and the pleasant accessories of a feast, and the dignity of the great lord by whose hospitality it is dispensed! The river and the sea, the field and the forest, are made to yield up their treasures; while sylvan boys are labouring, with hearty good-will, to gather in the grapes and other rich fruits that are to furnish the dessert.

As we have reached the Central Avenue, which divides the British from the Foreign departments, we will turn to our left, and go to the south entrance, in the Cromwell-road, whence we can look along this important avenue straight into the Horticultural Gardens, and, *en passant*, we can observe the more prominent objects that occupied this charming promenade; leaving, for a later notice, the great attractions on either side, and which belonged to the courts.

Beginning, then, at the southern end, we must record the great excellence of Benson's clock, the dial of which, as we have already mentioned, was placed over the Cromwell-road entrance. This Trophy Clock, which is valued at £3,000, is remarkable for the arrangement of the works, and the weights. The former, which were placed at a distance of 300 feet from the dial, and near the celebrated Gibson's tinted " Venus," were regarded as the finest clock-works that were ever produced in this country, the mechanism being adjusted with the accuracy of the finest chronometer. The weights, which amount to two tons, were placed in the eastern corner of the Exhibition; and it is scarcely necessary to remark, that as the machinery to connect these three elements of the clock—the dial, the wheel-work, and the weights—all had to pass under the floor of the building, the most accurate mechanism was required to secure the admirable performance by which this clock was distinguished. The five bells, recast by Messrs. Mears, besides being remarkable for the sweetness of their tones, had the great excellence of distinguishing each quarter of the hour by the peculiarity of their arrangement; so that those whose good fortune it is to live within sound of them, may always know the quarter they chime, even if they should forget to count them. It may be well also to add, that the pendulum, which is 15 feet long, vibrates once in two seconds; and, by means of a new double-lever *remontoir*, diminished the friction, so as to avoid all interference with the most satisfactory performance.

Near the entrance, in the Cromwell-road, stood the bronze colossal group of " Her Majesty, the late Prince Consort, and the Royal Children," by Mr. Durham; the busts being by Mrs. Thornycroft, whose admirable skill has secured a large amount of royal patronage. A peculiar and melancholy interest attaches to this celebrated group, which was designed for a memorial of the Exhibition in Hyde Park, having for its central figure the bronze statue of " Her Majesty;" while the Prince and the royal children were to be represented only in busts. This arrangement was changed by command of the Queen, who desired that the Prince should occupy the central figure.

The great attraction of the Central Avenue was the Grecian Temple, of which the tinted statue of the " Venus," was the principal feature, and on whose merits we have no wish to forestal the judgment of our readers. The perfection of the form presented by the triumphant goddess, as she holds her apple of discord in one hand, and the folds of her drapery in the other, admits of no dispute. The question for the public to decide, relates only to the effect of Mr. Gibson's experiment in adding the new element of colour to the sculptor's art. As we often gazed on this exquisite work—

perhaps the most successful production of our times—we had to listen to no small variety of opinions. Many a fair lady liked it; many thought it very pretty. As to the gentlemen, they were as much perplexed as Paris on Mount Ida—*tot homines tot sententiæ*. One of them, of a witty turn, resolved that the object was *marbleous;* a decision in which we are unable to concur, as the purity of the marble has been sacrificed by the tinting process of Mr. Gibson. Our readers must decide for themselves how much has been gained by the addition.

The Central Avenue had its other trophies, of a character about whose value there could be no dispute—the Cabinet of Imports into Liverpool, the Belfast Linen Trophy, the group of statuary in freestone, representing " Science and Practice equally Rewarded." Bearing in mind the miserable failure in the stone employed in the Houses of Parliament, we sincerely hope that the expectations formed of this Red Hall Freestone will be fully realised—that it will keep its colour, and prove to be most durable, *ære perennius*.

But we are now in the presence of another great work of the lamented Mr. Thomas—his " Shakspeare's Monument," of which we have given an illustration. If the artist assigned to his immortal subject an enormous bulk of material, it was only to suggest the great and growing space the poet fills in the minds of his countrymen, and of all people in whose language his imperishable works have been produced. There, on the summit of this noble monument, sits the Bard of Avon, having, on either side, the swan, which has become the emblem of his muse. The tragic and comic muses have taken their appropriate stand as the supporters of the monument, on which we have, in relief, a fine group of Shakspearian characters. The legend incised just above the plinth—" One touch of nature makes the whole world kin"—reminds us of one principal source of that ever-during popularity which attaches to the name of WILLIAM SHAKSPEARE, and will extend his fame to the remotest time

We have now arrived at the handsome Grecian vestibule that formed the entrance to the Horticultural Gardens, and of which our artist has preserved a faithful delineation. In this classical structure will be found some of the finest architectural details of a Grecian temple. The style we have employed is seen to great advantage in this illustration, in which the fine lines of the graver can be clearly traced; while the effects of light and shade are heightened by the neutral tints of chromo-lithography. The roof, divided into panels, highly enriched, is supported by clustered columns, and pilasters surmounted by Corinthian capitals; the whole forming a grand entrance to the gardens, into which the public passed through the three lofty arches in which the Central Avenue terminated.

We may next pursue our course through the foreign portion of the Nave, on our way to the Western Dome. Passing along the south side of the Nave, we had the great gratification, for the first time, to recognise a United Italy as an exhibitor. The great change which has passed over that land since the last Exhibition, has told, in a most remarkable manner, in the International Exhibition of 1862. Besides the statuary already noticed, the Italian portion of the Nave was rich in carved furniture, in glass candelabra, in vases of the purest design, and in Florentine mosaics. It is important to observe the difference between the Florentine and Roman mosaic; the

SHAKESPEARE'S MONUMENT BY THOMAS.

ENTRANCE TO THE HORTICULTURAL GARDENS FROM THE EXHIBITION.

latter being composed of minute tesseræ of stone, varied in form, but mostly angular; by the combination of which, the flowers and fruits, and all other objects are produced; while, in the mosaic of Florence, a figure is formed of one coloured piece, the *pietra dura* of the Florentine artist. The principal attraction of the Italian portion of the nave, consisted of works thus formed, by Barbensi, Torrini, and Viecchi of Florence. Italian artists indulge in more of romantic fancies than would be quite acceptable among our matter-of-fact countrymen. Candelabra, rich with prisms and stars, have adorned the Exhibition; but an English artist would be regarded as half-crazed if he made a candelabrum whose branches were formed of the bodies of grotesque-looking reptiles, having the sockets for the lights sunk in their heads. Such, however, were the candelabra in the Italian nave.

Among the beautiful productions in the Italian portion of the nave, was a mosaic table, exhibited by Dr. Salviati, of Venice, executed in the Venetian style—the price of which was 1,400 guineas—having for its subject the figure of the Redeemer, placed behind the altar-piece of the church of St. Mark, in Venice.

The trophies displayed by Spain in the nave, might be regarded as very fair exponents of the resources and characteristics of that kingdom, ranging as they did from the rich mineral treasures beneath the ground, to the models of the amusements to which the people are devoted; and among them that barbarous institution, the bull-fight, which we hope will be speedily doomed to destruction. The mineral treasures of Spain were displayed in great variety, and could not but excite much attention from the important fact that the railways, now in course of formation, must develop them, and render them sources of wealth, not only to Spain, but to our own, and every country to which they will be exported. Among the specimens of these valuable products, were coal, iron, copper, quicksilver, barytes, galenas, magnetic iron, cinnabar, native sulphur, antimony, nickel, salt in various states, marbles in great variety, and—not now to mention more—kaolin, a material which is being turned to good account in the manufacture of china. The trophy of arms included a rifled brass gun, made at Barcelona, but not remarkable for the high finish of its workmanship. There were saddles of exquisite beauty; and military accoutrements, on which much skill had been expended. Spain also showed a remarkably rich inkstand, the property of the Queen Isabella, with iron for the base, and inlaid with gold and silver. Various articles of this Damascene manufacture were shown, by no means attractive in appearance, but, at the same time, too costly to come much into use. The staple of cork appeared in some very beautiful models; and the industrial skill of Spain, in watches, pianos, articles of clothing, and very finely carved furniture, among which a rich side-board held a deservedly conspicuous place. The Spanish wood trophy was also rich and varied.

The great trophy of France might be described either as a screen, or as the grand gate of entrance into the French court. Messrs. Barbezat, of Val d'Ozne, displayed the finest taste in the design, and skill in the execution of this magnificent work; 148½ feet in length, and 25 feet high; formed wholly of cast iron, and serving to display the magnificent works of other exhibitors. The whole work was divided into three principal portions, and the ends were supported by lions on granite pedestals. The central portion was filled with a magnificent plate of glass, 16½ feet high, and 10½ feet broad, manufactured at St. Gobain; whose productions in plate glass are of the highest character—or key, to speak with technical propriety.

The tapestry hung on this magnificent screen displayed the great eminence which France has attained in this favourite art. Messrs. Braquenié, of Aubusson, hung up that exquisite work of "La Belle au Bois Dormant," in which the princess is represented waking up from her sleep, surrounded by a well-arranged group. The greatest praise has been bestowed on the border, which appears as if enriched by pearls, rubies, sapphires, and gold, all obeying the will of the artist.

Few of our readers can have failed to admire the elaborately executed ebony cabinet, placed beneath this tapestry. On the top are the figures of "Peace and Plenty;" the sides are enriched with figures of "Mars and Minerva;" on the upper folding doors are "Apollo and Diana;" and beneath them the "Rape of Proserpine." The whole work is covered with the most elaborate and beautiful carving, the effect of which is heightened by tablets of lapiz lazuli and blood-stone. We must notice, also, the great carved oak mantelpiece, which, as well as the preceding work, was exhibited by M. Fourdinois. In this elaborate work we see how French artists excel in producing a lively effect by the combination of different materials. Here *verde antique* and ormolu are united with oak, as a sort of base, in producing a work in which we have rarely found more than a single element; and still greater variety will distinguish this admirable work when the cornice and frieze are adorned with bronze. The "Hunting Scene," the figures of "Night and Morning," and the beautiful "Cupids," on the pediment, will never fail to renew the admiration which this production has excited among the thousands who have gazed upon it.

The decorations of satin damask, displayed on the western portion of the great French screen, were most beautiful in design, and rich in colour. Another mantelpiece, in marble and bronze, conceived in pure classical taste, and executed with the utmost artistic skill, formed an admirable counterpart to the work we have already noticed. This production of M. Eugene Piat was one of several, which displayed the taste of this distinguished artist, and the determination of France to give a higher elaboration to her works of industrial art.

The remaining portion of the south side of the nave was occupied with the productions of the Zollverein; a large portion being assigned to Prussia, the grandeur of whose capital was significantly represented by a model of the new Exchange at Berlin. The articles displayed in this portion of the building, will come sufficiently under our notice when we describe the courts and the classes.

We, therefore, now ascend the western daïs, which was occupied by treasures enough to render it one of the most attractive portions of the whole building The magnificent plate, presented by the city of Berlin to the Crown Prince and Princess of Prussia, on their marriage, could not but afford the highest pleasure to all who saw it, especially to the English people, who were gratified in witnessing this demonstration of the honour done to a beloved English princess. These splendid presents consist of silver candelabra, a table, a magnificent vase, and the celebrated Rhine shield. The former magnificent group is admirably commemorative of the royal marriage, and in the latter the four Rhenish provinces are historically depicted, offering their congratulations to the royal pair. The arms of all the subscribers to this costly present are figured in enamel round the rim of the shield, and add considerably to the fine effect of this elaborate work. The same exhibitors produced also the wedding presents from twenty-seven departments of Hessia, in the possession of the Grand Duke, and consisting of a dinner-service, in which, besides the table-service, there were four chandeliers with thirteen branches, and other rich silver ornaments.

Instead of lingering among the crowds always congregated on this favourite spot, we must be content just to notice the remaining objects it presented, leaving them for as full a description as our space will afford, in the classes to which they belong. It will be enough to enumerate the Prussian Breech-loading Steel Gun; the Arms' Trophy; the Telegraph Apparatus; the rich display of dressing-cases, and lamps of Austria; the shawls and woollens from Vienna; the Berlin lace; the walking-sticks from Hamburg; the Bohemian woollen manufactures; and the attractive collection of useful and ornamental works in buckhorn; the grand display of porcelain and china, of all the finest kinds, from Sèvres, Dresden, Vienna, and Berlin, to which the king of Prussia liberally contributed—all advanced by the stimulus of 1851 and 1855; and the greatest of all albums, now happily in possession of the city of London. Let us not omit that richly-carved Belgian pulpit, only a specimen of the elaborate carving expended on the pulpits of Belgium; and from which it is easy to imagine the faithful preacher looking over the costly display, and expounding to his vast congregation that ancient truthful text, "Vanity of vanities, all is vanity." For the present, we need say nothing of the organs, either Hedgland's or Walker's, which have had so many opportunities to speak for themselves.

We have yet to complete our survey of the Nave, where there were many things to admire, and others very unworthy of the noble sites they were permitted to occupy. Something approaching to a universal feeling of disgust was excited by the four collections of candles which were allowed to disfigure this important portion of the Nave; and the feeling was the more just, as the productions displayed were not of the new and beautiful quality—the Paraffine, exhibited in the Eastern Annexe. In one case, the coarse articles were so disposed as to resemble the pipes on the exterior of an organ; and in various ways they were formed into fantastic devices, but without, in any case, affording the least gratification to the millions before whom they were paraded. From these rude things it is not easy to make a transition to the plate-glass, for which Belgium has long been famous, and still has just cause to be proud; to the silver and diamonds shown by Holland; the carved work of Switzerland; the porcelain and sculptures of Denmark; the zinc, iron, and granite works of Sweden; the sledges, anchors, and minerals of Norway; among which was the famous block of silica; and the imperial trophies of Russian art.

Still, we must notice the noble collection of gems shown by Holland, the glory of which was the brilliant, found in Brazil, since 1851. This "Star of the South" is valued at one million sterling; and fortunate were they who saw it in the earlier days of the Exhibition, before the fears of the Company, who are its possessors, caused it to be removed, and replaced by a copy in glass.

The "Star of the South" was placed amidst a highly valuable collection of diamonds from different mines, and showing the various processes of the lapidary, as these most precious of stones pass from the rough state in which they are found, until they are cut and polished.

This may, perhaps, be the most suitable place in which to insert a brief description of the various forms into which diamonds are cut. A valuable pamphlet, recently printed for private circulation, says—" The two most common (forms) are the ' brilliant,' and the ' rose,' or ' rosette.' The latter, so named from its similarity to an unopened rosebud, was one of the earliest forms in use, and is applied generally to the cheaper form of stones. It is a sort of pyramid, with a flat base and inclined facets, terminating upward in a pointed apex. The flat base is imbedded in the setting; and, therefore, in the rose diamond, the whole of the stone appears projecting above. The ' brilliant' is the more valuable form; it may be considered as formed of two pyramids connected at their bases, with the apex of each truncated, or cut off, and the sides worked into facets, as in the case of the rose. The stone is held in the setting, or broadest part, or junction of the pyramids; one pyramid spreads upwards in sight, the other is hidden below, so that only half the stone, or somewhat less, appears; but the hidden part is most powerfully effective in adding to the brilliancy. The apex of the upper pyramid is cut off to a considerable extent; and the large facet, thus formed, is called the *table:* the corresponding facet below, formed by the truncation of the lower, or hidden pyramid, is much smaller, and is called the *collet.* The rim, where the setting takes hold, or, as we have described it, the junction of the basis of the pyramids, is called the *girdle.* There are thirty-two facets cut round the upper slanting of the surface of the stone—*i.e.*, between the girdle and the table; and twenty-four on the lower part, between the girdle and the collet. All these facets have names by which they are known to the cutters; and all the dimensions of the stone should, in order to produce the best effect, bear certain definite proportions to each other. The most favourable form of brilliant for exhibiting the lustre of the stone, is considered to be a square, having the corners slightly rounded off; but, of course, many stones will not admit of being cut to this form without loss; therefore round, oval, pear-shapes, &c., are, perhaps, more common. The stones lose about fifty per cent. in cutting, more or less; so that, to make a brilliant of one carat, a rough stone of two carats is required." It will be remembered that the Koh-i-Noor lost only $80\frac{1}{2}$ carats, out of $186\frac{1}{2}$, in its recutting; and it may be here added, that in colour it very far exceeds the " Star of the South."

The author of *Diamonds* also informs us, that " diamond-cutting, in the present day, is almost exclusively done by Jews at Amsterdam, where large diamond mills have been established; and it is calculated that 10,000, out of the 28,000 persons out of the persuasion living in that city, are dependent, directly or indirectly, on this branch of industry."

The Russian Trophy of 1862, like that of 1851, told of the great wealth and luxury of the imperial and the noble, and the absence of a prosperous middle class, to whom the manufacturer devotes his capital and the skill of his *employés.* Instead of again seeing those malachite doors, which drew forth the world's admiration, we had works of less magnitude, but of enormous cost. Russia is rich in porphyry, nephrite, jasper, lapiz lazuli, and many other materials admirably adapted for vases, obelisks, candelabra, busts, and the various objects that may be brought into shape by long years of hard labour; and the trophy of 1862 served to show how that labour is available for supplying the demands of imperial luxury. There was exhibited a Porphyry Vase, on which was an inscription, stating that it was begun in 1856, and finished at the close of 1861; a long time, in our estimation, but moderate in a country where a quarter of a century has not been deemed too long for the production of a single vase. This trophy was rich also in Florentine and Roman mosaics; and in a species in which Russia excels every other country. The mosaic in relief, copies, in the hardest stones, a variety of natural objects, which are imitated with the most perfect success. Currants, grapes, raspberries, apples and pears, are among the objects which might well deceive the sharpest eye.

This magnificent Russian Trophy included a number of well-executed bronzes; among which was a noble colossal statue of " Catherine II.," by Felix Chopin, imparting a vivid idea of the imperious lady who presided with such energy over the destinies of her vast empire. Russia, so famous for its porcelain vases, exhibited two of the finest of these productions: one containing a copy of Vandyke's painting of " Inigo Jones," and the other, Kneller's portrait of " John Locke;" and both designed for presentation to the Royal Society. We must not overlook the exquisite Nephrite Vase, five feet in diameter, whose handles are decorated with sculptured faces, most beautifully finished.

The Siberian Trophy, of plumbago (blacklead), exhibited this valuable mineral in large blocks, and in a variety of forms; in its native crudeness, and with the lustrous polish it imparts to other things, and of which it is itself susceptible. It was shown also in its various stages of preparation, until it reaches the point of perfection, in the blacklead pencil. At a time when this necessary product is dying out, in its old sources, in our country, it is gratifying to know that it is found in large quantities in Siberia. The Plumbago Trophy was accompanied by diagrams and drawings, showing the appearance of the country in which the mineral lies, a section of a blacklead mine, and the various uses to which it may be applied. It may yet be a long time before we shall want some inventive genius to give us a substitute for this important mineral, or repeat the natural process by which it is formed.

As the Western Transept, on each side of the western daïs, was occupied by the Zollverein and Austrian courts, we leave them for the present unexamined, and conclude our Walk through the Nave, by noticing some of the more attractive objects in the Eastern Transept, and which may be regarded as trophies, rather than as belonging to the various classes. Both Annexes will come under the class divisions to which they were appropriated.

The " Hereford Cathedral Screen," designed by G. G. Scott, Esq., R.A., and manufactured by Skidmore's Art Manufacture Company, was the principal decoration of the Eastern Transept. It is unnecessary to deduct anything from the praise bestowed on this beautiful production, soon after it was submitted to the public judgment, when every art critic made it the subject of his highest laudation. For the last twenty years, the greatest exertions have been made for the restoration of Hereford Cathedral; and it must afford the highest gratification to those who have so earnestly carried on the work, to have secured for the venerable edifice this appropriate decoration. In a most skilful manner, Mr. Scott has so designed his screen, as to blend into a whole his double arcade of five primary, and ten secondary arches, leaving to each part its own individuality. From the lofty centre arch, surmounted by the figure of the Saviour, to those smaller arches of the praying angels, we see one great design well carried out, of which it has been correctly said, that all the figures can be understood at a glance, without the aid of any inscription beneath the feet to set forth who and what they are. The screen claims our admiration for its size, being thirty-six feet long, and thirty-five high; "the largest piece of architectural metal work ever executed." It is admirable, also, for its combination of metals, consisting principally of iron, with brass and copper in the decorative details; the copper producing a beautiful result in its natural colour; while the effect of the brass is heightened by its intermixture with glass mosaic, and the addition of colour and gilding. This superb work will not be lost sight of by day or night, as might be learned from the beautiful gas corona which hung over it in the Exhibition, and will shed light upon it in the Cathedral of Hereford.

Towards the closing days of the Exhibition, a most valuable addition was made to the Eastern Transept, by Messrs. Defries, who erected there their magnificent Crystal Candelabrum. This noble pile of crystal seemed as if built up by fairy hands, which delighted to show all the beautiful effects this transparent material can produce. Based on a concave foot, hexagonal in form, and seven feet in diameter, the candelabrum towers to the height of twenty-two feet, throwing out eighteen crystal arms, for the support of as many gas-lamps. From the base rises a shaft, which is one large cylinder of glass, richly cut in flutes, and rows of diamonds, alternately; the whole being surmounted with a solid mass of the purest glass, cut like a pine-apple, and supporting a spire. The intermediate stages are so treated as to present nearly every form of beauty which the fragile material can assume, and to impart to it a perfect unity of design. The base of the main structure is composed of four rows of star-cut prisms; immediately above which are six large panels, tapering upwards, into which are let three large shields of cut-glass. Above is a magnificent dome, formed of cut bent prisms; over which is a fine tulip-shaped glass, feather-cut, and supporting a large cylinder, fluted and cut in diamond pattern. Another important feature is a great bowl, three feet in diameter—one of the largest pieces of work of its kind ever produced; and connected with which there is another tier of arms for lights; while another similar bowl bears the same relation to the upper tier of lights. Surmounting the whole is a cushion in crystal glass, sparkling with diamonds, having four crystal tassels and prisms, so falling as to represent fringe. On this cushion rests the royal crown, enriched with all its royal insignia—the *fleur-de-lis*, the Maltese cross brilliant with diamonds, the rich cut arches, and the oak-leaves, studded with diamonds and pearls. We may venture to ask that this praiseworthy production may hereafter be submitted to public inspection, as it was taken into the Exhibition too late to elicit the award of the jurors, or the approval of the visitors.

No one could look without some curiosity on the various specimens of steel manufacture, exhibited by Mr. Bessemer; among which was a portion of a rail, twisted as if it had been a hempen cable; and a huge bar, bent like a pair of sugar-tongs. These strange forms were impressed on the metal not only when it was perfectly cold, but when the ice lay thick about the ground. We have been accustomed to consider steel nearly as brittle as glass; but, as Mr. Bessemer tells us, "improvements in its manufacture have from time to time been introduced, and steel of a milder and less brittle character has long been made, capable of welding with facility, and working at a high temperature, without falling to pieces. Its uses have consequently been greatly extended, and the employment of cast steel for the best cutlery and edge-tools has now become universal." To Mr. Bessemer himself we are indebted for a process in the manufacture of steel, which secures some most important improvements in the metal, especially in the quality of softness; while the method he adopts greatly expedites the work of production, and dispenses with the necessity for many intermediate stages which have formerly been deemed necessary, and are at present in operation. This new process provides us with cast steel without requiring the use of wrought iron as its material, and thus dispenses with the lengthened processes of melting, refining, puddling, hammering, and rolling, which are employed in converting crude pig iron into a bar of malleable iron. Hitherto all these processes have been gone through for the purpose of driving all the carbon out of iron, and then of restoring to the metal a portion of the carbon, which is essential to the production of steel. If we speak of crude iron as containing five per cent. of carbon, we must regard the processes of steel manufacture as employed, first, to drive out the whole of the carbon, and then to restore to it one per cent. of that element. Mr. Bessemer says, instead of driving off these five portions of carbon, and afterwards restoring one, you had better drive off only four, and you gain your result in a more simple, direct, rapid, and, consequently, less expensive manner. This is really the *rationale* of the Bessemer method, which is silently revolutionising the process of steel manufacture, and must command the approval of every one who will take a little trouble to understand it.

To perceive the value of the Bessemer process, it will be necessary, first, to have some acquaintance with the method usually employed in the conversion of wrought iron into steel; of which Huntsman's process is, to say the least, one of the most approved, and very extensively practised. It should be remembered that the metal has previously passed through prolonged and expensive stages of preparation, to bring it from the condition of crude iron.

"In order to convert the wrought iron bars into blister steel, they are packed with powdered charcoal in large firebrick chests, and are exposed to a white heat for several days; the time required for heating and cooling them extending over a period of fifteen to twenty days. When thus converted into blister steel, they are broken into small pieces, and sorted according to the quality of the steel, which sometimes differs even in the same bar. For melting this material, powerful air furnaces are employed, containing two crucibles, into each of which are put about 40 lbs. of the broken blistered steel. In about three hours the pots are removed from the furnaces, and the melted steel is poured into iron moulds, and formed into ingots of cast steel, from 3½ to 4 tons of hard coke being consumed for each ton of metal thus melted. When large masses of steel are required, a great many crucibles must be got ready all at the same moment, and a continuous stream of the melted metal from the several crucibles must be kept up until the ingot is completed, since any cessation of the pouring would entirely spoil it: hence, in proportion to the size of the ingot, are the cost and risk of its production increased. The ordinary manufacture of cast steel is therefore obviously conducted at a great disadvantage. If cast steel is to supersede wrought iron for engineering purposes, it will be necessary to cease employing wrought iron as a raw material for this otherwise most expensive mode of manufacture."

Mr. Bessemer thus describes his own process, which can be sufficiently understood without the diagrams to which he refers in his pamphlet.

"Before commencing with the first charge of metal, the interior of the converting vessel is thoroughly heated by coke, with a blast through the tuyeres to urge the fire; when sufficiently heated it is turned upside down, and all the unburnt coke falls out. The blast now rushes upwards into the fluid metal from each of the forty-nine holes of the tuyeres, producing a most violent agitation of the whole mass. The silicium, always present in greater or less quantities in pig iron, is first attacked, and unites readily with the oxygen of the air, producing silicic acid: at the same time a small portion of the iron undergoes oxidation, and hence a fluid silicate of the oxide of iron is formed, a little carbon being simultaneously burnt off. The heat is thus gradually increased until nearly the whole of the silicium is oxidised, which generally takes place in about twelve minutes from the commencement of the process. The carbon of the pig iron now begins to unite more freely with the oxygen of the air, producing at first a small flame, which rapidly increases; and in about three minutes from its first appearance a most intense combustion is going on: the metal rises higher and higher in the vessel, sometimes occupying more than double its former space; and in this frothy fluid state it presents an enormous surface to the action of the air, which unites rapidly with the carbon contained in the crude iron, and produces a most intense combustion, the whole mass being in fact a perfect mixture of metal and fire. The carbon is now burnt off so rapidly as to produce a series of harmless explosions, throwing out the fluid slag in great quantities; while the combustion of the gases is so perfect that a voluminous white flame rushes from the mouth of the vessel, illuminating the whole building, and indicating to the practised eye the precise condition of the metal inside. The blowing may thus be left off whenever the number of minutes from the commencement and the appearance of the flame indicate the required quality of metal. This is the mode preferred in working the process in Sweden. But at the works in Sheffield it is preferred to continue blowing the metal beyond this stage, until the flame suddenly drops, which it does just on the approach of the metal to the condition of malleable iron: a small measured quantity of charcoal pig iron, containing a known proportion of carbon, is then added, and thus steel is produced of any desired degree of carburation, the process having occupied about twenty-eight minutes altogether from the commencement. The converting vessel is tipped forwards, and the blast shut off for adding this small charge of pig iron, after which the blast is turned on again for a few seconds.

"By this process, from one to ten tons of crude iron may be converted into cast steel in thirty minutes, without employing any fuel except that required for melting the pig iron, and for the preliminary heating of the converting vessel, the process being effected entirely without manipulation. The loss on the weight of crude iron is from 14 to 18 per cent., with English iron worked in small quantities; but the result of working with a purer iron in Sweden has been carefully noted for two consecutive weeks, and the loss on the weight of fluid iron tapped from the blast furnace, was ascertained to be only $8\frac{3}{4}$ per cent. The largest sized apparatus at present erected is that in use at the Atlas Steel Works, Sheffield, the converting vessel being capable of converting four tons at a time, which it converts into cast steel in twenty-eight minutes. In consequence of the increased size of the converting vessel in this case, no metal is thrown out during conversion; and the loss of weight has fallen as low as 10 per cent., including the loss in melting the pig iron in the reverberatory furnace."

This South-East Transept was the region of gates, great clocks, and bells. We must not forget the Coalbrook Dale Gates, and the Falkirk Iron-work Gates, which are fine specimens of cast iron work, rich in pattern, and faultless in execution: but the bells were so many, so varied in quality of tone, and so sweet in effect, that they seemed to transport us into that Canadian region celebrated by Edgar Poe, where, through the long night, they are heard—

> "Keeping time, time, time,
> In a sort of Runic rhyme,
> To the tintinnabulation of the music as it wells,
> From the bells, bells, bells, bells,
> Bells, bells, bells,
> From the jingling, and the tingling of the bells."

Messrs. Warner have the merit of introducing a new Chiming Apparatus, by which a lad may correctly play a great variety of chimes on peals of six, eight, or more bells, though he may have no knowledge of musical time. The hammers are so fixed as in no way to prevent the ringing of the bells, by regular bell-ringers, when their services can be obtained. As the good old institution of the bell-ringers' supper will not be damaged by this innovation, we must deprecate any clamour about violated rights on the part of the fraternity; for this invention " is not intended to take the place of ringing," being recommended " only for parishes where there are no good and steady ringers." Warner & Co. apply the principle of the barrel-organ to bell-ringing, and thus obtain their result by a simple but effective process.

The North-East Transept was given up to the British Colonies, whose productions will hereafter come under our notice. There was at one end the famous organ of Foster and Andrews, of Hull, which never failed to attract a large crowd of much-delighted listeners to the elaborate apparatus, the great powers of which will, perhaps, be understood by the following account of its elements:—It has forty-six registers, 2,475 pipes, six composition pedals, two sforzando pedals, and one pneumatic combination pedal. It is 30 feet high, 22 feet wide, and 14 feet deep. The pneumatic movement was applied to the great and pedal organs, and there were four pressures of wind. The bellows were blown by two of Jay's hydraulic engines, having a water pressure of 35 lbs. to the square inch.

Passing to the northern end of this Transept, we reach the case in which Messrs. Bell, of Newcastle, exhibited many exquisite specimens of the metal Aluminium, which has become known to the public since the Exhibition of 1851. The following are the properties of Aluminium, which have already commended it to public favour, and will secure its extensive application for useful and ornamental purposes. It is extremely light, its specific gravity being 2·6—about that of glass; while that of platinum is 21·5; and that of silver 10·5. It will thus be seen, that in comparing it with silver, the bulk of a given weight of Aluminium is nearly four times as great as that of silver. It is malleable and ductile; it can be reduced to very thin sheets, or drawn into very fine threads. Its tenacity is superior to that of silver; and, in a state of purity, it is as hard as that metal. It files readily, and is an excellent conductor of electricity. In air and oxygen it undergoes no sensible alteration. It is not affected by sulphur, or sulphuretted hydrogen, like silver. The vegetable acids have no effect upon it. It forms a variety of alloys, the most striking of which are those with copper; which are very hard, and capable of a fine polish, the colour varying from deep to pale gold. A very important property of this new metal is its sonorousness. An ingot of Aluminium, if suspended by a fine wire, and struck with a smart blow, emits a very clear and sharp sound; in consequence of which, it is already, and probably will soon be very extensively, applied to musical instruments. The price of Aluminium, which a few years ago was £60 per lb., is now only as many shillings—i.e., 60s. per lb.

As the greatest interest attaches to this newly discovered mineral, the following facts respecting it cannot but prove interesting. First, as to its discovery in 1827, before which time it was unknown as a metallic base:—

"Aluminium was discovered by Professor Woehler, of Goettingen, in 1827; and Professor Deville, of Paris, was led to the investigation of the characteristics of the new body, and to the discovery of some very curious properties. His first impression on their appearance was, that he had placed his hand on a metal destined to occupy

I

the intermediate position in the requirements of mankind, as soon as the means were found of removing it from the laboratory of the chemist to the workshops of the manufacturers. This prevision, which appears to realise itself every day, and the present state of the production of Aluminium, confirm entirely the conclusions set forth in his first account of this metal, published in the beginning of 1855.

"The following is a literal quotation of the opinions alluded to :—'From the facts related, I conclude that Aluminium is a metal destined to become one of the useful class, from its curious properties, by its power of under-going no change in colour or lustre by the action of the air, or of air charged with sulphuretted hydrogen ; by its resistance to the action of all acids, save hydrochloric ; by its fusibility ; by its beautiful colour, and its physical properties generally. Its density, so low as to be scarcely equal to that of glass, will insure for this metal special applications. Intermediate between the common and the precious metals, from certain properties it possesses, Aluminium is superior to the first group for domestic purposes, by the absolute inocuousness of its compounds with the feebler acids. When it is further remembered that Aluminium exists in considerable proportions in all clays, amounting in some cases to one-fourth of the weight of a very widely diffused substance, one cannot do otherwise than hope that, sooner or later, this metal may find a place in the industrial arts."

Then, as to the great advantage of its composition with other metals :—

"Aluminium, alloyed with 2 per cent. of Nickel, becomes less blue in colour, is harder, and rather more difficult to forge than pure Aluminium. For this purpose it must be heated to a dull red ; while pure Aluminium can be hammered with facility at a temperature sufficient to redden paper.

"The compound which Aluminium forms with Copper is especially worthy of notice. When these metals are alloyed in the proportions of one of Aluminium to nine of Copper, the bronze so obtained possesses great malleability and strength. Professor Gordon ascertained, that with wires of the same diameter, the strength of copper, iron, and Aluminium Bronze stood in the following relation to each other :—

Iron	. . . .	100
Aluminium Bronze	. . . .	155
Copper	. . . .	68

"Three compounds can be formed with Copper, distinct in their colours and properties.

"The first contains 5 per cent. of Aluminium, is of a beautiful gold colour, and takes a splendid polish. It is of great malleability ; and by being hammered, when cold, acquires great hardness, and a grain similar to that of copper.

"The second contains 7½ per cent. Aluminium ; is of that greenish gold colour which is known to be the result of an alloy of gold with silver ; it is very fibrous and malleable when cold, acquiring, like the bronze of 5 per cent. when hammered cold, great hardness. It is capable of a very beautiful polish.

"The third compound of Copper and Aluminium contains 10 per cent. Aluminium. It possesses great malleability and strength. These are much increased by a moderate amount of hammering when cold ; after which, owing to the greatly augmented hardness of the alloy, further action of the hammer becomes useless.

"At a red heat it very readily admits of being forged and rolled ; and if, when well heated to redness, it be left to cool down in the air to a dull red, and be then plunged into water, it becomes sufficiently malleable, when cold, to bear, without fracture, every kind of manipulation practised in the industrial arts.

"The several kinds of Aluminium Bronze melt at the same temperature as Copper. Plumbago crucibles should be used, and on no account any flux. A small piece of charcoal may be put on the top of the metal in fusion."

PRINCIPLES OF CLASSIFICATION—DISTRIBUTIONS—THE COURTS AND GALLERIES.

As we have already seen, the Commissioners of the Exhibition of 1862, found it altogether impracticable to arrange in classes all the multifarious objects entrusted to their care, so as to afford to visitors the opportunity of entering any particular class, and comparing the products sent to that class from all parts of the world. Each country claimed that its nationality should be represented—we will not assert for the gratification of vanity—but from various motives of a more excusable kind ; and, as the consequence, the whole contents of the Exhibition were distributed so as to effect a sort of compromise between the scientific and geographical principles of arrangement. An important advantage was, by this compromise, secured to the general public, for whom these national distinctions had a peculiar charm; while practical persons were able to pursue their investigations under some difficulties, which, however, could be surmounted by persevering effort.

It must be observed, also, that the classification of the Commissioners was not perfect in its character—a defect which does not imply any censure on the intelligence of those gentlemen and their officers; but is referred to, simply to show that it is next to impossible to classify a vast multitude of objects so as always to find the right thing in the right place, and at the same time render the distribution pleasing and satisfactory to the observer.

Nothing could appear more simple and systematic than the division into the four sections of—I. Raw Materials; II. Machinery; III. Manufactures; IV. Fine Arts: and yet it is obvious, that this division, in its practical working, proved inaccurate and defective. For instance, we ask why all the beautiful productions of Class XXXII., "Works in Precious Metals, their Imitations, and Jewellery," should be excluded from Section IV. of Fine Arts, and be reckoned only as "Manufactures?" Why should "The Slave," in ivory, or "The Child of Nature," in bronze, or the *repoussé* silver tazzi of "Night" and "Morning," be regarded only as manufactures, in the same section as "Cotton," "Flax and Hemp;" while works displaying no more taste, or artistic skill, though sculptured in marble, hold their high place in the section of the Fine Arts? The time has arrived when the boundary lines that separate between Manufactures and the Fine Arts must be revised; and it may be hoped that such a revision will be expedited by the incongruities to which the present division has, in so many instances, given rise in the late Exhibition. For the present, an engraving on a copper plate belongs to the Fine Arts; while the poetry of art, if expended on an Apollo, or a Venus, in silver, is a "manufacture," a "work in precious metals." Some feeble attempts were made to invade this order of things, which it would have been quite practicable to revolutionise, at the late World's Exhibition.

It will be seen, also, in looking into the contents of the first section of raw materials, that it embraces many manufactures which belong to Section III. The difficulty to which we allude was felt by the Jurors themselves; who state, that "a numerous collection of our most beautiful British marbles were catalogued in Class I., but afterwards handed over for adjudication to another class, from their having been manufactured into vases, inlaid tables, &c." Still we find the Jurors of this class dealing with mill-stones and grindstones, giving medals for "crucibles of graphite," for "Cornish crucibles," and for "a most elaborate piece of Derbyshire inlaid work, showing the great variety of mineral substances which may be employed in this kind of ornamentation, and the delicacy with which they admit of being cut into fine strips, and fitted."

We must, however, be content to follow the method laid down by the Commissioners, without attempting to readjust their plan; as any advantage that might accrue from a new arrangement, would fail to compensate for facility of reference. We shall therefore preserve the principles of classification adopted by the Commissioners.

Having a due respect to the compromise between the geographical and classification method which prevailed throughout the Exhibition, we shall, in the further prosecution of our work, first glance at the leading characteristics of each court, and afterwards review the whole collection, in the classes to which the various specimens belonged, having especial reference to the important work of comparison. Thus we shall traverse the Courts and Galleries, British and Foreign, and recall to the mind of the reader the scenes through which he passed, assuming that he was careful to follow a judicious plan, to economise time and strength, and do something like justice to the vast treasures spread out before him. We shall first examine—

The Courts and Galleries of Great Britain and her Colonies, beginning with the South Courts.

1. Civil Engineering; Architectural and Building Contrivances.

Supposing the visitor again to start from the daïs beneath the Eastern Dome, he will have to traverse the space enclosed by the Exhibition-road to the south-east corner, and the Cromwell-road as far as the Central Tower, and by the South Central Avenue as far as the Nave, which will bring him back to his original stand-point. If we send him also into the Galleries included in this space, he will have seen the principal objects exhibited by Great Britain. Let him make a second tour, through the corresponding portion of the edifice, being on the northern side, including the Eastern Annexe, and he would find himself among the Colonies and Dependencies of Great Britain, the mother country still holding place among her children in the large space devoted to furniture on the ground floor, as well as in the Galleries.

Passing first into the South Court, from the eastern daïs, the visitor would be surrounded by objects relating to civil engineering, architectural and building contrivances, all belonging to Class X.; and embracing the sub-class A, the sub-class B (sanitary improvements and construction), and sub-class C (objects shown for architectural beauty). The exhibitors in this class were 164, to whom a space was allotted of 13,962 square feet.

Bridges, displaying the greatest skill in their contrivance and execution, were here represented by several well-executed models, which, while assisting the engineer to perceive the principles of their construction, had a very pleasing effect for the general observer. There were models of the bridges at Chepstow and at Saltash, exhibited by Mr. Brunel; of the Clifton Bridge, by Messrs. Hawkshaw; the Boyne Viaduct, by Sir John Macneill; Mr. Bouch's bridge over the Valley of the Beelah, in Westmorland; of the bridges on the Central Indian Railway, by Colonel Kennedy; of the Viaduct across the Lune, by Mr. J. C. Errington; and a wrought iron girder bridge, supported on rollers, adapted for carrying railways or roads at a low level over navigable watercourses. In all the structures represented by these models, we have satisfactory proof of the progress of engineering science in our times, and of the ability of our countrymen successfully to compete with other countries in meeting the requirements of our railway age.

The late Mr. I. K. Brunel had to deal with a great difficulty in bridging over the Tamar, at Saltash, as it was necessary, in erecting the central deep-water pier, to sink to the depth of 82 feet, passing through a depth of soft mud to reach the underlying rock. This was accomplished by the aid of a wrought iron cylinder of 37 feet diameter, and 90 feet in height, which was forced down to the rock by the joint forces of gravitation and atmospheric pressure. To sink this cylinder, construct the foundation of masonry, to erect upon it the iron columns, and lift the tubes into position, were operations requiring no small skill; but they were successfully performed by Mr. Brereton, the able assistant of Mr. Brunel. The importance of this achievement, and of a similar success at Chepstow, will be seen from the fact that they were mentioned among the claims of the late Mr. Brunel to the medal awarded to his son as his representative. Both these bridges combine wrought and cast iron in their materials; the former in their superstructure, and the latter in their columns; while they combine the insistent and suspension principles in each work—a union which, however, was not deemed essential in either case.

The model of the Viaduct over the Boyne, near Drogheda, on the line of the Dublin and Belfast Railway, is the finest illustration of the lattice principle in the United Kingdom, and confers the highest credit on Sir John Macneill, by whom it was designed, and under whose direction it was constructed. Its total length is 1,750 feet, crossing the Boyne at a height of 90 feet from the water, in what is termed a " skeleton tube," through which the trains pass. Structures on this principle have been for some time employed in America, where they have been formed of wood; but it is the merit of Sir John Macneill that he has applied this principle in wrought iron, by which he has successfully combined the elements of lightness and strength with a due regard to economy. The total weight of iron work in the girders, and the line of rails, does not exceed 700 tons; although, in addition to the length already mentioned, we may add, that the span of the central opening is 264 feet, and the two side ones 138 feet 8 inches each.

The iron trellis principle is shown in the model of Mr. Bouch's bridge over the valley of the Beelah river, in Westmorland, on the South Durham and Lancashire Union Railway. This bridge, which is 1,000 feet long, and 200 feet high in the centre, affords a remarkable illustration of the rapidity with which a great work on this principle may be carried out, being completed in only four months.

A further application of this lattice principle was shown by Lieutenant-Colonel Kennedy, in a model of the bridges on the Bombay, Baroda, and Central Indian railways. In these bridges the piers are formed of cast iron columns, resting on screw piles firmly fixed in the bed of the river. For the extensive application of this method, a medal was awarded to Colonel Kennedy.

It is somewhat satisfactory to find that the long-delayed project of bridging over the Avon, at Clifton, is at last about to be realised, of which we have a promise in the model shown by Mr. Hawkshaw. The suspension bridge at the late Hungerford Market, is to span the distance of 703 feet over this chasm; and the work, when completed, may justly be regarded as a great triumph of our engineering skill.

As we have heard much of a proposal for uniting England with France, by means of a submarine railway, we must here notice a large sectional drawing of " The English Channel Railway," and also a model of the Metal Tunnel, by which it is proposed that this profound scheme shall be realised. The model represents an elliptical section of the tubular structure—clever enough as a model; and the drawing, by Mr. James Chalmers, shows how the rails are to be laid in a circular wrought iron tube. Nervous persons, who now dread the Box Tunnel, and can hardly breathe freely at the idea of being pent up in a tube running under the sea from England to France, will learn, for their comfort, that there is to be "a central ventilating shaft, rising above the surface of the water in mid-channel." As seen in the drawing and model, the arrangements for security and comfort are of the most satisfactory kind, and dreamy persons need ask for no more than the daring projectors of this undertaking venture to promise.

HARBOURS AND GRAVING DOCKS were represented by a number of models, exhibited by eminent civil engineers; among whom, the first place in this department must be assigned to Mr. Edwin Clark, for the skilful manner in which he has employed the principle of the hydraulic lift for the use of the Thames Graving Dock Company. Instead of floating a vessel into a dock, and then pumping out the water, or allowing it to float out with the tide, the inventor of the hydraulic lift employs a series of hydraulic presses for the purpose of lifting the vessel out of the water, on to a pontoon, on which it can be conveyed to the place where it has to be repaired. The presses employed for lifting the vessel are placed in iron columns, sunk into the ground, at such distances as to admit of its passage between the long rows. Several of these pontoons, varying from 160 to 320 feet in length, and capable of carrying vessels of from 500 to 3,000 tons, are now in use in the Thames Graving Docks; and the hydraulic lifts employed are sufficient to raise a dead weight of 6,000 tons. The operation of this system will, perhaps, be best understood by the following description in the Jury Report:—

"A space of water is enclosed, sufficient for the required pontoon, or floating dock, around which are firmly fixed a sufficient number of hollow iron columns, in each of which is an hydraulic press and piston, having chains attached to them; these chains are attached at the other end to transverse wrought iron girders, at the bottom of the enclosed water-space; the wrought iron pontoon which is to carry the vessel is then floated between the columns, and sunk on the girders, by admitting water into the compartments, until it rests upon the bottom of the enclosed water-space; the vessel intended to be repaired is then floated over the pontoon, and is placed accurately above it by means of girders; the girders and pontoon, with the vessel upon it, are then raised by the hydraulic presses, worked by the steam-engine and pumps, which act upon the pistons and the chains, attaching them to the cross girders; and as the pontoon rises with the vessel upon it, the water runs freely out of the compartments of the pontoon, and when the whole is clear, the valves are screwed down from the inside, and the pontoon is floated away into a basin, and another pontoon is placed in readiness for another similar operation, which generally occupies, for a very large ship, about forty-five minutes. Thus, one hydraulic apparatus, with its necessary upright columns, cradle, and basin, or deck space, will answer the purpose of as many dry docks as there are pontoons."

It is stated that the Thames Graving Dock Company, during the three years of their practical working, have most successfully docked upwards of 400 vessels, weighing 220,000 tons, by means of this apparatus, which, it may interest our readers to know, may be seen in constant operation at the works of the company, near the Victoria Docks.

In close proximity with Mr. Clark's model, were several models of improvements in Harbours and Graving Docks; one by Cory & Sons, of a float, designed for rapidly unloading screw colliers and other vessels, screening the coals, and depositing them in the barges without breakage; another, by Tod & Macgregor, representing the dock built by them on the Clyde, near Glasgow, the entry gates of which weigh more than sixty tons; and a model, also, of a Canal Sluice, so constructed (by Laurence Brothers), that the pressure of the water opens and closes the sluice-valve. In this sluice, a piston is placed above the sluice-valve; and the column of water, in the upper reservoir, is made to act, either on the upper or lower face of the piston, by a pair of small side-valves on the face of the sluice. We may here notice another model—which, although exhibited among the Naval models, Class XII., ought to have its place in the locality under consideration—that of Rennie & Sons, representing the large wrought iron floating dock they are constructing for the Spanish government. It is 350 feet long, 150 feet wide, and 37½ high, and will draw, when the largest vessels are in it, about 10 feet of water. The dock is divided into compartments, and is emptied by means of pumps, worked by a steam-engine placed on the floating dock, which can be lowered or raised, as may be required, by admitting or pumping out the water.

BREAKWATERS were duly represented among the models in this Court. When Mr. Canning went to see the celebrated Breakwater at Plymouth, he was so delighted with the works then in progress, that he said to his friends, " We must now make use of our eyes"—a piece of advice which was well worth following in the place our visitor has now reached; for, to quote the Jurors' Report, there were, " in this department, several works particularly worthy of notice." From that Report an extract deserves here to be introduced, for its obvious truthfulness, and the necessity that it should be duly regarded in the construction of this important description of public works. The Report says:—

"The breakwaters of the Carthaginians at Tyre and Sidon, of the Greeks at Athens, Halicarnassus, Ægina, and in numerous other places . . . . show that the simplest and most economical mode of constructing barriers, or break-waters, to resist the violence of ocean storms, was by throwing down and depositing rough undressed blocks of stone, as raised from the quarries, and allowing them to form their own slope, or inclination, by the action of the waves, until, finally, the masses thus thrown down became settled, when their permanence was further augmented by the growth of sea-weed, and the drift of sand into the crevices; so that these works have remained unaltered unto the present day."

The Jurors, when they add, that " the experience derived from these works, does not appear to have been taken advantage of until within a comparatively recent period," have lost sight of the excellent harbour of Kingstown (Dublin), which was formed on the principle they so justly commend. It is not always, however, that the best materials are within reach; and in their absence, every encouragement should be given to those who succeed in providing a valuable substitute. Notice ought therefore to have been taken of the models of Mr. Scott, showing a plan for constructing breakwaters of timber and stone, by a succession of frames, which, having been constructed on shore, are floated to their places, and then sunk; after which they are filled with stones. This timber is treated with creosote, and will protect the stones for many years. We must notice the Gridiron Breakwater, which consisted of a series of cast iron girders, laid on the top of a wall of rubble and concrete, with spaces through which the water might pass without battering the structure with all its force. A very valuable contrivance, placed near this model, is worthy of special attention, as it showed how, by means of brick cylinders, to construct a movable barrier for the defence of ports and harbours, by floating it to its place, and sinking it on the approach of the enemy. The model, although found in Class X., has its place in the Catalogue, Class XI., as a "sunken, but movable barrier, to exclude enemies' ships from ports." This model appears to have escaped the notice of the Jurors, but deserves the serious attention of the authorities to whom our national defences are intrusted.

RAILWAYS, though not belonging to the class of objects now under consideration, were represented, in one important instance, by the Tudela and Bilbao Railway, the beautiful and accurate model of which was executed by Mr. Stephen Salter, and for which he received a medal. This great work represents the line running between Bilbao to Tudela, and thence to Pampeluna. It crosses the range of the Cantabrian Pyrenees, passing through the Basque Provinces, at an elevation of 2,163 feet above the sea-level, with an inclination of one in seventy, for nearly twelve miles. The whole length of the line is nearly 160 miles, extending from Bilbao to a point between Alfaro and Tudela, whence other lines run to Madrid, to Barcelona, and Pampeluna. The model, which is $20\frac{1}{3}$ feet in length, by 12 feet in breadth, furnishes an area of nearly 250 feet, showing 36 miles of railway; and traces all the circuitous windings of the line, as it skirts the mountain sides, traverses artificial galleries, and runs over deep ravines, many of which are very steep, spanning, in one place, 700 feet of perpendicular rock. While this work properly found its model in our British Courts —where it stood as a proud trophy of English engineering skill—it also, much to the honour of the merchants and citizens of Bilbao, and the inhabitants of the towns on the line of railway, is aided by their friends and countrymen in the Havana and England; and they are, probably, the only subscribers to this most spirited undertaking.

LIGHTHOUSES were represented in the models of Mr. James Walker, displaying great boldness of design, and success in the construction of the Bishop's Rock and Small's Lighthouses; of Mr. Allen Stevenson, showing the Skerry Vore Lighthouse; and of Mr. George Halpin, showing the lighthouse on the Fastnet Rock, off Cape Clear, on the south-west coast of Ireland. A new era has been inaugurated by the introduction of cast iron and wrought iron, in the construction of lighthouses, which have become essential where stone was not found, and suitable native labour could not be procured. There ought to have been a more extensive display of models, showing structures of this class, which have been executed during the last eleven years, and must have proved of the greatest public service.

DIVING APPARATUS, whether bells or dresses, and all the important gear necessary for the safety of the divers, and the efficient working of the machinery, have been so long and so successfully employed, as to admit of very little improvement during the last few years. Still, these most valuable contrivances can never be viewed without much interest, as they show how man, instead of being the creature of circumstances, can overcome great natural difficulties, and quietly conduct his operations in the bed of the sea, instead of dreading the advance of its waves. While the principles of the diving-bell, as first employed by Mr. Rennie, in 1813, and of the diving-dress invented by Mr. John Bethel, can undergo no improvement, there have been recently some important additions to this kind of apparatus, of which the Exhibition furnished satisfactory illustration.

Messrs. Laurence exhibited the model of the diving-bell employed at Dover Harbour, for setting the stones in the foundations under water. The safety-valves and signal-apparatus, attached to the diving-bell, prevent it from filling with water, in case the air-tube should break. The aërostatic tubular diving-bell of Maillefert, exhibited by Fairfax & Co., shows the application of a large air-chamber to the bell, by means of which it could, in any emergency, be inflated like a balloon, and sent up to the surface. Mr. Scott showed an additional means of safety in the indicating cylinder he has added to the air-pump, which tells when any leakage or obstruction has taken place, and provides a remedy by having two air-tubes, one of which answers the purpose of a signal-line. Also, lest the glass window of the helmet should break, it is provided with india-rubber flaps, which would at once form a water-tight joint. Heinke, Brothers, also showed an arrangement for providing against a similar accident. Much interest was shown in the figure of a diver, in a complete diving-dress, with air-pumps and connecting-pipes; the helmet being provided with a segmental neck-screw, by means of which the head can be removed by one-eighth of a turn, and the cylinders of the air-pump surrounded by a water-casing, to prevent them from being unduly treated by the rapid compression of the air when at work.

THE METROPOLITAN MAIN DRAINAGE system was illustrated by the drawings and models exhibited by Mr. J. W. Bazalgette, the engineer to these important works. The method in which these vast substructures are to intercept the sewage, and carry it across the Eastern Counties Railway, and the Lea river, could be easily understood by the diagrams and models, to which were added a portion of one of the arches in brickwork, of the full size. To the inhabitants of London, it was very satisfactory to observe the admirable manner in which this great work is being carried out, the advantages of which are very soon to be realised, as it is rapidly approaching to completion.

BUILDING MATERIALS, natural and artificial, were represented among the numerous objects in this portion of the South Court. The former were shown chiefly as worked for ornamental purposes; and the latter consisted of artificial stone, and valuable cements used in architectural works. Among the objects shown for architectural beauty, were articles in terra-cotta; Italian and French marbles, in chimney-pieces; scagliola imitation of Florentine mosaics; Caen stone, in chimney-pieces; the model of a font in Maltese stone; a model of an inlaid pavement for Chichester Cathedral; enamelled slate, and marbled glass.

The terra-cotta productions have recently undergone much improvement, so that they now greatly assist the architect in the work of ornamentation; and among the specimens exhibited, the Jurors have, with much justice, referred to the ornamental columns, with bases, shafts, and capitals, well burned, and preserving the forms into which they were moulded. The value of terra-cotta, for architectural decoration, is now shown in the arcades of the Horticultural Gardens, where they drew forth the admiration of the public during the Exhibition. It is unnecessary to describe the beauty of Minton's encaustic tiles, of which it is not too much to say, that "they rival those of the Moors in the Alhambra of Spain." In the friendly rivalry for excellence in these beautiful productions, the firm of Maw holds a distinguished place,

K

directed as they have been by the skill of Mr. Digby Wyatt. Both these firms have shown specimens of mosaic pavement, which are unsurpassed in character by the best specimens preserved in some of our cathedrals. Mr. Blanchard's application of terra-cotta to the steps of a staircase, has probably suggested an application of this material which may be very extensively adopted. As there is likely to be a growing application of this material for decorative purposes, so we hope there will be greater care to secure the taste and experience of gentlemen, who will in future prevent the errors which manufacturers have, in several cases, committed, from their unacquaintance with the harmony of colours, and the essential principles of design. The manufacturer of this material has left nothing to be desired in his department; it is only required that he shall not act without the direction of the accomplished artist, and this branch of art will hold an important place among the industries of England.

The granite, serpentine, and marble in this Court, deserve notice only as valuable accessories to architectural purposes, in the form of fonts, pedestals, fountains, vases, and tombs; and even in such forms they betray that want of method to which we have already had occasion to refer. Vases, fonts, tables, and tombs, for example, are no essential parts of architecture, or architectonic ornamentation, although these items have obtained adjudication in Class X. We may, however, refer to the specimens of granite and serpentine, both of which show greater success in working the quarries, and securing a high polish. As materials, they belong properly to Class I., as shown in the Eastern Annexe, in which they will come under our notice.

Coloured Marbles, which are now being employed, with very fine effect, in English architectural embellishment, were properly shown in this portion of the British Courts, of which we had a very beautiful illustration in the shafts of the Norman window intended for the Digby mortuary chapel, and which are composed of a variety of beautifully coloured marbles. A medal was very justly awarded to Mr. W. Slater for his admirable mosaic pavement for Chichester Cathedral, distinguished as it was for high merit as to design, arrangement of the coloured marbles, and the execution. It is important to notice that, in this case, the committee felt they would be unjust if they did not award a medal to the mason as well as to the architect.

It is unnecessary to remark on the value of marble as a material for chimney-pieces, of which several beautiful specimens were exhibited. We cannot, however, pass over the exquisite work of the late Mr. John Thomas, enriched as it is with the lively *dramatis personæ* of the *Midsummer Night's Dream;* and showing, as has been correctly observed, how "ornamental designs for furniture and general articles of luxury are so closely allied to Fine Art, that they may be said to incorporate or blend into each other by inseparable gradations."

Artificial Stone, although not comparable with natural building materials, especially in durability, has its value as a substitute where stone cannot be provided. The best of such substitutes is, perhaps, the siliceous stone prepared by Mr. F. Ransome, who exhibited a block produced by his process, for which he received a medal in this class.

Artificial Cements are of such importance in building operations, as to have called into exercise a great amount of scientific skill in their production, and the satisfactory result is, that they are now produced where the manufacture was formerly unknown; in many cases, of improved quality, and generally so reduced in price as to encourage their extensive use.

Enamelled Slate, as produced by the Llangollen Slate Company, properly holds its place among the recent valuable accessories to architecture. Having all due respect for the Lamp of Truth in architecture, we cannot, in all circumstances, oppose the notion that, " if a Serpentine chimney-piece is too costly, the next best thing a man can do is to indulge his taste in the most perfect imitation," especially in this material, which is remarkable for hardness and strength, and will endure a heat of more than twice that of boiling water, and, if gradually and fairly treated, may probably bear a temperature of 600° of Fahrenheit. Certainly these imitations are as perfect as can be desired, " as the practised eye, at a little distance, cannot distinguish them from the originals ;" and, as far as they have been tested, they give great promise of durability.

As our great architectural and engineering works call for large supplies of artificial cements in great variety, we have had the satisfaction of finding, that, in the recent Exhibition—to quote the language of the Jurors—" the great scientific and practical skill which has been applied to this valuable department of materials, has already brought them to great perfection, and has materially reduced their price ; so that they can now be generally made and applied with great economy and advantage in building operations." The Jurors make honourable mention of many firms, and, besides, speak of others, whose works do them great credit. Captain Scott received a gold medal for " a good and cheap cement," which is remarkably well-manufactured by Messrs. Lee, Son, & Smith, to whom honourable mention was awarded for the process of manufacture of this article, the excellence of which the Jury were enabled to judge of in the construction of the building at the South Kensington Museum, where some instances of great strength were shown ; also to Messrs. White, Brothers, a medal for the great excellence, and extensive production of their Portland Cement, which, as in the previous case, the Jury were enabled to examine in the general construction of the building of the Exhibition, and more especially in the bases of the columns supporting the domes, and in the basin of the Majolica Fountain, where its power of hardening, and of impermeability, were satisfactorily tested by watching the progress of the construction, and the subsequent introduction of the water.

Sanitary economy having recently occupied a large share of public attention, it was by a very judicious arrangement that, in the section of the South Court (now supposed to be under examination), space was allotted to " Sanitary Improvements and Constructions," in which were included draining, sewering, making of earthenware for these, and cognate purposes; filtering of water, making of gas and water-pipes, baths and closets, gas apparatus, stoves, ovens, and various heating apparatus, as well as shoemakers' work-tables, and methods of window-making and cleaning.

Filters were exhibited in great variety ; and if they did not show improvements on the principles which have long been well known, they at least gave satisfactory proof that the necessity of filtration is increasingly acknowledged by the public. We may here notice the filter of Mr. Dauchell, which filters upwards, and through charcoal; the filters of the Silicated Carbon Company, who use the refuse of Boghead coal; and the carbon-moulded filter of Atkins & Son, the moulding being assisted by melted pitch. The Jurors also speak of globular vessels of charcoal manufactured by the same firm; the action of which is thus described:—"When this vessel is dipped in water, and the tube exhausted of air by pumping it, or by suction, the water rushes into the inside of the charcoal vessel, and becomes purified. If laid in a vessel of water while the tube hangs down by its side, the tube will act as a syphon, and a perpetual stream of filtered water be attained. When the pores are choked up—an occurrence, the frequency of which depends on the quantity of the water—they are readily cleared by a brush, until finally the smallest particles enter the very centre of the mass. The apparatus is not then finished, as it only requires to be made red-hot, and it is fresh again. This heating, however, must not be performed in a current of air, or the filter will burn and disappear."

The necessity of VENTILATION is now so well understood, that attention is readily given to every arrangement by which it may be promoted. Much importance is justly attached to the increased application of wire-gauze and perforated zinc, for the admission of fresh air, and, at the same time, for preventing the admission of dust; but a special interest attaches to the Glass-Louvred Ventilator of Mr. Moor, which is remarkable for simplicity and usefulness; and to the arrangement of Mr. M'Kinnell, for the ventilation of closed apartments in houses, and in the holds of ships, by means of concentric tubes. The method of this inventor is to place one tube within another; and its advantages are, perhaps, greater in the holds of ships than in any other circumstances. The method can be regarded only as a modification of the arrangement of Mr. Watson, of Leeds, who invented a double tube, or tube with a diaphragm, which, in favourable circumstances, will produce an upward and a downward current; an effect which is materially aided by having a square tube crossed twice diagonally, according to the method of Mr. Muir, of Glasgow.

Warming is very closely connected with ventilation, and will, it may be expected, be treated together before a perfect result can be obtained. The Jurors refer to various arrangements for warming part of the fresh air admitted into dwelling-houses, by means of the waste heat behind the fire-places. A very important principle, brought into action in the Houses of Parliament, by Mr. Goldsworthy Gurney, is deserving the careful consideration of all who are desirous of applying a good system of warming, especially in large buildings. The Jurors, who visited our Houses of Parliament to see Mr. Gurney's system in operation, thus report on his method :—"Mr. Gurney has shown the value of the vapour of water for conveying heat, which it does more thoroughly than warm air. He finds that air, loaded with vapour, mixes with other air more readily than it would do did it not contain vapour: heated dry, air rises, and its heat is lost to those below; but, when loaded with vapour, its tendency to diffuse produces an equalisation, which he makes use of. The Houses of Parliament have their air supplied from the central courts; it passes into the cellars, through a coarse gauze; it then passes over these Gurney stoves, rises up through gauze into a second apartment to make it equable, and thence into the Houses through the iron-grated floor. The House of Commons is kept, by this means, at a constant temperature of 62°—63° F.; the House of Lords, from 63°—64° F."

Gurney's stove cannot be more correctly and briefly described than, in the words of Mr. Robert Hunt, "as consisting of a plain interior cylinder, with an external series of perpendicular radiating wings. The stove is placed in a pan of water, the evaporation of which is regulated so as to produce the amount of vapour required for the due saturation of the heated air; the air, thus moistened, is passed over the external surface of the stove rising between the wings, and thus the air of the apartment is prevented from being 'burnt,' or over dried; for no air is allowed to come in contact with the heated metal without receiving an intermixture of water vapour."

An important move in the right direction has been made by different exhibitors, who provide for drawing air into the fire from the outside of the room, and heating it behind the grate. Edwards & Son bring it into the room below the fender, after being thus warmed. This warm air, being brought from the stove, does not rush towards the fire, having been already sufficiently rarefied. Mr. Woodcock conveys the air into the room through a space between the grate and the chimney-piece, covered with ornamental open work. Here, again, there is scope for improvement; for, as the Jurors' Report observes, "the air might be passed into the room above, near the floor, with great advantage, when it would rise and fill the room with that pleasant warmth which we find in lobbies heated with warm air from a cellar fire, or from an Arnott stove. The waste heat of one room would thus be economised by being used in the room above. It will well reward inventors to contrive the best and safest methods by which the heat we now waste in our chimneys may be utilised for the purpose of warming our bed-rooms."

There is too much truth in the statement of Dr. Angus Smith, in reference to the inventions shown in this department, that "the mechanical contrivance is behind our scientific knowledge." It is a remarkable fact, that while the Commissioners were overwhelmed with applications for space in almost every other part of the Exhibition, the Jury of Section B, Class X., should have to state, that "they have not been overwhelmed, as some have been, with the number of applicants." Very significantly they observe, that "they see the direction from which many contrivances must come;" and add, that "society is waiting for them."

Ingenious inventions are still wanting to give effect to the important discovery, long since published by Dr. Arnott, in his *Elements of Physic*, and which he thus describes:—"Any given quantity of water (it may be boiling), and an equal quantity of cold water (it may be freezing), can be caused to run past each other in separate channels, and shall not, thereby, become a double quantity, having a middle temperature, but the boiling water shall immediately be cooled to very near the freezing point, and the freezing water shall be heated to near the boiling point; in other words, the two shall wholly exchange temperatures." Dr. Arnott also found that the same interchange can be effected between quantities of air, so that foul air issuing from a breathing crowd, can be made to give pure warmth to an equal quantity of fresh air entering. It is certainly remarkable that, among the practical and inventive men of our country, "there should not yet have been found more than three who have taken patents for approximations to it (a good heat transferrer), and that those approximations should be very imperfect." Our readers who possess an inventive genius, will find a wide, and, it may be, a profitable scope for their talents in this department.

WINDOWS, on a new plan, were exhibited by Mr. Askew, so constructed as to present either side for cleaning in the room. By this plan, which the Jurors describe as "ingenious, and, perhaps, valuable," the sashes can be completely turned round, by simply lifting the brass knobs placed at the sides of the bars. The Jurors withhold from this invention the praise to which it seems entitled, because "one is afraid, on seeing it rapidly move round, lest, by leaning on it in an unguarded moment, it would give way, and leave you to fall." Ordinary care and prudence would prevent the danger thus apprehended; and, further to quote the Jurors, "it is a pity that such an objection should exist against a window which is the most convenient of all for persons who sit occasionally before a window, and prefer to modify the amount of air according to their pleasure, and not to be compelled to move their seats whenever the window is to be opened or shut." A much greater advantage to be gained by this mode of construction, is the removal of a most fertile source of accidents from persons cleaning windows in the ordinary way, and who are constantly tempted to break the law, and jeopardise their lives, by standing or sitting on the window-sill to do their work.

Gas Apparatus of various kinds, to assist in its manufacture, and to regulate and register its consumption, were shown in connection with the Court we have just examined. The exhibitors, in their different departments, all display much skill in design and execution. There was Mr. Bower's apparatus for the manufacture of gas, with the greatest regard to the economising of space; Edmundson & Co.'s portable gas apparatus, with the furnace so arranged as to make part of the heat available for cooking; Cookey & Son's regulating valve, as used in a large number of English gas-works; Simmons' arrangement, called the Gas and Water Connector, to prevent accidents in connecting service-pipes with gas-mains, by preventing the escape of gas during the change of the tools: but the most attractive of these objects was the copy of the Standard Gas-holder, manufactured by Messrs. Glover for the Exchequer. This apparatus, for which the manufacturer obtained a medal and the highest commendations, is remarkable for the great precision with which it registers the consumption of gas. The cylinder, or bell, is composed of an alloy of tin and antimony, which effectually resists the action of rust, being unaffected either by gas or water; and the finer subdivisions of the register are read off by an eye-piece affixed to the frame of the cistern. The Jury state that they have given him their warmest recommendations, and that, "no doubt, much ought besides to be given for the enthusiastic manner in which he has done his work, and the constant determination not to lose the smallest opportunity of making even the slightest improvement."

We shall not do justice to the public, nor to Messrs. Dauchell, if we leave this Court without noticing their Water-testing Apparatus, which is well adapted for domestic and manufacturing uses, as well as for the traveller and the emigrant. The patentees observe, with the greatest truth, that all natural water, from whatever source obtained, is more or less impregnated with impurity of some kind; and it cannot be too well understood, that water which has been esteemed as the best, is sometimes the most impure. This Water-testing Apparatus consists of seven small glass-stoppered bottles, containing readily-prepared chemicals, with test-tubes to hold the water; the whole being sufficiently compact to be carried in the pocket.

SOUTH COURTS.—MILITARY ENGINEERING.—Class XI.—The Court adjoining that through which we have passed was occupied with Military Engineering, Armour and Accoutrements, Ordnance, and Small Arms. Without repeating the regrets which we have already expressed, as to the causes which have produced a display such as was happily wanting in our First International Exhibition, we scarcely need confirm the statement that, " in no period of the same duration has so wonderful a progress been made in everything connected with the art of war, as that which has marked the course of the last ten years." It would, in some degree, have mitigated the uneasy feelings with which this display was contemplated, if all nations had agreed to a full and unreserved exhibition of the weapons with which they proposed to conduct the work of mutual destruction, as such a representation might tend to the settlement of inter-national disputes by the exercise of reason, and a better application of skill than for forging weapons of war. We had not, however, the satisfaction of so regarding the array of Arms and Ordnance made by various countries, inasmuch as (to quote the Jurors' Report) " the British Government is the only one which has attempted anything approaching a full and complete exhibition of its implements of war. In the Foreign Courts, the few specimens which have been produced are, with but rare exceptions, the contributions of private individuals; but few of the governments of Europe having forwarded any examples of their artillery." The Jurors ascribe this fact to the circumstance, " that more or less of mystery is still maintained, in almost all countries, on the subject of military armament; . . . . whilst the implements of war are, as at present, in a state of transition; whilst new trials and experiments are taking place daily, and new hopes are perpetually arising of attaining to a perfection not yet realised."

Sections A and B were devoted to Military Clothing, Accoutrements, Tents, Camp Equipage, and Military Engineering, and were supplied by but few exhibitors; but, in Section C—Arms and Ordnance—these were numerous, as the whole number amounted to 315. Our attention is claimed, not only by these individual exhibitors, but by important companies, and the highest governmental authorities. We had to examine the terrible engines of Sir William Armstrong and Mr. Whitworth; of Mr. Lancaster; of the Mersey Steel and Iron Company; the London Armoury Company; the Elswick Ordnance Company; and of the Royal Departments, under the control of the Secretary at War.

As the Whitworth and Armstrong guns were, at the time of the Exhibition, and still are, rival claimants for public favour, it may be well to state the peculiarities of each, leaving to others the responsibility of deciding on their claims. It is scarcely necessary to observe, that all the specimens shown in the Exhibition, were remarkable for the perfection of their workmanship, leaving nothing to be desired in exactness of measurement and finish of execution.

The Whitworth Gun, made of homogeneous iron, in character like hammered steel, and remarkable for toughness, is forged in a solid mass, and afterwards bored; and, to increase its strength, fortified with "jackets" of wrought iron, forced on by pressure. It is rifled on the hexagonal bore system; the projectile it has to discharge having also six sides to correspond with the chamber of the gun. In the official description, we are informed, that "the bore of the gun is really twelve-sided, one-half of each of the sides of the hexagon being cut away, to facilitate the passage of the projectile into the gun." The charge of powder required is one-sixth of the weight of the shot. It should be noticed, also, that "no special fuse is required when firing the shell, as the flash of the explosion ignites the fuse in the front, placed, and used like the ordinary time fuse." Mr. Whitworth exhibited a 1-pounder muzzle-loading rifle cannon; and a 6-pounder breech-loading rifled cannon—the breech action on the screw principle; a 12-pounder brass rifled field-piece; a 32-pounder rifled naval gun; a 70-pounder rifled naval gun; also, projectiles of various calibres, solid shot and shell, ranging from 1 to 70-pounders.

"The Armstrong Gun Trophy," of which we have preserved a faithful illustration, gives not only the weapon in its completeness, but in its various parts, and in the projectiles it has to discharge. The "coiled system," noticed in our illustration, is the most important and distinctive feature in the Armstrong ordnance, and cannot be more correctly stated than in the words of the Jurors, when they tell us that this "gun is made of wrought iron bars, coiled into hoops, which are then welded together, bored, and turned in a lathe, and built up into a gun, by shrinking one over the other, and arranged so as to give the proper amount of strength to the various parts, throughout the length of the gun." The object sought by this peculiar arrangement, is to secure the utmost advantage possible from the fibre of the iron, so that its greatest power of resistance shall be in constant use. The rifling has a number of small grooves, the number varying in different guns; and the "twist," or curvature of the grooves, ranging from one turn in thirty-eight calibres, to one in thirty. This gun is loaded at the breech, by means of a slot cut from the upper side into the bore, of sufficient length to admit the projectile and a charge of powder, and of a breadth a little larger than the diameter of the bore. A movable vent-piece fits into the space formed by the slot, and, being furnished with handles, can be easily lifted out of the space, or dropped into it. An efficient arrangement, also, is made for the escape of gas at the moment of explosion, by means of a circular plate of copper, which enters the bore behind the charge. We need not describe the arrangement by which the detonating cap is struck, the discharging cartridge fired, and its fire communicated to the main cartridge in the bore of the gun. There is an important difference, also, between the outward form of the projectile for the Whitworth and Armstrong guns, which, in the latter case, is surrounded by a leaden envelope, attached, by a zinc medium, to the iron shell it encloses. The Whitworth projectile, as we have seen, corresponds in shape to the chamber of the gun; but the Armstrong projectile has a larger diameter than the bore of the gun, from which it receives its size and shape by being forced in. It should be noticed, also, that the charge of powder required is only one-eighth the weight of the shot, instead of one-sixth, as in Whitworth's. Each of the

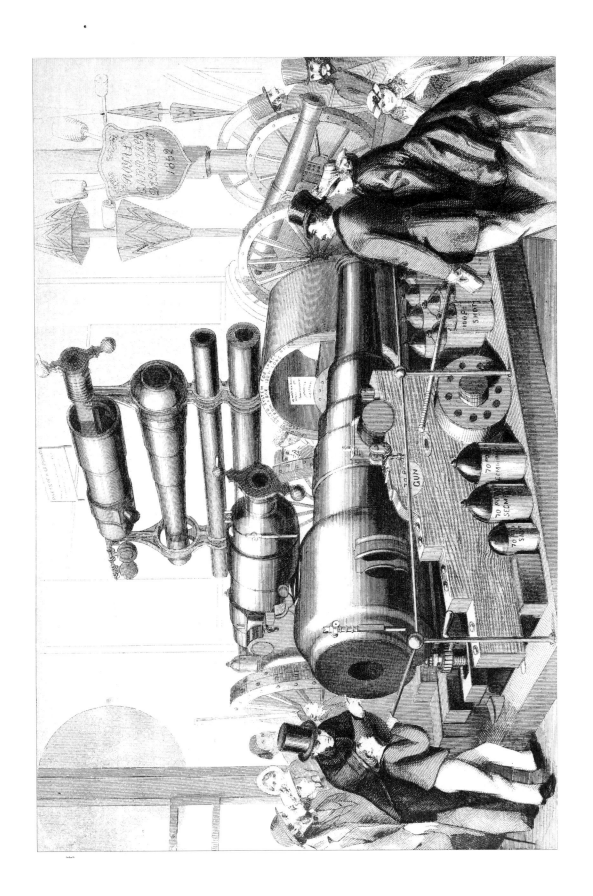

THE ARMSTRONG GUN TROPHY.

Armstrong guns is fitted with a set of sights for short ranges, and another set of side or tangent sights, for long ranges. This famous trophy contained tiers of coils, varying from twelve to thirty inches in diameter; they were shown in their different stages—coiled, welded, finish-bored, and turned. As "the workman is known by his chips," the great skill displayed in this manufacture was shown by a shaving of metal, which, if opened out, would extend to 1,200 feet in length.

To prove that the relative merits of these guns have yet to be decided, we may remark, that when we had written the above description, we observed the announcement that a committee had been appointed to test the merits of the Armstrong and Whitworth guns. By order of the War Department, six 110-pounders, on the Armstrong breech-loading principle, are immediately to be constructed, at the Royal Arsenal, Woolwich; and in their manufacture, steel coils are to be used. It has also been announced, that Mr. Whitworth is busily engaged at Southport in carrying out experiments, with a view of perfecting his gun, which is to be tested against one of Sir William Armstrong's, of similar weight.

The following tabular statements will serve as a record of the results these terrible pieces of ordnance have accomplished: it will be seen, however, that except in one case, that of a 12-pounder, charged with 1 lb. 8 oz. of powder, and at an elevation of 5°, they do not furnish the proper means of comparison, as in all other cases there are some important differences in the circumstances in which the guns were placed.

The work of the Armstrong guns is thus recorded:—

100-pounder—charge 12 lbs.

Elevation.	Range.	Time of Flight.
Point-blank . . .	345 yards . .	0·8 seconds.
1° . . .	680 ,, . .	2·0 ,,
5° . . .	1970 ,, . .	6·8 ,,
10° . . .	3470 ,, . .	12·3 ,,

40-pounder—charge 5 lbs.

Elevation.	Range.	Time of Flight.
Point-blank . . .	360 yards . .	1·0 seconds.
1° . . .	730 ,, . .	2·2 ,,
5° . . .	2160 ,, . .	6·25 ,,
10° . . .	3835 ,, . .	12·6 ,,

20-pounder—charge 2 lbs. 10 oz

Elevation.	Range.	Time of Flight.
Point-blank . . .	250 yards . .	·8 seconds.
1° . . .	510 ,, . .	2·0 ,,
5° . . .	1850 ,, . .	6·4 ,,
10° . . .	3250 ,, . .	11·9 ·,

12-pounder—charge 1 lb. 8 oz.

Elevation.	Range.	Time of Flight.
Point-blank . . .	330 yards . .	1·2 seconds.
1° . . .	680 ,, . .	2·1 ,,
5° . . .	1940 ,, . .	5·9 ,,
10° . . .	3108 ,, . .	11·6 ,,

Whitworth's 12-pounder field gun, in competition with a 12-pounder Armstrong at Shoeburyness, on the 2nd and 3rd of April, 1861, gained the following results:—

Number of Rounds.	Charge.	Elevation.	Mean time of flight.	Mean range of first graze.	Greatest deflection.
	lbs.	Degrees.	Seconds.	Yards.	
5	1¾	2	3·5	1290	Left—⅓ yard. Right—3 yards.
5	1½	2	3·5	1198	Left—nil. Right—2⅔ yards.
5	1½	5	6·9	2368	Left—1⅔ yards. Right—2 yards.
5	1¾	5	7·1	2471	Left—2⅓ yards. Right—nil. (Wind increasing).
5	1½	10	13·1	4400	Left—10 yards. Right—nil. (Wind changed and increasing, squally).
5	1½	10	12·7	4223	Left—4 yards. Right—nil.

The Mersey Steel and Iron Company, famous for its Horsfall monster gun, forged in 1856, exhibited another of its enormous productions—the "Prince Alfred" Gun, weighing 10 tons 15 cwt. 2 qrs. 14 lbs. This celebrated piece of ordnance was in all respects the great gun of the Exhibition, and never failed, in its peaceful state of repose, to attract large crowds; and we may feel assured that it was well prepared, if excited, to destroy them, as it can propel a projectile of from 500 to 600 lbs. The experience of the exhibitors has taught them, that in forging such large masses of iron, much injury is done to the weapon by forging it in a solid mass, as, in cooling, the metal contracts unequally, thereby causing cracks and flaws in the interior of the gun. These guns are therefore now forged hollow, and, in consequence, the metal cools, and contracts equally. The Mersey Steel and Iron Company, employing a patent of Mr. Clay, claim for their guns the merit of reduced cost, rapidity of fire (as they can give nineteen rounds in a minute), freedom of the screw from liability to foul (as it is completely covered), and great strength in the gun. Of this latter quality they have afforded a most satisfactory proof in the experiment they made with one of their 2-pounders. This gun was charged with an iron cylinder, 5 feet 7 inches long, weighing 88 lbs., and projecting eighteen inches out of the muzzle. This projectile was fixed without injury to the gun, but only to be followed by a more hazardous experiment; for the gun was then loaded with eighteen shot, and a six-foot cylinder, projecting five feet out of the muzzle. The projecting end was placed against the solid rock; and instead of the gun firing the shot, the shot discharged the gun, which it threw back; and although this experiment was made twice (the second time with 2 lbs. of powder), and the trial on the gun was calculated to be equal to firing 465 lbs. of powder, the gun was uninjured.

The power of all this terrific artillery, and the strength of materials by which their force is resisted, were shown by many remarkable illustrations sent to this department of the Exhibition. There was a wrought iron plate, $4\frac{1}{2}$ inches thick, broken by a spherical shot of 282 lbs., projected by a charge of 25 lbs. of powder, from the Horsfall monster gun, being the first armour plate ever broken. As we are now in the age of armour-clad ships, it has become necessary to create weapons sufficiently strong to penetrate, and to smash this formidable encasement; and hence the various specimens of ship armour broken by our guns. There was shown another plate, $4\frac{1}{2}$ inches thick, backed by a foot and a-half of solid teak, destroyed by a shot from the "Prince Alfred," by charges of 20 and 30 lbs. of powder.

The Lancaster guns have also displayed most terrific power in dealing with the mailed coating of ships. A target, representing the side of a corvette, was completely penetrated at a range of 4,800 yards, by a shot from one of these guns. The gun by which this result was obtained was a 100-pounder, of cast iron, the gun weighing 95 cwt. The shells fired are of wrought iron, weighing 82 lbs., in one solid piece. The Lancaster gun gives a rotation to the projectile by the twist in the oval boring.

Projectiles were exhibited in great variety as to size, purpose, and modes of operation. Sir William Armstrong's segment shells, and fuzees of different kinds, display the greatest inventive skill. The segment shell obtains its name from the numerous small segmental blocks in its interior, held together by a coating of lead.

which forms the receptacle for the bursting charge. On explosion, the shell disperses its contents into a vast number of fragments—as many as 112 of these segments being employed in the 110-pounder. The Armstrong fuzees are properly described as beautiful pieces of mechanism. It may be well to understand that, owing to the improved method of charging our guns, new conditions had to be met. The old smooth bore caused sufficient windage to admit of the flame of the powder passing round the projectile, which is not possible with Armstrong's gun. In that gentleman's time fuze, the composition is placed in a ring, round the outer portion of the fuze, communicating, at a point in its circumference, with the exploding charge in the centre. A small detonating charge communicates, by means of a movable passage, with the fuze composition, and can be set so as to form a connexion with it, at any point of the circumference. The time at which the shell will explode can be regulated by the distance between these two points of connexion. The ignition is produced by a needle pellet, fastened to the head of the fuze by a pin. This pin is broken by the shock of the discharge, and the pellet driven into the detonating composition, which explodes. There is great ingenuity in the concussion fuze, which is thus described:—It "consists of a needle pellet, suspended in the chamber of the fuze, by two brass wires. The shock of the explosion snaps these wires, and fires the pellet, which, during the flight of the shell, rests against the bottom of the fuze. On concussion, however, the pellet flies forward, into a small mass of detonating composition at the head of the fuze, which it ignites, thus causing the explosion of the shell."

One of the most astonishing of the missiles exhibited was "Mallet's" monster shell, which weighed about a ton and two hundredweight, its diameter being 36 inches. One of these shells, discharged at Woolwich, described a circle of about three-quarters of a mile in height, and penetrated the ground to a depth of eighteen feet.

The Parachute Light-Ball, of Colonel Boxer, is an object of great interest. It is designed to show the enemy's movements by night; and this it effects by throwing into the air a parachute, containing a composition which ignites, and throws a light on the surrounding country for a considerable distance.

In these days of target practice, attention is due to the arrangements for recording the hits at a target, without employing the time, and risking the safety, of the markers during the period spent in practice by a squad of men. Captain M'Neill exhibited his patent Self-indicating Targets, very ingeniously constructed. The face is made of half-inch wrought iron plates, firmly bolted to a strong iron or wooden framing. In a Regulation Target, six feet high by four feet wide, of Captain M'Neill's construction, the front or face is divided into four compartments, consisting of upper, lower, centre, and bull's-eye. Upon a bullet striking either of the plates, the blow will cause a hammer, placed behind, and in contact with the back of the plate, to rebound, and force back a lever to which it is connected. The motion of this lever will relieve a pin or crank attached to a shaft, which, being acted on by a heavy weight, will immediately begin to rotate; and, in so doing, will act upon another lever, and throw up a semaphore arm, which, by appearing above the top of the target, will indicate that the plate has been struck by a bullet. All the plates of which the target is composed, are provided with a similar arrangement of hammers, levers, and semaphore arms—the latter, however, being of different form or colours, to indicate the several plates. The Electric Target of Mr. Gisborne is designed to secure the same advantage—that of preserving a complete and correct diagram of a day's practice without the aid of a marker. It is divided into seventeen portions, each being of a different level, by which the evil of a double record, when the shot strikes the intersections between two plates, is avoided.

Small Arms were shown by a large number of exhibitors, displaying many improvements and great excellence of workmanship. All the small arms in use in the British Army and Navy, were shown by the Birmingham Small Arms Trade Association, by whom they are manufactured in large numbers for the Government, and whose trophy sustained the high character Birmingham has hitherto possessed in this department.

The Enfield Rifle, which may be purchased at £2 5s., and is manufactured at the rate of from 1,500 to 1,800 a-week, is an object of much interest; and the following description of the process of its manufacture may prove acceptable :—" The materials for the barrels of the arms made at the Government works, are brought to the factory in slabs half an inch thick, twelve inches long, and four inches broad. Those slabs of iron are carefully forged to insure the crossing of the fibres of the iron. They are heated, and first bent into a tubular form; they are then heated again, and, while white-hot, passed between iron rollers, which weld the joining down the middle, and, at the same time, lengthen the tube nearly three inches. This heating is several times repeated, and the process of rolling continued until the barrel assumes the form of a barrel about four feet long, having a bore down the centre, about a quarter of an inch in diameter. The muzzles are then cut off; the " butts " made up, and the process of welding on the nipple lump is begun. This operation requires much care, and is executed with great quickness and skill by trained workmen. The barrels pass from the smithy to the boring department: they are arranged horizontally; and the first-sized bore is drawn upwards from the breech to the muzzle. The second boring is effected with rapidity, but the third slowly; and after the fourth boring, the barrel is finished to within the $\frac{3}{1000}$ of an inch of its proper diameter. The outside is ground down to its service size, and the barrel is straightened; it is then tested by a proof charge of one ounce of powder and one ball. The next step is to fix the nipple-screw, nipple, and breech-pin. The barrel is then bored for the fifth time, and it passes to the finishing shop. In rifling the Enfield, each groove is cut separately, the bit being drawn from the muzzle to the breech. The depth of the rifling is 0·5 at the muzzle, and 0·13 at the breech; and the width of each groove is $\frac{3}{16}$ of an inch. After rifling, the barrel is again proved with half an ounce of powder and a single ball. It is then sighted, trimmed off, milled, levelled, browned, gauged, and at last finished so perfectly, that the steel gauge of ·577 of an inch passes freely through, while that of ·588 will not enter the muzzle."

We must here refer to the great improvement which has been recently effected in the tools and apparatus employed in rifled gunnery. Sir William Armstrong presented a remarkable assortment of the principal tools and gauges used in the manufacture of his guns. The gauges are properly described as models of workmanship, being constructed for dimensions, some of which consist of inches in three places of decimals; or, in other words, the one-thousandth part of an inch. Exquisitely perfect, indeed, must be the tools for work of such minute measurements.

The fame of the Whitworth Rifle will give an interest also to the description of its manufacture. "The length of the barrel is thirty-nine inches; it is uniformly tapering, being 1″ at the breech and 7″ at the muzzle; the weight of the barrel is 4 lbs. 7½ oz.; the bore is hexagonal, measuring across the angles 49″; and, across the sides, the spiral is one turn in 20, being uniform throughout. The cartridges contain the powder-charge, lubricating wad, and projectile, arranged in proper order, so as to be pushed down into the barrel by the ramrod in one operation, without reversing the cartridge."

The number of exhibitors of double guns and rifles was no less than forty-eight; and it should be observed, that the introduction of the breech-loading principle is the great novelty since 1851. The pieces shown were double guns and rifles, both breech and muzzle-loading, for sporting purposes; and single breech and muzzle-loading rifles for target practice. Guns of a cheap kind, for commercial purposes, were shown in great variety.

Mr. Storm's Breech-loading Rifle, which attracted much attention, and is regarded as one of the best rifles invented, has some very important advantages; not the least being the certainty that it will not fire accidentally, as the chamber must always be perfectly closed before firing. The principle may be applied to every description of fire-arms, as the connection between the barrel and the stock is not weakened: it is adapted to the use of the bayonet; and, what is most important, it cannot catch in the dress or the accoutrements. It is unnecessary to commend this advantage to those who have any idea of the numerous fatal accidents which have been occasioned by the lever catching in the dress of the sportsman.

After inspecting all this apparatus for the destruction of life, it affords some relief to notice the appliances invented for the comfort and restoration of the sick and wounded. Never before was so much skill and science applied to these benevolent ends; and it is due to a lady, whose name it is scarcely necessary to record—Miss Florence Nightingale—to the late Lord Herbert, and their associates—to acknowledge the benevolent aids they have recently afforded to the British army, by the attention they have devoted to the men who are disabled in our service. We may notice the model of a Wing Hospital, for use in the tropics, constructed by Major Moffat in India. This building, which allows 2,000 cubic feet space for each man, is raised three feet from the ground; slopes off to a distance of fifty feet on all sides, the roof being so pitched as to present the smallest area to the sun's rays, and, consequently, to secure a lower temperature than is obtained by any other arrangement. This important effect is, to a great degree, promoted by covering the main roof with two layers of one-inch bricks, and tiles three-fourths of an inch thick. The great benefit of a thorough ventilation is secured by flues, covered with large slabs, which, being heated by the tropical sun, tend to exhaust the air. Umballa, in which this hospital is erected, is intensely hot; but, by these combined arrangements, a great reduction of temperature is effected, not only in the interior of the building, but also in the verandah, where the men take their meals. The models of field ambulances also showed the great care which has been recently bestowed on the comfort of our sick and wounded soldiers. There were carriages of all kinds, from the small ambulance, to be wheeled by one man, to the large waggon, manufactured at the Royal Carriage Department, for the safe conveyance of a large number. The models showed how these carriages were to be drawn by horses, mules, or bullocks; and, in their variety of forms, displayed the application of the greatest ingenuity to the good work of mitigating suffering, and securing relief with the utmost despatch. It is, however, somewhat humbling to find, after the skill displayed in all these inventions, that, as the Jurors assert, "Amidst these varieties, the simple dhoolie, which has been in use for more than a century in Hindostan, would appear to be the most comfortable conveyance for a sick or wounded man, and would be universally adopted were it not for the number of porters required for it."

We regard with the same feelings of satisfaction the contrivances for furnishing to the soldier the best mode of suspending his knapsack. Colonel Trowbridge exhibited his plan of a metal yoke, passing behind the neck, curving under the arms, and bringing the load fairly on the shoulders. Colonel O'Halloran uses two small plates of soft iron, covered with leather, bent to the form of the soldier's chest, and affording points whence the straps pass over the shoulders; these plates being kept in position by small thongs of leather, proceeding from the bottom of the knapsack. The advantage of ventilation is secured by attaching a leather strap between the two arms of iron, by which arrangement, also, greater stability is given to the load. Volunteers and tourists may derive advantage from these inventions.

Works of defence have engrossed much attention during the last few years, in which so many minds at home have been haunted with the fear of invasion; and the introduction of the rifled musket, and rifled cannon, has produced a transition period in the history of British fortification. We had a military model of London and adjacent country, showing a line of defences, consisting of nine forts connected by redoubts and earthworks, and enclosing an area of twenty-two miles by fourteen miles. These forts and lines would mount 2,151 guns; and the forts would occupy Telegraph Hill, Forest Hill, Tooting Common, the Ridgeway, Richmond Park, Mortlake, Ealing, Hanger Hill, and Whembley.

Harbours and river mouths have also received attention; and among the methods proposed for their defence, is a battery, resembling a round tower, with a conical roof, rising a short distance above the water. This tower is enclosed in another, resembling a gigantic circular tank, completely hidden below the water-line, kept in position by rollers at the sides, and revolving on an axis in the centre. "From this tower a continual fire is supposed to be kept up at the enemy—the tower revolving as fast as the guns are fired.'

Fortifications, in which we could repose confidence before the introduction of rifled cannon, cannot now be regarded as equal to the wants of time. The experiments on the martello tower at Eastbourne, have shown that, "before such ordnance as will henceforth take the field, exposed masonry is little better than cardboard for the purpose of fortification." Hence the importance of the iron forts, of which a model was exhibited by Captain Du Cane. The parapet is constructed of two thicknesses of iron slabs, forming a wall of iron sixteen inches thick, by means of an ingenious method of interlacing. The same system is proposed to be applied to bomb-proof batteries, towers, and forts. It is stated that this mode of construction may effect such a saving as to counterbalance the higher cost of the material. It is to be regretted that the strength gained by this method was not properly tested before opinion was invited, as we can now speak of it only in the uncertain terms employed by the Jurors; who say—" If this iron wall be found strong enough to resist the heaviest guns likely to be used in field sieges, it can be readily applied to existing fortifications, for the purpose of protecting vital parts. In detached works, it might form an impregnable keep; and it might be used alone, in the shape of isolated towers, to occupy advanced posts of ground."

NAVAL ARCHITECTURE.—Class XI., including ships' tackle, is our next department of the South Courts, and includes sub-class A—ships for purposes of war and commerce; B—boats, barges, and vessels for amusement; and C—ships' tackle and rigging. Here, as in the Courts from which we have just passed, we were surrounded with proofs of the great revolution which has been effected in the British Navy and our mercantile marine since the Exhibition of 1851. " In that year," as the Jurors in this class state, "there was but one steam line-of-battle ship, the *Napoleon;* there are now, in this country and in France, extensive fleets of such ships, comprising both two and three-deckers. Not only have line-of-battle ships, of three and two decks, been designed and built especially as steam-ships, but many, indeed almost all, of our useful sailing line-of-battle ships have been adapted for the reception of engine and screw-propellers. Some of them have been lengthened, to give the additional displacement corresponding to the weight of the machinery and coals intended to be put into them. Thus," say the Jurors, " this country has, between the years 1851 and 1862, witnessed the mighty transformation of her sailing fleet into a steam navy of unrivalled power and magnitude."

An opportunity was given, by inspecting the series of models exhibited by the Lords of the Admiralty, to study the progress of our naval architecture from the time of Henry VII. down to the present day, including the royal and mercantile navies, sailing vessels and steamers, paddles and screws, mail-clad iron vessels, and those wooden walls which are rapidly losing their former glories.

Our space does not afford the opportunity to give more than a passing reference to the *Great Harry*, launched in the time of Henry VIII., carrying 50 guns, and of 1,000 tons' burden; or to the *Sovereign of the Seas*, with 100 guns, and built for Charles I.; or to the *Royal William*, launched ten years after the restoration in 1670; or to the *Royal George*, of 100 guns, built in 1756, and which foundered off Spithead in 1782, with the admiral and a crew of 800 men on board; or to the *Victory*, 121 guns, Nelson's flag-ship at Trafalgar; or to the *Queen*, 116 guns, built in 1838; or the *Howe*, 121 guns, the last three-decker built for the British navy. We must come to the iron-clad vessels of our own times, of which the first is the *Erebus*, 16 guns, and 1,054 tons' burden, launched in 1856. The *Warrior*, launched the same year as *La Gloire* of France, 1861, was our first armour-cased man-of-war, and its models attracted great admiration. By means of a transverse sectional model, and by the beautiful model of the whole vessel, shown in the Nave, the structure and interior arrangements of the *Warrior* could be well understood; but, much as she was admired, we are obliged to acknowledge the truth of the judgment, that, "though a ship of great dimensions and tonnage, and probably unequalled, certainly unsurpassed, in speed and general sea-going efficiency, by any ship of war afloat, (she) is still but a highly successful example of that series of unavoidable compromises with which all naval constructors are familiar." Nautical men perceived, in this mailed *Warrior*, the want of complete protection fore and aft, and of other sea-going qualities which were essential to perfection. Hence it has been resolved to construct three more of these armed vessels, of greater length, breadth, and steam-power; and a model of one of them, the *Northumberland*, had its place in the British Courts. This vessel, a model of which was exhibited by Messrs. C. J. Mare & Co., its builders, has the following dimensions:—400 feet in length, 59 feet in breadth, 21 feet depth in the hold, and a draught of 25 feet of water fore, and 26 feet aft. Her stern is coated with $5\frac{1}{2}$-inch armour-plates, backed by 9 inches of solid teak. The weight of her armour-plates is 5,320 tons, and her whole tonnage is 6,620 tons. Few visitors failed to admire her wrought iron crank-shaft, weighing 25 tons, and exhibited by the Mersey Steel and Iron Company in Class I.

Our mercantile navy was well represented by a number of excellent models, from which it was gratifying to mark the great progress that has been made, since 1851, in the science as well as the art of naval architecture. The degree of perfection to which our commercial navy has now attained, is shown by the fact, "that the very hour of arrival of our mail steamers, from continents thousands of miles from our shores, is now confidently looked forward to with expectations which are rarely disappointed. No language could express so forcibly as this fact, to people whose memory will carry them back a few years, the immense advance that has been made in naval architecture and marine engineering."

Not only have our first-class vessels been increased in dimensions, they have also been improved greatly in their proportions. The proper ratio of length to breadth is now much better understood than in former years. The dimensions of the *Great Britain*, built in 1851, the largest merchant vessel then afloat, are:—Length of keel, 289 feet; extreme breadth, 50 feet 6 inches; tonnage, 3,444. The dimensions of the *Himalaya*, built in 1853, are:—Length of keel, 322 feet; extreme breadth, 46 feet; tonnage, 3,542. On comparing these numbers, it will be seen that the changes thus indicated, relate as much to the relative proportions of the vessel as to the increase of bulk, and by which the conditions for an increase of speed are secured, those conditions being, "fine lines, and a small area of mid-ship section."

Mr. Scott Russell, who exhibited a number of vessels he had built on the "wave-line" principle, is entitled to a greater amount of honour than could be conferred by the Jurors, for the great service he has rendered to our naval architecture. The laborious, scientific researches of that gentleman, in connection with Dr. Whewell and other members of the British Association, led to the discovery of the great principle which he is now carrying into effect, and of which our navy is reaping the

MEADOWSIDE SHIP BUILDING YARD & GRAVING DOCK, GLASGOW,

FROM A MODEL EXHIBITED BY MESSRS TOD & MᶜGREGOR.

advantage. It is now well known that this principle admits of universal application, being adapted to ships of entirely opposite character, and intended for very different uses.

In our hasty survey, we regret that we cannot attempt anything like justice to the *Great Eastern*, the building of which has been properly described as forming an epoch in the history of naval architecture, and producing a monument of the mechanical skill and commercial enterprise of the nineteenth century. We need now scarcely state that she was designed by the late Mr. Brunel and Mr. J. S. Russell, and shows how well the wave-line principle may be applied to the largest vessels. This enormous mass of floating iron has a tonnage of 22,927, and 2,500 horse-power— 1,000 for the paddle-wheels, and 1,500 for the screws. The *Orleans* and *Lyons* have been particularly noticed, as showing how the wave-line principle assists to secure the best qualities a vessel can possess. Both these vessels have, for five years, run between Dieppe and Newhaven without any interruption from the weather, maintaining a high speed, and displaying the best sea-going qualities. The same principle is shown in the *Donna Maria Anna*, the *Bann*, and *Brune*, vessels of war; one being a deep, sharp-bottomed, capacious vessel, and the others flat, shallow-water, paddle-wheel gun-boats, designed for service in the Baltic.

The great attention now directed to the improvement of the lines on which vessels are constructed, was illustrated by a variety of exhibitors; among whom was Mr. Tovell, whose models claim the merit of a new invention, as every section of his ships, both longitudinal and transverse, forms part of a new circle. The *Margaret*, one of his vessels of 108 tons, beat the yachts *Phantom* and *Thought*, in running from Erith round the Nore light-ship and back, a distance which she is said to have performed, on another occasion, in four hours and twenty minutes.

One of the facts of which this part of the Exhibition furnished abundant proof, was the rapid substitution of iron for wood in our mercantile navy. Ship-builders are now training their hands to meet the requirements of the times; and it is gratifying to learn that they are readily overcoming the difficulties in the transfer of their labour from wood to iron. There can now be but little doubt, that, in a very few years, iron will be almost universally substituted for wood, as the material for ship-building. In favour of iron it is maintained, that a well-built iron vessel is practically indestructible, the decks being the only portions subject to early deterioration, and these probably not more than decks laid on beams of wood. Then it is stated, that, "with the same weight of material judiciously disposed and properly fastened, it is possible to make a much stronger fabric of iron, than could be made by any mechanical combination of wood."

These discoveries have an enhanced value, from the difficulty now experienced in obtaining English timber for ship-building at a moderate price. Our ship-builders are therefore, to a great extent, dependent on foreign markets, which might be suddenly closed against them; and the failure of the material would create a calamity much greater than the cotton famine has caused among the operatives of Lancashire. It should be stated, however, that we are still in want of the inventive genius who can discover the means of preventing the oxidation of the bottoms of iron ships, and the

N

adhesion of sea-weeds and shells. The latter of these evils is found to be greater than the former, as it retards the progress of the vessel, and necessitates an increase in the consumption of fuel.

An obvious change in the manner of propelling steam-vessels, since 1851, is in substituting the screw for the paddle-wheel. Nearly all the models of 1851 had paddle-wheels; and in 1862, nearly all had the screw-propeller. There were, however, some important exceptions in the *Persia* and *Scotia*—the former 360 feet long, 45 broad, and of 3,580 tons; the latter, 370 feet long, 47 feet 6 inches broad, and of 4,050 tons. Both these vessels are famous for the most regular and rapid passages across the Atlantic. The *Leinster* has the merit of making, as the average of four runs, 17·797 knots; but the *Connaught*, built for the Dublin Steam-Packet Company, has gained a higher speed, on her trial trip, than any vessel yet built. Her length is 350 feet; breadth, 35; her power, 700 horses; and her average speed, 18·097.

Life-boats have greatly improved in their form and equipments, and consequently in their efficiency, since 1851. None of those then exhibited, although they had done good service, combined all the qualities now deemed essential in a perfect life-boat; and which are—extra buoyancy, lateral stability, self-discharge of water, power of self-righting, small internal capacity for water, yet sufficient space for wrecked persons, and for the crew to use their oars; speed, and moderate, yet sufficient weight, with facility of transport along shore. We have the satisfaction of finding that there are 120 such boats, completely and efficiently equipped, stationed at all the prominent and most exposed points along the shores of Great Britain and Ireland. The Life-boat Institution exhibited the model of a row-boat, in which all these desiderata are combined, and which is very generally employed under its direction. A full-sized boat, with all its equipments, was shown in the gardens of the Horticultural Society. The Institution received a prize for models, and the important accessories of life-belts, boats, liquid compass, heaving-lines, and life-buoys. Other exhibitors—Mr. H. Twyman, Mr. A. Hawkesworth, and Mr. H. T. Richardson—sent life-saving apparatus, having several interesting peculiarities in their design and construction. The model shown by Hawkesworth and Annesley, represented the life-boat used at Hartlepool. It is a boat of excellent quality, has done much service, and is very popular among the seamen to whom it belongs. It has great stability, and maintains a high speed at sea; rights itself by partially filling with water the side air-cases; has a self-discharge of water, through an opening with two holes, and large valves; and weighs between four and five tons. The boat of Mr. Richardson, employed at Rhyl, consists of two parallel tubes of iron, two feet diameter, connected by a grating, or open-work deck, and thwarts above for rowers to sit upon. It draws only ten inches of water, and is therefore adapted for a flat beach.

The activity and the great value of the Royal Life-boat Institution, cannot be demonstrated better than by the following account of a meeting held on the first day of the present year, 1863, at its house in the Adelphi; from whose proceedings our limited space will allow us to give only the following brief extract:—

"A reward of £6 10s. was voted to the crew of the Institution's life-boat, stationed at Lytham, for saving, on Friday last, during a gale of wind, the crew of thirteen persons of the barque *Brazil*, of Liverpool, which, at daylight, was observed on Salthouse Bank. The poor men had hurriedly abandoned the ship in their boat, as the seas were rolling in fearful violence over the wreck. The life-boat came up just in time to save them from a watery grave; for in a few minutes afterwards the seas filled the ship's boat, and instantly sunk her. This valuable life-boat has this winter saved thirty-two shipwrecked persons. Amongst the number was a Liverpool pilot. On his relating to his co-pilots the narrow escape he had had of his life, and the noble exertions of the life-boat's crew, they voluntarily subscribed £14 amongst themselves, and handed the amount to the life-boat's crew, in gratitude for their services in rescuing him, and thirteen others, from the American ship *Annie E. Hooper.*— £6 9s. was also voted to pay the expenses of the Porthcawl life-boat, in saving, during a fearful gale of wind, ten persons from the schooner *Champion*, of Liverpool, which, on the dawn of the 20th ult. was observed, water-logged, on the Scarwether Sands, near Swansea. The cost of this valuable life-boat was presented to the Institution by a lady resident in Staffordshire; and her satisfaction must indeed be great that she has thus contributed to the saving of ten persons from an impending death.—A reward of £4 was also given to the crew of the Thurso life-boat, belonging to the Institution, for saving, on the 19th ult., during a gale of wind, the crew of three men of the schooner *Sisters*, of Wick. The vessel soon afterwards became a total wreck. The cost of this life-boat was presented to the Institution by A. W. Jaffray, Esq., of St. Mildred's-court.—Also a reward of £5 9s. to the Institution's life-boat at Plymouth, for assisting, in conjunction with a government steam-tug, in bringing to a place of safety the Dutch galliot *Aremana*, which was observed to be rapidly drifting on shore in a heavy sea. This valuable life-boat was the gift of Miss Burdett Coutts to the National Life-boat Institution.—A contribution of 2s. 6d., in aid of the funds of the Institution, was received from the wife of an old Scotch sailor. She was said to be a good sailor herself, and thought that everybody should give something to the life-boat fund."

Life-belts deserve to be mentioned in connection with life-boats. Some are formed on the principle of inflation, which, as we learn on inspection of the Assyrian monuments, is between three and four thousand years old, when inflated skins were used, as they are at this day, by persons crossing the Euphrates and the Tigris. Others are filled with cork shavings, or horse-hair. The best are considered to be those filled with cork cut in small pieces, and strung together, so as to be perfectly flexible. Captain Ward exhibited Life-jackets of this description, sufficient to support a man in the water with his clothes on, keeping his shoulders and chest above water, and so fastened on as not to interfere with his freedom while rowing. Four thousand of these excellent life-belts are distributed among the men employed on the stations of the National Life-boat Institution.

The Royal Humane Society deserves honourable mention in our pages for the models of its apparatus, such as Ice-ladders, and Drags for rescuing persons from drowning in lakes, harbours, and rivers, and for the means it adopts for restoring animation. The Society has 260 stations, chiefly in and about London; the principal being at the Serpentine, Hyde Park. It has been the means of restoring animation to 30,000 persons since its establishment; and of these cases, 222 occurred during the past year (1862).

When it is known that about 300 lives are saved each year on our coasts, by means of rockets communicating with the vessel in danger, it will be readily conceded that these instrumentalities deserve the greatest encouragement. Rockets and mortars for this purpose are supplied, by the Board of Trade, to the coast-guard around the coasts of the United Kingdom, under whose direction they are found to work admirably. The whole process of firing the line, and carrying the shipwrecked to the shore, was perfectly represented in the models. These rockets now attain a range of 350 yards in fine weather, and about 300 yards against a strong wind. We most cordially join in the recommendation, that every vessel should provide itself with the means of communicating with the land, instead of being dependent on assistance from those ashore. Lieutenant Nares has shown how this may be done by means of a kite. Mr. W. Rich exhibited a well-made kite, admirably adapted for this purpose; and the efficiency of this simple apparatus will be at once perceived, when it is remembered that the stranded vessel is generally on the lee shore, to which the wind would carry the kite; while the rocket sent from the shore has frequently to go against it.

In the interest of humanity, we claim particular attention to the method of reefing topsails exhibited by Mr. H. D. C. Cunningham, the inventor. The practice of sending men aloft to reef the sails in a gale of wind, has long been regarded as an unfair and unnecessary exposure of the lives of our seamen, and, under control of tyrannical masters, has proved the cause of fatal calamities at sea. A wish to remove the source of these frequent evils, has led to several inventions for operating on the sails without leaving the deck of the vessel; a design which is commended, not only by its humanity, but also by its economy of human labour—an object which ought to be desired in shipping as well as in every other kind of machinery.

Mr. Cunningham's method of reefing sails from the deck, was invented and introduced in 1852, and has commanded the unanimous approbation of the Jurors of Class XII. in the late Exhibition. By this admirable method, the topsails are so fitted that they can be reefed and unreefed by the men of the watch on deck; and not only are the men and boys relieved from the danger and exposure attending the operation of reefing, but the vessel is saved from a loss of speed which attended the old method. The advantage thus secured has a sensible effect in shortening the time of a long sea voyage, and is felt particularly in working in narrow seas in unsettled weather. It is an additional and very important advantage of this humane contrivance, that it is attended by much economy, durability, and efficiency, and a considerable reduction of the quantity of ropes to be worked aloft. Of the efficiency of the principle, we have a most satisfactory proof in the fact, that the ship *Champion of the Seas*, whose maintopsail-yard is upwards of eighty feet long by twenty-one inches in diameter, and weighing about five tons, has been fitted up and worked under its direction, for upwards of four years, with perfect success. It is stated that above 3,000 vessels belonging to this country, are now worked by this method; and that it is employed by other countries, from the clipper ships of 2,000 tons, to the coasting schooner of 50 tons. We cannot too strongly recommend the universal adoption of this great improvement, the claims of which ought to be recognised by her Majesty's navy as well as by our commercial marine; and, it may be hoped, will be importunately urged by those philanthropists who are earnestly endeavouring to remove unnecessary causes of suffering and a high mortality.

Our navy has, within the last five years, adopted an improved method of reefing topsails, in imitation of the example set by the imperial navy of France; the object being to secure a saving of material and labour, by the abandonment of the cumbrous method of reefing topsails with reef-points. Our wish is now, that the naval authorities may lose no time in recognising that improvement, which can be urged, not only on the ground of humanity, but of justice to our seamen, whose lives are unnecessarily, and too often from mere caprice, exposed to peril.

Compasses for nautical purposes must be mentioned among the omissions which the jealous apprehensions of inventors failed to supply; for, although Mr. J. Taylor exhibited a good Liquid Compass, fitted in a low binnacle, and well adapted for yachtsmen; and Mr. Gowland exhibited the introduction of the Vertical Card, for placing in elevated positions in iron ships, where the ordinary card compass cannot be seen; and the Lords of the Admiralty exhibited the model of a Binnacle, designed originally for the main-deck of the *Warrior;* also another arrangement in which magnets are introduced in the bottom of the compass bowl, and adjustments made for different latitudes by magnets of different powers; and other inventions were shown of very questionable claims to praise—there was a failure to display the most efficient compasses for supplying the want which has grown up in this "iron age" of ship-building. The use of iron in the construction of ships, has occasioned a want, the importance of which is literally immense. The fear has been created that the magnetic attraction which had swayed the needle in our wooden ships, would lose its power in our iron vessels, and that we should have to abandon all the advantages offered by this new material, in consequence of the sacrifice of the indispensable compass. So recently as 1851, to quote the Jurors' Report, "the laws and general principles affecting the compass in iron ships, were professionally unknown. They had seriously engaged the attention of a few leading men of science; and so far back as 1839, the present Astronomer-Royal of England had made an extended series of experiments in the iron merchant ship *Rainbow*. A tentative mode of adjusting the compass, published in 1840, by Mr. Airy, became the basis of a system of compensation since generally adopted in the mercantile marine."

A most melancholy proof of the importance of this subject, was furnished in the fate of the emigrant ship *Tayleur*, built of iron, and which, with a great number of the crew and passengers, was lost off the east coast of Ireland early in 1854, through "changes in the ship's magnetism," or "the imperfect action of the compasses." Since that period, scientific men have been engaged in the investigation of the subject; and it is now very satisfactory to find, that "a secure foundation of the theory and practice of compass management in iron ships is laid," which the intelligent seaman will understand. Recent improvements in the mariner's compass have been effected by the introduction of compound needles, and in the manufacture and fitting of liquid compasses, which have now become indispensable in any excessive motion of a ship. Many patents have been taken out for obviating entirely the effect of iron in the ship's compass; but the inventors are justly charged with overlooking the fundamental laws of magnetism, by dreaming that the interposition of a body between the magnet and the needle on which it acts, can intercept the action of the magnet. As it has been observed, it might as well be imagined that the interposition of a body between the earth and any other body, would intercept the action of the gravitation of the earth. We may, however, anticipate rapid progress in the practical application of discoveries which have been made during the last few years, by the scientific men who have investigated this most important subject. Inventors, however, will find that this desideratum, which our new circumstances require, will be obtained as the result of the growth of scientific discovery, and not of mechanical contrivance. In the meantime, it is most important to remember, that, "in every vessel with iron beams, every compass should be at least three feet six inches from the deck."

Lowering boats at sea from the vessel's side, has always been a dangerous and uncertain operation, and a fruitful source of accident. It was, therefore, gratifying to find in this department, several inventions for preventing accidents from this source, of more or less efficiency, but all well calculated to mitigate the evil. Mr. Clifford's method, which has been in use for several years, and to which a medal was awarded, affords the crew a sufficient degree of control in lowering a boat to the water, and setting it free at the right time. This method cannot be more correctly described than in the language of Mr. Robert Hunt:—"By Clifford's system, the boat is suspended from four points in the bow and stern, instead of from the keel, as hitherto, whereby the possibility of the boat's 'canting' is done away with. In the centre of the boat is a block, round which the lowering-line is wound, which is slackened out when the boat is being lowered. This line controls the movements of a roller round which the boat is suspended. The pendants run through two three-sheave blocks, which serve the purpose of a turn and a-half, and prevent the motion of the boat becoming too sudden. On the boat touching the water, the 'nip' is taken off the rope by the removal of the weight; the pendants run themselves out, and the boat is free." Mr. Watson employs slip-hooks, operated upon by a rolling bar running along the keelson, and moved by a lever, each end of the bar being furnished with a bayonet socket-link receptacle for the disengaging bolts, which are released by the turning of the bar allowing them to escape from slots in the socket. Honourable mention was well bestowed on a method invented by the late Captain Kynaston, the principal feature of which consists in the disengaging action being lodged in the hooks, while the slip action is produced by lines worked by the crew in the boat. It is a great recommendation of this method that its use is extending in the Royal Navy; and it should be remembered, that the test of experience must be applied specially to apparatus for this purpose, which may look well in a model, but fail when brought into use, in the difficult circumstances in which it has to be employed.

Under the simple designation of "Appliances connected with Ships" (2681), exhibited by J. W. Gray & Son, the exhibitors presented a model showing the method of applying tubular conductors in iron vessels and large mail steamers, for the purpose of preventing the destruction or the fatal damage of these vessels by lightning. They have been produced in consequence of the recommendation of Sir W. Snow Harris, to lessen the violence of the electrical discharge on the general mass. To this gentleman the country is indebted for his scientific researches in relation to the influence of metals on electrical discharges. It is due to him to assert, that he has carried out "a permanent system of lightning conductors in her Majesty's ships and in buildings on shore, the result of which has been the complete preservation of the Royal Navy from lightning." The conclusion to which his scientific investigations have led him is, that "supposing the ship's masts, rigging, sails, and hull, to be metallic throughout, no damage could arise in such a case, because, from the moment the explosive lightning-flash struck on any point, that form of action would vanish, and the discharge easily find its way in all directions to the sea." His object has been, therefore, to render the whole ship a lightning-conductor, by not allowing it to have any of those " explosive intervals" by which the natural discharge of the electric fluid is prevented. It has been his study, not to avoid the presence of metal, but to prevent any interruption in the passage of the lightning by a break in the application of this kind of conductor. His arrangements are all made in accordance with his own discovery, that " the lightning, when forcing a path through bodies which resist its progress, such as atmospheric air, glass, &c., violent expansive and explosive action results, attended with great evolutions of light and heat." The contrivances of Sir W. Snow Harris would, according to his well-established theory, have been unnecessary if our ships had been entirely of metal; but where the course of the metal has been interrupted—where the masts are of wood while the ship is of iron, or the iron-rope rigging has been occasionally covered with tarred yarn, or, from its construction, has not proved favourable to the transmission of heavy discharges of electricity, metallic tubular conductors are recommended, that the electricity might be conducted over the ship's sides to the sea. Hence the great value of the tubular conductors, already noticed, by which the continuous line of conduction can be preserved from the highest points of the vessel to the sea.

We must not, however, allow our readers to conclude that all danger, from magnetic sources, connected with the use of iron instead of wood in ships, has been removed. The words of the Jurors on this point have a very serious significancy. They say—" We have, in fact, yet to learn all the possible effects of heavy strokes of lightning upon vast masses of metal, more especially in cases in which fittings of wood, and other bad conducting material of an inflammable kind, are interposed between iron plates. It is quite certain that the whole ship, under the influence of a thunder-cloud, will have its natural electrical condition greatly damaged, and the conducting power of the iron mass may become interfered with." They also remind us of the remarkable instance of the magnetising influence of heavy strokes of lightning upon iron masses, which occurred in the brig *Tweedside*, of London, in April 1857, on the coast of Africa, when every compass in the ship was ruined, the magnetism of the needles being either destroyed, or so deranged, as to render them useless, while a corresponding damage was inflicted on all the steel parts of the chronometers. Even the after-part of the ship, although built of wood, was so influenced, that compasses placed on two portions of the deck, varied eight points at a distance of ten feet apart, and the vessel was with difficulty safely navigated to England.

GLASS was placed in the Court immediately on the east of the Naval Architecture, and had seventy-nine exhibitors. The repeal of the duty on this most valuable article of our manufacture, has led, as might have been expected, to considerable improvement, by assisting our country successfully to compete with others. It is the deliberate judgment of the Jurors in Class XXXIV., that the glass exhibited in 1862, shows progress, as compared with 1851; and this satisfactory judgment is expressed both as to " quality and manipulation." The favourable decision is thus given:— " The Jurors have great pleasure in stating, from their knowledge of the goods produced for several years past, in their various localities, and from their recollection of the goods exhibited in 1851, that laudable progress has been made in all branches of this Class."

Progress in the manufacture of glass may be regarded as one of the most satisfactory proofs of the advance of true civilisation. Our estimate of the civilisation of the Assyrians is considerably increased by the remains we have seen of their glass manufactures, among which we have evidence that they understood the structure of the lens, and the art of turning glass in a lathe. We could not walk through the Glass Court of the late Exhibition without a high degree of satisfaction, in contemplating the varied uses to which this material is now applied. Like many of the best inventions of man, glass is an imitation of a natural product—the crystal whose name it still bears; and whether we regard it as an accidental discovery, or as a scientific invention, or as both, we must always estimate it at once as the index and the instrument of civilisation.

The Exhibition contained glass for optical purposes—to aid the eye of the microscopist, of the astronomer, and of the ordinary observer; and now we find it often under our feet, sending light into the sub-structures of our crowded streets, and of sufficient strength to resist the heaviest foot-fall. Painted and stained glass may be regarded as among the arts once well known—then to some extent neglected, but now happily restored, and affording the most valuable aid to the designs of the architect. For all the ordinary purposes of life—for the table in the form of decanters and glasses, and other articles for use and ornament—for mirrors, for manufacturing and commercial purposes, we have this most valuable product, in improved forms, of higher quality, and, in many cases, at prices greatly reduced; while we see it applied to new uses, for which, a few years since, it was not supposed to be adapted.

As we are now attending only to the productions of our own country, we abstain from a comparison of British with foreign glass. We may, however, observe, that British glass ought to hold, as it does, a high place in its class, because the quality of our fuel, and the materials employed, generally speaking, are superior to those afforded by other countries. In the words of the Jurors—"The first enables the manufacturer to use a greater proportion of silica in his glass, thereby producing a closer and stronger texture of body, preventing what is technically known as 'sweating' in plate-glass; and, by the second, the greater purity and brilliancy of colour in flint-glass is obtained. Another advantage secured by the country possessing fuel of the greatest power is, that, in superior qualities of glass, the manufacturer is enabled to fuse his materials in covered and larger crucibles, entirely protected from the action of the fuel; and this is a great advantage, inasmuch as the colour of the glass is very much deteriorated by the carbon of the fuel passing over the fluxed materials, the carbon absorbing oxygen, and rendering the glass of a green tint. The same cause (the presence of carbon) prevents the use, in uncovered crucibles, of the oxide of lead, except to a small extent, the deoxidation of the metal resulting in the formations of metallic lead, which, by its own density, falls to the bottom of the crucible."

Mr. Apsley Pellatt, the talented reporter on the Glass Section, informs us, that the masters of his craft divide glass into simple and compound. The former contains only silica and flux, this flux being either soda, potash, lime, magnesia, alumina, or mixtures of some of them: in which case, the glass is simply a silicate of an alkali. To this "simple" glass belong plate, window, and bottle glass of every description. "Compound glass," besides these simple elements of silica and alkali, contains also the oxide of a metal; and it is known among us as flint-glass, and on the continent as crystal. It is employed for articles of luxury and domestic use. The oxide is introduced to give more refractive power to the glass, by not allowing the rays to pass through so freely as in simple glass, and the result is much greater brilliancy in the metal. This flint-glass, which is employed for achromatic purposes, and for articles of luxury, requires the utmost attention of the manufacturer, as its quality is of the highest importance. There is some difficulty in procuring the materials in a state of perfect purity, and, perhaps, a greater difficulty in regulating the escape of oxygen, while the elements are in a state of fusion. We are told, that "deoxidation alone, supposing all the materials to be perfectly pure, will affect the colour of flint-glass;" and that "if oxygen be not supplied, the materials, when fused, will produce, not a white, but a green tinted glass." It is for the purpose of retaining the requisite amount of oxygen, that the black oxide of manganese is employed in the manufacture of flint, as this substance has a strong affinity for oxygen, parting with it very slowly, and not until it has escaped from the other ingredients of the metal. A danger exists, on the other hand, of the glass being injured by the excess of oxygen, in which case it receives a light-purple tint, and acquires a more frangible character.

The "Stained Glass, and Glass used in Buildings and Decorations," were shown, not so much in the Court now under inspection, as in various parts of the building where it could be best seen to effect. It will be more convenient that we should here refer to these productions, that they may have their place in Section A of the Class to which they belong. No visitor could fail to observe how much the effect of the whole costly display was enhanced by stained glass windows, which adorned the edifices in various places; sometimes serving the purpose of windows to the building; and, in other cases, placed in favourable positions for being seen, and enhancing the general effect. Eight exhibitors of the United Kingdom obtained medals, and seven received "honourable mention" for "stained glass windows," for "painted glass windows," and "enamelled window-glass;" the awards being given "for excellence of ornamental work in cinque-cento style;" "for general excellence of design;" "for general excellence of production;" "for general excellence of design, colour, and execution;" "for general merit;" and "for general executive merit." The justice of these awards will be readily admitted by all who had the opportunity of looking at these noble specimens of the taste and artistic skill of our countrymen. A comparison of these modern productions with those of the archaic periods, which adorn our cathedrals, will confirm the statement of the Jurors, that the modern glass window is of "a brighter and higher key than the ancient; while it has less tone and richness, which, like the paintings of Titian and the old masters, may be viewed for any length of time without fatigue to the eye." It is remarked, also, that continental glass, being thinner, and of a higher key than the English, a fictitious surface and tone is obtained by enamel painting, which, while it reduces the glare of the modern work, produces too much dulness, instead of the subdued tone of the antique. We must fully concur with Mr. Apsley Pellatt in his judgment, that "modern windows, of inferior materials, being charged with bright colour at a higher key, transmit too readily, through the glass, bright rays of different colours antagonistic to each other, which fatigue the eye, and form an unpleasant contrast to ancient glass." This consideration is the more important, from the fact that paintings on glass are not toned down by time, like paintings in oil; although, as is justly stated by the authority whose words we have quoted, window-glass, whether coloured or of a greenish white, when long exposed to the action of the atmosphere, is liable to partial surface decomposition. Although glass, thus superficially acted upon, becomes less dazzling and more subdued, the effect obtained cannot be compared to that produced by time on oil paintings.

That effect which time cannot produce on coloured glass, can be secured in a manner described by Mr. Pellatt, who says, that "to succeed in making striated and bubbly-coloured glass, having a horny or gelatinous appearance similar to the ancient, the fining process must be arrested during the latter part of the fusion, by reducing the heat of the metal to a sufficient consistency for working, before the bubbles and the striæ are fully driven off: great attention is necessary, on the part of the manufacturer, to reduce the temperature of the furnace just at the right time to prevent the metal becoming too clear. This imitation of the ancients constitutes the chief improvement since 1851, as regards the vitrified material."

A careful inspection of the stained glass shown by our British exhibitors, discovered the characteristic tendency of our artists and manufacturers to seek for eminence in some particular branch, instead of being satisfied with mediocrity in every department—a circumstance which is sufficient to account for their present success, and gives promise of future progress.

The antique glass produced by the process already described, was exhibited by Messrs. Hartley, of Sunderland, and Lloyd, of Birmingham, to the great admiration of those who were prepared to appreciate its excellence. The early archaic style was well imitated by Clayton & Bell; also by Ward & Hughes, in their fine window for St. Ann's Church, Westminster, in which there is a happy combination of modern taste with the style of the thirteenth century. Several other exhibitors have also been successful in producing a material which rivals the antique in rich colour and low tone, showing richness and beauty, without the glare which it must be the study of our window-glass painters to avoid.

Although these beautiful art-treasures are all dispersed, yet many of them will be within reach of such of our readers as love the

> "Storied window richly dight,
> Casting a dim religious light."

As we have stated, Messrs. Ward's window is for St. Ann's, Westminster. Messrs. O'Conner's window, portraying "The Fall and Restoration of Man," "The Passage of the Red Sea," and various scenes in the history of the Israelites, is for the parish church of Aylesbury. The figures of "Isaiah," "David," and "Noah," are for a church in Stoke Newington. Messrs. Ballantine & Sons' figures of "St. John" and "The Poor Widow," will decorate the church of All Saints,' Kensington Park. The "Life of St. Peter," by Messrs. Lavers & Barraud, is to occupy the eight lower compartments of the great west window of Lavenham church—a beautiful combination of stone and glass, not sufficiently known to our far-travelled countrymen. Canterbury Cathedral is to receive the stained glass windows prepared by Hardman & Co., which are deemed suitable to replace the ancient subjects of which they are the successful imitation. " Passages from the Life of Joshua," by the same manufacturers, is for Worcester; and two of their windows were selected for the church at Whippingham, by the late Prince Consort. Travellers who go to the north, will find " The Wise Men's Journey to Jerusalem," by Forrest, in the crypt of Glasgow Cathedral; and the medallion heads of Wishart, Knox, Henderson, Erskine, Moncrieff, Thomson, M'Crie, Chalmers, and Cunningham (by Ballantine), in the Free Church Presbytery Hall, Edinburgh. Nor are these beautiful productions consecrated exclusively to the use of the church. Some of them will serve the purposes of domestic architecture, to which they are becoming increasingly adapted. Windows were exhibited by Ballantine & Sons, which they had prepared for the National Bank of Scotland, Glasgow, containing groups and emblems illustrative of " Commerce, Mechanics, and Agriculture." We must not conclude without noticing the great window of Messrs. Chance, representing " Robin Hood's Last Shot," of which an anonymous but very clever critic says—" I do not remember to have seen any modern painted window which, for boldness and originality of treatment and power of expression, can be compared to this work. The last dying effort, visible in every feature and muscle of the murdered outlaw—the indignant sorrow of the faithful Little John—the triumphant cruelty of his treacherous kinswoman and accomplice, are rendered with a force and directness which make the whole story clear at a glance; while a further examination of the picture only shows how completely the main idea has been carried out in the treatment even of the minutest details."

Our general survey of the Exhibition would be left very imperfect if we indulged in a distinct notice of the varieties in which glass was exhibited for household, useful, and fancy purposes. The Glass Court formed an exhibition of itself, with its chandeliers, lustres, candelabra, girandoles; its table services of vases, tazzas, decanters, wine-glasses, finger-glasses, and dessert pieces; its toilet services of bottles for perfume and smelling-salts, single and double, mounted in silver and gold. In some of these things, the favourite styles of the antique, and the most curious forms adopted by other countries, were successfully imitated; while, in many instances, they were far surpassed in richness of material, in beauty of design, and exquisite finish of workmanship.

British exhibitors were most justly commended by the Jurors for the advance they had made in the forms of articles for general use, which is properly attributed to the culture of taste in our schools of design, and the determination of our manufacturers to encourage a better appreciation of form on the part of the public. This portion of the Exhibition presented a gratifying proof, that the attention recently bestowed in this country on art knowledge, is now leading to very satisfactory results. It was particularly noticed by the Jurors, as it must have been by all visitors of taste, that great progress has been made in engraved glass. Many of the decanters and wine-glasses were exquisitely enriched by appropriate ornamentation, in which the vine, its grapes, leaves, and tendrils were so beautifully engraved as to render them objects for the eye to gaze upon, rather than for the hand to seize. Among the successful efforts at revival, we must place the Venetian glass, so much admired for its lightness—no lead being used in its composition—and for the beauty with which it is frosted, gilded, and threaded. Our exhibitors, besides presenting Venetian glass in sets of gilded bottles and glasses, have also successfully imitated the *mille fiore* work, which consists of bundles of threaded glass packed in a globe of clear white glass, or forming an ornamental paper weight. Crown, sheet, and plate glass occupied a prominent place in the Glass Court, where the inquirer might learn the process of manufacture, and mark the great excellence obtained in purity, brilliancy, in dimensions, and in the cost of production. It may be well here to guard the public against a deterioration to which plate glass is exposed; the nature and cause of which are clearly indicated in the following extract from the Jurors' Report:—After stating that "the manufacture is almost perfected," they "warn the manufacturers against the use of manganese, or other materials to whiten or destroy the greenish tint of the glass; because, in all cases in which extraneous materials are used for the purpose, the glass so heated, after continued exposure to light and the action of the atmosphere, rapidly becomes discoloured, and such productions obtain a bad character." The Jurors "caution the plate glass maker against an excess of alkali, to which he is tempted to save time in fusing;" as they state, that "such glass readily 'sweats;' that is, the alkali effloresces upon the surface of the glass, rendering it soon cloudy, and requiring constant wiping."

Some curious facts connected with the manufacture of glass bottles are deserving of notice, the forms of which have been greatly increased since the repeal of the duty on the material. Of these most useful articles there were exhibited no less than 800 sizes and shapes. It is to be regretted that no encouragement is given to the operatives to improve on the forms in which our glass bottles are produced, as, "however elaborate the pattern may be, the workmen are expected to produce as many for a day's work as others of a simpler shape." It is mentioned, also, that in the Aire & Calder Company's Works, about 20,000 bottles are made five days in the week; "that about the same quantity is made by three smaller firms in the same place; and about double the quantity in other districts in Yorkshire: giving a total weekly production, in that county alone, of 400,000."

We must congratulate the scientific world on the great excellence obtained in glass for optical, chemical, and surgical purposes; and the general public on its varied applications to useful and decorative objects.

A step further westward conducts us into the Court appropriated to—

POTTERY, Class XXXV., where sixty-nine exhibitors occupied 5,475 feet space, to the great satisfaction of the public, and much to their own honour; for if they were "bent on surpassing all former efforts," their honourable ambition was crowned with the most gratifying success. It is not easy to exaggerate the excellence of the productions made out of Bovey clay, Poole clay, the china clay of Cornwall, Stourbridge clay, the chert taken from the limestone formation of Flintshire and Derbyshire, and the other materials of the potter's art. The achievements of our exhibitors, besides filling the Court assigned to them, claimed a place among the splendid trophies in the Nave, where the finest works in Majolica, and the Queen's service in china, were displayed. The centre of the Court was filled with the richest specimens of porcelain, in all the beautiful forms in which it can be prepared. Minton's works were of sufficient importance to occupy a department by themselves; while the less attractive, but not less useful products of earthenware and stoneware were to be seen around the Court. Noticing the crowds of visitors who constantly lingered among the attractions of the Porcelain Court, and the unmistakable *furore* excited, we are unable to dissent from a writer who says, that, "noting all this excitement, it is not difficult to realise one of those great china crazes of the past, when some high and mighty personages became porcelain mad, and crowds of little people got porcelain mad also; that time, for instance, when Augustus of Saxony exchanged a regiment of dragoons for some old china vases; or the period when Charles, king of Naples, worked as a potter in his own palace, and had before the gates of that palace a shop, in which the productions of the royal manufactory were sold."

Porcelain, according to Dr. Johnson, is a term derived from the French *pour cent années*, in allusion to the absurd account given by the Chinese of their method of preparing this precious production; their statement being, that it was made of egg-shells and sea-shells, mixed in given proportions, and then buried *for a hundred years*. This great triumph of the potter's art was displayed, in the highest forms of excellence, by Messrs. Minton, Copeland, Duke, Binns, Kerr, Rose, Daniell, Wedgwood, Sharpus, and others, between whose meritorious claims the best Jurors and experts found it no easy task to decide.

Inverting for once the natural order of procedure, we shall enter the *sanctum* of this temple of art, formed of tiles and tesseræ by Minton & Co., for the reception of some of their finest works. The tiles of which this Minton Court was formed are of singular excellence, from designs by eminent artists and architects; among whom was the late Mr. Pugin. His ornamental work being produced by a process somewhat resembling that of block-printing, brings these beautiful works down to a moderate price, which will greatly extend their use in domestic as well as public buildings. The vases in this Minton Court were well calculated to realise the purpose of the exhibitors, which was, to show the great progress made in ceramic works since 1851, and in which they contemplate, with the greatest satisfaction, their success in producing the Rose du Barry, Turquoise, and Bleu de Roi, in as great perfection as at the royal establishment of Sèvres. Among the rival claimants to our admiration, it is perplexing to pronounce in favour of one set of objects, to the disparagement of the others. What could be imagined more beautiful than that Dessert Service, in which there was a centre-piece formed of four caryatide figures, supporting a large basket, with cameos in the cornices, and painted bas-reliefs at the base; four baskets for the corners, supported by cupids holding festoons of flowers, and a figure of one of the four seasons rising out of each basket, the exterior of the latter being painted with cameos and flowers? Another set of Dessert Plates most successfully imitated the style of Louis XVI.; while a third Dessert Service showed the reproduction of Palissy ware to a degree of perfection which would have afforded the greatest satisfaction to that enthusiastic artist, had he been "there to see." The wine-cooler of this service has four hunting groups arranged round the base; and the body is ornamented with the heads of wolves and bears, and bas-reliefs of a bear hunt. The whole, which is justly described as "a fine piece of modelling," is surmounted with a group of children sitting on each side a barrel. The Octagonal Chinese Lanterns, in green, and others in pink and gold, were among the attractions of this Court. So exquisite is the delicate workmanship in these fine productions, that we are told, the practical potter was astonished at the difficulties that have been overcome in the manipulation of such gems of art.

Majolica Ware—so called from a corruption of the word Majorca, the island in which the Moors first produced it—received its highest fame from the eminent artists by whom the decorations were designed. Among these artists was Raffaelle, who is said to have designed a set for the sideboard of the Duchess of Urbino. So far as the material is concerned, there is no reason why its imitation should be sought by our manufacturers, as it has been most correctly said, that the merit of Majolica is that of making, with bad material, by the aid of an enamel glaze, a fine-looking ware. We may advantageously imitate the work of the Moors, adopted as it was, in the middle of the 16th century, throughout Italy, by encouraging competent artists to furnish designs for our china ware. Of this Majolica ware, numerous specimens were shown by Minton & Co., proving how well they can imitate and surpass the Moorish school. There were many large dishes, containing representations of the triumphs of Julius Cæsar, copied from the cartoons of Mantegna. In this ware, also, were exhibited a magnificent pair of Vases, the handles formed of the ram's head, from which hung festoons of fruits—the Vases supported by four cupids. This species of ware is admirably adapted for fountains, as we have seen in the great Majolica Fountain on the Eastern Daïs; and as was shown in another large fountain, modelled from a sketch by Lady Marian Alford, in which the outer rim of the basin is ornamented with shells and corals, and three young Tritons do good service as supporters.

Alderman Copeland, who excels in every department of the ceramic art, well deserves the fame he has acquired from his wise selection of eminent artists to furnish the forms and pictorial decorations for his magnificent productions; and among those artists are the names of J. Gibson, R.A., Baron Marochetti, R. Monti, and E. M. W. Turner, R. A. To Mr. Thomas Battam, an artist employed by Alderman Copeland, we are indebted for the discovery of Parian, which is a very admirable imitation of marble; with this advantage—that it can be placed in the mould, and so brought into shape, without requiring the action of the chisel. When, in 1844, two years after the discovery, this new material was first shown to the eminent sculptor Gibson, he pronounced it "the best material next to marble," and desired to see one of his own works produced by this method. While duly mindful of the stimulus which this invention has given to the plastic artist, and having all due admiration of the fine specimens presented in the Exhibition, we cannot dissent from the judgment, that,

"After a very careful examination of the Parian figures exhibited, the conviction becomes stronger, that less care is taken in their production than distinguished the works exhibited in 1851. In many examples, this want of attention to the delicacy of outline, has produced forms which are in many respects offensive." Among the honourable exceptions, we concur in noticing the selection made by the Crystal Palace Art Union.

The caution thus honestly tendered, is the more deserving of attention, from the fact that a new process for the imitation of statuettes, busts, and other objects made in Parian, has been recently discovered, and brought into public notice in the Exhibition. It is a great disadvantage to Parian, that, in drying and firing, it contracts to the extent of one-fourth of its bulk, whereby the work is liable to great distortion, as well as to the loss of fine definition in its sharp lines and angles. In the new material, the loss by contraction is not more than one-seventeenth part; and consequently the cast is very nearly the size of the mould, and as perfect. The utmost care will, therefore, be required in the treatment of Parian, lest it should be displaced by its new rival.

In particularising the works of exhibitors or artists in the Ceramic Court, we are anxious to avoid all appearance of partiality, where, indeed, it is difficult even to have a decided preference. All the competitors have, in various ways, displayed the greatest excellence; and we could do justice to all, only by enumerating every work submitted to our notice; for which satisfactory act we have no space. Still, let us notice the Paul Potter's Tray, and the Dessert Service exhibited in the same case—both painted by Mr. Abrahams, whose chaste designs, correct drawing, soft touch, and mellowness of tone have given universal satisfaction. Most beautiful, also, were the many-coloured Vases produced at the Coalport Works, exhibited by Mr. Daniel; and the Vases of porcelain or Parian, presented to the Princess Alice by the Duchess of Wellington. There is now scarcely any style of the potter's art which our manufacturers have left untried, or any belonging to past eras which they have not reproduced to perfection; and among which we must not forget the beautiful bas-reliefs of Lucca della Robbia, the bright vitreous glaze of Palissy, and the enamels of Limoges.

In the humbler products of terra-cotta, of mosaic and other tiles, of stoneware and earthenware, there was not much to call forth the admiration of the great mass of the visitors, unless in the improved taste displayed in ornamental tiles, and mosaic pavement; in the greater size and excellence of chemical vessels; the superior quality of stoneware, and its adaptation to sanitary purposes; and one or two recent processes which it may be well to notice.

The first is the discovery of Mr. Prosser, of Birmingham—that if china clay be reduced to a dry powder, and in that state compressed between steel dies, the powder is condensed into about a fourth of its bulk, and converted into a compact solid substance of extraordinary density and hardness. This principle, which was applied, in the first instance only, to the manufacture of buttons, has been successfully applied to the making of tesseræ for ornamental pavement; and it may be expected that its use will be varied and extensive. The machine employed in giving effect to the principle, produces such enormous pressure as to bring the particles of clay within the limits of cohesive force; and while it converts to the use of man a primary natural principle, it may serve to give us some idea of those great natural forces which are in constant operation in keeping the elements of the material world together.

Next we may notice, as one method of carrying out this principle, the proposal to decorate the building of the Exhibition by mosaic pictures, which shall be as durable as the hardest terra-cottas. This new method of forming a mosaic work may be carried on in any locality; and it has the additional recommendation that it can be conducted by female hands. Some cartoons have already been prepared by eminent artists, with a view to these decorations; and it may be hoped that the funds will prove adequate to the accomplishment of this important design.

WORKS IN PRECIOUS METALS, AND THEIR IMITATIONS (forming Class XXXIII.), were deposited in the Court to the westward of the Pottery Court, and also in the Nave and the Eastern Daïs, where, in our first promenade, some of the most important and attractive have already come under our inspection. To this Court we cannot but refer with special satisfaction, as it demonstrated the enormous wealth of our goldsmiths and jewellers, and their readiness to furnish it forth to assist in producing an Exhibition worthy of our age and country. The wealth displayed by only three of the great exhibiting firms, was estimated at two millions sterling, a large proportion of which represents the taste of the artists by whom these fine productions have been designed. We must beg to dissent from some of the too severe criticisms pronounced on the great mass of treasures which this Court laid open to the world. It ought not to have been objected that there was a want of good taste in much that was exhibited, and that there was "a want of elegance," and "a meretricious character" in many things. If anything in this splendid Court deserved a censure of the kind, we can honestly give the exhibitors credit for their earnest endeavours to employ the highest talent in dealing with their rich jewels and gold; and we feel satisfied that all the exhibitors fully concur in the opinion, so well expressed by Mr. Harry Emanuel, that "the object of a silversmith and jeweller should not be to cram as many ounces of silver and carats of diamonds into a work as possible, but to make even the commonest and most ordinary articles of a beautiful form, and no heavier than the strength requires."

Among the exquisite specimens of the silversmith's work, directed by the skill of a consummate artist, we refer with satisfaction to Mr. C. F. Hancock's group of plate, designed and modelled by Signor Monti, expressly for the Exhibition. The object of the exhibitor was to do honour to the poets of Great Britain, by works so designed as to illustrate and embody some of the greatest and best known creations of our British poets. The dramatic, classical, romantic, lyrical, and popular poetry of the British Isles, found their appropriate representations in a Central Vase, dedicated to Shakspeare; and in two Loving Cups, and two Tazzas, dedicated to Milton, Byron, Moore, and Burns. The Shakspeare Vase is surmounted by a figure of the poet, in an attitude which would justify the lines of Ben Jonson :—

> "Thus, while I wond'ring pause o'er Shakspeare's page,
> I mark in visions of delight the sage,
> High o'er the wrecks of man, who stands sublime,
> Majestic mid the solitude of time."

The artist has contrived to group around this elaborate vase the principal creations of the immortal bard. Silvia, Viola, Isabella, and Helena, are on shields surmounted by laurels. Romeo and Juliet are among the characters that figure on the swelling of the vase; Falstaff, Mrs. Ford, and sweet Anne Page, have places on the opposite side; while "a local habitation" is found for each grand historical character, as well as for all the airy things of the *Midsummer Night's Dream*. The cup of Milton rests on a stand decorated with fruits and flowers, and bearing on its stem, heads, in high relief, of Dalila, Lycidas, the angel Raphael, and "Sabrina fair." The cover of the cup is surmounted by a figure of Urania, from the *Paradise Lost :*—

"Descend from heaven, Urania,
Up led by thee
Into the heaven of heavens I have presumed."

The precious stones exhibited by our jewellers, in a variety of ornaments, were the most valuable and beautiful ever submitted to public inspection. Messrs. Hunt and Roskell displayed, in *etourages* of brilliants, a fine sapphire weighing 680 grains; and a ruby of 323 grains, which formerly belonged to the kings of Delhi, has been cut to a shape similar to those forming the Queen's necklace, exhibited in Garrard's case. The same exhibitors presented a splendid sapphire and diamond suite, together with magnificent diamonds, pearls, and opals, the property of the Earl of Dudley; and a *pierre d'échantillon*, a large and very fine ruby, set with other rubies and diamonds, the property of R. S. Holford, Esq. Among the spoils of India, were the three large uncut rubies from the treasury of Lahore, and three very fine brilliant drops set in the Indian style. The centre ruby bears the following inscription in Persian :—" A ruby which, out of the 25,000 genuine jewels of the sultans of the world, the sultans, lords of the century, is come to this place from the treasury of Hindustan, in the year 1153. Ahmed Shah, the pearl of pearls, 1168." The same exhibitors had a ruby suite, the value of which is £12,000. More precious, however, was the Caversham sapphire, valued at £20,000. The emeralds of Garrard, Harry Emanuel, Hunt, and Hancock— some forming a cross; one weighing 156 carats, and making a noble brooch; another being a perfect hexagonal crystal, two inches long; most of them worked into jewellery, and others found in the matrix—were, in themselves, treasures worth a pilgrimage to see; but not more interesting than the varieties of precious opal, with its play of rich colours, displaying " the delicate complexion of a lovely youth." Among the quartzose gems, were the amethyst in several varieties, the false topaz, the cairngorm, the chrysoprase, the onyx, the rock crystal, the chrysolite, and cat's-eye. Pearls were numerous and magnificent, excelling in colour, lustre, form, and sizes; and among them was a row of thirty-two, each weighing upwards of thirty-nine grains; the whole valued at £8,000. Though we generally have to send far for these precious treasures, yet the Exhibition gave satisfactory proof that they are sometimes obtained nearer home; as there was shown a case of pearls found in the deepest part of the river Strules, at the town of Omagh, Ireland—being a product of the *Unio Margariti- ferus*, a mussel deriving its name from the fact of its producing pearls. Irish pearls have been worth as much as fifty pounds a-piece, but they are rarely very good in quality. The great demand for pearls, and the prosperity of the pearl trade, will be seen from a statement which has just appeared respecting the fisheries in Ceylon, which, it is expected, will yield, for 1862, a contribution of £100,000. The lowest estimate, which makes great allowance for disappointment, is £50,000 for 1863; while the net return for the next three years, is estimated at the rate of from £100,000 to £150,000.

Artificial pearls are now produced in great perfection; and many shown in the Jewellery Court, would, as far as appearance goes, successfully challenge comparison with the finest natural productions. The following account of the process of their manufacture will be read with interest:—"A French bead-maker, Jaquin, revived and improved the art. He observed that the small fish, called in France *ablette*, the bleak, *cyprinus alburnus*, filled the water in which they were washed with fine silver-coloured particles. The water, on standing, deposited a sediment which had the lustre of the most beautiful pearls; this led him to attempt the manufacture of the pearls from it. He scraped off the scales of the fish, and called the pearly powder, which was diffused through the water, *essence d'orient*, or essence of pearl. He first covered beads made of gypsum with this; but, as the ladies who wore them found the pearly powder left the beads, and adhered to the skin, the use of these ornaments fell off. The beads were then made of glass—a glass easily melted and made a little bluish, being drawn into tubes, which were called *girasols*, the word signifying opal. From these tubes hollow globes were drawn, and they were covered on the inside with a solution of isinglass, and the pearl essence, which was blown in warm, spread over the internal surface by rapid motion. When dry, the globules were filled with wax, bored through with a needle, and strung on threads. These beads are still made of all shapes and sizes; and many of the most perfect imitations are sold at good prices. The bleak is a fish of about four inches long, caught only in fresh water. To obtain a pound of scales, 4,000 fish are necessary; and these do not produce four ounces of pearl essence, to preserve which sal-ammoniac in solution is used. The optical effect is produced in the same manner as in real pearl, being represented by the inequalities of the laminæ, formed by those particles removed from the scales of the fish."

Coral has recently acquired an increased degree of public favour, and, in some of its finest forms, is the material on which the jeweller has successfully expended the resources of his art. Those who have examined the rich specimens of this material, exhibited by Mr. R. Phillips, will readily concur in the honour done to him by the Jurors, from whom he received a medal, "for a very fine collection of corals, some set in bracelets of Etruscan design, good diamond setting; and other works in jewellery and silver, of merit." This material appears to have been obtained recently, in richer qualities and finer colours than in any former period, perhaps as the result of the great encouragement given to those who dredge for it in the Mediterranean. The present rage is for the delicate flesh-coloured variety, which has obtained above £20 an ounce—more than five times the price of gold.

THE PROCESS COURT adjoined the Pottery Court, through which we have just passed, and afforded the visitor an opportunity of seeing the methods employed to produce the results which were shown in various portions of the Exhibition. Here, though on a comparatively small scale, our skilled workmen and workwomen displayed their rapid manipulation, and the admirable behaviour of the machinery placed under their control, to the no small gratification of those who were fortunate enough to get within sight of the operators. As it is no part of our plan to describe processes of manufactures, we shall not now undertake more than a notice of a few of the most remarkable operations performed in this Court, under the public eye.

The Albion printing-press, exhibited and worked by Mrs. Jones, of Bradford, furnished, on a miniature scale, the requisite apparatus for prosecuting the typographer's art, in such a manner as not only to furnish a source of amusement in parlours and libraries, but also to assist ladies in their attempts to learn the art of printing. The specimens of printing in various languages, shown by the exhibitor of the press, were extremely beautiful, and much to the credit of that lady, who, however, will scarcely undertake that the art and mystery of the printer shall be conquered by all ladies who wish to try their delicate hands on the Albion Press.

The manufacture of needles, as now conducted, showed an important arrangement to prevent the injury which this kind of work formerly inflicted on the operators. The men employed in pointing the needles, used to suffer damage from the fine steel dust that escaped from the grindstone, which might have been obviated if they had worn the magnetic masks prepared for their use, but which, from carelessness, or a wish to secure higher wages, they treated with neglect. Their power to suffer injury from this source has been removed, by means of a hood, connected by a tube with a fan, which revolves with great rapidity, and carries off not only the steel filings, but also the dust from the grindstone. The process for counting the needles is most curious, and is performed by a small wheel, which has a hundred notches on the circumference, each the size of a needle, so that it will pick up one, and no more. This wheel is divided into four parts by a stop. The needles are placed under the wheel on an inclined plane, and every revolution allows a hundred needles to pass through.

A Type-composing and Distributing Machine, in operation, was exhibited in the Process Court. Without deeming it necessary to pronounce on its practical value, and probable realisation of all the benefits contemplated by the inventor, we can refer to this very clever piece of mechanism as a remarkable display of skill and ingenuity. The compositor, in working this instrument, seems to have converted his serious business into a pleasant recreation, as, instead of standing up to his case, he quietly sits down to his piano. As he strikes the keys of the instrument, instead of bringing out a "treasure of sweet sounds," he operates on the mighty Twenty-four; each one, as the key is struck, being released, falls into a gutter, down which it slides into a sort of composing-stick (if so common a term may be applied to the receptacle provided for these letters), and into which they are received at the rate of 12,000 or 15,000 letters per hour. The long lengths are cut up by the compositor into the lengths required for his page, the line being depressed, as it is completed, to make room for each succeeding line, and which is done simply by turning a handle. This process is termed "justifying," and is performed at the rate of 4,000 types per hour. We have seen that the machine will deliver at least 12,000 types in that time, so that the services of three men are required to keep pace with its rapid action. Equally ingenious is the apparatus for the distribution of the types, or returning each type to the little box to which it belongs. To the uninitiated, this part of the process appears as mysterious as the wonders of the conjurer's art, as the type is held suspended in its groove, and refuses to drop until the little box arrives to which it properly belongs. This result is gained by a variety of notches made in the types, the operation of which can be properly understood only by inspection.

There were many other interesting operations conducted in this Court, very attractive to the visitors, but not requiring any special record in our pages.

IRON AND GENERAL HARDWARE next comes under our notice in the South Courts, returning eastward. We are now in Class XXXI., which, besides iron, includes brass, copper, zinc, pewter, and general braziery; and, if we add Class XXXII., consisting of steel goods, we shall have the great branches of our English manufacture conducted by Sheffield, Birmingham, and Wolverhampton. The exhibitors in this Court were 409, occupying 25,522 square feet; from whose numerous and varied objects we must select only those that are of the greatest general interest.

The Birmingham Court, occupied as it was by the leading manufacturers of that great industrial hive, showed how well it sustains the high character for which it has so long been distinguished. As iron is the most important element of the manufactures which now claim our attention, it may be well first to notice the proofs afforded of the improvements it has attained in quality. The specimens exhibited from the Earl of Dudleys' works, at Round Oak, showed one-inch, two-inch, and three-inch rods, twisted, while cold, into the Staffordshire knot; a twenty-seven feet rail, twisted, when cold, into the form of a corkscrew; and boiler-plates capable of standing a pressure of 513 tons on the square inch.

The wire of Birmingham, though a very simple production, may be noticed as remarkable, not only for its excellence of quality, but for the enormous lengths in which it is produced. Messrs. Webster & Horsefall exhibited two coils of steel wire without a weld, and weighing a hundredweight, the great merit of which will be perceived by a comparison with the length in which steel wire is usually produced—from ten to sixteen pounds—while the heaviest coil undertaken by a Sheffield house is not more than twenty-eight pounds. This, the heaviest coil of steel wire ever produced, and which taxed the power of the manufacturer's mill, is to be used as a pit guide, instead of the welded iron, which is subject to breakage at the welds. The same manufacturers exhibited a coil of No. 1 gauge wire, a portion of which was drawn from No. 1 to No. 2 Birmingham gauge, without undergoing the process of annealing after it was rolled into the rod from the ingot. The value of this test will be understood, when it is known that frequent annealing is necessary, in ordinary circumstances, in drawing wire to the finer numbers. The advantage thus gained—in which it is right to mention that many other manufacturers participate—is of the greatest importance, owing to the new purposes for which wire is now required. It is wanted for telegraphs; for the rigging of ships; for coal-pit ropes; for drawing heavy loads up inclined planes; for carding cotton, wool, silk, and tow; for covering ladies' bonnets; for artificial flowers; and for many purposes to which hemp has been formerly applied. Another illustration of the perfection attained in wire-drawing, was given by Messrs. Frederick Smith & Co., of Halifax, showing the process in its various stages. A piece of Swedish iron, weighing twenty pounds, and measuring only eight and a-half inches long, and three inches square, if drawn out, as it could be, to the finest wire, such as that shown in the case, would be extended to 110 miles in length. In the first stages down to No. 4, the wire is drawn while hot; after which it is drawn cold, through steel plates; but as the process hardens the wire, it has to be annealed, or softened, at different stages, and then drawn again; and this process will show the value of the achievement of Messrs. Webster, already described. Our manufacturers have, therefore, satisfactorily answered the question—" Cannot wire ropes be made of a more flexible nature than hitherto, and thus brought into use for purposes which they have been wholly unfit for ?"

Patent wire rope for collieries, and other important purposes, was exhibited by Whaley & Burrows, whose Compensating Winding-Drum may here be noticed as an invention of very great importance. This " drum" allows the ropes and cages in which the men are brought up, to balance at all points in the pit; and by this adjustment, when the pit is of such an arrangement that the weight of one rope is equal to the weight of the coals, half the usual power will suffice for the duty to be done. Stubbs & Fenton have invented a " Tell-tale," by which the weight on the ropes is registered so as to be read at a glance: and Burrows & Dougan exhibited a Clutch-Drum and Pulley, to facilitate the substitution of wire ropes for chains in working inclines.

These, and similar inventions, must be regarded with the greater interest, as they tend to the preservation of human life. The value of iron chains, instead of hempen rope, for lifting workpeople up the colliery shafts, has long since been proved; and it is much to be regretted that life has been so often jeopardised by the use of a material so easily worn out, and liable to be cut, as it sometimes has been, by the hand of a malicious person. The Madeley Wood Company state, that they " have substituted flat chains for flat ropes forty-six years." Chains of the same description are used in all the Shropshire collieries at the present time. The average depth of the collieries in this district is about 200 yards; but some reach 300 yards; and flat chains are found to answer most satisfactorily in them. Since their introduction, no loss of life has occurred from their breakage; and, though the first cost is more than that of flat ropes adequate to the same labour, the saving in the wear is very great. The beautiful and the ornamental are among the results secured by the improvements in the manufacture and treatment of wire. A medal was awarded to Mr. John Reynolds, for his ornamental wire-work, the effect being obtained principally by the use of machinery in twisting the wire. The ornamental Wire Aviary of Mr. Charles Dickie, of Dundee, was justly admired for its exquisite beauty. The aviary, built somewhat in the style of the exhibition buildings—the frame of mahogany, with domes of wire—stood on an ornamental wire table, embellished with carved figures. Much commendation is due also to a well-constructed Garden Stool, of ornamental cast-iron and wire-work, designed with griffins and dolphins.

Q

Chains, and chain-cables, which, so long since as 1811, were brought into use instead of cordage, by Captain Brown, were exhibited by several leading firms, showing the links in various forms, and with great improvement in the quality of the iron employed in their manufacture.

The philosopher who was content to define man as a " cooking animal," might have referred to these Courts as justifying his definition, at least in reference to human nature in Great Britain and Ireland, as this important operation appears to have taxed the resources of our exhibitors to the utmost. Kitchen ranges and cooking apparatus filled a large space in these Courts, and displayed a commendable anxiety, on the part of our manufacturers, to satisfy all the reasonable demands of the public. One great object has been to economise the use of fuel, to secure perfect combustion, and to prevent the waste of heat when it is generated; and it is due alike to all the inventors, to acknowledge the great regard they have shown to scientific principles, the ingenuity of their contrivances, and the exquisite finish of their workmanship. So numerous were the alleged improvements exhibited, that inventors must have been ingenious, indeed, to find places into which they could insert their specialities without ousting their predecessors; and yet it was apparent, that nearly every one of the inventions had an excellence of its own, worthy of public patronage.

As it is not within our power to notice every kind of cooking apparatus, from the Economic Cottage Range, up to the large range of Benham & Co., fitted to provide a dinner for 700 persons; or the larger range of Wright, to prepare a dinner for 1,500; we must be content with a selection, but without prejudice to any of the exhibitors, who all deserve the public favour for which they are candidates.

Leamington, determined to have its share in the honours gained by these inventions, put in two claims to public favour, by sending Young's Patent Smoke Consumer, the Leamington Cooking Range, and the Leamington Prize Kitchener. By the use of the first of these ranges, the smoke and gas produced by ordinary coal are consumed, and all unnecessary waste of the heat is avoided. As in the smokeless grate, by the same inventor, when the fire requires feeding, the coals are deposited in the trough, at the lower portion of the range, from which they are supplied beneath the fire, instead of at the top. Mr. Hewens, also of Leamington, exhibited his Improved Complete Apparatus, with various arrangements, to cook a dinner, and keep it hot; the most important feature being a " regulator" for lowering or raising the temperature, without loss of time.

Gas-cooking stoves were shown in great variety; and in one range, that of Ricketts & Hammond, the ordinary coal-consuming range was combined with the gas-stove.

Among the arrangements for preventing the waste of heat, the Empress Cooking Stove, by Smith & Welstood, deserves mention. It has four oven doors, lined with bright metal, leaving a space between it and the doors to prevent the escape of the heat; the bright surface of the metal being supposed to throw back the heat on the centre of the oven. The authors of this arrangement will do well to profit by the important suggestion which has already been publicly given, in reference to their internal metallic reflectors, which must gain their purpose, not by reflection, but by radiation. A surface polished like their reflectors, will retain the heat instead of giving it out, as its radiating power is represented by 15·; whereas, the radiating power of the plates, if covered with lamp-black, is represented by 100·. Here we have another proof that our manufacturers have to cultivate a greater acquaintance with the scientific principles involved in their art, or to invoke the aid of scientific men.

A special reference is due to Brown & Green, who received a medal for their Kitchen Range, fourteen feet in length, which contains four roasters, and three boilers, and secures the greatest economy of fuel. Before being placed in the Exhibition, this apparatus was tested by the inspector of cookery for the army, who conducted the trial by the command of the War Office. It is stated that the range is capable of doing plain cooking for more than 2,000 persons, with a consumption of less than one ounce of coal for each person. It professes, also, to be a certain cure of smoky chimneys, and to secure the ventilation of the kitchen, through an arrangement at the upper part of the range, for the benefit not only of those who are employed in the kitchen, but also of the occupants of the upper part of the house, who are frequently inconvenienced by the savoury odours of the *cuisine*. The upper portions of the apparatus are enclosed in white porcelain, fixed without the use of plaster or cement; and the whole work is, in all respects, most creditable to the exhibitors.

Roasting-jacks came in for their share of the improvements imparted to our cooking apparatus. Brown, Brothers, exhibited their Automaton Roasting-jack, which is kept in motion by the current passing into the fire; thus employing for this instrument a power which had been neglected. It supersedes the weight-jack, the spring-jack, and the bottle, or smoke-jack.

Grates, as well as stoves, have evidently occupied much attention among our manufacturers, with a view to the utilisation of heat, and with a most commendable desire to render these centres of our winter comfort as beautiful as possible, by the combination of rich materials and elegant forms.

The idea suggested by Dr. Arnott, of feeding the fire from the bottom of the grate, has been very extensively worked; and it would add much to the purity of the London atmosphere if it could be universally applied to domestic fires. This method, in some cases, has been modified, as in Mr. Leighton's plan for retaining the grating at the bottom, and supplying the fuel at the back and sides of the grate. The Patent Smokeless and Fire-Grate of C. Jeakes & Co., had peculiar claims to attention, as it will burn on for thirty-six hours without replenishing, and without smoke or waste; the consumption in a 15-inch fire being less than one pound of coal in the hour, and that of the cheapest kind. The fuel is stored in a chamber at the back of the chimney, when it is supplied at the lower part of the grate, thus securing the consumption of smoke.

Good examples of the method of utilising heat were given in Mr. John Taylor's stove, in which the smoke is consumed as it passes through a side flue, before it can escape up the chimney. On the sides of the grate are tubular slabs of fire-brick, in which the air is heated before being introduced into the apartment. In Mr. John Billing's grate, the smoke is made to pass through side flues, behind the back of the grate, and into contact with the fire, so as to be effectually consumed. An arrangement is made also for the purpose of securing a supply of heat for the adjoining rooms.

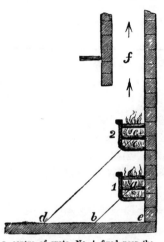

a, centre of grate, No. 1, fixed near the floor; a, b, direction of rays of heat impinging on the floor; c, centre of grate, No. 2, fixed higher than usual; c, d, direction of rays passing from it; e, back of the fireplace; f, chimney.—It will be seen from the above cut, that grate No. 2, radiates heat much further into the apartment than No. 1; in proportion, at least, to the difference of the length of the lines d, e, and b, e.

The error, long since introduced, of placing the grate nearly on a level with the floor, has not yet been corrected, as it should have been by this time. It has been imagined that, by this arrangement, the floor receives more heat than when the grate is placed at a higher level; whereas, the very reverse is the case. Heat propagates itself in straight lines, or by radiations; and the grate is the centre whence it issues, like spokes from the centre of a wheel. The annexed section of an ordinary fireplace, will show that, when the grate is brought down, the floor is deprived of many lines of heat which it would receive if that centre of heat were placed higher.

If this simple principle, for which we are indebted to Dr. Arnott, were duly considered by manufacturers, we should be relieved from the inconvenience which results from the unscientific method of which we complain.

Among the varieties of ornamentation now adopted in grates, we observe a tendency to return to the primitive method of placing the fire on the floor, and surrounding it with the antique decorations of the baronial hall. According to the quaint conceit of an old poet—

"The dogs, andirons, and the smoke,
They all to righteousness invoke;"

though in what manner, and by what law, it would not be easy to divine. We must, however, withhold our admiration from this, as well as many other illustrations which the Hardware Courts afforded of a tendency to worship mediæval types of our times. This slavish subserviency to the forms of a by-gone age, is the less to be commended at a time when our countrymen have acquired so much honour from their successes in the art of design, and when their taste is displayed to admiration in the Courts now under inspection. The boudoir stoves in blue and gold, the ornamental stoves in real bronze, the pillar grates of Mr. Hoole, show that we have no need to look back into past ages for patterns of beauty for our times; while the elegant grates and fenders of our numerous manufacturers, justify the commendation already given, that "it would scarcely be possible to give an idea of the nature of these beautiful objects, without describing each individual example: nearly every class of ornamental manufacture is laid under contribution for their decoration, giving a series of graduated effects—from those which strive to impress us by the beauty of the plain black castings, up to the most startling combinations of bright steel and gold, with encaustic tile mosaics, majolica, or painted porcelain."

Fire-screens, or guards, may here be noticed, on account of the exquisite taste recently expended upon them. Edwards, of Birmingham, displayed some which were highly ornamental, which, when dilated, are circular in form, and may be folded with as much ease as a lady's fan. It is their recommendation that they do not interfere with the cheerful appearance of the fire, or the diffusion of heat in the room, and that it is unnecessary to remove them from the grate when the fire has to be replenished.

LIGHT has given ample scope for the skill and taste of our manufacturers, whose object has been to secure perfect combustion, as well as improvement in ornamentation. As new materials for producing flame have been recently discovered, the best methods of using them have necessarily received much attention, and with results that are perfectly satisfactory to the manufacturers; and to a great extent, also, to the public. Great skill has been required in the use of the oils known as " paraffin," with a view of avoiding danger from explosion, and also to guard against injury from the products of its combustion. We may here repeat the important caution of Mr. Robert Hunt, that " those who burn paraffin oil, should be careful to select specimens which do not give off an inflammable vapour at 100° Fahrenheit, which is readily determined by placing the suspected oil in a spoon floating in hot water, and holding a light above it." The great object in preparing lamps for this material, as, indeed, for every other, is to secure the supply of a sufficient quantity of oxygen to render the combustion complete; and it affords us much satisfaction to add our testimony to that already given in favour of the Fumivore Lamp, as well adapted to this most important object. By an admirable contrivance, a current of air is supplied to the paraffin oil as it escapes from the wick of the lamp—which requires no glass chimney—and a secondary current increases the supply of oxygen, which completes the amount required by the oil. Although the flame thus produced is intense, it is another important advantage that the temperature is not materially increased; and thus one of the great objections to the use of mineral oils is obviated.

Of the success which has attended the endeavours to make each candlestick, lamp, chandelier, gaselier, and candelabrum, " a thing of beauty," it is unnecessary to speak, as the materials employed, and the artistic forms into which they are wrought, are well known to every one who has eyes to see; and as, where the price can be afforded, they have been fashioned under the direction of men of eminence, among whom Mr. Digby Wyatt consents to hold a place. It was no small treat to examine the bronze candelabra and porcelain chandeliers executed by Messrs. Messenger & Sons, directed by such superintendence. The lamps of Messrs. Gardner were distinguished by classical taste, and worthy of the distinction they acquired in 1851, when they obtained a prize medal. The chandeliers of Mr. Joseph Hill were deserving of equal praise; which is due also to D. Hulett & Co., for their gaselier in the *renaissance* style.

Here we must not omit to notice the important collection of patent Signal Lenses and Reflectors of Mr. William Nunn, whose starboard, mast-head, port, night-signal, and storm-warning signals, are fitted with powerful reflecting lenses, tested, approved, and adopted in the Royal Navy; so constructed that a new lens can be replaced in three minutes, by any person on board, when the old lens is broken. Another set of these lanterns is fitted with patent dioptric lenses, also constructed for refitting the new lens in three minutes, and made to burn oil, or stearine candles, as may be required.   The same exhibitor had also a valuable collection of railway lamps and reflectors, and ship and railway lenses in ruby, green, and white.

The "Sunlight," of Mr. W. Strode, which affords an excellent method of lighting public buildings, is much improved by an arrangement for self-ventilation, by which a valve for this purpose is opened when the gas is turned on, and closed when it is turned off.   Another important improvement in burning gas, was exhibited by Mr. W. Sugg, who substitutes lava instead of metal for a gas-burner, which is not oxidised, lasts longer, and produces a clearer flame.

Bedsteads were exhibited in great numbers, and in variety, in the Hardware Courts, from the light Iron Stump Bedstead, at the price of 15s., and the Iron Couch made by machinery in nineteen minutes, to the richly ornamented, and costly four-poster. Thus, to quote from one of the exhibitors, we have "French bedsteads in brass: one, with panelled head and foot-rails, and parallel twisted pillar; another, with ornamental head and foot-rails (black berry and poppy), and mountings on plain pillars; a third, with ornamental head and foot-rails (birds and oak-leaves), the vases and mountings to the pillars in imitation of precious metals and precious stones." As this material greatly promotes cleanliness, and so averts the great annoyances produced by the want of it, in this important article of furniture, its increased use is much to be commended.   The tubing of Messrs. Winfield is greatly valued, as giving lightness, combined with strength; while very beautiful effects are produced by applying to them the process of nature-printing, which, perhaps, most of our readers are aware, is the result simply of placing the object to be impressed between two plates of metal, which receive the impression by being passed between two rollers.   Some of these metallic bedsteads are ornamented by a coating of enamel, applied by a new and very effective process.

The horse comes in for his share of attention on the part of our hardware manufacturers, who seem determined to prove that there is nothing like iron for horse-stalls and boxes.   In all the iron structures exhibited for the safe keeping of the horse, due attention was shown to his health, comfort, and safety.   Mr. Carrington sent his Improved Horse-Stall, so constructed, that the animal cannot in any way injure himself, the fittings preventing the habit of crib-biting; while a system of drainage is introduced by which the stable is kept free from the effects of ammonia.   Also, by a new system of bitting, "the horse makes his own mouth; and, by so doing, makes his own temper."   Messrs. Cottam exhibited a model of Stable Fittings, showing some score of advantages which they offered to their patrons.   A great benefit is secured in all these iron stable-fittings, by the introduction of enamel, as a means of cleanliness; and it is a further recommendation, that they may be readily taken to pieces, and readjusted.

Iron Safes, and Safety Locks, were among the most important articles exhibited in the Hardware Courts; and so numerous and varied, as to justify the remark, that "if an attempt were made to describe them all, a small volume would be filled." It is now well known that fire-proof safes must consist of two cases, one within the other, and that the space between them must be filled with some non-conducting material, so that the inner lining may never become incandescent.   For this inner space, clay, or a chemical composition, and, in some cases, a stream of water is employed as the non-conducting medium. The numerous competitors for public favour in this department, are not satisfied with speaking of their safes as fire-proof; they are also " burglar-proof," " drill-proof," and " gunpowder-proof."

Messrs. Chubb & Son held, among the exhibitors, a position worthy the fame of the gentleman who formerly succeeded in picking one of Bramah's safety locks. They displayed a beautiful Jewel Safe, with ornamental sides and door, executed according to an Italian design, in dead and burnished steel, with gilt scrolls and ormolu mountings. This exquisite work was itself a jewel, and, in all respects, worthy of the treasures to be assigned to its safe keeping. Equally worthy of admiration, in its way, was their Banker's Safe, weighing four tons, made of wrought iron and hardened steel, forming a solid plate of an inch and a quarter thick. In this noble work, the makers employ, to great advantage, their famous wheel lock, which, by a single turn, throws out its thirty-one bolts in all directions, thus greatly multiplying the difficulties of the burglar, whose trouble is enhanced by the case-hardened scutcheon locks, the golden key of which the owner may, if he please, carry set in his finger-ring.

The Treble Patent Safe and Lock of Mr. G. Price, of Wolverhampton, well deserves the high commendation given by Mr. E. B. Denison, because it is as secure as Hobbs' " protector;" it cannot be blown open with gunpowder; its lock is too strong for any instrument to force its door; cannot be shut without using the key, which will prevent its being left open by negligence; and it has a solid key, which leaves no pipe to get plugged with dust.

The *Perauptic*, or changeable lock of Hobbs & Co., contains a comparatively new and distinctive principle, which, perhaps, cannot be correctly described in fewer words than are employed by the inventors, who state that, " the ' bits,' or steps, on the web of the key, that act on the levers inside the lock, are separate, instead of being, as in other keys, cut in the solid metal. These movable bits are fastened by a small screw on the end of the shank of the key, when it has the appearance of any other lever-lock key. There are, besides, spare ' bits,' to change when desirable. The lock has three sets of levers, and is so constructed, that, whatever arrangement the bits on the key may have when acting on the lock, the latter immediately adapts itself to the same arrangement, and will lock and unlock with perfect facility; but it cannot be unlocked by any formation of the bits except that which locked it." Thus, we can now possess a lock whose internal arrangement may be changed at the will of the owner, or the person in charge of the key, and which can be opened only by the key as arranged before the lock was last closed. The changes effected in the key, and by the key in the lock, may be counted by millions, or rather by thousands of millions, " every change virtually converting the lock into a fresh lock, by the simple transposition of the key." The permutations of which the lock is thus susceptible, give rise to its learned name of " Perauptic," which, in plain English, signifies changeable.

The Protector Lock of the same exhibitors is so constructed, that when any tampering is attempted on the lock, by pressure on the bolt through the key-hole, to discover the position of the levers, a "bolt-protector" comes into action, so as to prevent this pressure affecting the levers in any way, whereby they are rendered inaccessible to the clever person who attempts to pick the lock. This method of security was known previous to the Exhibition in 1851; but is now further improved by the addition of a movable nozle, just introduced, which affords a protection against fraud.

The "Letter," or "Keyless" Lock, originally invented by Viscount de Kersolon, has been improved, and the improvements patented by Mr. Loysel, who has carried out the permutation principle to an extent which must afford no little satisfaction to the arithmetically disposed. A lock having five cylinders, of twenty-four letters each, gives 7,962,624 combinations; one with six cylinders, each having twenty-four letters, affords 491,102,796 combinations; one with seven cylinders, of twenty-four letters each, gives 4,586,471,424 combinations; and it is calculated that, working assiduously ten hours a day, it would take about 2,000 years to put all these letters into the various combinations of which they are susceptible. Then it is further observed that, as there is no keyhole, no instrument can be introduced into the lock to pick it; while, for the same reason, it cannot be broken up by gunpowder. If the lock, the fore-part of which is called "the scientific key," were broken by extreme violence, the thief would have secured no benefit, the only result being, that the hinder part of this curious machine would be converted into an impenetrable block.

We have already seen that the horse comes in for his share of attention on the part of the exhibitors in the Hardware Courts. It will be observed, also, that the shoeing of this noble animal has been duly cared for, and with very satisfactory results. The racer, the hunter, and the cart-horse, have been carefully considered as to their various requirements, one peculiarity being the "bar-shoe," with the hinder ends joined by a cross piece, for a diseased hoof, into which the usual number of nails cannot be driven with safety. Mr. Dennis Woodin presented his Patent Shoes for preventing horses slipping on stone pavements, or ice, or other surfaces. They are said to give a strong, firm hold, and a level tread, to prevent cutting, or clacking; to be one-third lighter than the ordinary shoe, and equally durable. The Chillington Iron Company employ an improved machinery, patented in 1857; in working which, a bar of iron enters the machinery by a feeding-apparatus; a piece the length required for the shoe is cut off, and, by another operation, bent into the shape of the shoe. In a pair of dies the shoe is stamped and brought into its perfect form, that form being remarkable for exactness, and the true position given to the holes. This apparatus, when in good working order, produces more shoes in one minute than two men can make in a day. When thus prepared, they are largely exported; and are also much approved in the army of the Viceroy of Egypt.

Steel Pens, which were shown in every variety, now form one of the most important items in our steel manufacture. It is estimated that these most useful articles are now produced to the extent of sixteen tons a week. No remarkable improvement in the method of producing steel pens has been invented since 1851, when a description of the process was given in the Official Catalogue.

Another steel production, which, since that period, has come into much more extensive use—and in many cases, with fatal results—is the well-abused, but still highly fashionable, crinoline. It is computed that there are, at the present time, from 130 to 150 tons consumed weekly in this branch of manufacture.

The Cutlery and Edge-Tools of Sheffield, according to the report of the Jurors, maintained, and in some instances surpassed, the reputation they obtained in the Exhibition of 1851; but we must record the fact, that "the exhibitors were not so numerous, nor were their contributions on so large a scale as in the former Exhibition;" and the Jurors were unable to report any important discovery or invention, either as to the perfection of the articles, or the economy obtained in their production. Sheffield, however, is still to be regarded as the metropolis of our cutlery, file, saw, and edge-tool trades, although they have not kept pace with the increase in the population of that important town. The numbers of men and boys in the town in the file trade, are 3,940; in the saw trade, 1,115; in the edge-tool trade, 786. It should be observed, as perhaps somewhat explanatory, that since 1851, increased production has been secured by the extensive use of machinery.

CHAPTER III.

UNITED STATES.—THE AMERICAN COURT.

THE south-eastern corner of the building was appropriated to the United States of America; and, though that department of the Exhibition was but thinly occupied, yet the industry of the Western world was, to some extent, well represented. The unhappy and unnatural struggle that has, unfortunately, been devastating that vast country, and distracting that once mighty nation, prevented a greater display of the natural and utilising productions of the different states of the Republic; and, with respect to the southern people, they had no opportunity of taking part in the enterprise, and were wholly unrepresented.

Early in the year 1862, a commission, composed of eminent statesmen, was appointed by the president to represent the American people at the International Exhibition; who, too, were to act co-operatively with the officials from other nations in the execution of all measures having in view the advancement of the great enterprise—the promotion of industry and art throughout the civilised world. For reasons that cannot be satisfactorily explained, this official co-operation was withheld, and the people of that nation were, until almost the last moment, placed beyond the pale of international recognition. It does not become the character of this work to impugn the motives that dictated the sectional and ill-judged proceedings of the United States' government in declining to co-operate in an enterprise that was calculated to promote the welfare of its people, more than could possibly be realised by any other nation. It was a misfortune to the Americans; and the millions who attended the Exhibition felt great sympathy for a people who had been (we think unjustifiably) deprived of an opportunity of displaying their unrivalled genius and industry, especially in those departments of art wherein they have excelled the nations of the Old World.

As an evidence of the correctness of what we have stated with respect to the proceedings of the federal government, we quote the following from the Official Catalogue of the subsequently recognised volunteer commissioner for the United States:—

"For months it seemed as if no attention would be paid by our government to the call for contributions to this Exhibition; and when an effort was put forth, it was, in a great measure, paralysed by the ill-feeling made apparent by the leading English journals; and when congress was called upon for funds to meet the expenses of forwarding such contributions, and placing them properly in the building, the excitement of the Trent affair, and the belief current, from notices in the Southern journals, that the Royal Commissioners had granted space to agents of the so-called Southern Confederacy for the exhibition of Southern products, combined to defeat any appropriation for the purpose of aiding exhibitors, and compelled our government to withdraw all official support or encouragement, except the formalities that should give us a recognition by her Majesty's Commissioners."

The manifestation of *animus* on the part of the federal government, as declared by the commissioner, had no justification; and most surely it was not creditable to the dignity of a nation, nor courteous to the Royal Commissioners, who, in their laudable efforts, had nothing to do with political considerations. The object of the Exhibition was to give an opportunity to the people of all nations, tribes, or hordes, to display their genius in the useful arts, and the results of their discoveries in the sciences. It was immaterial to the Commissioners under what national banner this display was made, and it was left to the exhibitor to adopt or reject his legal nationality; and this was, to some extent, done by several Americans. Works of art, some of the highest order, executed by Americans, were found in various sections of the building. For example, in the department of Sculpture, the works of Story, Mozier, and Miss Hosmer, were exhibited in the Italian Court; the Cotton Gin, Printing-Press, Looms, and other improvements in machinery, were scattered throughout the Western Annexe; and, midway in the Central Avenue, stood, in full proportions, Lee's Fire-Engine, one of the last and most useful inventions of this wonder-teeming age.

With respect to the particular objects of interest in the United States' department, mention may be made of Mr. Jasper F. Cropsey's great picture, the "Autumn on the Hudson River," which most faithfully represented the golden hue of the October foliage peculiar to the American forest. "Looking from the coloured mazes of foliage on either side, the scene opens on a richly wooded country," through which the majestic waters of the Hudson rush onward to the ocean. This picture alone will give Cropsey a name that will live long after his own earthly career. Besides the "Autumn on the Hudson," he had several other pictures of great merit; and of these may justly be noticed, the "Cane-Brake in Louisiana," a vast plain on the delta of the Mississippi river, covered with the thrifty sugar-cane: far beyond, in the eastern horizon, the sun was seen to dawn, which gave an indescribable beauty to the scene. Through the cane-field, the deep and meandering bayous, so common in the "sunny south," were truthfully pictured: but the most natural features of this wonderful display of artistic power, were the cypress trees upon the margins of the streams, covered with the long tresses of grey moss, drooping from nearly every limb and bud. This department was also honoured with a few of Mr. Minor K. Kellogg's paintings, of which the "Bath Scene" was the most admired. This picture was remarkably well executed; and it exhibited powers of thought and artistic merit rarely displayed.

The scene depicted a lady of Circassian beauty, "reclining amidst the luxurious cushions of the divan, in an apartment adjoining the bath. The Narghili rests upon a stand near, after lending its mysterious power in provoking sweet dreams. Kneeling in front of the principal figure is a female attendant, who adds the charms of music to those already enjoyed by the bather." Kellogg's other paintings evidenced his masterly skill in the use of the pencil, especially in giving to his portraits a life-like truthfulness. Hay's picture of the "Herd of Bisons," crossing the grassy plains of the Upper Missouri river, was a truthful representation of those wild and furious animals of the Western world. They were seen in an immense herd, their heads down, indicating their fright and madness—all following, at full speed, the queen heifer, as she led in the stampede across the luxuriant grass and flower-covered prairie.

In sculpture, Kuntze's statue of "America" was a beautiful display of thought and artistic design. The proportions of the figure were perfect; and the combinations of symbolic representation were all in harmony; and, as a monument to Columbia, the statue should be placed in the Capitol of the nation, where it would receive the high degree of appreciation it so justly deserves.

The walls of the American department were ornamented with a large number of Brady's Photographs, including portraits of many eminent statesmen, generals, and men of enterprise. His "Army Views" were admirably executed, and faithfully represented the horrors of the civil war in Virginia, a country in which greatness and renown have been attained. The views from California, of the stupendous mountains and great valleys of the Sierra Nevada, were of more than ordinary interest, and enabled us fully to comprehend the vastness of the many peaks, rising like pyramids from the heavily-timbered plateaux, to the height of 17,000 feet above the level of the Pacific Ocean, and covered with perpetual snow. They also gave a perfect representation of the great California trees, some of which have been estimated to be at least 6,400 years old. The most interesting of the collection, were the pictures of the "Yo-hamite," the greatest natural wonder of the world—a vast gorge or cañon in the Sierra, through which flows the Merced, rising high up in the mountains. This cañon has a perpendicular wall of granite, nearly 5,000 feet high. It is a chasm not quite ten miles long, and less than a mile wide; its bottom is covered with grass; and over its walls plunge several cascades, one of which has an unbroken fall of 1,800 feet. These extraordinary natural wonders exhibit phenomena more stupendous than those produced by the volcanic burstings of the earth's crust in Iceland.

In the section of Metallurgy was exhibited a rare collection of unique and valuable specimens of Minerals, and some gems of Geology from the well-known cabinet of Mr. Joseph W. Feuchtwanger, of New York. The specimens were of the greatest variety, and displayed some of the most rare developments of the earth's formation. The Ores from the Pilot Knob, and the Iron Mountain of Missouri, were very interesting, and correctly exhibited the superiority of the different qualities of iron produced from those wonderful mountains. The Metals from the Pilot Knob are peculiarly fitted for stoves and cast iron implements; and those from the Mountain are of superior merit for wrought iron; and wire drawn from its best charcoal bloom, outrivals in toughness the purest Swedish bar. Professor Owen was of opinion, that there was iron enough in these two mountains to supply the wants of the world for 2,000 years. The Copper and Silver Ores, exhibited by Mr. Thomas Meads, of Lake Superior, were wonderful specimens of native purity; and the Gold and Silver Ores, from the Washoe mines of the Nevada territory, exhibited by Mr. J. Moshimer, were of great interest to the geologist: they evidenced the commercial value of the hidden treasures of the vast regions lying between the Rocky Mountains and the Sierra Nevada. The specimens of Galena Lead were complete, and fully exhibited the richness of that great "lead region," which occupies an area of about 2,200 square miles. The earth, in no part of the Galena country, rises to a greater elevation than 500 feet. The ore lies close to the surface of the earth, and the expense of working is comparatively nominal.

In connection with the mineral products exhibited in the American department, were samples of Petroleum Oil from the northern Appalachian ranges of the United States. Mr. M. H. Bagley, of New York, and Mr. F. S. Pease, of Buffalo, presented samples of the crude and refined oils from the springs of Pennsylvania, New York, and Ohio. The oil, in some districts, flows from the earth like water, and forms small rivulets. Within a few years the value of these springs has been discovered, and now they are of great commercial consideration. This novel product of the earth has been thus described by the late Commissioner:—

"The similarity of the products from coal, when distilled, to that of petroleum, points distinctively to a common origin; and I have no hesitation in attributing the large deposits of petroleum in the earth, in districts in Pennsylvania, Ohio, Virginia, and Canada, to condensed vapours once distilled from the anthracite and bituminous coal-beds of Pennsylvania, and other sections of the United States.

"Those at all familiar with the manufacture of gas, or the distillation of oil from coal, will easily understand the process by which this may have been accomplished.

"The theory is this:—1st, All our coal-beds, when first deposited, were similar in their composition to the cannel coals now used successfully in the production of coal oils; 2nd, At some period in the earth's history, after these deposits were formed, the earth has been heated to such a degree as to vaporise all the volatile properties of the coals known as anthracite, and the lighter portions, in greater or less degree, from coals termed bituminous; and, 3rd, That the vapours so eliminated and driven off by heat into the atmosphere, were moved about by the latter, till becoming so far cooled as to condense and fall in mist or rain to the earth, and, in the absence of water (which could not exist in its liquid state at the temperature necessary to vaporise the oil), would be absorbed by, and sink into the earth; and that these deposits were irregular, the heavy oil being condensed at a much higher temperature than the light oils. This theory, then, supposes that, by the action of water in floods and storms, the earth has been washed over these beds or deposits of oil, where it has remained for ages, except the gradual wasting from evaporation, and the oozing from the earth, through being displaced by water.

"The proofs of this theory are gathered, first from general admission of geologists that our coals are of vegetable origin, and the fact that the vegetable indications found in coal-beds are nearly the same, whether in anthracite, bituminous, or cannel coal. If the original composition were the same, it is safe to assume that the products from distillation should be the same; and as the character of petroleum, found in various places and in various degrees of density, corresponds identically with various products obtained from different coals of different degrees of density, and as there is no corresponding chemical product or compound *like petroleum* and coal oil (except from the distillation of vegetable matter), I deem the *identity* proved. I can so refine petroleum and oil from coal, that no chemist or chemical test can tell which is petroleum or which from coal; while no chemist can procure a compound (in which one or other is not incorporated) that cannot be distinguished from them. Assuming the identity proved, I state the following facts in support of the theory of deposits. *Good cannel* coal produces all the varieties of odour, colour, benzine, burning oil, lubricating oil, and paraffin, found in the different oil deposits in the earth. Bituminous coals produce some of the same varieties, but in less quantity, and vastly less of the light benzine and illuminating oil; and anthracite has none that can be rendered valuable or available for use.

"*Heat*, then, in the earth, has at some time been so great, that the anthracite beds have given off all their volatile matter in the form of vapour, and the bituminous beds have given off the lighter and more volatile portions; while the best cannel coals have been but little affected by heat, and retain, in a large degree, the elements that have so lately become the hope of millions for cheap light.

"It is known to all persons familiar with the distillation of coal, that the heat necessary to separate the volatile from the solid portions of the coal, varies from 300° to 800°, when produced in commercial quantities with economy ; and it follows, of course, that under such heat, all the waters of the portions of the earth, sufficiently heated to drive off the coal vapours, would be held in suspension in the form of steam, and would be so held as vapour till, moved by currents, it reached some point below 212°. The vapours of coal would be mixed and moved with those of water, till the various points of condensation would be reached, of 700°, 600°, or 400°, &c., as the temperature necessary to vaporise the various compounds was lost, and then the oil would be deposited nearly according to its gravity. In this way I account for the variation in the quality of the oil from various deposits ; and I am fully satisfied that a fair investigation of all the *known facts* in relation to coal, coal oil, and petroleum, will convince chemists, geologists, and scientific men, that the identity is established, and that they are of the same origin.

"Commercially, this subject rises to a commanding position. Cheap light, to those who inhabit the temperate and frigid zones, is one of immense importance ; and no known substance has yet been discovered that nearly approaches this for cheapness combined with brilliancy. It is produced so pure, that it does not offend the most delicate with its odour ; and so safe from explosion, that none need fear it : it is so much lower in price than other known substances, that all who care for expense in their living, will use it on the score of economy. *Good* oil is now produced at a price that, for the same quantity of light, costs but half as much as gas, and less than a quarter as much as candles or sperm oil."

It is premature to pronounce a positive judgment on this theory, or others, as to the causes by which these treasures have been deposited. We may, however, notice the opinion of Mr. F. S. Pease, of Buffalo, that "the oil is of vegetable origin, and the result of nature's chemical operations in the transformation of wood to coal, the different specific quantities showing the different stages of decomposition and transformation ;" and that "immense pressure forces the oil into different seams and springs far away from any unknown indications, and often in high and level districts."

We must also record the opinion of Sir William Logan, and several other learned geologists, given in the report of the Geological Survey of Canada :—"The oil-bearing limestone underlies an area of 7,000 square miles in Western Canada. The limestone is of marine origin, and contains no organic remains but those of marine animals ; so that we are led to conclude that these hydro-carbons have been derived from a peculiar decomposition of their tissues. These tissues, as is well known, differ but little from those of the plants, which, in many more recent formations, have given rise to bitumen. We may suppose that many soft gelatinous animals, and perhaps plants, whose traces have disappeared, may have contributed to form the petroleum of these coral beds."

COLT'S REVOLVERS.—One of the most prominent and interesting objects in the American department of the Exhibition, was, no doubt, the tastefully arranged show-case of "Colt's Patent Fire-Arms Manufacturing Company, of Hartford, Connecticut." It was in the Exhibition of 1851, that Colonel Colt, for the first time, produced his arms on this side of the Atlantic, and made them known to the English and European public ; but, although his invention was then a decided success, he could hardly have anticipated the immense extent which his business and the sale of his Revolvers reached in the interval—a success which the present lamentable civil war in America has tended to complete, but which the inventor did not witness, having died on the 10th of January, 1862. He contrived his first Revolver in the year 1829, which consisted of a number of long barrels to rotate upon a spindle, by the act of cocking the lock. Colonel Colt was not aware, at that period, that any arm more effective than a double-barrelled gun had ever been constructed. In the year 1835 he took out his first patent in the United States, for a pistol with a rotating cylinder, containing several chambers, to be successively discharged through one barrel by simply pulling the trigger. But these pistols, also, having been found more or less defective, he took out, in the year 1849, a patent for his improved pistol, as it is manufactured now, and which is as yet unexcelled by the Revolvers of his numerous imitators, in length of range, force of penetration, simplicity of construction, and durability.

These Revolvers differ from those formerly made, principally in their greater simplicity, and the better proportions of the parts of the lock and framework. Important improvements and additions were made in the loading lever ramrod, for forcing the balls firmly into the cylinder; the employment of the helical or spiral groove on the arbor, on which the cylinder turns—the sharp edges of which prevent fouling by scraping off any dirt accumulating on the cylinder; and the inclined plane leading to the recesses on the periphery of the cylinder, to direct the bolt below the opposite shoulder in the recesses. The lock is now composed of five working parts instead of seventeen, as formerly.

About 1856 another style of Revolver was introduced. It was called Colt's New Model Revolver, the main principles of which—namely, the rotating cylinder, the manner of loading, &c.—are, more or less, the same as in the former ones. This new model pattern is now exclusively used for Colt's Revolving Rifles and Shot Guns, and also for the pocket pistols of the smallest size.

We need scarcely inform our readers that Colt's Revolving Fire-Arms are now in general use all over the world, not only by officers, sportsmen, and travellers, but also in the armies, navies, and civil service of almost all existing governments.

Since the outbreak of the American war, Colt's armory has been increased to more than double its original capacity for the manufacture of revolving arms. Further additions have been made for the extensive supply of the United States' government rifle, Springfield pattern. The armory is now, without exception, the largest in the world. With all its offices, warehouses, and outbuildings, it covers an area of 250 acres; its value, £1,000,000; and the capacity of it is ample for turning out 1,000 weapons per day. The machinery employed in the establishment— much of it invented and manufactured on the premises, under the superintendence of Mr. E. K. Root, now president of the Company—is very ingenious and wonderful. From 1,500 to 2,100 men are employed in the different departments of the armory. All the accessories of arms, such as bullet-moulds, powder-flasks, lubricators, ammunition, &c., are also made there. Colonel Colt was the first who introduced the extensive use of machinery for the fabrication of small arms, and subsequently furnished large quantities, of his own make and invention, to several governments for their respective armories. It may not be amiss to mention, that the quality of Colt's revolving arms, which makes the same particularly well adapted for military and sporting purposes (especially in countries where gun-makers are not always at hand), is, that every part of the Revolver is made on the interchangeable principle, so that each piece of one weapon will fit perfectly well to every other of the same size. In providing oneself, therefore, with a duplicate set of the interior springs and the nipples, the simplicity of construction of Colt's Revolvers enables the owner to repair the arms himself without the least difficulty, should ever this become necessary. The prize medal of the Exhibition of 1862, was awarded to these arms by the Jury charged with the inspection of the fire-arms exhibited.

MARINE SIGNAL TELEGRAPH.—Passing from the department of fire-arms, we arrive at Ward's Marine Signals, arranged for semaphoric telegraphy, between ships at sea, either by day or night. One of the ablest Juries of the International Exhibition, awarded, for this most ingenious contrivance and combination of signals, the prize medal: and besides this distinguished mark of commendation, the inventor, Mr. William Henry Ward, has had meted to him the highest evidences of approbation from the most distinguished seamen of both continents. Nations have adopted, for their naval and merchant service, his system of signalling; and, in every practical manner, co-operated to effect its universal employment.

The art of conveying intelligence by the aid of signals has been practised for centuries; and, for aught we know, since Adam and Eve commenced their pilgrimage in the Garden of Eden. In the Old Testament we read, in chapter vi. verse 1, of the Prophet Jeremiah:—" O ye children of Benjamin, gather your-selves to flee out of the midst of Jerusalem, and blow the trumpet in Tekoa, and set up a *sign of fire* in Beth-haccerem; for evil appeareth out of the north, and great destruction!" The writings of Jeremiah date 588 years before Christ; and the above reference to communicating intelligence to others by the *sign of fire*, or by means of signalling, is the earliest on reliable record. In profane history and the classics, various methods of communicating by signals are mentioned. Homer is the first to mention the art of telegraphing. He compared the lambent flames which shone around the head of Achilles, and spread their lustre on every side, to the signals made in besieged cities by clouds of smoke in the day-time, and by bright fires at night, as certain signs calling on the neighbouring states for assistance, or to enable them to repel the powerful efforts of the enemy. Julius Africanus minutely details a mode of spelling words by a telegraph. It appears that fires of various substances were the means made use of. In Livy, in Vegetius, and in the life of Sertorius, by Plutarch, it is mentioned that the generals of certain epochs frequently communicated by telegraph. In Brumor's account of the theatres of the Greeks, it is stated that fire-signals were used to communicate the events of wars, and likewise to direct the commencement of battles. A priest, crowned with laurels, preceded the army, and held a lighted torch in his hand. He was respected and spared by the enemy, even in the heat of battle. Hence the old proverbial expression for a complete defeat, that " even the very torch-bearer had not been spared." The Chinese have, like the ancient Scythians, been in the habit of communicating intelligence by lighting fires or raising a cloud of smoke at different stations. The American Indians also, in the same manner, have, from time immemorial, signalled from the hill-tops, to distant tribes, the invasion of their lands by an enemy. In more modern times, the Chappé Semaphoric Telegraph has been the most successful, until the invention of the electric system within the last twenty years. At sea, however, it will never be possible to telegraph otherwise than by signalling, either in one form or another; and it only remains for each generation to determine what mode proposed is the best for the attainment of the desired end. A marine telegraph must be fitted for three states or conditions of things—viz., for the hours of light, darkness, and fog; and, after these circumstances are fully accommodated, then it becomes necessary to arrange the character and combination of the signals to communicate the greatest amount of information in the shortest space of time, and with the simplest appliances. With respect to day-time, flags have been the most acceptable style of signals, arranged as to colour and position, so as to express a number, letter, or arbitrary sentence. Mr. Ward has most successfully employed a combination of colours that can be readily comprehended, whether extended by the breeze, or drooping in a calm; and giving to each division of colour, an equal area of space in the same flag. The distant ship can easily distinguish each flag, and understand its signification with distinct clearness to define the signal and its reference to the vocabulary. For example, suppose a red flag represents 4, the yellow 1, and the black 7. These, combined, make 417. On referring to the vocabulary, the meaning of these figures will be found to be, "Steam-ship America;" and, in this manner, others are given and explained. It is not a new idea to transmit information by flag signals at sea; but it is new to realise the advantage of a system that can successfully operate in all its parts, as attained by Mr. Ward's arrangements. The old plans were complicated; but these are so simple, that an ordinary sailor can properly use the flags without the least liability of committing an error. The most important part of this new and truly valuable invention is the night signal, by which intelligence can be transmitted from ship to ship, even further than is possible with the flags. This great desideratum is accomplished by the use of coloured glass cylinders, encircling white-light lamps, with movable colours or screens for the glass globes. The inventor has adopted four lamps, of any required size, capable of transmitting the greatest degree of light possible to attain: around the fixed glass globes, he employs coloured glasses and metallic cylinders, arranged so that they can be moved up and down by small cords. For instance, the four lamps are suspended above deck at any height required; upon the deck a man has command of the small work cords attached to the cylinder covers and coloured cylinder lenses: if he wish to expose the red light, he pulls the red cord; if the white light, the envelope cord is slackened. The following is the official description :—

"The system consists in the use of four lanterns arranged at equal given distances in a vertical line, connected with each other and the deck, by means of jack-stays, and are as fixtures when properly triced up. Each lantern is provided with a movable screen envelope to hide the light, and cylindrical lenses to colour it, which are operated on, and brought into requisition, by means of small work lines coming down to the operator, who, at pleasure, screens or colours any one or more of the lights, thereby forming combinations indicating the numerals with the use of three lanterns, and the letters of the alphabet with the four, whereby continuous signal communications are maintained of any length, on any subject, with corresponding facility and correctness to that accomplished by the electric telegraph on the land, and applicable to any code of signals in common use, of whatever language, government, or nation. By the use of five of these lanterns, correspondingly arranged, the numerals are indicated without the aid of the coloured cylinder lenses; viz., by white lights only, affording great range of signal.

"These lanterns are so constructed, as to be divested of their work-gear, and used as ordinary signal lanterns by the flag halyards, whereby 4 signals are effected with two lanterns ; 23 with three ; 63 with four ; 160 with five ; and 384 with six : making a total of 634 separate, distinct, one-hoist signals, with six lanterns, and each signal displayed in a vertical line from any desirable part of the ship, with all the sails set ; showing the same at all points of the horizon ; to remain (if necessary) for hours, or till understood and correspondingly acknowledged—making its reception a certainty, which is not the case with signals that require any compound or other operation to complete a signification, as some of the changes pass unobserved to the most observing, or the difference in time-flashes disputed, and the signal misunderstood, leading to consequences the most serious.

"They are made applicable for steering, whereby instant signal directions are given by the pilot to the helmsman, by adding a green lens in connection with the ruby, and used in manner following:—The white light indicates 'attention,' or 'steady;' red, 'port the helm;' green, 'starboard the helm; and the metal or screen envelope (when brought into requisition) indicates 'all right,' or 'finished.'

"With one of these lanterns in the hands of the pilot and helmsman respectively, instant orders can be indicated by the pilot to the helmsman, who makes the lantern with him indicate the same as that of the pilot's, thereby signifying that he has respected the signal, and put the helm accordingly, amid driving storms, the blowing off of steam, or in action, when it would be almost an impossibility to have orders otherwise speedily and correctly given the ship's length, the very mistaking of which might endanger valuable lives, ship, and cargo."

Besides the system of flags for the day, and lamps for the night, Mr. Ward has arranged a code of sounds, to be used in time of fog, by the discharge of a cannon at fixed intervals, the number of seconds or minutes between the sounds to indicate the letter or figure desired. In this manner he has most successfully devised a system of marine telegraphy surpassing all others heretofore employed at sea, and deservedly won the high commendation accorded him by the Jurors of the Exhibition, and the universal eulogium expressed by the press and government officials both of the Old and the New World.

MAIZENA.—There was no article of food in the International Exhibition of greater importance than this new preparation of the American maize. It received the commendation of "Exceedingly Excellent for Food," from two different Juries, and was awarded a Prize Medal. The Maizena was exhibited by Mr. William I. Townsend, in behalf of the Glen Cove Company, of New York, and has been introduced most successfully by that energetic gentleman throughout Europe. As an article of food, the Maizena is one of the greatest blessings given to man by a beneficent Providence; for, indeed, it excels, in effecting beneficial results, the Iceland moss, arrowroot, sago, and all other species of farinaceous products. It is economically used for making puddings, creams, custards, blancmange, and various other preparations of food; and has been successfully administered to invalids and children. The best medical authorities recommend the Maizena as the most wholesome food that can be eaten.

Maize, or Indian corn, is a cereal of the greatest importance, although its real merit is but little known to Europeans generally. It is a plant, valuable in all its parts. The grain is eaten by man and beast; and to both it is unsurpassable as a nutriment. For man it is prepared in many ways; of which, Maizena, bread, and hominy are the most common. The stalk is eaten by horses and cattle, when green, or dried; and, in either condition, it is to them the most preferred "long-food." Horses, cattle, swine, and all kinds of poultry are partial to the grain; and it fattens more economically than any other kind of food. The best beef and bacon are produced by the use of maize; and they command the highest price in the American markets.

There are several species of maize, or Indian corn; and among them are the yellow and white flints, the pearl-white, gourd seed, stock grain, and pop or dwarf corn: each of these kinds is adapted for some special use. The yellow flint is a very hard grain, and grows in the northern states of America: it is not very luxuriant in growth,

T

nor nutritious as food. The white flint is raised in very large quantities in the western and middle states, and is the chief sustenance of the people, as well as horses and farming stock generally. Bread made from this maize is more wholesome than that prepared from the wheat, and is most generally consumed in the southern states of America. The pearl-white can only be raised in the middle states, where the long days and warm nights, with the heavy dews, unite in perfecting the growth of the grain by a steady and healthy process. During the day the sun expands the fibres of the stalk, and opens the bud-folds, that new parts may receive invigoration by its genial rays. At night the dews of heaven refresh the plant; the watery vapour penetrates each crevice, giving increased vigour to the stately stalk, luxuriant leaves, and beautiful tassel. While this progress is going on in the development of the fibre parts, the ear of corn is rapidly formed, and ripens to a state of perfection. Each grain grows without being injured by disease or drought, cold or heat, and attains fulness in due season. From this kind of Indian corn the Glen Cove Company manufacture their celebrated Maizena flour, and superior starch. This establishment now supplies all parts of the world with these two articles; and the superior merits of both have been fully acknowledged by various institutions.

Maizena flour is separated from the heart of the grain and its husky casing without the aid of chemicals; and thus, by this new process, the pure Indian corn flour is obtained, with all the native nutriment of that most important cereal. The maize flour was extensively used in the refreshment department of the Exhibition; its economy being fully realised by the contractor: and as an evidence that the visitors appreciated the merits of that particular kind of food, we need only remark, that there was a daily consumption of over 2,000 puddings, creams, omelets, blanc-mange, and custards, made from Maizena. Messrs. Huntly and Palmer, of Reading, use this flour in the manufacture of their biscuits, which are so extensively sold throughout the civilised world. The Maizena is an essential article of food in every family, and it is employed in a great variety of preparations. Messrs. Tomlin, Rendell, and Company, 33, Eastcheap, London, are the authorised consignees; and William I. Townsend is the general agent.

SEWING MACHINES.—Among the most remarkable novelties of the American Court, was the Sewing Machine, an invention that has come into very general use throughout the world, within the past twenty years; and, in fact, there were but few in domestic employment prior to 1852. There are several patented improved Sewing Machines; but the majority of them are only modifications and sectional improvements of the original, invented by Elias Howe, junior. There are, however, several machines based upon distinct principles.

The art of sewing is coeval with the creation of the world, as we learn from an edition of the Bible, printed in London in 1597; wherein it is stated, respecting Adam and Eve—" When the eyes of them both were opened, and they knew that they were naked, they sewed figge-tree leaves together, and made themselves breeches." How Eve sewed together leaves, and mantled her perfect form with the fig-tree foliage, we have not been informed by the ancient writers; nor have we the least authority for

WHEELER & WILSONS (PRIZE MEDAL) SEWING MACHINES.

supposing that the art of sewing was practised in the dim past in any other manner than by the hand, as originated, perhaps, by Eve in the Garden of Eden, upwards of 5,000 years ago. In ancient times, Tambouring Machines were employed for making and ornamenting fabrics of different kinds; and from time to time, since the creation of the world, improvements have been made in the form or make of the hand needle. In 1755, a patent was granted to Christopher F. Wiesenthal, of England, for an improved needle, which had for its novelty the eye in the centre; and, with a slight change, the idea was again patented, in 1842 (Fig. 1), for the purpose of facilitating

Fig. 1.

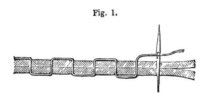

leather stitching; but, in the process, the needle had to be drawn "through and through" the leather with a pair of pincers. The next improvement was a needle for embroidering in a loom, with one, two, or more shuttles, which was patented by Robert Allsop, in England, in 1770; and, in 1804, a machine for embroidering with a combination of needles, was patented by John Duncan. In 1807, James Winter, of England, invented and patented an apparatus for stitching gloves; and, in 1834, a patent was granted to M. Thimonier, for a crotcheting machine, adapted for sewing purposes. A hooked needle was employed, and, when thrust through the cloth, caught the thread and brought back with it a loop. This needle carried the loop through the cloth a little in advance, where another was formed, and thus the stitches were effected. Various other steps were made, in Europe and America, towards the consummation of a useful and practicable sewing machine; but none of them obtained much notice prior to the invention of Howe. This ingenious inventor obtained a patent for his perfected machine in America, September 10th, 1846, in which was used a needle and a shuttle, combined with holding surfaces, and other auxiliary mechanism. The invention was a fully developed idea; and, as an apparatus, it worked successfully when brought to a fair test; and from thence it was but a short time before the grand achievement was appreciated by others. After the signal success of Howe, a great number of new contrivances followed, having in view the attainment of the great end, without infringing on the conception of the original inventor.

These various alleged improvements effected three kinds of stitches. 1st. The chain, or tambour stitch, used by Thimonier in France, in 1835, and latterly known as the Franklin single chain-stitch. This kind of sewing cannot be depended upon in fabrics intended for use, as it easily unravels. 2nd. The double-thread chain-stitch, being like the chain or tambour, except that two threads are used, one upon each side of the fabric. This process employs about six yards of thread for each yard of seam. The 3rd is the double lock-stitch, made by interlocking two threads in the fabric, and having a stitch upon both sides of the fabric alike, requiring about three yards of thread to each yard of seam. This latter process is the most substantial, and, in fact, the only reliable stitch for all kinds of articles intended for wear.

There were exhibited, in the American Court, several kinds of machines, each of which was alleged to contain some particular improvement with respect to mechanical combination; and of these were Wheeler & Wilson's, of New York, and 139,

Regent Street, London; for which a prize medal was awarded. I. M. Singer, of New York, and 72, Regent Street, London, for "his collection of well-constructed sewing machines," received "honourable mention." Willcox & Gibbs, for improvements in sewing machines, also received "honourable mention." A. Howe, representing an incorporated company, of New York, received a "medal" for their well-arranged collection of machines. L. A. Bigelow, of Boston, representing C. R. Goodwin, received "honourable mention" for a machine, constructed for sewing boots, shoes, and other kinds of leather work. The peculiar combinations of the various machines are not original, except with respect to some particular part, as all of them have the novelties of either the chain or the lock-stitch; and these, respectively, we shall briefly consider.

The single-thread "loop," or "chain" stitch, formed by the Franklin machine, is very objectionable, from its liability to ravel, as illustrated by the arrangement of the thread in Fig. 2. The double-thread "loop,"

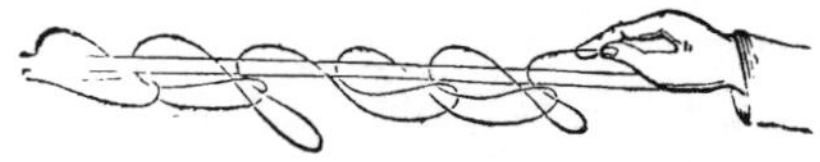

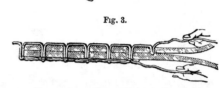

Fig 2.

or chain-stitch, represented by Fig. 3, is also liable to unravel; and, besides this fault, the thread makes an uneven surface of the fabric; and, ultimately, a contraction of the material on the line of the seam. This stitch requires at least six and a-half yards of thread to each yard of seam; about double the quantity required for the lock-

Fig. 3.

stitch, represented by Fig. 4. The illustration shows that the thread is interlocked in the centre of the fabric, and the surfaces of the cloth are left even. This stitch is decidedly the most serviceable, and suitable for all kinds of fabrics, whether of leather or fibre goods: it cannot ravel; the cloth is strengthened without the liability of contraction; and the interlocking thread practicably becomes a part of the

Fig. 4.

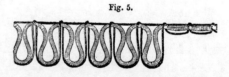

texture of the fabric. Besides this peculiar process, of uniting fabrics in the manufacture of garments, or other species of goods, the machine can be adjusted to make a gathering lock-stitch, as represented by Fig. 5, by which it will be seen that the most difficult of needle-work can be executed by the machine. This great achievement is effected by leaving the lower thread loose, which forms the gathering; and, singular as it may appear, the seam is not liable to ravel. The

Fig. 5.

advantages of the Lock-Stitch Machine have been considered to be—1st, Beauty and excellence of stitch, alike upon both sides of the fabric served; 2nd, Strength, firmness, and durability of seam that will not rip or ravel; and, 3rd, Economy of thread.

It will be seen from the preceding, that of the three combinations of stitches, the "lock" is the only one that can be considered of permanent utility. Now there are two kinds of machines that effect this great desideratum—namely, the "Shuttle" and "Rotating Hook" machines: the former was the peculiar characteristic of the

Singer machine, and the latter of the Wheeler & Wilson's.   The "Shuttle" machine
has been in use for nine years in America; and upwards of 60,000 of them have been
distributed throughout the Old and the New World.   They are well constructed, and
perform the work with neatness and considerable celerity.   The shuttle containing
the bobbin, moves back and forth, passing through successive loops, fixed by the to-
and-fro action of the needle.   This process of forming the lock-stitch, though perfectly
satisfactory with respect to a certain kind of sewing, was, however, found to be
imperfect in executing fine domestic sewing; and the inventive genius of A. B. Wilson
devised an important improvement, by dispensing with the shuttle, and adopting, in

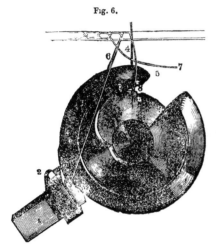

Fig. 6.

its stead, a "rotating hook," as represented by Fig. 6.
By this novelty, the sewing machine was brought
to a greater degree of perfection, especially for fine
work.   The combination of mechanical contrivances
of the machine, are the most simple and efficient
ever adopted to effect an end so important for the
industrial people of the world; and Mr. Wilson
will be justly acknowledged, by all industrial classes,
as having given to needle-craft an improvement of
inestimable value.

The inventor, Wilson, associated with himself
Nathaniel Wheeler; and, as a firm, they have manufactured a very large number of machines—amounting, in the aggregate, to at least 115,000.   The grand
novelty of this machine, as we have said before, is the rotating hook.   The machines
are represented in one of the illustrations of this work, as arranged in the Exhibition,
at the entrance to the American Court.   The mechanical parts—the treadle, lever,
needle arms, adjusting springs, and other auxiliaries—are well known; and therefore
we shall confine our description to that part of the machine known as the rotating
hook, which produces the lock-stitch, and is recognised as its essential part.

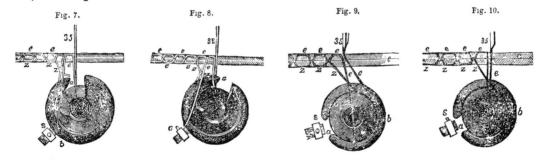

Fig. 7.   Fig. 8.   Fig. 9.   Fig. 10.

The stitch is formed by the combined action of an eye-pointed needle, 35,
carrying the upper thread, e, a rotating hook, 5, Fig. 8, and a double, convex,
metallic spool, carrying the lower thread.   The needle being threaded as in the
foregoing "directions," and the process of sewing being commenced, it will be
observed (Figs. 6 and 7), that the needle, having descended, as it rises, the line of
thread upon its right is slightly looped.   The point, a, of the rotating hook, reaches

the needle at this instant, passes close to its right side, and enters the loop of thread, as represented by Fig. 8. As it further revolves, it enlarges this loop, and carries it forward to the position indicated in Fig. 9, the upper thread extending from the eye of the needle along the groove of the hook, and thence to the fabric. Upon turning the hook further, the line of thread extending along the groove slips off, and falls in front of the metallic spool (Fig. 10), which contains the lower thread, and lies in the cavity of the hook, with the thread flowing from it towards the front of the machine. As the loop slips from the point of the hook, and is drawn up, it will be found to inclose the lower thread, and interlock with it. This loop is drawn up by the hook in the process of enlarging the next loop, as may be seen in Fig. 9. The loop slips from the hook when it has made little more than one-half of a revolution; and, as it is drawn up by the hook in enlarging the next loop, it is necessary to hold it until the hook shall have completed the revolution, and entered the next loop. For this office, the loop-check, 36, is employed. It consists of a small brush, or an equivalent, held in slight contact with the periphery of the hook as it rotates, and thus holds the loop, as in Figs. 6 and 7, and prevents it slipping until the hook has completed its revolution, and enters the next loop at the needle, as seen in Fig. 8. The chamfered portion of the hook then reaches this check, and relieves the loop, which is then drawn up, as seen in the same figure.

Among the advantages claimed for Wheeler & Wilson's Sewing Machine, are— 1st. Beauty and superiority of stitch, the seam being level with the fabric on both sides. 2nd. Strength of seam, not being liable to rip or ravel. 3rd. Economy in the use of thread. 4th. Simplicity and beauty of the machine. 5th. Speed, and variety of the kind of work that it can execute; such, for example, as stitching, hemming, felling, cording, embroidering, gathering, and, in fact, every kind of work that might be desired. It can not only be employed for coarse fabrics, but it may be used for sewing fabrics of the finest texture. The silk-worm may be disrobed of its silken covering, and the most delicate fibre of the cocoon may be introduced into the machine for embroidering. In fact, it is possible to use the coarsest or finest thread; a bullrush bag, a coffee-sack, or the finest fabric ever made by the ingenuity of man, can be successfully stitched, hemmed, or embroidered by this wonderful perfection of industrial art.

The Sewing Machine having been brought to a point of complete success, and perfected in its mechanical contrivances, it may be interesting to observe the product of its needle. According to an average computation, the following are the comparative results in the manufacturing of the articles mentioned. The time required for making a frock-coat by hand, is sixteen hours and thirty-five minutes; by sewing machine, two hours and thirty-eight minutes. By hand, a pair of trousers can be made in five hours and fifteen minutes; by machine, in fifty-one minutes. A silk dress requiring eight hours and twenty-seven minutes by the hand, can be made by the machine in one hour and thirteen minutes. These facts show the wonderful celerity attained in the making of fabrics, and the great saving of labour. In Europe, the Sewing Machine is rapidly being introduced into the domestic circle; and, ere long, it will be as common in the family service, as the ordinary needle has been since the art of sewing became a part of the handiwork of woman. We cannot but recognise the Sewing Machine as an achievement of great credit to the age in which we live—a blessing to the poor, and a convenience to the rich; and, we opine, it will redound to the honour and glory of the industrial world.

REAPING MACHINES.—In sacred history we are informed, that "Ruth, the Moabitess, said unto Naomi, Let me now go to the field, and glean ears of corn after him in whose sight I shall find grace. And Naomi said unto her, Go, my daughter. And she went, and came, and gleaned in the field after the reapers:" and thus, for 5,000 years, fair maidens have imitated their worthy exemplar, the reapers felling the corn by the aid of a sickle. It was not until the present century, and generation, that the tillers of the soil learned, by practical experiment, that the ancient mode of reaping could be superseded by a more economical and useful process for harvesting. A reaper could not cut, within a day, more than half an acre of an average crop of wheat with the sickle; and it is only within the past ten years, that the people of the Old World have even considered the propriety of an abandonment of the slow and toilsome process of gathering grain with the sickle-knife. In America, the "cradle" superseded the old method before the close of the last century; which was a vast stride in economical harvesting. It was a scythe about five feet long, fastened to a snath and a frame-work, consisting of six or eight fingers, or small rods, extending parallel with the scythe. Suspended by a strap from the shoulder, this apparatus was easily worked, and an expert hand could cut about two acres of wheat per day. It cut a swath about five feet wide; and the wheat was beautifully and evenly laid, ready to be raked in piles or heaps for the "binder." In the agricultural districts, it behoves the farmers to engage their labourers long ere the corn ripens to its golden hue; and as the demand for them is generally greater than at any other season of the year, they command a correspondingly higher scale of wages. The scarcity of labourers often occasions a loss to the farmer, as the delay in gathering the corn after it has fully ripened, in some instances, has inflicted upon the proprietor the loss of the crop by heavy storms, or by cereal diseases. The "cradle" lessened the expense of gathering the grain; but even in its employment, the delays in harvesting were found to be dangerous. This led the ingenious mind to contrive means to economise, with respect to time and labour, in the gathering of the ripened corn, whether wheat, rye, oats, barley, or buck-wheat; and this great achievement was accomplished by Mr. Cyrus H. M'Cormick, of the Valley of Virginia, in the production of his world-renowned "Reaping Machine." For more than a quarter of a century, the M'Cormick agricultural implements have been common to every farm in Virginia; and as the people of that great state spread, from time to time, throughout the west, they carried with them the improvements invented by their fellow-country-man. The wide-spread prairies, and vast, cleared woodlands of the great west, having become the wheat-producing regions of America, M'Cormick, about sixteen years since, located his manufactory at Chicago, where he has pro-duced for the agriculturists over 45,000 of his superior reaping machines. It is simple in its construction, and is capable of cutting fifteen acres of wheat per day; and, by the same process, delivers the straw in heaps, ready to be bound into a sheaf of convenient size. Two horses, walking in the last swath cut, draw the machine, which is fixed upon wheels; and the revolving of the wheels puts into motion a gearing, which produces a to-and-fro movement of a saw, teeth-like cutter. The straw falls evenly upon a plank-floor bed, and it is then pushed into the earth by a rake, which revolves synchronously with the wheels of the carriage. The invention of the raker has greatly enhanced the value of the Reaper, because it saves the expense of a labourer to do that particular work. It is easy to calculate the economy resulting from the use of M'Cormick's Reaper, in preference to the sickle. By the former, with one man and two horses, fifteen acres of heavy corn can be cut per day; and, by the latter, only half an acre can be cut and placed in small heaps for the binder. Besides the advantage of cutting thirty times more than can be accomplished by the sickle, the machine cuts the straw near the earth, and leaves a very short stubble.

M'Cormick's Reaper has been thoroughly tested, and impartially compared with other machines devised for the same objects. The result of an important trial is given in the following notice, which is extracted from the London *Times*, of August 16th, 1862:—

"In 1851, M'Cormick's American Reaping Machine, at the Exhibition, created a greater sensation, in its way, than either Power's statue or Hobbs' locks. Its fame at once, of course, raised up for it a host of antagonists and imitators; and it was not till the golden fruits of many autumns, in the fields of England, France, Belgium, and Germany, had been saved by this machine, that its superiority was tacitly acknowledged; and even competing agricultural implement-makers were compelled to own that, if not the best, it was certainly the most popular, and the most generally used. * * * *

"The new one consists in the addition of the automaton rake, which has two actions. During one part of the revolution of the gathering fans, it acts with, and as one of them, till its wooden teeth are level with the platform, where the cut corn lies. It then ceases to revolve, and, by a most ingenious piece of mechanism, makes a sudden horizontal movement, throwing aside on to the ground the entire sheaf, and instantly after resuming its motion as one of the revolving fans. This machine has been tried once before in England among some of the heavy Essex crops, when its performances exceeded the most sanguine expectations. Recently it has been publicly tried again, in the presence of a number of gentlemen farmers, on Mr. Dixon's farm, about three miles beyond Hemel-Hempstead. This trial was made under the most unfavourable circumstances; in fact, under circumstances which the farmers present contended should have prevented the machine being tried at all. The night and morning had been very wet, and the rain was still falling sharply, when the machine, drawn by two horses, and wielding its fans and rake in the most aggressive manner, was brought to a field of twenty-one acres, covered with a very heavy crop of red lammas wheat, completely saturated and bent down by the rain. Along the edge of this field, where the ground was very rough, and the corn straggling and beaten down, the machine was turned. Much misgiving was expressed before starting as to the power of the rake to act on such ground against wind and rain, and to remove the soddened crop from the platform into regular sheaves. A very few moments, however, sufficed to put these fears at rest. The Reaper went to its work at the rate of about three miles an hour, making a clear cut broad track of 5 ft. 6 in. wide, and turning out neat and remarkably large loose sheaves at intervals of about 15 ft. apart. The movements of the Reaper were exact and perfectly noiseless, and it was easily turned in any direction. An ordinary agricultural labourer at first drove it. Afterwards Mr. Dixon took the place of driver; but the results were the same in both cases. The bunches were well laid; the cut was clean and close to the earth; and the spacing between the sheaves as clear and accurate as if every foot had been measured. At one part the corn was tangled and badly flattened—badly enough to have offered difficulties to the ordinary Reaper; but the machine went through it with the same ease and regularity as through all the rest. The horses were then turned direct into and across the thickest part of the crop from corner to corner of the field; and though, as a matter of course, the passage of the animals drawing the machine trampled down a large portion of the stalks before its track, the Reaper still worked as cleanly and efficiently as ever. First came one of the fans, pushing its *quantum*, when cut, on to the platform; then a second, third, and fourth, when the rake swept round in a semi-curve, and turned the whole mass out in a thick sheaf on to the ground. The horses appeared to draw it easily—more easily, in fact, than the old machine; while, from the strength and simplicity of the improved mechanism, it was evident that, even in the most inexperienced hands, nothing but wilful damage could derange its slight but strong machinery."

The Reaper has been extensively employed in Great Britain, France, Germany,

Mᶜ CORMICK'S REAPING MACHINE

PRIZE MEDAL.

Hungary, Italy, Belgium, and Russia; and is being rapidly introduced into all corn-growing countries throughout the world. It was first exhibited in the Great Exhibition of 1851, and was originally patented in the United States in 1834, and improved in 1847. The invention was approved of by the "American Institute;" and it awarded to M'Cormick a "Gold Medal" in 1849. In 1851, the *Times* thus noticed the machine, then exhibited in the American department of the Exhibition:—

"It will be remembered that the American department was the poorest and least interesting of all foreign countries. Of late, it has justly assumed a position of the first importance, as having brought to the aid of our *distressed agriculturists*, a machine which, if it realise the anticipations of competent judges, will amply remunerate England for all her outlay connected with the Great Exhibition. The Reaping Machine from the United States is the most *valuable contribution*, from abroad, to the stock of our previous knowledge, that we have yet discovered."

And the "Council of Judges" awarded for it the Great Council Medal of the Exhibition, "on the ground of originality and value."

At the French Universal Exposition, in 1855, the Grand Gold Medal of Honour was awarded by the Judges, as follows:—

"In agriculture, the sole Grand Medal of Honour was awarded to C. H. M'Cormick, of Chicago, Illinois, United States of America, and inventor of the Reaping Machine that has operated the best at every trial, and is the type after which all the other Reapers have been made, with different modifications that have not changed the principle of the discovery."

In 1857, the highest prize of the Royal Agricultural Society of England was awarded for M'Cormick's Reaper; as also the Gold Medal of Honour, and Diploma of the United States' National Agricultural Society, at their annual fair in Syracuse, New York, "for the best Reaper," after a severe trial of several days.

In 1859, after a three days' trial on the imperial farm of Fouilleuse, near St. Cloud, France, the Grand Gold Medal of Honour was again awarded to M'Cormick's implement, "as the incontestably best machine among them all;" also the first prize as a Reaper, in competition with twenty-eight French and foreign machines.

An official report thus refers to M'Cormick's last improvement:—

"But the leading distinguishing characteristic of the present machine, is its automatic delivery of the cut corn at the side, in loose gavels or sheaves, out of the track of the horses in passing around, without being bound up or removed; this whole operation being performed by a driver with his team, and more perfectly than could possibly be done by manual labour.

"The new attachment may be thus described:—It consists in certain arrangements of mechanism in which a rake is used, and has motions given to it; so that, during one part of the revolution of the gathering reel, the rake acts as one of its vanes, bringing in the crop towards the cutting blades. When the rake reaches the cutting blades, in front of the platform, it ceases to revolve around the reel shaft—which continues its rotary motion—and is made to move horizontally, upon a vertical hinge, to which one end is attached, the points of the teeth being near the surface of the platform, over which it passes, sweeping the cut corn off at the side, and depositing it on the ground in sheaves, ready for the binder. Motion is then given to the rake, causing it to rotate around the shaft of the reel, and it is brought into a line with the reel shaft at that part of its revolution when it again begins to act as one of the vanes of the reel.

"The mechanism by which these operations are controlled is simple and durable—consisting of a roller, guided by an eccentric or cam, and the necessary parts to attach the rake."

In proximity to M'Cormick's Reaper was Wood's "Self-raking Reaper, Combined Reaping and Mowing Machine, and Grass Mowing Machine," invented by Mr. Walter A. Wood, of Hoosick Fall, New York. This improvement for the gathering of grass, has won the favour of many agriculturists of both continents. In America and Europe it has had a rapid sale since 1852—the number sold, in the aggregate, amounting to about 30,000; and, although the Reaping Machine did not receive a Prize Medal at the late International Exhibition, yet it is worthy of the most flattering consideration. The peculiar advantages of Wood's machines, compared with M'Cormick's last invention, were fairly tested on a special occasion; but it seems, from the report, that the latter was awarded superior merit. The Mower was highly successful in France in 1860, at the only trial of grass mowers ever held under the auspices of the imperial government; and, at that period, it received the "Grand Gold Medal of Honour," as the most complete machine on trial, either native or foreign; also, a gold medal and 1,000 francs, as the best foreign machine.

A "Reaping and Mowing Machine" was exhibited by Messrs. Russell & Tremain, of New York, but it failed to receive any especial commendation. Kirby's "Patent Combined Mower and Reaper," and his "Single Mower," received "honourable mention." The following is a description of the peculiar advantages of Kirby's improvement, viz. :—

"The peculiar features are an independent action between the driving-wheel and finger-bar when mowing, so that they may each follow their own ground, and each play up and down independently of the other. The driver's seat is so pivoted over the driving-wheel, that the weight of the driver balances the weight of the frame and the downward pressure on the horses' necks, and throws the whole upon the driving-wheel, thus adding to the power of the wheel, and materially lightening the draught of the machine. It has an adjustable overhanging reel, used in either mowing or reaping, or not, as desired, and a revolving track-clearer, which spreads the grass evenly. By means of a lever at the side of the driver, either or both ends of the cutting apparatus may be lifted to pass obstructions, or move from field to field."

It will be observed, from the brief sketch that we have given of this important invention, that M'Cormick has won unfading laurels in the production of his great "Reaper," and that agriculturists throughout the world have been most singularly blessed by this new stride in mechanics.

During the Exhibition period, M'Cormick's and other reapers were tested at Preston. The competitors were equally sanguine of success, and each anxiously aspired for the premium medal. The programme for the trials was impartially arranged; and, in its execution, each exhibitor endeavoured to honourably merit the reward for superiority. The grain was very heavy, and the surface of the ground traversed by the machines was calculated to fully test the utility of the inventions for general adoption by agriculturists. All were equally circumstanced, and each was impartially manipulated. M'Cormick was triumphant! His improved Reaper achieved a great success, and was recognised as a climax of agricultural invention.

Subsequent to the Preston trial, M'Cormick distanced his competitors at the International Exhibition held at Lille, France. There, too, his Reaper won the Great Gold Medal for superiority. Machines from England and other parts of the world were brought to the Exhibition to compete for the French honour, and they were fairly tried upon the fertile plains near Lille. The result was decidedly in favour of M'Cormick's machine in every respect. At the Hamburg International Exhibition, he was honoured with the Great Gold Medal, "for the practical introduction and improvement of the Reaping Machine." This was the only Gold Medal awarded to an American; and was one of the twelve distributed for the most useful inventions or improvements exhibited. The M'Cormick Reaper has attained a permanent position as a successful agricultural implement in both hemispheres; and, for the future, it will be as essential to farmers as the shovel and the hoe. It is in use throughout the civilised world, and universally recognised as the greatest labour-saving machine that has been devised during this most eventful century.

WASHING AND WRINGING MACHINES.—These singular domestic inventions have attained great perfection in economising labour, and in saving garments from the severe wear and tear so common to their cleansing by the rubbing process, heretofore practised. These machines *squeeze* the cloth, and expel from it the water and its dirty particles. The principle of washing by the machine is very similar to that performed by manual labour. The twisting or wringing of clothes by the hand, stretches or breaks the fibres; but the machine does not affect the thread; and, in fact, a piece of paper may be pressed nearly dry without producing the least tear. Of the machines exhibited, there were Sanborn's patent "Clothes Wringer, Starcher, and Mangler;" and C. E. Gray's "Little Giant Wringer, Washer, and Mangler." The two inventions, although not dissimilar in their operations, are quite different in their mechanical construction. For effectiveness and simplicity, Gray's patent has unquestionably the advantage. Figs. 1 and 2 are illustrations of his machine; the former representing it attached to a tray, as in process of wringing; and the latter shows its peculiar construction.

Fig. 1.

A A represent a horizontal wooden bar, each end of which rests upon the edge of a tray or tub, or across the corner of a table, to which it may be as easily fastened for mangling or starching; B B are solid india-rubber rollers, between which the clothes are made to pass; C C are galvanised iron levers, which hold the rollers in position; D is the handle by which the rollers are moved; E E are the rods which secure the machine to the tray, tub, or table, and are lengthened or shortened *ad libitum*, by means of a screw thread in the upper end; F F are the india-rubber springs, which hold the two sections of the levers, and regulate their action upon the material points between the rollers; through their agency the pressure is equalised, so that a small or bulky article is acted upon by very nearly the prime weight. All the iron parts of Gray's machine are coated with composition metal that does not rust; and, besides, it prevents softening of the india-rubber. Mr. Gray has attained perfection in the invention of a wringer; and, ere long, his machine will be regarded as one of the necessary articles of domestic service; while we are confident that it will be found economical, with respect to labour and the wear of clothing. The price of the machine is only 17*s*. 6*d*., and is sold by Messrs. Bostwick &

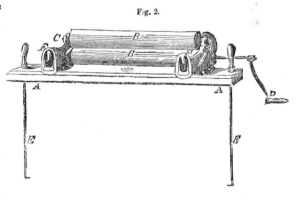

Fig. 2.

Co., 67, Blackman-street, Borough, London; who are the proprietors of the patent for the United Kingdom.

MANCUR'S COMPOUND SPRING SCALE.—This exceedingly novel contrivance was perhaps the most simple of the useful inventions exhibited in the American Court. The annexed figure represents one of the scales, gauged for two classes of measurement. The large ring and hook are employed when the article to be weighed is heavy, and the small ring and hook when it is light. The Scales are held in the hand by the ring, and the article to be weighed is attached to the hook: when suspended, the weight will open the circular or elliptical steel spring; and, as it opens, the pointer rises to the numeral indicating the weight of the article. These Scales have been carefully proved, and found to be most singularly correct, equalling the Roman balance. Each elliptic spring is practically tested and gauged, in conformity with the elasticity of the metal, which is tempered by a recently discovered process. By this new and important discovery the metal is mathematically prepared to present a given resistance or elasticity, alike in all climates. They are neatly constructed; and a scale measuring 200 lbs. is sold for the small sum of five shillings! Although only a short time has elapsed (June, 1863) since they were introduced to the British public, upwards of 18,000 have already been sold. They were exhibited by the proprietor, Mr. E. Mancur; and are on sale by J. A. Brown & Co., 11, Cullum-street, London.

BROWN'S LOCKETS AND JEWELLERY.—It was said by people of olden times, that "it was not all gold that glittered." There never was a more correct saying; and its truth is evidenced by Mr. Brown's new style of jewellery, exhibited in a case represented by the annexed illustration. These watch and miniature cases are manufactured and sold for almost nominal sums, notwithstanding their golden armour defies detection by acids; and they wear for many years. The inferior metal is thickly plated with 16-carat gold; and the articles manufactured therefrom, retain their original beauty in defiance of the rough usage of the hand of time. These superior goods are sold by the manufacturers, J. A. Brown & Co., 11, Cullum-street, London.

BLAKE'S STONE-CRUSHING MACHINE was another of the extraordinary labour saving inventions exhibited in the American department. The mechanism of this novel apparatus was exceedingly simple, and easy to be worked. The stone was placed between two iron grooved plates, which opened and closed upon it, and at each pressing it broke into pieces. These plates were adjusted to break a stone of any desired size. The machine will be found useful in all countries where there are macadamised roads, as it can crush the boulder or other stone to the size required, as "metal" for the road. It has been most favourably received in France, Russia, and other countries. It was exhibited by Mr. L. A. Bigelow, of Boston.

Besides the mechanical contrivances mentioned in the foregoing, there were exhibited, in this department, many others of considerable novelty; among which were the Cow Milker, California Pump, Gore's Belt Shifter, Emory's Cotton Gin, and Chickering's Piano. The Cow Milker attracted much attention; and it is a matter of infinite credit to the Americans, that this was, probably, the only "Yankee trick" presented on the occasion from their great country.

CHAPTER IV.

THE COURTS AND GALLERIES OF GREAT BRITAIN.

SOUTH-EAST GALLERIES.—According to the method announced (p. 42), we have noticed the leading characteristics of the South Courts, which were occupied by British exhibitors; to which, having reference to the order of arrangement in the building, we have added the Court occupied by the United States. In further pursuing this portion of the plan, our sketch must necessarily be brief and general, to afford the greater space to "review the whole collection in classes, having special reference to the work of comparison." Our visitor will therefore now hastily pass along the Galleries corresponding with the area we have already traversed. These Galleries were principally occupied with the textile fabrics of the United Kingdom; with cotton goods; flax and hemp; silk and velvet; woollen, worsted, and mixed goods; carpets, in the manufacture of which our country has greatly improved since 1851; woven, spun, felted, and laid fabrics, shown as specimens of printing and dyeing; tapestry, lace, and embroidery. In this department Ireland held a proud position, for richness of design and fineness of work; promising, at no distant day, to equal, if not to surpass, Brussels and Valenciennes. Spitalfields, Coventry, and Paisley here displayed productions of the greatest elegance, and ingenuity of design and execution, as much admired by our foreign visitors as ourselves. Scotland was specially rich in her tartans and hosiery; of which, one specimen was shown containing 1,060 diamonds, and in the manufacture of which no less than forty-two threads were used. Scotland, also, is successfully devoting attention to the manufacture of jute, of which numerous specimens were shown in the Dundee Case, where the manufacture is conducted with great activity. Clothing, also, was here represented, in boots and shoes, hats and bonnets, and the most exquisite dresses for ladies and gentlemen; the robes of the clergy, and the secular trappings of the laity. But we must not anticipate the description due to all these things in their proper classes.

NORTH-EAST COURTS AND GALLERIES.—A large portion of the North-Eastern Courts was filled with furniture, which will come under notice in Class XXX. Entering these Northern Courts from the Central Avenue, the visitor found himself in the Court filled with "musical instruments, and that of all sorts." Here were to be seen and heard all the recent improvements in organs, pianos, harmoniums, violins, drums, Æolian harps, brass instruments (as the cornet-a-piston, with the champion valves), flutes in wood and metal, concertinas, and all our national instruments for producing the "concert of sweet sounds." One great advantage offered in this Court, was the opportunity of marking the progress of improvement in a variety of instruments, from the earliest to the present time. Thus, in flutes, Messrs. Clinton showed some of the earliest, rising by gradual stages to their Eight-keyed Metal Flute, with new key mechanism designed for tropical climates. There was, also, a series from the old harpsichord, in which the strings are twanged by quills, to the iron grand piano of Broadwood, and their successful rivals.

The Courts of China, Japan, and the Ionian Islands adjoined our Music Court. The former two, by an act of welcome, trespass on our British domains. It was very gratifying to have such an excellent opportunity to examine the productions of the two foreign nations with whom we are now acquiring a growing intimacy, and an increasing commerce. The most remarkable object in this curiosity-shop was a human skull, mounted in gold, and alleged to be the skull of Confucius. As the historical veracity of Chinese antiquaries is not in the very highest estimation, the name assigned to this respectable cranium is not likely to impose much on the public credulity: it was certainly the most respectable the Chinese authorities could have selected for this very noble "dome of thought." Among the varieties shown in this collection there was very little of novelty, though there was much to call for admiration in the numerous exquisite specimens of carved works, of which the principal was the Screen taken from behind the emperor's throne in the Summer Palace.

The collection from Japan was, in many respects, more interesting than that from China, and served to sustain and enhance the favourable estimate we had previously formed of Japanese productions. Those who had formerly seen only the lacquered work, known as Japan ware, must have been much surprised at the large varieties of beautiful, rich, and well-executed works with which this little Court abounded. The porcelain vases, jars, bowls, grotesque figures, and egg-shell china; the bronzes, mirrors, and models; the intaglios and medallions; the arms and armour, including a shirt and cap of mail; the swords, bows and arrows; the paper, silk, crape, and cotton exhibited, all served to prove that the Japanese had attained a high degree of civilisation. Some insight into the science and literature of this interesting people, was afforded by their Quadrant and Sun-dial, a Pedometer, a Clock, Thermometer, and Telescope; an Encyclopædia, and several illustrated works on natural history. The so-called "Rice-glass," in this Court, excited no little sensation among those who imagined the glass to be what its name implied. The "Rice-glass" is composed of the same elements as any other glass—soda and silica; the latter being an important element of the husks of rice or wheat, or oats, all of which have siliceous coverings. To many persons, the most interesting objects in this Court were the two spotless solid Spheres of Crystal, from the "Holy Mountain" in Japan, remarkable alike for their transparent purity and their perfection of form.

As much interest is now taken in the silks of Japan (which will probably, ere long, form an important article of commerce with Europe and the western world), we here introduce an important notice which Mr. Robert Hunt has given, on the authority of Captain Howard Vyse; who states, that "twenty-one provinces produce silk. Eight or ten other provinces might be added; but their production is of too little importance to be noted. All the provinces between the east and north produce silk. Aussion and Montsen alone represent 45,000 bales—about 22,500 piculs* of annual production. In comparing the total production of Japan (which is about 67,500 piculs) with the principal silk countries of Europe, before the malady among the silkworms broke out, we find that the production of France was 2,000,000 kilogrammes; of Italy, 4,000,000 kilogrammes: of Spain, 300,000: that is to say, that Japan produces as much as Italy and Spain put together, and as much again as France."

The Ionian Islands were well represented in their geological features. There were specimens of breccia, containing the bones of animals, which easily have been mistaken for ancient petrifactions, but were probably of very recent date—perhaps not more than ten years old. There were also very fine specimens of stalagmite, which constituted the alabaster of the ancients. The wine, olive-oil, dried fruit, inlaid works in wood; the flaxes, sponges, silk, jewellery, and fanciful costumes exhibited in the Court, all proved highly attractive. We hope that cotton-seed, of the finest staples, will be soon introduced into the Ionian Islands, as very rich returns may be anticipated, instead of the inferior sorts now produced.

Passing, for the present, over the two Furniture Courts in this block, we reach the Courts of Hayti, Bahia, Natal, Western and South Australia, New Zealand, Queensland, New South Wales, and Victoria.

Hayti displayed some valuable natural products; as rock crystal, coal, copper, and iron ores; various kinds of wood; as lignum vitæ, and mahogany, of which there was a magnificent block—the manufactures having unimportant pretensions, if we except the embroidery and saddlery.—Bahia exhibited nothing calling for special remark, except its sugars; but Natal was properly described as one of the most picturesque and romantic Courts. It was remarkable for the contrast it displayed of savage and civilised life, in perfect keeping with a very well-drawn sketch of the country. Natal is remarkable for the range of its products, considering the limits of its area. There are the feathers; the land shells of intertropical climes; and the furs of cold climes—a strange diversity, produced by the differences of level, instead of the extensive range of area. Natal, from the great variety of the products shown in the Exhibition, is a perfect microcosm, affording a very good opportunity of studying the world in miniature.

Australia, including the western and southern districts, Queensland, New South Wales, Victoria, Tasmania, and New Zealand, were very fully represented by their varied products; among which gold held that highest place which it has always had in every country. As might have been expected, no part of the Exhibition proved more attractive to the mass of visitors, from the middle classes of British and Irish, than these Courts, filled as they were with the produce collected by their own friends and relatives, by whom these productive regions have been colonised. The mineral, animal, and vegetable products were shown as raw produce, and also as

* A picul = 133½ lbs.

manufactured articles, in such a manner as to indicate the vast natural wealth of these colonies, and the manufacturing skill of the colonists, who deserve the greatest credit for the pains they took in giving a fair representation of the wealth stored up for the enterprising settlers at the antipodes.

Western Australia displayed its rich ores of copper and lead; its metallic sands; its materials for pottery; its valuable woods, of which there was a very noble collection; its native silks, and wools, and wines; its grain of various kinds, which no English farmer could look at without admiration.—South Australia, also, established her claims to a high character for native wealth, making a rich return for the labour expended on her soil and mines, of which the Burra Burra have a world-wide celebrity; and showing, among her treasures, a malachite table of great beauty. One block of copper ore exhibited, weighed no less than six tons; and, among the wools, were the alpaca, angora, and other valuable varieties.—Victoria, as we have seen, was well represented in her obelisk of gold: she is also rich in silver, tin ore, and antimony, of which a block was exhibited, weighing half a ton. Iron ore, also, is plentiful, of which rich specimens were sent; such as are found, in tons, lying on the surface of the ground at Sandhurst. Kaolin, the valuable white clay used in making china, is sufficiently plentiful to have led to the formation of a company in Melbourne, by whom it is manufactured into different articles.

As the wheats and wines of this and the other Australian colonies attracted great attention, we may here mention that the Tuscan wheat weighed 69 lbs. per bushel; the Tartarian oats, 49 lbs. 4 oz. per bushel; and the barley, 58 lbs. 5 oz. per bushel. Twenty-five prize medals, and twenty honourable mentions (the largest number awarded to any British colony), were given for the grain of Victoria. The wines of the colony were highly commended; and it may be expected that, in time, they will gain a high celebrity. At present there are about 2,000 acres planted with vines, which are in a thriving condition; and new ground is preparing for this important growth. To facilitate the manufacture of wine, companies are formed to purchase grapes from the small growers, to assort them carefully, and preserve only the best. The price now paid for grapes is $2\frac{1}{2}d.$ per pound.

The Victorians boast that, since 1851, their country has exceeded all the British colonies in the increase of population. In 1861, the population of the Australian colonies was—in Victoria, 540,322; in New South Wales, 350,860; in South Australia, 128,000; in Tasmania, 89,977; in Queensland, 30,059; in Western Australia, 16,000.

New South Wales has, during the past ten years, yielded gold to the value of £11,683,857; and furnished to the Exhibition forty-eight samples from its various gold-fields. We must, however, regard its specimens of coal with as much interest as the most noble metal. Most important for the interests of commerce, in these times of locomotive and steam navigation, is the fact, that this important colony has its Newcastle, Wallsend, and other mines, from which hundreds of tons of coal are obtained daily; in all, about 20,000 tons weekly. The extent of the coal-field of this region is at present but very imperfectly known. It is ascertained that it runs from Queensland, in the north, to Tasmania in the south; and it is not too much

INTERNATIONAL EXHIBITION.—THE AUSTRALIAN GOLD NUGGET.

to expect that it very extensively underlies other Australian colonies. At present, the colony of New South Wales has eleven seams of coal at work, at levels as high as 1,500 feet above the sea, and down to 450 feet below it. When it is remembered that the produce of these mines, during the last ten years, has been 1,780,000 tons, and that the great field has been very partially explored, there is ample warrant for expecting that it will prove, in the future, a source of prosperity to our antipodal possessions, quite equal to their wants, as our British coal-fields have been to the old country. It should be noticed, also, that the neighbouring colonies, as well as India and China, have received more than half the coal raised in our Australian Newcastle and Wallsend.

Queensland, which has hitherto been distinguished by the export of wool, gives promise of yielding large supplies of cotton of the finest quality—the Sea Island cotton—which grows on the table-lands, 200 miles from the coast. Arrowroot, maize, sugar, coffee, silk, and Dugong oil, ornamental woods, and precious stones, were among the valuable products by which this Court was enriched.

New Zealand—no longer the abode of savage cannibals—is so changed by colonisation, that, " if a railway were made through the earth, the traveller, starting from London, would emerge close to the southern part of Otago, and, when he stepped from the carriage, would scarcely find a single specimen of those tattooed aboriginals who, in the imagination of the timorous, are supposed to cluster around the settlers in the middle island of New Zealand." This important colony approaches in size to Great Britain and Ireland, whose area is about 120,000 square miles; that of New Zealand being 90,500 square miles. The woods, wools, woollen cloths, dyes, gums, flax, cotton, hops, wheat, oats, gold and copper ore, from the five provinces of this colony, all justify the high estimate formed of its richness, and of the prospect it holds out to the emigrant. One very valuable product was the extremely fine Taranaki steel-sand, of volcanic origin, and from which cutlery of the best quality has been produced.

THE NORTH-EAST TRANSEPT, like the North-East Court, was devoted to our colonies. Here again we had Victoria, for the second time; Tasmania, Nova Scotia (which occupied also a square to the westward of this Transept), New Brunswick, Prince Edward's Island, and Canada. Returning towards the Nave, and on the eastern side, we had Newfoundland, Ceylon, Malta, Dominica, Jamaica, Trinidad, and Guiana.

Tasmania—no longer known as Van Diemen's Land—is an island nearly as large as Ireland, lying 120 miles south of our vast Australian continent. Being remarkable for the growth of noble timber, Tasmania was distinguished by a Timber Trophy, composed of planks and spars, for ship-building and architecture; also of beautiful woods for ornamental work. To show the length of ship timber in Tasmania, there were planks of the Blue Gum, measuring 90 feet; and of Stringy Bark, 80 feet in length, of equal width and soundness throughout. We are told that, " of large ship's knees—the want of which has even caused a modification of our naval architecture—an unlimited supply can be obtained from Tasmania, where the stumps of the large trees are left to rot after the trees have been cut up." A specimen of the Swamp Gum was shown in this trophy, which measured 230 feet in length. As no available ship could be procured to bring it whole to London, the plank had to be cut up into twenty-feet lengths; but it was done so as to show that the brand cut across in each transverse section, gave evidence of the former connection of the pieces severed. Coal, both bituminous and anthracitic; black and white marble; the beryl, pink, blue, and white; topazes; serpentine, veined with asbestos; sea-shells of great value; gold (not yet obtained in large quantities), and iron ore, abounding all over the colony, were among the numerous specimens of native produce. On this trophy were suspended two whaling-boats, for which some of the Tasmanian timber is well adapted. They were fitted up with all the gear (except lines and oars) necessary for the whale fishery, to which the Tasmanians are devoted, and of which, in the southern seas, they are likely to become the monopolists. The apex of the trophy was formed of the two jaws of the sperm whale. One whale produced oil worth £900; and the oil from the other was worth £1,150. We should notice also the oats, weighing 51 lbs. 10 oz. to the bushel; and seed wheat, which sells at a guinea a bushel.

The New Brunswick Court was remarkable for a new species of coal, highly bituminous, known as Albertite, and so called from the county in which it is found. Like the cannel coal, it is well adapted for the production of coal-oil, gas, and paraffin. In 1859, 15,000 tons were sold at £3 a ton. It has not yet been found to contain any vegetable remains, but the shale in the pits is rich in fossil fishes, from whose remains the Albertite is probably produced. Timber and fish were among the valuable products in this Court.

Nova Scotia showed specimens of coal, which is raised in large quantities; its oil-coal, which, in some cases, produces 199 gallons to the ton; its gold—above 10,000 dollars worth, and in a manufactured state, used for necklaces and brooches of beautiful workmanship, mounting Nova Scotia amethysts, and pearls. There were also wools, woods, furs, fishes, and models of ships, which are built very cheaply in Nova Scotia.

Prince Edward's Island exhibited samples of agricultural products and manufactures.

Newfoundland had its numerous specimens of fish, cod-liver, and seal oil; good models of ships, and ship-steering apparatus; valuable pharmaceutical preparations, as cochineal colouring, snake root, and poplar blossoms.

Canada, full of loyalty to the mother country, occupied a noble position among the colonies represented in the Exhibition. The minerals shown were numerous and well arranged. There were ores of iron, lead, copper, nickel, silver, and gold. Platinum and iridisomine were shown in grains, separated from the gold-drift. The rock oils of Canada, like those of the United States, are obtained from flowing wells, and are probably produced by the decomposed tissues of the coraline insect, as the rock from which the oil flows is composed of corals in a petrified state. It is gratifying also to find, that while our Cumberland lead is failing, plumbago is found in various parts of Canada. This colony is famous for its timber; among which the maple holds an important place, being productive of an abundance of excellent sugar.

Vancouver's Island displayed its woods, especially its Douglas pine, so useful for

PRINCE EDWARDS ISLAND & BRITISH COLUMBIA COURTS.

masts, and for the large quantity of turpentine it produces. It sent cereals and other vegetable products, and preserved fruits and meats; the oils of the whale, porpoise, and dog-fish; and particularly deserving notice, was the oil of the ulahan— a fish like a smelt, yielding its oil plentifully, which is considered to possess the valuable properties of cod-liver oil.

Our gold-bearing colony of British Columbia, which, in 1851, exported gold to the value of half a million sterling, has acquired great importance from its estimated possession of a large supply of the precious metal. It has other valuable products; among which is its native tea, used as a substitute for tobacco as well as for tea.

Our remaining American colonies, Jamaica, Dominica, Trinidad, and Guiana, were all duly represented: Jamaica by iron and copper, lead, zinc, and manganese, woods, fruits, sugar, and cotton; Dominica by its 170 kinds of woods, starches, cottons, tortoise-shell manufactures, sugar, cocoa, honey, and wax; Trinidad by its asphalt, iron ores, gypsum, lignite, and its exotic products; and Guiana by its fine collection of natural history, well preserved, and the cottons, which promise an ample reward to the cultivator of its extensive coast-lands.

Malta exhibited beautiful examples of sculpture, in its famous Maltese stone; of the finest silver filigree work; of its exquisite lace, mosaic work, and cotton produce.

Ceylon has the choicest woods for furniture and ornamental purposes; and many valuable products from the cocoa-nut, which seems to answer as many purposes in Ceylon as the potato in Ireland. Cinnamon, of the finest qualities, were shown, and the methods of its preparation illustrated. The country was well represented in its spices, pepper, vanilla, and nutmeg. Cotton is now receiving increased attention. Ceylon, also, will assist materially to supply us with plumbago, of which it showed fine specimens, and now sends us large quantities.

We may now ascend to

THE NORTH GALLERY, where we come first on the space allotted to India. Remembering the lamentable revolt of our great Eastern dependency, since the Exhibition of 1851, and the awful death-struggle through which the empire and its distant province have passed, it was with peculiar gratification that we saw abundant proofs not only of the wealth of India, but of its being still an integral part of the British empire. Notwithstanding that dreadful and sanguinary revolt, India made a most extensive display of her treasures in 1862, occupying well the space assigned to her in the British half of the building, and having, besides, a supplementary collection in the Indian Museum in Whitehall-yard. Dr. Forbes Watson, to whose care the success of this department may be principally attributed, anticipates that in a commercial point of view, its value to India, as well as to this country, will be very considerable, and that it will result in substantial advantages far exceeding those which followed the display of Indian articles in Hyde Park and in Paris.

As many of the objects in this department will claim our attention in the sections, we shall be satisfied, for the present, by noticing a few of the more prominent and attractive.

In the Topographical Model of India, the mountains and Highlands are displayed in relief, the mountains being divided into two groups by the valley of the Ganges. To quote from Dr. Watson—" On the north of the river extends the snow-capped chain of the Himalaya mountains, separating India from the Chinese dominions, and drained on all sides by the rivers Indus, Ganges, Brahmaputra, and their affluents. South of the Ganges is spread out an elevated table-land, including the Deccan. This Highland is bordered by the Western Ghauts, rising abruptly from the shores of the Arabian Sea; by the Eastern Ghaut, towards the Bay of Bengal; and by several chains of hills skirting the Ganges and its feeders." Maps produced by the geological survey of India, especially of Madras and Central India, were exhibited, and deserve great praise, as indicating its mineral resources.

The rich ores of India, the iron, copper, antimony, lead, tin, and the gold, and other native metals, were all shown, and are duly recorded in the Illustrated Catalogue; as were, also, the non-metallic mineral products, as coal, lignite, peat, and stone, for purposes of construction—siliceous and calcareous; freestones and flags; porphyritic and basaltic rocks and slates. The clays used for bricks, tiles, and the various kinds of pottery and porcelain, are of much interest, especially from their great variety of colour. The precious stones were not shown in sufficient abundance and variety, considering the large quantities in which they are exported, and which, in 1861-'62, amounted to £153,748. Plumbago, taken from a mine discovered in Goorgaon in 1861, by Dr. W. J. Thornton, was among the specimens which afford the promise that this essential mineral will be obtained in adequate supplies from our own possessions.

India had, also, a good collection of chemical substances and products; some used in manufacture—as impure carbonate of soda, saltpetre, alum, and salts of iron, copper, and lead; manufactured pigments, dyes, and chemical products; chemical substances employed in pharmacy—some metallic, and others vegetable and animal— used for nearly " all the ills that flesh is heir to," and some more calculated to produce disease than arrest its removal, as the churrus (*cannabis sativa*) of the Punjaub. It is a resinous exudation of hemp; and a small quantity placed in the hookah, and smoked, produces almost immediately an intoxicating effect. We are told that the dried hemp plant which has flowered, and from which the resin has not been removed, is called Gunjah, and is used only for smoking. The alcoholic extract is employed medicinally as an anti-spasmodic and anodyne, and is very useful in spasmodic coughs, in tetanus, and in hydrophobia. The large leaves and capsules, without the stalks, are called Bhang, Subjee, or Siddhee, and are used for making an intoxicating drink, and for smoking. Bhang is cheaper than gunjah; and though less powerful, is sold at such a low price, that, for one pice, enough can be purchased to intoxicate a person, though he be habituated to it.

Of agricultural produce, there were wheat, barley, oats, maize, millets, and especially rice, in great variety; peas and lentils. The peculiar fruits of the country were shown by very excellent imitations sent from Lucknow. The chutney, mango, and other produce, were shown as pickles and preserves. Of tea, no fewer than 153 different samples were exhibited, many of them of excellent quality, and all unadulterated with colour; thus showing how successfully tea can be grown in India, over a district above a thousand miles in length. To this important article much private enterprise is now directed, under the fostering care of our government. Coffee was shown in considerable variety, as it is being extensively cultivated in the Highlands of Southern India, where large tracts of the country are available for its growth. Its culture has been very beneficial to Mysore, many parts of which, from being wild and desolate, have become scenes of comfort and wealth. The natives are benefiting largely by the capital and example of European planters, who are learning the science of planting. Belonging to the starches, are the arrowroot, tapioca, and sago; and "Saleps"—a substance which, when pulverised, resembles arrowroot. It is used on fast-days by the natives, who prepare it in a variety of ways. They obtain it from the glutinous matter which issues from the stem of a jungle-plant, after being soaked in running water for some days.

The natives of India have several edible kinds of seaweed, lichens, and mushrooms, of which specimens were exhibited. Samples of sugar were not numerous; but some were of excellent quality, both raw and refined. Large quantities are obtained from the date-palm; and of the method in which it is obtained, an interesting description is given by Mr. S. H. Robinson, of Calcutta. He says—"Daily, at sunrise, throughout the goor season, the industrious ryot may be seen climbing his trees, and collecting, at a convenient spot beneath them, the earthen pots containing the juice they yielded during the past night. Under a rude shed, covered with the leaves of the date tree itself, and erected under the shade of the plantation, is prepared, the boiling apparatus to serve for the goor season. It consists of a hole about three feet diameter, sunk some two feet in the ground; over which are supported, by mud arches, four thin earthen pans, of a semi-globular shape, and eighteen inches diameter: the hole itself is in the furnace, and has two apertures on the opposite side for feeding in the fuel, and for the escape of the smoke. The fire is lit as soon as the juice is collected and poured into the four pans, which are kept constantly supplied with fresh juice as the water evaporates, until the whole produce of the morning is boiled down to the required density. As the contents of each pan become sufficiently boiled, they are ladled out into other earthen pots or jars of various sizes, from five to twenty seers of contents, according to local custom; and in these the boiled extract cools, crystallises into a hard compound of granulated sugar and molasses, and is brought to market for sale as goor."

Ardent spirits, as distilled from sugar-cane, and used by the Hindoos of the lower order, were shown; also aunish—a pure spirit, distilled from aniseed; and other spirits, as arrack, rum, and spirits of wine. Opium, and the instruments used in its preparation from the poppy seed, were exhibited; and a table, in the official Catalogue, shows that this vile manufacture, energetically pursued in 1860-'61, produced 63,490 chests, or 4,251 tons—the value being £10,184,713; of which, 59,405 chests were inflicted on China—the value being £9,428,887. This immoral and destructive trade is carried on by the government of India in despite of the loud protest of England; the only excuse for which, is the fact that it produces £5,000,000 of profit. With this produce we may associate the *datura hammatii*, the use of which is thus described:—"To facilitate theft, and for other criminal purposes, the seeds,

Y

mixed with sweetmeats, are very commonly administered in Bengal. The person who eats them sinks into a profound lethargy: the respiration is natural, but the pupils of the eye become greatly dilated; and these symptoms have been known to continue two days."

India exhibited animal and vegetable fats and oils in great variety, which, besides supplying the country, are extensively exported. Wool and silk, resins, indigo, madder, and other dyes were shown; among which was a new yellow dye in cake, taken from the petals of a flower which gives it out freely, and which attaches itself to the cloth permanently, without mordaunts.

Cotton formed a very important feature in the Indian collection. The specimens were arranged geographically, beginning with Bengal. These specimens from all parts of India, and many from new kinds of seed, justify the expectations which have been formed of ample supplies, and great varieties of produce. At the request of the Cotton Supply Association, space was afforded in the Indian Court for a complete series of specimens, illustrating the adaptability of the indigenous cotton of India to the manufacture, in this country, of goods of the first quality, and such as, until now, it was deemed impracticable to produce from Indian cotton.

Among the valuable fibres of India, Jute calls for special notice. There are two species—the *Corchorus olitorius*, and *Corchorus capsularis;* and both are largely cultivated. The quantity of jute and jute rope exported to all parts in 1850-'51, was 29,120 tons— value, £196,936; and in 1860-'61, 53,716 tons—value, £409,371; besides Gunny bags, and pieces of Gunny cloth (the same material); the value of which was £359,043.

Among the miscellaneous substances, the Soap Berry is deserving of attention, as it is admirably adapted for cleaning silks, and other fabrics, the colours of which are injured by the ordinary kinds of soap. It forms a lather with water, however hard.

The general manufactures from wood were very numerous and attractive, including specimens of turnery, carving, and modelling; as were also the manufactures from straw: and among them, a Leaf Cloak, worn in wet weather by the natives of Chota Nagpore. Of perfumes, of animal origin, the musk is of the chief importance. Of the vegetable class, there were various kinds of *attar :* the *odoratissimus* is extracted from the male flowers of the *Pandamus ;* its price in the bazaar being two rupees per tola—about a rupee's weight.

The machinery of India, for agricultural and horticultural, and all the ordinary purposes, displayed the usual primitive simplicity; in defence of which, it is said that the soils of India are of a character very different from those of this country, and do not require either the same amount or kind of mechanical treatment to produce the requisite effect.

Wood's East Indian Wages Calculating Machine, exhibited by the inventor, is deserving of special notice, and is suggestive to those who have much to do with the calculation of wages in this country. It is described by the exhibitor, who states, that he was led to the invention from having long experienced the labour of, and liability to error in, making up the weekly wages account in works where a number of hands are employed. The machine is so constructed that persons of ordinary capacity may be made familiar with its use in a few minutes. It will calculate wages in rupees, annas, and pice, at rates varying from six pice to twelve annas per day, and from a quarter of a day, to thirty-five days. Also for monthly wages, varying from a rupee per month, up to twenty rupees per month, or for any number of days during that time. If, for example, it were required to know the amount of wages due to a workman for $18\frac{3}{4}$ days, at the rate of seven annas and nine pice per day, it would be simply necessary to turn the rollers round until 7 9 turned up on the first row of large figures on the left-hand side, and then find $18\frac{3}{4}$ in the fixed index above the opening under the weekly wages table, immediately under which would be read 9/1/3 on the roller, being the amount—9 rupees, 1 anna, and 3 pice.

Military engineering and naval architecture had very little to attract; but, in photography, there were admirable portraits of distinguished persons, and groups of the natives, their country, and principal edifices. Musical instruments produced by the natives were very poor: but one of the finest things in the whole building, was the Ebony Case of a grand piano, carved by natives after an English pattern.

Our space will not permit us to do justice to the rich shawls of Cashmere and the Punjaub; the carpets and rugs produced by the prisoners in the gaols; the tapestry, lace, and embroidery, in gold and silver; the articles of male and female attire; the paper, stationery, and book-binding; the educational works, and appliances; the inlaid work, and other specimens of rich furniture; the works in precious metals, including beautiful examples of filigree work; the enamelling and Damascene work; and the many other specialties of Indian handicraft and manufacture. We must, however, refer to the numerous plastic models and figures sent by the Indian government; by which an Englishman could form a very correct idea of the occupations and costumes of the various native classes. The whole Court did the utmost credit to the exhibitors, not only for the extent of the display, but also for their skill shown in selection and classification, and was well calculated to increase the interest taken in the vast dependency they represented.

The remaining portions of the North-East Gallery were occupied by philosophical, surgical, and horological instruments; paper, stationery, printing, and carpets—all arranged according to the method of classification laid down by the Commissioners; and they will, therefore, be named in their proper places in the different classes. In order that this may be duly regarded as we proceed, we shall not occupy further time in traversing the Foreign Courts and Galleries, or in passing along the two Annexes or the open Courts.

We need scarcely state, that in a general review of the contents of the Exhibition, the attention of the reader has been but partially directed to subjects which have an extensive relation to the arts and manufactures, as well as to the necessities and luxuries of civilised life. Our future pages, which will be devoted to the consideration of the classes, will afford, as far as possible, a complete examination of those raw and manufactured products, &c., connected with the matters to which we have just referred. When essential to our plan, statistical and specific information on each class will be afforded, so that its value and importance may be duly appreciated.

The course we have followed in reference to the Courts and Galleries of Great Britain and her colonies, cannot be pursued, in reference to the foreign department, without occupying too much of the space required for the various classes. To a considerable extent, as far as Great Britain is concerned, some of those classes have been necessarily brought under notice; and the work thus done will not be repeated.

CHAPTER V.

CLASS I.—MINING, QUARRYING, METALLURGY, AND MINERAL PRODUCTS.

THE years which intervened between our first and second International Exhibitions, have been remarkable for the discovery of mineral treasures, some of them new to science and the arts; and, in consequence, Class I. has possessed a charm which was wanting in the former of these great collections. To quote the language of the Report on this class—"A series of changes has been brought about, which, but for the potency of the effect produced by mineral substances, would have required decades of years, if not centuries, to accomplish. Coal, the great basis of manufacture and of locomotion, has been extracted on a scale never before contemplated, and sought for and found in new countries, and under new conditions, with something like equal strides; it has been made to yield a variety of products, brought with unexampled rapidity into the applications of daily life. Iron and steel have been manufactured in masses, and applied to purposes equally unknown in former times. Metals, scarcely known except by name in 1851, have become the subjects of operations of commercial importance. And, lastly, the succession of gold discoveries in so many widely separated and enormous regions, has led to the exploration and settlement of vast tracts by myriads of men, with a facility which was impossible before the extended use of iron and coal had smoothed the way for so gigantic an emigration."

The extent of this class, as to the number of exhibitors, was 1,955: of whom 444 belonged to Great Britain; 237 belonged to Prussia; and the vigour of our own colonies was satisfactorily shown by Victoria, whose exhibitors were 106. The number of medals was 347; of honourable mentions, 222; making the awards 569. The space devoted to this class, for Great Britain alone, was the Eastern Annexe; while very large spaces were allotted to Class I. in the other countries, and especially in the German states, grouped in the Zollverein.

Through the labours of the Jurors and reporters in this class, all the varied products have been so divided into sub-classes, as to afford the greatest facilities for considering each sub-class by itself; and we shall thankfully profit by this subdivision, which groups all the objects of all countries belonging to the first class, as follows:—

1. Geological and Topographical Maps and Models, and general collections.
2. Non-metallic Mineral Substances, Coal excepted.
3. Working of Mines.
4. Coal, and other Mineral Fuels.
5. Iron.
6. Metals, other than Iron.

It will, however, be an improvement on this method, to reserve the subject of the working of mines until we have considered their various products.

1. *Geological and Topographical Maps and Models, and general collections.*—Geological maps, to be of any value, must be the results of protracted observations; and if they are not altogether made up of carefully collected facts, they must have such a basis of truth as will justify the geological reasoning of which the map is the record. Such maps were shown in numbers sufficient to speak most favourably of the state of geological science in our age.

Comparatively few among those who passed into the Exhibition, had the necessary time to examine the magnificent Geological Map exhibited at its entrance, or sufficient skill to appreciate its value. It records the labours of the Geological Survey of the United Kingdom, which has employed the skill of our practical and scientific men for many years—first under the late Sir Henry De la Beche, and then under Sir Roderick Murchison. The Ordnance Map, on which the geological survey is based, is on the scale of only one inch to the mile; but the map of the Lancashire coal-field is on the scale of six inches to the mile; as is also the Geological Map of Scotland. This map presents a vast collection of geological facts of the most valuable kind. They comprehend the whole of Wales; the whole of England, westward of a line running from the eastern side of Derbyshire to the Isle of Wight, and nearly all the counties south of the Medway. By means of this map and the accompanying sections, horizontal and vertical, the inquirer is informed as to the mineral contents of the country at various depths, and materially aided in scientific and commercial pursuits. The metallic veins are carefully distinguished by gold lines; the stream tin by gold dots; the coal-beds by black lines; and the faults, or dislocations, by white lines; and care is taken to distinguish each kind of metal by the use of chemical signs. The Geological Map of Ireland, by Sir Richard Griffith, gives the details of the southern half of that country. Particular districts were very carefully illustrated in excellent maps—as Derbyshire and South Yorkshire; the coal-fields of Northumberland and Durham; by the aid of which future coal-mining operations will be materially assisted, as also in the lead-mining districts south of Shrewsbury; and her Majesty's Forest of Dean, so celebrated for its coals, iron ores, bricks and clays, and building stones; also the district of Halifax, illustrated by its corporation. The high estimation in which the Jurors held accurate execution, was shown by the award of a medal to Mr. J. W. Lowry, "for the beauty and fidelity of his engraved representations of fossils, upon the faithful delineation of which so much depends in the modern exact comparison of the stratified deposits."

Our colonies are benefited greatly by the presence of scientific men, of whose diligent labours in geology the Exhibition presented the most satisfactory proofs in the excellent maps with which it was furnished. We had maps of the gold-fields of Australia, of an extensive area; of Victoria, on the scale of two inches to a mile, tracing carefully the golden veins (termed by the colonists *reefs*), which generally run north and south, at the rate of from fifteen to twenty in the breadth of a mile. Ballarat and Castlemaine districts have also been well surveyed, and were represented by excellent maps. Canada, however, excelled all our colonies in the attention paid to its geology by our loyal fellow-subjects. Sir William Logan, and his able associates, exhibited geological maps, plates, and descriptive works, which were highly satisfactory to every inquirer; and were most justly rewarded by medals, not only for assisting to develop the resources of the colony, but also for the ample contributions they have imparted to general knowledge. Natal had its geological map; so had New Zealand, Tasmania, and Trinidad; for which medals were conferred on the authors. All these productions must be viewed with the deepest interest, as they enlarge our estimate of the great value we ought to attach to our colonial possessions. Our East Indian dependency is not yet far advanced in geological exploration; and we must regard the maps of a part of the Himalaya, under the direction of the surveyor-general, and the maps and fossils of Professor Oldham, only as contributions to the great work which the geologists of India have yet to perform.

It should be remembered, that even the topographical survey of India has been conducted only to a very limited extent, and that no trustworthy maps exist even of the portions that have been surveyed. The Geological Survey, which was begun in 1856, is confined to the districts that have been mapped; and, in some cases, this work had to be done by the Geological Survey. The maps of the Raneegunge Coal-field are on the scale of an inch to the mile, and show, in the details they give, that a great amount of care and skill has been bestowed on this important work.

France, which, as far back as 1841, took the lead of all other nations in a geological survey of the whole country, fully maintained its high character in this branch of practical science, by exhibiting various geological maps of particular departments. There was a Geological Map of the Puy de Dôme, by M. Le Coq, detailing that important district; a Map of the Department of the Loire, by M. Grüner, illustrating the minerals abounding in that district—showing, among other features, the course of the porphyry dykes among the anthracite coal. The department of Haute-Marne was illustrated by M. Duhamel and M. Chancourtois, in a map of much scientific and practical value. The Subterranean Map of Paris, by M. Delesse, shows the character of the strata at various depths beneath that city, and is of the greatest value in its bearing on sanitary matters, as showing the sources from which pure water may be obtained, and indicating, also, the regions of vitiated streams, that they may be avoided. This important work is the result of careful observation of the numerous borings made for water at various periods, and other sources of information; and, according to the Report of the Jurors, the result is, that the contour of each level is given with almost as much detail as if it were the bottom of a lake, of which the soundings had been carefully recorded.

Austria, whose labours in this department date no farther back than 1850, furnished an admirable set of geological maps of extensive divisions of the empire, embracing Upper and Lower Austria, the Duchy of Salzburg, Styria, and Illyria; Bohemia, Tyrol, and Vorarlberg; Lombardy and Venetia; Hungary and Croatia; the Banat of Temeswar, Transylvania, and Galicia. These confer the greatest credit on their authors for scientific skill, judgment, and perseverance; who were justly acknowledged by the medals awarded to them.

Prussia exhibited a most important Geological Map of the Rhine Provinces and

Westphalia, comprising several valuable coal-fields. The Map of Upper Silesia presents the older formations—granite, syenite, and the coal-measures. Colonel Oesfeld, of the Prussian army, presented his comprehensive Map of Central Europe. Lower Silesia, in its rich mining treasures, was illustrated in a map on a very large scale, of much practical value to miners; and the chain of the Reisengebirge did great credit to Herr W. Runge, who, single-handed, executed his work with pictorial effect, as well as scientific fidelity.

Spain is becoming increasingly interesting by the development of its mineral treasures. M. Schulz exhibited a Map of the Coal District, and the metallic ores in the district of the Asturias, sloping down to the Bay of Biscay. Central Spain has been also well illustrated by diligent explorations. Portugal displayed maps of much interest to the geologist.

Denmark, Sweden, Bavaria, Hesse, Holland, Switzerland, and Italy, all contributed geological maps, showing the extent of mining operations, and marking, in a most gratifying manner, the progress of scientific investigation in geology.

2. *Non-metallic Mineral Substances, Coal excepted.*—Products of this kind included stone suitable for building, for ornament, for millstones and grindstones; plumbago, clays, and salt—a classification properly made for the sake of method; not altogether, however, without some disturbance in the first and second of these divisions, in which it would be difficult to find a place for paving and road-making. The great importance of giving more attention to building materials, and works of ornament placed in exposed situations, and intended to be durable monuments, has been shown by several recent instances of premature decay in our public edifices, especially in the Houses of Parliament. The high value of a fine specimen of granite for an obelisk in one piece, has been demonstrated by the failure to discover and convey, from any of our quarries, such a specimen as would form a suitable memorial for the late Prince Consort. The granite in the Exhibition was brought from various quarries in Cornwall, Scotland, and Ireland, and some from Lundy Island.

The Cheesering granite was well shown in the Obelisk by Bell, placed in the Nave; of which, we are assured that still larger specimens could be obtained. Other examples may be seen in the London Docks, Westminster Bridge, Rochester Bridge; in the tomb of the Duke of Wellington, under St. Paul's; and it has been sent as far as the island of Ceylon, for a lighthouse. Cornish granites have supplied Waterloo Bridge, the Portland Breakwater, the plinth for the railings of the British Museum, and its polished pedestals and pilasters. In the same building, the library pillars are the Scotch granite of Longhaven; the Duke of York's Monument is of Stirling granite, which appears also in the pillars of the Fishmongers' Hall.

As the granite of Lundy Island, shown in the Exhibition, has been but recently introduced, it may be well here to copy the example of Mr. Hunt, and quote the following passage, as given by the exhibitor:—

"It should be borne in mind, that, with the exception of No. 1, which was taken a few inches under the turf, all the specimens are merely surface stones, and have been exposed to atmospheric influence for perhaps hundreds, or even thousands of years; yet they are sound, and very hard. Much better are almost invariably found in depth, in a quarry, than on the surface, and (when?) any defects disappear. These specimens, therefore, should be considered as exhibited to show the fineness of the stone, not as the best of each sort; and yet they prove what is very desirable to know—that they can withstand exposure."

Hard sandstones from the coal-measures or grits, were exhibited in great variety, and are highly valued for the ease with which they are worked, as well as for their strength and durability. A particular interest attached to the produce of the Penmaenmawr quarries, on account of the arrangements made for conveying them to the harbour of Holyhead, to which a series of regular workings have been constructed. They are connected by self-acting inclines, and run the waggons down, over the Holyhead railway, shipping no less than 60,000 tons of paving-stones every year.

Slate, instead of being confined almost exclusively to the roofing of houses, is now produced in large slabs, for a number of more important purposes, and has risen greatly in importance. It is long since Carew, in his *Survey of Cornwall*, describing the slate of that county, says of it—"In substance, thinne; in colour, faire; in waight, light; in lasting, strong; and generally carrieth so good regards, as (besides the supply for home provision) great store is yearly conveyed by shipping, both to the other parts of the realm, and also beyond the seas, into Britaine and Netherland."

In 1584, the quarries of North Cornwall were described by Norden, as producing slates that were "thynn, beautyfull, and lighte, in great requeste, and verie vendible, as well in forraigne partes as at home."

The Welsh Slate and Llangollen Company exhibited some of the largest slabs of slate obtained. A slab belonging to the latter company weighed $4\frac{1}{2}$ tons, and was no less than twenty feet long by ten feet wide.

The Jurors mention, that, "less than a century ago, the slates were only made of very small size, not much larger than the hand; whilst the production of large slate has, in modern times, become a *sine quâ non* of success. In 1782, only eighty men were working in the Penrhyn quarry; now, no less than 3,000 find constant employment in that gigantic opening. At that period the Llanberis and Cilgwyn quarries appear to have been wrought, but on an inconsiderable scale." With a view of showing the great increase of the trade within the last few years, we may compare the amount of dressed slates shipped at the sea outlets of the chief quarries in 1826 and 1861:—

Shipping Port.	Quarries.	1826.	1861.
		Tons.	Tons.
Port Dinorwic	Llanberis Valley ...	20,600	91,080
Carnarvon	Cilgwyn & Co. Nantle	14,000	28,800
Bangor	Penrhyn	—	100,000
Port Madoc	Ffestiniog	11,396	65,741

Nearly 9,000 persons are employed, directly, in the quarries in this single corner of North Wales; but other slate-works, opened at intervals in the Silurian rocks, of a large area—as near Llanrwst, and north of Machynlleth—are as yet comparatively unimportant.

Among the stones for ornamental purposes, the serpentine of the Lizard has, of late years, acquired great distinction. This beautiful rock is generally a mixture of green and red in its colours; from which, and the dotted and striped forms in which they are disposed, it receives its common, and also its scientific, name of "ophiolite." It is very durable, as well as ornamental; and, by the aid of powerful machinery, is now formed into vases, obelisks, chimney-pieces, and many elegant articles, instead of being exported, as it once was, for manufacture to other countries.

Derbyshire furnished a large proportion of the ornamental marbles displayed in the Eastern Annexe; among which were all varieties of colour—the white, grey, dove, blue, black, and russet: many were varied by their fossil contents, as the bird's-eye, dog's-tooth, entrochal, shelly, and breccia. Of these, the entrochal (wheel-stone) is perhaps the most interesting. It is formed of the skeletons of the crinoidea, a form of life which was once very abundant. The encrinites (stone-lilies) were composed of bones so numerous, that one specimen is said to have contained nearly 27,000. They have been pasted together by the carbonate of lime contained in the seas in which they lived and died.

With many of these marbles—as the black marble and fluor-spars—the public have been so long familiar, that it is unnecessary to describe them here. The rose-wood marble (so called from its appearance) is much prized from its rarity, the high polish it receives, and its durability. A very precious marble, also, is the *rosso antico*, obtained principally at Newhaven, where it is found in small lumps, large enough only for small vases and other ornaments.

As plumbago is dying out in England, our exhibitors could produce it only as an article of manufacture. It was shown in the form of crucibles, by the Patent Plumbago Crucible Company, and by Mr. Juleff; and in a state of great purity for pencils, prepared by a highly scientific method by Mr. Brodie. Plumbago crucibles are in universal use in the European Mints, and government works.

Clays had an important place in this department, as they are products of great commercial value, for brick and tile-making, and for use as fire-clays, being highly prized for their power of resisting heat; while other clays were exhibited in great variety, as the materials of pottery, china, and porcelain. Mr. Hunt estimates the value of clays produced in England and Wales, in 1860, at £285,846; and that of clay manufactures at £2,911,980.

Devonshire and Cornwall furnished numerous specimens of their clays, maintaining the celebrity which had distinguished those products for more than a century—since they were first discovered in 1755, by Mr. Cooksworthy, of Plymouth. We had Porcelain Clay, Teignmouth Clay, Poole Clay, and clay from the numerous valleys into which the decomposed granite had been carried from the heights of the Dartmoor range.

The China-stone of Mr. Anstell ought to be mentioned in this connexion. It is a variety of granite, the felspar of which has been decomposed by the action of the atmosphere. The whole produce of Cornwall—the only county in which it is found—

is conveyed into Staffordshire, where it is ground and formed into a valuable glaze for the finest kinds of china. The annual consumption amounts to about £19,000.

The saliferous deposits of Cheshire and Worcestershire were well represented by specimens of rock and manufactured salt; the total production of which, for 1860, including a small portion from Ireland, was 1,570,972 tons—the ton of salt being twenty-six hundredweight. The Stoke Prior Salt-Works, in Worcestershire, are capable of producing three thousand tons of manufactured salt per week. A small quantity of salt is obtained from the Isle of Wight, where it is procured from the *salterns*—large shallow pits, into which the sea-water is received and evaporated by the heat of the sun, and afterwards boiled, like the produce of the brine-pits in Cheshire. The island also exhibited bricks, made of the clay near Arreton; hydraulic limestone, from the Binsted quarries, of which some of the ancient churches in the island, and Sussex, are erected; cement, also, from the nodules of septaria, in Alum Bay; and a beautiful pure and white sand for the manufacture of glass, from the same bay.

Our own colonies, and other countries, contributed to this department of the Exhibition with as much liberality as could be anticipated, considering the long distances from which these heavy materials had to be conveyed.

Victoria sent a series of building-stones, and specimens of china clay, very similar to that obtained from Devonshire. Specimens were also exhibited of limestone, gypsum, and fine clays for bricks and pottery.—South Australia furnished slabs of slate.—New South Wales, also, sent a series of building-stones, and a variety of polished marbles.—Canada exhibited building-stones of a valuable kind, formed into cubes of one foot, and slabs of 2 ft. 6 in. by 18 in. Gypsum, obtained by subterranean mining, was also sent from Canada.

3. *Coal, and other Mineral Fuels.*—The startling statement made by Sir William Armstrong, at the Newcastle meeting of the British Association for the Advancement of Science, that we have "much cause for anxiety" as to the continuance of our supply of coal, is one of the most important contained in his inaugural address, and does honour alike to his patriotism and science. It is true, that "the quantity of that invaluable mineral, which has been stored up throughout the globe for our benefit, is sufficient (if used discreetly) to serve the purpose of the human race for many thousand years;" and that, "in fact, the entire quantity of coal may be considered as practically inexhaustible:" but it is also true, that, "turning to our particular country, and contemplating the rate at which we are expending those seams of coal which yield the best quality of fuel, and can be worked at the least expense, we shall find much cause for anxiety."

It was necessary for some one whose scientific character and position would secure attention, to make such an announcement as that given by the learned president of the British Association. A few years since, those scientific gentlemen who ventured to estimate the probable duration of coal in Great Britain, gave us reason to expect that it would extend to such periods as to render it unnecessary to direct further attention to the subject. The delusion has prevailed that the coal-fields of England were nearly inexhaustible, and that it was possible, not only to discover, but also to work coal-beds at any depths to which they might descend.

Sir William Armstrong has taken the country by surprise, and awakened not a few scientific men from their slumbers, by his statement, that the entire quantity of available coal existing in these islands, will last only for 212 years, according to the present rate of consumption, and allowing, as we should, for a yearly increase of $2\frac{3}{4}$ millions of tons, which has been our rate of increase for the last eight years.

This announcement has not only excited a considerable amount of public attention; it has also set the British Association to work: in proof of which, we observe that it has voted £100 to Professor Phillips, for inquiries to be made into "the quantity of coal." The Association will do good service to the country by collecting all statistics of this subject, so as completely to dispel the delusions existing in various quarters, and form the basis of some important changes in our treatment of this most valuable mineral, so essential to the prosperity and greatness of our country. The returns which the learned professor has to collect, may, it is hoped, be in readiness for the Bath meeting of the Association next year.

Meanwhile the subject demands public consideration; for although there are those who care nothing for posterity, we may assume that most persons among us will take some interest in the prosperity of this country in six or seven generations from the present time, and would wish that England may not be blotted out in or about the year 2075.

Twenty years ago, the late Mr. Richardson, of the British Museum, wrote a passage in his *Geology*, which deserves attention at the present day; showing, as it does, the calamity we should suffer from the failure of our coal. "Not only (he says) should we lose, with this substance, the best means of maintaining the genial warmth of our personal temperament, and the health of our frames, as well as our cleanliness and comfort; but, from the scientific purposes to which our supplies of mineral fuel are now devoted, we should lose, with the coal, those advantages which, by the application of steam to the most essential wants of life, have raised us to our present eminent position as a people. No longer would our favoured country be the great factory for supplying the most important necessities of the whole family of mankind; no longer should we, with our commerce, convey the associate benefits of knowledge and civilisation to the remotest regions of the globe; no longer should we all but triumph over time and space, and traverse the island with a rapidity which excels all anticipation, and almost all belief, and the vast ocean with a swiftness and a certainty which brings the far East, or the New World itself, within the voyage of a few days. Our steam-power would be annihilated; and, with it, our prosperity and supremacy as a nation; our steam-engines would rust, disused for want of fuel and supply; our factories would be closed; our railroads would fall into disuse; our steam-ships would be dismantled; and the future historian of the revolutions of empires, would date the decline and fall of the vast dominion of Britain, from the period when her supplies of mineral fuel were consumed, and her last coal-field exhausted."

The "decadence" of Great Britain, as thus depicted, cannot be contemplated with patience by any of her people: nor may we anticipate these possibilities without inquiring how far they are well founded, and what means there may be of putting off the evil day, if not of altogether preventing its arrival. Such a caution which Sir William Armstrong has given, cannot remain unheeded by the intelligent and thoughtful people to whom it is imparted, and of whom it is not too much to expect that they will be ready to do whatever the circumstances of the country require.

We have not now to speculate on the notion, that, "before coal is exhausted, some other motive agent will be discovered to take its place." Speculations of this kind, and especially on the theory that electricity may hereafter supply the place of coal, are of very little value, and ought to be dismissed, especially after Sir William Armstrong has shown that, if we want to liberate either heat or electricity, "we must consume some oxidisable substance; and coal is the cheapest we can procure." The proper work of the day is to deal with our coal supply, and to look in the face the fact which has been seasonably introduced to our consideration.

Let there be, then, no uncertainty as to the fact, that the supply of coal for our own country is fixed and limited. Sir William Armstrong utters an incontrovertible truth, when he says, that "the phase of the earth's existence suitable for the extensive forma-tion of coal, appears to have passed away for ever." It will be observed, that this statement is not given without the qualification necessary to meet the doctrine of that class of geologists who maintain that the formation of coal is taking place at the present time. There is certainly no "extensive" formation of coal in our day; and, it may be added, that if the deposit of coal be now in operation on any part of the globe, it is in localities which will not be accessible until a change has taken place in the relative positions of land and water; so that when the coal now forming becomes available, many of the countries at present inhabited will form the bed of the sea. We need offer no objection to the opinion, that the trees annually carried down the Mississippi, and deposited in its delta, are forming the coal-field of some future and very distant generation; nor will any geologist encourage the hope, that as coal is being consumed in one part of the world, it is being produced in equal quantities in another. We may increase our vegetable and animal produce to an extent far beyond our present anticipations, but we may anticipate no addition to our available supplies of coal.

The origin of our vast treasures of coal has been, with philosophical truth, described by the late Sir George Stephenson, as the embodiment of the power originally derived from the sun; so that, when the miner sends us up a block of coal, he sends us the concentrated sunbeams of past days, which we may again excite and diffuse in light and heat at our pleasure.

Profiting by this noble thought, Sir William Armstrong refers the formation of coal to an era of greater vegetation, of higher temperature, and an atmosphere more laden with humidity and carbonic acid. We may continue to speak of the carboni-ferous period, and the carboniferous rocks, as of times and deposits distinctly removed from our age, and from causes which are not now, to any great extent, in operation.

The age in which the materials of coal grew, and were subsequently deposited in their beds, was long anterior to the secondary era, which was distinguished by the presence of enormous monsters of the deep, the shore, and the air—the age of ichthyosaurians and plesiosaurians; of lizards and crocodiles, such as the teleosaurus, the galosaurus, and iguanodon; and monstrous birds, which have left foot-prints twice the size of those made by the horse or camel. The carboniferous age has formed a tempting subject for those writers who have built up our geological literature: one of whom, the late Hugh Miller, thus describes the characteristics of this by-gone era:—"In no other age did the world ever witness such a flora: the youth of the earth was peculiarly a green and umbrageous youth—a youth of dusk and tangled forests; of huge pines and stately auricurians; of the reed-like calamite; the tall tree fern; the sculptured sigillaria; and the hirsute lepidodendron. Wherever dry land, a shallow lake, or running stream appeared, from where Melville Island now spreads out its ice-wastes under the star of the pole, to where the arid plains of Australia lie solitary beneath the bright cross of the south, a rank and luxuriant herbage cumbered every foot-breadth of the dank and steaming soil; and even the distant planets must have shone through the enveloping cloud with a green and delicate ray. Of this extraordinary age of plants we have our cheerful remembrances and witnesses, in the flames that roar in our chimneys when we pile up the winter fire; in the brilliant gas that now casts its light on this great assemblage,* and that brightens up the streets and lanes of this vast city; in the glowing furnaces that smelt our metals, and give moving power to our ponderous engines; in the long dusky trains that, with shriek and snort, speed dust-like athwart our landscapes; and in the cloud-enveloped vessels that darken the lower reaches of your noble river, and rush in foam over ocean and sea. The geologic evidence is so complete as to be patent to all, that the first great period of organised being was, as described in the Mosaic period, peculiarly a period of herbs and trees, 'yielding seed after their kind.'"

The atmospheric condition of our planet, at the commencement of the carboniferous ages, was marked by an excess of carbonic acid far beyond that which now exists. Dr. Rogers states, that "an estimate, carefully made from the best data, of the sums total of coal within the principal coal-fields of the world, indicates, that the aggregate of carbon buried under the soil, cannot be less than some six times the quantity still resident in the air."

An acquaintance with the great geological facts thus described, will leave undisputed the position, that our world has long since passed the period for the formation of coal available for the use of man. No one anticipates the deposit of more gold, silver, copper, iron, tin, or lead, or any metals precious or base in our mines; and it is equally opposed to experience, and the deductions of science, to anticipate the renewal of our black diamonds where they have been exhausted in our country, or in any other region to which man can have access. It is possible that the investigations of Professor Phillips will result in the discovery, that the quantity of coal in Great Britain and other countries is somewhat above our present estimate; but no scientific man indulges the hope that, as the result, we shall feel authorised to expect that our present supply, when once exhausted, will ever be replaced.

The Duke of Newcastle has earned for himself the praise of the Jurors in the late International Exhibition, for his perseverance in sinking, at the distance of several

* The extract is made from a lecture delivered in Exeter Hall.

2 A

miles away from the visible coal-field, through new red sandstone and magnesian lime-stone, to the "top-hard" coal, at the depth of 515 yards. The Jurors state, that this confirmation, at Shireoak, of what geological reasoning had predicted, although too costly an undertaking to be imitated for the present, may be looked on as the first step to the development of a probable coal area of 300 or 400 square miles. Great experiments of this kind may lead, in fresh cases, to the extensive discovery of new coal areas; but we must rest in the conclusion already arrived at, that the formation of coal is among the great creations that have long since passed away.

The considerations that have been adduced being sufficient to prove that we have to deal with a limited quantity of coal, to which no additions can be made—the amount of our supplies, compared with the rate of consumption, becomes a practical question of the deepest interest. We have been furnished, by the Exhibition, with the opportunity of seeing specimens of the various kinds of fossil fuel obtained from our own country, our colonies, India, and other countries; and the information thus recently imparted will be regarded as of the greatest value.

The large blocks placed in the open Court of the Eastern Annexe (one of them weighing 38 cwt.), were calculated to give the visitors the impression of our enormous wealth as a coal-producing country, and to encourage the notion which has been so prudently dissipated, that this kind of wealth was inexhaustible; nor was that impression effaced by the great varieties of coal sent from our numerous mines. The competition and liberality of our great coal-owners, secured the ample representation of our most important coal-fields—those of Scotland and Ireland, Durham and Northumberland, Yorkshire, Derbyshire, Lancashire and Cheshire, Staffordshire, Gloucestershire and Somersetshire, Monmouthshire and South Wales.

The consumption of coal from all these districts, amounted, in 1851, to 52,000,000 tons; and, with some fluctuation, has since proceeded at an increasing rate, as follows:—In 1854, 64,661,401 tons; in 1855, 64,453,070 tons; in 1856, 66,645,450 tons; in 1857, 65,394,707 tons; in 1858, 65,008,649 tons; in 1859, 71,929,765 tons; in 1860, 83,208,581 tons: and the statistics collected by Mr. Hunt, of the Mining Record Office, show that, at the end of 1861, the quantity had reached the enormous total of 86,000,000 tons. On the authority of such facts, Sir William Armstrong states, that the average annual increase in the consumption of our coal, has amounted to $2\frac{3}{4}$ millions of tons during the last eight years. Here it is important to notice the fact, that about one-twelfth part of this great total—more than 9 per cent.—is exported to other countries; the amount of that export, in 1860, being 6,788,060 tons.

While we are called upon to look very attentively at this fact, which tells with such force on the rapid reduction of our fuel, we should at the same time observe, that some of those countries to which our coal is exported have been carefully examined, and with much success, for the discovery of that valuable mineral. On this point the Jury Report has the following important observations:—"Not only has the total quantity annually consumed been increased beyond all expectation, but new applications in manufactures have been invented; and materials, little valued a few years ago, command the highest prices of all their kindred. Only a few years ago, the nations of the south derided our evil-odoured coal, and pitied us for its dirty smoke; now we have not only France, Prussia, and Austria vying in the amount of mineral coal which they can raise, but Spain, Portugal, and Italy assuring us that they produce some thousands of tons a year; and even sub-tropical India, and Brazil and Trinidad —proud to show that they have other means than the sun's rays of generating heat. Each country, in fact, puts in a claim to consideration, and tacitly appears to consider that the production of coal is, more or less, a criterion of manufacturing prosperity."

The estimated quantity of coal accessible to our miners, has been stated with as much accuracy as can be attained in our present circumstances. How far the estimate may have to be modified, as the result of the scientific investigations under Professor Phillips, and by discoveries in the cooling of deep mines by ventilation and other processes, we have yet to learn. For the present, it should be noticed, that the estimate which gives us little more than two hundred years for the consumption of all our coal, makes its whole bulk to amount to about 80,000,000,000 (eighty thousand millions) of tons.

This estimate is not intended to apply to all the coal contained in our coal-measures, and resting in those depths to which it is assumed we can never penetrate. It supposes that 4,000 feet is the greatest depth at which it will be possible to carry on our mining operations; and it also rejects all seams of less than two feet in thickness. In support of his data, Sir William Armstrong refers to Monkwearmouth Colliery, which reaches a depth of 1,800 feet below the surface of the ground, and nearly as much below the level of the sea, where the temperature of the air in the workings is about 84° Fahr., and considered to be nearly as high as is consistent with the great bodily exertion which the miners are obliged to employ.

At present we are not shut up to any conclusion as to the depth below which it is practicable to work our mines. Some objections are made to the theory that the increase of heat is one foot for every sixty feet in depth. It is objected that the temperature increases only when the mine is working; and we are referred to the Oatfield engine-shaft, which, at a depth of 182 fathoms, had a temperature of 77° while the mine was working; but, on being abandoned, in a few months had cooled down to 66°; and, in a month after, had reached the equilibrium of 54°. Several other cases are adduced: among which is that of the Herland shaft, the temperature of which being 54° at the depth of sixty feet, was not more at the depth of 1,150. It remains now to inquire whether there be any foundation for the opinion that the increasing temperature, ascribed to increasing depth, is to be attributed to chemical action, produced by the oxidation of the substances newly exposed to the action of the air; and whether we may add to this cause, "the friction in extricating the ore, the presence of the miners, the heat of their candles, blasts, and electric currents."

There must be investigations, also, as to the possibility of cooling the mines by some process which is not beyond the reach of our practical science. At present, the arrangements for the ventilation of mines are very imperfect, and the necessity of making a provision for cooling down the mines has scarcely been considered. It is very possible that the difficulties produced by high temperature may be overcome.

If, however, some method should be discovered by which the high temperature of our mines may be checked, still, we cannot anticipate the probability of their being worked to a much greater depth than that which has been assumed by Sir William Armstrong as the basis of his calculation. He assumes 4,000 feet as the greatest depth at which it will ever be possible to carry on mining operations; and half that depth has not yet been reached in our deepest coal-mine. We cannot, therefore, venture to hope that our available coal, if the increasing rate of consumption is to be maintained, will extend over the term of 212 years. If that increasing rate can be avoided, our supplies will last for 930 years, instead of only 212; and we may very safely leave the question to posterity.

The Exhibition afforded an opportunity of viewing specimens of the coal obtained in other countries; where, however, the produce, as at present ascertained, is very small as compared with that of our own kingdom. We speak without reference to the United States, which exhibited none of its fossil fuel, of which it has most extensive treasures, being thirty-seven times greater than our own.

France obtains its coal from fifty-two coal-fields; the whole produce of which, in 1859, amounted to 7,482,570 tons. This quantity, which was seven or eight times the amount obtained at the beginning of this century, is not sufficient for the requirements of that country, which is supplied largely by ourselves, by Prussia, and Belgium. The production in 1859, was about one-tenth of that of the United Kingdom; the quantity imported being 5,759,387 tons. The late alterations in the French tariff have led to a steady increase in the imports of coal into France. The estimated imports for 1860, are 8,400,000 tons. France is active in its search for coal, and anxious for the greater development of the trade. M. Pougnet, who, in 1855, obtained a Paris medal for his perseverance in exploring at a great depth in the coal-measures in Saarbrüken, appeared, in 1862, as the sinker of the first shaft at Carling, in the department of the Moselle. The two chief seams discovered were at the depths of 230 and 280 mètres. In consequence of the great excess of water, the seams were lined, for 180 mètres in depth, with tubing; and an engine had to be erected, at the cost of £72,000. The French coal-owners have now the satisfaction of supplying their own navy, instead of being dependent on English coals.

The perseverance of France in seeking for coal in its own fields, was illustrated in the case of M. Sens, who exhibited specimens obtained from the Pas de Calais, strongly resembling those of Belgium. After twelve years of energetic efforts, this new district has produced 500,000 tons per annum; but it appears likely, since the new tariff, to suffer from the competition with our coal, unless further improvements are effected in the transit. The largest colliery in the world is at Anzin, near Valenciennes; producing 1,200,000 tons per annum, and employing 8,000 persons.

Belgium.—The Belgian coal-field is but a narrow strip of land; but it is worked with such industry and intelligence, that the production, in 1860, amounted to 9,650,000 tons; and it is much to the honour of the Belgian miners, that the Puits Ste Marie has reached the depth of 850 mètres.

Austria.—The employment of coal in manufactures and household economy, is comparatively recent in Austria, but its progressive use is very rapid. There are fine seams in North Bohemia, fifty or sixty feet thick; and those in Styria and Carinthia are of greater thickness, in some few instances. There are excellent coals in the lias formation of Southern Hungary, and in the carboniferous beds of Bohemia, Moravia, and Silesia. The quantities raised have been—

In 1831	200,000 tons.
„ 1851	1,200,000 „
„ 1860	3,500,000 „

Great credit is due to the exhibitor, Bergrath T. Fœtterle, who presented 239 good specimens of Austrian coal, and gave, in distinct labels, the particulars of the formation, the owner, the annual quantity raised, the number of engines and people employed; the thickness of the seam; the proportions of ash, water, and coke; and the caloric units, or the number of units of water which may be raised by the combustion of one unit of fuel for 0° to 100° centigrade.

Prussia.—The utmost credit is due, also, to the exhibitors in the Zollverein department, and to the compilers of the catalogue; whose specimens in Class I., and their description of them, cannot be too highly praised. This comprehensive document describes all the coal-measures throughout the Zollverein, and important particulars as to the produce of each mine. The quantities raised in the whole of Prussia, in 1860, were—of coal, 43,283,626 tonnen; brown coal, 21,021,961 tonnen: total, 64,305,587 tonnen, or about 14,860,000 tons English, valuing the tonnen at 4 cwt.

The Jurors, in their Report, make special references to the coal-field of Westphalia, on the Rhur, where, but a few years since, only three partial synclinal troughs, or basins, were known; the most northerly of them hemmed in by the overlying chalk formation. Subsequent researches have shown as many as eight additional, more or less parallel, basins; being neither more nor less than a series of convolutions, or foldings of the measures, repeated on the northward, under the constantly thickening cover of the cretaceous rocks. The coal has thus been followed to the distance of 6,000 or 7,000 fathoms from the visible edge of the carboniferous formation, and at a depth of 182 to 194 fathoms. In this whole area, it is estimated that there exists no less than 39,200,000,000 tons of coal, the knowledge of half of which is due to explorations made since 1851.

Prussia, and other members of the Zollverein, are rich in brown coal, the distillation of which yields highly valuable products. The seams of this coal are found to crop to the surface at a vast number of points; frequently running to from six to forty or fifty feet in thickness, and therefore yielding large masses of fuel within a small compass.

Upper Silesia has a coal-field, untouched before 1784, which at present appears in patches only. The borings show, that to the south-east of the Riesengebirge, and near the head of the Vistula, there is one of the greatest and richest coal-fields in Europe, extending into the adjoining provinces of Moravia and Silesia.

Italy, Spain, and Portugal give very little promise of coal. The fossil fuel alleged to be discovered in patches in Italy, "always ends in proving to be lignite;" and the quantity obtained is only 60,000 tons. Some small quantities of anthracite have been worked in the valley of Aosta. It is hoped that the cuttings for railways in Spain, may develop, on a larger scale, the coal-fields of the Esturias, of Cordova, Valencia, Leon, and Catalonia, from which specimens were sent. Portugal exhibited anthracite from the Douro, and lignites from the oolitic series at Cabo Mondego, and elsewhere. It is very evident that we have no reason to expect that these countries will produce coal to any considerable extent.

The colonies of Great Britain are now being carefully examined, with a view to the discovery of coal; but, at present, they by no means encourage the large expectations that have been entertained respecting them.

New South Wales has an extensive coal-field, but its limits remain unexplored. Coal is found in Queensland, and reappears in Tasmania. These colonies have their Newcastle and Wallsend; the former at the mouth of the Hunter, sixty miles north of Sydney. The total produce of coal for the last ten years, has been 1,780,000 tons; of which, more than one-half has been shipped to India, China, and the neighbouring colonies. The people at Newcastle can raise and ship 20,000 tons weekly, at the price of 12s. to 14s. a ton. Mr. Keene, the government examiner of coal-fields, states that there are eleven distinct seams of coal; and that most of those now at work are from six to nine feet in thickness, the levels at which they are worked being from 450 below, to 1,500 feet above, the sea. The Wallsend colliery sends to the wharf 500 tons daily; the Minnie Company raise 300 tons; the Tomago Company, from 100 to 150; and from the mountain side, the daily supply varies from 100 to 200 tons.

Tasmania has produced coal for the last twenty-five years; and it is to be obtained in various parts of the island. The seam which crops out at several points on the side of Mount Nicholas (locally known as the Killymoon seam) is highly bituminous, and is believed to be well suited for gas, steam, and household use. The bed is estimated to occupy an area of fourteen miles. The coal-bed of the Douglas River and Long Point is good: it is supposed to extend over an area of fifteen miles; and, at Douglas River, is above eight feet thick. This coal is rapidly rising in public estimation, and a company has been formed to work it. Beds have been discovered in the Mersey River, and have been profitably worked, being easy of access. This coal has been used for the coasting steamers, as also for exportation to Victoria. Anthracite is abundant on the southern side of the island, of which several specimens were exhibited. The labours of Mr. Gould, the government geologist, have been carefully directed to this important subject; and, as the Parliament has voted a sum of money for its investigation, and a commission was formed in March, 1862, to take charge of experiments on specimens in bulk, it may be expected that Tasmania will be found highly productive of various kinds of coal.

Victoria has carboniferous rocks to an extent of 3,000 square miles, though very few seams of coal have been discovered; and respecting them, very little is known as to the possibility of their being economically worked. The seams discovered at Cape Patterson are not more than three feet nine inches thick. It is still uncertain whether the coal in Victoria will pay for working; but more light will be soon thrown on the subject, as the Victoria Coal Company has received the government authority to raise 500 tons of coal.

New Zealand, which has hitherto produced but very little coal, and of an inferior quality, now reports that the geologist of the colony of Canterbury has discovered coal "in large quantities, of a very excellent description, suitable for steam and every other purpose, about forty miles from Christchurch, and accessible by a sound level road. The exploration is still proceeding, and promises to be fertile of further important results." For the province of Otago, nothing more is said, than that "lignite abounds over large spaces; and carboniferous coal, despite the surmises of superficial observers, has been discovered."

New Brunswick is one of our North American colonies from which specimens of coal were sent to the Exhibition. For want of sufficient capital, no adequate exploration for coal has hitherto been made in this colony, where much success may be anticipated, as the carboniferous system covers an area equal to more than one-third of the entire province. Within a few years a new species of coal has been discovered in Albert county, whence it has received its name of Albertite. It is highly bituminous, and suited for the production of gas and coal oil; and, at the pit's mouth, 15,000 tons were sold, at £3 per ton. A vein of pure cannel has been discovered in the same county, and preparations are being made to work it on an extensive scale. It is evident that justice has not yet been done to the coal-fields of this province, which, in 1858, yielded in value, £13,743; and in 1859, three times that amount.

Nova Scotia invites the enterprise of the miner, where the General Mining Company is at present obtaining about 70,000 tons per annum. Its coal-fields were represented by a pillar of coal, thirty-four feet in height—a slice from the great Picton seam, one of the largest in the world, varying, as it does, from thirty-three to thirty-six feet, and well adapted for gas, for generating steam, for manufactories, and for domestic use. Good specimens were sent from several other mines. The amount of coal raised at the Picton seam, in 1860, was 165,055 tons; at Sydney mine, 100,098 tons; at Lingan, 35,300; at Joggins, 5,295; and at Glass Bay, 7,625 tons (in 1861). The amount of coal in Nova Scotia has been very imperfectly estimated, and may for a long time remain unexplored, owing to the sparse population, and the abundant supply of wood.

India was well represented in its coal produce by Professor Oldham, who exhibited a map of the Geological Survey, and a series of coals, with their analyses, from several Indian coal-fields. The Raniganj coal-field has produced, from forty-nine collieries—in 1858, 217,136 tons; in 1859, 324,754; in 1860, 304,094 tons. The total average return for the three years preceding the Exhibition, from all India, was 320,631 tons; but a fairer average would be, above 1,000 tons a day during the whole year. The produce is gradually on the increase from year to year, and is of much importance, although only about a two-hundredth part of the quantity raised in Great Britain.

PATENT FUEL—which has been recently introduced for the purpose of utilising the small coal—must be regarded as a great improvement on the former state of things, in which vast amounts of that valuable material were utterly wasted. The small coal, pasted together with pitch or tar, is shaped into square blocks or cylinders, and is conveniently stowed away on board our steamers. It is now manufactured at from

9s. 6d. to 12s. 6d. a ton. The small anthracite can be used in the same manner. The shapes into which this artificial coal is moulded, render them liable to cake together into a solid mass, which would be avoided if they were formed into balls, as it would then be impossible to pile them up so as to prevent the free passage of the air. It might, however, be an objection to this shape, that it would require too great a space in stowage on shipboard. We are told, that "its advantage over coals for steamers on long voyages, arises from its cubical form and density, as it occupies less space by about 10 per cent. than ordinary coal. A great advantage in this kind of fuel is its density, which exceeds that of many kinds of coal. The specific gravity of one kind of brown coal is 1·126; while the several kinds of block fuel are, 1·271. 1·267, 1·275, and 1·315."

Moulded Peat Charcoal deserves great attention; as, although the Jurors could not pronounce on the value of the specimens exhibited, it was only for want of satisfactory statistics on the economy of the processes employed.

One kind was exhibited, the raw material of which is obtained from Fen Moss, Salop—moulded by machinery, dried by artificial heat, and then carbonised; when it becomes a hard charcoal, of great value in making pig-iron. It is used with great advantage in preparing bars for wire, and plates for tinning, and in the manufacture of phosphorus. It has also great sanitary properties. By Buckland's process, the peat, when taken from the bog, is passed through a straining machine, by which it loses its fibrous character. In this pulpy state it dries quickly; and, without pressure, becomes as hard as oak, and nearly as heavy as coal. If this material will justify the strong recommendation of the exhibitor, Mr. Brunton—who says it is good for gas, steam, for domestic use, and for melting iron (being free from sulphur)—it ought to be much encouraged. It is cheaper than coal; and it would be well if our bogs in Ireland could be used up, so as to prevent the excessive drain on our coal mines.

France has produced this agglomerated coal for the last twenty years, and it is now manufactured in large quantities.

Austria afforded much competition in this important article. One of the exhibitors, A. Riegel, showed "a compressed coal, which may be obtained in any required form and size, with presses constructed according to the systems of Middleton and others; and has been found, by practical proof, to be highly appropriate for domestic uses, for the heating of locomotives, steam-boats, and boilers. The connecting substance, composed of organic and inorganic ingredients, is combustible, without leaving a residuum of ashes."

Prussia is duly sensible of the value of compressed coal, and artificial charcoal obtained from peat; of which the peat district of Miesten sent some excellent specimens. This artificial charcoal is produced without pressing or washing—simply by heating the peat in an oven of a new construction, invented by the exhibitor, and from which 10,000 lbs. are delivered in twelve hours. It has been used with satisfactory results in blast-furnaces at Gemünd, and is applicable for puddling, and re-heating for boilers and locomotives.

4. *Iron—Iron Ores.*—The United Kingdom could scarcely be regarded as making the greatest use of the space allotted to its iron ores and produce, in the Eastern

Annexe, as there were many important iron-making firms by whom no contribution was made. The display, however, was quite sufficient to show that this portion of our mineral wealth is very extensive and varied, and that it is being developed in enormous quantities. This fact is the more important, from the circumstance that, of late years, one valuable species of our iron ore—the argillaceous or clay-band ironstone, which is found in our coal-measures—had become scarce, either from the beds dying out, or else having to be worked at greater depths, and consequently at greater expense. Hence there has arisen a necessity for obtaining supplies of ore from other districts; without which our British resources would not have been able to meet the enormous demands made upon them. Those other districts have not been explored in vain; and the result has been an enormous development of our iron trade during the present century. The following table, given in the Juror's Report, shows the increase in our manufacture of pig-iron:—

Years.	Tons of Pig-iron.	Years.	Tons of Pig-iron.
1800	180,000	1850	2,250,000
1825	600,000	1852	2,701,000
1830	678,000	1854	3,069,838
1835	1,000,000	1856	3,586,377
1840	1,396,400	1858	3,456,064
1845	1,512,500	1860	3,826,752
1849	2,000,000		

The last amount, as sold at the pit's mouth, is valued at £12,703,950; and was produced by 582 furnaces in blast in 1860, being an average of 6,575 tons per furnace, or about 126 tons per furnace per week.

This portion of the Exhibition divides itself, first, into iron ores, which group as follows:—

Red Hematite, from Whitehaven and Ulverstone.

Brown Hematite, from the Forest of Dean, Cornwall, Devonshire, and South Wales.

Spathose Ore, from the Brendon Hills, and Exmoor.

Argillaceous Carbonates, and Clay Ironstones, from the Coal-measures.

Black-band Ironstone, from Scotland and South Wales.

Hydrated Oxides, from Westbury, in Wilts, Oxfordshire, Northamptonshire, Lincolnshire, and Staffordshire.

Carbonates of Protoxide of Iron, as from the Cleveland district.

The Red Hematite—so called from its blood-red colour, and which is found at Whitehaven and Ulverstone—is not an original formation like the ironstone in the coal-measures, but had been first formed in the older rock, whence it has been carried by the action of water in the cavernous openings in rocks, where it is now found. At the Parkside mines (of which a section was given), near Whitehaven, it has a thickness of 70 feet. The quantity used, in 1860, at the Cleator Moor and Working Iron-Works, was 466,851 tons, valued at £256,768. That from Ulverstone, 520,829 tons, was worth £260,414. Fine samples of this red hematite, as well as of the brown, were exhibited in the Open Court. The latter, which supplies the greater number of the French iron-works, and all the works in Belgium, has hitherto not been much worked in this country, where it is very scarce. Some good specimens were sent in from Ladock, in Cornwall.

Spathose Ore, or Sparry Carbonate of Iron, is a highly important metal, as it affords natural steel with the greatest facility, being known formerly under the name of Steel Ore. These ores are found in a valley in the county of Durham (the Weardale), near the springs which form the sources of the river Wear, and in a region fifteen miles in extent from west to east, and from six to seven miles wide. The ores in Weardale have been deposited in the condition of sparry carbonates; but, in some cases, have passed into the state of a brown hematite. This ore, as well as the calcareous hematite, and the ironstone of the Devonian series, was shown by Mr. Rogers, of Abercarne.

The Coal-measure Iron Ores, the Argillaceous Carbonates, and the Black-band Iron Ores, have been, and still are, contained in abundance in our principal coal-fields. The wealth and industry of Glasgow are attributable, in a large degree, to the black-band ironstone, to which attention was first directed at the beginning of this century. Good specimens were exhibited by the Scotch masters.

New sources of iron ore have recently been discovered in this country, the specimens of which commanded very great attention, as forming new contributions to our national wealth and industry. We refer first to the

Cleveland Iron Ore, as illustrating, in a remarkable manner, the fact that treasures of great material value may long lie unappreciated under our sight. We allude to the large blocks of a greenish and weighty stone strewn on the north-east coast of Yorkshire, which were at length found to contain iron, and then taken to the smelting furnaces at Witton Park, Durham. It was proved that these "tumblers" formed a regularly stratified bed in the Cleveland Hills, and showing along the coast towards Whitby. In 1851, mines were opened at Easton; and beds were discovered, fifteen feet thick, of solid ironstone. This thickness prevailed at Middlesborough, whence these treasures ran to Guisborough, where they were found to be six feet in thickness, and gradually thinning thence far south. As the geologist is aware, these beds are the "marlstone" of the Lias, which is easily bored or broken. These important discoveries have led to the excavation of extensive mines, the erection of furnaces, and all the active industry connected with extensive collieries. From year to year new furnaces have been erected on the river Tees, and along the lines of railway— the trains carrying iron from the mines, and taking back coke in return: thus, to quote the words of the Report, revivifying "moribund works which had exhausted the clay-bands of the western outcrop." From this document we learn, that the total quantity raised, annually, from these Cleveland Hills, for the last two or three years, has varied from 1,800,000 to 1,470,000 tons of ore, representing above 400,000 tons of pig-iron. Towards the southern end of this region, and where the Easton and Guisborough bed appears to thin out, other beds of iron ore, in the oolite, make their appearance; and near them, in Rosedale, a remarkable mass of magnetic iron ore.

This valuable ore is chiefly a carbonate of iron with a little clay, a considerable per-centage of soluble silica, and about 33·6 of iron. The materials for making a ton of pig-iron from the Cleveland ore, are—

Ironstone	3 tons 3 cwt.
Coke...	1 ton 10 ,,
Coal (for boilers, &c.)	4 ,,
Limestone	13 to 15 cwt.

And the cost of making a ton, from 40s. to 42s.

The great importance of the Cleveland ore is further seen in the fact, that it furnishes material for above one-tenth part of the annual production of Great Britain. The number of furnaces were as follows :—

Year.	In Blast.	Out.	Total.
On May 1, 1858...	43	20	63
,, ,, 1859...	56	11	67
,, ,, 1860...	53	16	69
,, ,, 1861...	50	26	76

To Messrs. Bolckon and Vaughan, who have principally developed this great department of our mining industry, the Jury awarded a medal. The Jurors state, that this firm exhibited products which "it is not pretended are from Cleveland ore exclusively, but which evince a quality far superior to the character which has been assigned to the Cleveland iron by rivals, and which does, probably, attach to those samples of it which have been turned out with less care and attention."

Hydrated Oxides of Iron.—In the Exhibition of 1851, there were three specimens of silicious ironstone: two from near Northampton, accompanied with the notice—"The clay ironstones of the Lias are only just beginning to add to our iron-making resources." The Jurors record the interesting fact, that "the very day after the closing of the Exhibition in 1851, Mr. S. H. Blackwell—whose attention had been called to the subject, not only as an iron-master generally interested in it, but as the collector of a series representing all the British ores then worked—visited Northampton, and found it at Higham Ferrars, and soon commenced working certain beds of brown iron ore, which he at first imagined to be the Cleveland ore, but which subsequently proved to belong to the oolite." This discovery has already led to important results, as the ore can be raised at a very cheap rate, and extended over a very large district of country. Objections have been made to the use of the ore, on account of the large quantity of silica it contains; but, in the words of the Jurors, "It has been sufficiently proved, that a portion of it, along with other judiciously selected materials, will produce an excellent iron." It appears that, already, the total quantity raised from the workings near Wellingborough, Heyford, Market Harborough, &c., may be about 150,000 to 200,000 tons per annum.

We are obliged to Mr. Robert Hunt, F.R.S., for the following table, giving the analysis of this newly discovered ore, which adds much to our national wealth, and will greatly enhance the value of an extensive district in our midland counties, in which, until recently, it was not imagined that mineral treasures were contained.

	1	2	3
Peroxide of Iron	45·10	58·00	44·67
Protoxide of Iron	1·25	.....	0·86
Protoxide of Manganese	·62	3·11	0·44
Lime	......	0·91	9·29
Magnesia	·50	0·45	0·66
Alumina	4·00	......	8·95
Phosphoric Acid	......	1·32	0·55
Carbonic Acid	2·28	......	6·11
Silica	10·20	4·10	12·22
Water	26·00	27·82	16·31

An experienced iron-master gives us the following estimate of the cost of producing a ton of pig-iron from this ore:—

	£	s.	d.
Iron ore, 2 tons 15 cwt., at 2s. 6d.	0	6	10
Coke ... ... 25 „ 18s. 6d.	2	2	6
Limestone ... 20 „	0	2	0
Wages, &c.	0	10	0
Cost of steam, heating blast, &c.	0	5	0
	£3	6	4

The quantity produced in Northamptonshire was 96,664 tons.

The discovery thus made by Mr. Blackwell has been followed up in other directions. It was found at Westbury, in Somersetshire, in the coral rag, where furnaces have been erected; and subsequently in North Lincolnshire, where enormously thick masses of ironstone were discovered. An interesting section was exhibited, made of the stones in the Lincolnshire strata. One very interesting fact, elicited in the search for these oolitic ores, is, that although new to us, they were worked in the old days of the charcoal furnaces, and subsequently abandoned and forgotten; and it appears, from coins and pottery, that they were known to the Romans.

The Ebbw Vale Company were exhibitors of a variety of interesting products, including "magnificent samples" of ores of iron, and excellent iron from their new mines in Somersetshire; and a series of puddled steel products, made from a mixture of thin Welsh stone, Ulverstone hematite, and Brendon Hill spathose ore. Following the example of the Jurors, we have the gratification of referring to the new iron mines of Somersetshire, as a fresh instance of the advantages flowing from the Exhibition of 1851, and of the success which has rewarded exploration for mineral treasures in Great Britain. The Report tells us, that Mr. Rogers, of Abercarne, taking the hint from the appearance of the spathose ores, or carbonates of iron, then exhibited by Austria and by the Prussian province of Siegen, proceeded to the Brendon Hills, in Somersetshire, and secured the leases of a highland of Devonian rocks, in which, at several points, abortive attempts to find copper had been made by Cornish miners. Where the search for copper failed, this "prospecting" for iron had proved a great success.

The Report states, that, "running nearly parallel to the shore of the British Channel—or, in other words, to the beds of the Devonian slate, which, over a very large area, have a tolerably uniform dip to the southward—a group of several lodes, more or less interrupted in places, has been traced, and worked at intervals, from a place called Raleigh's Cross, south of Watchet, over a length of nine miles to Eysen Hill." It is remarkable that this name, the *eisen* (iron) of our modern Germans, should furnish a record of mining operations of former years, left by their predecessors, by whom our mining works were conducted. This important tract having been secured by the Ebbw Vale Company, is connected with the sea by a railway, and worked with much activity. At Raleigh's Cross the mine is 274 feet in depth; the lodes varying in thickness from three to twenty-six feet. This spathose ore is found also at Goosemoor and Gupworthy, though varying much in thickness. The Report adds, that, "along the whole range, it is pretty clear that, as in Styria and Siegen, the oxide of iron has been produced by the change from the surface, downwards, of the spathose carbonate; and the manganese present in the latter is met with as black oxide mingled with the former." This company, in 1861, raised 2,794 tons of spathose ore, and 20,993 tons of oxide: being a total of 23,787 tons, of 2,520 lbs., or 26,787 ordinary tons. A medal was awarded to the company for its interesting products.

The discoverer of these mines, Mr. Rogers, having learned in Belgium the position of the pisolite (peastone) red iron ore, searched the corresponding strata in South Wales—the bottom of the carboniferous limestone; and there, at Cwm Noddi, discovered a precisely similar bed of pisolitic iron ore, red and flaky, and abounding in stems of encrinites.

There are other discoveries of iron ore in new localities in our country, of which the Eastern Annexe furnished many instances; and are triumphantly referred to, as evidence "that the story of the rapid exhaustion of our iron ores is altogether wrong." We can fully concur in the satisfactory conclusion of Mr. Robert Hunt (perhaps our best authority on these subjects)—that "these islands possess the best iron ores, in unlimited quantity, for manufacturing the finest varieties of iron."

It is unnecessary to notice all the kinds of ore exhibited. We may, however, not pass over the black-brush of the Forest of Dean, of which there were two kinds, sent by Mr. H. Crawshay, from the sandstone vein and the limestone vein. The total quantity of this ore raised in the forest is about 90,000 tons; the greater part of which is consumed at the Cinderford and Parkend furnaces. Considering, also, the great value of hematite, it is important to notice the specimens of this ore, remarkable for size and beauty, sent by the Parkside Mining Company, from Cleator and Ulverstone, and of which the annual yield is 1,000,000 tons.

Our colonies, though furnished with iron ores, have not yet utilised or exhibited them to any extent; but Canada is evidently a large repository. The Survey, as reported by Sir W. Logan, describes the occurrence of fine blocks of magnetic ore in the Laurentian, the most ancient of the Canadian stratified series, ranging from 200 to 500 feet in thickness.

The iron ores of foreign countries can be most conveniently noticed in connection with the iron and steel produced from them.

Iron and Steel, as distinguished from the Ores.—Conjointly with the increased production of iron ore from old and new sources, we have now to record the improvement in the iron manufacture of Great Britain of late years, which has been "more remarkable than any other branch of human industry." Pig-iron, in 1750, was not produced to a greater extent than 30,000 tons; fifty years later, in 1800, it reached 180,000; and, in 1825, 581,000 tons. From 1826, when the duty on foreign iron became merely nominal, the increase has been as follows:—

Year.	Furnaces in Blast.	Pig-iron made.	Year.	Furnaces in Blast.	Pig-iron made.
		Tons.			Tons.
1835	...	1,000,000	1857	628	3,659,447
1840	...	1,396,400	1858	618	3,456,064
1847	433	1,999,608	1859	607	3,712,904
1852	497	2,701,000	1860	582	3,826,752

Our great manufacturers furnished the Exhibition with the most satisfactory proofs of their skill and enterprise in the production of iron and steel. The Report justly observes, that the axles and tyres, bars, bent and knotted, and plates, tortured into all conceivable shapes, prove that good quality of iron can be obtained when a proper price is paid for it. The specimens thus referred to were principally West Yorkshire; but the works of Shropshire and Staffordshire well sustained the reputation of these places; while Thompson & Co. received the highest commendation for their galvanised sheets and tin plates. The visitors could not but look with admiration, if not with wonder, at some of the specimens of heavy work brought before them. The Mersey Steel and Iron Company sent a Double-throw Crank-shaft, intended for the *Northumberland* or *Minotaur*, of 1,350 horse-power, and weighing, as it came from the hammer, 24½ tons. They showed also some armour plate, 26 feet long, 6 feet wide, and 5½ inches thick. The Butterley Company sent some very large plates of iron; and a rail, 117 feet long, which was placed in the Open Court. The Principality was not behind in the great competition; and among its productions were fine specimens of tin plate, by the Margam Company. The Aberdale Company exhibited a model of a blast-furnace, which produces from 400 to 426 tons a week. The Ifor furnace has yielded as much as 441 tons a week. The process of rolling, on a very large scale, was illustrated by the Blaenavon Company, which exhibited a bar of bulb-iron rolled into one piece, above 42 feet long, by 11 inches deep; and by the Dowlais Company, which showed remarkable samples of rolled girders, having also made arrangements for exhibiting them of larger dimensions than any of those sent to the Exhibition.

Steel.—Messrs. Hawksworth & Co., who furnished most valuable specimens in the improvements in steel, give the following interesting description of the process they are working with great success:—"First come various shaped tubes and rifle-barrels, made under Christopher Hawksworth and Harding's patent, without join or weld, out of a solid bar of cart-steel, by a process of *cold* drawing and rolling—one or the other of these processes, or a combination of both, as follows:—We take a piece of properly prepared steel, from six inches to a foot long, by from two to six feet diameter, through which a hole of a certain size is drilled; and afterwards, by a series of drawings through a wordle and over a mandril (both of peculiar construction), the metal is elongated and highly polished at the same time, and reduced to the given shape and size, internal and external. Should the tube be desired for a gun or rifle-barrel, it is afterwards passed through the elliptical roll, and the desired cone given; then placed in a matrix, and the mandril drawn through to straighten the bore, and bring it to the proper size. One machine, worked by five men, will turn out 600 barrels per week. The process is simple, expeditious, and cheap: cast-steel rifle-barrels made under it can be sold at little over the cost price of the present ordinary iron ones. The principle is applicable to all ductile metals."

The steel products of Mr. Bessemer, and his truly scientific process, have already been described in " Our Walk through the Nave."*

France.—The industry of France, in her iron manufactures, deserves the highest commendation, especially when it is remembered that her ores have to be taken from a variety of formations, and that among them are several kinds which have received little attention in this country. These ores, which were but sparingly exhibited, are obtained in the form of hydrated oxide, from the middle Tertiary formations, which cover the elevated plains of Champagne and the Berri; and in the form of red and brown oxides, in the regular beds and cavernous deposits of the oolite at La Voulte, in the Ardèche, and other districts; and in masses of pisolitic grain, in the green sand in the Bas Boulonnais. We must recollect, also, the difficulties of the French iron manufacturers as to fuel, of which, as we have seen, a large proportion has to be imported. Notwithstanding these drawbacks, the iron-produce of France is rapidly on the increase. In 1819, the quantity of coke-made iron was only 2,000 tons; of charcoal iron, 110,500 tons. In 1847 it had risen to 522,000 tons; and, in 1859, to 900,000 tons. The French manufacturers have gradually substituted coal and coke, and have consequently been able to reduce their prices.

The various manufacturers presented a fine series of wrought-irons, especially girders of great length, and numerous patterns for buildings; steel products, prepared on the Bessemer principle; excellent wire, rolled to various fine gauges; a good class of rod-iron and wire, from the brown and ochry ores of the Dordogne; which, notwithstanding their poor appearance, are described as " sufficiently good to have been long treated in the old Catalan forge." Honour is done to De Rostaing, for an ingenious method of applying centrifugal force to granulate metals. Among the specimens was cast-iron, divided, at will, either into spangles or into fine grains— some to the gauge of twenty-five wires to the inch; others to fifty and to 120.

Algeria sent fine blocks of magnetic iron ore, containing 68 per cent. of iron.

* See *ante*, p. 38.

The deposit whence these specimens were taken is estimated to contain 100,000,000 tons; and after being conveyed twenty miles to the coast near Bona, it may be there obtained at 12s. per ton.

It is due to France to mention, that some of the largest manufacturers, such as Creuzot and Commentry, did not send anything to this Exhibition; and we must also give record to the following explanation respecting a meritorious firm:—" It may be a matter of surprise to those conversant with the attempts to produce wrought-iron and steel by a direct process, that Messrs. Chenot go unrewarded; although, in 1855, the great gold medal was awarded to their father, the late Mr. Adrien Chenot, for the ingenuity and success of his method, which a great authority in France did not hesitate to pronounce the greatest metallurgical discovery of the age." The Jurors' Report adds—" It has been represented that the Jury, on that occasion, awarded the medal unanimously; but having been present at meetings where the Foreign Jurors negatived the proposition, the reporter considers it right to state that the medal was only awarded when all the objecting Jurors had left Paris, and when M. Chenot's countrymen were persuaded, by additional statements, that the manufacture had now attained a sound commercial footing."

Belgium has greatly improved in its iron manufactures, and in the amount of its production, of late years. Its smelters have set a good example to other countries in the economising of fuel. In 1851, the number of coke furnaces in blast was thirty; idle, thirty-five: the charcoal furnaces, in blast, were sixteen; idle, forty. The tons of coke-pigs were 153,919; charcoal-pigs, 13,790. In 1860, the coke furnaces were forty-three in blast, and thirty-four idle; the charcoal furnaces, in blast, eight; idle, thirty-nine. The tons of coke-pigs were 314,672; tons of charcoal-pigs, 5,272. It will thus be seen to what a great extent the Belgian smelters have introduced coke instead of charcoal. This is effected by the construction of ovens, in which the bottoms and sides are heated, and in which some of the drier coals can be used—the yield of coke being from 70 to 78 per cent. on the weight of coal.

Medals were gained by M. Amand, of Nettel, Namur, for samples of excellent charcoal-iron, specially adapted for gun-barrels and hardware; being delivered at Liège at from thirty-six to fifty-two francs per 100 kilogrammes. The Providence Company is distinguished for its fine wrought-iron, and especially for girder-beams of great depth. This company (to which also a medal was awarded) exhibited a rail thirty-four mètres long. The plates and axles of the Société de l'Heure were of the first-rate quality. The sheet-iron of Belgium was distinguished by an equable, smooth, and dark surface: some specimens being shown as they came from the roller, and others highly polished.

These productions are the more creditable to the Belgian manufacturers, as they are obliged, by the poverty of their country in ironstones in the coal-measures, to search elsewhere—among the irregular masses of hydrated oxide (limonite), found in connection with the sub-carboniferous limestones, yielding from 30 to 40 per cent. An important accession to their supplies has been obtained by the discovery, within the last ten or twelve years, of a bed of red pisolitic ore (peastone, oligiste), at the base of the carboniferous limestone, and traced from east to west to a great extent.

Austria is rich in iron ores, and skilful in working them. The Austrians tell us that, with the exception of Upper Austria, the Littorale, Dalmatia, and Venice, all the provinces of the empire yield quantities of iron. Styria and Carinthia furnish more than two-fifths of the ores; Hungary above three millions; Bohemia more than two millions and a-half cwts. of ores. From the different nature of the iron ores, the northern provinces may produce many cast-iron wares; whereas the southern provinces are principally engaged in the production of pig-iron, for being worked into refined iron and steel. At present, nearly all the Austrian smelting-works use charcoal; but some few coke. Pit-coal and turf are nowhere exclusively used; but in Bohemia, Moravia, and Silesia, coal and coke are the principal fuels employed.

About 1,000,000 tons of iron ore are annually used in the Austrian furnaces; consisting of carbonates and red and brown oxides—some not very rich in iron; while others are of excellent quality. These iron-works are conducted in mountainous districts, remote from the great centres of consumption; which, in consequence, is less rapid than it would be under more favourable circumstances; and yet the aggregate quantity of pig-iron, from 1851 to 1860, has risen from 179,184, to 274,118 tons: the ratio of production, including castings as well as pig-iron, having increased from 100· to 146·6.

It is to the credit of the Austrian Exhibitors that they were not anxious to astonish the uninitiated by gigantic specimens; being content, instead, to send such bars and other objects as would show their ordinary work.

Among the exhibitors was Prince Schwartzenberg, the owner of the old-established work at Muran; famous for the varieties of steel known as Roman, Brescia, Mock, and Münz: as also F. Mayr, who first introduced the *treppen-rost*, or step-grate, for furnaces; the use of brown-coal gas, for making cast-steel; and Siemen's ingenious furnace. He produces 12,000 cwt. of cast-steel, and 20,000 cwt. of other steel, and boiler-plate, of cast-steel, five feet wide. The Austrians, who have paid much attention to economy in the use of fuel, have, in some cases, saved 25, and, in others, as much as 40 per cent.

The steel-works of the Austrian empire produced, of—

Raw Steel, for sale	110,000 cwts.
Hammered Steel and Refined Steel ...	112,000 ,,
Cemented Steel	18,000 ,,
Cast Steel	20,000 ,,

The quantities of refined iron and steel far exceed the demands of home industry, furnishing important items of export.

The Zollverein exhibited a scientifically classed collection of the ores found in its several geological formations—embracing the spathose ores of the Devonian rocks; the crystalline and botryoidal red and brown ores of Siegen, of the same formation; the argillaceous stone and black-band of the coal-measures; the pisolite from the oolite, and the light-coloured clay-band stone from the Tertiaries.—Prussia is celebrated for a beautiful variety of silvery lamellar pig, for steel-making, which is produced now, as formerly, by smelting with charcoal. The Westphalian coal-field being now connected with the Siegen by railway, has led to the employment of coke in the furnaces; but it is said to leave the quality of the pig-iron unchanged. The iron of Prussia is now rendered accessible to a much greater extent than formerly, by the construction of railways; and the consequence has been, an increased development of this portion of its mineral wealth. The entire production of the Zollverein, in 1844, was only 150,000 tons; and, in 1859, the amount reached 561,900 tons, of which Prussia furnished above two-thirds. In 1860, the Prussian make amounted to 394,000 tons.

The Köln-Müsener Mining Company, to which a prize was awarded for the superior quality of its spiegel iron, raises, from the celebrated Stahl-berg, 30,000 tons a year of spathose ore. The Phœnix Company sent many fine specimens of rolled iron; and, amongst them, a girder $18\frac{1}{2}$ inches deep; and axles, one of which, five inches thick, was sharply bent without injury. The curious fact now occurs, that the black-band, extensively used as an ore for the production of iron, is now claimed by the agriculturists, as it yields 25 per cent. of phosphoric acid. A bed of this black-band has been discovered at the Josephine mine, as much as sixty-seven inches thick.

The most popular exhibitor of the Zollverein was Herr Krupp, of Essen, who received a medal in this First Class, in recognition of the astonishing advance made by him in the production of homogeneous masses of cast-steel. In 1851, he astonished the visitors by his great block of 4,300 lbs.; but, in 1862, he exhibited a mass of 40,000 lbs.: as, also, a cylindrical ingot of cast-steel, without any forging or workmanship, weighing twenty tons, being forty-four inches in diameter, and eight feet long. It had been broken in the middle, in a cold state, for the purpose of showing that the manufacture of even the largest pieces is perfect, and that the ingots, in a rough state, are quite free from honeycombs or faults; also that the purpose of hammering is not to condense or weld the imperfections, the existence of which would be a serious defect. Another fine specimen, weighing four tons, was a square ingot of cast-steel, one-half of which was in the cast state, and the other half forged. The whole piece was broken longitudinally, in order to display the fine grain, soundness, and toughness of the steel in the cast state, and the improvement gained by forging. This quality of steel, as well as that of the larger specimen, is the softest and toughest produced in these works, and is much employed in the manufacture of guns.

Spain is rich in mineral ores, cropping to the surface; and the cuttings for railways have brought to light numerous treasures that were previously unknown; many of them being within easy distance of fine coal. These minerals are still, to a great degree, neglected; and the Exhibition, in London, illustrated the want of systematic industry in the Spanish people, rather than of the mineral wealth of their country. Durbo & Co., of Langres, exhibited some fine specimens of pisolitic ores (arenisca ferruginosa): but these, with other samples from the Silurian formations, were much injured in the transit; and the confined and slovenly manner in which they were shown was quite unworthy of the occasion. Notwithstanding this great want, the annual production of Spanish pig-iron is about 50,000 tons— not a tithe of the amount that might be obtained if justice were done to the country.

Sweden maintains its celebrity for steel and iron, and is doing great justice to its valuable produce. During the last ten or twelve years, experiments have been made on the hot-blast; from which it has been found that it may be applied, without detriment, to the smelting of iron intended to be refined or wrought—a great improvement, by which considerable economy is effected. Attention has been paid, also, to the best method of calcining the ores in kilns. Mr. Bessemer's method has been brought into use in six of the Swedish metallurgical works. The total produce of Sweden in pig-iron, for 1859, was 215,000 tons. Among its exhibitors we have many medalists: some "for good pig, used for iron guns;" several "for the successful use of peat;" others for "gun-barrel iron." Motula is noted for the production of ship-plate. An iron steamer, covered with these plates, struck on a rock, while going at the rate of eight or nine miles an hour, in a fog; and although a number of the plates were "crumpled up," reached her destination in safety. A medal was awarded to Messrs. Aall & Sons, for their complete collection of good iron products; and another to V. Eggertz, of Fahlun, for new methods of determining, approximately, the amount of sulphur and phosphorus in iron.

The active energy of the Swedish iron-masters and manufacturers is much to be commended. They have an association, which meets once a year in the provinces; and, by their metallurgical staff, render assistance in testing and improving the details of their great trade. At these meetings, and at those which take place in the capital, papers are read, and discussions held, on points of commercial and scientific importance, by which the interests of this branch of industry are considerably advanced.

Russia exhibited many excellent varieties of iron, quite in keeping with the qualities for which it has long been distinguished. The beautifully surfaced sheet-iron, the cast-steel, the fine hammered bars, were all highly satisfactory.

Italy sent numerous specimens of iron ore and iron; but the trade is evidently retarded for want of fuel and a good method of working. A highly prized description of iron was sent from the Val d'Aosta, from the magnetic ores of Traversella and Cogne. Splendid ores of Rio, and of several other unworked localities, were sent from Elba, where there are many of the oldest and grandest mines in the world. The total quantity of pig-iron from Italy does not exceed 38,000 tons per annum. Elba produces, on the average, 48,000 tons of ore, of which, 20,000 are smelted in Fullonica and other places in Tuscany; a small portion is sent to the forges in Catalan, and the rest exported. The works in Lombardy are much retarded by a mischievous custom, handed down from ancient times; according to which, each shareholder has his own number of smelting days, and takes his own mineral and fuel to the furnace. A medal was awarded to And. Gregorini, of Bergamo, for the successful introduction of peat in puddling iron and steel. This was given with special reference to the difficulties caused by the neglect of forests, and the want of fuel. It was honourable to several of the smaller manufacturers that they were found to contend, with much perseverance, against the difficulties occasioned by the recent tariff in favour of imports.

5. *Metals other than Iron.—Gold.*—To maintain the prescribed order, we must, in

the first place, notice the specimens of gold produced in the United Kingdom, although we have, for the present at least, very little reason to expect that these islands will furnish this precious metal to any very large extent. Notice must be taken of the Clogan Mining Company, to which a medal was awarded for their ingots of gold, procured through the meritorious exertions of their then captain, John Parry. The company, up to April 5, 1862, had obtained 2,795 ounces of gold, from 392 tons of vein stuff; and it has been found that, during the two past years, the yield has gradually increased. The other experiments made in Great Britain, go rather to illustrate the adage, that " we may buy gold too dear."

Canada sent specimens of the gold obtained in 1851—'52; the whole profit of which amounted to no more than 182 dollars in the former year, and 508 in 1852.

New South Wales, from which gold was brought away twenty years ago, yielded, in 1851, £461,366; in 1855, £1,781,172; in 1859, £1,698,078; and in 1860, £1,876,049. The total quantity, in ten years, was 3,281,000 ounces troy, equal to a value of £11,683,857.

The Colony of Victoria represented the value of its gold by a tall pyramid, of which we have already given a description.* The number of persons occupied in alluvial workings, is stated at 91,887, aided by 311 engines, with a power of 4,398 horses; besides 18,339 engaged in mining auriferous veins, with 465 engines, of 7,365 aggregate horse-power.

New Zealand sent numerous samples of gold from the alluvial deposits in the fields of Otago, and for which medals were awarded.

Nova Scotia was represented by its provincial government, which sent characteristic specimens from Tangier, Sperhooke, the Ovens, and other places, where the precious metal occurs in the quartz veins.

British Columbia exhibited a large case of stream-gold, from the Cariboo workings. Gold was first discovered in this colony in 1856, but the exploration did not commence until 1858.

Brazil sent various specimens of gold. The St. John del Rey mine, from March, 1861, to February, 1862, yielded 96,612 tons of ore; of which 71,902 were stamped, the produce of which was 62,672 ounces troy.

Austria.—The gold of Austria is obtained from the streams, which, in the tenth and eleventh centuries, employed thousands of persons, and now yield only a few pounds. The quantity from the Hartz and Saxon mines is very small; while those of Hungary and Transylvania produce about 32,000 lbs. weight per annum. It is an important feature of these workings, that some of them belong to the Tertiary period, and the oldest to the latest Secondary.

Silver.—This precious metal has not, of late years, been discovered in remarkably large quantities, corresponding with the enormous increase of gold; and, with only a few exceptions, it has been obtained principally from the ores of lead.

The United Kingdom produces, yearly, from half a million to 600,000 ounces, obtained from lead ore, at the rate of from eight to thirty ounces per ton of lead.

* See *ante,* p. 17.

There are some kinds—those of the Foxhole lode—which yield as much as 200 ounces to the ton; but they are regarded as exceptional. True silver ores are sometimes obtained. A bunch of horn-silver was recently found at North Dolcoath, a few fathoms in length and depth; and recently, magnificent crystallised argentite, or sulphide of silver, with other ores of silver, have been raised, of several thousand pounds value.

France received honourable mention for a series of interesting products obtained by the persevering exploration of argentiferous lead veins, running through the gneissose granite, near the volcanic district of Auvergne. The French production of silver is about one-third that of England.

Austria—whose silver mines, after being for a long time abandoned, were brought into work at the end of the last century, and have lately been worked with much vigour —sent many valuable examples of its produce to the Exhibition. Among these specimens were ore of the Adalbert lode, found in one foot width of galena, containing thirty-three half ounces of silver to the cwt.; and other specimens from various levels. One sample, from the Barbara lode, contained native silver, argentite, stephanite, and polybasite. The experience of the Austrian mines contradicts the theory that the proportion of metal decreases with the increasing depth. In the Przibram lodes the reverse is the case, to the depth of 200 fathoms. The total yield of the Austrian states is from 68,000 to 69,000 lbs. per annum.

Prussia obtains its silver chiefly from galena, from the Devonian up to the deposits of the Muschelkalk; and some from copper of the cupreous schists of Mansfield and Eisleben. There is scarcely a lead-ore in the Zollverein without traces of silver. Too much praise cannot be bestowed on the scientific manner in which the production of silver has been attended to by the justly-famed miners of the Erzebirge. Carried on uninterruptedly for the last seven centuries, and under increased difficulties as each lower level was reached in succession, the operations have had a great influence in the art of mining throughout Germany. During the last century, the workings of these royal mines have shown what science and industry combined can accomplish, in securing for man the treasures hid in the earth.

Norway exhibited splendid specimens of native silver, crystallised and wire-form, from the Königsberg mine, and for which a medal was awarded.

Spain.—The chief mining officer of the Guadalaxara exhibited two specimens of the lode of Hiendelaencina mines, which have been highly prosperous during the few years that have elapsed since their discovery. One of the specimens contained a fine group of crystals of Freieslebenite, which was regarded as among the rarest natural productions until it was found in this district, where it constituted a large part of the vein. This discovery has led to regular workings, carried to the depth of 180 fathoms; the erection of steam-engines, and the taking of three or four hundred other setts in the neighbourhood.

California sent a remarkable group of rich silver ores from Nevada, consisting of granular masses of mixed argentite, stephanite, and other silver minerals; and we are assured, that if half that is said of the thickness and extent of the veins can be accepted, the "territory" is destined to play an important part in enabling the production of silver to maintain its place against that of gold.

Lead.—Many of our productive mines having been worked and closed, it is satisfactory to find that others have been discovered and opened, of which we have some instances in the United Kingdom.

The largest lead-mining establishment in the world—that of Allenhead—belongs to Mr. Beaumont, M.P.; and of which Mr. Sopurth furnished an excellent model. The maps and sections showed the progress of a new adit, "the Blackett level," which is to extend six miles and 567 yards, and will facilitate the working of the veins in the valley. It is seldom that an individual can accomplish so great a work.—A medal was awarded to Messrs. Baker and Rawson, of Sheffield, for a series of specimens showing the process of refining common lead, and exhibiting its various products—white, red, and orange lead.

The following extract from the Juror's Report is given, as it contains a valuable notice of this important process :—

"Mr. W. Baker has shown that only two-and-a-quarter ounces of copper per ton, or 0·0071 per cent., communicate a distinct pink tinge to the corrosions of white lead.* The samples which illustrate the refining process are as follows:—*Hard slag lead*, produced from smelting the slags from the ore furnace in a blast furnace. The higher temperature employed enables lead to take up various impurities, the chief of which are sulphur, antimony, copper, arsenic, and iron. These communicate a hard and brittle character to the metal. Antimony also imparts a silver-white appearance. On submitting a pig of lead to a heat approaching the melting point, it may be readily broken, disclosing a fracture which varies with the quality of the lead, and affording a valuable indication of its character. Hard slag lead generally possesses a granular fracture, but is often fibrous, the fibres being small and of a white colour.

"The first step is the softening of the slag lead. At the Alport Smelting Works this is done by Baker's patent process, which is very suitable for the Derbyshire smelting district, as only a small proportion of antimony is present. It consists in stirring into the lead, immediately after it is tapped, about one per cent. of nitrate of soda. All the impurities are oxidised, except copper, and, of course, silver. Where antimonial leads are worked, as at Newcastle and Bagilt, the improving furnace is adopted. This is a reverberatory furnace, in which the lead is submitted to an oxidising flame for a length of time until it is softened. This lead breaks with a fibre having a purple and yellow tarnish.

"If the lead now contain only five ounces of copper per ton, Pattinson's desilvering process would economically reduce this quantity † But there is a limit at which copper remains in the lead, though submitted to many crystallisations, which necessitates a special process. The lead is decopperised by a process not yet made public. A single operation reduces twenty-one ounces per ton to two-and-three-quarter ounces. The sample of decopperised lead breaks with a coloured fibre about the same as before treatment, and then equals in quality the very

---

* *Vide Phil. Mag.* June, 1862.   † *Vide Chem. Gazette,* 1856.

best ore lead. Pattinson's process is finally effectively employed to remove all but a trace of copper. The lead then assumes a whiter surface, and the fracture exhibits bold columnar masses. The surface of a pig poured out at a low temperature, is covered with brilliant arborescent forms of crystals, which appear peculiar to the purest lead, and which the addition of copper would totally destroy."

A coil of lead-foil, said to be a mile long, was exhibited by the Metal Foil Company—prepared by a process invented by Mr. Wimshurst, by which lead is reduced to sheets, of any length, and of a thickness varying from four to ten ounces per superficial foot, and at the rate of twenty linear feet per minute. This is a great improvement on the old method of reducing the cast-plates by rolling.

The lead of the United Kingdom, in 1860, amounted to 62,525 tons. It is gratifying to find that our colonists in South Australia and Canada, are successfully pursuing their lead mining and metallurgic operations, for which medals were awarded.

Belgium has a mine that is, perhaps, the richest in the world; the value of which was increased threefold three years since, by the discovery of an extraordinary mass of galena. The mine—that of Bleyberg, at Montzen—is not worked without much difficulty and expense, as it is necessary to pump out nearly 1,000 cubic mètres of water per hour, from a depth of 120 mètres.

France has its extensive lead mines at Pontgibaud. From Kefoum Theboul, in Algeria, it sent a full series of specimens, illustrating the manner of dressing ores in that important colony. Fine ore was sent, also, from the mines of Gar-rouban.

Austria has mines producing lead of the finest quality. Those of Nötch, in Carinthia, have, for the last fifty years, produced about 40,000 cwt. a year of the purest lead in the world, the yield being at the rate of 6,500 of pure lead, from between 50,000 to 60,000 cwt. of raw ore. The total amount of lead produced in Austria, in 1860, was 125,019 cwt., and 22,627 cwt. of litharge.

Nassau, also, is rich in lead, of which fine specimens were sent from Holzappel and other places.

Prussia has lead mines, which, in 1861, produced 3,000 tons of lead, and 4,400 lbs. of silver, besides importing and smelting 10,482 tons of lead from purchased ores. The district of Schleiden sent specimens of *Knoten-erz* (knotty ore), with illustrations of the manner in which it is dressed. This knotty ore is found mixed with the sand, in a district of about four-and-a-half miles in extent. In the same district 300 persons are successfully employed in dressing old waste heaps and slags.

Italy would be very poor in lead were it not for Sardinia, where several mines which were wrought in Roman times have been again brought into activity; and where the production, instead of being a mere trifle (as it was in 1851), reached 15,000 tons of galena in 1861. This valuable ore contains 70 per cent. of lead, and 25 grains of silver to the 100 kilogrammes. Of these mines Monteponi is the most productive, being celebrated also for the cerussite and anglesite, found lining cavities in the galena. The mines of Monteponi, in 1861, yielded 6,383 tons of dressed ore: and the total was 10,000 tons of galena, sold abroad; 5,000 tons of lead, smelted in the country; and three tons of silver.

Portugal has its mines at Aveiro, where 350 persons are employed, producing 1,750 tons of *metallic* lead, not rich in silver; and Spain has mines which are estimated to produce nearly as much lead as the whole United Kingdom.

Zinc.—Mining for the ore of zinc is not remunerative in the United Kingdom; but three different methods of smelting are carried on at Swansea, where, however, the production is small. Large quantities of calamine have recently been discovered in the carboniferous limestone in Ireland; and honourable mention was made of the General Mining Company of Ireland, which sent large samples from its mines.

Belgium showed fine specimens of calamine and blende, sorted by a wind apparatus, instead of being dressed by water—the exhibitors being the Nouvelle Montagne Company.

Prussia has mines and furnaces in full activity; the production of rough zinc, in 1860, being 1,106,930 cwt. Ruffer, of Breslau, exhibited excellent plates of rolled zinc, of unequalled size, for which he received a medal; as did other Prussians for the excellence of their productions.

Spain is rich in zinc, having recently discovered calamine in a district extending for miles along its north coast, from Santander into the Asturias, and which have proved a large source of wealth to the shareholders in France and Belgium, and of employment to the people in the district. These treasures are spoken of as existing in "quarries" rather than mines, and the ore is obtained at small depths. They give employment to from 800 to 1,500 persons, and promise to last for ages. Some of the ores are smelted in Spain, by the Royal Arsenal Company, but the larger quantity is smelted at home.

Copper.—This metal has lately become an object of unusual interest, in consequence of the discovery of extensive mines in our colonies, as well as in other countries. Lake Superior, South America, Central Africa, and Australia, have come to our help at the time when some of our own mines are nearly exhausted.

Great Britain.—Swansea has long been celebrated for its copper-works, and holds its position still, notwithstanding the activity of rivals near Liverpool, in France, Chili, Australia, and in North America. If some of our mines have gradually failed, others have proved increasingly productive; and, in 1860, the British production was 236,696 tons of copper ore, raised from nearly 200 mines; the quantity of metallic copper being 15,968 tons. The products exhibited by the Swansea Committee—the tough cake, ingots, solid rollers for calico-printing, and large sheets, were all of the greatest excellence.

Ores were sent by the Devon Great Consols Company, which, in 1862, employed 1,098 persons; by the proprietors of extensive mines in Western Cornwall; and by the Mona Mining Company, the latter being of a very high character, and illustrating, also, the process of cementation and smelting adopted by the company. Large quantities of iron pyrites (mundic) are often found mingled with the copper pyrites; and is employed for the manufacture of oil of vitriol—the quantity sold in England, in 1860, being 135,669 tons.

South Australia has now many powerful rivals to its celebrated Burra Burra mine, from which many ponderous specimens were sent; and New South Wales showed very valuable results of the explorations to which it has been subjected, and from which continued perseverance may produce substantial benefits hereafter.

In Canada, the mines of the Montreal Mining Company, and the Wellington mine of the West Canada Company, give promise of good returns; the former having produced, in 1861, 472 tons of ore, of 17 per cent.; and the latter, 1,175 tons, of 19 per cent.

Jamaica contains copper in the cretaceous formation—much to the surprise of the older geologists, who find that these secondary rocks have been subjected to metamorphic action.

Newfoundland sent some rich and showy ores from several localities, which have to be explored by experienced persons before the mineral value of the country can be satisfactorily ascertained.

Belgium has, mixed with its copper ores, a vast quantity of iron pyrites, of which 18,000 tons were exported in 1861. It was exhibited in blocks as well as dressed.

France, and its colony Algeria, produce very little copper; but it turns its coal, in the extreme north and south, to good use, by working up ores from other countries.

Austria prosecutes its copper-works with activity. A company which smelts the ores of Iglo, in Hungary, and produces between 18,000 and 19,000 cwt. of metallic copper per annum (with about 600 cwt. of mercury), sent a very complete collection.

Bohemia has reopened the mines of Grasslitz, which were very prosperous three centuries ago.

Prussian copper was well represented by the Mansfield Company, whose works are conducted in such a scientific manner as to claim the high appreciation of the mining world. It employs 4,580 men; and produced, in 1860, 30,480 cwt. of copper, and 15,690 lbs. of silver. The most celebrated products of this company are its hammered copper pans, for the manufacture of beetroot sugar.

Italy is said to produce 1,100 tons of copper annually.—Portugal yields 50,000 tons of iron pyrites.—Russia has a high reputation for the copper of the Uralian mines and the Government of Perm.—Spain sent specimens of cement copper, and the very rich ores of Santiago de Cuba.—Sweden produces 15,000 tons of copper, half of which comes from the ancient mine of Fahlun.

Tin.—Great Britain retains its predominance as a tin-producing country; the quantity raised, in 1860, being 10,462 tons of dressed ore—equal to 6,695 tons of the metal. It is a curious fact, that large quantities of tin have been found in deep mines, where, for a time, only copper had been obtained. The great produce expected from India and Victoria has not yet been realised; and the export from Australia, hitherto, has not reached more than 500 or 600 tons a year. Samples were shown from Bohemia, but the quantities are very small. There were specimens, also, from Spain and Portugal. The Perseverance Society sent examples from the district of Porto; but the workings are on a small scale.

Nickel was exhibited in alloys, and cobalt as an oxide for colouring pottery—both by Messrs. Evans & Askins. Good specimens were sent, also, from Prussia and Italy, the latter in magnetic iron pyrites.

Mercury was sent, in noble specimens, from the Royal Spanish Mines of Almaden, where the lode sometimes attains the thickness of eight or ten yards. France sent cinnabar, from the province of Constantine; the Zollverein, from the Ludwig mine; and Italy, from the Val Sassina, and the mine del Sile.

Platinum was exhibited by Messrs. Johnson, of Hatton Garden, who sent an ingot worth £3,840, which had been melted by the intense heat of combined gases, according to the method of St. Claire Deville. They displayed, also, a platinum boiler, of novel construction and design, for the concentration of sulphuric acid, and which had been employed to rectify vitriol at the rate of three tons per twenty-four hours. They exhibited, also, a platinum alembic for the use of mints refineries for the refining of gold and silver, as well as other purposes. The total value of the platinum sent by this firm, in pyrometers, crucibles, wire, gauze, &c., was £5,180.

Iridium was exhibited in a pure ingot, melted by oxy-hydrogen; and, also, mixed with osmium, for the manufacture of pen-points—the value being £6 6s. per ounce; and among the rare metals were rhodium, ruthemium, and palladium.

The aluminium of Messrs. Bell, of Newcastle, has been already described in " Our Walk through the Nave;" and very beautiful results were presented, also, by M. Morin & Co., of Nanterre, in France. The newly discovered bauxite (so called from a commune in the south of France, where it was first observed) may be regarded as the ore of which aluminium is the metallic product. It is found in deposits, from near Tarascon almost to Antibes, a distance of 150 miles.

6. *The Working of Mines.*—The products of our mines were accompanied by many most important illustrations of the skill and enterprise employed in working them. The models exhibited were designed to show the method of sinking shafts; the description of underground conveyance; the mode of raising and lowering in shafts; the important subject of ventilation; the dressing of minerals; and other attendant subjects.

The vast expense incurred in sinking shafts is shown by instances related of the county of Durham, where the miner has to sink through the mountain limestone, and the quicksands at its base; of Lancashire, where the shaft is quarried through the new red sandstone; of Westphalia and Belgium, where the shaft runs through the cretaceous rocks, and a watery stratum more difficult still to overcome. Shafts, in these circumstances, have cost as much as £80,000.

Among the most attractive objects in this part of the Exhibition, were the cages for raising ore, which have been substituted for the corves (baskets) of the old Saxon times. The winding-engines have undergone great improvement, as well as the ropes that coil round the improved cylinders, many being of wire instead of hemp, and some of steel wire. By the improved apparatus, a shaft can now send up from 1,000 to 1,200 tons a day. The invention of safety cages shows the earnest desire to save human life, as well as to improve the working of mines at home and abroad; although it is much to be regretted that none of those exhibited have solved the great problem with which they have to deal. In many cases the result depends on the efficiency of a spring, which must lose its value in two or three years. The Jurors state, that the "safety-clutches" are still on their trial, and that these attempts to provide them are deserving of encouragement. They are therefore mentioned *causâ honoris*. The best apparatus of this kind—the "man-engine," which is successfully worked at several of our Cornish mines, as well as in Belgium and Westphalia—was not in the Exhibition. It is well adapted to mines where a number of men are employed, and at different levels.

Mr. Calon exhibited a method of releasing safety-clutches, which is properly characterised by the reporter as "very ingenious." The spring, instead of being held in tension, as usual, by means of a rope, is kept down by a weighted cap. If the rope breaks, the cage begins to fall; but the cap, having the force of gravitation diminished by the upward pressure of the spring, allows it to expand, and thus brings the clutch-levers into play.

The necessity of increased attention to the best methods of preventing accidents in mines is but too evident, from the accounts with which we are furnished of the loss of life in connection with the raising of coal. The following is a summary of the returns of the official inspectors:—

> Total tons of coal raised in Great Britain in the ten years, 1851 to 1860 .... } 605,154,940.
>
> Total number of lives lost .... 8,466.
>
> Average of tons of coal raised to each life lost ...... 71,480.

The proportions thus given are, however, very unequal in different mines. In South Staffordshire, one life is lost for every 30,000 to 39,000 tons of coal raised; while in South Durham the proportion is as high as 130,000 to 180,000 for one life lost. Much attention has been directed to one of the principal causes of these calamities—the want of the proper ventilation of mines. The practice of splitting the air into numerous runs, and avoiding the necessity of a number of doors, has been extending, and exertions have been made to render one portion of the works independent of another. Besides, there have been improvements in the adaptation of the furnace, and of mechanical ventilators. The safety-lamp has also received great attention, with a view to secure a good light, and prevent the removal of the safety-gauze. It is an important fact, that the lamp of Mueseler, which gives such good light that the men have no temptation to open it, has so well satisfied the miners of Belgium, that upwards of 22,000 are now in daily use in that country. It has also been, to some extent, introduced into England.

A strong claim is presented in favour of the Patent Combination Lamp, which is thus described by the proprietor:—"*It has now no lock that can by any possibility be unfastened, or even touched, until the light is extinguished and the gauze chimney removed;* the only movable part (when the lamp is closed) being the pin by which the wick is raised or lowered, and which, at the same time, answers the purpose of the lock and the extinguisher; for, until this pin is turned, so as to lower the wick into the oil-vessel sufficiently to extinguish the light, there is no means of removing the gauze, which, when placed on the lamp after it is lighted, *locks itself;* nor is it possible that the gauze chimney should be in its proper place on the lamp, and unlocked whilst the lamp is alight."

A very interesting model of a Section of Excavations in a large Colliery, was exhibited by Messrs. Wood and Daglish, which illustrated the port-and-stall and pillar-and-bord systems. The model showed how the whole or unbroken coal is attacked, and when the men may work with candles; and the other method, in which the pillars are to be got, soon after being formed, when the safety-lamp must be used. From the lines of railway, round the borders of the table, we learned how engine-power is applied to convey the coal to the pit from the inner workings. The rails are so laid as to permit the running of two trains—the carriages, or "tubs," being attached to a wire rope, with coils upon a drum worked by an engine near the shaft bottom; and when the inclination of the road is so slight as not to enable the empty "tubs" to run down by their own weight, a tail-rope is employed, passing round a horizontal sheave at the inner end of the workings, for the purpose of thus forming an endless rope. By these arrangements many of our northern collieries have been able to dispense with horses in their main roads.

A valuable Ventilating Apparatus was represented by the model of Mr. Nixon, of Aberdare, showing how large rectangular pistons are employed to extract 45,000 cubic feet of air per minute.

The extent to which large quantities of mineral can be raised, was shown by a model of the Railways and Inclines of the Iron Mines at Upleatham, belonging to Mr. Pease. By the arrangements thus represented, from 300,000 to 500,000 tons of ore are raised every year; and it is stated that, if necessary, a million tons per annum could be raised from these mines.

The model of a large Colliery in Belgium, with its range of handsome buildings, its fine pumping engines, its two cages for taking the tubs of minerals, and the men in separate compartments, and its ventilating apparatus, drew forth the remark, that such " an extensive and carefully arranged plant could be erected only under the favourable circumstances of extensive royalties, long leases, and the prospect of remunerative prices."

France has shown the most admirable perseverance in seeking for coal by boring operations, which have been carried on for a hundred years, during which time 400 bore-holes and shafts have been made. The appliances used by Mulot and Dru in making the artesian well of Grenelle, were exhibited by those gentlemen: among which were their screw-joint lining-pipes, the free-fall borer to be released by a jerk, and not needing the water in the bore-hole, as in Kind's invention, which requires water in the bore-hole. Great honour is due to Herr Kind, the inventor of the free-falling borer, for his artesian well at Passy, which was commenced in September, 1855, with a diameter of 1·1 mètre, and completed on the 27th of September, 1861, by cutting, at the depth of 586½ mètres, a feeder which throws up 6,200 cubic mètres of water in the twenty-four hours. The enormous expense of such works is shown in the case of Carling, in the department of the Moselle, where the many watery strata had to be lined for 160 mètres with continuous wooden tubbing.

The expense of the Carling shaft, including the powerful engines employed, was £72,000. It is hoped that the cost of such operations will be greatly reduced by Kind's method of boring, and Chaudron's method of sinking tubs.

CHAPTER VI.

CLASS II.—CHEMICAL AND PHARMACEUTICAL PRODUCTS. III.—SUBSTANCES USED AS FOOD. IV.—ANIMAL AND VEGETABLE SUBSTANCES USED IN MANUFACTURE. V.—RAILWAY PLANT. VI.—CARRIAGES NOT CONNECTED WITH RAIL OR TRAM-ROADS. VII.—MANUFACTURING MACHINES AND TOOLS.

THE products exhibited by Great Britain and Ireland, in the first of these classes, were in the Eastern Annexe, beyond the mining class, and before reaching the articles of food. On the western side were the organic chemicals; on the eastern, the finest specimens of pigments; and going from south to north, we had pharmacy, dyes, and manufacturing chemicals.

Among the chemicals used in manufactures, one of the most important is sulphuric acid, as it is essential to the production of many other chemical substances. By mixing it with nitre, and distilling it at a gentle heat, we obtain nitric acid; and by mixing it with common salt, and distilling it, we obtain hydro-chloric acid.

Borax is of great importance, from its extensive use in the manufacture of various kinds of glass. It is employed, also, in soldering and in glazing stone-ware. We import, annually, 26,000 cwt. of boracic acid; 6,500 cwt. of refined borax; and 13,650 cwt. of tincal. This last article, which is an impure bi-borate of soda, and is used in the production of borax, is found in Thibet, China, and Persia. Borax is prepared from the borate of lime, which is found in its native state in Peru. The lagoons of Tuscany furnish large supplies of boracic acid, in the form of vapours, which spread over them to an extent of thirty miles, producing an intolerable heat, and nearly suffocating the population. These hot vapours are passed through water, to absorb the acid, and are afterwards evaporated by the steam from the springs; their produce being from seven to eight thousand pounds troy daily.

Acetic acid, the product of the dry distillation of wood, and known in commerce as pyroligneous acid, forms a solid mass—in appearance like ice—at an ordinary temperature; and in this form is used extensively in photography.

Iodine—of which we now hear so much, and knew nothing before 1812, when it was discovered by Courtois, a French chemist—was exhibited in various forms by several of our best manufacturing chemists. It is prepared from seaweeds, the chemistry of which was shown in the case of Mr. E. C. C. Stamford. Iodine is also largely employed in photography.

The phosphorus and amorphous phosphorus, exhibited by Albright and Wilson, are objects of great interest, not only on account of the extent to which they now minister to the uses of life, but also from the melancholy effect which the manufacture of lucifer-matches produces on the workpeople engaged. They are so saturated with

2 F

the fumes that their clothes become luminous in the dark; the cartilaginous and bony parts of the body are diseased and softened; and, in time, the lower jaw is destroyed. It is lamentable to know that the useful lucifer-match is produced at such a fearful price. We hope there is truth in the statement that the introduction of the amorphous variety would remove this dreadful infliction.

Carbonate of soda, on account of its extensive use, had numerous exhibitors, who produce it, and its various products, on a large scale. It is an important fact in the history of our manufactures, that, in 1823, common salt was relieved from taxation; when Mr. Muspratt erected his works at Liverpool, in which salt was decomposed by sulphuric acid, for making sulphate of soda, to be used for the manufacture of carbonate of soda. Our Exhibition included caustic soda, the alkaline ley of the soap-boiler, and one of the principal ingredients of glass; phosphate of soda, most valuable to the calico-printer; stannate of soda, much used in dyeing, and made direct from the native peroxide of tin; tungstate of soda, formed by the union of tungstic acid and soda, and used to render clothing non-inflammable; silicate of soda, used in calico-printing and by soap-makers; hyposulphate of soda, used by bleachers, paper-makers, and photographers; and, also, aluminate of soda, employed in printing and dyeing operations.

Sodium was exhibited, in a crystalline form, by Mr. Bell, of Newcastle, by whom it is employed in reducing aluminium, according to a method thus described by Mr. R. Hunt, who says—"An intimate mixture of carbonate of soda and charcoal is made by igniting in a covered crucible a salt of soda, containing an organic acid, as the acetate of soda, &c., or by melting ordinary carbonate of soda in its water of crystallisation, and mixing with it, while liquid, finely divided charcoal, and evaporating to dryness: this mixture is mixed with some lumps of charcoal, and placed in a retort, which is generally made of malleable iron; but owing to the difficulty of getting these sufficiently large, earthenware or fire-clay retorts have been used with success; and sometimes these are lined with, or contain, a trough of malleable iron. These retorts are so placed in a furnace that they are uniformly kept at a heat approaching to whiteness, and sodium distils over. The receiver contains rock-naphtha, and is surrounded by cold water. The sodium which comes over is mixed with some impurities; and in order to separate the metal from these, the sodium is melted under mineral naphtha, in a cylinder, into which is fixed a piston, worked by a screw or hydraulic press; and when this is forced down, the metal forms in a mass above it, while the impurities remain at the bottom of a cylinder." By this process, the metal, which formerly was a rare curiosity, employed to enliven a chemical lecture, by inflaming on hot water, is now produced in large quantities.

Potash was exhibited in various interesting and valuable compounds—the hydrate, being the most powerful of alkalies; the chlorate, of intense oxidising power; the nitrate, better known as nitre or saltpetre; the carbonate, our potash or pearlash; the bichromate, extensively used in dyeing and colour-making; and the two prussiates, from one of which is prepared the cyanide, much used in photography and electro-plating. Potash, it may be mentioned, is prepared from felspar and fluor-spar, by a process described by the inventor.

Chloride of lime had many exhibitors. We are now well acquainted with it as a deodoriser, and, what is more important, as a disinfectant. It is one principal agent in our manufacturing industry, as we use it to bleach " the thousands of miles of cotton fabrics produced in this country annually." It is obtained by passing a stream of chlorine gas over a quantity of fresh lime.

Alum, of which many noble specimens were exhibited, has become an object of increasing interest, from the new sources from which it is obtained—from the shale of our coal-measures, which, until the discovery of Mr. Spence, was regarded as of no value. After the loss of many thousand pounds in experiments, success has been obtained, and there are extensive manufactories along the coast, near Whitby, where the aluminous shale is found, in connection with the lignite beds.

Sulphate of copper, in very large crystals, obtained directly from the copper ore; the nitrate of lead, used as mordants for dyeing and printing red and scarlet; and the chloride of gold, and nitrate of silver, now extensively used by photographers, occupied this part of the Exhibition.

Benzole, which is now much used for removing grease and fatty matters from wool, silk, and mixed fabrics, is an object of much interest, not only for the uses to which it is applied, but on account of the source whence it is obtained, being one of the many beautiful productions of coal, now known as the aniline series. Ordinary coal-naphtha is produced by the distillation of coal-tar; and benzole, which was formerly obtained from benzoic acid, is now procured from coal-naphtha, by careful processes of distillation. It can be rendered perfectly pure by freezing, when it resembles camphor in its appearance. The products of coal show the most beautiful results of our modern chemistry, and illustrate the extent to which the value of a raw material may be enhanced by science and manufacture—as the pure aniline violet, in powder, is worth from 3,000 to 4,000 francs per kilogramme of 2 lbs. $3\frac{1}{4}$ oz.; while the same weight of coal is worth only four cents. " Thus," it is observed, " with coal carried to its tenth power, we have the price of gold." There is a little innocent sophism in this statement, which we must not severely criticise. The whole of this aniline series (so called from the native Indian term for an indigo plant) will be again mentioned among the " pigments."

The fine chemicals and rare substances exhibited by several skilful manipulators, could not fail to interest those who wish to mark the progress of chemical science. Dr. Crisp exhibited a piece of iron made from the blood of an ox. Mr. Crook's case showed a specimen of the new metal *thallium* (so called from θαλλος, a green twig), which he discovered by means of the spectrum analysis. Its spectrum is a remarkable green band, of great beauty and brilliancy. It can be obtained from iron pyrites, from oil of vitriol, hydrochloric acid, and other sources; but in very small quantities—ten ounces only out of a ton of the richest pyrites. It is easily fusible, melting at a temperature of 555 Fah., and it may be distilled at a full red-heat. It burns brilliantly in oxygen, and small fragments of the metal take fire when thrown into a gas flame, giving rise to an intense green light; for which reason it will, when obtained in large quantities, prove very acceptable to the pyrotechnist.

As the spectrum analysis is now being diligently applied to the discovery of new metals, the following account of the manner in which it is applied may be read with interest:—"If any salt of soda is burnt in a flame, it gives a yellow light; and if a beam of this monochromatic light is passed through a prism, it produces a well-defined yellow line. The red flame of strontium gives a well-defined series of red lines; lithium another set; and thus it is found that every substance produces its own peculiar spectral image.   Bunsen, on examining the alkalies contained in the waters of the Dürkheim, in Rhenish Bavaria, saw, on looking at the spectra they produced, some lines which he had never seen in the spectra of any other alkalies.   Bunsen further states, in a paper on the two new metals, cæsium (from *cæsius*, a greyish colour) and rubidium (from *rubidus*, red)—owing to the lines of these colours being characteristic of the presence of these two metals—that from the 30 grammes of the mother-liquor, he obtained only 1·2 milligrammes of the impure salts of these two new alkaline metals.   This was all he had to begin with—about the one-hundredth part of a grain; but so certain was he that his spectrum never failed him, that he set to work at once, and evaporated down fifty tons of water to get some more of this substance: forty-four tons yielded him only 105 grammes of this chloride of rubidium, and 70¼ grammes of the chloride of cæsium; so that out of forty-four tons of water, he got only about 200 grains of the mixed chlorides of these two new metals."

The proximate principles discovered in lichens and seaweed; the rare vegetable acids—tolnic acid, suberic acid, picric acid, and their salts; the vegetable alkaloids (such as strychnine) and their salts, were all exhibited in such quantities as can be rarely seen.   Among these curiosities were the chemical elements obtained from tea (*theine*), from coffee (*caffeine*), and an extensive series of the products of opium.   The collection of Mr. E. F. Langdale gave an attractive display of essential oils and fruit essences; and a curious composition, known as the essence of gin and the essence of brandy—a pound of which, mixed with fifty gallons of pure spirit, will convert it into London gin, or Cognac brandy, as we are assured by the exhibitors.

Paraffin, the products of which were first brought before the general public in 1851, was exhibited by Mr. Young, of Bathgate, in Scotland, whose chemical works are said to be the largest in the world.   His specimens of paraffin were made from many different kinds of coal.   Millions of gallons have since been produced; and, in the solid state, if made into candles, is finer than the purest wax; while the liquid products are used as oils for lubrication as well as combustion.

Under the head of dyes, pigments, and varnishes, the most attractive were the new products which constitute the aniline series, which have yielded our fresh and attractive mauves and magentas.   The anilines at first were obtained from indigo, by the application of hydrate of potash; though the source of these beautiful hues is itself destitute of colour.   It was then found among the products of the dry distillation of coal; and, in 1856, Bechamp discovered a method of obtaining it from benzole.   The first colour produced from aniline was mauve, discovered by Mr. Perkins, while endeavouring to make artificial quinine.   Aniline, when treated with bichloride of tin, nitrate of mercury, and chloride of carbon, produces many magnificent colours, such as fuschine, or rosaniline, indisine, azaleine, and other modifications of the same beautiful element. Pure rosaniline, when first produced, is perfectly clear; but, by the addition of an acid, it assumes its well-known exquisite colour.

The discovery of this new source of new and beautiful colours, the produce of coal-tar, will have a mighty influence on the chemical manufactures of England, as we have the material in unfailing quantities; so that we shall be able to export, to a large extent, finer hues than we have heretofore had to obtain from abroad.

Dyes, from lichens and madder, are very beautiful; and it is no small commendation that they bear any comparison with the aniline series. Alizarine and garancine are obtained from madder-root, which is treated with oil of vitriol.

The lac-dye, as exhibited by Marshall & Co., is obtained from a species of coccus; and, from the vivid and permanent quality of its scarlets, is a good substitute for cochineal.

Indigo, the most important of our blue dyes, was shown in all its varieties, as sent from Bengal, Oude, Benares, Madras, Manilla, Java, and Guatemala. The mode of preparation by the native growers is thus described:—" The green plants are placed in troughs, and covered with water; fermentation takes place, ammonia and carbonic acid being disengaged. The liquor is drawn off into other troughs, and a small quantity of lime is added; the mixture is stirred briskly, and the indigo separates as a deep-blue granular powder, which is drained, pressed into cakes, and dried." The specimens were free from the brown and red colouring-matter found in the indigo of commerce. The finest Bengal indigo is sent in cubical pieces, being light, brittle, and of a clean fracture; soft to the touch; of a fine, bright, blue colour; porous, and adhering to the tongue. The Madras indigo is inferior in quality. Our imports of this important dye, in 1860, were 77,321 tons.

The pigments exhibited by Messrs. Winsor and Newton, worth more than a thousand pounds, are regarded as the finest display ever made in this country. The collection included the most beautiful specimens of ultramarine, prepared by calcining the *lapis lazuli*. This precious article, in consequence of its extreme value, has been in a great measure superseded by the artificial ultramarine, made of fine china-clay, sulphate of soda, carbonate of soda, sulphur, and charcoal; of which admirable specimens were shown by Gaskel and Deacon. Ultramarine formerly fetched as much as five guineas an ounce; the artificial may now be obtained for little more than a shilling a pound. It is manufactured in Paris, in Meissen, and in Nuremberg.

Among the medical and pharmaceutical products, there was the valuable collection prepared by Professor Redwood for the Pharmaceutical Society, and which the visitor had the opportunity to handle and examine, under the supervision of the curator. There were, besides, numerous valuable specimens sent by eminent manufacturers. The collection of Peruvian barks—properly cinchona barks—was placed in front of excellent drawings of the plant; and, near them, some growing plants.

Ether has acquired, within the last few years, an additional value from its employment in the preparation of collodion, for the use of photographers. It is obtained by dissolving gun-cotton in ether. Chloroform, so extensively employed as an anæsthetic, is obtained by distilling eight ounces of chloride of lime, twenty-four ounces of water, and one ounce and a-half of alcohol, at a gentle heat, in a half-gallon retort. The first products are crude, but they acquire the requisite purity by washing and re-distillation.

An important object in this class was the hard, transparent, vitreous material (silicate of alumina), exhibited by Messrs. Bartlett, of Camden Town. Silicate of potash, known also as liquid flint or water-glass, has for years engrossed the attention of the chemists; and the dissolution of that hard and imperishable substance, flint, promised for the discovery a most important future : but the energetic action of the material itself, in the presence of acid re-agents, rendered it inutile for many purposes for which it appeared to be especially destined. If the original state of insolubility were sought to be restored, this end could be accomplished by the use of the ordinary re-agents; but with such energy was the reaction effected, that a disruption of the product was the result, and the silica was at all times presented as a pulverulent mass, without any coherence or properties of cohesion. In the presence of an alkaline solution of a re-agent, however, the case is reversed; and in this fact lies the sum of the invention. The silica and alumina are both dissolved by an alkaline solvent; and, when brought together, the menstruum being the same, the two minerals are left to act on each other. This action takes place so slowly, that the solution may be applied to any body sought to be indurated; and, after the lapse of a few hours, a solid substance is produced by the perfect union of the silica with the alumina, forming that hard and enduring substance so often found in nature under the names of jasper, ruby, and garnet; all of which are silicates of alumina, or combinations of silica, alumina, and potash, in varied proportions. This valuable material has been selected for restoring the decaying stone-work of the New Houses of Parliament.

THE SUBSTANCES USED AS FOOD (Class III.), were divided under the three heads of Agricultural Produce; Drysaltery and Grocery; and Wine, Spirits, Beer, and Tobacco. The best opportunities were afforded by several exhibitors, British and foreign, for comparing the various productions belonging to this class, they sparing no expense in collecting, as they had shown the utmost taste in the display of their cereal produce. The Jurors, with the greatest justice, speak of " the scientifically arranged and instructive collection sent by Vilmorin Andrieux, of Paris," who presented the most complete collection in the Exhibition, including samples of nearly every raw produce of Section A in this class. Specimens in straw, of nearly all the wheats cultivated in Europe, were named by M. Louis Vilmorin, the first authority on this subject. M. Vincent Janeo, of Pesth, sent 200 small collections of the farm produce cultivated in Hungary, and for which he received a medal. Russia gave an interesting collection of cereals, flour, groats, pulses, oil, grass-seeds, nuts, chicory, &c. Prussia sent a neatly arranged collection of cereals in ear, with about seventy kinds of kidney-beans in seeds and pods; and Algeria sent two very extensive collections of cereal grains, pulses, and oil-seeds of excellent

.quality, well arranged, and showing the rapid progress of this great French colony.

The *Common European Cereals* were presented in numbers far exceeding those shown in 1851, as nearly every country was represented. Britain and her colonies, with the northern continental countries, sent principally the *Triticum sativum*, of which the best specimens came from Australia; and the *Triticum durum* was sent from Spain, Italy, Greece, and Algeria, some examples weighing 68 lbs. per bushel. Spain also sent the *Triticum polonicum;* and Germany several specimens of spelt wheats. The power of wheat to endure the rigours of a cold climate was shown by the specimens sent by Sweden, grown within ten miles of the Arctic Circle. From this country we had also excellent samples of barley, peas, rye, and vetches, sent by the Agricultural Society of East Gothland.

No peculiar interest attached to the oats, rye, and inferior cereal produce of our own or any other country. Of barley, shown in great perfection by Germany, Denmark, Great Britain, Victoria, and Tasmania, the best example, weighing more than 59 lbs. per bushel, was sent from Prussia, by Captain Von Grunow.

It may be well to record the following observations on the production of malt from barley—that "a quantity of good barley, which weighs 100 lbs., being judiciously malted, will weigh, after drying and sifting, 80 lbs.;" and that, "since the raw grain, dried by itself at the same temperature as the malt, would lose 12 per cent. of its weight in water, the malt process dissipates, out of these remaining 88 lbs., only 8 lbs., or 8 per cent. of the raw barley. On the other hand, the bulk of good malt exceeds that of the barley from which it was made, by about 8 or 9 per cent."

The specimens of English wheats most admired, were the *Talavera*, adapted to gravelly soil; the *Chidham*, for rich-bearing soil; the *white turnip*, sown principally in southern counties; and the *red nursery*, suitable for limestone or chalky districts. The effects of artificial selection were strikingly shown in the great improvement of the English wheats; and particular notice was taken of the Case 714, showing very large ears, procured by preserving for seed, from year to year, only the largest ears produced, thus obtaining an increase in the number of ears as well as in their size. Now—not so much as in the time of Dr. Johnson—oats and other grain are much " used as food by the people in Scotland," especially in the form of Scotch or pearl-barley, which were shown in great perfection; as were also groats, and oats for oatmeal, ground to various degrees of fineness. The English exhibitor who tried to astonish the natives of all countries by his sample of barley " grown from oats," is very justly censured by the Jurors, who express their surprise " that such a delusion should gain credit at the present day." The specimens of compressed hay, packed in bands of iron, excited much attention, as showing perfect samples of the manner in which our troops can be supplied with fodder in their distant campaigns.

The colonists of Australia have sought to compete with their native land in the culture of wheat, in which they have not only maintained a friendly rivalry with each other, but, in some important respects, have excelled the mother country. South Australia surpassed New South Wales in the quantity of wheat to the bushel, estimated by weight; though only by a kind of neck-and-neck race—the former being 68 lbs. 1 oz.

to the bushel, and the latter 68 lbs. in weight. From the analysis made by Mr. Dugald Campbell, it appears that the average weight of South Australian wheat was 65¼ lbs. to the bushel; whilst the per-centage of flour was 83·5, and that of bran, 16·5; the proportion of the latter being remarkably small. It was also found that the moisture in "dried" South Australian wheat was only 12·57, against from 15 to 20 per cent. in the wheat of Great Britain. Tasmania had the credit of producing the heaviest oats shown in the Exhibition, weighing 51 lbs. 10 oz. to the bushel; and some very fine specimens of wheat for seed, which sold at a guinea a bushel.

Indian corn, or maize, was sent in numerous samples from Spain, Portugal, France, Australia, and North America; and Modena sent a fine collection of 200 varieties. Good specimens were sent from Algeria, and the white-seeded kind from Peru. This product requires, for its growth, a higher temperature than that of the United Kingdom.

The *Cereals of comparatively rare cultivation in Europe*, were rice, broom-corn, and Chinese sugar-cane. Rice was shown in its clean and "lurked," or *paddy*, state. The principal specimens were from Brazil, Ceylon, and the East Indies; it was sent, also, from the southern countries of Europe. Indian millet-broom corn was shown in great varieties from France, Italy, Spain, and Portugal, and from Africa, where it is used extensively as bread-corn. The Chinese sugar-cane, widely cultivated for its saccharine matter, and for fodder, was exhibited in excellent samples of grain.

Millet, and other small Grains, which are not cultivated in Britain, were important items from other countries. Millet makes a favourite article of food in Germany and South Europe, whence it was sent; as also from the Portuguese colonies in Africa. Fine examples of the canary-seed were sent from Italy. Peruvian millet, which is said to be suitable for growth in the English climate, was shown by the consul for Peru.

Pulse, the Pea and Bean family, occupied a place in nearly every European collection. Sweden, Germany, and Russia sent samples of peas and beans of the common kinds; and the first of these countries, a fine specimen of mazangan. Canada and Britain sent the best samples of the small horse-bean. Windsor beans, the large and broad, were shown by Canada, and the medium size by Spain and Portugal. The latter country sent thirty varieties of kidney-beans: many were also forwarded from France, Prussia, and Italy.

Hops were exhibited, not only by our own growers in Kent, Sussex, Surrey, Hampshire, Worcestershire, and Herefordshire, but by growers in Bavaria—so famed of old, and still, for its beer; also Belgium, Bohemia, France, Würtemberg, Poland, and Russia. The influence of climate and soil on the quality of this delicate and uncertain crop, as affecting taste, smell, colour, and size, was remarkably shown in the specimens exhibited. English hops were found to maintain their high reputation in regard to delicacy of flavour, brightness, and perfection of colour; while there were many points of interest in the hops sent from the twelve European countries, the two British colonies of South and Western Australia, and the Northern States of America. The hops of Bavaria and Bohemia were distinguished for the amount of "lupuline," and the excellence of curing; those of Alsace and Lorraine for fineness of flavour, though somewhat deficient in strength. More attention must be given to the picking of the plant; to avoiding green leaves; and to its curing, so as to prevent the smell of smoke in foreign hops, which will make them more acceptable in the London market. The disagreeable flavour of the Canadian and United States' hops renders them unsuitable for our fine ales. Portugal might evidently become a good hop country, as was proved by the excellent samples of the wild plant sent from that kingdom.

Among the exhibitors of agricultural produce, there were, we may notice, the "Hellenes," who represented each *demos*, or commune; many samples being of fair quality, though not commended. Besides wheat, or Indian corn, there were barley, common beans, kidney-beans, peas, chick-peas, broom-corn, vetches, lentils, oil-seeds, such as sesamum, colza, and linseed; and other seeds, such as tobacco, anise, cumin-fennel, and coriander. Turkey sent about 250 specimens, from forty-seven exhibitors. They are valued as the foundation of good samples, but show "proofs of inferior cultivation and bad dressing." Egypt had a medal for her collection of wheat, barley, rice, Indian corn, sorghum, flax, carthamus, sesamum, fermgreek, tobacco-seed, lentils, beans, cotton-seed, coriander, lupins, nigella, and Alexandrian clover. In reviewing this important section, it is gratifying to observe the stimulus given to the produce of agriculture, and to see the evidence afforded, since 1851, that it is receiving more of that earnest attention which has secured the fuller development of commerce and manufactures.

Chick-pea, chickling vetch, and lentil occupied an important place in the French, South of Europe, and Algerian collections.

The *Grasses* principally cultivated were shown in seeds and bunches, in the British French, German, North American, and Russian collections.

The *Forage Plants* were sent principally from the countries where they are an article of commerce. There was red clover from France, the Netherlands, and the American colonies; the yellow-seeded variety, and very fine alsike from Sweden; white clover from Germany; the yellow and scarlet clover from France, and sainfoin from Germany. Agricultural roots were well represented by the potatoes of Belgium, France, and Algeria, and by well-executed plaster models, not only of this root, but of the mangold-wurtzel, carrots, and turnips, which were exhibited by France and Germany. Models of fruits, beautifully executed, were very numerous in this class. An extensive collection was sent from Paris; casts of fruits and vegetables from Victoria, in coloured plaster; and *papier-maché* casts from Guiana. The whole fruits of Jamaica were represented by wax models. The fruits and vegetables of Nova Scotia were also well represented by specimens preserved in spirits of wine.

Under the head of *Flour and Preparations from Cereal Grains and other Seeds*, it is due to Austria to mention that she carried the day in the production of flour, her German milling being "magnificent." The Jurors say—"It was not only the outward appearance, and the intrinsic value of the flours exhibited, but also the exhibition of the different kinds of grains from which the flour was produced, together with the bran, accompanied by statistical notes, carefully made, and very instructive. . . . . . The samples of the first quality are all of an excellent fineness and colour; and those from Hungary full of body." "Compressed flour," and "compressed bran," were among the new products under this head.

The Section B comprehended Drysaltery, Grocery, and preparations of food, as sold for consumption; and included dried fruits from the Ionian Islands and Greece. These are the only places from which we can obtain our supply of currants, and which were larger than in 1851, owing to the practice of "ring-cutting." Raisins were sent from Spain and Turkey, as the principal, but not the only sources of supply; and they have increased in quantity, notwithstanding the fearful blight, the *oidium Tuckerii*, which originated in 1851. No method of resisting this fearful blight has been found so useful as the application of flour of sulphur at particular periods during the growth of the plant, together with the system of training the vines on the ground in dry situations, instead of allowing them to grow to the ordinary height. It has been supposed that the efficacy of the sulphur is due to the presence of minute traces of sulphurous acid in the powder, and it is hence recommended to try a weak solution of sulphite or hyposulphite of an alkali instead. The show of dried fruits was regarded as creditable to the exhibitors; but the specimens suffered much from being packed in small bottles or boxes, and subject to atmospheric influences.

The attention now paid to the growth of tea in the East Indies, and with most encouraging success, gave great interest to this part of the Exhibition. There were 142 samples of Indian teas, some sent by the government, and others by twenty-eight exhibitors from India. The black varieties were pekoes, souchongs, pouchongs, bohea, and congous; and the green, hysons, hysonkin, and gunpowder. They were adjudged to be free from any colouring matter, and every other kind of adulteration. The awards were all made in favour of private individuals; while the government produce was found to be "deficient in strength, and generally of indifferent flavour." Assam teas stood high in point of strength and depth of colour in infusion.

The colonial teas were from Natal and Victoria, but were remarkable only as being new products from these colonies. The Java teas showed skill in the manipulation, but they were harsh and bitter in taste, as were also the Brazilian specimens. There were fine examples of Chinese teas, in illustrative series, shown by the firms of Dakin and Phillips.

Chocolate, manufactured from the cocoa-plant, and now coming increasingly into use in England, was a very attractive article in this department. France is foremost among the countries in which it is manufactured; Spain (where it got into extensive use immediately after its introduction into Europe) being second, but scarcely inferior in the order of merit. The French chocolates are not flavoured, except with vanilla; but those of Spain receive the addition of cinnamon. Switzerland exhibited pure chocolate in tasteful forms. The Zollverein and Austria were excellent in the finish of their best chocolate, and the great variety of figures into which it was formed, as well as in the common kinds, which are consumed extensively by the German peasantry. Italy displayed much taste in its chocolate; but that of the Netherlands was shown principally in powder. England is paying increasing attention to this manufacture, and importing the berries which give to the French chocolate its peculiar flavour.

Arrowroot was sent from Jamaica and other countries, and especially from Queensland, where many tons were manufactured in the year preceding the Exhibition. The samples of white arrowroot from that colony were considered equal to the best kinds from Bermuda. Medals were given for arrowroot to Mr. Lamport, of Natal, and Mr. Robertson, of New South Wales. The canna variety, sent from Victoria, is said to be of little value, on account of the abundance of supply.

Sugar, though more extensively illustrated than in 1851, showed very little marked improvement since that period, "notwithstanding the use of the turbine or centrifugal process, whereby the molasses is more quickly separated from the crystallisable sugar"—as stated in the report.

Besides the old sources of supply, it was interesting to observe the good specimens sent from Natal, which were "very creditable, and promise well for the future." Liberia also sent a good illustrative series, which "promises well for the future prosperity of its free population." Beetroot-sugar was exhibited by France, Belgium, Austria, Prussia, and Russia; and so considerable is the amount of produce in these countries, that, in Austria and Prussia, very nearly the whole of the want of the population is supplied by inland labour. The consumption of this article, in Austria, has increased considerably during the last few years: it amounts now to nearly five pounds per head per annum, and is much on the increase.

Among the *Confectionery and Sweetmeats*, Dr. Hassall had a case to represent the various kinds of adulteration practised about the time of the first Exhibition, when every comfit and *bon-bon* contained an amount of impurity which would now shut them out from the market: these impurities consisted of chalk, plaster of Paris, flour, and poisonous pigments. The quantity produced in 1855, in this country, was 8,000 tons, which has now risen to no less than 25,000 tons per annum. The chief cause of this increase is said to be the application of steam-power to the several processes of manufacture, which reduces the cost of production.

It is a curious fact, that, in 1848, "French" confectionery was first made in England by Messrs. Schooling, of Whitechapel, who had to employ French workmen, and could not, with every attention to economy, afford to sell their produce for less than 3s. 6d. per pound. After seven years' experience, the process has been so far perfected, that every species of confectionery can now be produced at 1s. 4d. per pound. Although previous adulterations are now rejected, except by the inferior manufacturers, who "still employ the yellow and red compounds of lead for colouring materials," yet the most respectable manufacturers are of opinion, that "a small quantity of flour is necessary in some cases to bring up the colour, and make the comfits freely soluble in the mouth:" and in the manufacture of almonds, it is found that a certain proportion of gum and flour must be used, as a ground or coating over the almond for the adhesion of the sugar. British manufacturers have become the masters of this trade, as the finest variety of French confectionery is still produced by hand-labour, and cannot compete in price with our own, which is manufactured by steam-power. There are about thirty houses in this trade, producing nearly the whole of the sweetmeats consumed in this country, the colonies, and a large portion of the continent. It is curious to observe how this new branch of trade has its separate divisions. " One house will devote its attention to jams and marmalades, making hundreds of tons in a year; another produces medicated lozenges; a third nothing but ' dry goods'—that is, various seeds, &c., coated with sugar, and lozenges; another house will produce 'boiled goods,' as acidulated drops, &c.; another, ' gum goods,' as jujubes, gum-pastiles, &c.; and another, 'liqueur goods'—that is, sugar crystallised in forms, and holding various liqueur flavours within them. A few manufacturers devote their attention to every variety of goods; but the result is not so satisfactory as when the attention is not divided."

Marmalade, Jams, and Preserved Fruits, were well illustrated by England and foreign countries. Orange marmalade was sent from Glasgow and from Dundee, where Keiller and Sons produce 250 tons in the season. Batty and Messrs. Crosse gave fine examples of preserved fruits and jellies: the jellies of Batty were from the currants of 1850. France sent numerous specimens from several manufacturers, all of whom received honourable mention. Prussia was well represented; as were several British colonies, Tasmania, Queensland, and New South Wales.

Pickles have greatly improved since 1851. France and Belgium have demonstrated that bright colour may be given to pickles without the aid of copper. English houses exhibited pickles of great beauty, in which not a particle of copper could be traced; and a medal was given to Batty & Co., who use " colouring materials from vegetables and green foliage." The French producers set off the colours of their pickles by the aid of bottles of a brilliant glass; respecting which the Jurors remark, that " it is a matter for consideration whether the practice is or is not deserving of imitation in this country."

Mustard had many claimants to public favour. It is, happily, now ascertained that it can be prepared for sale without the aid of flour and turmeric; and that a good article can be produced by the admixture of the white and black varieties of seed. It was difficult to decide between the merits of Colman and Harrison; but the award was given to the first-named firm, only " after careful examination, chemically and microscopically, as well as by the test of flavour." Good specimens were shown by France, Austria, Prussia, and Norway.

Other Condiments were shown—such as powdered English herbs for flavouring purposes, by Makepeace, of Merton; sauces and essences by numerous makers. Honourable mention was made of the vanilla essence—a spirituous solution of the active principles of the fruit, prepared by Hexter.

Preserved Meats were exhibited by McCall & Co., who seek to improve on the former methods, by introducing into the tin case a small quantity of the sulphite of soda, to remove the remaining oxygen, by which the over-cooking is avoided. Messrs. Jones preserve their food uncorked, by perfectly exhausting the air from the tin case in which the food is placed. Our colonists are endeavouring to provide the mother-country with the productions they possess in abundance. Turtle, and turtle soup, were sent from Jamaica; salmon and lobster from Newfoundland, New Brunswick, Nova Scotia, and other places. Uraguay sent dried beef, in excellent condition. The foreign exhibitions were chiefly articles of luxury—such as game-*pâtés*, sausages from France, dried and compressed vegetables, and dried soup; the *pâté de fois gras*, from Strasburg; new butter, from Paris, preserved in patent bottles, quite fresh, and of good flavour, although it had been kept eight weeks.

Cheese, of a rich flavour, was sent from France; Gruyère and Emmenthal, from Switzerland; and Parmesan, from Italy. The Netherlands, Denmark, Norway, and Germany, also competed; the cheese from Mecklenburg being specially mentioned: most of the specimens sent from Portugal were preserved in oil.

Isinglass, Gelatine, and Jellies.—Vickers sent an extensive collection of every variety, imported from Russia, Brazil, East and West Indies, and America. Gelatine is an article of growing importance; whilst, in 1851, it was a novelty. Batty & Co. now produce about eighty tons per annum.

Tobacco in various states—in the leaf, cut up for the pipe, ground into powder for snuff, and rolled into cigars for smoking—had its place in this class. British manufacturers obtained much credit for their perseverance and skill, as shown in the variety of their productions; while they could not, in point of flavour, rival tobacco-growing countries. Hungary sent ten sorts of tobacco. The leaf forms an important article of Austrian revenue. Belgium and Holland were represented by some of the best cigars, of which large quantities are manufactured in Antwerp. Kylberg exhibited some leaf grown near Stockholm. Other specimens were shown from Sweden; but most, used for manufacturing, is imported into that country from Bremen and Hamburg. France exhibited largely, but not the finest kinds, such as were sent from Brazil. The tobacco products of the Mauritius included a dozen bottles of snuff, seven boxes of cigars of the Coringby kind, and one of the Faham leaf.

Wines, Beer, and other drinks, will conclude our record of this class. Ale and porter, of the greatest excellence, had many British exhibitors; among whom were the well-known brewers, such as Bass, Salt & Co., and many continental firms. A greater interest was taken in the variety of wines, not only from the old sources of Portugal, Spain, France, and Germany, but also from our own colonies, Hungary, Italy, and Greece. The following table records the effect of the late legislative measure in favour of the use of wines in Great Britain.

Wines cleared for Home Consumption.

Origin.	1860.	1861.	1862.
Spain	2,975,906	4,031,796	3,956,213
Portugal . . .	1,776,172	2,702,707	2,349,954
South Africa . . .	426,597	331,483	176,732
France	1,125,816	2,229,038	1,900,344
Germany	222,726	345,652	316,440
Naples and Sicily . .	204,969	227,266	214,125
Madeira . . .	28,941	28,814	28,550
Canaries . . .	4,015	3,756	3,356
Other countries . .	592,147	886,589	858,332
Total gallons . . .	7,358,189	10,787,091	9,803,046
Annual revenue . .	£1,174,105	£1,219,533	£1,123,605

ANIMAL AND VEGETABLE SUBSTANCES USED IN MANUFACTURES (Class IV.) This class was divided into four sections, of which Section A included *Oils, Fats, and Wax, and their products*. This section embraced—1. Animal and vegetable oils and fats, including wax in the unmanufactured state. 2. Products manufactured from those substances—such as the fatty acids, glycerine, spermaceti, bleached wax, and the different varieties of candles. 3. Soaps. 4. Wax flowers. In reference to the first of these four heads, the idea was expressed, in the Report on the Exhibition of 1851, that among the numerous little-known oils of tropical countries, there were many as well suited for manufacturing purposes as those then employed. Producers were also reminded, that "the value of such oils depended on the care bestowed on their preparation, in the cleanliness of the seeds, and the exclusion of all impurities in the preparation of the oils." This important suggestion has not been neglected, and the good results have now appeared. India exhibited a novelty, under the name of "illoopa oil," the produce of the *bassia longifolia*, one of the most beautiful trees in India, and as hard as teak. This oil, which might be denominated a butter, is solid at 84°, liquifies at from 90° to 95° Fah., and is used for illuminating purposes and the manufacture of soap. Queensland exhibited wax, which was remarkably hard, well bleached, and brittle. Some excellent produce, from the west coast of Africa, was exhibited by M. Pilastre—a small nut named m'p'oga, very abundant at the Gaboon, and used as food. The oil exudes freely on pressure by the finger. The dika almond was exhibited in four states: the first being a cake, formed of the bruised almonds, which, on strong pressure, yields from 65 to 70 per cent. of grease, resembling the butter of cocoa, fusible at 125° Fah., and fitted for the manufacture of soap. Ten kinds of oil, in good condition, were sent from the French Indies; but, at present, the amount exported is limited. The cocoa-nut and sesamum oils are sufficiently obtained to give rise to a good trade. The produce of fatty matters at Tahiti has been doubled in less than two years; the most remarkable being the nut and oil of tamanu, used medicinally for rheumatism, and well adapted for the manufacture of soap. The Report of 1851 must be referred to, for an account of the ordinary sources of oil and grease produce.

The second head under this section included wax, and candles made from it; spermaceti and sperm candles, which have reached a high degree of perfection in the process of extraction, refining, and moulding; and the manufactures of glycerine and paraffin. Great improvements have been made in these substances, and in the economy with which they are obtained. The manufacture of stearine by means of sulphuric acid, is rapidly displacing the old process of saponification. The economical advantages obtained by the new process are—the saving of time; the comparatively small quantity of sulphuric acid required; and the power given to the manufacturer of using cheaper materials, without producing inferior articles. No great improvement has taken place in the manufacture of glycerine since 1851; but such is not the case with paraffin. A few years ago, the candles made from it were greasy to the touch; were sufficiently soft to bend slowly when supported at the two ends; guttered when burned in an atmosphere but slightly disturbed; and gave out smoke copiously when carried about. These disadvantages are now overcome. Their dryness and hardness are considerable;

FINISHING CARDING ENGINE,

BY PRATT BROTHERS

they do not become dirty from dust, nor soften or bend more than good stearic candles.

A medal was awarded to Messrs. Field, of Lambeth, who are the refiners of the paraffin extracted from the "boghead" coal, the purification of which is adjudged to be perfect. Their candles were distinguished by whiteness and transparency, hardness and dryness to the touch, as well as by the exquisite beauty of their aniline colours. The same award was given to Barclay, of Regent Street; Ogleby; Tucker; Langton; and Taylor, of Leeds.

A fine collection of candles, made from pressed and bleached tallow, sent by Quelch, of Victoria, also obtained a medal. The candles and soaps of Austria were rewarded in the same manner. One Austrian medallist was F. A. Sarg, who exhibited stearic acid from aqueous saponification, under the pressure of twelve atmospheres; stearin, and church candles; two qualities of glycerine, one of which was nearly colourless, and chemically pure; and glycerine soap.

De Roubaix, of Antwerp, exhibited stearic acid from lime saponification; acids obtained by this process, followed by distillation; acids from Buenos Ayres; tallow, and palm butter; refined paraffin and palm oil. Medals were deservedly given, also, to manufacturers in Brazil, Denmark, France, Italy, Greece, the Netherlands, Prussia, Russia, Spain, Sweden, Turkey, and the American States. The Jurors say—"We are not acquainted with any manufactory which can produce fatty acids and candles superior in quality to those of the (Netherlands) Stearic Candle Company. Honourable mention was made of numerous manufacturers in these countries. The candles and toilet soaps of De Roubaix, of Brussels, and De Roubaix Oedenkover, of Antwerp, are largely imported into London; also Brandon's Neva stearine, by Wymark & Co.

Soaps formed the third head of this section. It appeared that the soaps more generally used in England, are mottled soap, produced from kitchen-stuff, and pale yellow soap, produced from tallow and North American rosin. The yellow soaps of the continent are inferior to those of England; being of a dull, dingy colour, retaining the *nigre*, which is removed by the English process. Palm oil and cocoa-nut oil are extensively used in the manufacture of German soaps; but the latter material is regarded as quite unsuited to the purpose, from its taking up an excess of water and alkali. Dr. Ure found a London cocoa-nut-oil soap to contain 75 per cent. of water; whereas 25 per cent. is a large quantity for any but potash soaps; and these generally have less than 50 per cent. The public should feel thankful for the information given on this point by the reporter; who says—"When it is considered that soft soap contains less than 50 per cent. of water, what should be thought of a soap capable of containing 75 per cent. of water!"

The oleic acid soap is now extensively used in England by dyers, who formerly employed mottled and soft soap. This soap is less troublesome in use, and leaves the silk far softer and easier to work than other kinds. It is also used by woollen-cloth millers.

It is found that the soaps of the United Kingdom have greatly improved since the repeal of the duty. The reporter says—"Soaps from the most inferior materials are now turned out in a very creditable manner, which is due to the judgment employed in their manufacture, as well as to the many recent and important discoveries." He tells us, also, that "there is still an unfortunate tendency to adulteration, owing, in a great degree, to the ignorance displayed by the public in preferring light-coloured soaps, as being, in their opinion, the purest: consequently, in order to gratify this mistaken judgment, the soap-maker has to reduce the quality of a pure soap, of rather brown colour, by the copious admixture of salt and water, or other adulterants. There is still a more objectionable mode of adulterating soap by baking it, the soap being mixed with large quantities of water, and an outer skin of hard soap produced by the baking process. Large quantities are manufactured in this manner. Silicate of soda is also used extensively as an adulterant."

The colonies sent mottled and yellow soaps; and Natal, marbled soap for the toilet. New Zealand sent, from Wellington, well-made yellow soap; but the curd soap, from Auckland, was better in the manufacture than the materials.

France exhibited soaps made of olive oil, with the occasional mixture of sesame and other seed oils. A method has recently been invented of extracting oil from the useless pulpy residue of the olive, by treating it with bisulphuret of carbon.

The Jurors give a specimen of their impartiality, and freedom from a determination to praise everything, in their remarks of the soaps sent from Brazil, when they say—"The samples from this country came so badly arranged, that it was impossible to make out to whom they severally belonged. The majority of the specimens are very bad, exhibiting an enormous excess of alkali; so much so, that, in one case, crystals were formed on the top of the soap; while in others, from the same cause, the soap was actually crumbling away. Taken as the exhibition of a country, Brazil offers, unquestionably, the worst samples shown. Italy shows excellent soaps manufactured only from olive oil; but those were very inferior into which cocoa-nut oil and rosin were introduced."

Wax Flowers and Fruits had their place in this section, being principally the work of British hands. Miss Lambert's bank of wild flowers was, in many respects, unrivalled; and beautiful groups were exhibited by Mr. Austin, Mr. Pierson, and others. Mr. Black sent an interesting collection from Nova Scotia, chiefly of wax fruits. Other countries also gave specimens.

The Section B, occupied with *other Animal Substances used in Manufacture*, embraced a very miscellaneous variety of objects, which may be noticed in the alphabetical order in which they were reviewed by the Jurors.

Albumen derives its importance from the property of becoming solidified, and being rendered insoluble in ordinary menstrua by heat, as well as by many chemical re-agents. It has been found very important in calico-printing and dyeing; and its use has become still greater since the discovery of the aniline colours. These colours have a strong affinity for animal substances, and but little for those of a vegetable nature; so that, without a mordant, they cannot be imparted to linen and cotton fabrics. Albumen, applied to these fabrics, animalises them, just as black-lead mineralises a vegetable basis, and thus these exquisite colours may be transferred. The albumen may be passed from the liquid to the solid state, simply by drying at a temperature of 90° Fah. The principal sources from which it is obtained are blood, hen's eggs, and the roe of fish.

A specimen of albumen from fishes' roe was sent from Sweden. It was not, however, quite satisfactory, as not being perfectly soluble. The solution was turbid, and had a strong and unpleasant fishy smell, perhaps from not having been entirely deprived of the oil, contained in large quantities in the roe of the fish.

Bone is spoken of under "Horn" and "Ivory;" but bristles were exhibited in great perfection from the wild boar, and some varieties of the domestic hog. Examples were sent from Belgium, Holland, Prussia, Russia, and the United States. Bristles are now sorted by machinery. Russia was the best exhibitor of this article, having sent samples of okatcha—7½, 7, 6½, 6 inches long. White, bronze, black, and grey, at £15 18s. per pood (36 lb.) First quality—5½, 5, 4½, 4, 3½ inches long, at £7 19s. 4½d. per pood. Long—8, 7½, 7 inches, £7 14s. per pood. Second quality, from 5½ to 3 inches, at £5 12s. per pood. The United States obtained a medal for their excellent specimens.

Cochineal and Kermes.—The importance of these insects will be seen by the fact, that, in 1850, no less than 2,154,512 lbs. of cochineal were imported into this country, varying from 2s. 6d. to 5s. per lb. The best kinds are the *Lecanium ilicis*, used by the ancients, and still by the Turks and Arabs. The kermes live on the roots of the scleranthus, and are sent principally to Poland.

The cactus is a principal source of the kermes; and where it will grow in the open air, and the climate is not rainy, the cochineal may be cultivated. It is found to prosper in Spain, Italy, Algeria, Madeira, and Java; and there is every reason to believe that it will be produced abundantly in Greece and Asia Minor. An important species has its habitat in Mexico, where it feeds on the *Cactus opuntia*. The "grains," as the dried insects are termed, were sent from New South Wales, where the insect feeds on the acacia; and from Peru, where 50,000 lbs. are obtained annually.

Gelatine (not alimentary) and Glue were regarded specially in reference to the sources whence they are obtained. The gluten, or true gelatine, is obtained from the skin, tendonous parts, and bones of *adult* animals; while *cartilage-gelatine*, known as *chondrin*, is obtained only from young animals. The glues, presented by nine exhibitors of the United Kingdom, were all remarkably good, showing a great improvement since 1851. Particular notice was taken of the coloured gelatine used for tracing purposes, and as wrappers for confectionery. An extensive assortment of glue was sent from Victoria. It is suggested that it would be better to export the materials of glue from hot countries, than to attempt the manufacture on the spot. Very excellent preparations of glues and gelatines were sent from France. Much praise is due to Holland, which retains its character as a country famous for its glue.

Goldbeater's Skin is a skin stripped from the outer surface of the intestine of the ox. It is a manufacture of great importance. A medal was given to Puckridge; and to Tucker, for some excellent specimens of ornamental and coloured varieties.

Horns and Antlers, used for numerous purposes, are imported in large quantities: deer antlers from different parts of the East, afforded by numerous species of the *ceroidæ*. The fallow-deer yields a good annual supply; as do the reindeer and moose from Canada, and other northern countries. Rhinoceros horns were sent chiefly from South Africa, and some from the East. The finest horns are those of the Cape ox, the great buffalo of India, and several other species. Buenos Ayres exports largely. The greatest number and variety of horns was presented in the Natal Court. There were many, also, from the French possessions in India, and from Cochin China.

Ivory is derived principally from the teeth, the tusks, or lateral incisors of the elephant—two species from Asia, and one from Africa. The finest "*transparent ivory*" is collected on the western coast, within 10° of each side of the equator. The *white* ivory is from the eastern coast, from Bombay, and, of late years, from the island of Madagascar. The African ivory is more valued, for several qualities, than that of Asia. Other sources of ivory were represented—as the walrus and hippopotamus. Among the beautiful works in ivory, were carvings of exquisite beauty—billiard-balls, handles for sticks, parasols and umbrellas; and turnery works. Russia sent an image of the Saviour crowned with thorns, carved out of a mammoth tusk, in the space of two years and a-half; the value being £480.

Shells were sent from Manilla, the Sandwich Islands, and Singapore; new Caledonia, Costa Rica, Japan, and the Dutch colonies. The United Kingdom exhibited artificial flowers and coloured shells; and fine collections, beautifully arranged. The Bahama collection contained illustrations of uncoloured shell-work—"the most delicate and beautiful things of the kind in the building." The Tasmanian Court had some exquisite and most valuable shells and necklaces.

Silk Cocoons occupied much attention on the part of the Jurors, in consequence of the destructive effects of the disease which appeared among the silkworms in 1856, by which the *Bombyx mori*, the insect most in repute in France, Italy, and Spain, has been almost entirely annihilated. The enquiries made into the causes of this calamity, show that too much "breeding in-and-in" has produced excessive delicacy in the worm; and that, "in departing too widely from the natural conditions under which the silkworm exists, we have caused it to lose what may be termed its rusticity." Great satisfaction was created by the supplies of cocoons from India, to which a medal was assigned, to mark the success of the efforts to render the different varieties of the cocoon economically useful. From New South Wales four exhibitors sent cocoons of China silkworms, "pointed in form, but poor in silk." The worms were fed principally on the black mulberry, although the white has been successfully introduced. Natal sent some cocoons; but it is hoped that "they will be supplied by some of more vigorous forms." France had many exhibitors, who were rewarded with medals. The specimens from Algeria were also rewarded with medals and honourable mentions. The island of Réunion sent excellent specimens, reared in the open air. The Silk-rearing Company of Silesia exhibited cocoons, remarkable from the circumstance that they had been produced in a comparatively high latitude, and were very rich in silk. Prussian cocoons, bred in the high latitude of Stettin, were very excellent. Greece sent some of large size and good quality. Even Russia exhibited excellent cocoons of the Florentine, Chinese, and Italian breeds.

Sponges.—These "horny skeletons of certain species of a large group of creatures belonging to the lowest division of the animal kingdom," differ greatly in degrees of closeness, fineness, and softness, and their capacity for absorbing water—all which qualities affect their commercial value. They are supplied from the Mediterranean, Trieste, and the West Indies. The Bahama Islands produce a great variety of useful kinds, though not comparable to the Mediterranean. The West Indian kinds are distinguished by their large size, sub-globular or massive form, and coarseness of character. The Natal sponge, which can be procured in great abundance, resembles in appearance that of Turkey, but is not so absorbent, and is hard and unyielding, and possesses little absorbent power compared with the Turkish, although fine and of close texture. Medals were awarded to the *demos* of Voen and the *demos* of Ægina, for sponges they sent from Greece.

Tortoiseshell was exhibited on a very limited scale. The finest kinds are from the scales of the *Chelonia imbricata*; but those of the *Mydas*, the green or edible turtle, are also used, though of very little value. Those of the loggerhead turtle, though in use, are also of inferior value. Specimens of different kinds were sent from Jamaica, French Guiana, Martinique, Senegal, Mayotte, and New Caledonia. In Mayotte and Nossibe the turtle fishery lasts from September to March; and the export of the shell (*C. caretta*) amounts to from 4,000 to 5,000 kilogrammes annually, at the price of about 50 francs per kilogramme. Each turtle affords twelve scales, weighing, at the maximum, $2\frac{1}{2}$ kilos. Coloured horn is much used to imitate tortoiseshell; but a better imitation was exhibited by Pinson, of Paris, in gelatine, mother-of-pearl, and ivory; the gelatine being protected against damp, and capable of resisting exposure to the air.

Wools.—A table given by the reporter, shows the enormous development to which the culture of wool has attained, especially in the British colonial possessions, which afford half, and, together with the East Indies, considerably more than half the entire quantity of wool imported into this country. From 1852 to 1862, the increase of bales imported into Great Britain has been as follows:—South Africa, 21,011 to 66,841; Australia, 145,767 to 226,015; Portugal, 7,746 to 11,482; Russia, 13,687 to 40,302: from the East Indies the supply has declined; from Germany also— 36,114 to 29,238. In connection with Australia, the curious fact is mentioned, that, in 1797, Captain John M'Arthur took out to Australia three merino rams and five ewes; but that so slow was the early growth of this little flock, that it was not till 1807 that M'Arthur brought home the first bale to England. The number of exhibitors were— from Great Britain, 36; New South Wales, 28; South Australia, 7; Queensland, 11; Tasmania, 18; West Australia, 1; Victoria, 76; New Zealand, 30; Natal, 6; Eva, 2; Algeria, 37; France, 41; New Caledonia, 3; Spain, 19; Portugal, 1; Uruguay, 6; Austria, 46; Zollverein, 24.

Sub-class C was occupied with *Vegetable Substances used in Manufactures;* and, as is candidly confessed, "was made to receive the rejectamenta of many other more precise classes and sections," in which meerschaum pipes, works in amber, ladies' fans, fishing-tackle, &c., found place. The number of objects disposed of was more than 14,000, sent by 2,242 exhibitors.

Cotton wool was the most important of these articles, and was, of course, regarded with peculiar attention in the year of the cotton famine. A large space was devoted to cottons from India, one principal source to which England must look for her future supplies. Ceylon sent three specimens of middling cotton, each worth about 1s. per lb. Queensland sent cottons of the highest quality, and brought forward in an excellent manner. Some samples shown were worth 3s. 3d. per lb. Natal promised well, and sent samples worth 2s. per lb. West Indian was worth 1s. 6d., 2s., 2s. 7d., and 3s. 6d. per lb. Excellent cotton was sent from Barbadoes, Trinidad, and British Guiana, of the best kinds. The samples from Malta and the Ionian Islands were only sufficient to show that cotton is cultivated in those islands, but of middling quality, though the staple is longer than Surat cotton. New South Wales sent cotton worth 3s. 6d. per lb., and can raise plenty of the best kinds. Algeria has colonists who are alive to the importance of the cotton culture, and many of their contributions proved very satisfactory. The quality was considered the best in the building, and the quantity is rapidly increasing. Oran promises to be a highly productive region for the Sea Island and New Orleans variety. Italy promises very good and useful kinds. The quantity at present raised is small; but " in Central and Northern Italy large tracts would be suited to the growth of cotton, were they only drained; indeed, it might be easily made one of the staple products of Italy, without in the least degree interfering with the present agriculture." The samples exhibited were generally worth about 1s. per lb. Brazil sent few specimens, and those not remarkable for goodness—valued at about 1s. per lb. Venezuela had one bale worth 2s. 5d. per lb., but the rest worth only about 1s. Peru sent some worth 2s. per lb., the remainder only from 1s. 2d. to 1s. 6d. Good specimens were sent from Turkey, worth from 10½d. to 1s. per lb., and the promise of a large supply.

Flax and Hemp showed great excellence in most cases, the result of admirable management. Attempts have been made to use flax for the purpose of cotton; but flax is intractable, and will be treated only as flax. It is found, that "nothing succeeds so well in the disintegration as water-retting, provided the water is clear and pure." The Belfast Local Committee had an admirable display, showing the choicest specimens of the Irish looms, and the various stages in the preparation of the material. There were good specimens from Hants, Toronto, and Ceylon. India sent only two sorts, which were not remarkably good. New South Wales sent a well-dressed and very good sample of flax, prepared from the native plant, which may prove of great value to the colony at no distant period. Belgium stands highest among the foreign countries for flax; and her hemp is good; many specimens of the flax being remarkable for their beautiful silky fineness, and the even regularity of their fibres. France ranks next to Belgium for flax, and has tried to substitute mechanical means for water-retting; but the Jurors remark, that "it requires long and extensive experiments to prove that the strength and durability of the fibre are unimpaired by this process." The Italian exhibition of hemp was highly excellent. "The garden-hemp of Italy is the kind best known in commerce; its staple is the longest known—often over six feet; the colour is light and bright; the fibre beautifully soft and flexible; and it is raised on rich, well worked, deep soil." Russia sent fifteen sorts of hemp, and twenty of flax, and obtained medals for both. The exports for fifteen years (1846—'60) were 150,592 tons. The high character of the Russian hemp and flax is owing to the universal application of the water-retting process and hand-scutching, no machine processes having been yet introduced."

"*Other Fibres*" included the East Indian *Bœhmeria nivea*, which has been introduced into Jamaica, and will be of great use for cordage and paper-making; silk-cottons, adapted for common paper, but not suitable for spinning, owing to the extreme brittleness, although it might do for gun-cotton and collodion. The miscellaneous fibres from Trinidad were principally *bast*, useful for coarse cordage and for paper-making. Western Australia sent, among other things, the bark of the paper bark tree—"worth the notice of paper-makers." New South Wales presented fibres prepared from the barks of trees. Queensland sent good fibres for paper. India sent a large collection of useful fibres, the specimens being very varied, including some for paper and mats. Among the materials from the British colonies, an important one was the husk of the cocoa-nut, called *coir*, which, since its first introduction, fifteen years ago, has given rise to a large industry, and the employment of considerable capital. It makes excellent mats and brushes for house use, and dyes well in various colours. The besoms of former times are being superseded by a fibrous product of the palm tribe, the *piassava* or *bass*. The *Agave Americana* produces a fibre now much used instead of bristles, in the manufacture of cheap clothes-brushes, nail and scrubbing-brushes, and is said to have some qualities superior to hog's bristles. As shown by the Agave Patent Hair Company, it is much used as a substitute for curled horse-hair, for stuffing furniture, cushions, and the interior of first-class railway carriages. Similar materials were sent from our colonies and foreign countries.

Woods, Manufacture of Wood, and Basket-work, included specimens of timber, and other woods; turnery, and small wares in wood; coopery, sticks, and canes; woods for cabinet-making, building, ship-building, and numerous other purposes. This portion of the world's display was very attractive and important, and we regret that our limits will not afford it due space.

Vegetable Exudations, and Manufactures therefrom, included gums and resins, gutta-percha, caoutchouc, and their various applications to the arts and manufactures.

Tanning Materials were exhibited for the first time, but only two or three specimens were remarkable as novelties. It is satisfactory to know that an "abundant supply may be had from all parts of the world, of materials more or less useful in converting hides and skins into leather;" and that "many are equal, if not superior, to our own oak bark."

Starches were, from some mistake in arrangement, found in Class III. as well as Class IV. The produce of the *Arum italicum* and *Pancraticum maritimum* is very abundant, and can be sold at $3\frac{1}{2}d$. per lb. Potato starches were very good.

Sub-class D—Perfumery.—Through the exertions of the London perfumers, their valuable and pleasant productions were no longer mingled with the contents of other classes—with miscellaneous products, as in 1851, or with chemical products, as in

1855. The distinction thus accorded to the manufacture was well deserved, by its peculiar nature, by the number of the exhibitors, and the interesting character of their productions. There were no less than 232 exhibitors of perfumery—109 sending perfumery materials, and 123 displaying manufactured perfumery and toilet soaps.

It appears from the elaborate report of Mr. Rimmel, that the materials used in perfumery vary from as little as sixpence per lb.—the price of the "expressed oil, emulsion or meal of the bitter almond of North Africa—to £192 per lb., the price of the essential oil or otto, the Indian otto of roses." We learn, from the same authority, that perfumery is now divided into two distinct branches—the preparation of the materials, and the manufacture of perfumes, cosmetics, and toilet soaps; the former being carried on chiefly in the south of France, Italy, Spain, Turkey, Algeria, India, and other warm countries, where the climate imparts to flowers and plants an abundance of odour. At the same time it is remarkable, that England (especially in Merton and the neighbourhood) produces better lavender and peppermint than can be obtained in any other part of the world.

Some perfumes consist simply of the materials in their natural form, as in the dried flowers of the *Rosa centifolia*, grown in the south of France. Others undergo various kinds of preparation; the following four kinds according to the elements to be treated, and the results to be obtained—distillation, expression, maceration, and absorption. In distillation, very frequently the same water is re-distilled with fresh flowers; and, as in the case of rose and orange-flower, is sometimes of sufficient value to be kept. In expressing the essential oil from the rind of the *cibrine* series, in some places they rub the fruit against a grated funnel, and in others they press the rind against cloth bags. Maceration is employed to extract the aroma of flowers for pomades and oils, by means of fatty bodies, from which it can afterwards be transferred to alcohol. It is applied to the less delicate flowers, such as the rose, cassia, orange-flower, jonquil, and violet, which can bear a tolerable degree of heat without losing their scent. Absorption, which the French term *enfleurage*, is chiefly confined to the jasmine and tuberose flowers. Square glass frames are covered with purified grease, on which fresh-gathered flowers are strewed, and renewed every morning, as long as the flowers are in bloom, and until the grease is saturated with the flavour.

Two of the Paris perfumers availed themselves of the opportunity to show two new and very beautiful methods of obtaining the odour of flowers: the first "invented by M. Millon, a French chemist, who places the flowers in a percolating apparatus, and pours over them some ether or sulphuret of carbon, which, after a few minutes, is drawn off, carrying with it all the aroma of the flowers." The ether process, invented by M. Piver, consists of placing in a pneumatic apparatus layers of flowers on perforated plates, alternately with layers of grease, and causing a current of air to pass through several times, until the aroma is all transferred to the grease. It is doubtful whether these methods can be employed at a cost low enough for commercial purposes. May they not, however, be applicable to domestic use, in a country where the materials can be obtained in good quantities, and the flowers are in excess of the demand for them?

Our British colonies in Australia are already producing the materials of perfumery, and will probably yield them in novelties and in large quantities. Victoria sent some new essential oils, principally extracted from the leaves of the trees of the *Eucalyptus* family, which abound in Australia. The Jurors regarded some of them as of "a sufficiently grateful fragrance to render them available for perfumery purposes." Their price will also commend them greatly, being only six shillings a gallon—about one-fourth the cost of the cheapest essential oil used for scenting soap.

It was owing to a sad misfortune that nearly all the samples of essential oils sent from Ceylon were lost on the voyage. They would have made a large display, as Ceylon is the source of the great bulk of Indian essential oils used in England. India, of course, sent a rich supply of materials; of which, with the exception of patchouli, jasmine, and sandal-wood, very few are known in England.

Turkey exhibited fragrant oils and waters, comprising otto of roses, principally distilled in the neighbourhood of Adrianople; rose and orange-flower water; peppermint; essence of geranium; sage; sandal-wood; laurel; rosemary; aloes; bergamot; and the celebrated balsam of Mecca, which, sad to tell, is now reduced to such small quantities as to leave none for use after the Sultan has been served. Turkey is not duly attentive to the preparation of these delicate wares, many of which are adulterated, and others not prepared with sufficient care. We may hope that our Turkish merchants will profit by the gentle rebuke administered by the Jurors of the Exhibition. Particular notice was taken of some specimens of Turkish pastiles, called kours—round, flat, gilt discs, used in the harem for sweet fumigations, or by smokers, to give a finer flavour to their tobacco. There were, also, chaplets and bracelets made of scented paste; kohl for darkening the eyelids; and various other cosmetics used by the ladies of Turkey. It is remarked, however, of the Turkish perfumes—and the observation is applicable to most of the perfumes of the East—that they "exhale a strong odour of musk, ambergris, and sandal-wood," which are "too strong and oppressive for European nerves."

Paris is a great centre of the manufacture of perfumes, which form important items in the "*articles de Paris*." In that capital there are 120 working perfumers, employing about 300 men and women, whose united returns are estimated at not less than forty million francs a year. Other parts of France are busily occupied with the materials of perfumery. "Grasse, Cannes, and Nice, are the principal towns where the maceration and absorption processes are in use. There are about 100 houses engaged in these operations, and in the distillation of essential oils; giving employment, during the flower season, to at least 10,000 people."

The French perfumery trade has greatly increased within the last thirty or forty years. The average of—

Exports for ten years, from 1827 to 1836 were	6,000,000	francs.
" " " " 1837 " 1846 "	8,000,000	"
" " " " 1847 " 1856 "	10,000,000	"
The exports in.................. 1858 "	12,000,000	"
" " .... 1860 "	31,000,000	"

The principal exports of French perfumery are to various parts of Europe, and to North and South America; while England exports chiefly to India, Australia, and other British colonies.

Mr. Rimmel, to whom we are indebted for the elaborate report on perfumery, appears to have done justice to every one but himself. He is evidently the most enthusiastic and successful of perfumers, and it would have been gratifying to record his numerous achievements in the art. We have room only to notice his "Perfume Vaporiser," for diffusing the fragrance of flowers, and purifying the atmosphere in apartments, ball-rooms, theatres, &c. Its effects are very superior to those produced by burning pastiles, papers, ribbons, and other means of imparting fragrance. The vaporiser is a beautiful urn, designed with great taste, in bronze or china, and has been used with satisfactory results at the Lord Mayor's banquets, on board the great steam-packets, and at the theatres.

Class V. was taken up with RAILWAY PLANT, LOCOMOTIVE ENGINES, AND CARRIAGES; and its objects were supplied by 169 exhibitors, among whom were distributed thirty-nine medals, and thirty-four honourable mentions. These awards are the more valuable from the circumstance that the Jurors were instructed to be careful in admitting claims for "novelty of invention without sufficient scrutiny, but to reward fitness for the object sought to be attained, economy in first cost, durability, economy in maintenance, and excellence in workmanship."

It should be observed, that of late—since the first great Exhibition—there has been a general increase in the weight of locomotives; that the competition for traffic has led, in many cases, to an increase in the distances between the stopping stations for the express and fast trains, which has rendered it necessary that the capacity of the tender for carrying water should be increased, so as to enable the fast trains to run for much longer distances without stopping; and that some other means should be devised by which a supply of water could be obtained by the tender while on its journey. The increase in the weight of engines has necessitated an increase in the strength of the permanent way for the narrow-gauge system of railways—a heavier rail, and a greater number of sleepers per mile, which sleepers should be of a better description. It was also found that the engines should burn coal instead of coke, in those districts where economy could be thus secured.

To the twenty locomotives sent to the Exhibition, ten medals were awarded: to five of this number for excellence of workmanship; to two for excellence of workmanship combined with the adaptation of the engines for their purpose; to two for varieties of construction, suited to particular requirements; and to one for the goodness of arrangements. One—the best of the engines—that sent by the London and North-Western, was not allowed to receive the award to which it was entitled, from the circumstance that Mr. McConnell, the talented engineer at Wolverton, under whose direction it was made, was himself one of the Jurors. It had been decided, that "if exhibitors accept the office of Jurors, or assistant Jurors, or experts, they cease to be competitors for prizes in the class to which they are appointed; and these cannot be awarded either to them individually, or to the firms in which they may be partners."

A medal was awarded to Beyer & Co., for a six-wheeled express passenger locomotive, weighing 28 tons 6 cwt. when full; whose tender carries 1,750 gallons of water, and $1\frac{1}{2}$ tons of coal; the maximum weight of a pair of wheels being 11 tons 12 cwt. It was an inside cylinder engine, fitted with straight-link motion, and ordinary pumps; the cylinders being 16 inches in diameter, with 22 inches stroke; the diameter of the driving-wheels 7 feet, and that of the leading and training-wheels 3 feet 9 inches. The total length of the wheel base, which is equally divided on each side of the driving-wheel, is 15 feet 4 inches, the centre of gravity being in front of the driving-wheel. The heating surface of the fire-box is 104 square feet, and that in the tubes (215 in number), 1,233 feet; making up a total heating surface of 1,337 square feet.

A more interesting object, to which also a medal was awarded, was the model of an apparatus for supplying water to tenders while running on a journey. A trough, filled with water, is sunk between the rails, and into this trough an apparatus connected with the tender falls while the engine is running on its journey. The water begins to flow into the tank as soon as a tube is lowered into the trough. To secure the advantage of this arrangement, the engine must travel at the rate of twenty-two miles an hour. The London and North-Western Railway Company had practically tested this system at Crew about fourteen months before the opening of the Exhibition, and with results sufficiently satisfactory to induce them to bring it into operation at other stations. During the time the trough had been laid down, 1,366,000 gallons of water were taken up by the engines.

A medal was awarded to a "four-wheeled coupled locomotive coal-burning tank-engine," exhibited by Manning & Co., of Leeds. It was well adapted for the mineral traffic at iron-works and collieries, and for contractors' purposes, where there are sharp curves and steep inclines. It was stated to be capable of carrying 260 tons on the level, with 60 lbs. practical pressure on the pistons. Another remarkable locomotive engine was exhibited by Sharp and Stewart, of Manchester, which is said to have taken a load of 350 tons on a line which has inclines of 1 in 100, at a speed of twenty-three miles an hour; the consumption of coal being 22 lbs. per mile.

A Belgian engine obtained a medal "for the successful introduction of M. Belpaire's fire-box, which is stated to be well adapted for burning very small coal." A medal was awarded to La Compagnie du Chemin de Fer du Nord, for an eight-wheeled coupled goods tank-engine, weighing 41·6 tons with full supply of water and fuel, and a maximum weight of 10 tons $11\frac{1}{2}$ cwt. on a pair of wheels. The heating surface is 1,770 feet. It is one of a class which attracted much attention among French engineers. Its total weight, as compared with the steam-producing power, is much less than in the ordinary coupled goods engine with tenders, as it does not exceed 53 lbs. per square foot of heating surface. A goods tank-engine was exhibited by the State's Railway Society of Austria. It had ten wheels coupled, specially adapted for taking a load of more than 100 tons up inclines of 1 in 50, where the curves are very sharp (370 feet radius), at a speed of nearly ten miles an hour. This noble engine received a medal for its adaptation to these special purposes, as

2 K

well as for excellence of workmanship.   A. Borsig, of Berlin, received a medal for a
six-wheeled engine, which could carry 460 tons, independent of the tender, on a line
having many gradients of 1 in 200, going at the rate of $16\frac{1}{2}$ miles an hour, and
consuming 43 lbs. of coal per mile.   R. Hartman, of Saxony, received a medal for
an engine adapted to take a load of 73 tons up an incline of 1 in 40, at the rate of
twenty miles an hour.   The prize was given for good workmanship.

The *Railway Carriages* scarcely admitted any particular novelty, but medals were
awarded to five.   Mr. Beatie, Mr. J. Gibson, and Mr. C. Mansell, were awarded
medals for their respective inventions in the mode of securing tires, welded or
unwelded, on railway carriage-wheels, by which the liability of the tires to open out
or fly off from the rim of the wheels, when they break off, is almost entirely avoided.
A medal was given for a first-class carriage intended for the Egyptian railway; and
another for a goods-waggon, manufactured from the raw material—pig-iron, and
timber in the log, including the conversion, forging, and finishing of the iron-work in
the short space of $11\frac{1}{2}$ hours.   La Compagnie Générale de Matériels du Chemin de
Fer, of Belgium, obtained a medal for a six-wheeled carriage with compartments at
the ends, and an intermediate open space.   It weighed 9 tons 17 cwt., and was
intended to carry twenty-four persons.   It had a very light and luxurious character,
and was considered well adapted to the picturesque district in which it is used.   Its
price was £520, and its exhibitors received a medal.

In wheels, axles, and tires, there were many improvements since 1851, to which
much importance was properly attached, as they bear on the safety of the public
travelling on railways.   Brown & Co., of Rotherham, received a medal for "a good
process of making solid and unwelded wrought-iron tires."   Larne & Co. had a
medal for excellence of material and workmanship, and the "proved durability of the
cast-iron hollow wheels."   It ought to be noticed, that accidents from the breaking
and flying off of tires, which are numerous in some countries at certain seasons of the
year, are said never to occur in France; and, at the same time, we call attention to
the medals awarded for solid wrought-iron wheels and unwelded steel tires, of
superior quality and workmanship, which are generally used in France for the
carriages of fast trains.   An Austrian manufacturer—Ganz, of Buda—was rewarded
"for the proved durability of certain chilled cast-iron hollow wheels for railway
carriages in use since 1855," weighing about 5 cwt., and manufactured at a very low
rate in comparison with wrought-iron wheels.   The cast-steel tires and axles of
railway carriages, exhibited by the famous Krupp, of Essen, obtained a medal "for
excellence of the quality of the materials."

Railway Carriage-Breaks properly occupied much attention, and to various improvements medals were awarded.   A medal was given to Fay, of Manchester, for
"improvements by which breaks fitted on to several carriages in a train may be
worked by one guard, from a break-van placed at the ends or in the centre of the
train."   These continuous breaks are much in favour with experienced engineers
and guards, as are also those of Newall and Bury, to whom also a medal was
awarded.

The miscellaneous objects in this class included several of great interest; among which the two following deserve special notice:—Bateson, of London, obtained a medal for a Feed-water Heating Apparatus, by which "the dangerous tendency of water to assume the spheroidal condition when confined in a small space, as in tubes, and subjected to intense heat, is avoided." The object is accomplished by means of an internal perforated tube, connected at each end with the water-space of the boiler. When there is any tendency in the outer tube to the spheroidal condition, a small jet of water is forced, by the pressure of the water in the boiler, through the perforation nearest the spot, which at once restores the circulation. To M. Giffard a medal was awarded for an Injector, "by which the supply of water into the boiler of a locomotive engine is kept up, whether the engine be still or running." It is said that this invention appears likely to prove useful for the supply of all boilers; while it is specially adapted to locomotives.

Class VI. consisted of CARRIAGES, not connected with Rail or Tram-roads. There were 167 exhibitors, and 140 carriages contributed by them. Medals were given to thirty-five persons, and honourable mentions made of fourteen. Foreign and colonial contributors, being less than half the number of British, gained rather more than half the medals; but the British obtained nearly all the honourable mentions. The objects presented under this class included great variety—Phætons, landaus, Broughams, sociables, waggonettes, sleighs, barouches, vans and waggons, coaches, chariots, private Hansom cabs, dog-carts, public omnibuses, curricles, state coach, dress chariot, droski, Irish car, town car, gig, clarence, basket carriage, and cart. Besides the carriages, there were exhibitions of various especial portions of such; and of drawings and designs, as of springs, axles, heraldry, wheels, models, chasing, ornamental painting, and shafts. Several perambulators and invalid chairs, and one velocipede, were added to this department. British contributors in this fragmentary part of the class numbered twenty-six, and foreigners but eight.

In the preliminary Report of the Jury to the Council of Chairmen of Juries, disappointment is expressed with the display of articles under this class. There was, contrary to the expectation of the public, an entire absence of decorative, court, or even town carriages, such as were present in the Exhibition of 1851; and at that time afforded such pleasure to the visitors. This is accounted for from the loss occasioned to those who sent carriages of superior ornament to the Hyde Park Exhibition. The painting and trimming were irreparably damaged by the dust to which they were exposed from the place assigned to them. During the Dublin Exhibition of 1853, the exhibitors of carriages experienced nearly as unfavourable treatment, although the manufacture has obtained in that city, both for home use and export, considerable importance. At the Paris Exhibition there were continued grounds of complaint, so that many were disheartened, in 1862, of having a fair opportunity to display their workmanship. There are conditions as to light, essential to a proper display of varnished and highly-painted manufactures, which the coach-builders who sent the products of their taste to Paris, Dublin, and Kensington, did not obtain. There is much diversity in national style in this class of manufactures. The English are deficient in lightness of build; the Americans and Australians carry it to excess; indeed, the extremely light build of American carriages is so acceptable to the British colonists of Australia, that they import them in preference to the best workmanship of London or Dublin.   The Russians, on the other hand, desire a heavy and strong-built vehicle, rendered necessary by the sudden and extreme changes of their climate in spring and opening winter.   The stout-built carriages of England are, therefore, in favour in the Russian metropolis; and English skilled workmen are employed to some extent upon native constructions.   In Europe, probably, the most tasteful specimens of carriage-building are to be found in Paris; and that city stood high in the competitions of 1851 and 1862.   The countries which sent specimens to Kensington, were Scotland, Ireland, Belgium, Denmark, Hesse, France, Prussia, Mecklenburg, Italy, Netherlands, Norway, Sweden, Russia, and the United States. There were several besides from the British colonies.   Six waggons and vans, and a cart, were sent by English exhibitors.   There was considerable improvement in the English department, as compared with former occasions, for competition at home and abroad.   Prussia contributed a richly-decorated state coach, which had been built for the king.   In Berlin much attention has been paid to carriage architecture of late years, and some of the productions of that city have rivalled those of Paris.   One of the most beautiful carriages was a highly-finished dress chariot, sent from Italy.

In deciding on the awards, the Jury arranged for themselves a programme upon which their decisions should proceed:—1. As to suitability for the purpose intended, giving comfortable accommodation for those who use the carriage.—2. As to good general design and proportion.—3. As to soundness and accuracy of workmanship, combined with good materials.—4. As to improvement or novelty.—5. As to the construction, that it shall be so carried out that no part be unnecessary; and that every part shall be best adapted for its intended use.—6. As to harmonious combinations of colours.

Although the arrangements for exhibiting this class were superior, in 1862, to those in 1851, and better in Kensington than at Dublin and Paris, there were serious defects, which ought to warn the administrators, on all future occasions, of the necessity of studying the accommodation required for each department on its own merits. The tone of colouring on the walls was too uniform in the building at South Kensington; and the successful exhibition of this class depended upon a skilful adaptation in this respect, which was not afforded.   The effect of the uniform crimson blinds, which ran along the whole gallery, was injurious to the harmony of colour in the articles they were designed to protect.

It was observed, as a proof of changing taste, that no carriages were fitted with hammer-cloths, which give, or used to be considered as giving, an air of dignity and grandeur.   It was also noticeable that not one specimen of a travelling-carriage was to be seen, probably arising from the general use of railways, rendering such less necessary than formerly.

Specimens of good street-cabs were also *desiderati.*   London is much behind Paris, and several provincial cities, in this description of vehicles.   Manchester has, undoubtedly, better street-cabs than any town in England; and Glasgow will alone rival her for omnibuses in Great Britain.   But the ingenuity and industry of these places were not well represented at South Kensington.

There was no proper arrangement to obtain specimens of *all* descriptions of vehicles; the discretion of each exhibitor alone determined the quality of carriage presented. The Jurors, in their Report, therefore, raised the question as to the propriety, at future exhibitions, of considering high quality in design and construction rather than mere quantity, or even variety.

It was a marked feature in the works exhibited in this class, that many of them were only in " a partially finished" state. This was occasioned by the desire of the coach-making trade to convince the public that unsuitable or inadequate material was not concealed by paint, varnish, or decoration of any sort.

Several new woods have been brought into use by the English coach-builders, the principal of which are Canadian black walnut, and American hickory. The black walnut is suitable for panels, and is a good substitute for mahogany. The hickory is used for light wheel-spokes.

It is becoming customary to import not only American timber for wheels, but wheels manufactured in America by peculiar machinery. These are admirably adapted to Broughams, and certain other carriages of a light construction.

Originality of construction was not presented generally, but there were several instances of original detail which were striking. The duchy of Hesse displayed a self-acting, double-fold step, which was considered ingenious, and much admired. But the carriages of Russia were more dissimilar to those of England, than were any others in the gallery. On a Brougham, sent from Russia, there was a double-action spring door-lock, so that the inside and outside handles act independently, reducing the friction and wearing of the spindles.

The Droski (the national carriage of Russia) showed to great advantage. The mode of attaching the horse is very peculiar, and of harnessing him. The harness is so adjusted as to prevent the horse from falling, and to render him considerable support; yet the Russian harness is light in construction and appearance, so as to surprise any Englishman who sees it for the first time. The manufacture of harness leather, in Russia, is contrived so as to unite great strength and lightness.

One of the causes which contributed to a lighter make in English carriages, in the decade between the two exhibitions, arose from the use of smaller horses by the public. Some attributed this to a mere fashionable caprice; others to deterioration in the breed of horses for draft purposes, which is alleged to be produced by the passion in this country for breeding race-horses.

There are few occupations of the British workman, not immediately connected with the fine arts, which give more scope for taste than panel-painting and coach-trimming. The general coach-painter's work is simple; but the employment of devices and arms requires a high degree of refined judgment, and delicate touch. Artists of eminence have begun their course as " coach-body painters;" and one of the most eminent sculptors of the day—M'Dowel—thus commenced his career. The coach-trimmer has excellent opportunity for studying and displaying good combinations of colour. The most excellent carriage, for construction and painting, may be spoiled, as to its effect, by bad trimming. The arrangement, style, and mounting of harness, must also harmonise with it. The English manufacturers attained to more perfection in the mounting and make of harness, than in trimming and arrangement of colours; but, in all these respects, improvements were visible at South Kensington, notwithstanding that the most elegant and costly description of carriages were not sent by contributors.

Amongst the many trades to which this business gives employment, that of the coach-smith is one of much importance; and here, also, utility and taste have great scope. Tough steel has supplanted iron, especially in very light fabrics. A tough, hard, and dense iron, capable of being welded, is much used for screws, nails, bolts, and clips.

Since 1851, the English have adopted, from the French, panels of fancy wood, interlaced with basket-work. By the use of more skilful machinery, the English have improved this manufacture, so as to surpass the French original. Means have been adopted for the preservation of this description of work from the injurious influence of rain and mud.

The use of the old " drag-shoe" has been generally displaced by a lever-brake of hard wood, saving time, expense, and effecting simplicity of arrangement, with additional security. In connexion with this invention some cognate improvements have made progress in the trade.

The Landau is a description of carriage suitable to the climate of the British Isles, especially to the west of Scotland and the west of Ireland, the variableness of the climate making it an advantage to have a vehicle which may be used closed or open, at pleasure. They were seldom either elegant in outline, or ingenious in general construction; but, in the " Great Exhibition," these disadvantages appeared to be overcome, the specimens produced uniting all the attributes desirable to a good and tasteful landau.

The Waggonette was considered a great improvement, so far as accommodation to a greater number of persons on a carriage of a given weight. This is effected by adjusting places in back-seats for the sitters, sideways, and *vis-à-vis*. This invention is attributed to Prince Albert, who desired a carriage suitable to a hilly country, when in Scotland, by which the large family of her Majesty might be accommodated in their drives without employing a second vehicle. From this circumstance it became fashionable, as it was also found to be convenient. It first appeared in the Exhibition in Hyde Park; and, from that time, became much used.

The South Kensington Exhibition building became famous, in the class of which we are now treating, by a splendid four-in-hand coach, built somewhat upon the old lines of the almost extinct stage-coaches. Since then improvements have been made, which give greater command of the team, and afford a firmer seat to the driver, which will make this description of carriage still more popular among the very wealthy, to whom, of necessity, its enjoyment must be confined.

Artistic designs in manufactures have been an occupation in London long since the manufactures themselves have found their almost exclusive seat in the provinces. This was the case in the production of silks, printed calicoes, china-painting, &c. Coach-building is pursued in various cities of the British Isles with success—as Dublin, Edinburgh, Glasgow, Birmingham, Manchester, Derby, Preston, &c.; but drawings and designs for the provinces are still, to a great extent, supplied in London. Dublin and Edinburgh are more independent in this respect than other cities; and the Irish and Scotch provincial builders generally look to their own respective capitals for the requisite aid. The excellently-managed schools of the Royal Dublin Society, especially in the "ornament" department, have turned out many excellent designs for the decorative department of the trade, and have produced many superior heraldic painters. The continental carriage manufacturers look to London for assistance in these particulars.

What has been written above of other departments of designing, will apply to the chasing of metals used in carriages; but, in this particular, Edinburgh falls behind, and Birmingham assumes prominence.

Expense is a serious consideration in the production of so costly a manufacture as that of carriages. Leather has enhanced in value; and, as this was a substance largely required, substitutes of a cheaper sort have been found in various elastic substances. Waterproofs for seats have secured drivers and outside riders from the dangers attending seats that readily absorbed moisture.

It is not generally known that the coach-builders have an *Art Journal*. France led the way in this effort to influence the progress of the trade; America followed; and now the English manufacturers have adopted the idea with spirit and success.

The art of photography has enabled those desirous of improving this branch of manufacture to extend a knowledge of the best complete equipages, and of model details. The facilities afforded by the enlightened measures of Sir Rowland Hill, in the Post-Office, for transmission of artistic and printed papers, have aided the spread of correct tastes and opinions in this as in other branches of British industry. In the French department, in the main building of the Exhibition, there were exhibited two photographs of a state railway-carriage, built for the Pope, which drew the attention not only of the trade, but of the public.

There was one deficiency in the building at South Kensington, in connection with this class, to be regretted. It was thought that wheelwrights, body-making carriage-makers, smiths, &c., should have sent in specimens in detail, and drawings of their respective productions. On and along the walls there was space for such a display. There is a great export of this fragmentary character from London and Birmingham to Ireland; and a continental trade of the same nature might have been opened by a successful representation of what can, in this way, be performed in England more cheaply than anywhere else.

The omnibuses require improvement, probably more than any other description of vehicle used in London. Several patterns of improved carriages, under this head, were introduced to London during the Exhibition, such as are adopted with comfort and success in Manchester and Glasgow. One enterprising proprietor, in the Lanca-shire metropolis, sent up a number of these omnibuses, which were very popular. But even these need improvement, as the open end, in winter, is unpleasant to Londoners. The breadth of this public carriage was somewhat of an inconvenience in the great city thoroughfares; but, on the whole, it was an improvement which has not been adopted with the alacrity it deserved.

From our colonies there was sent a " well-balanced car," used for passenger-traffic in Victoria. It was heavy, and roughly moulded; but it possessed an ingenious canopy roof, which could be set up, or lowered, with facility.

An attractive object in the English gallery of architectural state drawings, was presented in the form of her Majesty's state carriage. Concerning this there was much diversity of opinion; some regarding it as the very best specimen of a court carriage; others deeming it obsolete in form and style. The writer of these lines has examined the " state coach" itself with care, and is of opinion that there is room for improvement both in the carriage and harness.

There was a very numerous collection of woods appropriated for this class of manufacture, exhibited by the English colonies, and admirably arranged.

Tasmania.—Blue-gum, for wheel felloes and shafts; black wood—spokes and reaves; myrtle—panels; stringy bark—felloes.

Ceylon.—Iron-wood was especially noticed; but Ceylon abounds in wood admirably adapted to coach-building, both for strength and beauty. The products of this colony were not well arranged, as it respects the class of which we treat.

Canada.—Black walnut, for panels; shell-bark hickory—spokes, poles, shafts, and tool-handles; white pine—bottoms, roofs; plane-tree—foot-boards, common panels, rockers; white ash—spokes, reaves, boot-bottoms; white wood—common panels; white ash—felloes, and bending purposes; smooth bark-hickory—spokes, poles; bark elm—reaves; black birch—foot-boards, rockers; butter-nut—common panels; pepperidge—reaves; wild black cherry—panels; red pine—bottoms, roofs; red oak—spokes, boot-bottoms; case-wood—light boot-sides, panels. Canada sent a few other woods less specially suitable.

Trinidad.—Fustic, for reaves, &c.

Jamaica.—South American acacia, for under-work; white lance-wood—shafts; fustic—reaves.

British Guiana.—These woods are not generally reported as to their special application, but they are of great variety, and answer for panels chiefly. Locust, tonquin bean, hockia, hyabella, hoobaballa, tataboo, warrenara, mora, tornenara, bullet-tree, purple-heart, green-heart, wallaba.

Victoria.—The wood from this colony is applicable to spokes and felloes. Red-gum, iron-bark, black-wood, stringy bark.

Queensland.—Bark, blue-gum, cypress pine, stringy bark, iron-wood, black iron-bark, red iron-bark, forest oak, blue-gum, silky oak, jambosa.

New South Wales.—Cherry, buranna, forest oak, flooded gum, red box, Moreton-bay chestnut, yellow box of Camden, hickory, yellow-gum, spotted gum, tallow, black wattle, blue-gum, white myrtle, teak wood, red iron-bark, swamp mahogany.

Auckland—New Zealand.—Tauri, tannekapa, ribbon-wood, mairi, kohekohe, white tea-tree, marpaw, tortara, mihu.

Natal.—Red ivory-wood, sterile-wood, white pear-wood, red pear-wood, assegai, red speke-wood, umealota.

Western Australia.—Jarrah and tookart. These woods are very hard, and the latter of great weight and strength, fit for hard-working waggon-wheels.

New Brunswick.—Birch, white pine, white ash, black oak, oak, beech.

Mysore—India.—Bellawar, tratany, tampensis—generally resembling mahogany.

Penang—India.—Klat—like mahogany.

The recent adoption of hand-machinery, in the use of which the operatives cordially comply, will enable the manufacturer to work up the very hard woods suitable for heavy work.

The road vans and waggons, included in this class, exhibited improvement.

In 1851, the perambulator was unknown; or, at all events, not exhibited. In 1862, there was a single specimen, which attracted attention by its beauty, and its skilful adaptation to its purpose.

MANUFACTURING MACHINES AND TOOLS.—In this department, the improvement, as compared with 1851, was very signal. The ingenuity shown, of late years, in the manufacture of tools for working metals, greatly conduced to an advanced facility for making machinery in almost every branch of its application.

Class VII. was divided into various sections, alphabetically arranged. Under the letter A the first of these sections was placed, and related to machinery employed in spinning and weaving. The section itself was arranged under sub-divisions. The first of these was "Conversion of Fibrous Raw Material into a Continuous Thread." In the cotton trade, the machines sent were far more automatic and complete than any ever exhibited before, either in this or any other country. Section A (manufacturing machines and tools) gives one mention to Victoria, and twenty-five to foreign states. Section B, in the same class (machines and tools employed in the manufacture of wood and metal), gives no mention to the colonies, but thirty-nine mentions to foreign states. In Section A there were accorded twenty-one medals to the United Kingdom, and twenty to foreign states. In Section B, forty-two medals to the former, and forty-eight to the latter.

Although, under Section A, the machinery for manufacturing cotton was more ingenious and perfect than that applied to the manufacture of other textile fabrics, there was no branch of this description of industry that did not exhibit well.

The exhibitors, in the English department, who gained most attention were Messrs. Dobson and Barlow, of Bolton. They presented a complete system of machines for preparing cotton yarn for spinning in fine numbers, and for spinning the cotton thus ingeniously prepared for the purpose. Messrs. Hetherington and Sons, Manchester, were equally successful in their machinery for coarse numbers. The same firm gained a medal for a combing machine in fine numbers. They introduced several novelties in carding machines; amongst which, the daffing-knife was considered as most original. Higgins and Sons, Manchester; John Mason, Rochdale; Platt Brothers, Oldham; Walker and Hocking, Bury, all obtained medals for their varied and successful inventions tending to save labour, cheapen production, and ensure accuracy of detail, and general perfection in the work.

In the cotton machinery department, the foreign exhibitors—there were but two —made no impression.

The second article in the list, under this section, was wool. Here the foreign exhibitors were more numerous; and, as might be expected, France, Belgium, and

Saxony comprised nearly all. The English exhibitors who were most successful, were—Apperly & Co., Strand; Perrabee & Co., Strand; Maclea and March, Leeds; Mason, Rochdale; Perry, Bradford; and Platt, Oldham. The most ingenious exhibition was probably that made by Vouillon, of Louviers (France). It was a machine in which the threads were composed by a felting process, instead of by twisting—a new system.

Flax and Hemp.—This exhibition was inferior to that of machines for wool, and still more inferior as compared with that of machinery for working cotton.

In the United Kingdom, the Irish exhibitors were foremost; Messrs. J. Combe & Co., Belfast, excelling all others. Messrs. P. Fairbairn, of Leeds, and Messrs. Lawson and Sons, also of Leeds, obtained honourable mention. Belgium presented several machines which were more ingenious than practical.

Silk.—This department was of small extent, but of some importance. Messrs. Wren and Hopkinson, of Manchester, presented a numerous array of machines of every sort used in the manufacture of silk. Winding, sizing, cleaning, spinning, doubling, throwing, self silk-winding, and stringing machines; a throstle with patent revolving weight; a bobbin-reel, hank-winding, balling and spooling machines; cubing and bundling presses, and a pirn-winding machine. In this great array from one house, there were some striking and useful novelties. A French, and also an Italian house (the latter an English firm settled in Naples), obtained a medal and an honourable mention respectively.

Sundry Machines and Accessories.—There were numerous displays of ingenious and excellent workmanship, and, in some cases, of useful inventions. Carding machines; machines for curling hair; a self-acting machine for winding, on cards or bobbins, sewing-silk or cotton thread. The foreign department of this branch of the section showed more zeal than that of the United Kingdom.

Weaving of all kinds, and Connected Machines.—Looms.—As many of the looms were exhibited at work, they were objects of attention to the visitors, sometimes attracting considerable crowds around them. Silk, wool, flax, cotton and mixed fabrics, were all produced within the building, and in the presence of numerous spectators. Some of the most interesting of the processes thus presented to the public, were in connection with carpet-weaving. Tuer and Hall, of Bury, showed a loom of cheaper construction than produced by any other exhibitor, and yet capable of turning off a greater quantity of work, and also of superior quality. Messrs. Smith and Brothers, of Heywood, who obtained a medal, presented a very complete and original loom; as did also Mr. A. Smith, of New York, one adapted to the weaving of Axminster carpets.

There were some silk and ribbon looms which fixed the attention of many visitors by their operations, and the beautiful work they contained. Messrs. Wahl and Loein, of Basel, Switzerland, had a medal awarded for two looms for weaving figured ribbons. The designs were complicated, and so were the looms; but by persons skilled in that manufacture, they were considered remarkably simple for the production of such elaborate work. M. G. Bonelli, of Turin, obtained a medal for a very scientifically-prepared loom. He applied electricity to Jacquard-weaving. The pistons had two conical heads, and were so disposed that one portion remained in connection with a voltaic battery, while the other portion is in connection with the horizontal needles which act on the hooks of the Jacquard. It is alleged that superior richness of design is the result of this invention.

In the *Stocking and Hosiery Department* there were but few novelties. A French house, E. Tailbouis & Co., presented the most ingenious improvements, and obtained a medal. They produced a rectilinear loom, in which they can weave from four to six stockings at one time in a frame: the narrowing is performed automatically, and the needles are supported by bars. The Jurors pronounced the manufacture good.

Sewing and Knitting Machines.—Few of the industrial departments attracted more interest, or excited so much surprise as this. The exhibition was vast as to number, interesting as to variety, and marvellous for perfection. In 1851, only two sewing machines were presented. Indeed, the invention was introduced to the public so recently as 1845-'6, by Mr. Elias Howe, of New York. Mrs. Rogers, in the machines of Messrs. Newton and Wilson, produced beautiful embroidery. M. Calle-caut, of Paris, exhibited very ingenious machines of varied adaptations, and obtained a medal. Inventions, suitable for tailors, boot-makers, saddlers, glovers, and different ornamental processes, were brought forward by M. Callecaut. M. de Celles, of Paris, also attracted much attention to his invention of " the secure knot." This is effected by a double rotatory hook, which so knots the thread, that the stitches are made independent of one another, and the sewing is nearly indestructible.

The House Sewing Machine Company, of New York, obtained a medal. Amongst their ingenious contrivances for machine-stitching, was one for forming eyelet-holes.

Wheeler and Wilson, of New York, also obtained a medal. Their collection was remarkable for a machine producing the lock-stitch. Newton, Wilson & Co., of London, obtained honourable mention for their ingenious processes and high finish. Mr. Lenay, of Brussels, received honourable mention for a machine adapted to sewing button-holes. C. R. Goodwin, of Boston, United States, exhibited machines specially applicable to boot and shoe-making. He presented a very ingenious plan for sewing continuously round the soles of the boots, and following correctly the hollows and flats of the soles. This obtained honourable mention. Another American contributor obtained honourable mention—Messrs. Wilcox and Gibbs, of New York. They introduced an improved needle—a " spur-hopper"—to tighten the thread; and a treadle-motion, which admits of stopping or starting the machine by the action of the feet only. Mr. H. C. Lee, of London, had an honourable mention for a simple and effective knitting machine, for all sizes of stockings, socks, and, indeed, for hosiery articles generally. The loops were made larger or smaller by a loop-regulator.

A medal was given to M. Villain, for the sewing and twisting action of his fringe-making machine.

In this department, the award of superior excellency must be accorded to the United States of America. The Jurors declared that some of the English sewing machines equalled any foreign production; but the Americans were numerous as exhibitors, and their mechanism was adapted to a greater variety of objects than that of any other nation. The French were also prominent for ingenuity and high finish of work.

Section B.—Machines and Tools employed in the Manufacture of Wood and Metal.—The heading of this section, in the Report of the Exhibition, imperfectly conveys the subjects which it really embraces. All machinery not intended for thread spun from fibrous materials, was comprised in it—such as tools and machines for working in stone, clay, coal, leather, paper, flour, sugar, liquids, and various other things. This section was too vast to treat with amplitude. There were 442 exhibitors, who presented no less than 1,800 machines. Ninety medals were awarded, and ninety-three honourable mentions. Neither in the Crystal Palace of 1851, nor in the Paris Exhibition of 1855, was there anything approaching, in vastness and completeness, to this splendid display of machinery. The different means of construction, adopted in various countries, for the same end, were exceedingly instructive and curious. Although the English machinery was greatly in excess of the foreign, the awards to the latter were in greater proportion. This is accounted for by the exertions of different foreign governments, which, by the appointment of skilful commissioners, eliminated the common or inferior specimens submitted to their decision before being sent to London. More than half of the contributors, from all parts of the world, were English: considerably less than half the medals were obtained by the British; but somewhat more than half the honourable mentions were given to them. It was authoritatively admitted that, on the whole, the Exhibition of 1862 was inferior, as to originality, to that of 1851, in general machinery. If there were not, however, any great increase in novelty, there was considerable improvement, especially where scientific engineering was brought into requisition.

1. *Machine Tools for working in Metal.*—M. Ullhorn, of Dusseldorf, had the good fortune to present the best coining machine in the Exhibition. Whitworth, of Manchester, who has achieved a world-wide fame, exhibited an extraordinary collection, both as to number and excellence; iron sawing machine; punching and screwing machine; hand drilling machine; pillar-drills; radial-drills; machines for shot-drilling, slotting, shaping, milling, bolt and nut-shaping, wheel-cutting, bolt and nut-screwing, and planing; lathes—screw, gap, and double plate; presses for forging and mandril-forcing; hand screwing-tools, and cylindric gauges. Peter Fairbairn, of Leeds, also made a large and admirable display. Greenwood and Betley were remarkable for originality. Nasmyth showed effective contrivance. Sharp and Stewart, great perfection in arrangement. Shepherd and Hill evinced very superior workmanship in their tools, especially lathes. Peacock and Tennent, Hartman and Zimmerman, won also the high opinion of engineers, and men of general science. M. Tusseaud surpassed, in some directions, all competitors. His system for cutting plates of any length or width, was original and most useful.

2. *Machines for working in Wood.*—These comprise sawing, planing, moulding, morticing, drilling, and turning. Nine medals were awarded in this department, six of which were won by the United Kingdom; three by France; and one by Saxony. Nine honourable mentions were made—three in favour of exhibitors of the United Kingdom; one each of exhibitors from Belgium, France, Hanover, Mecklenburg, Prussia, and the United States.

The most remarkable machine, in connection with wood-working, was shown by

Mr. Worssam, and entitled the "general joiner"—a name which seems admirably appropriate, for it performs nearly all work which the joiner can accomplish by hand. It saws, grooves, tongues, rebates, tenons, moulds, bores, cross-cuts, and squares-off.

3. *Machines for working in Stone.*—Only two medals were awarded under this head, and they were carried away by France and Italy. The honourable mentions were four, all of which were won by the United Kingdom, except one, which was claimed for the United States of America.

Sommeliere, of Turin, obtained a medal for his remarkable boring machine, now employed in tunnelling the Alps.

4. *Machinery for working in Coal.*—One honourable mention.

5. *Machines for working in Clay.*—Six medals were awarded. Three to the United Kingdom; one to France; one to the Grand Duchy of Hesse; and one to Prussia. One honourable mention only, which was obtained by W. Wilson, of Glasgow. Machinery for brick-making was prominent amongst this description.

6. *Machinery for working in Leather.*—Three medals were awarded, which were merited by England, France, and the United States. An honourable mention was also accorded to a Paris firm.

7. *Machinery for working in Paper.*—The exhibitors in this department of the section were numerous and ingenious, and represented a great many different nations. Eighteen medals were adjudged. Of these, eight fell to the United Kingdom; France obtained four; and the remainder were distributed among the representatives of this industry, from Belgium, Switzerland, and Germany. The number of honourable mentions was as large as the number of medals, and there were only five which were not taken by the United Kingdom. France, Switzerland, Germany, and the United States obtained the residue. The objects under this number of the section were various, comprising machinery for paper-making, paper-folding, type-casting apparatus, type-composing and distributing, and printing machines. The space allotted to these descriptions would render it impossible to give, in detail, the nature of the different forms and apparatus exhibited. The paper bag-making of Youngman; the type-casting of Besley; the type-composing and distributing of Mitchell, were especially interesting.

8. *Machinery working in other Fibrous Materials.*—Here there were five medals given, of which three were taken by the United Kingdom. Germany won the other two. Seven honourable mentions were accorded; of which the United Kingdom received two; France and the United States each one; and Germany the rest. Machinery was comprised under this number, for making sugar, for laundry purposes, telegraph wire-covering, bristle-sorting, cigar-making, calico-printing and dyeing, telegraph rope-making, electro copper-printing, mat-making, tobacco-spinning, and scutching. There was much ingenuity in the exhibition of this part of Section 8.

9. *Machines for working in Flour.*—Six medals were given; of which France won four; the other two fell to Switzerland and the United Kingdom. The only English victor in this honourable contest was T. T. Vicars, Wheatsheaf Foundry, Liverpool. The French have paid great attention to every department of this industry—biscuit-making, bread-baking, confectionery, preparation of kneading machines, manufacture

2

of ovens, &c.   The English public have not afforded encouragement to those millers and tradesmen who, by improved systems, have produced better flour, biscuits, and bread, by cleaner processes.   The old mode of kneading, which is still mainly pursued, is inexpressibly filthy, the kneading being carried on by perspiring men, and sometimes employing their feet for the purpose.   Well-adapted machinery was shown in the Exhibition building, by which all the processes of grinding and baking can be performed with purity.   It would appear that, in order to obtain clean-made bread, the public should resort to large establishments, the proprietors of which can afford to employ the requisite machinery.   Almost all the small establishments work on the oldest and worst methods.

There were eight honourable mentions.   In respect to these, the United Kingdom was more successful than in the competition for medals—winning six, and leaving to France and Austria the other two.

10. *Machines for working in Sugar and Liquids.*—A large volume might be produced in stating the details of this number under Section B, of Class VII., and in discussing the chemical, mechanical, and commercial questions incidental to the subjects involved.   Twenty medals were awarded; of which the United Kingdom did not secure quite half.   The remaining eleven were divided among the French, Prussian, and Belgian exhibitors; France taking "the lion's share."   The honourable mentions were seventeen; of which Great Britain conquered over one-third: France, Germany, and Russia claimed the rest; France here, also, obtaining the greatest proportion. Under this number, machinery for various ingenious processes was presented—apparatus for sugar-refining, distilling, brewing, aërated water, and ice-making.

The machinery for refining sugar was well represented.   Its importance demanded that such should be the case.   The refining of sugar is an exceedingly prosperous and increasing business, the tendency being to the exportation of refined sugars from England, even to the best sugar-producing countries.   Jamaica sends us her raw production, and receives it back again, when refined, for her own use.   The great consumption of sugar by all classes of persons in the British Isles, and the large contribution which the commodity makes to the revenue, compel attention to its production, refining, and commerce.   The late Daniel O'Connell—a shrewd observer of national peculiarities, and the habits of men, on a large scale—frequently observed, that the proportionate consumption of sugar by a people, might be taken as a test of their *status* in civilisation.   The largest and most powerful sugar-mill was exhibited by Mirelles and Tait.   It will produce 4,000 gallons of cane-juice (equal to two tons of sugar) per day.   For refining sugar, the favourite process for the concentration of the juice is "the vacuum pan."   There were many displays of this machine; but that which attracted most notice was made by Forrester, of Liverpool.   In the display of distilling apparatus there were some interesting machines.   One of these was wonderfully successful for its purpose: it was exhibited by Normandy & Co., London, and produces, from ordinary sea-water, pure, aërated, wholesome, sweet water, equal to that of the best springs.   Even from foul water, it will produce that which is free from all contamination.   The distillation of alcohol is conducted with great advantage by the machinery of M. Ergot, of Paris.   The brewing department

PATENT ICE MAKING MACHINE

THIS MACHINE IS CAPABLE OF CONVERTING 269 GALLONS OF SPRING OR
RIVER WATER INTO BLOCKS OF SOLID ICE WITHOUT THE USE OF CHEMICALS

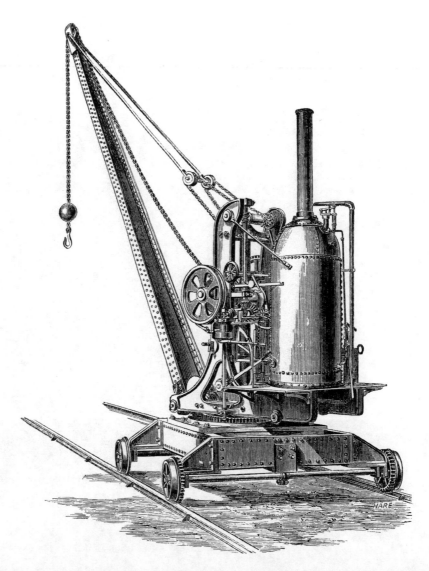

APPLEBY'S PATENT PORTABLE STEAM DERRICK CRANE.

These Cranes are usually made to lift 1½ or 3 tons at high speeds, and 3 to 6 tons at slow speeds.

Fitted with Appleby's Patent Steam Travelling and Steam Derrick motions, the Crane is travelled backwards or forwards along the road, and the radius of the jib is altered by steam at pleasure; either operation being performed with or without the load suspended. They have hitherto been used principally at Railway Stations, Steam-Boat Piers, Stone Quarries, and for Stone Setting; but it is obvious that, with these improvements, they are especially valuable in all situations where the radius is variable; as, without them, the load would frequently have to be brought up to the Crane, requiring a gang of men to do it, whilst, with these improvements, the work is done with greater speed and economy by steam power than by manual labour.

PORTABLE CRANE TO LIFT AND RADIATE BY STEAM.

This Crane has two Cylinders, fitted with Link-motion for reversing, single and double purchase-gearing; the radiating motion can be given in either direction, without stopping or reversing the Engine, and the lifting and radiating motion can both be at work at the same time.

presented a good Hop-Separator, by Handyside, of Derby; a Yeast-Press, by Needham and Kite, of Vauxhall; a Refrigerator, by Vanginderstaelen. Ice-making has, of late years, become an important business, and various exceedingly ingenious contrivances were exhibited for this purpose. Carré, of Paris, effects the purpose of his machine by the continuous circulation of ammonia. He exhibited apparatus of two distinct sorts —one for domestic use, and a great industrial apparatus.

CHAPTER VII.

CLASS VIII.—MACHINERY IN GENERAL. CLASS IX.—AGRICULTURAL AND HORTICULTURAL INSTRUMENTS AND MACHINES. CLASS X.—CIVIL ENGINEERING; ARCHITECTURAL AND BUILDING CONTRIVANCES. CLASS XI.—MILITARY ENGINEERING; ARMOUR AND ACCOUTREMENTS; ORDNANCE AND SMALL ARMS. CLASS XII.—NAVAL ARCHITECTURE, INCLUDING SHIPS' TACKLE. CLASS XIII.—PHILOSOPHICAL INSTRUMENTS, AND PROCESSES DEPENDING ON THEIR USE.

THE machinery of 1862 was marked by less of originality than that exhibited in 1851. This was not only the case in several sections under classes already treated upon, but was generally so. There was improvement in details, workmanship, and invention, but no extensive introduction of new principles. In material, the most striking improvement was the more general use of steel, and of iron approaching steel in its properties.

Class VIII. was divided into five sub-divisions, each of these being further divided into sections, displaying remarkable method, order, and contrivance on the part of those who had the management of the arrangement.

The first sub-division included "Prime Movers;" and under this, the first section referred to boilers, furnaces, &c. With few exceptions, the boilers exhibited belonged to traction-engines, or to portable and semi-portable steam-engines. Economy of space, and means to facilitate cleansing and repairs, were the chief aims of the projectors. The models and drawings were more ambitious, making greater pretension to originality. The newest style of boiler exhibited was an American invention, manufactured by Mr. Harrison, a British exhibitor. In the boiler-yard of the Western Annexe, Mr. H. Cater set up, too late for an award, boilers presenting a peculiar arrangement of tubes. In the same locality, Mr. D. K. Clark (United Kingdom) set up an apparatus for promoting perfect combustion, preventing smoke by using very small steam-jets for blowing streams of air into the furnace. This apparatus might be seen at work with well-established success. Several of the exhibits in this section seemed as appropriate to Class VII. as to that under which they were arranged; while others appeared more suitable to other sub-divisions in their own class. There was, in fact, great difficulty in effecting a perfect classification; and objects of machinery were removed from one class to another, and one section to another, in their respective classes, during the progress of the Exhibition, up to a very late period of its existence. The objects were too numerous for separate notice even where the merit was signal; but it is useful to observe generally, that, in comparison with that of 1851, the exhibition of steam-engines showed an increased employment of high-pressure, great expansion, and super-heating; an increased use of surface condensation; a tendency towards simplicity; a higher perfection of workmanship and finish; and a general construction more conducive to economy in fuel, power, and repairs.

The traction-engines were especially worthy of notice. Those made by Bray, Taylor & Co., and Tunford and Sons, received awards: they were all capable of working well on common roads. Mr. Yarrow's steam-carriage obtained extensive notice; and the Jury were about to test it on one of the roads leading to the Exhibition; but the fatal habit of moving objects from one class to another, up to a late period of the Exhibition, defeated this purpose, and deprived Mr. Yarrow of honours to which all believed him entitled.

Section 3.—Marine Steam-Engines.—These, as compared with the same objects in the Exhibition of 1851, showed even a greater practical improvement than appeared from a comparison of the land-engines. Horizontal screw-engines, as best suited for ships of war, and therefore also more easily spared for exhibition, were in a great majority. Moving models were extensively presented. Paddle-engines were represented by working models. Messrs. Rennie made a good display. The horizontal trunk marine screw-engines of Mr. Penn, C.E., London, showed great perfection in material and work; but no award could be given, Mr. Penn being one of the Jurors.

Section 4.—Windmills.—This scarcely deserved to be called a section, so small was the array. Wentworth and Jarvis, of the United States, were the best exhibitors.

Section 5 was also on a limited scale, and comprised *Water-wheels and Turbines.*

Section 6.—The same remark is applicable to this section, which consisted of *Water-Pressure Engines.*

Section 7 bore a very limited relation to the general exhibition of machinery. It consisted of a *Vacuum Power-Engine*, to which the Jury could not, with propriety, apply the name.

Section 8—Electro-Magnetic Motive Power-Engines—was also a failure.

Section 9—Miscellaneous Prime Movers—contained little of importance.

Sub-division II.—Separate parts of Machines; Specimens of Workmanship; Miscellaneous pieces of Mechanism.

Section 1.—Heavy Castings or Forgings in the Rough.—Castings or forgings, plain, intricate, or beautiful, in the rough, made up the display of this section, which was greatly superior to the corresponding one of 1851. This improvement was mainly due to the Nasmyth and other steam-hammers. The minuter, and more scientific specimens, under some of the heads detailed, showed exquisite workmanship, and great ingenuity. Separate parts of machines, miscellaneous pieces of mechanism, metal turnings, specimens of filing in finished work—such as surfaces and irregular figures, valves, cocks, pistons, &c., were exhibited in spacious array, and attracted the attention of scientific men and amateurs.

The *Air-Pumps* were principally represented by exhausting machines for creating a vacuum for the evaporation of syrups in the manufacture of sugar. They are constructed on nearly a uniform model; but this very circumstance brought into view, more distinctly, superiority of workmanship. Several *Water-Meters*, of very ingenious adaptation, were exhibited. The weighing and measuring machines were also

MORRISON'S PATENT DOUBLE ACTING STEAM HAMMER.

THIS HAMMER WILL STRIKE A BLOW EQUAL TO 20 CWT AND IT CAN BE EASILY ADJUSTED TO SUCH A NICETY THAT A WAFER CAN BE TAKEN
OFF A WATCH WITHOUT BREAKING THE GLASS AS ABOVE REPRESENTED OR IT WILL CRACK A NUT WITHOUT INJURING THE KERNEL

RANSOMES & SON'S 15 HORSE POWER HORIZONTAL STATIONARY HIGH PRESSURE STEAM ENGINE.

RAVENHILL, SALKELD & COMPANY'S PADDLE ENGINE.

THE FARMER'S FIRE ENGINE IRRIGATOR AND
AGRICULTURAL FORCE PUMP

IMPROVED HOSE REEL

MERRYWEATHER'S IMPROVED FIRE ESCAPE.

GARRETT & SON'S IMPROVED STONE MILL FOR GRINDING WHEAT.

GARRETT & SON'S PATENT COMBINED THRESHING & DRESSING MACHINE.

W. CROSSKILL'S IMPROVED LIQUID DISTRIBUTOR OR WATERCART.

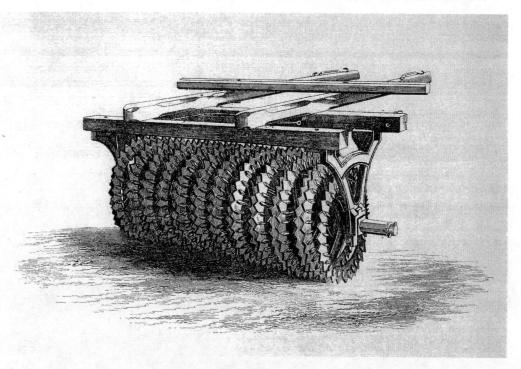

W. CROSSKILL'S SELF CLEANING CLOD CRUSHER & ROLLER.

"THE SUTHERLAND" STEAM FIRE ENGINE,

BY MERRYWEATHER & SONS

remarkable for their practical utility. Few objects showed more contrivance, on the part of the makers, than registering machines. Some of these were for commercial purposes, and a smaller number for private employment. Gauges, indicators, "tell-tales," &c., constituted the detail of these ingenious instruments.

There was an appendix to Class VIII., a special Jury having been appointed for fire-engines. A strong party of the officers and men of the fire-brigade were in attendance during the experiments by which the relative merits of the engines were tested. Two hundred men of the Guards were present, and worked the manual engines; and they were aided in keeping order by an equally numerous body of police, as the experiments excited considerable public interest. Five medals were distributed, four of which were given to exhibitors of the United Kingdom, and one honourable mention to a foreigner. There were some improvements in design; but only one exhibitor, Mr. Fowke, was rewarded as an inventor. Good workmanship, compactness, effectual performance, durability, and simplicity, were the qualities which won awards. Lee's American Steam Fire-engine showed much ingenuity of design. There were thirty-seven English, and six foreign engines in the building, about half of which were offered for trial.

The number of awards, under the head of "General Machinery," was very great; the variety of objects presented to the judgment of the Jurors being so vast, and the exhibitors, British and foreign, very numerous. There were 67 medals granted to inhabitants of the United Kingdom. To Victoria was awarded, 2; Austria, 3; Baden, 1; Belgium, 6; Bremen, 1; France, 29; Hesse-Cassel, 1; Norway, 3; Prussia, 9; Saxony, 1; Sweden, 2; Switzerland, 7; United States, 19. There were honourable mentions accorded—To the United Kingdom, 50; to Canada, 1; New Brunswick, 1; Nova Scotia, 1; Victoria, 5; Austria, 6; Bavaria, 1; Belgium, 2; France, 28; Greece, 1; Hanover, 1; Italy, 2; Mecklenburg-Strelitz, 1; Prussia, 12; Saxony, 2; Sweden, 2; Switzerland, 3; United States, 8; Würtemberg, 1. Mr. Bodmer, of the firm of R. and L. R. Bodmer, United Kingdom; and Mr. J. Penn, of J. Penn and Sons, also United Kingdom, being Jurors, could not obtain the awards of which their exhibitions were deemed worthy.

AGRICULTURAL AND HORTICULTURAL INSTRUMENTS AND MACHINES (Class IX.)— Including *Implements of Tillage, and of Carriage; Tools directly connected with the Cultivation of Plants, and Implements used in harvesting the Produce; the Machinery of the Barn; and the Tools and Implements of the Feeding-house and the Dairy.*—These different sub-classifications comprised a long list of useful objects, such as the plough, cultivator, barrow, and roller; carts and waggons; machines, whether of manure or seed; horse-hoes; reaping and mowing machines, hay-tedders, and horse-rakes; threshing machinery, winnowers, corn-separators, weighing machines, &c.; corn and cake-crushers, flour-mills, turnip-cutters and pulpers, chaff-cutters, steaming and cooling apparatus, and dairy utensils.—Most of these were well represented.

This part of the Exhibition was placed in the Eastern Annexe, the least advantageously situated portion of the building. After the first three weeks the access was made more easy, and the contents became better known and more popular.

The number of medals given in this department, was—To exhibitors of the

United Kingdom, 47; Canada, 7; New Brunswick, 1; South Australia, 1; Victoria, 1; Austria, 4; Belgium, 5; Denmark, 1; France, 11; Italy, 6; Netherlands, 1; Norway, 2; Prussia, 1; Russia, 1; Sweden, 6; Switzerland, 1; United States, 6; Würtemberg, 1. The honourable mentions were thus distributed:—To the United Kingdom, 59; Canada, 2; India, 3; New Brunswick, 1; Victoria, 1; Western Australia, 1; Austria, 9; Bavaria, 1; Belgium, 6; Denmark, 2; France, 18; Italy, 12; Mecklenburg-Schwerin, 1; Netherlands, 5; Norway, 4; Prussia, 2; Russia, 2; Sweden, 12; Switzerland, 1; United States, 5; Würtemberg, 2.

M. Prutus (of the firm of J. Prutus & Co.), Zollverein, being a juror as well as an exhibitor, could not receive the award to which, otherwise, he would have been entitled.

One of the great objects of the Exhibition was to test the improvement in various matters of art, manufactures, and commerce, during the decade from 1851. There was, in the department of agricultural machinery, a very marked improvement during that period. This indication of progress was shown in four particulars, each signally proving that the advance was decided and encouraging. The first of these was the increased use of the movable steam-engine: this is used for threshing corn. The flail has almost entirely disappeared, and the steam-engine used in its stead. This circumstance has effected an entire revolution in the winter employment of English farm labourers, and even in the farm buildings in which they are employed. The old "barn" is rapidly passing away, and the homesteads are influenced by the change. The second indication of progress was the cultivation of the land by steam-power. In 1851 it was just thought possible that such a change might come to pass. In 1862 it was an accomplished fact: steam-ploughs and "cultivators" were leading features of the class. A third mark of improvement was the exhibition of reaping and mowing machinery. The idea of employing this description of agricultural machinery seems to have been caught from the few specimens presented, in 1851, by the Americans. The fourth proof of advancement was the display of machinery for pulping the food of live stock.

In other respects, the agricultural machinery of 1862 was not so much in advance of that exhibited in Hyde Park.

A vast trade has been opened in the manufacture of farming implements in England, not only for English farms, but for other parts of the British Isles, for our colonies, and for foreign countries. The list of articles in this manufacture, largely exported, is a long one, consisting of steam-engines, ploughs, cultivators, corn-drills, corn horse-hoes, reaping machines, hay-tedders, threshing machines, chaff-cutters, and corn-bruisers. All these articles are made by thousands, and some by many thousands, annually.

The British colonies exhibited well in this department. Ploughs and reaping machines were especially successful.

The United States, as in 1851, gained great renown in its display of agricultural implements and machines. There were two remarkable novelties in this section. One was Messrs. Kinshaw and Colvin's *Cow-milker*. The Jury were of opinion that this invention would be extensively introduced to English dairies. The other was

GARRETT'S PATENT HORSE HOE.

GARRETT & SON'S IMPROVED ELEVEN ROW. SUFFOLK LEVER, CORN & SEED DRILL.

IMPROVED PORTABLE STEAM ENGINE BY GARRETT & SONS.

GARRETT & SONS DOUBLE-CYLINDER STEAM PLOUGHING ENGINE AND TACKLE

M'Cormick's new "Self-acting Reaper." Both these American inventions are ingenious, exceedingly practical, and economical of labour.—The French section was not largely filled, although occupied by remarkable proofs of progress. France, as well as England, has established an export trade of these articles; and, in all the departments of the former, there are small manufactories, carried on with economy and ingenuity. This section contained reaping and mowing machines, threshing machines, mill-work, drawings, and various contrivances for irrigation.

One of the most important discoveries ever made in connection with the preservation of agricultural produce, was that of M. Deyère, of Paris. The object is to repress the chemical action which sets up fermentation in corn when stored; and, to preserve it from insects, M. Deyère has completely succeeded in both these objects. He has formed vessels of thin sheet-iron, coated with a particular kind of varnish, and enclosed in concrete or masonry. By this discovery any amount of corn can be stored, without requiring movement of any kind, such as has formerly been deemed essential. A warehouse has been built at Brest to store 70,000 hectolitres.

It is a remarkable circumstance connected with Class IX., that no report was received from any of the sections but those above-named. The Commissioners were enabled, through the Juries, to adjudge medals and honourable mentions to the foreign exhibitors; but, with the exception of France and the United States, no reports were made of the general or comparative excellence of the articles displayed by the various nations. The space, therefore, allotted to this class must necessarily be short, unless it were occupied by a minuteness of detail not given in the description of other classes.

CIVIL ENGINEERING; ARCHITECTURAL AND BUILDING CONTRIVANCES (Class X.)—Probably there was no part of the Exhibition more difficult to appreciate, as a whole, or of which it is less easy to write a descriptive history. A weekly journal, devoted to architecture,* thus noticed this class:—

"It is divided, but not on any principle that we can discover in arrangement of the objects, into three subclasses—viz., A, 'Civil Engineering and Building Contrivances;' B, 'Sanitary Improvements and Constructions,' which are under the galleries at the south-western angle of the eastern dome, and adjoining in the South Court; C, 'Objects shown for Architectural Beauty,' on the opposite side of the South-eastern Transept; which last division contains works that might have found place with those in the Mediæval Court of the Class XXX."

Section A was arranged under ten sub-divisions:—I. Bridges. II. Harbours and Docks. III. Movable Barriers or Weirs. IV. Compensating Reservoirs. V. Lighthouses. VI. Railways. VII. Diving Apparatus. VIII. Building Materials, in their natural state. IX. Artificial Building Materials. X. Contrivances and Machinery for facilitating Engineering work.

The awards under Section A were very numerous. Medals were given to exhibitors—Of the United Kingdom, 19 in number; Canada, 2; New South Wales, 2; Victoria, 1; Austria, 8; Bavaria, 1; Belgium, 1; France, 30; Hanover, 1; Italy, 4; Mecklenburg-Schwerin, 1; Netherlands, 1; Norway, 1; Prussia, 7; Russia, 1; Sweden, 1; Switzerland, 1; Würtemberg, 1. The great superiority of France, not only over other foreign exhibitors, but over all competitors, British, colonial, and

* The Builder.

foreign, is very striking. Of late years, England has become the rival of France in military engineering, in which the French were formerly universally acknowledged to be superior. It was not suspected that France could make a near approach to English excellence in civil engineering; but the display at South Kensington, and the awards won by her, prove that she is a rival in this fair and friendly competition.

The honourable mentions accorded were—To the United Kingdom, 13; Canada, 3; and what is called by the Jury, a collective honourable mention to four gentlemen engaged in the construction of "the Victoria Bridge;" India, 1; Queensland, 1; Natal, 1; New Brunswick, 1; New South Wales, 1; Nova Scotia, 2; South Australia, 1; Tasmania, 1; Victoria, 5; Austria, 1; Bavaria, 1; Belgium, 1; France, 28; Hanover, 1; Italy, 1; Netherlands, 2; Portugal, 2; Prussia, 3; Würtemberg, 2.

It will be seen, that in this class of awards, as well as in that of medals, France is pre-eminent.

In the sub-divisions under Section A, the first is—

Bridges.—These comprised much, if not every, variety: viz., tubular; plain and lattice girder; turning, or "balanced principles;" stone; brick; timber; and iron, cast or wrought. In this department works of the greatest merit were exhibited by means of models and drawings. The wrought-iron tubular girder bridge, thrown across the St. Lawrence, at Montreal, received general commendation. This bridge was constructed by the late Robert Stephenson, M.P., after the model of the Conway and Britannia bridges, on the Chester and Holyhead line of railway. A medal was awarded.

The bridge across the Wye, at Chepstow, and the Albert bridge across the Tamar, at Saltash, constructed under the direction of the late Mr. Brunel, also attracted great attention. These bridges are of wrought-iron, with cast-iron columns. The arrangement is upon the insistent and suspension principles combined. Medals were given for these works.

The lattice bridge across the Boyne, at Drogheda, on the line of the Dublin and Belfast railway, was warmly eulogised by professional men. It was designed by Sir John M'Neill, and constructed under his direction. By far the largest of the kind erected in the United Kingdom, it was regarded as a work of national importance. Similar structures of timber were built in the United States of America, and suggested the formation of an iron bridge to Sir John M'Neill. Another bridge of identical construction has been thrown over one of the streets of Dublin, on the same line of railway. Medals were accorded for these.—France was richly represented by models of bridges and viaducts. The largest turning or balanced bridge ever attempted, is that across the Penfold, near Brest. It was constructed by M. Matthieu, who received a medal for another of his bridges—that of Fribourg—the erection of which was characterised by a series of simple, yet ingenious and novel contrivances, never surpassed in this department of civil engineering.

Harbours and Docks.—Under this head, models or plans were exhibited of the " Digue" of Cherbourg; the new port of Marseilles; the lock-gates of the docks at St. Nazaire; the lock of the citadel at Havre; the new naval graving-dock of the arsenal at Toulon; the graving-dock of the dockyard at Rochford; and the coffer-

GWYNNE & C⁰ˢ CENTRIFUGAL PUMP.

dam for the construction of the dry dock at the arsenal of L'Orient. There were various specimens of floating docks; but, in this department, Mr. Edwin Clark, C.E., showed more originality, ingenuity, and boldness of conception, than any of his compeers.

Movable Weirs.—The object of these contrivances is to dam up water in summer and dry seasons. The invention is French, and it has been reduced to practical utility, almost exclusively, upon the rivers of that country. The Jurors report, that "this system may be applied with success to the rivers and streams of Great Britain."

Compensating Reservoirs, &c.—Their object is to provide bodies of water for irrigation of lands exhausted of their moisture, and pure water for other purposes, when rivers are polluted with sewage. France almost exclusively exhibited in this sub-division, such reservoirs having been practically adopted in that country.

Under this head sewerage was arranged, various plans and maps for which were exhibited. The French were here much inferior to the British; the magnificent schemes set on foot in London, were matters of surprise and admiration to all.

Lighthouses.—Smeaton was the inventor of the system now adopted by the United Kingdom. It consists simply of dovetailed masonry, thoroughly well banded together, horizontally and vertically. The tower is circular, tapering upwards from a curved base. The Eddystone Lighthouse is a perfect illustration of the principles upon which Smeaton proceeded. Rennie improved this plan in the erection of the Bell-Rock Lighthouse, on the north-east coast of Scotland.

The most important improvement in the system of lighting, is the invention of the celebrated M. Fresnel, of France. It consists in a series of solid cut-glass lenses surrounding the light. The rotating machinery of another French gentleman, M. Lepante, is a great improvement.

Railways.—The Jury admitted that railways were as unsuitable as the lights in lighthouses to Class X.; but they appear not to have known where to place either. This sub-division was uninteresting.

Diving Apparatus.—There were no improvements, in this sub-division, upon the Exhibition of 1851.

Natural Building Materials.—These consisted of stone, clay, and wood, in great variety.

Artificial Building Materials.—This sub-division was interesting, and it included in it so many specimens of what was exhibited in Sub-division VIII., that both might be properly treated together under this head. The following notice was written by one of the ablest men of the day, in connection with the scientific and practical knowledge of a subject which it would be impossible to elucidate in less space:—

"Amongst the beautiful order of works, none deserve more attention than some already referred to, of those which are classed in the first (A) division. Mr. George Maw, of Broseley, has arranged a most interesting 'Court,' with a 'collective series of architectural productions, illustrating the clay manufactures of the Shropshire coalfield,' acting on behalf of his own firm and Messrs. W. B. Simpson and Sons, Messrs. J. and E. Burton, G. Davis and Co., R. Evans, W. Exley, G. W. Lewis, and Doughty, Mrs. Thorn, and the Colebrook Dale and Madeley Wood Companies. The productions of the Benthall Works, which are chiefly from the designs of Mr. M. Digby Wyatt, hold the most prominent place. The divisions of the series comprise 'roofing materials,' which include tiles, common and ornamental; unglazed, glazed, and enamelled; plain tiles and pan-tiles; roof-crestings, plain and flanged, and with fixed and loose ornaments; ventilating roof-crest tiles; hip and gutter tiles, and flanged hip crestings; 'paving materials,' including illustrations of the revival of pictorial mosaic, consisting of a pavement, the subject 'Apollo and the Four Seasons,' which is equal to anything that could be produced, but does not reconcile us to the pictorial treatment of flooring; a facsimile head from the pavement at Bignor, and various works in *tesseræ*, geometrical mosaic, and tiles, plain and encaustic, and their combinations; Moresque mosaics and majolica tiles for wall linings, some of which may be fixed by ornamental brass-headed nails, without cement; 'Draining Materials,' 'Fire-bricks, Furnace Materials, and Stove Fittings;' 'Bricks and Materials used in the Construction of Walls;' 'Accessories to the Decoration of Buildings;' pillars and square shafts effectively treated in colour, and with ornamented capitals; and 'Raw Materials,' illustrated by a section of the Shropshire Coal-field, and specimens, some of which show the relative shrinkages of the clays. It should be recollected that there are other, and perhaps higher, aims in architecture, than demonstrating the serviceableness and scope of any one material: in other words, interests and feelings of manufacturers, and the taste of architects, are not what should lead to the same conclusions; but the geometrical mosaic is doing excellent service in the decoration of houses; and some of the credit for the obvious future of popular taste will be due to manufacturers and to those whom they have called to their assistance. The Italian and other roofing tiles; bricks, red, green, black, and white; and ornamental ridging, of Mr. R. Brown, of Surbiton, are well known; as are also the articles sold by Messrs. J. and W. Eastwood, of Lambeth. The collection of clay manufactures is too large for complete enumeration. The class includes articles which, like some of those (excellent of their kind) manufactured by Messrs. John Cliff and Company, of Lambeth, might have come appropriately into the 'Pottery' class; and the clay retorts for gas-making, which, with fire-bricks, drain-pipes, and chimney-pots, are exhibited by Messrs. Joseph Cliff and Sons, of Wortley, near Leeds. It would be of little service to give the numbers in the catalogue. The invert blocks of the last-named firm are provided with longitudinal tubular channels, with which lateral openings communicate, to take the land drainage. The productions of the Brownhills Blue Metallic Tileries and Fire-brick Works (Messrs. Garrett Brothers, late H. and R. Haywood), are well known as consisting of drain-pipes, flue-linings, as used in London, at Buckingham Palace, and Bridgewater House, and the houses of Mr. H. T. Hope; the Duke of Buccleuch, Whitehall; and Mr. R. S. Holford, Dorchester House; roofing tiles and ridges, plain and ornamental; and paving tiles. They also include Clarke's ventilating ridges; alcove fern bricks for placing in recesses of conservatory walls, or for the formation of hexagonal columns or fountains for the growth of ferns and lycopodiums (Dr. Watson's patent); white glazed bricks; wall diapering; and circular shafts in red terra-cotta, as used in the church in Baldwin's-gardens, Gray's-inn-lane. Equally well known are the terro-metallic bricks and tiles of Mr. T. Peake, of Stoke-upon-Trent. Messrs. Henry Doulton and Co. exhibited a good selection from their articles for sewerage and other purposes. Amongst them are sections of sewers built of hollow blocks. Information respecting the application of this method of construction, and the cost as compared with brick sewers, should have been given. We are compelled to endorse the expression of regret, in another quarter, that prices of articles are not generally supplied by the British exhibitors. In the same class are the facing-bricks and tiles of Mr. W. Basford, of Burslem; the sewer-tubes, fire-bricks, and retorts of Mr. E. Brooke, of the Field House Fire-Clay Works, Huddersfield; the ornamental tiles of Mr. J. G. Colla; the retorts and bricks of Messrs. Joseph Cowen and Co., of Newcastle-on-Tyne; and the similar articles of Messrs. Fisher, Brothers, and Co., Stourbridge; and the building-blocks, facing and fire-bricks of Messrs. Fayle and Co.; the ornamental bricks and tiles of Messrs. R. and N. Norman, of Burgess-hill, Sussex; the glazed stoneware sewage-pipes, fire-bricks, and terra-cotta of Messrs. Gibbs and Canning, Tamworth; and the roofing and paving tiles of Mr. W. Jones, of Newcastle, Staffordshire."

Portland cement; galvanised metals for tiles; wire fences; indurated stone, and means of preserving stone from decay; railway sleepers, of great utility, novel form, and material, were all to be found in this sub-division.

General Machinery.—The managers of the Exhibition seem to have been wholly bewildered on the subject of machinery. Again and again the same description of subjects recurs under the most diverse classifications; and it seems unavoidable, so various are the uses to which the same tools and machines may be applied. It is, however, somewhat surprising to find the subject of traction-engines, and steam-power on canals, reappear under this sub-division: and various matters, such as zinc roofing, methods of preserving wood, and varnished metals (all properly belonging to Sub-division IX.), are here introduced in connexion with honourable mentions.

Section B.—*Sanitary Improvements and Constructions.*—Prominent in this section were Beaumont's sanitary tubes, and the sewage-pipes of the Bourne Valley Pottery Company. The Jurors directed their attention to filters, ventilation, water and gas-pipes, smoke consumption, dry water-closets, water-supply, baths, sanitary bricks, improved traps for street-drainage, clay retorts, windows, earthenware pipes, tressels, shoemakers' tables, paints, water-pipes, effluvia-traps, and warming. Generally, in this section, mechanical contrivance was behind scientific knowledge.

Medals were awarded, in this section—To exhibitors of the United Kingdom, 10; Austria, 3; Belgium, 4; France, 5; Hamburg, 1; Russia, 1; Sweden, 3; Switzerland, 1. Honourable mentions were conceded—To the United Kingdom, 7; France, 2; Sweden, 1.

Section C.—Objects shown for Architectural Beauty.—Medals were awarded—To the United Kingdom, 22; and also a collective medal to the Colebrook Dale Company, for the excellence of the encaustic tiles, and various other articles; Malta, 3; Austria, 2; Belgium, 4; Denmark, 1; France, 14; Greece, 2; Italy, 2; Netherlands, 2; Prussia, 6; Russia, 3.—Honourable mentions were conceded—To the United Kingdom, 8; Malta, 2; Bavaria, 1; Belgium, 1; Denmark, 1; Greece, 1; Italy, 1; Prussia, 1.

The difficulty of making a perfect classification was much felt in this section. Many of the exhibitors here were actually rewarded in other sections of this class, or in other classes, for similar productions, which thus found their way to diverse places. The Jurors were very severe in the general opinion expressed of the English branch of this section, for the want of taste and judgment by which it was characterised. There was, as to form, colour, design, and special adaptation, a marked want of the æsthetical, with rare exceptions. Mr. Digby Wyatt redeemed this part of the Exhibition from disgrace. The objects shown for architectural beauty were, to a great extent, depending upon richness of material, such as marble, plain and coloured; serpentine, Oran onyx. Some good displays were made in carved wood. Russia surpassed all other countries, in proportion to the number of objects presented, for the very highest class of excellence, whether considered for tasteful design, preciousness of material, or perfection of execution. Exquisite maps, plans, and illustrated publications were placed by the French in this section.

MILITARY ENGINEERING; ARMOUR AND ACCOUTREMENTS; ORDNANCE AND SMALL ARMS (Class XI.)—This class was originally divided into three sections, A, B, and C; but the number of exhibitors was so few in the first two, that, in the reports, they were grouped together, so as virtually to make only two sections—one marked A and B, and the other C.

Section A and B.—Clothing and Accoutrements; Tents, Camp Equipage, and Military Engineering.

Military Clothing.—A scanty display; that of Switzerland and Russia the best.

Accoutrements.—There was nothing worthy of notice.

Camp Equipage.—Some new patterns of tents and ambulances were shown, improvements upon the old forms.

Barracks.—Some models of barracks and barrack hospitals were sent by the British war department. Hitherto, gross neglect of the comfort and health of the soldier has characterised the building and government of barracks in the British empire, especially in England and in India. It would be impossible to imagine dens more filthy, or places of abode in every way more wretched, than some barracks in the United Kingdom have even very recently been. The late Lord Herbert gave attention to this subject; and, under public pressure, the War-office now shows more concern for the soldier's health.

Field Engineering.—Draw-bridges, which, as the reader has seen, were exhibited under another class, are again presented in these sections. Barriers to prevent an enemy entering a post, which seems hardly appropriate to field engineering, were displayed. Pontoons, by Captain Fowkes, and an excellent camp fire-engine, by that officer, constituted the chief objects in these sections.

Fortifications.—In the English Court only were there any models of this nature. The introduction of weapons of precision, and of long range, rendered the old fortifications valueless. Lines of defence must be formed at a greater distance from the places defended, and be adapted to bear guns of larger calibre. Cover for the men, from the deadly certainty of modern field and battery fire, was also a desideratum. Models of fortification for all these objects were presented.

Military Topography.—In this department, the United Kingdom and Spain alone presented models or maps. Medals were awarded—To the United Kingdom, 10; France, 4; Spain, 1; Switzerland, 1; Turkey, 1.—"Honourable mentions" were awarded to the exhibitors of the United Kingdom in five instances; Brazil, 1; France, 2; Algeria, 1; Russia, 1; Switzerland, 1.

Section C.—Arms and Ordnance.—The novelties of this section were of great practical importance, and very numerous. Medals were given to exhibitors—Of the United Kingdom, 28; Austria, 1; Belgium, 7; Brazil, 1; France, 14; Italy, 6; Prussia, 5; Russia, 3; Spain, 2; Sweden, 2; Switzerland, 3; Turkey, 2; United States, 1.—Honourable mentions—United Kingdom, 16; India, 19; New South Wales, 1; Victoria, 1; Anhault-Dessau, 1; Austria, 4; Belgium, 8; France, 12; Hanover, 2; Italy, 5; Lübeck, 1; Netherlands, 1; Norway, 1; Prussia, 4; Sweden, 3; Switzerland, 2; Turkey, 2.

In perusing this list, any one acquainted with the subject, unless his knowledge of it be most intimate and extensive, will feel surprise. Places from which the best weapons and most numerous exhibitors would be expected, figure but moderately; while medals and honourable mentions have been justly given to exhibitors from places where it would be supposed the production of military weapons of any kind would be unlikely. Great Britain, France, and Belgium have been properly regarded as the countries where productions of this sort are chiefly manufactured; and these countries made a considerable display. England might be expected, with good reason, to have taken the honours in a far greater proportion, as compared with the rest of the world. The United States of America had obtained great fame in Europe for the manufacture of pistols and rifles, but not for artillery. Since the civil war commenced in the United States, and more especially since the close of the Exhibition, ordnance have been manufactured there of great weight and power, both smooth-bore and rifled. Guns have been employed, in the siege of Charleston, of great magnitude and range, and of most destructive efficacy; yet only one medal has been awarded to that country—to Colt, for his celebrated revolving arms, more especially the pistol; and not one honourable mention. Italy has not been found as an arms-producing country: but Prussia has; and, in the recent bombardments of Danish defences, has given proof of the effective power of her ordnance; yet Italy won a medal more than Prussia; and, in the honourable mentions, stands high as compared with Prussia. The fact is, that of late years, especially since the Italian war against Austria, Italy has paid great attention to the fabrication of arms, more especially to artillery. The Italian exhibition of swords and gun-barrels was beautiful for artistic skill, and judicious selection of material. The Cavalli gun was also worthy of distinction. Since the Exhibition closed, Italy has brought forth several cannon of formidable efficiency. The accurate gun-barrels of the Prussians, and their cast-steel ordnance, merited warm eulogy. The Russians showed an unhammered steel cannon, of enormous strength; and their sword-blades were superior. During the Crimean expedition, the swords of the English cavalry were made of such inferior material, that they bent against the buff jackets of the Russians; while the swords of the latter were literally "true as steel." The Turkish sword-blades in the Exhibition were of the finest temper, and keenest edge. The ordnance of the Turks has been chiefly made in Prussia. The small arms were rather collections of curiosities than specimens of progress. The Belgians excelled in every department, and were especially successful in cheapness of production. Their material for manufacturing powder was the purest in the Exhibition. They supply England with great numbers of her Enfield rifles. Of all places in the world, the reader would probably hesitate to look for honourable mentions in connexion with India: that country, it is true, has attained celebrity for its sword-blades; but, of late years, and in late wars, the native soldiers of India used old English blades, tempered and sharpened by themselves, and which they made more effectual weapons than they were when turned out from our factories. The long list of honourable mentions given to India, related to a single feature of merit—collections of arms. Some of them belonged to native princes; one to the imperial government; a few to natives; and the rest to British officers. Victoria sent an interesting collection of aboriginal arms, which accounts for its single honourable mention. One would not expect to find New South Wales receiving honourable mention for sword-blades. Austria is well provided with arms: she has a splendid rifled gun, supposed by many to be the best in Europe; but her appearance at the Exhibition, in this department, was poor indeed. There was very little originality in the productions of France, from which much in this respect was looked for; and not a single cannon, notwithstanding that France led the way with rifled ordnance. She exhibited, however, what was not expected—very excellent specimens of guns used by sportsmen. The most remarkable and valuable contributions were made by the English government, and English manufacturers. Amongst these the Armstrong guns were especially noticed. Much controversy has been maintained as to the efficiency of these kinds of ordnance: many defects were discovered, and remedied; still the discussion as to superiority proceeds. The smallest Armstrongs exhibited were 6-pounders; the largest, 100-pounders. Since then, Sir William has fabricated

2 o

far heavier metal. His seven-inch howitzer was considered a serviceable gun. The charge of powder is, in many cases, one-eighth the weight of the ball. Some of his guns are breech-loaders; some muzzle-loaders. The largest range of any of his ordnance exhibited is that of the 40-pounder, which, at an angle of ten degrees, has a flight of 3,855 yards in twelve seconds. Several pieces, since manufactured by him, far surpass that range. The rifling machines used by Sir William, are wonderful specimens of accurate mechanism. The machines for making the rifle-ball, or bullet, are also curious for their ingenuity and efficiency.

The *Royal Carriage Department* presented various gun-carriages of admirable construction and adaptation. Ambulance-waggons and barrows, which appeared in other departments, found space again in this. Shells, fuzes, bullets, round cannon-shot, and a vast variety of *matériel*, were shown by the British government.

The Whitworth guns were objects of great interest; and discussions as to their merits, as compared with the Armstrongs, were warmly maintained by spectators, professional and non-professional. The general feeling was in favour of Whitworth. Some of his small rifled cannon were very beautiful, especially the smallest, the 1-pounder. Whitworth's guns only require powder one-sixth the weight of the ball— an advantage over Armstrong's.

Mr. Lancaster exhibited two fine guns; but his system not having proved successful in the Crimea, they did not attract much notice. The guns of the Mersey Steel and Iron Company, like those of Whitworth, were favourites with visitors from the County Palatine. Mr. Bashley Britten's invention of attaching the end-coating of an iron ball, for a rifle cannon, to the ball, by a zinc medium (now adopted by the government), was examined by officers and gun-founders with interest.

In small arms, a comparison between the Exhibitions of 1862 and 1851, shows a marvellous advance. " Old Brown Bess" has been supplanted in the British army by the Enfield rifle. This is by no means an accurate weapon at long range; the ball ascends, and loses accuracy of flight in proportion to the increase of range. It is also too heavy. The short Enfield is made " top-heavy" by the increased length of the sword-bayonet.

Mr. Whitworth is a rival of the government manufacturers in rifled muskets, as well as rifled cannon. His musket has obtained a great reputation.

The breech-loading rifles of Westley Richards, especially carbines suitable for cavalry regiments, were much admired. Mr. Richards, being a Juror, was debarred from the prizes his excellent productions merited. Sheffield, noted as it is for cutlery, did not send the best specimens of swords. London, Birmingham, and several foreign cities surpassed it—thus furnishing another surprise to many.

None of the foreign governments sent specimens of ordnance, small arms, ammunition, or gun-carriages. It was supposed that an apprehension as to any secrets in their system of arms being discovered, led to this reserve. These governments, however, gave another reason as the real one—that they did not wish to compete with private persons of their respective nationalities.

It was a disadvantage in the way of a full report of the Jury, that they could not see the different weapons tested. In various branches of machinery, opportunity was possessed by the public to see them at work; and when that was not the case, it was practicable, in many instances, for the exhibitors to present to the Jury some form of test which enabled them to come to a decision. But it was not possible to fire off Armstrong and Whitworth guns, nor discharge volleys of Enfield and Whitworth rifles. The Jury could therefore only give their decision by a judgment formed as to the adaptation of the weapon, from its form, power, and manufacture,.and from the report of trials and experiments made elsewhere.

There was an excellent opportunity of testing the quality and workmanship of the gun-carriages, and other wood-work connected with arms, exhibited by the British government, as the wood was not painted.

Several private English companies made a good display, as " The Birmingham Small-Arm Trade Association," and " The London Armoury Company of Bermondsey;" both of which firms manufacture Enfield rifles for government.

There was a large display, by the British government, of appliances connected with artillery, such as carriages, wheels, platforms, slides, sponges, rammers, handspikes, powder-cases. Specimens were also shown of cutting in wood, proving the capabilities of the hand-saw; each word—" Royal," " Carriage," " Department," being sawn out of a piece of wood by one continuous cut.

One of the most curious contrivances in the section was that of Colonel Boxer, R.A., called the " Parachute Light-Ball." It consists of two hemispheres, in one of which is packed a canvas parachute, and in the other the light-ball, with the cords which attach it to the parachute. These hemispheres are united by a layer of paper, sufficiently strong to bear the shock when fired from a mortar. A thread of quick-match is fixed within the shell, completely round the line of junction of the hemispheres, and communicates with a fuze in the upper half of the shell. The fuze is regulated to explode on the shell attaining its highest elevation. The quick-match, when fired, burns through the layer of paper that unites the hemispheres, and they consequently separate, the parachute is set free, and, from its form, opens immediately —thus checking the descent of the light-ball, which has also been ignited by the quick-match.

NAVAL ARCHITECTURE, INCLUDING SHIPS' TACKLE (Class XII.)—This portion of the Exhibition was divided into three sections; and certainly in no department of science or of material progress, was there such an advance, since 1851, as in this. Vessels of war have been constructed which can compete with forts in the heavy guns they carry, and in power of resistance. Gun-boats drawing a small draft of water, bearing heavy armaments, can penetrate shallows, and ascend rivers, which no gun-carrying ship could have attempted before 1851. Ships of enormous size, made of iron, are engaged in the commerce of nations (especially in the service of Great Britain), which, for fleetness and tonnage, were never before approached. So completely independent of winds and tides are the modern passenger-ships, that vessels sailing from the other hemisphere, or from the remotest east, or Australia, are expected to arrive to a day; and some of the regular packets between England and the United States are looked for to the hour.

Section A (Ships for purposes of War or Commerce) produced fifteen medals and thirteen honourable mentions for the United Kingdom; five medals and four mentions for foreign states; and none for the colonies.

Sections B and C.—Life-boats, Barges, Vessels for Amusement, and Ships' Tackle and Rigging.—Seventeen medals and thirteen honourable mentions were awarded to the United Kingdom; one mention to Victoria; and four mentions to foreign states. Four medals to the colonies, and thirteen to foreign states.

In 1851, there was but one steam line-of-battle ship, the *Napoléon:* now large fleets of such are possessed by England, France, Italy, and the United States of America. The paddle-steamers of 1851 have been supplanted by screw-propellers, or transformed into such by simple but ingenious contrivances.

In the Exhibition of 1862, models of line-of-battle ships and frigates were presented, showing the increased dimensions, and especially increased proportionate length of modern steamers, ensuring fleetness and general capacity.

The emperor of the French, to whom so many improvements in the art of war are to be attributed, was the originator of the iron gun-boats which were so formidable in the Crimean war, and also of the large armour-clad ships of war, which are now mainly relied upon for maritime aggression; and, to a considerable extent, for maritime defence. The cupola steam-ships, and rams, originated in the United States, constitute a more formidable defence than the armour-cased ships invented by the French emperor. These rams and cupolas draw little water: the former are extraordinary in their swift-sailing power, and both carry the most formidable armaments ever seen in the history of war.

Ships, available alike for aggressive and defensive purposes, are at present being constructed, built wholly of iron. Divided into compartments, they are less liable to wreck in case of striking, and cannot founder. Models of the *Warrior*, as a fast-going iron-clad, and of the *Northumberland*, a ship of more width, much greater length, more horse-power, and with iron casing to protect the armament, were exhibited by the Admiralty.

It cannot be denied that, notwithstanding the vast increase of resisting power of the most recently-produced plates, new artillery has been also fabricated, by which the thickest plates a ship would bear and float, and of the hardest metal, have been penetrated.

Probably the swiftest ships in the world, excepting some of the river steamers of the United States, are the *Connaught* and *Leinster*, belonging to the Dublin Steam-packet Company. The *Connaught* has performed 18·079 knots per hour; the *Leinster*, 17·797 knots per hour. The performances of all the mail steamers between Dublin and Holyhead, are such as to excite admiration and surprise at the vast progress in rapid sea-going within the last decade.

Under Section A, Captain Coles, R.N., received a medal for inventing revolving cupolas for protecting ships' guns, and enabling the vessel, without changing its position, to shift its direction of attack. This invention is not conceded to Captain Coles by the Americans, who lay claim to it, they being the first to bring it into actual use, and having had the earliest opportunity of testing its power in war. It has been found terribly efficient, but not wholly free from disadvantages. Captain Coles maintains, that however dexterous and wise the Americans in making the contrivance available, the invention is his; that he first proposed it, but received only neglect or repulse from the British Admiralty, whose slowness to adopt any new thing is proverbial. Notwithstanding the bad reputation of the British Admiralty in this respect, a medal was awarded to the Board, for improvements in ship-building since 1851.

One of the most important awards was to G. Rennie and Son, for a floating dock, executed for the Spanish government. The necessity of floating docks has become evident if the use of iron continue to be general in the construction of ships. The bottoms oxidise; weeds, and other injurious things, collect below the water-line, entailing expense for cleansing, and increase of the ratio of wear. As yet, no scientific remedy for this has been discovered.

Most of the medals awarded were for models of existing vessels, which, however skilfully and tastefully executed, hardly seem to be performances entitled to first-class rewards.

An ingenious steam-steering apparatus, exhibited by F. E. Sichles, of the United States, justly won a medal.

It is remarkable that the Russian government appeared to great advantage by their designs for ships of war, carrying away a first-class honour.

Sections B and C were united; the former comprising only boats, barges, and vessels of amusement; the latter, ships' tackle and rigging.

Since 1851, the improvement in the rig and tackle of ships, in the construction of boats and yachts, and their fitting-out, has kept pace with the improvements in naval architecture.

It was regretted that so few models were presented of boats, canoes, and their multitudinous diversities, as known on all coasts and in all great rivers. This was the more a disappointment as there exists no complete collection of such, or of their models, anywhere. Some of the boats, canoes, and haws, bagalas, junks, praos, baidars, gaélettes, lancions, smacks, yawls, &c., are of marvellously skilful construction, experience seeming to teach even the most savage people to adapt the form and quality of the vessel to the exigencies of their circumstances. Many, also, are beautifully constructed, carved with rude but laborious art, and manifesting great devotion, on the part of those peoples, to life on the water, and attachment to their vessels, which are often almost their homes. Such a display would have enriched the Exhibition, which presented rather the products borne over the great world of waters, than models of the peaceful media by which man and material are carried from one country to another.

Even the models of British boats were not near so numerous as those exhibited in 1851. A description of these would therefore be rather an essay upon the subject, than a memorial of the Exhibition.

Since 1851, wonderful improvement has been made in life-boats; so much so, that not a single model, in 1851, presented the qualities now deemed indispensable, and which are possessed by probably 150 of these useful vessels stationed around our coasts. Medals and honourable mentions were given for models, plans, and apparatus connected with this department. The specimens were sufficiently numerous and interesting to enable humane persons, and those whose business is upon the great waters, to satisfy curiosity, gratify their benevolent feelings, and afford instruction for efforts of practical utility.

The Royal Humane Society exhibited ice-ladders, drags, and other implements for rescuing persons from broken ice, lakes, rivers, ponds, &c. These specimens of apparatus for benevolent purposes received *very* honourable mention.

The Lords Commissioners of the Admiralty exhibited charts which have been useful in preventing shipwreck: 130,000 of these useful guides were issued, within the previous twelve months, from the Hydrographical Office of the Admiralty.

In the rigging of ships, the objects of inventors have been to economise labour, preserve life by rendering it comparatively unnecessary for men to go aloft, incurring risks of accident and drowning, and, in very hot or cold climates, of excessive exposure; and also to facilitate generally the sailing and anchorage of ships, and general health and convenience on board. Thus sails can now be reefed from the deck by very simple yet ingenious contrivances.

In the models were exhibited new arrangements of masts, depending upon increase of number, made necessary by the vastly enlarged structures of modern naval architecture. Thus many ships in the commercial marine have four masts, and the *Great Eastern*, six. Several of the new ships of war have four. Masts and yards are now very generally constructed of iron, and the yards not unfrequently of steel. Iron masts and yards were first introduced by the Dutch. By the adoption of this material, lightness, strength, and incombustibility are secured.

Iron has been substituted for wood in blocks, "dead eyes," "hearts," and other minor appliances. Galvanised iron now enters largely into the equipment of vessels both for war and commerce.

Mr. H. D. F. Cunningham invented a mode of reefing, of great facility and rapidity, which can be used in all weathers without checking the speed of the ship, or unduly taxing the strength of the crew. It is now in use in 3,000 ships belonging to the United Kingdom. Mr. Cunningham being a juror, could not receive an award; but his invention was universally admired and praised.

Among modern improvement in the minor arrangements—working, loading, and unloading of ships—the employment of steam-power is very remarkable, and has effected changes of great utility, such as, in 1851, could not have been expected. "Steam-winches" now receive and discharge cargo; and steam-power works the sails and yards, cables, and anchors, and is applied to other ponderous operations which formerly oppressed the crews.

Fewer sailors, in consequence of all these improvements and new appliances, can work a ship, and work it better, and with more safety to property and human life, and less of suffering from exposure to sun, and cold, and storm.

It is now allowed, by scientific men, that iron ships are less in danger from lightning than wooden ships, iron being a better conductor; but a new system of copper conductors arranges for still greater security, as iron has only one-sixth the conducting power of that metal.

Anchors, in 1851, were objects of interest to professional men: in 1862, the

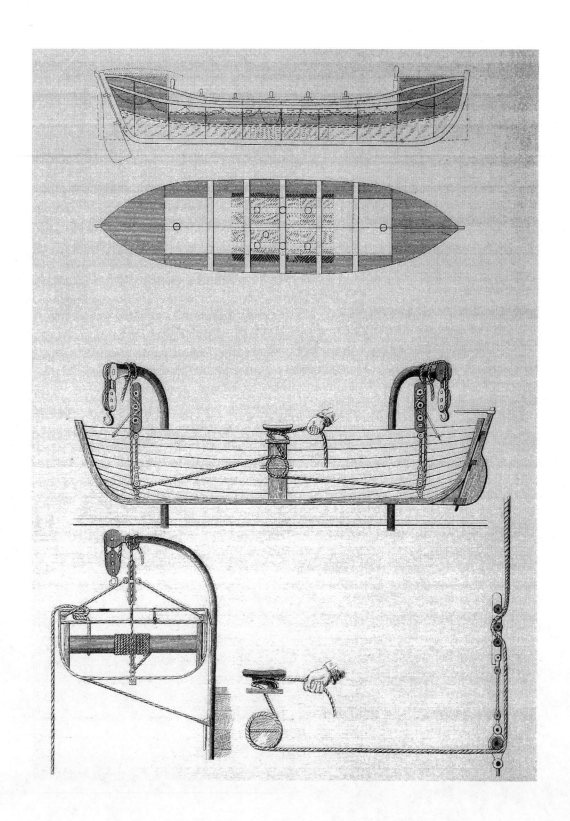

LIFE BOAT OF THE ROYAL NATIONAL LIFE-BOAT ASSOCIATION,
AND TACKLE FOR LOWERING BOATS.

improvements effected were considerable. Lighter implements of this nature are now used, with stronger hold, and surer operation.

Chain cables, their necessity, quality, and the impositions practised in their manufacture, have much occupied the minds not only of professional men, but of the public during the last decade. The legislature has been invoked to secure, under penalty, the quality supplied by manufacturers, and to compel the use of such cables in all sea-going ships. This single appliance will save many lives: deficient cables have proved a common cause of shipwreck.

Under Class XIX., ropes and cordage suitable to marine purposes, will come under consideration. It is here, therefore, only necessary to refer to the fact, that among the improved material for rigging and working ships, this department had some prominence.

Probably in no respect did the transition from wooden to iron ships involve so much practical difficulty as in connection with the mariner's compass. The material of which the new class of vessels is composed, caused deviations in the compass, as every one foresaw must be the case. There was, therefore, scope for ingenuity to prevent so dangerous a result. The magnitude of the danger was made plain by the actual loss of ships, attended by sacrifice of human life; and the inventions, devised as preventives, were failures. This subject would require too much space to give even a cursory view of the principles it involves, and their practical relations. It is enough for the present purpose to state, that a secure foundation for the theory and practice of compass management has, it is believed, been laid, so that iron ships may now be steered with impunity by the guidance of the needle. The display of compasses was ample, and made by nearly all European nations possessing a seaboard.

Buoys and beacons are important matters connected with shipping; and both, but much more especially buoys, have been very defective as to material, conspicuousness, and security in all parts of the United Kingdom, and still more so in, probably, every other country in the world. During the parliamentary session of 1861, a commission made a report to that effect; and this circumstance drew the attention of scientific men and mariners to the subject: so that short as the time was from the presenting of the report to parliament, until the Exhibition was held in 1862, there were various new forms of buoy invented, and contrivances for making it conspicuous, preventing it rolling, and securing it from being swept away by the violence of the waves. Mr. Herbert seems to have discovered a mode of mooring which prevents the rolling, and enables the buoy to be made a beacon. The general scheme of his manufacture and placing of buoys has met with the approval of the government and the shipping interest. Captain Peacock has proved a worthy rival of Mr. Herbert: his buoy is of iron, and very conspicuous, bearing a light; easily approached, and the lamp accessible for adjustment. These iron buoys are, however, sure to rust, and are liable to be mistaken for one particular class—red buoys: they are also more frequently "stove-in," but are more cheaply kept in repair.

A frequent cause of loss of life at sea, even in calm weather, has been the clumsy apparatus for lowering boats. It was difficult to cut, simultaneously, the rope at each end. Mr. Clifford discovered a mode of obviating this difficulty, and of lowering and "releasing" the boat at will, by the seamen waiting for the favourable moment to let the boat touch the sea gently and safely. Mr. Clifford deserved, and had awarded to him, a medal. Various gentlemen obtained honourable mention for inventions in this direction.

Logs, sounding machines, and nautical instruments, in much variety, were represented by novel specimens, deserving and procuring honourable mentions. The "Nautical Instrument Manufactory of St. Petersburg," sent specimens of sounding apparatus, by which whatever covers the bottom of the sea can be taken up. Ships' lights, and night telegraphs, were also well represented, especially from America. Captain Ward, R.N., received a medal for an efficient description of cork jacket.

PHILOSOPHICAL INSTRUMENTS.—This department of the Exhibition is, perhaps, of less general interest than many others; but its importance is equalled by few. We shall chiefly select such objects as may most familiarly be known in their uses, and are of general application.

Electrical Instruments, both for research and practical use, were exceedingly numerous, especially those devoted to telegraphic purposes. In a former page an account has been given of many ancient modes of communicating intelligence to a distance, all of which have long gone out of use—such as fires, or beacons, on hill-tops, &c. Within the present century, the chief means used were an upright post fixed at a great elevation; and on the post, arms, moving on pins, were so arranged that they could be placed at right angles to the perpendicular post, either singly or in combination. By a pre-arranged code, these arms spelt words, and a distant observer read them by aid of a telescope. By stations placed at a distance of a few miles apart, intelligence was conveyed between the most distant places. Of a similar nature is the use of flags at sea, by means of which ships "speak" with each other, and naval signals are conveyed. But all such methods are useless in foggy weather; and this often occurs at the very moment that a message of great importance has to be conveyed. The electric telegraph has, however, supplied a complete and (with rare exceptions) a constant means of communication. Its action depends on the fact, that two metals and a liquid, properly arranged—as, for example, a piece of zinc and silver in water containing an acid—will afford an electric current. The current, again, will traverse a metallic wire to any distance, at a speed certainly exceeding 5,000 miles per second. The last element in this method is the power which such a current has of acting on a magnetised body—as, for example, the needle of the mariner's compass; for if the current be passed over the magnetic needle, it will deflect or turn it right or left, according to the direction of the current. For example, if the electricity passes from north to south, the needle turns to the right; and, *vice versâ*, it will move to the left if the current pass from south to north. By an ingenious contrivance called a commutator, the direction of the current can be changed very rapidly, and then the needle can be simultaneously deflected either way with the same rapidity. It is on this principle that the *needle telegraph* is constructed, an instrument mostly employed in this country for telegraphic purposes. In America a different system is used, Morse's instrument being employed; as it is also largely done on the continent. By this plan the message is conveyed by the electric current producing dots and dashes on prepared paper or cloth, the lengths and intervals of these forming an alphabetical code of signals. One of the advantages of this plan is, that the message is fixed, and can always be read ; indeed, it may be recorded in the absence of an attendant, which could not be done with the needle telegraph, for that requires the eye to read it as it is spelt. By other instruments, the *sound*, produced by electro-magnets, is equally available as a means of telegraphic communication.* Other methods we shall notice as we proceed.

Amongst numerous exhibitors of telegraphic arrangements, we may select the following for a short description of their plans :—Mr. Allan, of the Adelphi, London, has long been identified with such subjects, and has also invented most ingenious instruments for the purpose of converting electricity into a moving power. One of these engines he exhibited ; and it depends for its action on the attractive power of a series of magnets placed vertically, exerted on circular plates of soft iron. These act successively on rods attached to a crank, and ·so the rectilinear is converted into a circular motion. As far as we have seen, this is the most successful attempt yet made in applied electro-dynamics.

His code and cable, especially adapted for Atlantic telegraphy, were so highly thought of by the Jury of this Class as to have induced them to give Mr. Allan a prize medal. His system, although resembling in part that just described as Morse's, differs from that in the use of the dot alene. At the signalling extremity of a telegraphic line, whether on land or submarine, he uses the following method :—A ribbon of paper has dots punched into it by a machine ; and on this prepared message, when passed into the apparatus for transmission, and the automatic action once commenced, each single punch-hole, as it passes over the tooth of a small rotating spur-wheel, permits of electrical contact being made with the sending machine, and of thereby inducing a perfectly synchronous movement at the receiving extremity of the telegraphic wire (no matter how distant), and also of causing a puncture in the ribbon of the receiving instrument through the automatic apparatus there. Thus, whilst a hole ready exists on the paper at the *sending* instrument, an exactly similar hole or emboss is made simultaneously on the paper of the receiving instrument at the distant station. The punching of the message for the sending instrument is effected by an ingenious contrivance called a "Composing Machine," of so simple a construction that any one may use it with half-an-hour's instruction. We regret that our limited space forbids a description in detail of this part of the arrangement. Mr. Allan claims for this instrument its great certainty, accuracy, speed, and simplicity of action ; whilst it is also possible, by the same sending instrument, to send messages simultaneously to several stations—a circumstance of extreme value and advantage in reporting political and general intelligence for the newspapers.

Submarine telegraphy has of late years acquired great interest in all circles, more especially owing to the two unsuccessful attempts to lay a cable across the Atlantic. The following is a short description of the cable proposed by Mr. Allan for the purpose ; but which, despite its valuable qualities, and the high recommendations given it, was

---

* For a complete description of the philosophy and practice of electric telegraphy, the *Circle of the Sciences,* brought out by the publishers of this work, may be consulted.

not adopted in the recent (1865) attempt to connect Ireland and America electrically. Before describing this cable, however, it may be desirable to state that the ordinary submarine cable consists chiefly of three parts, viz.—1. The internal copper wires that carry the electric current. 2. The non-conducting material—gutta-percha or india-rubber—which insulates those wires; or, in other words, which prevents the dispersion or loss of the electric current: and, last, is the external covering of coarse iron wire, intended as a protection to the cable from injury by rubbing on rocks, or by vessels raising it by the anchor, as has sometimes happened with cables laid across the English Channel. It need scarcely be stated that such a cable is necessarily heavy: those laid between Dover and Calais weighed seven tons to each mile; whilst the Atlantic Telegraph Cable, an attempt to lay which was made in July, 1865, weighed nearly two tons per mile. The latter contained seven fine copper wires, twisted together, as the conducting medium.

Mr. Allan adopts a single solid copper wire, of the best possible softness and quality. This wire he surrounds and covers by means of a spiral of thin steel wires—a complete novelty in all respects. This forms not only the core, but tends to give resisting strength to the arrangement. The insulation of the core is effected by coating it with either india-rubber or gutta-percha; preferring, however, the latter material. The insulated core is then covered with hemp saturated with marine paint, and the deep-sea cable is complete.

On testing such a cable, it was found that, with a weight equal to 7,500 fathoms of itself, it did not elongate more than 1 per cent.; and, according to the government report, the steel wires not only afforded increased security, but greatly additional conducting power. The weight, per nautical mile, is thirteen hundred-weight; specific gravity, 1·7: in water it will bear nine miles of its own weight, and not elongate more than at the rate of one foot in every 100, and even then without danger of breaking.

Of late years, house or private telegraphy has greatly extended; and it is now a common occurrence to find electric wires not only under our feet, but over our heads, reaching from roof to roof between two distant stations—perhaps the counting-house and factory of a large firm, situated in different parts of town. The Universal Private Telegraph Company exhibited the instruments they employ for sending messages; and these were invented by Professor Wheatstone, to whom the world is indebted not only as the pioneer of telegraphy, but as one who has been the chief contributor to its development and success.

The Magneto-Alphabetic Telegraph, for private or railway use, employed and supplied by the Company, is illustrated in the annexed engravings, copied, by permission, from the original. It consists of two instruments—the communicator and indicator; the former sending, and the latter receiving the message. On each, the letters of the alphabet and numerals are engraved, in the form of a disc. A needle, actuated by an electro-magnet, spells the word, letter by letter, simultaneously on both communicator and indicator as the message is sent; the electricity, induced by magnetism, being employed so as to save the necessity of chemicals, &c., required in the voltaic battery. The wires between the two stations are made into a kind of rope; and, so arranged, they may be distributed, in individual pairs, to any number of separate telegraphic districts or houses. This prevents the necessity of raising fresh wires as each new customer requires the use of the arrangement.

No. 1.—The Communicator

No. 2.—The Indicator.

Round the discs of each instrument are as many keys—like those of the concertina—as there are letters and numerals; and by pressing down that corresponding to the letter of the word being spelt on the communicator, the same letter is indicated to the attendant at the distant station by the indicator. The instruments, &c., are charged for by an annual rental; and the system is so simple and complete that it may actually be used in the house, between the parlour and kitchen, in place of the bell; having also the additional advantage of at once conveying the message intended to be communicated.

The great interest now attached to electric telegraphy, will form an apology for the extent of space here devoted to the consideration of such matters, as illustrated in the Exhibition of 1862. Amongst numerous other exhibitors of electric invention, we may mention Mr. Brett's submarine cables, and Roman Type-printing Telegraph; and, by the latter, the message is printed in bold type as it is sent: telegraphic instruments, cables, &c., by the British and Irish Magnetic Telegraph Company; Clark's improved cables; Cheyne and Moseley's electric check on signal-men and engine-drivers; Glass, Elliot, and Co.'s submarine cables—the firm who prepared the last Atlantic telegraph and many other cables; W. S. Henley's magnets, magnetic instruments, &c.—another name identified with electro-telegraphy; Reid, Brothers, who exhibited various telegraphic materials; Siemens, Halske, and Co., whose telegraphic instruments created great interest, some being kept in action; the Submarine Electric Telegraphic Company; Varley's telegraphic apparatus, insulators, electrometer, &c.; C. V. Walker, Esq., the telegraphic manager of the South-Eastern line, exhibited his system of train-signals; Tyer's train-signalling telegraphs, for preventing accidents by collisions, &c. The Gutta-Percha Company, who have had committed to their charge the insulation and manufacture of several submarine cables, also exhibited interesting specimens.

It will be unnecessary to enter into any description of instruments intended solely for the use of the philosopher in each branch of science. There were numerous, and, in some cases, highly elaborate pieces of work. Amongst these we may class astronomical instruments, microscopes, telescopes, induction coils for obtaining intense electricity from coils of insulated copper wire by the agency of the voltaic battery: measuring and dividing-instruments, &c., &c. We shall rather take a general view of such objects amongst these philosophical productions as may be of general interest, selecting the following.

A singular discovery has been recently made, in the fact, that the human breath, when received on a suitable surface, produces crystalline appearances, which, when viewed by the microscope, may be taken as indications of health or disease; and illustrations of these were found in this Class. Numerous interesting objects for the microscope were also shown; amongst the most important of which, were specimens of blood-globules. To explain the use of them, it may be remarked, that each species of animal has a distinctive globule, which, if placed under the microscope, is as readily indicative of its source as the face of a man indicates his difference from another. It is thus perfectly easy to find out the nature of blood-spots on the dress of a supposed murderer, and to state at once whether they be those of the human species or of other animals. This curious discovery has been of incalculable advantage in legal inquiries; and, on more than one occasion, has tended to ensure the conviction of the criminal. In another case, a gentleman was completely cleared of a foul charge, made by a woman who, ignorant of these facts, had sprinkled sheep's blood, to give the idea of violence having been offered her. This is one of the most striking instances of the depth of research involved in modern scientific investigation.

Bestall's Polariscope, exhibited in this Class, is a most simple and effective apparatus for exhibiting the beautiful phenomena of polarised light; and it places in the hand of even a child, illustrations of some of the most beautiful of optical phenomena. Mr. Darker, of Lambeth, exhibited some interesting illustrations of the action of polarised light on crystalline bodies.

Considerable general interest has been excited in meteorological subjects, owing to the numerous ascents of Mr. Glaisher, and meteorological instruments were accordingly well illustrated in the Exhibition. Messrs. Negretti and Zambra, who have supplied Mr. Glaisher with his instruments, and received so many prizes for their inventions, were amongst the leading exhibitors. They are the inventors of excellent minimum and maximum thermometers for self-registration of the temperature. The British Association, at the Kew Observatory, where standard barometers, thermometers, &c., are tested, also exhibited in this department. Dr. Bagot, of Dublin, sent a Nephelescope, for viewing the upper strata of the clouds.

Mr. Warren De La Rue, who has done so much for photography, as applied to astronomy, furnished some beautiful photographs of the eclipse of 1861, which deservedly attracted great attention. By this gentleman's labours we can now

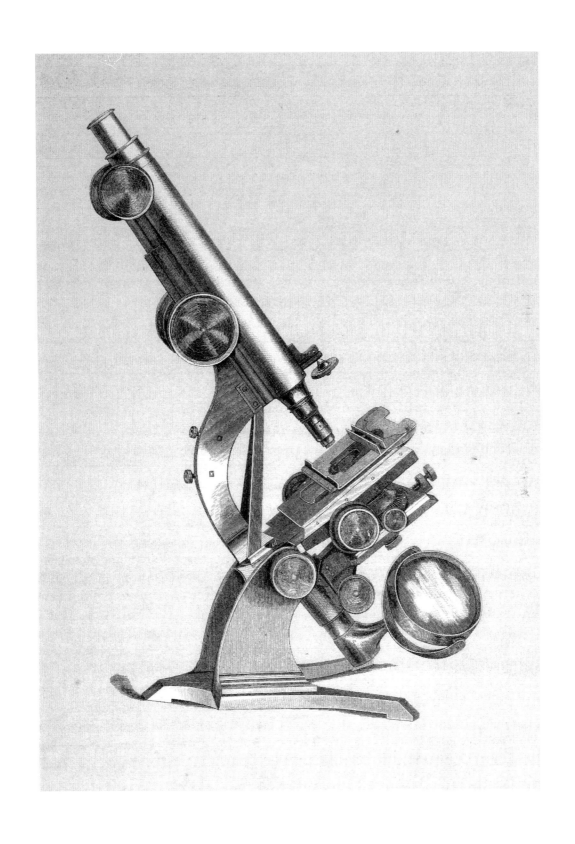

PILLISCHER'S IMPROVED COMPOUND MICROSCOPE.

HOLMES MAGNETIC-LIGHT MACHINE.

EXHIBITED IN THE INTERNATIONAL EXHIBITION 1862

IMPROVED ANTI VIBRATION STEERING COMPASS FOR STEAMERS.

study the face or disc of the moon, on paper, with a far greater sense of accuracy of delineation than an ordinary engraved map of the world. The moon has been made to delineate herself so completely by the aid of photography, that every peak, mountain, and valley, with all the beautiful effect of light and shadow, may be perfectly studied. Messrs. Chance, of Birmingham, who are largely engaged in the manufacture of glass, and have supplied that material to the "Crystal Palaces" which have been erected, exhibited some of their dioptric sea-lights and lanterns. Here it may not be out of place to mention Holmes' Electric Light Apparatus, which was exhibited in the Western Annexe, and which, in broad sunshine, gave a brilliant and overpowering light. The inventor does not employ the voltaic battery; but by the revolution of numerous permanent magnets opposite to iron cores, surrounded with covered copper wire, obtains an immense quantity of induced electricity, which, at two terminals or poles of charcoal, affords a light admirably adapted for lighthouse purposes. His instrument was long used at the South Foreland Lighthouse, where its brilliancy was so great as to permit of the light being distinctly visible at the opposite French coast. The electric light has the advantage of possessing a penetrating power, which is of incalculable value during fogs, when other lights are useless. An illustration, on steel, of Mr. Holmes' invention, is given with this work. Lighthouse apparatus was also exhibited by Messrs. Wilkins, of Long Acre.

Amongst instruments for taking specific gravity, weight, &c., may be mentioned those exhibited by Messrs. De Grave, Short, and Fanner; and balances by Ladd and Oertling, for chemical, assay, and other purposes; hydrometers, saccharometers, &c. A fine equatorial instrument for observatory use (achromatic), and having an aperture of twelve inches, was exhibited by Mr. Grubb, of Dublin; ship and azimuth compasses, by Messrs. Dent, of the Strand; surveying instruments, by Elliot, Brothers, also of the Strand. There were several useful modifications of the smaller class of instruments used for taking observations at sea, as sextants, compasses, &c. The International Decimal Association exhibited illustrations of a decimal and metric system for all nations—a scheme which, if successfully carried out, would afford incalculable advantages to commerce, by the simplification of all kinds of calculations; and which, it is to be hoped, will be eventually adopted in this country, as it has long been in France.

Amongst scientific curiosities and varieties, may be named Pulvermacher's Galvano-Piline, for producing a constant but insensible voltaic current for medical purposes; Sugg's Photometer, and apparatus for determining the illuminating power, specific gravity, &c., of coal-gas; Armstrong's (Sir W.) Hydro-Electric Machine, for obtaining frictional electricity from water, or rather steam; an ebonite or india-rubber Electric Machine, exhibited by Messrs. S. W. Silver and Co., who are largely engaged in india-rubber manufactures at Silverton, near Bow; a machine for drawing ellipses and other oval curves, by Mr. Hall, of Clerkenwell; Peters' machine for microscopical writing, exhibited by the Microscopical Society of London; tables calculated and stereoglyphed by the Swedish Calculating Machine, and exhibited by the Registrar-General; models of crystals in glass, by Professor J. Tennant, of the Strand, &c., &c.

2 Q

In the Foreign Department, Class XIII. was well sustained; but we can only spare a brief space for a general *résumé* of the numerous, interesting, and useful matters which were exhibited in connection with philosophical instruments, and allied objects.

As a specimen of native workmanship from India, Sir Proby Cautley exhibited a Troughton's improved level and prismatic compass. Electrical apparatus, electric clocks, batteries, telegraph instruments, and other philosophical arrangements, were sent by firms in Belgium, resident at Liège, Brussels, Ghent, &c.; as were also similar productions from Denmark. France has long been noted for the excellence of its philosophical instruments; and French makers were well represented in all variety of electrical, optical, telegraphic, and other instruments. Without making invidious distinctions, where excellence was so generally shown, we may particularise the various instruments exhibited by M. Breguet, in horology, electricity, &c.; the optical apparatus of M. Duboscq, also, of Paris, who has done so much in the practical extension of optical science; balances of aluminium, which have the advantage of resisting the action of many chemical vapours, liquids, &c., exhibited by Collot, Brothers, of Paris; a safety-lamp and gazoscope, both for use in mines, by M. Chuard, of Paris; a magneto-electric machine for producing the electric light, by Berlioz and Co., of Paris; with other apparatus and instruments, as opera-glasses, mathematical instruments, telegraphic apparatus, balances, thermometers, microscopes, &c., too numerous to detail. Amongst similar articles sent from Austria, we may notice the optical instruments of Voigtlander and Son, of Vienna, who have gained much renown in that department of scientific instrument manufacture. Prussia was chiefly represented by firms resident at Berlin, in all departments of scientific instruments. From Italy, a large telescopic lens, and a reflector, with numerous and ingenious astronomical and optical instruments, were exhibited by Professor Amici, of Florence; and the University of Pavia made a very interesting contribution in various electrical apparatus once used by the celebrated Volta, who laid the foundation of that branch of electrical science generally called after him. Switzerland exhibited several optical, telegraphic, mathematical, engineering, surveying, and similar instruments. The United States was represented by one exhibitor only in this Class.

CHAPTER VIII.

CLASS XIV.—PHOTOGRAPHIC APPARATUS AND PHOTOGRAPHY.   CLASS XV.—HOROLOGICAL INSTRUMENTS.   CLASS XVI.—MUSICAL INSTRUMENTS.   CLASS XVII.—SURGICAL INSTRUMENTS AND APPLIANCES.

WE are quite at a loss to account for the reason why, at least, the first Class (XIV.), mentioned above, was not included in that of " Philosophical Instruments, and processes dependent upon their uses," by the Commissioners of the Exhibition; but in this, as in many analogous cases, we must bow to a decision which it is certainly too late to mend; although we must remind our readers that numerous photographic apparatus are actually included in the preceding Class, especially lenses, so important to the photographer.

Comparatively, but few years have elapsed since the first practical branch of photography was made public. It was that of the Daguerreotype, by means of which views, likenesses, &c., were taken on silver plates, or copper plates with a silver surface. The silver was made sensitive, in that process, by the action of iodine in vapour, and the image was developed by the vapour of mercury. Many objections existed against this process, which we cannot here stop even to point out. Suffice it to say, that by the careful investigations and experiments of numerous scientific and practical men, the *collodion* process was discovered; and this may now be considered as the only one followed in the present method of taking all kinds of photographic pictures.

A short description, or rather outline of the process, may assist our readers to comprehend the uses of the instruments, &c., exhibited in this Class. Collodion is made by dissolving gun-cotton in ether, and adding to it solutions of iodine, bromine, or their salts. When used, the collodion is poured on to a clean glass plate, so as to leave an exceedingly thin film; and the glass, thus coated on one side, is dipped into a bath containing nitrate of silver in solution. By this means a film of a salt of silver is formed on the collodion surface, that is exceedingly sensitive to the action of light, and which accordingly receives in the camera an exact impression of the lights and shades of any object reflecting light through the lens. On removing the glass into a dark room no image is visible; but on pouring a solution of a salt of iron and other substances on to it, the image is developed—that is, it becomes visible to the eye. The next process is that of fixing it, which is done either by a solution of hyposulphite of sodium, or cyanide of potassium, either of which removes the silver salt that has not been acted on by light; leaves that which has been so acted on untouched, and so produces an accurate picture of the object on glass. A *negative* picture is that which has its lights and shades the reverse of nature; and it is from these that all *paper* positives, such as *cartes de visite*, &c., are printed. A positive picture is that in which the lights and shades are the same as those of nature. This class of pictures on glass used to be those chiefly taken, until the negatives were improved, and the present method of printing them positively on paper was brought to perfection. *Stereoscopic* pictures are those in which two views are taken, at an angle equal to that of the difference at which *each* eye sees an object. Accordingly, when they are viewed through the lenses of a stereoscope, the two images overlap each other, and produce all the appearance of real solidity. With these preliminary remarks we may proceed to notice the novelties exhibited, rather than the ordinary landscapes, likenesses, &c., with which every photographic studio now makes us so familiar. The Amateur Photographic Association exhibited various photographs by members of the society. Mr. Beard, a name identified with the first public photographic, or rather Daguerreotype attempts, contributed coloured and plain photographs; and here we must, at the same time, mention Mr. W. H. Fox Talbot, to whom the art of photography is so much indebted, as a scientific and practical man, and who exhibited engravings produced solely by the action of light. M. Paul Pretsch, formerly of Vienna, also contributed specimens of engravings produced entirely by the action of light. It has been long a desideratum to employ photography to the engraver's art; and a short description of M. Pretsch's process may prove interesting, as a successful instance of the kind. A glass plate is carefully coated with a solution of gelatine, in which iodide of potassium, bichromate of potass, and nitrate of silver, have, in certain proportions, been dissolved. When dry, an engraving or photograph to be copied, is placed face downwards on this prepared plate, and exposed for a day or two to the action of day or sun-light. On removing the plate, and dipping it into water containing a little common salt, those portions —corresponding to the dark part of the copy—that have been unacted on by the light, swell up, leaving those which have been acted on quite untouched; and, being hardened, they do not rise beyond their previous position. Thus a kind of engraved glue-plate is produced. A copy of this is then taken in gutta-percha, or any other suitable mould; and on this being blackleaded and exposed to the usual electrotyping process, an accurate engraving is produced, from which a considerable number of copies may be printed by the ordinary method of copper-plate printing. Thus an engraved plate is produced by light and electricity, without any artistic aid on the part of man whatever.

The London Stereoscopic Company exhibited many interesting views, stereoscopic likenesses, &c.; some taken instantaneously. And here we may mention that photography has made such rapid strides, that we are now enabled to take views in far less than a second of time. Thus a horse may be photographed whilst galloping; the very foam of the sea may be photographically fixed on paper at the instant it is formed; and still more wonderful is the fact, that a cannon-ball may be accurately photographed during its passage from the muzzle of the cannon to the target. The scientific reader is well aware of a still more astonishing fact, that the heavenly bodies have had their likenesses taken, despite their rapid speed through space. In the preceding chapter we have mentioned some excellent lunar photographs, taken by Mr. Warren De La Rue, as well as others, representing the phenomena of a solar eclipse, accurately, at the moment of their occurrence. It should here be named that the publishers of this work are indebted to the London Stereoscopic Company for the originals of many of the engravings illustrating it, which were taken during the time the Exhibition was open.

A considerable difficulty long existed, in the fact that, according to the usual collodion process, the plate should be used shortly, or rather immediately, after its preparation. To obviate this, several processes have been invented, which have been denominated " wet," " dry," " Fothergill," &c., according to the method adopted. In all these the photographer is enabled to prepare his plates a considerable time beforehand, without diminishing the sensitive state of the plate, or exposing it in the camera. Specimens of landscape views, taken by these means, were exhibited by several professional and amateur photographers. Photography has lately been largely used to illustrate works, in place of steel, copper, and wood engravings; and this method was also plentifully illustrated in this department. Coloured, enlarged, microscopic, and other photographs, were numerously exhibited.

Amongst other photographic exhibitors not already named, we may instance the productions of Mr. Fenton, Mr. Vernon Heath, and Mr. Mayall, who have earned the highest reputation in the practice of photography. Amongst the curiosities of this art, the methods of copying maps, writings, &c., adopted by Colonel Sir Henry James, in connection with the Ordnance Survey, were well worthy of inspection, as being most valuable in producing cheap copies, engraved on zinc, of such objects for sale. We regret that our space forbids a full description of this ingenious process.

M. Joubert exhibited some beautiful photographs burnt into glass, and, therefore, quite imperishable. His process promises to come largely into use for ornamentation, or for door-plates, table-plates, and other purposes. A curious and interesting use of the art was seen in the photographs taken during, and illustrating, the eruption of Mount Vesuvius, in 1861-'62. Photographs enlarged to the size of life, and others reduced to extreme microscopic dimensions, were numerous; and, without mentioning individuals, we may state that all the leading London, and numerous provincial firms, did ample justice to their able pursuit of the art. Similarly, the manufacturers of photographic apparatus, such as lenses, cameras, stands, collodion, and other articles in constant request, were fully represented.

The government of India contributed a large collection of photographs of individuals of the different native tribes, interesting alike to cursory examination and the student of ethnology. Amongst specimens sent from Belgium, were some by M. Fierlants, of Brussels, representing the master-pieces and monuments of Belgium, executed by order of the government of that country. M. Dupont, of Antwerp, contributed others, illustrating " The Antwerp School," in respect to portraits. From Brazil were photographs of the imperial family, and views of the botanic gardens of Rio Janeiro. Denmark sent photographs from the works of the celebrated sculptor Thorwaldsen. France was almost as extensively represented as our own country, both in respect to photographic productions and apparatus. Austria; Prussia; Saxony; Italy; Holland;—whence were sent photographs of the etchings of Rembrandt and others: Norway, with specimens illustrating Norwegian dress and scenery: Rome, affording interesting views of paintings, ancient and modern sculpture, &c.: Russia, Switzerland, and the United States (see p. 93)—all were, more or less, represented in this Class.

HOROLOGICAL INSTRUMENTS (Class XV.)—In our earlier pages (see pp. 17, 29) a general description has been given of some of the largest clocks in the Exhibition—as those of Messrs. Dent, and Mr. Benson's. It may not be out of place to make a few remarks here on the general construction of clocks, watches, &c. Their action depends on the regulated movement of either a weight or spring—the former method being commonly employed in house and observatory clocks; and the spring is used in some kinds of clocks, such as eight-day, &c., watches, and chronometers. The weight and main-spring are only useful as sources of power; and, if left to themselves, they would speedily cause the hands to revolve over the face, and the clock would be useless as a measurer of time. To regulate, therefore, the speed of the hands, either the pendulum or balance-wheel is employed. The pendulum acts on the principle of gravitation; that is, a body, if let fall towards the earth, will, by virtue of the gravitating or attracting force of our globe, pass through a definite space in a certain period—e.g., $16\frac{1}{3}$ feet in a second of time in our latitude. And if a pendulum be

made of a length a little exceeding thirty-nine inches, it will take just one second of
time to make a complete oscillation. Such a pendulum, however, if working at the
equator, would move slower, because the earth's surface is then at a greater distance
from its centre than in London, and hence the attraction of gravitation is less;
whilst, at the poles, the same pendulum would move faster, because there the
surface and centre are thirteen miles nearer to each other than they are at the
equator. It hence follows that pendulums must be made of different lengths in
various latitudes, to beat exactly a second of time. The pendulum, when it oscillates
in a clock, therefore, both retards and regulates the falling of the clock-weights; and
by a proper train of wheels between each and the hands, an accurate measure of
time may thus be constructed. A watch and spring-clock have the same train of
wheels; but their motive and regulating power are different. The main-spring is
fixed in a barrel, and from this to the fusee is a chain, which is alternately wound
on both. When the watch is wound up the chain is on the fusee, and the elastic
force of the spring inside the barrel, gradually winds the chain from the fusee on
to the barrel. On this being effected, the watch stops, because all the motive force is
exhausted. In watches the main-spring is comparatively small, and the chain short;
hence they generally "go" only about thirty hours: but in some clocks both are
made longer, and hence they only require winding once a week, or even during
longer periods. The regulating power of the watch, &c., is a small spring, acting on
a wheel; and the oscillations of this, caused by the fine wheel, produce a regulating
power as effective as the pendulum of a clock.

A chronometer differs materially in the details, although not in the principles of
its construction. Extreme accuracy is essential; and hence the utmost care is required in the execution of the workmanship. It is a common error to suppose that
the value of a chronometer depends on its *never* varying. On the contrary, the best
chronometers do so, considerably, in an astronomical point of view. But their
excellence rests in the fact that they do so *regularly*. Thus if it be known that a
chronometer loses or gains *exactly* a second per day, allowance is easily made for this
clock-error. This loss or gain is called the *rate* of the chronometer, and it is carefully ascertained at some observatory before being sent to sea. In England, Greenwich Observatory is chosen for this purpose. The uses of a chronometer are to find
the *longitude* at sea, east or west of Greenwich—so far as British sailors are concerned:
and this is thus found. The earth takes twenty-four hours in rotating on its axis;
and supposing its surface to be divided into 360 parts called degrees, it follows that
fifteen of these must pass the sun in each hour of time. Now fifteen degrees of space
must, therefore, be equal to one hour, or sixty minutes, of time; hence if a ship be
sailing on the west coast of Ireland, which is ten degrees west of Greenwich, it
follows that noon will happen there about forty minutes *later* than at Greenwich—
ten degrees of space being equal to forty minutes of time. If, therefore, the captain
of the ship takes an observation, and finds it twenty minutes past eleven o'clock,
he will, on looking at his chronometer, find that it will be noon, Greenwich time.
There is hence a difference, between his and Greenwich time, of forty minutes, he
being that much too slow by the sun. This being converted into space, gives his

longitude ten degrees west of Greenwich—four minutes of time corresponding to a degree of space, and being equivalent to the ratio of 15° to an hour of time. If he had been travelling to the *east* of Greenwich, then his time at noon would have been shown by the chronometer as twenty minutes to one o'clock, for he would be forty minutes *faster* than Greenwich. By this means, combined with observations of the moon, Jupiter's satellites, &c., a commander may find his place at sea on the earth's surface with as much accuracy as a railway traveller traces the stations as he is travelling on his journey.

From this short explanation, our readers will discover the necessity of the utmost anxiety in the workmanship of chronometers, and will still further understand the keen competition which subsists between the makers of these valuable instruments, so many of which were exhibited in 1862.

Amongst the numerous exhibitors of horological instruments, watches and chronometers formed the chief articles of display. The names of many will be familiar, as those of Bennett, Benson, Barraud and Lund, Dent, Frodsham, Losada, Parkinson and Frodsham, and numerous others. Timepieces of every kind were exhibited, from the simple workmen's watches, to the most beautifully finished, jewelled, and even microscopic form of those articles. The various details of watch-manufacture were fully represented, as springs, escapements, &c.; and it may be here stated, that the value of workmanship in respect to springs for watches, forms so great an item, that a pound of steel, worth a few pence, is converted, by the watch-spring maker, into articles worth several hundred pounds. Amongst the curiosities of clock-work, were the trumpeter and cuckoo clocks of Messrs. Camerer, Kuss, and Co., of Bloomsbury; an astronomical clock, impelled by gravitation, and which requires no oil to the escapement, exhibited by Dr. Clark, of Finmere; silent clocks, by Captain H. B. Coathupe, of Kensington; a clock showing time and longitude at important places, by Mr. C. W. Davies, of Notting-hill; electro-magnetic clocks, in which the force of electro-magnetic attraction takes the place of gravitation; a "regulator," by Mr. Hawleys, of High Holborn, requiring to be wound once in twelve months; "clocks" working by the resistance of the air in tubes of small bore; a chime clock, with fifty changes, by Mr. Quaife, of Hawkhurst, Kent; a clock by Tanner and Sons, of Lewes, affording a perpetual register of the day, week, and month; Black Forest clocks, with English movements, &c., &c. Tools, horological instruments, &c., were sent by the committee of exhibitors of Prescott. From France, the chief contributors were residents of Paris and Besançon; watches being the most numerous articles. Chronometers, ornamental timepieces, materials, tools, &c., however, were well represented; and some, of great elegance, were much admired. These objects give full scope to French taste, and have been always a favourite production of the artists of that country. Austria was represented by contributions from Pesth, Vienna, &c. Berlin similarly represented Prussia. Dutch clocks, from the Black Forest, were sent from Wirtemberg. Switzerland has long been noted for the production of horological instruments; and it took one of the foremost positions in the Exhibition in this respect. The contributions of separate parts of watches, tools, &c., were both very minute in character, and large in number, and comprised cases, screw-plates, screws, machines for cutting and rounding the teeth of wheels, springs, keys—in fact, every minutiæ of the watch and its settings. As a practical illustration of the construction and manufacture of watches, the Swiss department was most valuable, and unequalled by any other in the Exhibition.

MUSICAL INSTRUMENTS (Class XVI.)—This class naturally attracted much attention in the Exhibition: in fact, in many cases it was over-attractive for the studious visitor; because many a young lady, fresh from school and music-lessons, was anxious to show her prowess in pianoforte playing. As these instruments abounded in most parts of the building, music, either with or without charm, was more than abundantly supplied. In many cases performers were engaged to show the peculiar qualities of the instruments, so far as the organs and pianofortes were concerned; and the performances on the grand organs had a thrilling effect, at times, on the multitude of hearers attracted to them.

Musical instruments are chiefly of two kinds—namely, stringed, as the harp, pianoforte, violin, guitar, &c.; and those in which a current of air of different lengths is employed. Of this kind are organs, flutes, wind-instruments generally, as the cornopean, horn, &c. The concertina and harmonium take a mid-place, for in them the vibrations of metallic tongues, set in action by a current of air, are the cause of sound. In stringed instruments the sound is regulated by the length of the wires; the shorter producing shrill, and the longer wires the bass notes. The simple inspection of a piano or harp will illustrate this. In the violin the performer shortens the length of the strings at will, by pressing them by his fingers, and hence he makes his notes; whilst, on the piano, they are ready-made for him. The violin-player has the advantage of producing a far greater number, and, therefore, a more pleasing variety of sounds than can be obtained from either the harp or piano. In the organ, similarly, the length of each column of air is regulated by the length of the pipes; whilst, on the cornopean and other wind-instruments, the player has a similar advantage to that of the violin performer, in being able to make his notes by lengthening or shortening the column of air at will. An important part of the harp, pianoforte, violin, &c., is the sounding-board, by which the sound is largely diffused in the surrounding air. The pedals of the harp and pianoforte, and the stops of air-organs, modulate the sound by either lessening or permitting the full flow of the sound produced by the instrument. By the *soft* pedal we diminish the sound produced by the vibration of the strings; whilst the loud pedal, removing the hammers from the strings, allows them full power to act on the surrounding air. We may add that air is absolutely necessary to convey sound to the ear, as in an air-pump vacuum no sound is conveyed. Hence the varying effect of the atmosphere on the sound of church-bells heard at a distance. It is by the air receiving and propagating waves of sound to our ear, that we are enabled to exercise the faculty of hearing the vibration of musical instruments, and all other sounds whatever.

A description has already been given, at page 39, of one of the large organs, which was exhibited by Messrs. Foster and Andrews, of Hull; and we need not here extend on that subject, except so far as to state, that the large organ-builders, as Messrs. Bevington and Sons, Messrs. Walker, Willis, and others, fully maintained their high character in this manufacture. Pianoforte manufactures were also largely represented; and the instruments of Messrs. Broadwood, Collard and Collard, Chappell, Cadby, and many others, whose names are familiar to all, were found amongst the exhibitors of high-class instruments. Skeleton pianos, and the materials, individual parts, and tools used in their construction, were abundantly illustrated by other makers. Amongst exhibitors of wind and military instruments, were Mr. Distin, Mr. Chappell, Rudall Rose and Co.; M. Köhler, Metzeler and Co. Amongst the flutes and similar instruments, an "Omnitonic" Flute, adjustable at will to any key, was contributed by Mr. Wilson, of Camberwell; and the Peri Campanula, or fairy bells, exhibited by Mr. Locke, of Manchester, excited much interest. Violins, and other like instruments, from the real "Cremona" to the most modern make, were numerous. Harmoniums and concertinas were also in considerable number. In the foreign department, Belgium, and many small kingdoms, sent specimens of musical instruments. France, as might be expected, especially Paris, ranked high in the exhibition of musical instruments of all kinds; but especially of pianos and brass instruments. Austria was similarly represented by Vienna; and amongst the curiosities were wind-instruments, made of wood; citherns, harmonicas of glass, &c. Berlin sent numerous instruments; and amongst them were several polysander pianofortes. Some curious instruments were contributed by firms in Italy, from Naples, Milan, and Padua; and, amongst them, were a piano-melodium, with two rows of keys; a vertical one; and a new kind of flute. Musical bells, Turkish cymbals, melodiums, pianofortes, &c., were sent from the Netherlands. M. Ebermayer, of Ellwangen, in Wirtemberg, contributed a novel instrument, called the "Tastenblas Jupwüment." Even from the far north pianos were sent—from Sweden, and Christiania, in Norway; and from Bergen, one of the most northern of civilised towns in Europe. M. A. Heldal forwarded a Hardanger fiddle, of the kind used by the Norwegian peasantry. A viol and violin were the only contributions from Portugal—both from Braga. Spain was represented by a grand piano, a picolo, and strings for musical instruments. A pianoforte from St. Petersburg, and musical instruments from Warsaw, represented the musical proclivities of Russia; whilst Switzerland, noted, as we have already seen, for watch and clock-work, sent numerous musical boxes from Geneva, besides accordions, brass instruments, pianos, and a church harmonium. Turkish musical instruments and kettle-drums were exhibited, as sent from Constantinople; and America contributed to this Class, in the shape of grand, square, boudoir, and other pianofortes, from New York.

Before concluding this *résumé* of articles exhibited in Class XVI., we may remark, generally, on the absence of what we may term native articles in the Exhibition; which, had they been more numerous, would have formed a most interesting study for the general observer and the ethnologist. Music is, perhaps, the most refining of all the arts practised by man; it alike soothes his sorrows, stimulates his joys, and, at times, may excite the worst passions of our nature. No nation has yet been discovered which has not had, in some form or other, a musical instrument; and war-songs are far too well known to leave any doubt, that if music does not always soothe the savage breast, it may have a directly opposite effect. Again, it is remarkable what similarity exists between the music, musical instruments, dances, &c., of nations or tribes similarly circumstanced. Amongst many others, we may call the bagpipe common to the mountainous region of our own country and Spain. In like manner, the music, dances, &c., of inhabitants of hilly countries, are all, more or less, of similar character. The musical instruments of China have, in some respects, an identity with our own—especially in the shape of a kind of guitar, much used by the Celestials. Without further extending these remarks, we cannot help expressing the opinion, that such a collection of native musical instruments, throughout the world, would not only have been curious and interesting, but would also, to a large extent, afford a kind of indication or key of the finer or other sentiments actuating, generally, each people. We judge of the refinement of ancient and decayed nations chiefly by their poetry—the only remains of their musical or harmonic tendencies. Even in our own day, it has been well said, that if we know the songs of the people, we may know what they are; and, for this reason, the collection we have hinted at would be an invaluable addition, either in a temporary or permanent Exhibition of All Nations.

SURGICAL INSTRUMENTS AND APPLIANCES (Class XVII.)—This Class, although of the highest utility and necessity in life, is not of such general interest as to require detailed description. In fact, we cannot help remarking on the rapid manner in which most visitors passed the cases in which the articles were exhibited. A temporary curiosity was more than satisfied by a glance at objectionable instruments for extracting teeth, sawing off a limb, and the like. Doubtless many a shudder was felt, and hurried prayer for deliverance from all such machinations uttered by some who nervously peered at such articles. To the professional man, however, and acute sufferers, these objects have no such repulsive characteristics; but for them, mainly, must this Class be of interest and study. We may possibly, however, call attention to some ingenious and invaluable inventions.

Artificial teeth were prominently exhibited, together with appliances for fixing them in the gums. At the present day, the churchyard, or dentist's shop, are *not* the sources of artificial teeth, so far as these have had a previous use by previous owners. Teeth are now made of hard mineral substances, and have all the appearance, in shape, texture, &c., of the best natural kind. In fitting them into the gums, an india-rubber or vulcanite base is used, which affords a similar elastic feeling to that naturally produced by the gums; and numerous other inventions were exhibited, all tending to add to the comfort of those compelled to use artificial organs of mastication: we may add, also—to their safety; for instances have occurred of a row of teeth escaping, during sleep, from the proper place, and nearly choking the wearer. In one instance, at least, we have heard of a fatal accident thus arising.

Amongst the artificial class, we may name that eyes, arms, hands, and legs, were freely exhibited—the former ornamental, and the latter useful. There were also numerous instruments for correcting deformities of various parts of the human frame; elastic stockings, trusses, &c., &c. Instruments for strictly surgical purposes, and of ingenious character, with excellent workmanship, were very numerous. Amongst others, we noticed excellent water-beds, cushions, and lifts, for invalids, exhibited by

Mr. Hooper and others. By the invention of the water-bed, Dr. Arnott has rendered incalculable benefit to the suffering and bed-ridden patient. It consists of a water-proof or india-rubber cloth "tick," in which the water is placed; and the bed being under an ordinary feather-bed, affords a *perfectly* elastic "mattress," allowing of any motion in any direction by the patient. Vulcanised india-rubber is now largely used in surgical appliances; and some of these were exhibited by Mr. Macintosh, of Cannon Street, London.

Respirators, acoustic instruments, bandages, supporters and suspenders; medicine-chests; inhalers for chloroform, and vapours generally; slings, crutches, spectacles of peculiar make; apparatus for feeding children; breast-drawers, syringes, arm-splints, baths, artificial palates, &c., &c., were all represented. Amongst the curiosities, we may notice Caplin's Electro-Chemical Bath, by which the patient, immersed in a suitable solution, has mineral and other substances eliminated by the pores of the body, by virtue of the chemical action of voltaic electricity. Mr. Pulvermacher exhibited his minute batteries for the application of free electricity to any affected part of the body; and a magnetic chain and battery were exhibited by Messrs. Welton and Monckton, of Grafton Street—in which invention we are not believers.

We have omitted mentioning the names of the British contributors, in most instances, for the simple reason that they are too numerous; and still further, because it would have seemed invidious had we made a selection where excellence was the rule. The French department was well filled; and, whilst including many of the articles already specified, had the addition of preparations, models of parts, taxidermic objects, plans of sanitary and other erections; a curious substitute for the leech, exhibited by M. Damoiseau, of Alençon; movable artificial eyes, &c., &c. Vienna, and other cities in Austria; Bavaria; Berlin, Breslau, and Bonn, in Prussia, also contributed. From Hamburg, a paralytic and valetudinarian's self-acting mahogany arm-chair, with wheels, was exhibited. Numerous instruments, models, apparatus, &c., were sent from Italy; and, amongst other matters, we may notice drawings illustrating the development and diseases of the silkworm, by Dr. Maestri, contributed from the Zoological Museum of the University of Pavia. Spain and Sweden also appeared amongst the exhibitors.

CHAPTER IX.

CLASS XVIII.—COTTON MANUFACTURES. CLASS XIX.—FLAX AND HEMP MANUFACTURES. CLASS XX.—SILKS AND VELVETS. CLASS XXI.—WOOLLEN AND WORSTED GOODS, INCLUDING MIXED FABRICS. CLASS XXII.—CARPETS. CLASS XXIII.—WOVEN, SPUN, FELTED, AND LAID FABRICS, AS SPECIMENS OF PRINTING OR DYEING. CLASS XXIV. —TAPESTRY, LACE, AND EMBROIDERY.

IN this chapter we shall embrace all those goods or articles, whether of use or ornament, which are produced from fibrous substances as their raw material; and for that purpose shall include wool and silk, which, although not strictly "fibres," in the exact definition of the term, are dealt with in manufacturing processes in an exactly similar manner as cotton, flax, hemp, and their substitutes.

We need not remind our readers that, to a large extent, the prosperity of our country has, in a great measure, arisen from the enormous expansion of this class of manufacture.   At the time of the Exhibition, the unfortunate civil war in America had already broken out, and great anxiety was manifested in all quarters as to the effect it might have on our national resources, and also, even, on the existence of the manufacturing districts of Lancashire.   The effects of that war have been already too largely known in our own country to require of us any details whatever.   By the generosity of their fellow-countrymen, the operatives of our cotton districts were at least saved from starvation; and now it is to be hoped that, the evil being past, they will soon regain that prosperous condition in which they had so long previously existed.

But the circumstances to which we have just alluded had a powerful effect in calling out the productive energies of countries in which cotton, flax, and hemp had not before been cultivated; or at least, if so, they had not been staple commodities of such countries.   Hence an immense number of specimens of such articles were forwarded; a notice of which, in respect to cotton, has already been given at page 178. The high prices then asked for cotton wool also caused a great effect; and thus, although the calamity which first fell on the cotton districts was heavy, it has been productive of great eventual good in giving us a more varied supply than that on which our mills had previously depended.   In this respect alone the Exhibition of 1862 was a national blessing.   In fact, one of the chief objects which such exhibitions generally have, is that of diffusing specimens of products previously unknown. These catch the eye of the manufacturer, and frequently enable him to make useful and profitable selections.

All statistics in reference to the manufactures of cotton subsequent to the year 1861, would, of course, be valueless: but before entering into a detailed description of them, we may afford some statistics of interest in 1860-'61, and previous to the breaking out of the civil war in America.

In the year 1860, no less than 12,420,000 cwts. of cotton were imported into the United Kingdom from *all* sources.   Of this quantity, 9,970,000 cwts. came from the United States—an amount which, in 1862, fell to only 120,750 cwt.: an enormous decrease, and amply sufficient to account for the distress of our cotton districts.

In the United Kingdom there were about 6,300 factories, of which 2,862 were engaged in the cotton manufacture.   Of spindles, there were working, throughout the kingdom, 36,500,000, of which no less than 30,000,000 were employed for cotton. Out of 490,000 power-looms, 400,000 were devoted to cotton weaving; and 450,000 persons, out of a total of 780,000 factory operatives, were engaged in the cotton manufacture.   The preceding numbers, we need scarcely state, refer to the year 1861; but are now equally correct, owing to the re-establishment of spinning, &c., in all our cotton districts.

In 1861, Lancashire alone employed 316,000 persons directly in the manufacture of cotton; and no less than 1,980 cotton factories existed in that county.   In fact, three-fourths of the entire cotton trade are carried on, and an equal proportion of operatives are employed, in its towns, out of the total for the United Kingdom.   The

W. G. TAYLORS PATENT POWER LOOM CALICO MACHINE

OBTAINED THE PRIZE MEDAL 1862

following are the chief statistics of the cotton manufacture for Great Britain and Ireland for 1861:—

	Number of Factories.	Spindles.	Operatives.
England	2,715	28,351,925	407,598
Scotland	138	1,915,398	41,237
Ireland	9	119,944	2,734
Total	2,862	30,387,267	451,569

In reference to foreign countries, we may add that France has one-eighth; Russia, one-fifteenth; Germany, one-fifteenth; Austria and Switzerland, each one-twentieth; and Italy and Belgium, each one-sixtieth of the number of spindles in operation, compared with our kingdom.

We may now proceed to detail the manufactures of cotton in reference to the specimens exhibited in 1862, making a few preliminary remarks on the raw material of cotton, and its manufacture, which are the subject of Class XVIII. And, first, we may observe that there are three chief points on which the value of cotton depends for manufacturing purposes; and by these the specimens sent to the Exhibition were fairly tested—the colour, cleanliness, and length of staple. The difficulty in finding a substitute for American cotton, lay in the fact that it eminently possesses all these qualities; whilst most other kinds are deficient in one or other of them. As nearly all the Lancashire machinery has been made to spin American, it was of importance that the staple—that is, the length of each fibre of the specimen—should equal, but not much exceed it; and, for this reason, the East India grown cotton was with difficulty used at first, because its staple is so much shorter than the American species. Again, until very recently the Indian growers were exceedingly careless, not to say fraudulent, in the cleaning and packing of the cotton—a circumstance which has, justly, much militated against their interest. We have frequently seen sticks, even lumps of iron, stones, and an immense quantity of seeds, in a bale of Surat or Madras cotton, packed inside of a much inferior quality, and, therefore, seriously diminishing its value. The colour of East India cotton is another objection. Instead of being a rich creamy or glossy white, like the American, it is usually of a dull yellow tint, and, therefore, bleaches badly when made up either into yarn or cloth. We noticed some beautiful specimens from Queensland, Venezuela, Trinidad, Japan, Italy, &c.; but remarked both the variety and cleanliness of that sent from Algeria. If this colony would enter, in an enterprising manner, into the growth of a similar article in bulk, there is no doubt but that it would speedily equal in value, to France, some of the best colonial possessions of Great Britain. We cannot here refrain from observing, by way of parenthesis, on the astonishing variety of products exhibited from Algeria; and fancy that, if British capital and enterprise were encouraged in that region, the results would be astonishingly profitable.

There are, chiefly, four species of the plant grown for economic purposes. The shortest staple is produced from the *Gossypium herbaceum*, chiefly cultivated in India,

China, and the east generally; its full height is from sixteen to twenty inches. The Brazil kind is obtained from the *Gossypium Peruvianum*, which, by careful treatment, can produce a variety almost equal to the best kind used in the cotton manufacture—the Sea Island. The American cotton is mostly the product of the *Gossypium Barbadense*; and of this the true Sea Island cotton is produced. That grown in Alabama and the Southern States of the United States, is the kind on which we primarily depended before the American war. It is of a rich white silky appearance, and loses but little during the process of manufacturing. The Sea Island variety is produced by the saline marshes of Florida and Georgia—common salt, or some other saline substance associated with it, being always necessary for the production of the best cotton. The sea air, in fact, has always a most decided influence beneficially on the colour and staple of cotton. The reason of this, however, is, as yet, not explained.

After the cotton is packed it has to be cleaned from seeds and shell; and the machinery employed for this purpose, and for carding, spinning, &c., has been already alluded to at page 191.

In the articles exhibited in Class XVIII. great variety was shown; in fact, most articles manufactured from cotton were represented. Our lady readers would not fail to notice the names of many exhibitors with whom they are familiar, in such articles as the sewing-cotton of Brook, Brothers, of Meltham Mills, Huddersfield; Clark and Co., of Paisley; Clark, of Mile-end, Glasgow; J. and P. Coats, of Paisley; Evans, of Derby; Manlove, of Chesterfield, &c. In sewed muslins, the largest firm engaged in their production—Messrs. Copestake, Moore, Crampton and Co.—were exhibitors. This firm alone, directly or indirectly, employ the services of some hundred thousand workers, chiefly resident in Glasgow and the north of Ireland. In fact, a change of fashion in this respect, would, perhaps, affect not less than half a million females now depending on it for their daily bread. The cotton manufacture has its special localities; and the exhibition of calicoes and shirtings from Manchester, Preston, and Blackburn, was very extensive; whilst counterpanes and coarse cotton cloth are more generally produced at Bolton and other towns in Lancashire. Several specimens of sewing and other cottons were exhibited in a glazed state—a condition which much facilitates their use for sewing purposes, and renders them as easily worked as silk, and without "fraying." Cotton cord, to replace hemp cord, than which they are 30 per cent. lighter for the same length; cotton-mill bands, candle-wicks, and other coarse yarn manufactures, excited considerable interest. Amongst the great variety of cotton articles shown, we may name muslin for dresses and window-curtains, dimities, towelling, blankets, India twills, China sheetings, toilet-covers, imitation velvets, damasks, velvet ribbons, embroidered collars, sleeves, &c.; a variety of astonishing extent when considered as produced from one fibre.

FLAX AND HEMP (Class XIX.)—This class of manufacture had received, in the year of the Exhibition, an enormous stimulant, owing to the deficient supply of cotton, which we have already noticed. The chief localities in which it is carried on, are the north of Ireland, as Belfast, Lisburn, Coleraine, &c.; Dundee, Arbroath, and Forfar, in Scotland; and various parts of the West and North Ridings of Yorkshire. The Irish district is celebrated for its linens, cambrics, &c.; the Scotch manufactures, for coarse goods, as Hessians, sackings, sail-cloth, towellings, &c.; whilst yarns, for sewing, tailors, shoemakers, and other purposes, are mostly produced in Yorkshire.

A general idea of the varieties of raw material sent to the Exhibition, has been given at pages 178, 179; but we may here enter, advantageously, somewhat more in detail on that subject, both in respect to flax and hemp, and the numerous substitutes which are employed for them. Flax is chiefly grown in Russia, Holland, and Ireland, so far as our supply is concerned. The plant is familiar as an ornament of our gardens, growing to a height of about eighteen inches, and producing a pretty little blue flower. The seed forms the "linseed" of commerce, which affords an excellent oil, and the refuse of which becomes the oil-cake used for fattening cattle. After the plant is gathered, which is done just as it is becoming ripe, it is "retted;" that is, the solid matter is separated by steeping it in water until all the fibre becomes free. This is then coarsely cleaned, sorted, and becomes ready for the processes of manufacture. There are two species chiefly grown—namely, the common flax, or *Linum usitatissimum* of this country, and the Siberian flax, or *Linum sibiricum*.

Hemp is coarser in fibre than flax. It is produced from the *Cannabis sativa*, a native of most parts of Europe. In India a variety of this plant is cultivated; not for economic purposes, but to produce an intoxicating liquor called Bhang, and a solid substance, or extract, called Gunja, which is largely used for smoking by the natives of the East Indies. The common jute, so much used to mix with hemp, and the useful properties of which have been so much developed since 1862, is a native of India. China-grass is produced from a plant of the nettle kind, and is much adapted for producing cambrics, linens, pocket-handkerchiefs, &c. New Zealand flax, Zercum fibre, Pita fibre, Maroot and Neyanda fibre, Banana and Plantain fibre, Manilla hemp, Sunn hemp, &c., &c., figured amongst the substitutes for flax in the Exhibition; and are all, more or less, employed for textile purposes. Parenthetically we may state, that the museum at Kew-gardens now contains a vast number of these and other natural products, as woods, fibres, &c., which were exhibited in 1862; and still, therefore, affords an opportunity of personal examination to those desirous of pursuing this inquiry further than our limits will permit.

From the coarsest sail-cloth to the finest cambric, articles of all kinds were exhibited. The Belfast Local Committee, by their trophy, &c., gave a full exposition of the manufactures carried on in the north of Ireland. Other exhibitors from Belfast and neighbouring towns, sent damasks, table-cloths, napkins, diapers, drills, cambrics, sheetings, &c. From Arbroath, Dundee, Dunfermline, Kirkcaldy, and other towns in the east of Scotland, sail-cloth, or canvas, duck, tarpaulins, carpeting, Hessian or packing-wrapper, fishing-nets, yarns, thread, bed-ticks, &c., were abundantly contributed. Smaller articles were also sent from other parts of the country. From Yorkshire (especially Messrs. Marshall, of Leeds), yarns, threads for sewing, manufactured goods, &c., were exhibited. Specimens of felt, by Messrs. Croggon and Co., of London, showed how the waste of the manufacturer could be utilised: it is also employed in the manufacture of paper.

In respect to marquees, tents, rick-cloths, sacks, tarpaulins, water-buckets, portable water-tanks, seamless hose for conveying water, ship-sheathing, ropes, twine, sail cordage, fuse for miners, coir yarn carpets, and matting; rugs, door-mats, wool and guano sacks, the contributions were large and numerous. Amongst other articles we have named above, it may surprise our readers to find that water-buckets and tanks can be made from hempen cloth, to hold water. This, however, is easily explained. As soon as moisture touches the fibre it shrinks it, and hence all the interstices left in weaving become closed up, rendering the article completely waterproof. By the same cause ropes are broken when tightly stretched, and left out thus during a shower of rain; and, for the same reason, a cotton or gingham umbrella protects the user far better when it is thoroughly wetted, than when first opened out dry in a shower.

In respect to the statistics of the linen manufacture, we may observe that, as an object of export, it ranks next to metals; those of cotton and wool preceding it in value. In 1861, we exported, of all kinds of linen goods, a total in value of £3,850,000. But so great was the stimulus given to the trade by the cotton famine, that, in 1863, the total value of our exports, in all kinds of linen manufacture, amounted in value to £6,510,000; and of this increase much was due to the extension of fibre-supply induced by the Exhibition of 1862, the manufacturers having been able to obtain a greater variety and quantity of the new material.

SILK AND VELVETS (Class XX.); and WOOLLEN AND WORSTED, INCLUDING MIXED FABRICS (Class XXI.)—It will be unnecessary for us here to enter into any statistical detail of the raw material of wool imported into this country, as that has already been done at page 177 of this work. All wools may be divided into two classes, according to their fineness and staple. The fine and short-staple kinds are employed for making cloth; whilst the coarse and long-stapled are used chiefly in making worsted, hosiery, gloves, shirts, &c.; hence the manufactures themselves are also distinct, and are generally, if not universally, carried on by separate firms.

The west of England, and the West Riding of Yorkshire, are the chief localities in which the woollen trade is carried on, so far as cloths are concerned; and, formerly, Wilts, Somerset, and Gloucester shires were the chief homes of the trade. But, gradually, the Yorkshire manufacturers so improved the quality of their productions, as to rival, and, eventually, surpass the productions of the west: and hence Leeds, Bradford, Huddersfield, &c., figured most numerously in the Exhibition. In Scotland, the manufacture of tweeds, hosiery, &c., is largely carried on; especially at Galashiels, where the tweed manufacture for trouserings and shawls is chiefly located.

We may here remark that wool has certain properties which vegetable fibres generally do not possess. Wool fibre contains on its surface numerous minute hairs, which tend to entangle with each other; and, by taking advantage of this, the process of "felting," on which the stability of cloth depends, is carried out. We must here add that this property is somewhat improperly taken advantage of. Old carpets, on being broken up in a "devil," produce a short-fibre wool, with which, if some longer stapled fresh wool be mixed with oil or soap, it can be spun into yarn, and woven into pilots and other cloth. The original stuff is called "shoddy;" and many a well-to-do personage walks through the streets, at the present day, wearing, apparently, a good broadcloth coat, which, however, has thus had its origin in old carpets.

In respect to commerce, woollen goods rank next in importance to cotton. In the year (1861) preceding the Exhibition, we exported to foreign countries and our colonies, woollen goods, of all kinds, to the value of £11,130,000. But, like the linen trade, that of wool was stimulated by the cotton famine; and accordingly, in 1863, the exports had risen, in value, to £15,520,000.

The number of exhibitors in this Class, at the Exhibition, was very great; and goods were sent from all the districts in which the manufacture is carried on. The Bradford local committee afforded an excellent exposition of the products of their district, in every variety of goods, including alpacas, mohair, Orleans cloths, Cobourgs, Paramattas, reps, gambroon, camlets, moreens, damasks, shawls, delaines, fancy goods, umbrella cloths, worsted goods, &c., &c. We have already stated that the West Riding of Yorkshire is the centre of the woollen trade in our country; and hence its towns, as Leeds, &c., were well represented.

It would be a difficult matter to enumerate all, or each class of articles which were sent to the Exhibition. As we have already mentioned, Scotland was represented in tweeds, shawls, trouserings, &c.; and each article of dress for either sex was fully illustrated. Running cursorily over the catalogue of contributions from other places, we should have to mention so many objects that the patience of our readers would be exhausted; whilst we should have to write the almost entire history of the woollen manufacture. Suffice it to say, that from the finest cloth which " becomes" the aristocrat, to the coarsest yarn employed in making the mop, wool was completely and fully represented.

SILK AND VELVET (Class XX.)—We have ventured to invert the order adopted by the Commissioners, preferring to describe the woollen manufacture before that of silk; because the former more properly ranks under the head of "fibrous substances," and hence may be safely classed with cotton, flax, and hemp: silk, on the contrary, is not a fibrous substance. If we could take the filament as produced by the worm, we should find a continuous thread of several hundred yards in length. There is hence a great distinction between cotton, flax, and hemp, when compared with silk, not only in the character of each, but also in the mode of manufacturing them. It will be here convenient that we should describe the sources and preparation of this valuable material, before we enter into a description of the various articles which illustrated its uses in the Exhibition of 1862.

The eggs of the silkworm are of about the size of a pin's head. They are obtained from the moth of the previous year, and are carefully kept unhatched until the mulberry-leaf is fully developed, otherwise the worm would be without food. Of course we are here speaking of the Chinese method of dealing with the worm, which is, indeed, the type of that followed in Italy, Greece, France, and other countries where raw silk is produced.

The worm, when hatched, has a length of about the tenth part of an inch, and resembles a thin black thread. If plentifully supplied with food it rapidly increases in size until mature.

An ounce of the eggs, after hatching and until death, produces worms which eat about half a ton of mulberry-leaves. The worms producing one pound of cocoons, eat about fourteen pounds of the leaves. One hundred eggs weigh about one grain; and the worms increase so much in size, that, at the time of spinning, they become upwards of 9,000 times the weight they had at their birth. The worm is forty times longer at the spinning-time than when born. It requires about 3,000 worms to spin as much silk as would supply the material for an ordinary dress; and at the present rate of import of the raw material into this country, at least 20,000,000,000 of worms would be required to keep up the supply. The food of the worm is chiefly derived from two species of the mulberry—the *morus alba* and *nigra*. The tree is indigenous to Asia Minor; but is now grown in most temperate climates.

The manufacture of the raw material much differs from that we have already described in respect to wool, cotton, and flax. The cocoons are small oval balls, produced by the worm, just preceding its change into the chrysalis state; and we have the analogues of these in many productions of spiders in this country. Indeed, spiders' webs have, ere now, been spun and woven into ladies' dresses.

The cocoons are preserved from the destruction which would ensue, by allowing the insect to enter into its *imago* state. This is done by heating a certain proportion of the cocoon to a high temperature, by which the insect is killed. It would otherwise eat its way out of one end of the cocoon. Some of the moths are kept so as to provide eggs for the ensuing season.

When the process of reeling the thread is commenced, the cocoons are thrown into a vessel of hot water, which has the effect of dissolving off the gummy substance with which the thread is enveloped. The end of the cocoon being found by means of a small wisp, numbers of them are wound together on a reel; but each thread is carefully kept apart, so that they may not adhere to each other. By this process they are formed into hanks, in which state silk is imported into this country from China, Persia, India, &c.

The subsequent processes are those of reeling, twisting, or throwing; and, in this respect, silk differs from cotton, as it is neither spun nor carded. "Spun silk" is the waste of the material, obtained either from the outside of the cocoon, or from the ends and piecings produced as waste in throwing or reeling the silk. The colour of the raw silk varies from a rich white to a dark orange, and seems to arise from some individual peculiarity of the worms which produce it. Silk takes a brighter dye-colour than cotton, flax, or wool; hence the beauty and variety of dresses, ribbons, &c., produced from it. It has also the power of absorbing a large amount of tannin—as obtained, for example, from sumach, employed in dyeing it black. This properly gives rise to the practice of "weighting;" that is, permitting it to absorb in the sumach vat a large quantity—nearly 25 per cent. of the tannin. Its weight is thus not only increased, but the silk obtains a better and "fuller" body. The practice, however, is largely used for fraudulent purposes, and opens out a considerable source of gain to the perpetrators of this deceit.

We cannot enter into the process of weaving silk, which is done in a Jacquard loom, and of which there is an illustration given in this work. In making velvets,

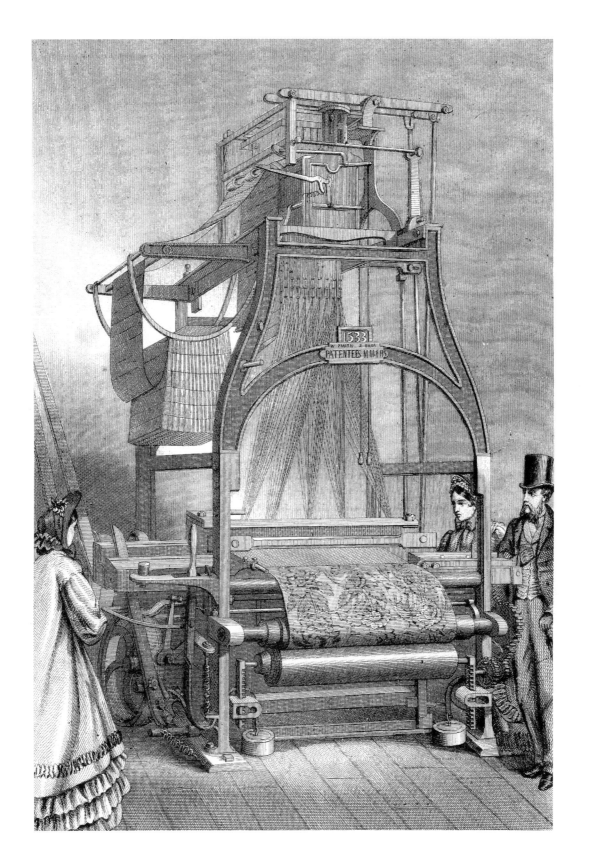

SMITH BROTHERS PATENT JACQUARD LOOM

OBTAINED THE PRIZE MEDAL 1862.

the nap or pile is produced by loops in the thread left above the surface of the web. These loops are cut horizontally by a sharp knife or razor-like instrument, and thus the delicate and dull-looking "pile" is raised.

London, Coventry, Derbyshire, and Manchester, are the chief seats of the silk manufacture in England; and the contributions of the products of each locality, indicate that some branches are confined to certain localities. Thus from Leek and Macclesfield, silk-throwings, twist, &c., were sent by various firms; whilst London-made goods were chiefly broad silks, employed for ladies' dresses; velvets, reps, brocades, crapes, aerophanes, tissues, satins, &c. Galloons, bindings, &c., were sent from Derby, Leek, &c. Coventry has long been celebrated for its ribbons; and whilst many firms of that city exhibited, most of the ribbons nominally sent from other places had been manufactured at Coventry.

Amongst the general variety of articles of this class besides those named, we may mention elastic webs, braids, serges, handkerchiefs, scarfs, flags, dress trimmings, thrown silk, and "waste" goods, in producing which jute is often mixed with the silk; hat-plushes, for making silk hats; _moire antiques_, carriage lace, "mohair" yarns, embroideries, cravats, neck-ties, shawls, and, last, a respirator-scarf, from Sudbury. Of late years, many of the London firms have established manufactories in various parts of Essex, where hundreds of hands are employed.

We need not state that France was conspicuous in this Class: in fact, we regret that it is absolutely impossible to give any idea of the beauty of many of the French productions in silk. Not only were they the object of admiration by the sex destined to wear them, but the richness and beauty of design and colour were equally attractive to the sterner sex; and, in many cases, reminded us of the gorgeousness so vividly described of the dress of Eastern nations. Lyons figured most in respect to broad silks, velvets, handkerchiefs, &c. It is the chief locality in France for making those articles; and some idea of the extent of the French manufacture of silk, may be gathered from the fact, that apart from the amount consumed at home, upwards of 300,000,000 of francs' worth of silk goods were exported in 1861; and in 1863, this rose to upwards of 375,000,000 of francs— a circumstance in part arising from the stimulus given to the manufacture by orders consequent on the Exhibition, and also to the extra quantity of silk goods used, owing to the "cotton famine." The ribbon manufacture in France is chiefly carried on at St. Etienne, in the department of the Loire; and some of the articles exhibited were of exquisite taste and beauty. Paris firms contributed both broad and sewing-silks. Numerous specimens of silk plush, for hats, were sent from that city, and also from various manufacturers in the department of Moselle, especially from Sarreguemines, where much of the hat-plush is produced for the use of French and English hat-makers.

Thus, the usual silk goods were similar to those we have described as produced in this country; but among the specialities, we may mention, as sent from many towns in France, the following—viz., taffetas, Chambery gauze, silk for umbrellas, furniture silks, embroidery, cotton and silks worked in imitation of straw and wood; silk lace, some of which was extremely beautiful; ribbons made of raw silk, which had a very pretty effect; waistcoat silks; silk articles for church ornaments, crapes and muslins, fancy silk thread, spun silk, wadding for lining dresses, silk fabrics for "bolting" flour; silk articles with portraits wove in the web, printed silks, &c. The raw material was also largely exhibited; an immense quantity of worms being reared in the south of France, but not producing sufficient silk for the manufacturers of that country, who consequently import a large quantity from Italy, China, and India. There were also exhibited, in the French department, some woven fabrics of Algierian silk—a new product of that colony.

Our space will not permit of a lengthened description of the silk products of Austria, Prussia, and German towns generally, all of which were well represented. We must, however, devote a few lines to describing those of Italy, which is a great silk-producing country. Raw silk was largely contributed from Florence, Turin, Terni, Milan, Lucca, Novi, Sienna, Messina, Ancona, &c.; and, generally speaking, the details of the silk manufacture were best learned from a study of this department; the production of the material and its manufactures being simultaneously carried out in most parts of Italy. Amongst the curiosities, we may notice a contribution of 6,000 tints of sewing-silk, by Messrs. Levinstein and Co., of Milan. Belgium, Greece, Holland, and many other European countries also exhibited; and amongst the most numerous contributions, were those of raw silk, shawls, and other goods from Turkey, some of which were of great beauty, and gathered from various places in European and Asiatic Turkey—extending even to Persia. Many most beautiful articles of lace, &c., were sent from Malta. India contributed largely in raw silk and silk goods: those of the latter kind, worked by hand, being greatly admired. Numerous articles of silk from China and Japan were also exhibited; and most of them were of great richness.

CARPETS (Class XXII.)—Under this head a great variety of material was aggregated by the Commissioners; including carpets of all kinds, floorcloth, &c. At page 192, general reference has been made to some looms; and one of these is illustrated on steel in the plates of this work. The carpet mostly in use in this country is that called "Brussels;" and at Tournay, near Brussels, large quantities are still made. Amongst other kinds exhibited, were some from Axminster, Kidderminster, and Scotland. Velvet-pile carpets, of great beauty and richness of design and material, were also contributed.

In other articles, the variety, as we have stated, was considerable, and included rugs, blankets, seal-skins, carriage rugs; floorcloths of various designs, some imitating mosaic pavement tiles, &c.; stair-coverings, table-cloths, alpaca coat-linings (by the way, rather a singular article to "class" with carpets); silk and wool curtains, &c., &c. Kamptulicon was also exhibited: and as it is now so largely used, we may give a short account of its manufacture. It consists of india-rubber and cork, in the proportion of three pounds of the former to seven pounds of the latter. The cork is first ground into a coarse powder in a mill; and, meanwhile, the india-rubber is "masticated," or worked, in a hot cylinder by strong iron teeth; the effect of which is to remove dirt, &c., and to give it the requisite softness: the cork is then mixed with it, and the two are rolled together until they gradually extend to a

MOXON & C? PATENT CARPET LOOM

OBTAINED THE PRIZE MEDAL 1862.

sheet about twenty feet long, and from three to four feet wide. This sheet, when cool, is fit for use; and in laying it down, the edges are joined together by means of a solution of india-rubber spread on strips of thick calico. Many public buildings are thus "floored:" and Kamptulicon has the advantage of being noiseless, and a bad conductor of heat; hence the feet do not become cold whilst standing or walking over it. It is also printed, like floorcloth, by wooden blocks, on which the pattern is cut in relief. As many blocks are required as there are colours; and any design may thus be produced on the sheet material.

In the foreign and colonial department, we may briefly notice the following:— From India some beautiful specimens were sent, including carpets from Arcot, &c.; woollen carpets, of Persian patterns; carpets made by Thugs at Lahore; native imitations of British carpets; coir and rattan matting; mats from Pandang-leaf, from Java; palm-leaf mats; straw grass, rush, wild palm-leaf matting, &c. Similar articles were sent from Ceylon; including, also, skins of lions, tigers, monkeys, &c., used as hearth and carriage rugs. The Carpet Company of Tournay contributed articles illustrating the manufacture of that district, and to which we have already alluded. The productions of France, especially the tapestry carpets of the imperial manufactories of Gobelins, &c., were beautiful: indeed, many visitors mistook one specimen of great size for a painting, so richly and exactly was the pattern worked. Firms at Aubusson, Nîmes, Neuilly, Paris, and other towns, also contributed some rich and beautiful articles. Austria, Prussia, and several of the smaller German states were represented; oil-cloths for table-covers, and other purposes, being predominant. From Greece several carpets were sent; and there were a few exhibitors from Italian towns. The quiltings of Norway were included in this Class. Turkey, as might be expected, largely exhibited the peculiar class of carpet for which it has long been noted. Damascus, Broussa, Akhia, Saraoukhan (chiefly), Angora, Crete, &c., all contributed; and the designs, sizes, and uses of each kind were very various.

WOVEN, SPUN, FELTED, AND LAID FABRICS, AS SPECIMENS OF PRINTING AND DYEING (Class XXIII.)—In this Class a heterogeneous combination of manufactured goods was made for the purpose of showing the effects of after-processes. Most of the articles have been already described; including, as they did, printed calicoes, chintzes, furniture-hangings, embroideries, printed silks, woollen goods, worsted yarns for knitting, printed lawn muslin and other dresses, delaines, challis, printed ribbons, corahs, sewing-silk, felted carpets, bandanas, Turkey-red goods, &c., &c. These constituted the chief of the articles exhibited; but the interest of the collection did not lie in them so much as in the colours that were produced. We need not enter here into an individual description of the articles exhibited from each country. In respect to beauty of design, richness of colour, and general excellence, we must give France the palm of merit—a character long sustained by French dyers and printers: so much so, indeed, that we have seen one of the largest cotton-printing firms in *our* country, label its goods, fresh from the printing-works, as "finished at Paris"—a successful, but, to the purchaser, a fraudulent device. The various articles, pigments, dyewoods, &c., used in dyeing and printing, have been already described at p. 160, *et seq.*, in this work; and to those of our readers desirous of further inquiry into this interesting subject, we recommend the perusal of the section on Economic Botany, in the *Circle of the Sciences*, which may be had of the publishers of this work.

TAPESTRY, LACE, AND EMBROIDERY (Class XXIV.)—In this Class a great variety of objects was included—from the fine lace for ladies' attire, to the "coach-lace" and ornamental work of the artisan. In former times the hand manufacture of lace was extensively and profitably carried on in many towns of this and other countries; and from this circumstance have arisen some of the names familiar to our lady readers— as "Honiton," "Irish point," "Valenciennes," "Brussels," &c. At the present time the hand manufacture is almost entirely superseded by that of machinery, which is of the most ingenious and yet complicated description. In this country Nottingham is the chief seat of the lace manufacture, although it is also largely carried on at other places. Glasgow is especially noted for its "sewed muslins;" and immense numbers of young women find employment in making that well-known article of female attire.

Without entering into a detailed examination of the various articles exhibited in this Class, we may instance such as were of special interest. Amongst these were— A cover for articles used in Jewish synagogues, exhibited by Messrs. Abraham and Son, of Lisle Street, London; Valenciennes, Maltese, Honiton, and other laces, manufactured in Nottingham; lace shawls, falls, &c., from the same city; some beautiful specimens of silk embroidery on muslin, handkerchiefs, sewed muslin, ladies' under-clothing, &c., from Ireland; an excellent *resume* of the lace manufacture by that eminent, and, we believe, largest firm in the trade, Messrs. Copestake, Moore, Crampton, and Co., of Bow Churchyard, London; pillow, Irish point, Buckingham-shire, and other hand-made laces; fancy and gold-lace embroidery; hats made on the pillow-lace principle, and straw embroidery from Wycombe, in Buckinghamshire; trimmings for coach and upholstery purposes; curtains, flounces, parasol covers, &c., &c.

Belgium was largely represented in "Brussels lace" in every variety of object and design. The articles from France, however, were, perhaps, of the most *recherché* character of any shown in the Exhibition, the greater portion being sent from manu-facturers in Paris; but which, perhaps, like similar articles sold in London, had been really made in provincial towns. Amongst the curiosities in this department were lace articles made of aluminium thread—the "new" metal already described in our previous pages.

We cannot enumerate here the various countries which contributed to this depart-ment. In most of the large cities of Europe the lace manufacture is carried on: and amongst contributions from other parts of the world, India deserves chief notice; some splendid specimens of embroidery and lace-work having been sent. It is remarkable that, despite the astonishing improvements which we have made in machinery at home, the natives of Hindostan far outstrip us in producing fine cotton thread; and hence the Dacca muslins, spun and woven by hand, are far finer and more delicate in texture than the best kinds produced in Europe. The Indian collection embraced a great variety of articles. The government contributed embroidered work from Surat, Agra, and Benares; embroidered muslins from Scinde; lace, lappets, veils, berthas, sleeves, &c., from Tinnevelly; embroidered caps from Peshawar, Benares, and Lahore; embroidered muslin from Madras, &c., &c. The native princes were large contributors; and slippers, shawls, table-cloths, Dacca muslins, saddles, parasols, Cashmere work, purses in lace and gold embroidery, raised the ardent desire of possession, and caused a frequent breach, in heart, of the tenth commandment amongst the many admiring lady visitors who thronged this, to them, deeply interesting department of the Exhibition.

CHAPTER X.

CLASS XXV.—SKINS, FUR, FEATHERS, AND HAIR. CLASS XXVI.—LEATHER, INCLUDING SADDLERY AND HARNESS. CLASS XXVII.—ARTICLES OF CLOTHING.

IT reflects somewhat sarcastically on civilised human nature, to observe that the objects which are so largely adopted as matters of ornament amongst ourselves, are just those which are eagerly sought for by savage nations; and hence the feather is considered equally *apropos* for the head-dress of the court lady and for the Indian chief. The ultimate motive of each wearer is the same—that of increasing or setting-off supposed personal attractions; but we may possibly ascribe to ourselves a deeper appreciation of ideas of beauty and grace in the use of such articles, and thus palliate that which, it cannot be concealed, must arise from " vanity of spirit." In Classes XXV. and XXVI., we shall find, however, articles of great utility as well as of ornament: and disposing of the sub-class B (XXV.), which only included ostrich feathers (certainly of great beauty, and exhibited respectively by De Costa, Andrade, & Co., and Sugden, Son, and Nephew), we proceed to describe articles of fur, skin, hair, &c., applied to so many useful purposes in daily life. Respecting this Class we must remark on the peculiar mode of classification adopted by the commissioners, who included in it such heterogeneous materials as skins, furs, ostrich feathers, wigs, hair-brushes, brooms, &c.—the generic term, hair, having been considered sufficiently categorical to embrace articles which have not the most remote connection with that material.

The sub-class A (Class XXV.) included a great variety of the skins of animals " worked up " as furs. The " warmth " of these articles arises from the fact that the hair or fur on the skin encloses a large amount of air, which, being the worst conductor of heat when *perfectly still*, affords thus an excellent material for warm clothing. It must be borne in mind, therefore, that it is not the fur which causes the sensation of warmth therefrom: on the contrary, this arises solely from the air which the hair retains on the surface of the fur. This is readily proved by wetting an ordinary fur article on the hairy side, when its value as an article of warm clothing is entirely removed, because the air which its parts contained has been driven off.

Again, it is the fine inner hair of the skin which is most valuable; and hence, generally speaking, the smaller animals produce the warmest kind of fur.

Sable is obtained from the skin of an animal of the marten kind. It is a native of Siberia. An American species likewise affords a good sable. Furs are also obtained from the mink, weasel, pole-cat, ferret, stoat, or ermine; the valuable fur bearing the last name being chiefly got from the white skin of a British animal. Otters, hares, rabbits, bears, beavers, the musquash, chinchilla, squirrel, and numerous other animals, are sources of skins which, in the hands of the furrier, become useful as articles of dress or ornament.

The exhibitors in this department were all of eminence in the trade, and included Messrs. Bevington and Sons, Mr. Ince, Mr. J. M. Meyer, Mr. Nicholay, Messrs. Poland and Son, Messrs. G. Smith and Sons; with others, who unitedly represented the department to the best advantage. The articles exhibited included all kinds of ladies' furs, rugs, boots; and there were some very valuable cloaks, made from the skins of the seal; furs in different processes of manufacture, &c., &c. In the Russian department a large collection of skins, including those of the sheep, lamb, fox, reindeer, seal, &c., were shown. In that country fur is essential as an article of winter dress; and hence, whether in the raw or manufactured condition, the Russian department was, *par excellence*, the representative of this class of goods. The articles of dress, as used in Russian daily life during winter, were curious and much admired. We may add that fur is mostly produced where mostly wanted—namely, in cold countries. Hence the lower animals and human beings of those regions are thus both providentially supplied with a real necessity of life. For beauty of skin, however, the products of warmer climates are more noted; and the contributions of the government of India, and private firms of that country, were much admired. They included tiger, chamois, and other skins, with many articles of manufactured furs.

In this sub-class, the contributions from most European countries, besides those already named, were very good; but, as objects of natural interest, those from Denmark were the most remarkable. They consisted of female Greenlanders' costume (Greenland being a dependency of Denmark); Esquimaux hunting-dress, and other articles; seal and other skin mats; bird-skins, used for dress, &c. Our readers may still see a similar collection, made, some years ago, by J. Barrow, Esq., so well known through his energetic endeavours in connection with Arctic research, in respect to which he has been a worthy successor of his father, Sir John Barrow, formerly secretary of the Admiralty. This collection is now in the British Museum; and as each object of dress, &c., is fitted on representations of Esquimaux, the whole forms a most interesting illustration of the use of furs, &c., by native tribes.

Manufactures from Hair (Sub-class C).—In this sub-division of Class XXV., the various articles produced from hair, bristles, &c., and their substitutes, were exhibited; and a great variety of matters must be enumerated to give our readers an idea of the numerous purposes to which the raw material is applied, for domestic and other purposes. The sources of the raw material are also numerous, and extend through a long list of animal and vegetable substances, which are employed in the manufactures included in this sub-class. We have previously remarked on the heterogeneous nature of the goods categorised in it. They include brushes; brooms; feathers; petticoats; crinolines; wigs; horse-hair, for stuffing chairs, mattresses, &c.; wool, used for the same purpose; combs; eider-down; perfumery; painters' brushes; artificial scalps, for the bald head; human hair, worked into devices of all kinds; hair-cloth seating for chairs, &c., &c.

We need not detain our readers in describing this sub-class more in detail. The great variety of goods exhibited would demand too much of our space for that purpose; whilst the interest attached to them is not so great as to require our closer examination.

LEATHER, INCLUDING SADDLERY AND HARNESS (Class XXVI.)—Most interesting results might be obtained, were we enabled to trace the various steps by which our present modes of preparing many kinds of raw material have been arrived at. In this, as in most other matters, however, we must be generally content to admit that "necessity is the mother of invention;" for it happens, even in instances where the history of a process has been fairly arrived at, that its initiative arose in some "accident," turned to account temporarily; and as fresh wants arose, improvements gradually became introduced, until approximative perfection was at last attained. The use of skins for clothing has, doubtless, been common for ages past; indeed, savage tribes of our own day, especially in cool climates, have, of necessity, availed themselves of this ready means to preserve them from the external cold. As we have already remarked, the lower animals of those countries are provided by nature with exactly that sort of clothing which our most advanced scientific knowledge suggests as the most proper. And man, for whom all things were made, avails himself of this provision, and so participates, abundantly, in that universal "fitness of things," observed in every phase of animate and inanimate creation.

The tanning of skins, to convert them into leather, however, is so peculiarly a scientific process, that we cannot class its discovery amongst the "accidents" of life. Besides, until recently, it was an extremely slow process, and required an intelligent supervision and careful manipulation, to fit the raw material for the numerous purposes to which it is applied. The early methods of preparing skins consisted, chiefly, in drying them, either by sun or artificial heat. In that state they were still unchanged *skins;* but by our methods, the process of tanning takes away every vestige of animal substance, converting it into a solid, insoluble, waterproof, and, comparatively, indestructible material. A short description of the process, and of the materials used, will, doubtless, prove interesting to our readers, as being descriptive of the preparatory steps which have to be taken in the manufacture of leather, saddlery, harness, &c., to which Class XXVI. was devoted.

The skins employed are obtained from the ox, buffalo, calf, sheep, horse, &c. In fact, any quadruped's hide may be converted into leather: and, by the way, we have seen a book bound, as a curiosity, with tanned *human* skin. Generally speaking, the younger the animal, the softer and more pliable is its skin; and, for this reason, the calf affords the best material for our boots, so far as the upper leather is concerned; whilst the ox, buffalo, or other full-grown animal, is chosen for its skin to produce thick, heavy leather, such as is used for soles, harness, machine-straps, and similar strong articles. Still, this rule does not always hold good. For example: the tanned skin of a young rhinoceros is much harder and thicker than that of the oldest amongst our domestic animals. The choice of these skins, after tanning, is, therefore, of great importance to all engaged in the various branches of manufacture in which leather is employed.

From whatever animal the skin, or, as it is more usually termed, the *hide*, is obtained, it consists chiefly of two parts—viz., the external hair, or *fur* (of which we have spoken under the head of Class XXV.), and the *skin proper*, which, alone, is of value to the tanner. With these, however, is a little animal fat, which is removed during the process of tanning. The skin consists chiefly of *gelatine*, a substance exactly similar to isinglass, which, in fact, is nearly pure gelatine. The waste portions and the hoofs, &c., are commonly converted into glue, which is another form of gelatine, in an exceedingly impure state.

The process of tanning converts the gelatine into an insoluble substance; and is effected by impregnating it with *Tannin* — a substance found in a variety of vegetable products. An extensive collection of these was shown in Class IV. (*Animal and Vegetable Substances used in Manufactures*); and as they have yet been but simply named in this book, a short description of those chiefly in use may be here given.

Oak-bark was long the only material used by the tanner. It is obtained by making a slit, lengthwise, from the top to the bottom of the tree, after this has been cut down. The bark is then removed, in strips of about three feet in length, and packed up in bundles. That obtained from the branches is similarly collected, and is equally useful. Cork-tree bark is also employed, and is obtained from a kind of oak. Similarly, the bark of the willow, chestnut, alder, larch, mimosa (or wattle) tree, hemlock spruce, mangrove; the leaves of the sumac tree, grown in Southern Europe; the root of the common barberry, and even the heather, or ling, of our moors—all are used in tanning. Besides these, terra japonica, catechu (or cutch) —both extracts of the wood of Indian trees; valonia, the cups of a kind of oak; divi-divi, the pods of a South American tree; myrobolans, the fruit of an Indian tree; Boomah nuts; kino, obtained as a resinous substance from some trees in India and Australia, abound with tannin, and, accordingly, rank amongst the numerous sources of that substance.

Whatever materials are used, a strong infusion is made from them, in water, for the purpose of extracting the tanning principle, and of introducing it, in a soluble state, into the substance of the skins. The liquor thus made is called " ooze ;" and pits dug in the ground of the tan-works are used to contain it.

The skins, before being immersed in it, are first completely cleared of hair, fat, &c., by lime and other agents. They are then laid in the tan-pit with a portion of the tanning material between each; and the pit is filled with the ooze. In this condition the hides gradually absorb the tannin, which converts the gelatine into an insoluble substance. Our readers will better understand this process by trying the following experiment :—Add a little tincture of nut-galls, which contain much tannin, to a weak solution of either size, glue, or isinglass. A flocculent brown matter will fall down; and this is really *leather*. If the bark of a species of birch be employed in tanning, its oil imparts a peculiar smell to the leather; hence that noticed in Russian leather, which is tanned by that agent.

The process of tanning takes a long time, because its progress is its own retarder; the outside of the skin being rendered impervious first, and thus hindering the further introduction of the "ooze" into the centre. The practical methods of obviating this, and the new inventions which have been introduced to hasten the process, are exceedingly ingenious; but are beyond the sphere of our duties to describe. We have restricted, indeed, our description solely to the usual method of producing shoe-leather. Other kinds, such as morocco; chamois or "shammy;" kid; lamb; rat; &c., undergo entirely different processes; in fact, they are rather "cured" than tanned. The skins for kid gloves are prepared by means of alum, and the yolk of eggs, which renders them soft and pliable.

After the hides of the larger animals are finished in the pit, they are sent to the currier, who, by means of hammering, scraping, cutting, rubbing with tallow, &c., reduces them into a fit state for making the various objects included in the Class which we have now to describe.

Bermondsey, as most of our readers know, is the great London locality of the leather manufacture and trade. It announces its existence by the unmistakable smell of tan, which spreads on all sides through the atmosphere. Amongst the largest firms engaged in the trade, are Messrs. Bevingtons; Hepburn; and many others who exhibited leather of various kinds, and of different modes and stages of preparation. The leather trophy of Messrs. Bevington and Sons was well worthy of close examination. The "raw material" of the leather trade included not only that article, but vellum; parchment; skins prepared for boots, machine-straps or belting, and hose pipes; enamelled, grained, and other fancy leathers; with many varieties, showing the great progress which has, of late years, been made in the conversion of all kinds of skins to so many purposes, despite the large use which has been made of gutta-percha and india-rubber as substitutes. In this Sub-class A, there were also exhibitors from Edinburgh, Leeds, Dublin, Newcastle, and many provincial towns, where tanning and currying are both largely carried on.

Sub-class B included articles manufactured from, or to be used in connection with, the various kinds of leather we have been describing. The exhibitors were numerous, and from every part of the kingdom. Saddles and harness generally had pre-eminence in respect to number; and saddlers' ironmongery, such as bits, snaffles, stirrups, and other metal objects, used by the saddler, were included. Horse-clothing, holsters, saddle-bags, whips, canes, &c., made up the *miscellanea*.

In Sub-class C, the more refined manufactures of leather were found, as snuff-boxes, ornamental wall, screen, and other furnishings; potichomanie; with articles for embroidery, gilding, and other purposes of embellishment. Modelling in leather is an art of recent introduction; and it is astonishing to what numerous ornamental and pleasing purposes the material may be applied. Amongst them we may especially notice copies of leaves, fruit, flowers; animals, especially *crustacea* (as the lobster tribe), all of which have been much patronised as house ornaments.

In the foreign departments Class XXVI. was well represented. India contributed some beautiful specimens of horse-trappings, saddles, harness, &c. Belgian firms chiefly contributed articles for heavy use. From Brazil, the lighter kinds of leather, &c., were sent. In the French department, the "elegancies" of leather, in respect to boots, shoes, &c., were remarkable; attended, however, by large collections of more solid articles. The same remarks also apply to objects sent from Vienna, and various Austrian towns; and from other parts of Germany. In the Prussian collection, a considerable variety was exhibited both in solid and fancy articles. Italy also appeared to advantage, especially in the collection of the Parma sub-committee for the Exhibition. Amongst contributions from Russia, were chamois-dressed reindeer skins, Morocco, and other leathers. Spain exhibited leather, manufactured and in hides; and an Andalusian horse-harness created some curiosity. From Sweden and Norway the articles were chiefly those required for heavy work. Turkey ranked amongst the largest contributors in this class; Morocco leather being abundantly represented, and collected from all parts of the empire. The saddlery, and other manufactured goods, were very interesting specimens.

ARTICLES OF CLOTHING (Class XXVII.)—From the early days of our history, when dress was made of the simplest materials, to the present time, in which both man and woman "have sought out many inventions," our habiliments have doubtless been the subject of an almost endless variety in respect to material, colour, size, shape, and other conditions. Class XXVII. alone contained so many forms of dress, from the hat and bonnet to the shoes and boots, as to defy any possibility of presenting our readers with an epitome of its contents. To do so, would be equivalent to cataloguing the contents of the hatters', milliners', drapers', hosiers', glovers', and shoemakers' shops in Regent Street, or Oxford Street; a task which we shrink from even contemplating.

The articles embraced in this Class were, first, hats and caps; secondly, bonnets and general millinery; thirdly, hosiery, gloves, and clothing in general; fourthly, boots and shoes. We can only spare a few lines for remarks on each of these subclasses.

Of late years, beaver, which formerly was the chief material for the manufacture of hats for men, has been almost entirely replaced by silk plush, that can be produced for even less than half the cost of the old felted hair. It is not only that the material is less expensive; but the amount of work needed to produce the article is but trifling compared to that required in the various successive processes of beaver hat-making. They consisted of shaving the hairs from the skin; sorting them, so as to select the finer sort; bowing them; felting, heating, rolling, dyeing, &c., so as to form the body of the hat; and, finally, blocking this into shape. The silk hat, of modern use, is a much simpler affair. The body is made of thick brown paper, cork, felt, willow, hair-cloth, or some similar material, stiff enough to maintain its shape; and, being covered with a solution of shellac in spirit, the plush (already described in connection with the French department in Class XX.) is spread neatly over it. A hot iron soon moulds the whole into shape, and, with the addition of inside and outside trimmings, the hat is completed. Numerous exhibitors were found in this department; and, amongst the oldest firms in the trade, we may name that of Messrs.

Christy, of Gracechurch Street, who exhibited illustrations of felted and silk hats, &c. The curiosities in this sub-class, included ventilating and air-chamber hats, cork and felt hats for India, expanding hats, &c., &c.

In respect to bonnets and general millinery, we shall preserve a decorous silence. These are articles of too exalted a nature to permit of the profanity of male description. Crinoline must also be left unnoticed for the same reason, with the brief observation, however, that the largest desires of the female sex might have been satisfied in respect to the *extent*, quality, colour, &c., of the articles exhibited.

In Sub-class C, including hosiery, gloves, and clothing in general, an immense variety of articles was embraced. For example, there was hosiery of all kinds, in shirts, gloves, stockings, &c., a business now extensively carried on in Leicestershire and Nottinghamshire, where machinery has completely superseded the old method of hand-making. In articles of male attire, we noticed shirts, leggings, gloves, collars, fronts, web braces, belts, ecclesiastical and academical robes; wearing apparel, made of paper, and seamless felt; articles of waterproof and elastic materials, exhibited by the well-known firms of Macintosh and Co., S. W. Silver and Co., and others. Ladies' clothing, of all kinds, was included; and to complete the heterogeneity of the sub-class, umbrellas, sun-shades, parasols, were embraced in its category.

In the last sub-class (of boots and shoes), in addition to the ordinary articles of that kind, which were exceedingly numerous, we may notice, as partly or entirely new, the following :—Adjustable and detached heels, which can be so arranged as that, when one part is worn away, that which is unworn can be turned round to replace it; self-adjusting leather clogs; various novel boots; others to prevent splashing; ventilating boots; "easy" boots—a great advantage, we presume, to all wearers; new kinds of overshoes, or goloshes; chameleon, or colour-changing shoes!! boots with sole and heel moulded solid, *cum multis aliis*—a long list, which we must leave undescribed.

We turn briefly to the foreign departments included in this Class, noticing first the Indian collection, in which were numerous rich articles, and of great beauty. Amongst the most interesting were those sent by the government of India, native princes, and others, illustrating the clothing used in that country generally. Most European nations contributed; and, in many instances, the peculiarities of costume in each were exceedingly well illustrated. The French department carried the palm in number, variety, and elegance, especially in respect to gloves, and articles of lady-attire. Vienna, and other parts of Austria, largely contributed; and the same observation applies to Prussia generally. From Greece and Turkey many beautiful objects were sent, especially those in embroidery. The Chinese and Japanese collections contained many rich articles of this class, which were greatly admired. In the Portuguese collection was a beautiful silk mantle, worked with lace made from the fibres of the Guinea aloe. The Russian collection was interesting in an ethnological point of view, bringing before the spectator vivid representations of the kind of clothing used in various parts of the empire; and, to some extent, the same may be said of articles contributed from Spain, many of which were highly characteristic.

CHAPTER XI.

CLASS XXVIII.—PAPER, STATIONERY, PRINTING, AND BOOKBINDING.   CLASS XXIX.—EDUCATIONAL WORKS AND
APPLIANCES.

IN this chapter we shall include but two classes, because the matters they comprise are, in general, mutually related; Class XXIX. being, in fact, illustrative of the numerous applications of those processes, objects, &c., embraced in the preceding one. We may first take a glance at the various uses to which paper is now applied, the methods of its manufacture, and the materials from which it is made—subjects which will doubtless be of interest to all our readers.

Amongst the earliest methods of obtaining a material suitable for communicating knowledge by writing, we may class the papyrus paper, vellum, and other prepared skins. There is little doubt but that the Chinese have been longer acquainted with the uses and manufacture of paper than any other existing nation; and at the present day they employ it for far more numerous purposes than western nations. The well-known rice-paper must not here be confounded with the ordinary material. It is obtained from a tree growing in Formosa, of the ivy kind—the *aralia papyrifera*. For this purpose the pith of the tree is cut into sheets of extreme thinness, by means of large knives. It is extensively used for making artificial flowers, and is beautifully painted by the Chinese, who sell it, in the raw state, at the rate of about three-halfpence per hundred sheets, each three inches square. The ordinary paper of that nation is felted like our own, but made by hand, and is an exceedingly cheap article.

Paper manufacturing, in our own country, is carried on chiefly by machinery; only a small portion, comparatively speaking, being made by hand. The favourite material is worn-out rags, either of linen or cotton; but, of late years, owing to the scarcity of rags, many other sources have been tried. Straw, grasses of many kinds, especially Esparto grass (*lygœum spartum*), grown largely in Southern Europe; many fibres obtained from Indian plants, sugar-cane, rice, straw, &c., &c., have all been used with varied success, and, in some cases, to a very large extent. There is, however, an objection to using the raw material not existing in rags. It is, that in breaking up grasses, &c., in the preparatory processes, much loss is sustained, from the harshness or brittle nature of the fibre. Many, however, of the low-priced daily and weekly journals, both in London and the provinces, are printed solely on paper obtained from varieties of the grass tribe. In India, the fibres of the *Daphne papyracea*, and the *Edgeworthia gardneri*, are largely employed for paper-making. The paper is porous, and somewhat resembles our "whitey-brown." It is strong and durable; being highly suitable for the purposes of the engraver.

In our brief notice here of the manufacture of paper in Great Britain, we shall confine our remarks to that made from rags. These, on being received at the mill, are carefully sorted by women, in respect to their colour and quality. They are then cut to a nearly even size, and passed through a "dusting-machine," to remove all loose dirt, &c. Boiling and washing are the next processes; and, as the latter is carried on, the rags are torn to pieces by iron knives revolving in a kind of cage, through which clean water constantly and abundantly passes. By these means the rags are converted into a coarse pulp, which is afterwards bleached in a close chamber by chlorine gas. On being removed, the pulp has attained a beautiful white colour. It is then broken up still further by knives revolving in a machine, as before described; and at last becomes so comminuted, as to make, with the water, a liquid somewhat resembling milk in appearance: this is caused by the extremely fine fibres being completely detached from each other by the violent mechanical processes to which the rags have been subjected. At this stage, a little size is added to the pulp, to give a gloss on the surface of the paper, and also to prevent it absorbing the ink when used for writing purposes. The varieties of paper, from that used for printing, to the highest class of writing-paper, depend partly on the quantity of size added. In the absence of any, "blotting-paper" alone would be produced. At this stage, also, the colouring matter is added—only a minute portion, if any—for "cream-laid," and greater proportions for paper desired of a blue tint. "Smalts," and artificial ultramarine, are the chief colouring matters used.

It is impossible to describe the paper-making machine accurately without a drawing; but the following will give a general idea of its construction and mode of use. At one end is a large vat, into which the pulp is introduced; and this is kept in constant motion by arms revolving inside the vessel. From this the pulp passes into a square trough, and thence it slowly overflows in a thin but continuous stream, on to a horizontal wire sieve, kept constantly in a jerking kind of motion. The water gently drains off this wire, which, revolving on rollers, gradually carries the pulp to others that press the remainder of the loose liquid from it. By this time the pulp has gained a certain consistency, its fibres having felted together, and, proceeding onward to other rollers and cylinders filled with steam, it becomes dry and glossy. As it is thus produced, it is wound on to another cylinder, and is ready for cutting into sheets. In this condition it leaves the mill, and falls into the hands of the merchant, to whom belongs the duty of sending it out for the numerous purposes to which it has to be applied. Hand-made paper is produced at the rate of a sheet at a time, by a process similar in principle, but different in certain details; and it is after this method that Bank of England, and other notes, are produced at the present day. Of course this is a slow process; whereas by the machine, all that is required to keep up an incessant production of paper, consists in supplying, constantly, the pulp at one end, and removing the paper at the other, as each cylinder or roller becomes filled. Thus the process is kept on night and day without interruption, and a web of paper measuring miles in one continuous length, may be obtained.

Having thus described the raw material, and processes of paper-making, we may dispose of the first sub-class, which was devoted to various kinds of paper. Messrs. Burgess and Ward, of the Mendip paper-mills, near Wells, Somerset, afforded a very interesting series of illustrations respecting the manufacture and applications of paper made from straw. Writing-paper of all kinds, both hand and machine-made; drawing, card, and mill board, &c., were included: and amongst the novelties, were paper and mill-board made from hop-bine.

Under the head of Stationery, a great variety of articles comes under our notice. Ink, black-lead pencils, paper of many kinds, seals, sealing-wax, elastic bands, tracing and copying-paper, envelopes, account-books, tablets, playing-cards, pencil-pointers, drawing-papers, waxed papers for wrapping greasy substances, gold and other pens, &c., &c., are but a few of the articles we have to enumerate. The names of many of the exhibitors would be familiar to most of our readers; and we shall not lay ourselves open to the charge of being invidious by making a selection from them. Nor can we stop to describe the methods of making any of the objects we have named, although some of them present great temptations to that course.

In respect to the next sub-class, devoted to plate, letterpress, and other modes of printing, a few explanatory remarks may be acceptable. Under this head was classed type-printing; engraving, and printing from wood, copper, steel, &c.; lithography, chromo-lithography, and, generally, the production of illustrations on paper, so far as the mechanical part of the processes is concerned. With respect to the art of " printing," it is known that the Chinese were the first to use blocks for producing impressions on paper; and they have possessed that art, together with that of making paper, for at least 2,000 years. About the year 1440 of our era, Guttenberg, of Strasburg, commenced printing from blocks in Europe, and after-wards became partner with one Faust, or Faustus. The two succeeded, in 1450, in publishing an edition of the Bible. In England the art first became known about the year 1470, and the name of William Caxton is historically associated with its first practice; whether justly or no, has, however, been disputed. The invention of movable types, and the improvements in the printing-press, led to the rapid progress of the art, which has now culminated, in the diffusion of knowledge, to an extent that the wildest visionary would have considered as Utopian in its early days.

None but those who have engaged in literary pursuits are aware of the amount of trouble involved in producing a printed work. The setting-up of the " copy" in " type," correction of " proofs," stereotyping, preparation of wood and steel illustra-tions, printing, folding, stitching, binding, &c., are some of the most essential steps, and are carried on in the order here named. Despite every care on the part of author and reader, some error or blemish is sure to appear in every work: and woe be to the luckless wight whose name appears on the title-page as the " re-sponsible party," should his production fall into the hands of adverse critics. The only consolation he possesses, under such circumstances, is, that at some future day his enemy may write a book, when, being in turn severely handled, he may learn to temper justice with mercy. The mistakes of " compositors," to whom it falls to set a manuscript in type, are frequently ludicrous in the extreme, and would afford far more " fun," in the perusal of an uncorrected page, than even a lively number of *Punch*. As a rule, publishers are not their own printers and bookbinders; but in large concerns, such as that from which this work is issued, every branch of the business of "book-making" is carried on; the sub-division of labour being so arranged, that each step progresses in separate departments, from the reception of the manuscript from the author, to its distribution, as a book, amongst its readers.

We shall not enter here into the details involved in producing the illustrations of a book, as that will be more conveniently considered under the Fine Art department in our subsequent pages. It will be sufficient to say, for the present, that there are chiefly three methods of producing illustrations—namely, on wood, stone, and metal. Wood engravings are obtained on that material by cutting away such portions as are to afford the light parts of the engraving; whilst the shaded portion is effected by raised surfaces. Hence printing from cuts is precisely similar to the same operation from ordinary types. Thus, the illustrations at pages 100, 103, &c., are from wood-cuts fixed with the type in the "forme," which produces the page. Steel or copper engravings, on the contrary, are printed from the plates of metal, *in* which the dark portions are cut; and hence the operation of metal engraving and printing is exactly the reverse of that followed in wood engraving. From the qualities of the material employed, the metal-engraved process affords a far better opportunity of bringing out the gradations of light and shade; and hence the great beauty of copper and steel engravings. Lithography and chromo, or coloured lithography, is pursued on an entirely different plan. A tracing of the design or illustration is first made on prepared paper, and then transferred to a peculiar kind of stone, which has the property of retaining ink only on those portions where greasy matter has been introduced. The stone, on being wetted and "inked" by a proper kind of ink, will then readily afford impressions to damp paper. This is the ordinary method of lithographic printing; but in chromo-lithography, ink of various colours is employed. This method, which is of recent invention, has arrived at such great perfection, that pictures can now be produced rivalling both water and oil-colours in beauty and correctness. By a somewhat similar process "nature-printing" is carried on, and thus exact *fac-similes* may be had of leaves, and other vegetable products.

The art of electrotyping has been of essential service to the various trades embraced in the sub-class now under consideration. Copies in copper are obtained from wood-cuts by the action of electricity on a salt of copper; and as these can be multiplied to any extent, great expense is saved, because the original wood-cut is not in the least injured, its only use being that of affording a mould from which any number of electro-copies may be taken. This advantage is still further enhanced, because much time is saved, not only in the rapid production of the copy, but also in the fact, that a number of machines may be worked at the same moment, throwing off the illustrations at the rate of thousands per hour. In large illustrated periodicals, such as the *Illustrated News*, &c., this process has now become essential.

Photography is another branch of applied science, which has been of great service to all the trades embraced in this sub-class, for it affords *exact* illustrations of an object. The steel engravings embellishing this work are mostly from photographs, which served as the originals for the exercise of the engraver's art. Hence our readers are put into possession, not of fanciful pictures of the objects, but of representations, conveying a truthful idea in every respect.

We now refer to the various details of the sub-class, the production of which results from some of the processes we have briefly described. Specimens of types, for ordinary printing, were exhibited by Messrs. Besley, Caslon, Figgins, and other type-founders. The Electro-Printing Block Company contributed enlargements and reductions from copper-plates, wood-blocks, &c.—a result obtained from a most ingenious and successful process. Amongst specimens of chromo-lithography, &c., we must especially notice the productions of Messrs. Day and Son, who have attained so high a reputation for this kind of illustration. In bank-note printing, Messrs. Bradbury and Wilkinson held a first place. The Bank of England contributed, also, specimens of surface-printing, by which their notes are partly produced. In the ordinary operations of printing, we have much pleasure in noticing a specimen sent by Miss Faithfull, whose exertions in finding suitable employment for females at the Victoria Press, entitle her to the greatest praise. In polyglot typography, Messrs. Bagster maintained their world-wide reputation. Messrs. Leighton and Leighton illustrated the various processes connected with the methods of wood-engraving and the peculiarities of printing-surfaces; whilst the processes of surface-colour printing by machinery were effectively exhibited by Messrs. Leighton, Brothers. Amongst other curiosities, were a reprint of the first edition of Shakespeare; a letterpress *fac-simile* of ancient manuscript; a method of engraving by clock-work, to prevent forgery; specimens of the new art of auto-typography, &c., &c.

We pass over the remaining articles included in this sub-class—consisting, as they did, chiefly of books, tools, and other matters illustrating the production of books— by remarking, that in it and the next sub-class (devoted solely to bookbinding), most of the leading firms, in all parts of the kingdom, ranked as contributors; all running, as best they could, the race towards the goal of public favour, whether the *contents*, or the *exterior* of their works were considered. *En passant*, we cannot help expressing the opinion that, at the present day, the attention of many a book-buyer is chiefly caught by the *external*; illustrating, *literally*, the sound philosophy of an old Latin poet —that the organ of sight is the nearest road to the mind—a result not accordant with the sense in which he would have had his aphorism understood and acted on.

EDUCATIONAL WORKS AND APPLIANCES (Class XXIX.)—"What to teach," and "How to teach," have afforded problems (so far as the young are concerned) which have puzzled the wisest heads for centuries past; and the directions, plans, "systems," &c., which have been given, are, indeed, "legion." Within the memory of many of our readers, books were issued for the special use of "children of the age of four years and upwards," which certainly defied the comprehension of those even in mature years. Now, however, this is entirely changed; and if the royal road to learning be not completed, its pathways have been well paved for facilitating the progress of the young.

The Class to which we have now to direct attention is entirely devoted to educational objects, and embraces Books, Maps, Diagrams, and Globes; School Fittings and Furniture; Toys and Games; and, lastly, Illustrations of Elementary Science.

The range of these matters may be guessed at by our readers, when we state that the Commissioners included in the Class, as a whole, the instructive subjects of—Versions of the Holy Scriptures; Baby-jumpers, and Perambulators! Educational sets of Scientific Apparatus; and Fossils discovered at Peckham and Dulwich—certainly a congeries which, from its ludicrous nature, may afford the amplest apology for any defects in its description on our part. We are puzzled, in fact, as to whether we should commence with the jactatory apparatus devoted to the benefit of the infant, and so gradually trace its physical and mental development until it could appreciate "Books, Maps," &c., or follow the example of the Commissioners, and begin where the child should end. Out of respect to their authority, the last is the only course left open to us.

Amongst the contributors of educational books, diagrams, maps, &c., we notice the names of most of the leading publishers in the kingdom; and, pursuing the plan we have hitherto adopted, shall not make invidious selections. The collection of " one hundred and ninety-one versions of the Holy Scriptures, in various languages," may be, however, particularised as a noble example of the benefits arising from individual talent being utilised and aided by combined public effort, as shown in this contribution of the British and Foreign Bible Society. Had it not been for the energetic perseverance of this valuable institution, a great proportion of the heathen world would have been deprived of the best of books; for no private individual could have undertaken the work which has been so successfully accomplished through its instrumentality. In a similar way the greatest benefits have been conferred on a large class, who, from physical infirmity, are practically shut out from the world. We refer to the deaf and dumb, for whose special benefit works have been prepared, and of which several were exhibited in this class. The *miscellanea* and specialities of this sub-class, included, besides books, atlases, globes, maps, chronological charts, geological maps, instruments and apparatus for musical instruction; drawing-books; arithmetical, geometrical, and algebraic diagrams, with numerous devices for teaching elementary knowledge in general, for home and school use.

Sub-class B was devoted to the illustration of School Fittings and Furniture, and embraced all kinds of educational apparatus. A prize-medal was awarded for educational models and apparatus, to Joseph, Myers, and Co., who have long occupied a first position in simplifying science by models, &c., for the instruction of young people, on the plan of converting amusements into objects of an instructive nature. The British and Foreign School Society contributed valuable educational appliances; and similar articles were sent by the Congregational Board of Education. We would especially draw attention to the contributions of the Blind Asylum of Bristol; the Association for Promoting the Welfare of the Blind; the London Society for teaching the Blind to Read; the School for the Indigent Blind; and those of Viscount Cranbourne. Nothing can be a greater deprivation than a loss of sight; and it is truly gratifying to notice how successful have been both public and private efforts, not only in the attempt to communicate knowledge to these sufferers, but also in utilising their labours. Amongst other public bodies contributing generally to this sub-class, were the Home and Colonial Training Institution; the National Society for the Education of the Poor; the Philanthropic Society's Farm-school, at Redhill; the Reformatory and Refuge Union; the Society for Promoting Christian Knowledge; and the Sunday-school Institute. The Science and Art Department, South Kensington, sent illustrations of the course of instruction in schools of art, &c.; and these were exceedingly interesting, as representing the system enjoined by that department on schools and school-teachers connected with it. To further particularise objects included in this sub-class would be impossible, they being of too varied and numerous a character.

Sub-class C comprised Toys and Games of every possible variety, whether for in or out-door amusement, and for both sexes and ages. Dolls, cricket, perambulators, rocking-horses, baby-jumpers, chess, backgammon, with almost every other game, were represented, and most sources of juvenile amusement had been cared for. We shall draw attention only to the following:—The "Kindergarten" is an ingenious method, imported from Germany, for the amusement and instruction of very young children. It assists in calling out their latent faculties; materials are given by which the youngsters may make or copy any object that strikes the fancy: and from what we have seen of the system, we have no hesitation in strongly recommending its use in the families of our readers. Musical games were also exhibited by M. Van Noorden: their object is to teach the elements of the art in an easy manner. Whilst dealing with the subject of amusements, we cannot help remarking on the facility which exists on turning even the toys of our childhood into sources of instruction to even the youngest child. In many cases, a direction may be given to the bent of the mind at a very early age; and in recounting the biography of some of our greatest inventors, engineers, and men of science, we may often trace the germs of the future, as having been evidenced in the days of their childhood.

These observations lead us to the consideration of the last sub-class in this Class—namely, "Illustrations of Elementary Science." Certainly not a quarter of a century has elapsed since it was considered that a study of any branch of practical science, except by those who intended to make it a profession, was decidedly inimical to the progress of the young man in business pursuits. Such an idea is now scouted: indeed, science is universally reckoned as a necessary basis of many businesses; and an acquaintance with its principles has become essentially requisite in numerous instances. In any case, it has the advantage of calling out both the observant and reflecting faculties; and also affords, what is a universal advantage to every young person, a kind of hobby, which, in its encouragement, can not only lead to no harm, but must positively be productive of some good. The objects comprised in this sub-class represented many branches of scientific study: amongst them we may name the specimens of stuffed birds; vivaria and aquaria; geological cabinets, and mineral collections; chemical, optical, and other apparatus used in pursuing experimental sciences; ferneries; zoological series; orreries, &c., &c. At the present day, all these articles are supplied at so low a rate, that even the hard-working man may easily and cheaply employ his spare time in some branch of scientific study. In numerous cases, such a pursuit will not only be valuable as a means of mental recreation, but may be an aid in many of the occupations of life, and hence prove of even money value to those engaging in it.

In this chapter we have varied from the plan hitherto adopted, of glancing at the foreign department of each Class immediately after describing the articles contributed by British exhibitors. We have done so because the objects included in the two Classes are, with a trifling exception, so nearly related as to make it more convenient to deal with them collectively.

From India some very interesting objects were sent: amongst them being—bark used by former kings of Assam as a writing material; Thibetan works and printing-blocks in that character; paper from Madras and Nepaul, &c. The government contributions were of a most valuable nature, consisting of samples of paper from bamboo, old rags, hemp, aloe fibre, plantain fibre, the *Daphne cannabina*, &c., made in various parts of our Indian possessions. Some beautiful illustrations of caligraphy in Persian, Sheekista, Nagree, &c., also formed part of the collection.

Commencing with Belgium, amongst continental exhibitors, we may observe, that the paper-makers of that country can successfully compete with us on our own ground; hence the various kinds manufactured were well represented. The miscellaneous articles in Class XXVIII. were of a similar character to those of Great Britain. The educational portion contained a collection of objects formed under the superintendence of Professor Braun, and sent by the government; illustrations of the method of teaching writing adopted in Belgian schools, &c. The French department of Class XXVIII. came in formidable competition with our own, in respect to all kinds of paper, printing-tools, engraving, lithography, &c.; and the contributors were very numerous, but chiefly from Paris: the variety and taste of the articles displayed, in many cases, outstripped those produced by us. In Class XXIX. a most valuable collection was exhibited by the imperial Commissioners, embracing works, apparatus, &c., for teaching the young; which reflected great credit on the "paternal" government pursued in such matters by our neighbours across the Channel. From Algiers, as a French colony, some interesting matters were also sent.

Austria appeared to great advantage in many respects, but especially in Class XXIX.; the educational department being both varied and valuable: and the works which were sent showed an eminently practical tendency in the mode adopted for the early training of young people. The specimens of paper, lithography, typography, &c., were numerous. One remarkable feature was, the number of " Chambers of Commerce" figuring as exhibitors. From Bavaria, numerous objects, in both Classes, were shown; and the same may be remarked of other of the German states. Prussia vied with France and ourselves in respect to Class XXVIII.; the variety of objects exhibited in paper, engraving, lithography, stationery, &c., being great. The educational department was also excellent; and many of the methods, formerly peculiar to Prussia, are now largely diffused in Great Britain. Leipsic and Dresden (Saxony) amply sustained their long-known character in connection with Class XXVIII. The contributions to both Classes from Italy were numerous, and consisted of paper, engravings, books, &c. The educational collection was highly instructive, and indicated a general tendency to teach from natural objects rather than representations.

Amongst the Japanese general contributions, we noticed an Encyclopædia, illustrated works, story books, and a collection of toys, &c. From China specimens of paper were exhibited.

The collection belonging to the Netherlands, contained books printed in the Japanese, Chinese, and other languages (of peculiar character in respect to type), sent from Leyden and Amsterdam, besides numerous articles of stationery, engraving, and ornamental printing. One of the prominent objects of Spanish contribution was "smoking-paper," used, we presume, for the manufacture of cigarettes. The educational class was *not* represented—a significant fact in connection with the state of that country. On the other hand, that department of Norwegian and Swedish models, &c, was well worthy of inspection, as was also that of Switzerland. Even Turkey had a place in Class XXVIII., as was seen by the papers, pens, specimens of printing, engraving, &c., sent from Constantinople.

CHAPTER XII.

CLASS XXX.—FURNITURE, PAPER-HANGING, AND DECORATIONS.

WE are accustomed to estimate the civilisation of any people by the articles of domestic furniture which we find common amongst them. This test is certainly correct in principle, because a civilised condition of society has the tendency of stimulating the production of articles which minister not only to the wants of daily life, but also to its tastes in respect to art-application. Decoration is, at all times, an expensive fancy to gratify; and its extent is only measured by the possession of pecuniary means, and a refined disposition of mind in the individual who indulges in it. In a normal state of domestic life, such as the savage state, or during the early struggles of a colonist in a new settlement, nothing but the necessities and bare comforts of existence are sought for: on the other hand, in highly civilised countries, luxuries are not only common, but, by habit, become necessaries; and hence the great encouragement which is given to the skilled workers in the production of such articles.

The Class which now comes under review, combines both the useful and ornamental; and the variety of its objects is, perhaps, unequalled in any other branch of human industry illustrated in the Exhibition. It comprises all kinds of "furniture," whether domestic or ecclesiastical; and our readers can only arrive at an idea of the nature or number of articles which were contributed, by considering the manifold objects which the mansion requires for its complete furnishing—for the hall, drawing-room, library, bed-rooms, &c.

Daily habit familiarises so much with the objects surrounding us in our houses, that it requires some effort to estimate the amount of labour, &c., involved in producing them. The "raw material" of our house-furniture may, however, be chiefly divided into wood, metal, glass, and paper. Of these we shall select only the first, as manufactures of metal and glass will be considered under future Classes. The manufacture of paper we have already described; and we shall only have to notice it here as used for decorating walls, and similar purposes.

The Exhibitions of 1851 and 1862 have been productive of great advantage to the cabinet-maker. At each of them, woods of the most beautiful and useful nature were introduced into this country for the first time, and hence a fresh stimulus has been given to the production of ornamental furniture. We shall give a short account of some of these, and also of others generally employed; and those of our readers who may be desirous of pursuing the subject further, may have the opportunity of seeing a collection of woods from all parts of the world, which was transferred from the last Exhibition, and is now arranged in the Museum of Economic Botany at Kew. The Australian and Asiatic woods generally, in that collection, will well repay a careful examination, some of them being exceedingly curious and beautiful.

Furniture wood may be divided into two classes—namely, that used in the solid, and such as are suitable for veneers; the latter, however, embracing many kinds available also for solid work. Beech and birch (both natives of temperate climes), oak and mahogany, are the staple woods of the cabinet-making and allied trades; whilst rosewood, walnut, bird's-eye maple, the "curled" or feather kinds of mahogany, are often used for overlaying cheap woods. Veneers are made by cutting extremely thin leaves from ornamental woods by means of a circular saw. They are laid on the cheaper article by means of glue; and, when well done, they defy detection, except by an experienced eye. Many of our readers will readily understand this from painful experience; having, perhaps, purchased what was palmed on to them as "solid mahogany," &c.; but which turned out, after a little time, to be nothing better than veneered. Inlaying, which is commonly done for making ornamental tables and other furniture, is a species of veneering. For this purpose woods in great variety are used; the chief being cedar, cherry, ebony, holly, lignum-vitæ, maple, apple, pear, plum, satin-wood, tulip-wood, &c., besides some already named. In choosing a wood for useful or ornamental purposes, its colour, grain, hardness, and durability have all to be considered; and, as oak and mahogany combine all requisites in these respects, they have become largely used. Formerly, oak was much employed for house furniture, panelling, &c.; at the present day, its use is chiefly for ecclesiastical furniture, specimens of which we shall have to refer to hereafter. Our supply of mahogany is derived from the West Indies, especially Cuba and Honduras. The wood of the Australian *Eucalyptus* will, doubtless, become a cheap and abundant substitute. It resembles teak, a material which has been, of late years, also adopted by cabinet-makers. Both woods are hard, durable, and susceptible of a good polish.

To enumerate the various articles exhibited in this Class, and its sub-divisions, would be equivalent to making out a list of the furniture of a well-appointed household. Tables, chairs, bedsteads, plain and ornamental; bagatelle, billiard, and backgammon tables; sideboards, book-cases, reading-stands, &c., &c., with all their modifications, abounded. Some beautiful specimens of wood-carving were exhibited;

amongst which we may specially notice a Library Chimney-piece, by Trollope and Sons : a steel engraving accompanying this work illustrates this elegant production. A handsome marble Chimney-piece, by Leclercq, is also the subject of a steel engraving. Papier-maché articles were numerous; this material being exceedingly suitable for the manufacture of ornamental objects for the household. Messrs. Betteridge, of Birmingham, were large exhibitors of trays, tables, chairs, caddies, inkstands, made wholly or in part of it; as were also Messrs. Bielefield, of London. Parqueterie, marqueterie, buhl, encaustic, and mosaic work, tiles, and other productions of a similar nature, were amply represented; and some specimens of fret-work and curvilinear sawing were highly creditable to the ingenuity of the modern cabinet-maker. Buck-horn hall furniture attracted much attention amongst the designs of furniture in general. There were some of the Louis XIV., mediæval, and other admired kinds, not excepting even specimens of the Pompeian style. Camp, barrack, military, ship, and portable furniture and equipages were also contributed, some of the articles being exceedingly applicable to the conditions and purposes for which they were intended.

In respect to " church furniture," we must especially notice the contributions of the Ecclesiological Society, in which the various matters connected with church ornamentation were exhibited. Although anticipating our remarks on the foreign department of this Class, we here mention a splendid Gothic Pulpit, as a specimen of Belgian oak-carving, which attracted universal attention, although in a style to which we are quite strangers in this country. The Hereford Screen, designed by G. G. Scott, and executed by Skidmore and Co., was an object of much curiosity and admiration. It consisted of wrought iron; and hammered copper foliage, by way of ornamentation. The central figure represented our Lord rising from the tomb : there were other figures on either side; and the panels were filled with mosaic, composed of various coloured stones. The pulpit and screen here described are the subjects of steel engravings illustrating this work; and they have been accurately rendered from photographs of the originals.

Having pointed out some of the prominent objects in the British department, we must omit the endless variety of *miscellanea*, and turn for a moment to the sub-class embracing paper-hangings, and decorations for similar purposes. It is not too much to observe, that we are yet far behind the ancients in this class of ornamental work. Until recent years, our paper-hangings were on a par, as to their designs, with the crude willow pattern of our pottery; and in both respects we have had much to learn from our neighbours across the Channel. The variety of designs in the paper-hanging, in 1862, was great, and in many instances the specimens were exceedingly beautiful. Imitations of marbles, woods, &c., were very numerous. Methods of staining common woods, to imitate the more expensive kinds, were very good, and are now largely adopted, both for house and church fittings. Amongst curiosities connected with this method, we may mention the art of Pyrography, or carving on charred wood, for decorative purposes. If carefully executed, exceedingly pleasing effects are produced, as was seen by the specimens contributed to this sub-class. Washable papers for wall-decorations; Marmography, produced by chemical means,

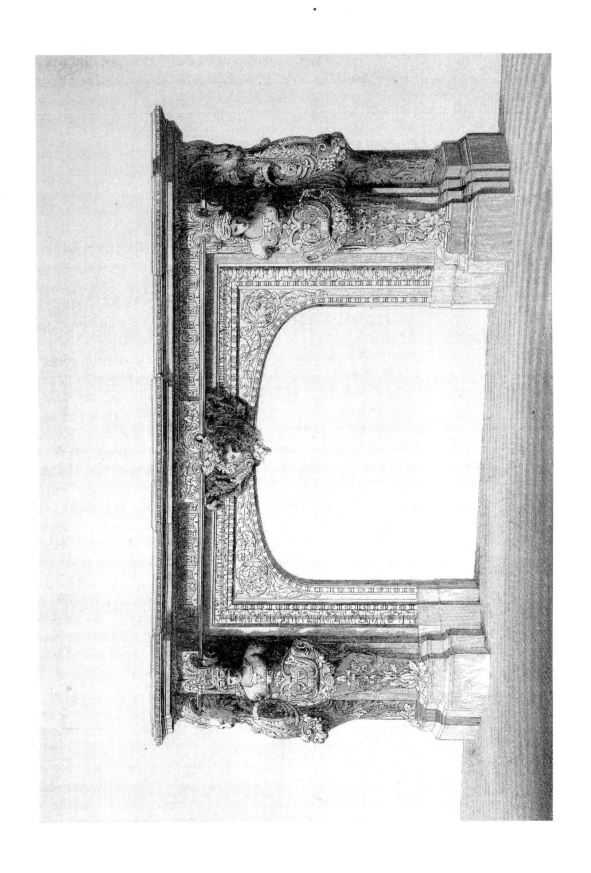

MARBLE CHIMNEY PIECE BY LECLERCQ.

GOTHIC PULPIT - SPECIMEN OF BELGIUM OAK CARVING

LIBRARY CHIMNEY PIECE BY TROLLOPE & SONS.

THE HEREFORD SCREEN

on transparent articles; and ornamental wood-work, printed by the agency of heat, may be ranked amongst the curiosities of this sub-class.

It is, unfortunately, impossible to give a description of the articles contributed from foreign countries to this Class, so as to contrast them with our own, without entering into technicalities that would be anything but interesting to our readers. Indeed, the nature of the objects, which can only be appreciated by being seen, prevents the possibility of our doing so, independent of any other consideration. We must, therefore, be content with noticing such as were either novelties, or of special value.

The government of India sent a considerable variety—in sandal-wood writing-desks, jewel and work-boxes, from Surat; inlaid tables, writing-desks, &c., and a collection of ivory inlaid work, from Bombay; articles in carved sandal-wood, from Coompta, Surat, and Mysore; carved black-wood furniture, lac-ware work and boxes, horn-work, from Vizagapatam; carved and inlaid work from Bareilly; papier-maché articles from Cashmere and Lahore, &c., &c. Contributions from private individuals, and of a similar nature, were also forwarded from Madras and other places. A grand piano, in rosewood case, elaborately carved by natives of Madras, and exhibited by Messrs. Kirkman and Sons, of London, was much admired. Sandal-wood was the chief material on which the carving was worked by the natives. From Japan there were some beautiful specimens of lacquer and inlaid-work, cabinet-stands, trays, bowls, &c.; articles in ivory; flower-baskets; carvings in ivory, wood, and other material; screens, vases, &c. We have already spoken of the Belgian pulpit: the remaining contributions were of a similar kind to those exhibited by our own makers. Brazil sent some very interesting objects made of woods grown in that country.

In the French department, the contributions were mostly of an ornamental nature, and did ample justice to the character for taste and elegance, which is always a feature in the productions of that nation. The exhibitors were chiefly resident at Paris, although the objects had, in many instances, been manufactured at provincial towns famed for certain classes of goods. The inlaid and gilt furniture, of old and modern styles, was rich in the extreme; and, in this respect, far exceeded that of any other nation. In paper-hangings some of the patterns were exceedingly beautiful; the variety and harmony of the colouring being not only extremely pleasing to the eye, but correct in taste and in the delineation of natural objects. Perhaps one secret of success in many French productions, is the accurate following of nature, in cases where designs have been thence drawn. Our perception of beauty is never outraged by the introduction of fanciful creations in such matters; and thus our operatives have frequently to become learners in all matters of decoration and embellishment, when they are put into competition with the French. The ingenuity displayed in the construction of many of the articles, was as credit-able as the taste shown in their decoration. Some excellent specimens of wood-carving, marqueterie, mosaic-work, trellis, &c., were exhibited.

The productions of France and other European nations were distributed in various parts of the Exhibition building, independent of the localities assigned to each nation; and some of them have been already named in the general glance at the contents of the Exhibition, in the early part of this work. We shall, therefore, confine our future remarks to matters of special interest only, as, generally speaking, the objects named in our description of the British and French departments, were, more or less, repeated in all others. From Munich, a specimen of flooring inlaid with twelve kinds of wood, showed excellent artistic skill. Household furniture, made from hart's horn, and sent from Frankfort-on-the-Maine, was much admired. Amongst the numerous contributions from Prussia, we may specially notice, as cheap and curious, the domestic articles made from wicker-work; and an ornamental chair, exhibited by the Board of Directors of the Penitentiary at Sonnenburg. As chimney-pieces have been already named in this Class, we must mention one sent from Meissen, and made at the Royal Saxon China Manufactory. It is the subject of a steel engraving in this work, and properly belongs to Class XXXV. As a work of art, especially in pottery, it received much attention. The contributions from Hamburg were both numerous and valuable. We specially noticed, as being extremely pretty, the fancy furniture made from stag's antlers, and articles of amber. Solidity and utility were the general characteristics, also, of the objects exhibited from that city. The basket and wicker-work evinced great skill in the treatment of that cheap material, and which is largely employed, in Northern Germany, for many domestic purposes. In the Italian department, the ornamental and decorative work was of the highest character; and, perhaps, as a whole, was not excelled in any other Court. The mosaic tables, from Florence especially, were of great beauty, and formed centres of admiring groups. The inlaid cabinet-work was very finely executed. In illus-trating the mosaic-work, we may mention that the "Royal Manufactory of Mosaics in Pietre-Dure," contributed numerous articles of their manufacture—vases of Egyptian porphyry, and a collection of 121 siliceous stones, used in the production of Florentine mosaics, tables, &c. The marqueterie views of Rome, Venice, Florence, &c., were of great beauty, and excellent specimens of artistic skill. Utility chiefly characterised the Netherlands' Court—a remark also applicable to those of Denmark, Norway, Sweden, and Switzerland. The tables from Rome, in marble, imitation malachite, lapis-lazuli, porphyry, and alabaster, were gems of art; and, amongst the curiosities, was a table made from a rare stone found in the ruins of Rome; and others from breccia, obtained from Adrian's Villa. The Spanish collection comprised, inter alia, some fine arabesques; a group of animals in mother-of pearl; and a curious bedstead, convertible into a column. In the Turkish collection, a great variety of articles was found. Mother-of-pearl was a favourite material of ornamentation; and table-covers, embroidered work, perfumed waters and oils, inlaid work, ottomans, cushions, &c., gave a lively picture of the household goods of the better class in Constantinople, Damascus, and other cities of the empire.

Our colonies—the products of which were not generally included in the syste-matic classification of articles which was adopted in respect to foreign countries— contributed many valuable objects, especially in respect to the "raw material" of this Class. South Australia exhibited specimens of malachite and native wood. The Bahamas contributed yellow wood, green ebony, cedar, mahogany, &c. From

CHIMNEY PIECE BY THE ROYAL SAXON CHINA MANUFACTORY.

Canada we noticed a considerable variety of woods; and our attention was specially drawn to an invalid bedstead, in which, by an ingenious contrivance, a sick person could easily lift or turn himself, independent of the aid of an attendant. Some very pretty articles in ebony were sent from Ceylon; also a pair of tamarind card-tables, and articles made from the wood of the cocoa-nut tree. Dominica supplied upwards of 150 specimens of ornamental woods indigenous to that island. Most of them were polished; and they formed an excellent collection of material for fancy and ornamental cabinet-work. We must here conclude this cursory account of the contents of Class XXX. In the following six Classes, other articles, both useful and ornamental in the household, will be detailed; our division of them having been adopted in respect to the material of which they are made, rather than with regard to the objects to which they are applied as matters of daily domestic use.

CHAPTER XIII.

CLASS XXXI.—IRON AND GENERAL HARDWARE. CLASS XXXII.—STEEL, CUTLERY, AND EDGE-TOOLS.

BIRMINGHAM and Sheffield, the two great centres of our iron and steel manufactures, may be considered to almost monopolise the production of articles included in the two Classes which form the subject of this chapter; for although contributions were sent from all parts of the kingdom, still the two towns just named may be viewed as affording the material of all our hardware and cutlery manufactures, though these are carried on at other places. It will be unnecessary for us to enter into any account of the production of iron from its ores, or of steel from iron, as this has already been given at p. 139, *et seq.*, and to which we accordingly direct the careful attention of our readers. The new process invented by Mr. Bessemer, and which has produced so great a sensation in the trade, and profit to himself, is described at p. 38. It well merits a careful study, more especially as it was not the result of "accident," but rather of pure experiment, and correct scientific induction. He has had to contend with prejudice, and opposition of "vested interests;" but the merits of the invention have been confirmed by experience, and its adoption is becoming largely extended. The old methods of preparing steel are still largely followed, especially in Sheffield; and to these we shall have to allude incidentally, as we describe the cutlery manufacture.

The variety and extent of Class XXXI. defies the possibility of selection or arrangement. Almost everything to which iron is applicable was included. Bird-cages; cooking apparatus; locks, bolts, and bars; stoves and ranges; roasting-jacks; scales and weighing machines; gates, staircases, chains, fences, and hurdles; ships' iron furniture; wire ropes and lightning conductors; smoke-jacks; anchors; safes and locks from Bramah, Chubb, and other eminent makers; enamelled iron-work for domestic utensils; buttons; tanks and cisterns; nails, &c.; galvanised iron-work; shoe-heels and tips; bellows, forges, anvils, &c.; ink-stands; corkscrews; fire-bricks and tiles; crinoline fire-protectors!!—a valuable article for modern use; knife and boot-cleaners; spectacles, eye-glasses, &c.; horse-shoes and nails; fenders, scuttles, and fire-irons; bedsteads; "kitcheners;" hooks and eyes; wire plant-stands; springs, axletrees, and other carriage fittings; bottling machines; builders' iron-work; wire-cloth for meat-screens, &c.; coins, complete and in progress; hand-cuffs, leg-irons, and dog-collars; drinking fountains; lamp-posts; block-tin work; pins, needles, and thimbles; powder-flasks and shot-pouches; goffering machines and laundry utensils; fish-hooks; wrought-iron tubes; vermin-traps; mincing and sausage machines; saddlers' ironmongery; gas-cooking apparatus; coffee-mills; glass ena-melled hollow ware; hat and umbrella-stands; gas bath arrangements; rat and mouse-traps; cord, picture, and sash-lines made of wire; refrigerators or coolers; railway iron-work and fittings; sea-water distilling apparatus; lamps, gas-burners, &c.; copying presses;—all these afford but an imperfect idea of the variety and number of articles included in the first sub-class devoted to iron manufactures. We must call special attention to two matters—namely, the splendid iron gates exhibited by the Colebrook Dale Company (which were greatly admired), and the improved stable-fittings contributed by Messrs. George Smith and Co., of Glasgow; steel engravings, representing each, being given in this work. The Norwich gates, by Messrs. Barnard, of that city, have been already described at p. 23.

In looking over the imperfect list of objects just given, we cannot help feeling surprised at the enormous variety of articles which are manufactured from iron. To us, as a country, our mines of that material and coal are of infinitely greater value than we should have gained had they been mines of gold; for it is not the value of the raw material which can measure that of the manufactured article; a few ounces of iron being convertible into articles worth upwards of £100 in value—as, for example, in the instance of watch-springs. It is rather the price paid for skilled labour, and, by consequence, the large number of persons employed, that must be taken as a commercial estimate of the value of our mineral fields. The dis-coveries of new sources of the precious metals do not tend to enrich a nation per-manently; for their use is chiefly confined to representing the value of other com-modities; whilst iron, on the other hand, the cheapest of all the metals, has such qualities as fit it for nearly every purpose; and hence its possession as a mineral tends to bring about a greater augmentation of capital than perhaps any other pro-duction of our earth.

Sub-class B was devoted to manufactures in brass and copper; and although not so extensive as that just described, comprised a large number of useful and orna-mental articles. Gas-meters were included; and most of the leading manufacturers were represented. Mr. Thomas Glover, of Clerkenwell Green, received a prize medal for excellence of manufacture as regards dry-meters. In chandeliers, &c., Messrs. Defries' productions received the unqualified approbation of all visitors to the Exhibition, especially for the glass candelabrum (Class XXXIV.), which has been already described at p. 36. Great variety was shown in various articles of gas-fittings for house and other purposes.

IRON GATES

EXHIBITED BY THE COLEBROOK DALE COMPANY

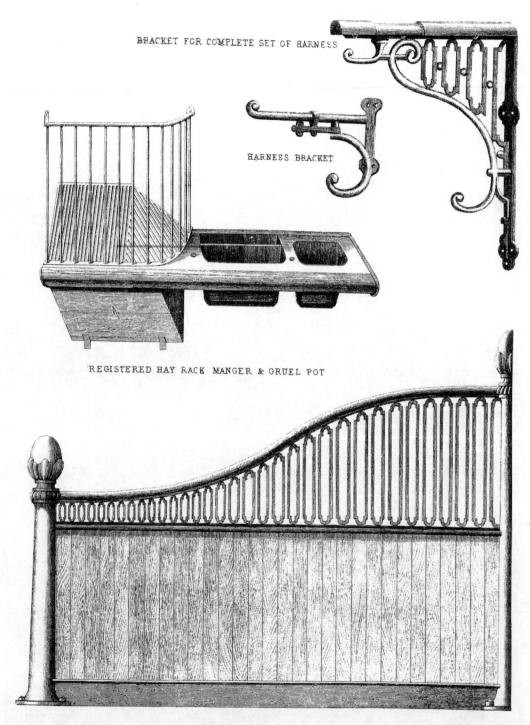

BRACKET FOR COMPLETE SET OF HARNESS

HARNESS BRACKET

REGISTERED HAY RACK MANGER & GRUEL POT

ORNAMENTAL STALL DIVISION.

IMPROVED STABLE FITTINGS BY MESS.ᴿˢ GEORGE SMITH & Cᵒ GLASGOW.

In this sub-class were also included bells, made from bell metal; and some of the leading founders exhibited. The screen for Hereford cathedral has been already described: it was contributed by the Skidmore Art-Manufactures Company, with others of a similar kind. Other articles for ecclesiastical decoration were numerous in this sub-class, and chiefly in brass-work. Mediæval, Gothic, and other old styles were included.

Amongst the *miscellanea*, were inlaid, gilt, and enamelled plates for decoration; lamps, in great variety, for oil and gas, and for household, railway, ship, and other purposes; musical inventions applicable to clocks; tea-trays, urns, kettles, &c.; various articles for gas and water-works purposes; brass and plated harness furniture; gas, steam, and water-cocks; safety-indicating gas chandeliers, and safety-taps for gas; moulds for confectioners; weathercocks, &c.; coffee-pots on the percolating principle (Loysel's); brass knobs, beading, &c., for house furniture and door-handles; coal-scoops; brewing and distilling apparatus, contributed by the eminent firm of Pontifex and Co., of Shoe Lane, London; lamps for the oxy-hydrogen or lime-light; with other articles in copper, brass, and alloys, too numerous and various to detail.

The Sub-class C included manufactures in tin, lead, zinc, pewter, and general braziery. The articles were generally those of common daily use, and we shall only particularise one contribution—namely, that of Mr. Lovegrove, of Isleworth, which afforded specimens of plumbing from the fourteenth century to the present time.

STEEL, CUTLERY, AND EDGE-TOOLS (Class XXXII.)—Before proceeding to notice the foreign Courts, in respect to the Class just described, we shall take a glance at the contributions to Class XXXII., including objects of steel manufacture carried on in this country; commencing with the Sub-class A, which was restricted to matters not relating to cutlery and edge-tools, of which Sub-class B was constituted.

In the early part of this chapter we mentioned the Bessemer process of producing iron and steel as one of the greatest improvements of our age, and as being gradually adopted wherever those materials are required. It must, however, be remarked, that, at present, the old methods of iron and steel production are still largely followed, especially in the neighbourhood of Sheffield; and an outline of them will therefore be desirable before we enter into a description of the cutlery articles included in Sub-class B.

Pig-iron, as produced in the first stage of the *ordinary* smelting process, is charged with a great variety of impurities, such as silica (or the matter of flint), phosphorus, and carbon or charcoal; and to remove these, the process of refining (which Mr. Bessemer's method supersedes) must be gone through. To effect this, the pig-iron is broken up into pieces, which are thrown into a shallow trough, and exposed to an intense heat in a suitable furnace. The iron melts; and, in this condition, atmospheric air, which is allowed to pass over its surface, burns away, by degrees, a considerable proportion of the carbon. The melted metal is then run off, and, after becoming solid, is again broken into pieces, and conveyed to the puddling furnace. Here it is brought into a softened condition, and just up to the melting-point. At this stage it is constantly kept stirred-up by the workman until it becomes of a pasty consistence, and then removed in masses called "blooms," weighing about sixty pounds. The metal now possesses the properties of malleability and tenacity, which it has acquired during the processes just described. Previous to this, and in the pig-iron state, it is brittle, and has little or no tenacity.

A "bloom," at nearly a white heat, is placed on an anvil, and struck with heavy hammers driven by a steam-engine. It thus becomes converted into a flat bar. After being re-heated, it is repeatedly passed through powerful rollers, and, at last, acquires all the characters and properties of "wrought-iron." Bar, rod, railway-bars, &c., are produced by rolling together rods of the metal; iron having this property of "welding" or uniting in pieces at a red heat, which is alone possessed by it and platinum.

For producing steel, the best English, or, what is often preferred, Swedish iron is used. Steel differs from iron chemically, and in many of its physical characters. In a chemical point of view, it contains more carbon than wrought-iron; and its physical differences consist in greater tenacity, ductility, and the property of being tempered—that is, of receiving and maintaining any degree of hardness and elasticity properly communicated to it. To effect this conversion, wrought-iron bars, of the best quality, are packed in boxes, with layers of charcoal, and exposed to heat: gradually the carbon, and also a small portion of nitrogen obtained from animal substances (also introduced occasionally), or from the air, are absorbed. The workman carefully watches the process, and, at times, takes out a bar to judge of its progress. When complete, the bars present a blistered appearance; and, in fact, are converted into what is technically termed " blistered steel," which is chiefly used to make cheap articles, and is of an inferior quality.

"Shear-steel" is produced by breaking up the bars just described into pieces of about a foot long, and exposing them to the action of a powerful hammer. Their particles are thus brought into closer contact, and the tenacity of the metal is increased. The next step is to make them white-hot, when they are hammered together, so as to form a solid mass. The process of "tilting" is then pursued; and this consists in hammering the bars, heated to a comparatively low temperature, so as to give an even and close texture to the metal. The steel is then cast into ingots, and afterwards rolled into sheets or bars, according to the purpose for which it is required, when it becomes the raw material of the cutler and other workers.

It would be impossible for us to describe the various processes adopted in manufacturing steel into the numerous articles of cutlery. We will, however, select a few, which may be interesting to our readers. Table-knives are forged either out of shear or cast steel. To effect this, a piece of the metal, of about the size of the intended article, is made red-hot, and hammered into the required shape; the end or tang, which secures the knife to its handle, being made separately, and afterwards welded to the blade. The "tempering"—that is, giving it the requisite degree of hardness—results from heating the blade to a red heat, and then plunging it into cold water. It is subsequently ground on a grindstone, polished, and is then ready to receive the handle. Razors are made in a similar manner; but in this, and many other steel manufactures, much depends on the tempering; and according to the purpose for which the article is to be used, so its "temper" is suited by heating it to temperatures varying from about 250° to 600° Fah., by which means all degrees of elasticity, hardness, &c., are imparted to it. This is one of the most valuable qualities of steel, especially in the manufacture of watch-springs and steel pens; the value of both of which depends entirely on their elastic qualities. In judging of the temper, the workman is partly, or, in many cases chiefly, guided by the colour which the steel acquires. This varies from a light straw to a deep blue; and an illustration of it may be seen in an ordinary watch-spring. Besides springs and pens, needles, fish-hooks, buffers for railway carriages, crinoline steel, busks, wire for musical instruments, swords, and many other steel articles, are entirely dependent on tempering for their value; not forgetting, also, the numerous tools of the engineer, carpenter, and other artisans. A good sword, for example, if of the best steel, and of the right temper, may be struck against an object, and bent so that the handle and point are nearly in contact, and yet, on being removed, it will regain completely its original shape. This is, perhaps, an *experimentum crucis* in the manufacture of steel, and one which the celebrated Damascus and Toledo blades are said to bear with impunity.

Nearly the whole labour or art of the cutler, and other workers in steel, consists in the operations we have described—namely, heating, hammering, grinding, and tempering; to which may be added filing and polishing. The production of files is still one of handicraft; and, as they are most important articles, a short description of making them may not be out of place. A piece of bar-steel, of suitable length, is heated and forged into the required shape, which may be either "square," "half-round," or triangular—names applied to files as sold in the shops. The metal is then *annealed* by heating it, and cooling it gradually—a method always adopted to soften steel. When quite cold, it is ground so as that it may acquire a level surface on all its sides. The teeth are formed by holding a tool of hard steel across the softened bar, and striking it with a hammer, when a "dint" or shallow cut is formed, the edges of which produce the "tooth." The entire bar is similarly treated, and all the teeth are made. The file then requires hardening, which is effected by making it red-hot, and plunging it into water containing ale-grounds, &c. It is then dried; and having thus become of the right temper, is ready for the use of the machinist. Saws are made from sheets of "cast steel," which are cut up into strips of the requisite width and length. The edge on one side is then ground down, and the teeth are cut out by punches, or, rather, are left on the steel by the action of the punch. The blade is hardened by heating it in an oven, and plunging it, whilst still hot, into a trough containing oil. Hammering and planishing are the next steps; and the teeth are afterwards ground to the requisite sharpness, on a large revolving grindstone, and "set" by beating every other one out of a straight line. The handle is then fitted on, and the saw is completed.

The operation of grinding causes two sources of danger to the health and lives of the workmen. Occasionally, the stone, which revolves on a horizontal axis, suddenly flies to pieces by centrifugal action; and as the operative sits almost on it, and in front, he may be instantly killed by this accident. The other source of danger is, however, the most to be feared, because it is insidious and constant. It arises from the fine particles of steel, which are inevitably inhaled, and that tend invariably to produce consumption. Inventions have been introduced to diminish this, such as magnetic masks, &c.; but their adoption is but partial; and hence "grinders" are generally short-lived, and occasionally somewhat dissipated in their habits—a result arising partly from the high wages they obtain, and from the depression of feeling engendered by the causes mentioned.

This brief account of some of the most common manufactures in steel, and the conversion of iron into that material, will serve as an introduction to the two sub-classes. Many of the articles included in them have been already mentioned, and we shall therefore only notice such as are of special interest. The two methods of steel manufacture were amply illustrated by the Acadian Charcoal Iron Company, of Sheffield, and Mr. Bessemer, of London. The leading manufactures of steel pens, needles, fish-hooks, &c., were represented. Heavy steel works were numerous; and we must draw attention to the contributions of Messrs. Naylor, Vickers, and Co., of Sheffield, whose bell trophy, consisting of nine cast-steel bells, suspended in a Gothic bell-tower, and various specimens of steel, showing its application to the manufacture of ordnance, and every kind of arms, &c., is the subject of a steel engraving given with this work. Crinoline steel—a most important article of Sheffield manufacture, consuming some tons of iron weekly—was not forgotten; and its analogue, umbrella ribs, showed how extensively whalebone and cane have been substituted by metal. Saws, files, engineering tools, &c., were amongst the specialities of the trade.

A few words on the manufacture of needles and pins may prove of interest to our lady readers. They were included in Sub-class A. In olden times needles were made of bone, bronze, gold, &c., and were exceedingly expensive articles: so much so, indeed, that estates have been held in this country subject to the annual payment of one or two of such costly articles. Ridiculous as this may appear to us, it must be remembered, that, even now, the Corporation of the City of London holds certain lands on conditions of a similar character. A very interesting collection may be seen in the British Museum, of ancient needles, gathered from various places in this kingdom. The present centres of the trade are chiefly Redditch and Studley; although the manufacture is carried on in other places.

A very instructive illustration was made in the Exhibition by Mr. A. Morrall, of Studley, to whose family and to himself we are indebted for many improvements in the manufacture of needles; an outline of which is as follows:—The needle-maker receives the wire in the form of rolls, three feet in diameter, the size or thickness depending on that of the needles to be made. He places two or three of these rolls side by side, and cuts them through with a large pair of shears, in lengths sufficient to make *two* needles from each piece of wire: this point is essential to be remembered, because the speed, &c., of the process depends on it.

The wires are then straightened by placing several thousands of them between two iron rings, which retain them in the form of a bundle. This is placed in an oven, and made red-hot; and in this condition the bundle is rubbed with a curved

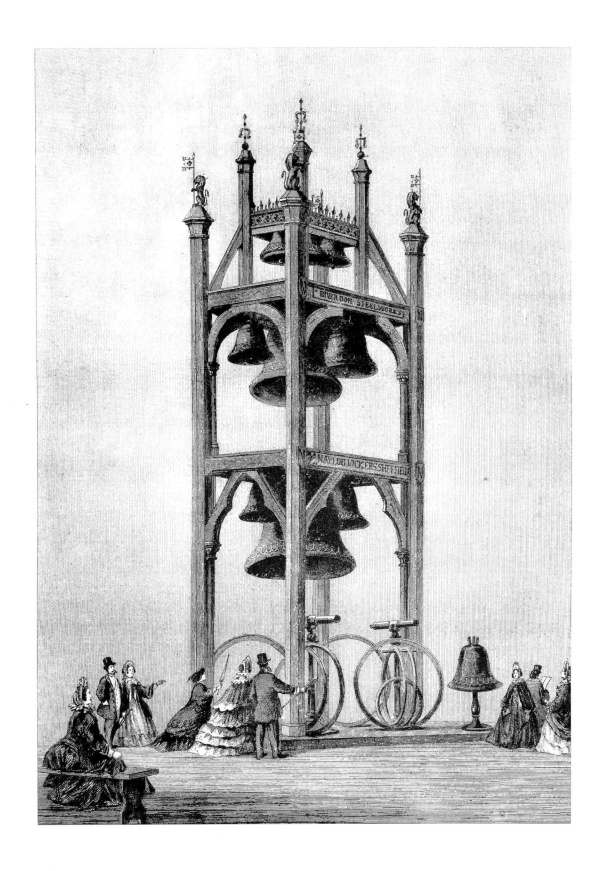

MESS.RS NAYLOR VICKERS & COMP.Y BELL TROPHY &c.

bar of iron, until all the wires are forced into a straight condition. The ends of each are then pointed by pressing them against a dry revolving grindstone; after which they are washed, dried over a fire, and placed, singly, between two dies or stampers to flatten the middle, and to form the head of each needle, into two of which the wire is shortly to be made. At the same time, the place of the eye, and that at which the wire is to be broken, are also marked.

The wires are then taken to a hand-press, and the eyes of the two needles punched out at one stroke. The wires are next given to children, who gather together about fifty at a time, so that the workman may remove, by means of a file, all rough edges produced during the operation of punching. They are then broken at the middle, and thus two rudimental needles are produced. After the tops of the heads and the inside of the eyes have been filed, the needles are "tempered"—a process, the importance and nature of which we have already frequently spoken. The needles are ranged on iron plates, and heated in a furnace. When red-hot, they are taken out, and thrown into a vessel of oil or water, in which they are afterwards heated, and allowed to cool gradually. Such as have become crooked are straightened on an anvil, by means of a small hammer. They are afterwards polished, by putting a large quantity into a canvas bag with oil, soft soap, and emery-powder, in which they are kept constantly in motion for about a week. On being removed, they are washed in hot water, and dried in sawdust.

After being sorted, and spread out in a line on a piece of wood, the eyes are burnished, so as to prevent them cutting the thread when they are in use. The heads are first softened by placing them on a red-hot iron, and are then rubbed with the burnisher. The finishing process is that of completing the polish, which is done by pressing the needles against a wheel covered with prepared leather, and called a "buff," which is kept in rapid movement. They are then packed in paper, and are fit for the use of our lady friends.

We have already mentioned how much labour enhances the price of manufactured iron; and on the authority of Mr. Morrall (to whom we are indebted for some of the facts here given), we may add that one sovereign's worth of steel is converted into about £70 worth of needles. About 100,000,000 are made, weekly, in the needle district; and upwards of 10,000 persons depend on the manufacture for subsistence. Various names are given to the different articles. Thus, "sharps" are those commonly used for sewing purposes; "short sharps" are a coarser kind; and, amongst the rest, are "blunts," "straws," "harness," "darning-needles," "netting-needles," "bodkins," &c.

Pins are made from brass wire, as they do not require the elasticity so necessary in needles. The wire is, at first, cut into lengths sufficient to make several pins. The ends of each piece are sharpened by turning them round, whilst they are, at the same time, pressed on the edge of a revolving grindstone; and, when sufficiently sharp, as much of the piece is cut off at each end as will be enough to make two pins. The remaining portion is similarly treated, until all the wire in each piece has been converted into headless pins; or, at all events, wires blunt at one end and sharpened at the other, and of the length of one pin each.

The heads of pins were formerly put on by twisting a piece of thin wire round another of the size of the proper pin, so that a little bead, hollow in the centre, was formed. These beads were then pressed on to the pin at its pointed end, and fastened on the blunt portion by a few gentle taps of a hammer. "Solid-headed pins," now in universal use, are made by cutting the pin a trifle longer than it is intended to be. The blunt end is then compressed in a machine having a cone-like opening; and the wire, expanding as it is pressed, forms the conical head of the pin. These are "whitened" by "pickling" them in acid-water to remove dirt, &c., and then boiling them in a vessel containing tin and a coarse kind of cream of tartar. By a chemical action, the tin becomes dissolved and thrown down on the brass wire of the pin, which is thus rendered beautifully white. After being washed and dried in hot bran, women sort them, and fix them in rows on paper, or pack them in quantities when they are to be sold by weight.

Sub-class B, devoted to cutlery and edge-tools, we have already anticipated. Knives and forks; razors; carpenters', engineers', and tools of all kinds that are made of steel; scissors; corkscrews; scythes; sickles, &c.; pruning-knives, and horticultural instruments generally; carriage and railway-springs; files; watchmakers' and jewellers' articles; lancets and other medical instruments, &c., &c., give some idea of the variety of objects exhibited, although many which might have otherwise been included in this sub-class, being devoted to special purposes, have been already referred to in other Classes.

The Foreign and Colonial Courts, of Classes XXXI. and XXXII., must now be briefly glanced at, which we shall do in nearly alphabetical order, omitting matters that have been already described except for the purposes of comparison. Connected with Class XXXI., India contributed numerous articles for domestic use, chiefly of brass and copper; and in Class XXXII. were gold and silver-mounted swords, knives, specimens of Assamese cutlery; and similar articles from Bangalore, Bokhara, Cuttack, and Salem. Messrs. Halliday, of London, exhibited some Burmese razors, tweezers, and an areca-nut cutter. From Sydney cutlery was sent, and a few specimens of other steel manufactures, surgical instruments, &c. Mining-picks, hammers, and other metal articles, arrived from Victoria.

Belgium was largely represented in Class XXXI.—a matter of no surprise when we remember that it is similarly circumstanced with ourselves in respect to coal and iron; Liège and Charleroi being as noted for hardware and steel productions on the continent, as are Birmingham and Sheffield with us. Among the curiosities may be named a lock sent by Mathys Declerck, of Brussels, having 629 fixed, and 414 movable pieces, with a key possessing eighty-four different divisions—a monument, indeed, of patient and persevering labour. The specimens of rolled and other iron, showed how extensively and successfully the manufacture is carried on in Belgium. The cutlery and other steel goods were not numerous. Brazil contributed various articles in wrought-iron and steel. Denmark also exhibited, to a limited extent, in Class XXXI.

France ranked next to ourselves in the extent and variety of objects exhibited in both Classes. The contribution of Messrs. Barbezat, an armour trophy, &c.,

which is the subject of an engraving in this work, was especially worthy of notice. "Bronzes" were exhibited in great numbers, both real and imitative; and the articles already mentioned, as found in the British Courts, were equally represented in those of France. Cutlery of all kinds was largely contributed, together with tools, steel surgical instruments, pens, ornaments, &c.; some of the fancy cutlery being very elegant. The contributions of Austria were exceedingly large and varied in both Classes; the collective exhibition of iron and steel wares, of manufacturers at Waidhofen and Ybsitz, and from the district of Stadt Steyer, in Upper Austria, deserving careful attention: and here we may note, that the empire, generally, is greatly favoured in mineral riches, in respect to iron and most of the commonly used metals. The manufactured articles of iron, steel, copper, &c., were, in general, similar to those of our own country. Bavaria, and several of the smaller German states, exhibited in both Classes. Prussia was also extensively represented, especially in Class XXXI. The Berlin Royal Iron Foundry contributed a monument of Frederick William III.; busts of the Prince and Princess Royal; a chandelier; and various smaller articles. The number of exhibitors, and the variety of goods, were large. A butcher's knife represented Greece! Italy made a respectable show in both Classes. The Netherlands exhibited, but to a moderate extent, in Class XXXI. only; and the same remark applies to Norway. Russia contributed a small variety of articles in iron, steel, bronze, and yellow metal. Spain and Portugal were barely represented. The contributions of Sweden do not require special notice, although that country supplies us with large quantities of excellent iron, used here for conversion into steel and other purposes. Copper wares constituted the chief collection sent from Turkey in Class XXXI.: the articles in steel were mostly knives, daggers, and scissors.

CHAPTER XIV.

CLASS XXXIII.—WORKS IN PRECIOUS METALS, AND THEIR IMITATIONS; AND JEWELLERY.

WHATEVER "moral" effect the Exhibition of 1862, as a whole, may have had, this Class must be excepted, its general tendency having been that of producing a constant breach of the tenth commandment, especially in the fair sex. It was scarcely possible, at any time, to catch even a glance at the articles exhibited in the cases of the leading jewellers, so thronged were they with eager visitors. As far as the jewellery is concerned, we shall refer our readers to pp. 19, 25—27, 33—34, and 78—80, where some of the leading productions are described; and devote our space here to the more practical part of the subject—viz., the material, and modes of manufacturing.

The metals employed in the articles exhibited, were chiefly gold, silver, and silver plate; electro-gilded and plated copper or other metals; Britannia metal, aluminium, and bronze. The jewels embraced diamonds, rubies, emeralds, and most precious stones; pearls, both home, and obtained abroad; pebbles, granite, coral, &c. It must be remarked, that although most of these "materials" are costly, still, in many cases, the value of the articles exhibited was enormously enhanced by the price paid for the skilled labour involved in their construction; and perhaps no class of workers are higher paid than those in jewellery and plate manufactures. The sources of most of the different metals used have been mentioned in Class I., p. 149, *et seq.*; and we shall therefore chiefly describe the methods of their manufacture into plate and jewellery.

Gold and silver, except for very special purposes, are never manufactured in a pure state, because they would be far too soft, and consequently wear away rapidly. They are therefore alloyed or mixed with copper, which gives them the requisite degree of hardness. The English standard of gold, according to which sovereigns are coined, is such, that one ounce is worth £3 17s. 10½d.; the ounce containing 480 grains, troy weight. In this condition the metal has twenty-two parts of pure gold, mixed or alloyed with two parts of copper. A carat weighs twenty grains; and hence the term, in the trade of the goldsmith, of "carats;" standard gold being twenty "carats fine." By the same rule, the proportion of gold in plate, watch-cases, &c., is measured by "carats;" the number expressed indicating the proportion of gold to the alloy, whatever that may be. Plate, watch-cases, &c., are usually made of eighteen-carat gold; but chains and low-priced jewellery vary far below this value.

Standard silver consists of twelve parts of the pure metal mixed with one part of copper; and this alloy, generally, is used in making silver plate, although the proportions are occasionally altered. German silver—a common imitation of the real article—is an alloy of nickel, zinc, and copper; whilst Britannia metal is an alloy of brass, tin, bismuth, and antimony. Sheffield plate is made by soldering a plate of silver on one of copper: the two are then rolled out so as to form a sheet, having silver on one side, and copper on the other; but, in making an article from this material, an extra portion of silver is soldered on to the edges, so that, as they wear rapidly, the copper surface may not be too quickly exposed. Whatever material be employed, the usual mode of "plate" manufacture is as follows:—A design of the intended pattern is first drawn on paper; and, according to this, a mould, or model, is formed in some pliant material, as wax, &c. From this the operative works as a model. Occasionally a cast is made in a mould, which, of course, is the reverse of the model. In other cases the metal is pressed into the proper shape or design by dies, in which are engraved the reverse of the intended pattern. When the required shape or design is so impressed, each part is neatly soldered together, and afterwards polished and burnished.

Of late years, electro-plating has been largely adopted in making articles for domestic use—imitative of, but really covered with, the precious metals in a *pure* state. A short outline of the process may interest our readers, as objects thus made are universally sold in our large towns. The principle on which the process depends is easily explained.

If a piece of zinc be placed on one side of the tongue, and a half-crown rest on the other side, no sensation will be felt; but if the two metals be made to touch each other, then the nerves of the tongue will be affected, because a current of electricity is generated. This proceeds, in its effects, from the zinc, over the tongue, to the silver, and back again to the zinc, at the point where the two metals touch. A simple arrangement, of a similar kind, is formed by immersing a plate of copper and zinc in a little water, to which a small quantity of any mineral acid has been added: and this forms what is called a galvanic cell—a number of them affording a " galvanic battery." If a wire from each plate be dipped into a vessel containing a solution of blue vitriol—or, as it is chemically called, sulphate of copper—it will be found, that the wire attached to the zinc will become gradually coated with copper, provided wires of that metal be used. If, however, the wire from the copper plate be of pure silver, immersed in a silver solution in a separate vessel; and if, further, a plate of copper, attached to the zinc plate by a wire, be placed in the same vessel containing the silver solution, then the silver wire will be gradually dissolved, and a coating of pure silver will be deposited on the copper plate. Similarly, if other solutions of metals, and their wires or plates be used, they may be deposited on others; and thus, as a *general rule*, any metal may be coated by another through the chemical action of electricity.

The practical working of the electro-plate art consists in first carefully cleaning the article which is to be plated or gilded; in using the proper solution, and plate for solution therein; and, lastly, in polishing or burnishing the surface when sufficient metal has been deposited thereon. In connection with this subject, and the Class with which we are now dealing, we must specially name Messrs. Elkington, who have so long been identified with electro-plating and gilding processes; and amply sustained the reputation of the art by their contributions to this Class.

The art of setting stones—that is, gems of all kinds—is one of the most delicate and " tasty" in the whole range of art-manufacture. The details are too intricate and technical to permit of description; besides, they are of too minute a character even to interest our readers. The manufacture of rings, chains, bracelets, brooches, and other varieties of this kind, must therefore be passed by without further notice.

There is, however, one branch of the manufacture of the precious metals which may demand our attention for a few moments. It is that of converting them into thin leaves; and which, so far as gold is concerned, is termed " gold-beating." The leaves so formed are largely used for many purposes, and were included in this Class. The gold is not used in the pure state, but alloyed with about 1 per cent. of copper. This is done by melting the two metals together in a crucible, by means of a blast furnace. The fused mixture is then cast into ingots, which, on cooling, are passed between steel rollers until they are flattened out into a kind of ribbon. This is cut up into pieces, and hammered on an anvil, until an inch square does not weigh more than six grains. These squares are then made up into a packet, and a piece of vellum, nearly four inches square, placed between each. About 150 are then piled together; and the whole being covered with parchment, the bundle is beaten on a smooth stone by a heavy hammer. Each square of gold is thus extended to sixteen times its former size; and is further expanded by being placed between

"gold-beater's" skin, and hammered until the requisite thinness be obtained.
The extent of this may be imagined, when we state that 300,000 of such leaves, on
completion, would be required to make one inch in thickness. With this material,
picture-frames, chimney-glasses, sign-boards, and a vast variety of objects are
gilded, the thin leaf being affixed to the object by means of a little gold size.

Having thus detailed some of the leading manufactures of precious metals, and
their imitations, we need scarcely enumerate the articles displayed in the British
Court comprising this Class. Knives, forks, spoons, watches, jewellery of all kinds,
electro-plated goods of a similar character, brooches, ear-rings, rings, chains, &c.,
&c., are a few of the objects exhibited. The Birmingham Committee made an
ample display of articles produced in that town; and we have already referred our
readers to previous pages, where the contributions of the leading jewellers are
described. It is only needful to observe, that British artists fairly competed, in
most respects, with any other; and, regarding the question of money value alone,
were not equalled.

We must give a general glance, however, at the colonial and foreign contributions to this Class. From India numerous elegant articles were sent, including
an ornament of pearls, taken at the siege of Seringapatam; various manufactures
in gold and silver; jewellery; a necklace of 122 pearls, nine emeralds, topaz
and diamonds; filigree-work, &c. The government collection embraced gold
filigree-work, bracelets, &c., from various districts; coins and miscellaneous articles
of jewellery: some Burmese jewellery was also exhibited. Numerous specimens of
gold and precious stones were forwarded from our Australian colonies. The Belgian
Court was but slightly represented. An eye glass, the property of his imperial
majesty, of Brazil; the imperial arms; and gold lace, came from that country.
In the Chinese collection were various silver, ivory, and other articles; with
which we must include a human skull, richly set in gold, and said to be the skull of
Confucius! The emperor's jade-stone, used to stamp documents certifying literary
proficiency, &c., was amongst the miscellaneous objects. From Costa Rica some
pretty filigree-work was sent. Various articles, chiefly in silver, represented Danish
manufactures in this Class.

We next notice the French Court, which, as might be expected, was largely
filled with objects of great beauty, richness, and elegance. Paris was the chief
place of contribution; and the jewellers and goldsmiths of that city were numerous
as exhibitors. The articles, in general, were similar in character to those shown
in our department; but although most tasteful in the setting of stones, &c., the
value in money was far below that of works exhibited by the London jewellers:
the fancy objects, in which the highest skill of the workman was elaborated, were
greatly admired. The number of exhibitors in the Austrian Court was not large.
A curiosity was seen in a contribution from Dr. Zloch, of Prague, consisting of
eighteen large rock-crystals set in silver, for a candelabrum of five feet in height.
The jewellery from Prussia, and many of the small German states, presented
no point of special interest. The Italian Court, on the contrary, was characterised
by great variety, especially in red coral-work, filigree, and small articles of jewellery:

INTERNATIONAL EXHIBITION.—THE FRENCH COURT.

THE SWEDEN & NORWAY COURT.

THE FIGURES AT THE ALTAR REPRESENT A NORWEGIAN BRIDE & BRIDEGROOM

INTERNATIONAL EXHIBITION – JAPANESE COURT

CARVED IVORY JUNK

among which was a curious ring, serving as a perpetual calendar; also galvano-plastic imitations of ancient shields, helmets, &c. In the Japanese collection was a beautifully carved ivory junk, the subject of a steel engraving in this work; two polished spheres of rock-crystal, contributed by Messrs. Baring; and numerous objects in ivory, &c.—all of exquisite workmanship. In the Dutch Court, were rough, cut, and polished diamonds; and various articles of gold and silver, including Netherlanders' gold and silver hair-dresses. The Russian department contained various works, chiefly in silver. Switzerland was amply represented by the productions of many of her towns, especially in regard to gold and gems, intended for the manufacture of watches, for which Geneva is so celebrated: other small objects, of much beauty, were found in the collection. The productions of Turkey were gathered from Constantinople, Beyrout, Vidin, Conia (or Konieh), Damascus, Lebanon, Crete, and Trebisond; and hence were exceedingly interesting, coming, as they did, from countries famed for gold and silver productions from the earliest periods of history. A steel engraving, given with this work, represents a Norwegian bride and bridegroom attired in ornaments used at marriage ceremonies.

CHAPTER XV.

CLASS XXXIV.—GLASS FOR DECORATIVE AND HOUSEHOLD PURPOSES. CLASS XXXV.—POTTERY.

In the early part of this work, a general account has been given of the two Classes which we shall include in this chapter. A more detailed description of the manufactures may be therefore given here, so far as they relate to the objects which were exhibited in the British and Foreign Courts.

The raw material of both glass and pottery is exceedingly abundant in most countries. In an impure state, sand and clay, respectively, may be considered as its type; and as these substances are so universally diffused, we are not surprised that articles of both kinds have been long in common use. The manufacture of each dates from an early period of human history; but the improvements that have been effected during the present century, have made both, comparatively speaking, of recent date, so far as their present condition is concerned. Indeed, 300 years ago, glass windows were scarcely known: the panes consisted of small pieces fixed in leaden frames, something after the style now adopted only in church windows; and although plate-glass was manufactured, to a small extent, so far back as the end of the seventeenth century, it will be quite within the memory of many of our readers, that this material was, thirty years ago, very expensive, and of imperfect quality. The great impetus given to the glass trade by the abolition of the duty on the material, and that on windows, has been the chief cause of the present advanced condition of the manufacture. The fiscal regulations were not burdensome, as a pecuniary question, so much as in the restrictions which they imposed on the working of the material; and which were considered necessary for the purpose of charging and collecting the tax.

The principal centres of the two trades are in the north of England, especially Newcastle; St. Helen's, in Lancashire; Glasgow; Dublin, &c.; and the "Potteries" of Staffordshire are too well known to require more than a passing allusion as the seat of the trade for which they are celebrated. Lambeth, in London, has long been noted for the coarse kind of pottery; whilst Worcester has had an equal fame for the finer kinds; and its reputation was amply sustained in the Exhibition of 1862. We are chiefly indebted to Mr. Wedgwood (whose descendants still carry on works at Etruria, Staffordshire) for the rapid improvements in material and design which have taken place during the last forty years in ceramic productions, and which have enabled us to compete successfully with the best foreign makers; not excepting the Chinese, from whom it is said we derived an early knowledge of china-ware.

The making of glass depends on an intimate union, effected by intense heat, of pure sand, or flint, and an alkali. The sand contains an acid, called the *silicic*, or *silica*, which, when fused with soda or potass, unites to form a salt of the latter, insoluble in water when certain proportions of the material are used. An oxide of lead is added to make the glass more readily fusible, and easier worked. Numerous precautions have to be taken to produce the "metal," as the glass is termed, of a white and clearly transparent appearance; some of which are named at pp. 70, 71, of this work.

The glass-house in which the fusion of the materials, and the earlier stages of manufacture are carried on, has an immense furnace in the centre, of a dome-like shape. Inside of it is a crucible, which contains the materials, and in which they are melted, small coal being used in great abundance as fuel. At its sides are openings, by which the workman is enabled to withdraw the "metal" as it is required. As the materials melt, they unite and form a mass, having the consistence of treacle whilst hot: and it is this quality of glass—its extreme readiness to take any form in that condition—which makes it so valuable as an article of manufacture, and applicable to so many purposes.

The operations of converting the "metal" into the required shape are various: that of pressing it in moulds being a recent invention, and one now largely adopted; for, by this means, any ornamental form can be instantly given. A more common process is that of "blowing;" and thus decanters, jugs, goblets, and, indeed, most articles of common use, were formerly, and are at present, made. The tools are of the simplest kind, and consist of a long iron tube, through which air is blown into the pliant material; a flat table on which the article is partly shaped; iron rods, pincers, &c. In "blowing" a hollow vessel, for example, the workman dips one end of the iron tube into the "metal" in the crucible, withdrawing a sufficient portion for his purpose. By blowing through the tube into the shapeless lump of glass, he gives it a globular form; and, by turning the whole rapidly in his hands, the centrifugal motion equalises the shape on all sides. The "metal" has by this time become cooled down; but is soon sufficiently heated again, by holding it in the top of the crucible. On withdrawing the glass globe thus made pliant, it is again blown and shaped by rolling it on the table, and thus a cylindrical figure is given. By repeating these processes, any form may be obtained; and the vessel is easily removed from the blower by touching the hot glass at the neck with a cold iron rod, wetted with water. This cracks the glass at the part touched, and so separates the article and the iron tube. Bearing in mind the facility with which glass is thus worked, and made into any shape, our readers can easily understand how wine-glasses, tumblers, decanters, &c., are formed. When the method of moulding is followed, metal moulds are used, in which the external shape of the article has been cut: the "metal" being pressed or forced into them, instantly takes the intended figure. It is by these means that so many cheap glass objects, in common domestic use, as tumblers, cream-jugs, sugar-basins, &c., are made, and resemble the more expensive articles known as "cut glass."

When the vessels have acquired the desired shape, they require "annealing"—a process which, in some respects, is analogous to that of "tempering," described at p. 265, as necessary for steel. Without this the glass would instantly fly to pieces on hot liquid being poured into it—a result which commonly takes place, as our lady readers too well know, when inferior articles are washed in hot water. This effect is wholly due to the unequal expansion produced by heat, which tears away one part from another. A very curious result is obtained by dropping a piece of melted glass into water. The pear-shaped piece thus formed may be struck by a hammer without risk of fracture: if, however, it be scratched by a piece of sand, a diamond, or file, it instantly flies into dust, for reasons similar to those which cause the destruction of glass vessels by hot water. Annealing is performed by placing the articles, after leaving the hands of the blower or moulder, in a kiln, where they are gradually heated to a high temperature: they are then allowed to cool very slowly; and thus the particles are so arranged, that the mass can more safely stand a sudden expansion, to which glass is constantly subjected in daily life.

Window-glass—that is, thin crown—is made by blowing; but during the process, the workman, instead of making a hollow vessel, dexterously throws the "metal" in such a manner as produces a circular thin sheet. Plate-glass, on the contrary, is manufactured by machinery, and rolled on a long table. It is subsequently polished. Tiles, and other sheet-forms of thick glass for windows, &c., are manufactured in a somewhat similar manner, or by one of the methods already described.

Glass-cutting is an art which makes the material so valuable and beautiful for ornamental purposes. The process and tools are both remarkably simple. A rapidly revolving wheel, covered with emery or hard sand, against which the glass is pressed, produces a roughly-cut surface. By turning the object in various directions, and pressing it against the edge of the revolving wheel, any device or pattern may be thus cut; and where a polished surface is afterwards required, this is produced by rubbing it against a wheel covered with putty-powder. Another method of ornamenting glass, is that of acting on its surface by means of hydro-fluoric acid. The parts which are not to be acted on are covered with wax, the rest being exposed to the action of the acid fumes, obtained by adding sulphuric acid to fluor spar or fluate of lime, and by applying a gentle heat. By such means, the "ground" gas-globes, or "moons," flat and engraved sheets of glass, for window and other screens, &c., are produced. As the pattern can be made in every variety by removing portions of the wax with which the plate is covered, before it is exposed to the acid, this plan has strongly recommended itself for simplicity and beauty.

Amongst other important uses of glass, is that for optical purposes; and this branch of the manufacture has become of great importance during the last twenty years, not only in respect to spectacles, telescopes, &c., but for apparatus of a scientific character, especially microscopes. A peculiar kind of glass is employed for these purposes, having a high refractive power; and the lenses of which such instruments are made, are produced by grinding the glass in a lathe until it has gained the required curvature. A hollow mould is used, having a concave corresponding with the convex surface which is to be formed on the glass. The inside of the mould is lined with emery laid on resin; and by pressing it on the glass, the face of the lens is gradually formed by the action of a lathe employed and constructed expressly for this purpose.

Looking-glass-making, or silvering, is a process of great importance in connection with the glass manufacture; and forms a distinct business, which is largely carried on in the metropolis. The process depends on coating the back of a piece of plate-glass (although the inferior kinds are also used) with a metal having a highly-polished surface, and therefore capable of reflecting light. As no metal can be reduced into a sufficiently pliant state to adhere perfectly to a glass surface so conveniently and cheaply as an amalgam of tin and mercury, that is exclusively employed in making looking-glasses for sitting, bed-room, and other uses. The surface of the glass is carefully cleaned before the tin-foil is applied; and on this, mercury, or quicksilver, is spread, by means of a hare's foot or fine brush. Heavy pressure is used to cause the amalgam thus formed to adhere to the glass surface, and also to drive off any excess of mercury. Another method, chiefly used for coating the inside of glass globes, is that of putting into them a weak solution of the nitrate of silver, and one or two common essential oils. These being exposed to the action of sun-light, gradually reduce the silver to the metallic form, and so produce a bright reflecting surface. This process is really "silvering;" whilst the former is so called by the trade, from part of the commercial name—quick-*silver*—of the mercury used.

Glass staining is an art to which we owe much of the beautiful decoration of our churches, and many other public buildings. It must not be confounded, however, with the method of simply painting the surface of glass with transparent colours, which, in the course of a very short time, would wear off, and destroy any design formed by it. The stained glass used for decorative purposes is produced by incorporating with the material a transparent colour, obtained chiefly from the oxides of metals. These are burnt into the glass by heat, the colouring-matter spread on the surface of the glass being gradually absorbed into its substance. Oxide of iron thus produces a green or brown; oxide of copper, red; cobalt, blue; oxides, of chromium, green, which is also obtained by using oxides of uranium; the latter affording a more yellow tint. By suitable mixtures of these and other oxides almost any tints may be obtained; but their beauty, brilliancy, and other qualities, depend on the skill of the workman; and hence, till very recently, the practice of the art has been kept in comparatively few hands, and chiefly to certain places on the continent.

We have thus briefly described some of the chief processes involved in the manufacture and subsequent treatment of glass for domestic use, decoration, &c. Class XXXIV. was divided into two sub-classes: the first being devoted to *stained glass, and glass used in buildings and decorations;* and Sub-class B included *glass used for household and fancy purposes*—a mode of dividing the class which, whilst highly characteristic of the system we have already had occasion to animadvert on, was by no means conducive to a full study of this interesting manufacture. Sufficient has been said of the stained glass in the British department, at pp. 72, 73. The remaining articles included, in the Sub-class A, crown, sheet, plate, painted, and other flat glass specimens, glass shades, &c. An interesting contribution was made by Mr. Warrington, of progressive examples of the art of staining glass, from the twelfth century to the present day. We may add, that the numerous stained glass windows admitting light into the Exhibition building, added materially to the general effect, and were, we believe, entirely produced by British firms.

Sub-class B will naturally be more interesting as a whole. It included most of those articles of daily and domestic use with which we are all familiar. One of the most brilliant of these was the chandelier of Messrs. J. Defries and Sons, previously described in this work. And, as another similar specimen of glass-cutting, we may refer to the contributions of Messrs. Osler. The variety of articles exhibited was great, and comprised jars, wine-bottles and glasses; chandeliers, lustres, and chimney ornaments generally; goblets, tumblers, and other drinking-vessels; toilet-glasses, and table decorations; ornamental writing, photography, engraving, &c., on glass; medical, surgical, and chemical apparatus; optical and photographic glass; lamp-glasses and globes, &c., &c.

The foreign department will next engage our attention; and it will be scarcely necessary to remark, that those countries which exhibited largely in this Class, must necessarily be favoured, like our own, with abundant material—coal and cheap labour. Belgium, where all these conditions prevail, maintains about 6,000 persons, directly employed in the production of glass and earthenware. Various articles of this class were exhibited, especially that used for windows. The Société des Manufactures de Glaces, Verres à Vitres, Cristaux et Gobeleteries, of Brussels, contributed numerous specimens, including plate and window-glass, bottles, drinking-glasses, silvered glass, &c. Table-services, goblets, and drinking-glasses, were also shown by the Société Anonyme, of Herbatte, near Namur. Several private firms from Brussels, Liège, and other places were exhibitors. From Rio Janeiro (Brazil), ornamental glass was sent.

The French department came in formidable competition with our own. Most of our readers will remember the splendid specimens of French plate-glass. The Joint-Stock Company of the Manufactures of Glass and Chemical Products of St. Gobain, Chauny, and Circy, hold a high position in reference to flint-glass manufacture generally. Glass-making, as a trade, seems extensively diffused over France; the exhibitors being from various parts of the country, and not so much confined to

Paris as we have found to be the case in other instances of manufacture. Each branch of the art was represented, including stained and painted glass, with other kinds for ornamental purposes.

In respect to Austria, we may remark that Bohemia has been celebrated for its glass manufactures ever since the thirteenth century; and especially for the hard or potash glass, which is extremely valuable for many of its qualities. Numerous articles of flint-glass were exhibited from various parts, the greatest proportion being from Bohemia. Our own workers in ornamental glass have derived many useful hints from those of that province, especially in the art of producing cut-glass, with two or any number of colours on one object. This is done by coating successively the inner portion with glass of each required colour; and accordingly, as the out-coatings are removed by the operation of grinding, so any one or more beneath may be brought to view. A branch of the French establishment of St. Gobain (already mentioned), exhibited plate-glass, as the Mannheim Looking-Glass Manu-factory. Bavaria was represented in the products of Munich, Furth, &c., by looking-glass plates, silvered and unsilvered; photographic, cut, muslin, and ornamental glass. The St. Gobain French Company again appear as exhibitors of looking-glass plates, in connection with the Prussian department. Various articles, in-cluding plate, stained, ornamental, and other glass products, were contributed by private firms at Berlin, Aix-la-Chapelle, Halle, Liegnitz, Breslau, Posen, and other towns in Prussia. The Italian collection embraced several objects of interest, sent from Venice, Florence, Naples, and Bologna; the ornamental kind being prominent. Amongst them were articles in artificial aventurine; a painted glass window, in the style of the fourteenth century; the "Three Graces" of Canova, engraved on gilt glass; beads, mosaics, &c. The Russian glass manufacture was represented by the productions of the Imperial glass-works at St. Petersburg, and works belonging to Count Tchernishof; the former sending mosaic pictures of St. Nicholas, and two angels; and the latter specimens of window-glass. The contributions of Spain and Portugal were of no importance. Manufactured glass and materials were sent from the Bromö glass-works, and other firms in Sweden; Norway not being repre-sented in this Class. Turkey was also absent.

POTTERY (Class XXXV.)—As an extended account has already been given of the contents of the British department of pottery, we need not repeat the subject to any extent in this place; but shall rather enter into some details of the history and processes of an art identified with the most ancient people of which we have an account either in sacred or secular writers. And here it may be remarked, that the potter's wheel of our day has scarcely been the subject of any improvement for ages; its present form agreeing with the kind used long ago, so far as we can learn from written and sculptured illustrations.

China is generally considered as the birth-place of the higher productions of the pot-ter's art. By its history we find the first porcelain furnace was set up in that country in the seventh century, in Kiang-si province. The most celebrated works, however, at Kin-te-Chin, on the east of Lake Poyang, were not originated until about 1000 A.D.; and here all the best kinds of china-ware are still made; upwards of 500 kilns having been, up to a recent account, in active work. The Chinese use a pure kind of white clay, which is called *Kao-lin* (whence our terms applied to the finest kinds of pottery clay). The native derivation is from Kaouling, signifying a "lofty ridge;" and this points out the geological and mineralogical sources of the material, which consists of felspar, obtained from granite and other volcanic rocks. The action of air and moisture gradually disintegrates the felspar, which contains silica (the matter of flint) mixed with alumina (the matter of clay): with these are soda, potass, and mica—all removed by careful washing. The glaze used by the Chinese is obtained from finely-pounded quartz, called by them *pe-tun-tse*, which they mix with the ashes of a kind of fern. This affords the alkali requisite to make the quartz fusible. In respect to hardness, clearness, and fineness of fracture, the ware made in China has long been highly celebrated, although its ornamentation is often ludicrously grotesque.

In Europe our material is drawn from similar sources as that of the Chinese, being chiefly decomposed felspar, obtained from beds of that substance, especially (so far as we are concerned) from parts of Dorsetshire, Devonshire, and Cornwall. Bovey Tracey, in Devonshire, possesses extensive beds of the clay, of which immense quantities are sent to the "Potteries." Staffordshire, Worcestershire, and other places afford large supplies of pottery clay. It may be interesting here to state, that the so-called new metal, *aluminium*, is a constituent of pottery clay, and of some of our most valued gems; the alumina being united with silica, and coloured by the oxides of metals. The emerald is an example, being composed chiefly of alumina, the pure matter of clay, and an oxide of aluminium, combined with silica. Alum again, the common clay of the brick-maker, and the material of low kinds of pottery, all contain that metal in the state of oxide.

The pottery manufacture has, like many others, its special localities; the chief, in England, being the Potteries of Staffordshire. The district is situated in the north-west portion of the county. Stoke-upon-Trent is the great seat and centre of the Potteries: here, in Hanley, Burslem, and the remaining towns of the district, upwards of 30,000 persons are engaged in the earthenware, china, and porcelain works. Etruria, a village in Staffordshire, is celebrated as the place where Wedgwood established his works. We have previously referred to him as the author of most of the improvements which have been adopted by English potters, and that raised the art to its present perfection amongst us. The lower kinds of pottery are generally made near places where the clay can be obtained. Thus Lambeth, in London, is noted for this class of ware, the material being obtained not far distant from the locality. Of late years, the immense demand for sewage and drainage pipes has much increased this branch of the earthenware manufacture; hence factories have sprung up in localities favourable to it in every part of the country. On the continent, the trade is similarly localised. Meissen, near Dresden, in Saxony; Berlin, in Prussia; Sèvres, in the department Seine-et-Oise, in France, but deriving the clay or kaolin from a granite district at St. Yrieix, near Limoges, are instances of the kind.

Although strictly depending on scientific principles, the art of the potter, in its early stages, is of the most simple kind. The " wheel" consists of a large wheel, connected, by a strap or band, with a smaller one; on and above which is a table, intended to hold the clay; and as this table is made to rotate rapidly, the clay being soft, has a tendency to fly off in all directions by centrifugal action. It is the business of the potter to modify this, and so shape the article he is making.

The clay is prepared by grinding the materials—the clay proper, and burnt flints—under large stones, with water. This is done until it is very soft, fine, and plastic, and of the consistence of thin putty. A lump of this is transferred to the potter's table, which is made to turn rapidly. He then gradually shapes it into a cone-like heap; and by means of a piece of flat iron, hollows it out, gradually shaping the mass into the desired form. The ease with which this is done cannot be described on paper; but fully justifies the old saying, " As clay in the hands of the potter:" so readily is any vessel produced. Handles, ornaments, &c., are made separately, and affixed to the article whilst still moist; pieces of the clay at once adhering to each other if kept in that condition. The potter constantly "tempers" the clay, by wetting it if too dry, or adding some of the dry material if it be too wet. Simple as is this process, all depends on the dexterity of the workman, in respect to perfection of shape and symmetry, at this early stage of the manufacture.

After the vessel has thus been formed, the next step is to dry it before baking; and these two operations are the most serious and uncertain in the whole art. It must be stated, that at the conclusion of these processes, the clay will have contracted to at least two-thirds of the bulk with which it left the wheel; and if the materials are unequally wet, or, indeed, by their own weight, the form may be completely destroyed, and all the labour previously expended will be lost. The drying is effected by lengthened exposure to the air; and the articles are then placed in vessels called "seggars," in which they are transferred to the kiln. This is a tall furnace-like building, wherein the ware is exposed to an intense heat. After some time it becomes hard, tenacious, and solid; and if broken in this condition, presents no appearance of a clay texture; the fracture more resembling that of glass, but without a polish on the surface. The glaze has now to be applied to overcome the porous condition of the vessel. This is effected by washing it over with a suitable liquid, and a second exposure to heat, when a partial vitrification takes place. This forms the glazed surface noticed in china and other ware.

Another process, however, must be named, on which depends much of the beauty of our best porcelain: it is that of ornamenting its surface. The design is first sketched on paper, and then transferred to the ware; the colours being applied before the surface has been glazed. Mineral substances are employed as colouring-matters; and some of them, and their properties in this respect, have been described at p. 276, when we were dealing with stained glass. The design is then burnt into the ware, and the glaze is afterwards added. The beauty of the pattern depends on the taste and skill of the designer, the purity of the colouring materials, and the care taken to prevent these running into each other, which would utterly spoil the design. Lengthened, experienced, and careful watching, are the only conditions likely to ensure success in this delicate branch of the art.

The terms applied to various productions of the potter, are generally intended to indicate their quality. Thus, "delph," "crockery," "earthenware," &c., are used to denote the lower kinds. "Ceramic" is a name given, generically, to all the higher qualities, which are separately designated as "China;" "Porcelain;" "Parian;" "Majolica;" "Palissy;" "Sèvres;" "Dresden;" "Worcester," &c. Terra-cotta is an article much sold, of late, in the form of tiles, out-door ornaments, vases, &c.

The preceding outline of the manufacture of pottery in general, may be followed by mentioning some of the articles displayed in the British Courts. They varied from the lowest to the best kinds; and for a description of many of them, we again refer our readers to p. 74, *et seq.*, in this work. Tiles, plain and ornamental; "pots and pans," of coarse materials; draining and sewage pipes; filters; breakfast, dinner, dessert, tea, and toilet-services; statuary; lamps; chemical apparatus; chimney-pots; tobacco-pipes; works in terra-cotta; jet, jasper, mosaic, and antique wares; jars, bottles, butter-cups, water-bottles, and other minor domestic articles;— these give a general idea of the "pottery" manufactures of our country, as represented in the Exhibition. In the main avenues of the building, Minton's great fountain in modern majolica ware; Copeland's porcelain collection; her majesty's dessert-service, made at the Worcester porcelain works, and exhibited by Messrs. Kerr and Binns; porcelain belonging to the Emperor of Russia; and another collection of the King of Prussia; Spanish porcelain; Swedish terra-cotta; Danish porcelain—were amongst the leading objects of attraction in connection with this Class, which created as much interest, or perhaps even more, than any other in the Exhibition, so far as visitors in general were concerned.

The colonial and foreign departments of this Class were also exceedingly interesting; for, like that of furniture, it gives us an insight into the domestic affairs of other countries; and, to a considerable extent, forms a test of their progress in the arts of civilised life. We shall therefore give an extended notice of each country's contributions. The Class was represented by the following articles sent from India. The government exhibited collections of pottery from Allahabad, Gyah, Patna, Moradabad, Bellary, and Lucknow; also specimens made at the Bangalore Industrial School. From the School of Industrial Arts of Madras, Dr. Hunter forwarded articles of pottery made at that institution; and private individuals contributed other objects of interest. Some specimens were even sent from Victoria, New South Wales, and Tasmania, with potter's clay from the last named colony. Brazil was represented by earthenware tiles, bricks, and other common pottery goods. China-ware, direct from that country, appeared in the form of vases, tea, and other services, enamels, &c. Similar articles were seen in the Japan Court.

Returning to Europe, we first notice the productions of Belgium, which consisted of table, coffee, tea, and other services, crockery for ordinary use, and various designs in porcelain. The Royal Porcelain Manufactory, at Copenhagen, and Bing and Gröndahl, of the same city, exhibited numerous objects in porcelain, biscuit-ware, domestic articles, ornaments, vases, &c. Of the coarser kind, were modelled and pressed bricks, stoves, tiles, figures, and vases of baked clay.

The Imperial Manufactory of Sèvres, near Paris, has long placed France in the highest position in connection with the manufacture of the finest kinds of pottery; "Sèvres china" being considered as amongst the choicest and most valuable kinds. The collection contributed from those works, of course, attracted great admiration on the part both of the public and connoisseurs. The ordinary articles of domestic use were numerous, varied, and, in many cases, exceedingly beautiful, whether considered in respect to shape or ornamentation. Many fancy applications of the potter's art were also exhibited, especially imitations of ancient pottery. Amongst the curiosities were enamelled ceramic pastes, imitating mother-of-pearl, ivory, the emerald, &c.; soft porcelain, in imitation of old Sèvres; flint-glass enamels, encrusted with engraved gold and silver, &c.; kaolin; refractory fire-bricks; articles for chemical and general laboratory use.

In connection with Austria, the Prague Porcelain and Earthenware Manufactory, and that of Vienna, contributed general porcelain goods: various towns in Bohemia, Hungary, and other provinces, also contributed to a moderate extent. Bavaria was represented by painted porcelain from Munich and Bamberg, and pressed graphite crucibles from Nuremberg. The Royal Porcelain and Gesundheitsgeschirr manufactories sustained the reputation of Prussia for the higher class of pottery; besides which, private firms and individuals contributed articles in baked clay, terra-cotta, coal-tar retorts, refractory fire-bricks, stoves, crucibles, glazed tiles, conduit-pipes, ornaments for churches, &c. One of the contributions of the Royal Saxon China Manufactory, of Meissen, the chief locality for the manufacture of fine pottery in Saxony, we have already mentioned. It is a beautiful chimney-piece, of which an engraving is given in this work. In an early part of this chapter, we also referred to Meissen as one of the chief localities of the continental pottery productions; although Dresden has had its name applied to the articles made at Meissen. Other contributions from these places, Leipzic, Pirna, &c., consisted of painted china, articles for chemical uses, which have been long prized by the practical chemist; mirrors, lustres, candelabra, pendule cases, vases of porcelain and serpentine, tea and other services, bowls, cups, pots, water and butter-coolers, &c.—a list showing the variety and extent of the pottery manufactures of this comparatively small kingdom. Some porcelain articles, chiefly of an ornamental character, were sent from towns in Saxe-Meiningen, Schwarzburg-Sondershausen, Würtemberg, and the free town of Hamburg.

The Italian collection was varied and interesting, especially in respect to vases, of which there were imitation Pompeian and Egyptian, sent from Messina; terra-cotta vases, imitating those of Etruscan and Greco-Siculean styles; articles of domestic porcelain; stoves, furnaces, &c. From Florence there was a collection of majolica, in imitation of that of Urbino and Pesaro, of the fourteenth and fifteenth centuries; similar copies of Lucca della Robbia ware; and earthenware of various kinds. The Roman articles were pavements, imitating marbles, porphyry, granite, &c., sent by the Societá Anonima dei Marmi Artificiali.

The pottery manufactures of the Netherlands, so far as the articles that were exhibited afforded any indication, were mostly confined to the coarser kinds, such as earthenware, stone-ware, &c.; tobacco and cigar-pipes having the largest number of contributors. We presume that utility characterises Dutch pottery productions, and therefore lessened the opportunity of the makers taking a striking position in respect to this Class. Norway was but poorly represented; but numerous articles in porcelain were sent from Sweden: the Gustafsberg Porcelain Manufacturing Company, of Stockholm, contributing porcelain tables, dinner-services, &c. Portugal pottery was almost entirely of the inferior sorts; consisting chiefly of earthenware, stone china, drainage-tubes, pots, &c. From Spain the objects were of a similar character; but they included, also, some in porcelain, ornamental glazed tiles, Malaga figures; with raw material, such as refractory and white clay. The Imperial China Manufactory, at St. Petersburg, exhibited china figures, ornaments, and tea-services; and there was also in this Court a collection of common earthenware, used by peasants in some parts of the empire. Switzerland was represented chiefly by articles of general utility. Turkey appeared strongest in pipe-bowls, and ordinary domestic earthenware.

CHAPTER XVI.

CLASS XXXVI.—TOILET, TRAVELLING, AND MISCELLANEOUS ARTICLES.

THE Commissioners of the Exhibition of 1862, did wisely to introduce the saving-clause in the term "Miscellaneous" to this Class; for although the British department maintained pretty accurately the character of the two sub-classes of "Dressing-cases and Toilet articles," and "Trunks and Travelling Apparatus," we think that the Foreign Courts contained, under the above class-heading, almost every imaginable object. In fact, so far as these were concerned, it might properly be denominated the "waste-basket." This name, however, must not be applied derogatorily, in respect to the value of the articles: on the contrary, we shall find many of them useful, curious, ornamental, and valuable.

It will be equally impossible and unnecessary for us to make any introductory observations on the objects included in this Class, because they are mostly *sui generis;* and, except in the British department, are incapable of proper classified arrangement. What we have to say must be a kind of running commentary on such as may prove generally interesting to our readers.

Sub-class A was devoted to dressing-cases, travelling-bags, despatch-boxes, writing-cases, and similar productions; most of the exhibitors being resident in London, and representing the chief manufacturers of such articles. Sub-class B embraced portmanteaus, trunks, waterproof dress and bonnet baskets, leather bags, and travelling requisites in general. As none of these require any explanation, we shall proceed to detail the miscellaneity of the Colonial and Foreign Courts.

The Indian department illustrates the remarks we made on the variety of objects included in this Class. The government sent children's toys from Mysore;

punkahs, &c., from Nepaul; chess and draughtsmen, from Cuttagh; fifty-seven figures representing different trades from Kishnaghur; figures from Lucknow; inlaid turnery-ware, from Burhampore; walking-sticks, shell bracelets, small wares in ivory, table-mats, fans, &c., from various localities; and Burmese figures from Assam. Combs, "ivory back-scratchers," necklaces, spice-boxes, sandal-wood spoons, &c., fishing-lines, weights and hooks, modelling in wax, mats and boxes of palm-leaf, bird-cages, &c., were contributed by private individuals; making, altogether, a varied but interesting collection of minor articles, yet exhibiting the taste of native workmen in all parts of Hindostan. The objects belonging to this Class, sent from Jamaica, Malta, Mauritius, Natal, New Brunswick, Newfoundland, New South Wales, New Zealand, Nova Scotia, and the rest of our colonies, not having been at all classified, prevent us detailing many which would have been of general interest, as showing skill and taste in miscellaneous matters. The same remark also applies to the Chinese, Japanese, and African Courts. Brazil was represented by some jewellery cases; Costa Rica, by cigar-cases, and purses made of pita fibre; halters of cabuga; calabashes, and a cocoa-nut goblet.

The French miscellaneous articles were almost innumerable; and consisted of work in ivory, porcelain, malachite, &c.; snuff-boxes, pipes, combs in great abundance, and beautifully ornamented; photographic albums; portfolios; fancy articles made of the sawdust of exotic woods, hardened and compressed; cabinet goods in morocco, tortoiseshell, ivory, aluminium, gold and other materials; spectacles; mechanical toys, and automata; dolls; "atmospheric" playthings; cigar-cases; morocco articles for toilet, tea, coffee, and other services; designs for shawls, dresses, lace, paper-hangings, furniture-stuffs, silks, carpets, cabinet and goldsmith work. The Austrian contributions may be summed up generally by the term "fancy goods;" under which head most of the objects were exhibited. From Bavaria, we noticed a *bouquet* made of sugar; steatite or soapstone wares; gas-burners; xylochromic and xyloplastic objects; dyed woods, and pressed objects in dyed woods. Offenbach, in the grand duchy of Hesse, largely exhibited in leather purses, cigar, dressing, and other cases, pocket-books, work-boxes, glass bracelets, wallets, game-bags, &c.

The Prussian Court contained a great variety; and we must especially notice the works in amber—a gum-resin, of a fossil character, which is found on the shores of the Baltic: occasionally it contains insects, now extinct. This fossil, the remains, without doubt, of old pine forests now submerged beneath the sea, is made up into bracelets, brooches, and other jewellery, pipe and cigar tubes, &c.: the waste of the manufacture is employed in making amber varnish, in use for a great variety of purposes. Leather-work, whips, gold bordering, looking-glass frames, razor-strops, imitation marble, and tortoiseshell articles; toys and wares for domestic use, made of polished wood-carvings; chess-boards; india-rubber articles, beads, &c., sustained the miscellaneous character of the Prussian Court in respect to Class XXXVI.

The Hanse towns of Hamburg exhibited kites, walking-sticks; paper, meerschaum, and cigar-tubes; brooches of pink and green shells, ivory flower-baskets, &c.; and from Lubeck, were cigar-boxes, portfolios, porte-monnaies. A portmanteau was the sole Italian representative; and trunks performed the same duty for Holland.

INTERNATIONAL EXHIBITION - PRUSSIAN COURT

WESTERN DOME

Norway figured largely in this Class; and some details respecting the collection may be of interest, as showing the life and industry of the Norwegians generally; for which purpose, a special contribution was made by W. Christie, of Bergen—at least in relation to peasant life. The objects were nearly all of practical utility; and included artificial flies for fishing, an occupation of great importance where salmon and other fish, caught by the fly, are so numerous; Finmark dresses, and a cradle; carvings in wood; Fin-shoes; turnery, coopers' and basket-makers' work; a collection of national costumes from Finmark; maps for schools, and sea-use; fishing apparatus in general; and models of fishing-boats. An instance of the Norwegian method of economising criminal industry, was found in the collection sent from the House of Correction, Agershuus. It comprised an economical, adjustable oil-can; an apparatus for communicating with divers by the voice; articles in polished granite and porphyry; and objects illustrating the life and customs of the Laplanders.

The Portuguese department was also of considerable interest, exceedingly varied, and characteristic. For instance, there were artificial flowers made of thread, obtained from the Guinea aloe; brooms made of maize straw; tobacco; razor-strops; articles in cork and horn; wax flowers and fruit; umbrellas, parasols, and sticks; baskets; artificial flowers, made from shells and sea productions; cloaks made of straw; models of casks; gourd-bark fruit-stand and sugar-pot; toothpicks; goat-skins'dressed to carry wine; chocolate-pots; ropes made of various vegetable fibres, horse-hair, &c.; mats in great variety, and numerous specimens of plaited straw. From some of the Portuguese colonies, were walking-sticks of sandal-wood; tobacco and cigars; pipes; feathers; teeth of the hippopotamus; palm-wool; horns of animals; and various vegetable fibres, useful for manufacturing or other purposes.

The *miscellanea* of Rome comprised a tazza of Giallo, and rosso antiquo; lamps in the Pompeian and other styles; statuettes, &c. The Russian department exhibited articles for travelling. From Spain, soaps, fishing-nets, candles, &c., were the chief objects of this Class. The Swiss collection was confined to travelling requisites. The Turkish contributions, always highly characteristic, and truthful in indicating home habits, were mostly of pipes, amber mouth-pieces, ornaments pertaining to smoking requisites, purses, sticks, &c.

With this Class we conclude our general survey and detailed examination of the Industrial Department of the Exhibition of 1862; and it may be remarked, that whilst a personal inspection must, doubtless, at first be most inviting and interesting, still the after-study of such a collection, in its relation to our own wants, manufactures, arts, &c., and those of other nations, taken individually and relatively, must prove of greater value, and therefore of more permanent interest, to every thoughtful and reflective mind. The idea of comprising, in one building, specimens of the world's natural and artificial products—of giving, as it were, a *coup-d'œil* of terrestrial creation, was a sublime thought; and, in its realisation, a grand fact. The details of such a collection are far too vast to be comprehended by any one mind, despite all the aid afforded by systematic classification, could that be made perfect. Another difficulty also presents itself, which affects every visitor to a large exhibition. It is the mental blinding effect that arises from seeing so many novel objects brought together in so small a space, and calling, in rapid succession, for notice if they be passed by ever so cursorily. The eye, in such cases, works too rapidly for the brain; and even the strongest mind, and persons long experienced in such matters, suffer from a confusion of ideas, and loss of memory, that are, at times, distressing. A great advantage is therefore gained by a perusal of a work like the present, in which a sufficient, although imperfect, outline is given; and which may serve as a guide to further inquiring into subjects directly or correlatively bearing on the objects for which our great exhibitions have been held.

It would be quite out of place for us to attempt any comparison between the Exhibitions of 1851 and 1862, in regard to the industrial progress of our own or other nations. The subject is one on which individuals could not agree; and, still further, would have no chance of arriving at a correct judgment, unless blessed with a faculty little short of omniscience. Independently, again, of other considerations, the wants, fashions, habits of a nation, necessarily change; and this change stimulates the production of objects of similar materials, but in other forms. Whilst the *new* is before our eyes, we naturally like and praise it for that novelty, from our partiality preferring it for the moment; although, perhaps, in a comparatively short time, it will become distasteful, if not offensive to the sight. These and many other considerations should lead us to judge with lenity of the past, and caution in respect to the present. In many departments, our material progress, during the intervening years, is not a question of opinion, but one of fact, especially in regard to chemical and mechanical processes connected with manufactures, agriculture, military and civil engineering, &c.; and the improvements have been so evident, that those unconnected with such subjects may justly give a decision.

Human nature, especially the operative portion of it, is necessarily imitative—the degree of that power varying with the individual; but being of greatest social benefit in him who combines with it a measure of original and combinative utility. Hence the value of exhibitions in spreading abroad a general knowledge of particular processes, &c., or special modes of carrying them out in all localities. An excellent system prevails on the continent, of making the artisan travel and work in each part of the country during a period of three years. He thus not only loses local prejudices, so common amongst workmen, but, by comparing his ideas with others, learns new methods of doing; or, what is still more common, finds better and easier processes as substitutes for those he had previously followed. It is by this plan, on the small scale—by the visits of our operatives to our exhibitions—that great benefit arises to our country after such have been held. Designs, plans, forms, and other conditions of a novel kind, have been presented to the eye of the expert; and, on returning to the scene of his labours, he infuses his new-gotten knowledge in future work, and proves, by fresh productions, the value of a comparison of ideas, effected by such collections as have been brought together in recent years. They make, in fact, experience a common property, in place of being a monopoly; and thus break down barriers which, in former times, limited skilled workmanship to a few, with whom it very often died, to the loss of mankind at large.

The Exhibition of 1862 may properly be called that of all nations; for all were, more or less, represented. Africa, Belgium, Brazil, China, Costa Rica, and adjacent countries, including states in the north of South America; Denmark, France, and its colonies; Austria, Prussia, and most of the Federal States of Germany; Bremen, Lubeck, and Hamburg; Greece, and the Ionian Islands; Hayti, Italy, Japan; Liberia, the new free negro settlement on the west coast of Africa; Madagascar; the Netherlands; Norway and Sweden; Peru, Portugal, Rome, Russia, Siam, Spain, Sweden, Switzerland, Turkey, the United States, and Uruguay, form a list of foreign contributors.

Our colonial possessions, besides India, included South and Western Australia, the Bahamas, Barbadoes, Bermuda, Canada, Cape Colony, Ceylon, the Channel Islands, Dominica, Jamaica, Malta, Mauritius, Natal, New Brunswick, Newfoundland, New South Wales, New Zealand, Nova Scotia, Prince Edward's Island, Queensland, St. Helena, St. Vincent, Tasmania, Trinidad, Vancouver, and Victoria.

From all these the contents of the building were derived; and with all of them we have an extensive export and import trade. The value of our foreign and colonial commerce is enormous, and is the chief source of employment to a large proportion of our working population. In 1862, the year of the Exhibition, we exported to our colonies, including India, produce to the amount of £42,000,000; and our total exports to all countries reached £124,000,000. In the same year, our imports from all countries, amounted, in value, to £226,000,000: and uniting the two totals, our foreign trade reached the sum of £350,000,000. We manufacture for at least 1,200,000,000 of the human race; and, at our present rate of foreign trade, we have a commercial interest amounting to about two shillings for each man, woman, and child on the face of the globe. In 1863, our customers ranked in value as follows; the figures expressing the export values in millions of pounds sterling—viz., India, 20; United States, $15\frac{1}{2}$; Germany, including Prussia, $13\frac{1}{4}$; Australasia, $12\frac{1}{2}$; Turkey, $11\frac{1}{3}$; France, $8\frac{2}{3}$; Netherlands and Italy, each about 7; and China about $5\frac{1}{2}$ millions. These figures constantly vary; but, taken for the year following the Exhibition, they have their relative value in that respect.

The previous pages of this work have served to give a *résumé* of the goods, products, &c., represented in value by the preceding figures, as the objects of British trade. Hence a visitor to the Exhibition might, in a commercial sense, have considered it as the "sample-room" of our imports and exports. The wildest dreams of a Phœnician, Carthaginian, or Roman merchant, must have fallen infinitely short of the realisation presented in the counting-houses and warehouses of thousands of our modern merchants. Their vessels trade with all parts of the world; and neither the tropical heats of the Indies, nor the frozen lands of Siberia and North America, present difficulties which enterprise and industry have not overcome, and almost annihilated. In our days everything bends to commerce: politics are ruled by it; science is its handmaid; our literature takes a tone from it. Years ago, an aristocratic noble would have felt his position lowered by contact with it. Now, it is well known that the capital of hundreds of the upper ten thousand is employed largely in it: and with respect to the masses, it is the source of their daily sustenance, and a stimulus to the increase of their numbers. It at once centralises and diffuses; and, by its centrifugal action, gradually has spread, and still spreads, civilisation to the most remote corners of our globe.

We have occasionally adverted to the benefits which have accrued to us, nationally, by the introduction, mainly through the two Exhibitions, of new raw materials, and new sources of raw materials previously known; and our remarks extend, in this respect, to the animal, vegetable, and mineral kingdoms alike. It is impossible to point out the numerous instances of this kind which have affected so many branches of our manufacturing industry. Australia, Japan, and Eastern Asia, generally, have been prominently brought forth, in the Exhibition of 1862, in this respect, especially in regard to cotton, timber, ornamental and dye-woods, fibrous materials for the hemp, paper, and other manufactures. If we consider this point alone, the value of such periodical collections cannot be over-estimated. Much as may have been done in this respect, however, far more remains yet to be accomplished. We have, hitherto, only had a sample or glimpse of what we may rationally expect. Commercially and politically, we have relations with China and Japan; but, as yet, of a limited nature. We know little of these countries, in which a great proportion of the human race exists in a state of civilisation far beyond that common in western nations 500 years ago. Their national products, whether raw or manufactured, excited deep interest in the Exhibition of 1862, although their number was exceedingly small. Similar remarks apply, in certain respects, to other parts of the world. Thus South America, one of the richest countries in the world, if we regard it in relation to the products of nature, is almost unexplored. It may hence be expected, that, surprising as was the collection at South Kensington, it has yet to be eclipsed, at no distant day, by others, not only of far greater extent, but also in the nature and economic value of the articles to be exhibited.

In bringing these remarks to a conclusion, we cannot refrain from offering a few observations on the value of these great exhibitions, as stimulating others, on a smaller scale, but of a permanent character, in special localities. If our manufacturing industry has benefited already, how much more advantage may be expected to arise from collections on a similar plan, at which the artisan or operative may study, at his leisure, the products of competing countries, in towns where he has to earn a daily sustenance. We are happy to find, that, to a certain extent, the plan has been, or is about to be, acted on. It is the natural and due fruit of that which we have attempted to perpetuate in this work. Such institutions could easily be made self-supporting; and in respect to obtaining the requisite specimens from home, colonial, and foreign parts, our past experience has proved that the difficulty has only existed in our not seeking them, rather than in their being granted when sought for. Nationally and locally, such museums would be of incalculable advantage; and, stirring up the spirit of emulation, would soon remove all hindrances from which British enterprise has, for want of them, materially suffered to the present time.

THE FINE ARTS DEPARTMENT.

CHAPTER XVII.

CLASS XXXVII.—ARCHITECTURE.   CLASS XXXVIII.—PAINTING.   CLASS XXXVIII. A.—ART DESIGNS.   CLASS XXXIX.—
SCULPTURE.   CLASS XL.—ENGRAVING.

ON entering the second great division of the contents of the Exhibition, we find ourselves in very different circumstances, and with different conditions imposed in respect to description and criticism, to those under which we were placed when dealing with the contents of the Industrial Department.   In each of its Classes we had objects on which, from certain fixed data, we could arrive at definite conclusions. The qualities of strength, colour, size, and others, were such as to permit of accurate detail; and, on certain points, all could agree in expressing a correct opinion.   It is not so with art-products; for, although we may have the rules of each school to guide us, still, we cannot forget that these " institutions" differ so much in their estimate of a work, that even authorities on each subject arrive at exactly opposite opinions in expressing a judgment on the merits of a production.   In respect to the public at large, a picture or sculpture gallery is a kind of Babel of opinions, each person viewing the contents in the light of his own fancy and prejudices; and as no two persons see the same colours simultaneously in a rainbow, so no two uninitiated mortals can arrive at the same results in judging of any of the products of the painter, sculptor, architect, or engraver.   Our task is, therefore, an exceedingly difficult one.   We have on one side the Scylla of artists; and, on the other, the Charybdis of popular judgment: to steer between these will defy the ablest judgment, and the best pen.

It must be remembered, also, that we have to deal with no ordinary gallery of art.   Even our national collection, comprising, as it does, some of the first productions of early or modern times, is small and imperfect compared to the great gathering which presented itself in the Exhibition of 1862.   Then the schools of our own country, France, Germany, Austria, Holland, Sweden, Norway, Denmark, Russia, Belgium, Spain, Switzerland, Italy, Rome, Greece, &c., were placed in competition with each other, all claiming admiration, not from one, but from many stand-points.   In fact, the Exhibition presented a kind of art Olympic game, in which the contest for public favour was hidden by the multitude of rivals.

There are, however, some general principles on which all, more or less, agree; and we cannot do better than quote the remarks of an able critic.   He says—" To draw thoroughly, and colour truly, are the first fundamental necessities of painting as an art; nor will graceful feeling, or depth in thought, or sense of life and humour— no pictorial intention, in a word, however excellent—atone for want of these primary requisites."   Now, if we divest this quotation of all technicalities, and translate it into the language of the *profanum vulgus*, we shall agree with the writer, by saying that he who would paint to please the masses, must do so *according to nature*. And, without pretending to any great degree of art-knowledge, belonging to no "school," but exercising the principles of common sense, we cannot help expressing the opinion that such a qualification is the great secret why certain productions live, whilst others lie neglected, valued only for their age, or some adventitious circumstances. For example, the cartoons of Rafaelle, and the paintings of our Hogarth, alike appeal to our natural sentiments and experiences. We do not look at them as pictures, but as faithful transcripts of circumstances in which, despite ourselves, we are forced to take a part, and sympathise with.

But we have already extended these introductory remarks too far. They have been made simply to excuse the numerous shortcomings which our attempt to detail the Fine Arts department must be the subject of. To this duty we shall at once proceed ; simply remarking, that, following the plan of the Commissioners, the British departments must first occupy our attention ; and these will be followed by those of foreign countries, in the order they were arranged in the galleries of the Exhibition.

ARCHITECTURE (Class XXXVII.)—It will prove somewhat difficult to interest our readers in a subject which is far from being popular, in the usual sense of that term. To a large extent, architecture becomes an historical study, the commencement of which should date from an exceedingly early era of our history. The various steps through which the art has progressed to its present condition, can only be occasionally perceived, owing to the breaks occasioned by lapse of time. With little exception, the splendid edifices which must have existed in ancient Syria, and antecedent to the days of Greece, are all passed away ; and hence we have slender means of judging what must have been the state of the art, compared with modern schools, at that remote period. What we do know is mixed with fable. Much of interest, however, has been discovered, of late years, in the ruins of Nineveh ; and, perhaps, still more may be brought to light by future explorations.

The origin of a house or building, of course, depends on the objects to which it is to be applied ; and if we take a lesson on the subject from savage nations of the present, as a guide to our study of remote periods, simplicity, rather than style, would be the chief characteristic. As in the time of the early Israelites, so, at the present day, the boughs of trees are often employed to afford shelter in wild regions. As, however, social, rather than gregarious habits become common, " tents in the wilderness" are laid aside, and habitations, possessed of some degree of comfort, are erected. The villages of Dahomey, Ashantee, and many parts of Africa, indicate this tendency, and give us modern types of the early attempts at house-building. The climate of a country must not be left out of consideration ; for it materially modifies or directs style in architecture. With us, the constant changes of temperature and weather necessitate an entirely different class of building, whether for shelter or prolonged residence, compared to what would be required in Egypt, Syria, Palestine, Greece, or even Italy ; and, as necessity is the mother of invention in most arts, it is, doubtless, of great importance in architecture, the object of which is to provide against those necessities which must have given it origin.

Modern schools are more the result of ancient forms than of new beginnings: we have built on, rather than laid the foundations. To quote the remarks of a clever critic—" This story [of their history] must begin far back; for in architecture, from its essential nature, and from the similarity of wants which it provides for, practical experience has been the source of the changes generally made, and established types have always held a strong hand over free imagination. Nothing is more curious than to watch the slow steps by which men learned the simplest expedients, and the persistency of a few forms through every age between Nebuchadnezzar and the nineteenth century. We are indebted here, as for the elements of almost all human knowledge, to ancient Greece. The Greek style was itself, indeed, founded on the earlier practice of Assyria and Egypt; but it was only by the reduction of African or Asiatic architecture to European ideas and climate, in Greece, Italy, and Sicily, that it was able to influence later races." The writer then points out, how, whilst adopting the simplest expedients, such as of laying single stones from pier to pier, the Greeks yet initiat d a delicacy of design, and completeness of finish, which resulted in the Doric, Corinthian, and other styles, for which we are indebted to them.

Following, and derived from, the Greeks, the Roman school appeared. " Throughout those wide provinces, which were held almost identical with the world, Roman architecture, as displayed in buildings of civic utility — the bridge, the aqueduct, the city gate, and theatre—shared in the dominant influence of the ' masters of all,' and covered the empire, in length and breadth, with trophies of colossal commonplace. * * * * The style of ornament, from Syria to Spain, from Trèves to Tunis, exhibits no radical change from that of the Greeks, except a gradual descent through floridity to coarseness; no vital feature whatever, so far as appears, was invented or developed. * * * * A sense of power, an emanation from the Majesty of the empire, given by vast masses and a construction of weighty simplicity, is [however] the one redeeming quality of the Roman style. The Romans, commanding the resources of the world, were able to build higher piles than any other nation; and, in so doing, a great amount of constructive ingenuity was brought into play. But this cannot blind us to the fact, that their imperial architecture is barbarous in the true sense—a bastard and tasteless style, without even the merit of such originality as may be found in Japan or Mexico. Sense and feeling alike would set one fragment of the Parthenon of Athens before all the palaces which Nero roofed with gold, or the halls within which Diocletian gathered the population of the whole world's capital."

We have liberally quoted these opinions, because they were issued with the sanction of the Commissioners of the Exhibition, and hence come upon us with a high degree of authority. If our space permitted, we should have been glad to have transferred a larger portion to these pages; conveying, as they do, not only a free and able opinion of Roman architecture, but also a powerful hit at the same evils, so common in the construction of many modern erections in our own country. The remarks, however, are chiefly intended in regard to the early history of the Roman school; and justice is done to the great improvement which originated in the later years of the empire; and to the influence of the spread of Christianity, is ascribed the marked and elegant changes which resulted in the *Romanesque* style of western Europe, and the *Byzantine*, in the eastern division of the empire; Rome and Constantinople being the respective capitals.

The Gothic style originated from the Roman, Romanesque, and Byzantine, by what we may term the modifying influence of the taste of northern, or Teutonic Europe, and was that chiefly adopted between the years 800 and 1500 of our era. The style is divisible into two—viz., the *circular* and *pointed;* the latter of which was chiefly followed subsequent to the middle of the twelfth century. In respect to the pointed style, the writer already quoted, remarks—" It is certain that no style has ever excelled the pointed Gothic in picturesque and lavish beauty of plan and of ornament; in the poetry of its lines; in the romance with which our associations invest it"—a result, however, much due to the mollifying influence of time.

We cannot here detail the various styles which have either ornamented or defaced more recent architecture, and which have sprung, more or less, from those already alluded to. In reference to many of them, our critic remarks—" Palladian, Renaissance, Italian, Louis XIV., Louis XV.; whatever name it bears, it is still but the copy of a copied architecture—a galvanised pedantry."

The modern architecture of the great cities of western Europe, at the present day, must be of the " composite" order, at least, taking the metropolis as an example. In vain do we seek a really magnificent building erected within this century: we have to fall back on productions of two or three centuries ago for instances of the kind. Incongruity and want of harmony characterise our buildings, and the streets which they form. House and "villa" architecture, as a rule, is simply a caricature; whilst its variety is endless. Much of this may be accounted for by the enormous price of land: but even with every allowance on that score, it is not too strong an assertion, if we aver, that an almost universal want of taste is displayed in modern erections, whether churches, government offices, theatres, or other public edifices.

In looking over the official catalogue of this Class, the great number of designs exhibited for public buildings, especially churches, indicates the direction in which the talent of our modern architects is chiefly running. For private houses, and, still more, dwellings for the working classes, the competitors were few. This is a fact, the existence of which might be expected from the comparatively small pecuniary return that designs for buildings of moderate pretensions are likely to produce.

We feel considerable difficulty in selecting from the numerous contributions which were sent to the Exhibition in connection with this Class. Were we to confine such to high-sounding names, we should omit those of many rising individuals, whose merits have yet to be decided by their works. We shall, therefore, make the objects that were designed our guide, and so attempt to give an impartial illustration of the value of the architectural department.

The following contributions will thus come under our notice:—A design for a National Palace of the Fine Arts—Garden-front; and the same—Elevation-front. The Mausoleum at Halicarnassus, restored according to recent discoveries; by

J. Fergusson. The Entrance Hall at the Grosvenor Hotel, Victoria Station; and the Exterior of the Grosvenor Hotel; by J. T. Knowles. The principal Façade of a National Institution of Science and Art; adapted for the site of Burlington House, Piccadilly; by J. B. Waring. In reference to a proposition of this kind, we need hardly remind our readers of the great advantages which would arise from such a localisation of our learned societies. The Town-halls of Hull and Leeds; by C. Brodrick. A design for covering the Royal Exchange, London; and designs for Government Offices; by R. Kerr. Proposed High-level Road and Viaduct, from Hatton Garden to St. Sepulchre's Church, looking east and west; by F. Marrable—a proposition which, in another form, is now about to be carried out by the Corporation of the City of London. A Study in Polychromy; showing how Coloured Marbles and Terra-Cotta may be ornamentally used in external architecture; by S. Smirke: on which we may remark, that the adoption of some such plan would materially alleviate the monotony of our street-frontages. The Palace Hotel, Buckingham Gate; and the new Custom-house, Folkestone; by J. Murray. A design for the new Foreign Office; by Banks and Barry: for which the second government premium had been awarded. The Interior, showing the East-end, of St. Paul's; and the Altar-piece, as intended by Sir Christopher Wren; also a design for the Decorative Completion, with Mosaic Paintings, of the Interior of St. Paul's; by F. C. Penrose. The Hartley Institution, Southampton; by J. W. Green and L. De-ville. The prize design for the Rev. C. Spurgeon's Tabernacle; by E. C. Robins. Interior of Chester-le-Street Church, Durham, showing the Restorations; by M. Thompson. The West-front of Llandaff Cathedral; by Prichard and Seddon. Works of Ecclesiastical and Domestic Architecture in Great Britain, Russia, and France, executed or designed between 1851 and 1862. Interior of the Examination Hall, Queen's College, Cork; and design for the War Offices—Staircase-angle; by Sir T. Deane, Son, and Woodward. Interior of St. Michael's, Cornhill; by G. G. Scott and H. Williams. Numerous designs by G. G. Scott—including the Martyrs' Memorial, Oxford; Restoration of Westminster Chapter-house; designs for the new Government Houses; Reredos, Lichfield Cathedral, &c. Design for proposed Memorial to George Stephenson, at Newcastle; by A. M. Dunn: and one for the Wedgwood Memorial, at Burslem; by Morris and Wigginton. View of the Royal Insurance Offices; and Assize Courts of Manchester, with Interior of the latter; by A. Waterhouse. Some interesting architectural selections; by H. H. Collins. Proposed High-level Railway Bridge over the Thames, below-bridge; by Ordish and Le Feuvre. Designs for the Thames Embankment; by T. Allom. Designs for a Metropolitan Institution of Fine Arts; of Metropolitan Sea-water Baths, &c.; by A. Allom. View of London, from the Victoria Tower, Westminster, showing a proposition for the embankment of the Thames. The contributions of Mr. Digby Wyatt and Mr. Owen Jones were exceedingly numerous; and it will be sufficient to mention their names for our readers to be assured of the value of their designs; their professional connection with so many public and other works being well known. An interesting series of sketches of buildings, designed and executed between 1844 and 1862, were exhibited by P. C. Hardwick. The designs of the Imperial Insurance Offices, London, were shown by J. Gibson; together with those for the National Bank of Scotland, Glasgow; and house for F. R. Pickersgill, Esq., R. A., Highgate. We must also notice a prize design for Agricultural Cottages, built by the Royal Agricultural Society, and exhibited at their meeting in 1861. Mr. Godwin exhibited a view of the South Porch of St. Mary, Redcliffe, Bristol, as restored. Our space is now almost filled up with details in respect to architectural matters; and we can only further notice that the remaining exhibitors were, more or less, of note. The executors of Sir C. Barry contributed the following designs or views:—An Entrance-front of Bridgewater House; design for the construction of new Government Offices; Sketches in the East; proposed Government Houses; Plan of Improvements connected with the New Palace, Government Offices, and Thames Embankment, Westminster; Hichclerc Castle, Hants; the River Facade of the New Palace, Westminster; and original Sketches in the East, made in the year 1818-'19. The Old Abbey Church of Paisley; and the same restored; by James Salmon, of Glasgow, were worthy of notice; and the Perspective View of the General Post-Office at Edinburgh, on the site of the old post-office, was a specimen of one of the latest instances of Scottish architectural skill; but it is still uncompleted at the time this is penned.

There were numerous other specimens of architecture in Scotland, which we regret that our limited space forbids us to notice; but we must confess that, generally speaking, the edifices erected, of late years, in Glasgow and Edinburgh, far exceed, in most respects, those of which the metropolis can boast. This may, in part, be due to the fact, that building materials in London are chiefly of brick; whilst, in the north, the best freestone is almost always at command, immediately adjacent to, and often beneath, the site of the intended erections. Hence our northern friends have an advantage which gives them far greater opportunities of architectural display than those we can possibly avail ourselves of, except at a much greater expense.

A sub-class, in respect to architecture, was devoted to models. These comprised the following:—The Portico (Western Façade) of the Royal Exchange; a Rifle Drill-shed; Saltaire, a new Village and Factory, founded by Messrs. Salt & Co.; Versailles; the Crossley Orphan Schools, &c., of Halifax; a Drinking Fountain; St. Paul's Cathedral; Arcades and Terraces of the Horticultural Gardens, South Kensington (designed by J. Smirke, Esq.); Salisbury Cathedral; Chichester Cross; Windsor Castle; Broadway Church, Westminster; Ealing Church; buildings for the poor, erected by Miss Burdett Coutts, in Charles Street, Hackney Road; Gloucester Cathedral; Lincoln Cathedral, &c., &c.

With these we must bring our notice of the architectural portion of the Exhibition to a close. We have endeavoured to make such a selection of the numerous designs and models as would exhibit the general tendency of our leading architects in respect to improvements of all kinds. In doing this we have been guided by utility and ornament, rather than by the names most noted as producing *chef-d'œuvres* in such matters. We can only hope that their " works may follow them ;" and that the result may be of great public gain, both in respect to artistic display, and convenient arrangement for business, domestic, and other purposes.

PAINTING (Class XXXVIII.)—Our introductory remarks on the Fine Art department will prepare our readers to expect little or no criticism, on our part, in respect to the relative value of each school of painting As our attention must first be directed to the productions of British artists, it will lie within the range of our duty to give a slight sketch of those who have chiefly founded our reputation in delineating on canvas the characteristics of our national peculiarities; and Hogarth pre-eminently demands our earliest notice. He, perhaps, of all others, is the one to whom we are indebted for the formation of the British school. To quote the words of one to whom we have already been indebted for able criticisms on art—"In his life, not less than in his works, Hogarth presents a sturdy protest against all previous styles. No man more distinctively, and decidedly, and creative—not even Phidias of Athens, or Giotto of Florence—ever handled art; no one, for good or for evil, was ever less affected by pre-existing influences, or by contemporary criticism. The modern art of Europe began as completely with him as its modern poetry with Dante; and, as Dante's fellow-countrymen were at first unable to believe that a great poem could be written in their mother-tongue, so Hogarth's were credulous that England could produce a painter." In fact, to him we are indebted for the foundation of what we may term the British School of Oil Painters.

We must now turn to the contemporaries and successors of Hogarth; and of the former, were Wilson, Reynolds, and Gainsborough, names long familiar in the history of art. Respecting two of these, the remarks of the author already frequently quoted, will again be of aid to us. He says—"The sense of beauty, the love of innocence—no artists have enjoyed these more deeply than Reynolds and Gainsborough; nor in the management of colour, in light and shade, in gracefulness of line, and delineation of character, have they been often equalled. Their art, in technical points, was based on that of their great foreign predecessors. In them ended, in fact, that noble style of portraiture which began with Giorgione and Titian in Italy, and was continued by Velasquez in Spain; in Flanders by Vandyke and Rubens. It is to these latter men, however, that their likeness is most visible. Rubens and Vandyke began the modern manner in portraiture, introducing greater variety in colour, dress, and furniture; and, as sacred art was declining, giving their portraits a more ornamental and independent character. Gainsborough and Reynolds fell short of these artists in thoroughness of work." His further remarks tend to a general comparison of these painters with those of other schools in the early part of the eighteenth century, or of what we may call the Hogarth-Gainsborough era of British painters, extending from 1697 to 1788.

We cannot here enter into a detailed history of the progress of British art from that period to the present; but must simply name some of the leading painters with whose names our readers will be familiar. Wilkie, who stands next chronologically, and in importance also, owing to the peculiarity of his artistic creations, reminds us, in many points, of Hogarth, although the range of his subjects is narrower. The charm of his productions lies in their close copy of nature, and hence they have been ever favourites with the connoisseur and the masses—a proof of which is seen by the large number of cheap wood-cuts which have been spread all over the land, and have found their way even to the humblest cottage, the inhabitants of which require no art-instruction to help them to estimate the humour of "Blind Man's Buff," &c.

We must pass over many great names—Etty, Millais, Haydon, Maclise, Landseer, &c., &c.—to notice, last in these introductory remarks, that of Turner, respecting whose productions so great a variety of opinions has been expressed. Sympathising little with the enthusiastic admiration which the following remarks convey, we think it only right that our readers should be put in possession of the opinion of one whom the Commissioners entrusted with the duty of making introductory comments on each Class of the Fine Arts department; and to whom we have often paid that deference which his position deserves in art-criticism. He remarks, respecting Turner—"'The name of Shakspeare,' says Mr. Hallam, 'is the greatest in our literature—it is the greatest in all literature.' Turner is one of the very few men to whom similar words might be applied without exaggeration. He is the greatest of the English landscape painters; he is the greatest of all landscape painters. Others have rivalled him in quality of colour, others in fidelity of detail; he has failed at times from over-ambition of attempt, at times from obscurity of purpose; he trusted, occasionally, too much to facility in execution; he was led away by caprice of fancy—yet he is still the Shakspeare of another and a hardly less splendid poetical kingdom. No one has penetrated so deeply into the soul of nature; no one has so surprised her in her sympathy with man; no one so nearly rendered her infinite mysteriousness, her multitudinous variety. Aspects, which to others almost singly engrossed their strength, are but modes and moments in the torrents of his prodigal creativeness; yet each of them is treated with a vitality and a fulness which the best masters had not attained to. Compare him with Titian in the forest, Rubens in the meadow, Rembrandt in twilight, Cuyp at mid-day—with the storms of Salvator, or the repose of Claude; Stanfield's sea, Linnell's woodland, the coast-scenes of Hook, the glens of Landseer—but this one has included and surpassed them all. Yet if praise ended here, Turner's most peculiar merit would hardly be expressed. For whilst he has made the closest approach to painting the infinity of nature, he is almost alone in his rendering of her deeper poetry. That deeper poetry springs invariably from the presence of human feeling—either contrasted with, or embodied in nature: nor, without the touch of humanity, are our profoundest sympathies ever awakened. To impress on his work this sentiment, the painter does not necessarily require that man should form a part of his representation. There are pictures by Turner more peopled in their waste wilderness, than the most elaborate figure-landscapes of Claude or Canaletti. But it is still the sense of the human element which gives loneliness to the desert, and splendour to the city; which recalls the past in the ruins of Rome, and speaks of the future in the fields and coasts of England. There is a terrible seriousness about his work — a moral sadder and deeper than Hogarth's: 'the riddle of the painful earth' flashes out through many of these scenes of more than earthly loveliness. Everywhere he contrasts the fate of man, his passions, and his achievements, with the landscape around him, or makes the landscape itself a reflection of the drama of life, on the more august theatre of nature. Birth and death, stories of man's strength and degradation, passion and despair, are written in the scarlet and azure of Turner's skies, or revealed by the seas, hill-sides, and rocks he painted so lovingly. In his art there is a spirit-stirring in the tree-tops, and a voice of more than what we rashly name Inanimate Nature in the torrent :"—

" The light that never was on sea or land ;
The consecration, and the poet's dream."

With this passage, which, although intended solely as eulogistic of Turner, is an excellent guide to, and an epitome of, art-criticism, we must conclude our introductory remarks. We shall name some of the productions of the chief painters of the British school; it being impossible, in our limited space, to mention all exhibited, the list of which occupied upwards of thirty pages of the official catalogue. We shall take them in the order in which they were numbered in that work, and in which they were hung in the picture-gallery. A steel engraving, representing the entrance to the principal gallery, Cromwell Road, is given with this work. Owing to the paintings of many artists being distributed in various parts of the gallery, their names, in frequent instances, appear more than once : we shall, however, omit re-mention of them where possible.

Hogarth's works—comprising a Portrait of himself at his Easel; " The Harlot's Progress ;" " Scene from the *Beggar's Opera*;" " The Mall;" " The March of the Guards to Finchley ;" " The Election ;" " Portrait of Mrs. Hogarth ;" " The Rake's Progress ;" " Portrait of Captain Coram ;" " The Shrimp Girl ;" " Portrait of Lavinia Fenton, as Polly Peachum in the *Beggar's Opera* ;" " The Marriage A-la-Mode"— early met the gaze of visitors, and attracted an amount of attention which proved that innate merit is recognised by all classes. The productions of other eminent painters were also associated with them ; such as those of T. Gainsborough, Sir Joshua Reynolds, Opie, Wilson, Wright, J. S. Copley, James Barry, &c. We again notice the paintings of Hogarth, in his " Southwark Fair ;" " A Conversation ;" " A Conversation at Wanstead House ;" " The Strolling Actresses ;" and " Portrait of Mrs. Doughty." Continuing our running list of names, there were exhibited paintings by B. West, J. Zoffany, R. Wilson, E. Morland, De Loutherbourg, Mason, Chamberlayne, Hoppner, Northcote, Singleton, Stothard, Ramsay, Crome, Runciman, F. Stone, Sir H. Raebum, F. Danby, P. Nasmyth, W. Glover, Sir Thomas Lawrence, Sir A. W. Callcott, R. Smirke, T. C. Hofland, J. J. Chalon, R. Westall, J. Jackson, W. Hilton, R. P. Bonnington, Sir M. A. Shee, H. F. Briggs, T. Uwins, H. Fuseli, Sir W. Allan, A. E. Chalon, D. Scott, R. Cook, Sir William Beechey, C. S. Lidderdale, G. C. Stanfield, D. Macnee, B. R. Haydon, J. Constable, Sir David Wilkie, W. Collins, William Etty, J. M. W. Turner, F. R. Pickersgill, G. S. Newton, W. Mulready, R. S. Lauder, C. R. Leslie, P. Westcott, J. Partridge, Sir J. W. Gordon, D. Maclise, D. Roberts, Sir C. L. Eastlake, J. Meadows, J. Graham Gilbert, W. Delamotte, J. N. Paton, Sir E. Landseer, Barnes, Carrick, Mrs. Wells, Müller, Hughes, Cooper, C. Marshall, H. Le Jeune, Mrs. Carpenter, J. Faed, E. J. Cobbett, C. E. Hering, R. McInnes, J. Archer, C. W. Cope, A. L. Egg, F. Goodall, R. Redgrave, Holman Hunt, E. M. Ward, D. O. Hill, W. Dyce, T. Creswick, C. Landseer, J. E. Millais, F. Dillon, W. P. Frith, G. H. Thomas, &c., &c.

In this partial list of oil painters, we find a large number of artists whose productions have long been familiarly known; and regret that we have not space to mention others rising into fame. We must, however, now turn to the British school of water-colour painting, in which many of the leading oil painters also hold a high place; but especially Turner, whose water-coloured paintings were exhibited in large numbers. There can be no doubt that the art is the oldest form of painting; but, like that of illumination, it has been comparatively laid aside until recent years. At all events, so far as gaining popular favour, its rival—oil painting—has had a much higher position.

In this sub-class, works of the following water-colour painters were exhibited—viz., those of Cozens, R. Westall, T. Girtin, Hills, Gainsborough, Sandby, Robson, Hearne, Barrett, Uwins, Stothard, Glover, A. E. Chalon, Liverseege, Prout, Sir A. W. Callcott, P. De Wint, J. J. Chalon, Samuel Prout, Constable, Joshua Cristall, Armitage, J. Varley, R. P. Bonnington, Blake, Wilson, Cox, G. A. Fripp, J. M. W. Turner, as we have already said, in great numbers; W. Hunt, Weigall, Burton, J. Nash, E. H. Corbould, Jutsum, W. Turner, G. Cattermole, Copley Fielding, J. F. Lewis, J. R. Herbert, Carl Werner, F. Stone, R. Thorburn, H. T. Wells, W. Essex, Sir W. C. Ross, Linnell, W. Goodall, F. W. Burton, E. A. Goodall, K. Meadows, Clarkson Stanfield, D. Roberts, Miss F. Corbaux, Sir E. Landseer, C. Martin, W. Mulready, G. Richmond, Holman Hunt, &c., &c.

ART DESIGNS FOR MANUFACTURES (Class XXXVIII. A.)—This Class was devoted to designs of a vast variety of objects for manufactures of materials of all kinds, and for numerous purposes; and it will be impossible to enumerate them, as they included nearly every subject capable of artistic decoration or ornament, from a ceiling to her majesty's state-coach; candelabra; vases; furniture; porcelain; works in precious metals; picture-frames; wall, statuary, pavement, and similar matters; lamps, chimney-pieces, and ornaments; chandeliers; printed calicoes, and other woven materials; paper-hangings; needlework; watch-cases; jewellery; carpets; stained-glass windows; gates; book-covers; ecclesiastical decorations; lace; harness; illumination, &c., &c. The designers were divided into two classes—deceased and living; and included Sir F. Chantrey, Sir W. Chambers, J. Bacon, Flaxman, Pugin, Stothard, W. Wyon, Wedgwood, amongst the deceased artists; and a long list of well-known names, to whose art-contributions we are now indebted for constant improvement in ornamentation and decoration. It will be unnecessary for us to enter into any detailed examination of this Class; for the Industrial department has already afforded numerous instances of the advantage which a correct knowledge of art-productions affords to the manufacturer generally. The establishment of schools of design, in localities where our pottery, cotton, and other textile works are carried on, evidences that we are making rapid progress in the right direction in this respect. The collection at the Exhibition afforded abundant means for study, and also facilitated the comparison of art-designs of modern and remote periods.

SCULPTURE, MODELS, DIE-SINKING, AND INTAGLIOS (Class XXXIX.)—This division of the Fine Arts department was comparatively small in extent, although, generally speaking, highly attractive and interesting. At the present day it unfortunately happens that the art of sculpture is but little patronised by those whose means might be advantageously devoted to its encouragement. In the early history of civilisation, and in ancient times, sculpture stood first in rank as a fine art: in fact, painting was then but little practised and patronised. Fashion thus governs all things: but still we must not forget, that although the art of producing objects chiselled in stone is in decadence, we have yet its equivalent in the noble metal castings which modern science and art produce in such great perfection. It is therefore the material, rather than the art, which has suffered in disuse; and, so far, we retain the taste for the effect of, rather than the work of, the sculptor. We are, indeed, as much advanced in working metals, as were the ancients in the art of sculpture; and hence stone-carving, which requires qualifications possessed by few, is but little followed in our day.

Modern times, however, need not be ashamed of those who have practised the art: and the objects contributed to the Exhibition of 1862, showed, that although the public patronage formerly bestowed may be on the wane, there are yet living many who can give, and have given it vitality; whilst others, during the last century—such as Nollekens, Bacon, Flaxman, Westmacott, Chantrey, &c.—have left behind them works which, in many respects, will bear comparison with some of the best productions of olden times.

In respect to the present condition of the art of sculpture, we shall quote some remarks from the introduction to this Class in the official catalogue of the Exhibition. The writer observes—" One branch of sculpture, however, remains, which has always maintained more or less of life; and to this, with the recovering of a more vital manner in architecture, and the reunion of the arts so long divorced, we may fairly look with hope for the future. Portraiture, since mastery in it was first reached (hardly before the age of Alexander), has remained, and must always remain, the foundation of excellence in sculpture, as it will finally be recognised in regard to painting. The corrupting influences of popular taste * * * * * act with less immediate force on the bust than on the statue. Men are here a little less unwilling to compare the semblance with the reality; and wanderings from nature are more easily traced, or censured with greater freedom. It is true, that here, also, the general false position of the art appears. How few public or ornamental statues can be named which do not fail, often utterly, from the conventional classic style, bringing with it feebleness in modelling, and tameness in outline—from meretricious trick, or shallow artifice—from vacuousness and slovenly execution! Conspicuously placed as they are, how few have any interest or influence over the thousands who would be ' moved, as by a trumpet,' by the real effigy of a Richard, a Wellington, a Newton, a Napier, a Peel—even of the sovereigns in their succession, or men of local mark and position! To foreigners who visit Trafalgar Square or St. Paul's—to Englishmen who know Berlin and Paris, the Louvre, and the Santa Croce—it will be needless to add more, or give the list of recognised too-familiar failures. But Foley, Rauch, and Rietschel, may be properly named amongst the few honourable exceptions.

" These remarks apply to the larger and more difficult style of portrait statues. But, returning to the bust—a series of heads, occasionally figures of real excellence, may be traced during the last hundred years, rising to high and severe perfection

3 c

in design, most rarely to vitality in execution, yet often proving, that men whose ability was sacrificed in imaginative art, with better opportunity would have rivalled better times. Amongst those Englishmen who rank thus, are Nollekens, Banks, Chantrey, Flaxman, Watson, Foley; Canova, Danneker, with many more less known here, in France, Germany, and Italy. The work of Nollekens, though not rising to genius, is careful and life-like. No one will fail to find truth and grandeur in Rauch, Foley, and Watson. Canova brought to his busts the smoothness and elaboration, Flaxman the poetry, of his ideal groups."

Leaving now the critical part of our subject, we hasten to name some of the leading sculptors—deceased and living—whose works were contributed to the Exhibition of 1862; remarking, that whilst, in many instances, the originals were shown, still, in some, plaster and other copies formed a portion of the collection. In naming the artists, we shall also give the period during which they flourished, as was done in the official catalogue.

The works of T. Banks (1735—1805); of Nollekens (1737—1823); Bacon (1740 —1799); J. Flaxman (1755—1826); Rossi (1762—1839); Hills (1765—1844); Sir R. Westmacott (1775—1856); Sir F. Chantrey (1782—1841); J. Gott (1785— 1860); T. Campbell (1790—1858); S. Joseph (1791—1850); R. J. Wyatt (1795— 1850); G. Rennie (1801—1860); M. L. Watson (1804—1847), and P. Park, were those of deceased artists, exhibited in the British department. The names of living sculptors who exhibited, or whose works were contributed by the owners, included G. G. Adams, Ambuchi, Armstead, E. H. Bailey, W. Behnes, J. Bell, C. B. Birch, A. Brodie, W. Brodie, T. Butler, H. Cardwell, J. E. Carew, Mrs. Bonham Carter, B. Cheverton, E. H. Corbould, J. D. Crittenden, E. Davis, Miss S. Durant, J. Durham, T. Earle, J. Edwards, E. A. Foley, J. H. Foley, G. Fontana, Mrs. Freeman, C. F. Fuller, A. Gatley, J. Gibson (whose beautiful tinted Venus formed one of the leading attractions of the Exhibition), Miss Grant, J. Hancock, Sir G. Hayter, J. E. Jones, J. Lawlor, Lough, Lynn, P. Macdowell, W. C. Marshall, F. Miller, T. Milnes, A. Munro, M. Noble, W. J. Doherty, E. G. Papworth, Hiram Powers, H. Ross, T. Sharp, J. Steele, W. Theed, Mrs. Thorneycroft, Thrupp, H. Weeks, J. S. Westmacott, R. Westmacott, T. Woolner, E. Wyon, &c. A case of intaglio gems, by J. Wilson, with specimens of medals, by J. S. Wyon and L. C. Wyon, were included in this Class.

In illustration of some of the specimens of sculpture—viz., of "The Resurrection," a bas-relief, by F. Redfern; "Love Resting on Friendship," a marble group, by E. Fantacchiotti, exhibited in the Italian Court; a view of the entrance to the Picture Gallery, Cromwell Road, in which a piece of sculpture is a prominent feature; and the "Veiled Vestal," which, at the Exhibition of 1851, created so much interest and admiration—steel engravings are given in this work.

ENGRAVING (Class XL.)—This Class included both etchings and engravings; and was primarily divided into two sections, containing, respectively, the works of deceased and living artists. Before detailing their names, &c., it may be interesting and instructive to many of our readers if a short sketch be given of the different kinds of engraving, which is, perhaps, the most popular and widely-diffused of all the Fine

ENTRANCE TO THE PICTURE GALLERY – CROMWELL ROAD.

ITALIAN COURT — LOVE RESTING ON FRIENDSHIP

Engraved by T. Pound from a Daguerreotype

THE VEILED VESTAL

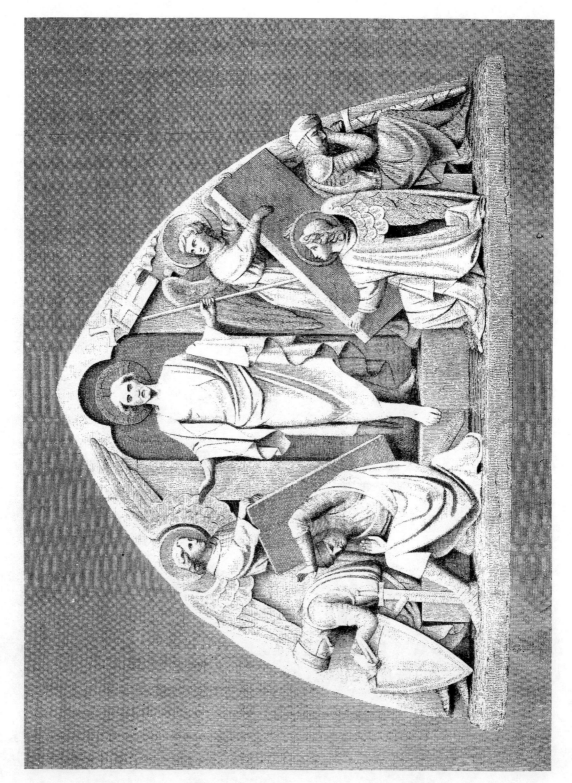

Engraved from a Photograph by the London Stereoscopic Company

THE RESURRECTION - BAS RELIEF BY F. REDFERN.

Arts. Of late years, indeed, so far as wood engraving is concerned, the productions have been enormously extended, for which we are, in a great measure, indebted to the practice of electrotyping. By this the original may be multiplied to any extent, without diminishing the beauty or accuracy of outline: in fact, the most delicate portions are perfectly reproduced.

The materials on which engravings are made, consist of wood, metals (chiefly copper and steel), and stone, which gives rise to the art of Lithography and Chromo-lithography, the latter being now greatly employed for producing coloured illustrations, vying in beauty with the best oil or water-colours.

Wood-cuts were, doubtless, the earliest means of reproducing copies of art-designs, &c. The early productions were frequently of a grotesque character, representing allegorical subjects with a literalness which often becomes amusing, especially in illustrations of scripture relation. The work, however, was generally coarsely executed; and it was not till Bewick, of Northumberland (1753—1817), applied his skill, that wood-cuts became popular, and extended in use. "The older wood-cuts had rarely attempted more than to reproduce drawings. Bewick added an effectiveness in light and shade, a delicacy and variety to his works, which gave wood-cuts henceforth an independent existence in pictorial expression. This great change —one of the most decided in the history of art—he effected by his unusual good sense, truth to nature, and tenderness in feeling. * * * * * * Bewick's other gifts are shown in the exquisite simplicity, truth, and invention of his well-known wood-cuts. These cannot be too carefully studied: they have a directness in reaching their point, a breadth and largeness in style exactly analogous to the qualities of Velasquez. So little are perfection and greatness in art dependent on size or material."

In making a wood-cut, the design is first traced on the material by means of a pencil. Box-wood, from its hardness, even texture, and other qualities, is most generally employed. Lines are then cut into the wood to produce the light parts, whilst the raised portions thus left form the printing surface. Hence printing from wood-cuts and ordinary type is a precisely similar operation; and they can thus be carried on simultaneously in a page at the printing-press. Wood-cuts are multiplied by taking a mould in gutta-percha, &c., from their face. This, on being removed, is blackleaded, to make the surface a conductor of electricity. The mould is then immersed in a solution of sulphate of copper, and attached by a wire to the zinc plate of a voltaic battery. From the other battery-plate a wire is carried, and attached to copper immersed in the metallic solution, and facing the blackleaded mould. After a few hours' action the copper of the plate dissolves off, and becomes precipitated on to the surface of the mould. When the metal is removed, it presents an exact copy of the wood-cut; it is then soldered on to a metal back, and can be printed from. Thus any number of copies, all precisely like the original, may be obtained: indeed, the latter is often not used at all in printing after a first proof has been taken from its surface. It is this application of electrical action which has tended to produce so many illustrated periodicals; for, whilst the original cut may have cost many pounds, the electro-copies may be obtained for a few shillings, and, indeed, pence in the case of small cuts. Among our leading British producers of wood-cuts, we may especially name the brothers Dalziel, with whose engravings many of our readers will be familiar; and who contributed " English Landscapes," " Illustrations to the Parables," after Millais, &c., to this Class in the Exhibition.

Lithography is pursued on entirely different principles to any other form of engraving: indeed, it deserves to be ranked in that art, from its effects, rather than for the process itself. The design is first traced on prepared paper, with a kind of ink containing soap or other greasy substance. The paper is then placed face downwards on a stone, which has the property of attracting the greasy matter only, and which is thus transferred to it after the stone has been properly prepared. A roller, covered with suitable ink, is run over the stone; and wherever the grease has adhered, there the ink remains. A sheet of damped paper is placed over the inked surface; and the whole is then passed through a press, when the design is transferred to the paper. By the ordinary methods, black ink alone is used; and thus impressions from wood or metal may be transferred to stone, and printed from. Chromo-lithography is a precisely similar invention; but in this colours are used—one stone being needed for each colour, and the process of printing being required to be repeated for each colour in succession, until all are laid on. This method has almost entirely replaced hand-painting, which was formerly necessary in producing coloured surfaces in illustrating books, &c.; its cheapness, ease of application, and beauty of result, all rendering it exceedingly available. Both at home and on the continent the art is largely practised; and constant improvements are being introduced, stimulated by the great sale which such productions have commanded.

Engraving on metal, however, is by far the most perfect and efficient means of reproducing, on paper, art-designs of all kinds. It is properly divided into *Line*, *Mezzotint*, and *Etching*. Copper and steel are the metals employed, and in the form of perfectly level plates, the surface of which is entirely free from the slightest scratch before being operated on: for it must be remembered, in this mode of printing the hollows receive the ink, and produce the shaded portions; whilst in wood-cuts and lithography, the same are printed from surfaces raised beyond the surrounding parts. Copper being the softest metal, is much easier to work; but, of late years, steel has largely replaced it: for, whilst comparatively few impressions can be obtained from a copper surface without injuring it, many thousands may be printed from steel before re-touching is required. The art of electrotyping has been applied in two ways to metal engraving. Copper copies are produced in a way we have already explained in regard to wood-cuts; but the metal being much softer than rolled or hammered copper, would soon wear away: in fact, 300 or 400 impressions completely spoil an electro-plate. An ingenious process has been invented to cover such plates with a thin coating of pure iron, through the action of electricity; and thus ordinary copper or electro-plates may be made as durable as those composed entirely of steel.

Line-engraving is that now most largely practised on metals. It consists of cutting into the plate, by means of a hard steel tool, lines intended to receive the ink during printing. These lines are fine or deep, according to the amount of shade required; and the depth of shade can be graduated to any desired extent, owing to the peculiar texture and qualities of the metal—qualities which wood is unsusceptible of. The art has long been practised; and is especially adapted to reproduce valuable paintings, photographs, &c. The steel illustrations of this work belong to this style of engraving. " The artists who probably contributed most to the final advance in line-engraving, are our countrymen Strange, Sharp, and Woollett, who, towards the middle of the eighteenth century, were among the first to take definitely successful steps in the larger manner. Strange is not always faithful to the expression of his originals; but in a blended tenderness and brilliancy of effect he is yet unequalled; and to his invention is due that curious network of lines by which modern engravers aim at representing every surface, however varied. The ' Charles I.' (after Vandyke), the 'Sleeping Child and Angel' (Guido), are amongst Strange's master-pieces. Sharp's work has more severity and meaning; his ' John Hunter' (after Reynolds) is of the highest merit. Woollett's prints, from Wilson and Claude, exhibit the beginning of that art, which, within fifty years, became capable of rendering the infinite sweetness and magnificence of Turner. * * * * * Much as we owe to an art which has placed so much of beauty and nobleness within the world's reach, it must be, however, owned that line-engraving rarely has succeeded in a complete conquest over its besetting sin—the sacrifice of the sweet largeness and repose which mark all good painting, to the display of mechanical dexterity in the conduct of the lines. The single line-engraver who appears to have given his style variety and vitality sufficient to render not only the design, but the very touch and manner of the original, is Schiavone, of Venice. His two prints, from Titian's ' Assumption,' and ' Entombment,' are almost alone in the art for painter-like qualities, and show the breadth, freedom, and tenderness to which true feeling may carry it."

Etching is effected by first covering the metal plate with a thin coat of resinous substance, to protect it from the action of the acid afterwards employed. By means of proper tools, fine lines are cut through this coat, and then the surface of the metal is exposed; and on acid being poured over it, it acts by dissolving away the metal, and produces hollow lines correspondingly with those afforded in line-engraving; the acid, in fact, taking the place of the graver. The depth of the lines, in etching, is regulated by the strength of the acid, and the length of time during which the metal is exposed to its action. Etching has been largely followed by many painters in oil, who have been desirous of reproducing their own works on paper, from Hogarth to many living artists; and differing little as it does from drawing, it possesses great advantages in the freedom with which the original artist can work. " Every European nation, in turn, has been successful in this art. The etchings of the school of Overbeck in Germany, of Goya in Spain, Pinelli in Italy, are more or less known or appreciated. But in our days, the brilliancy of the French, and delicacy of the English artists, have carried out the method to an excellence which, except by Rembrandt of old, has never been equalled. Nor has even he surpassed the spirit, variety and pic-turesqueness of Cruikshank—since Hogarth, our greatest Humorist in etching."

Mezzotint, which was invented in or about 1640, is an entirely different and almost reverse process, compared with line-engraving and etching. The plate is first evenly covered with lines, which, if printed from, would give a completely black impression on paper. The artist, by polishing and scraping away this roughened surface on the metal, produces the lights, and any required amount of shade; the latter being diminished as the roughened parts are removed. "Mezzotint is one of those branches of art which, for the last hundred years, have flourished most in England. Lupton and C. Turner in pure mezzotint, C. Landseer and Cousens in a mixed style, are our most conspicuous recent masters: but even these excellent works do not appear to equal that great series, mainly from the paintings of Sir J. Reynolds, which was produced in the eighteenth century, by S. Reynolds, McArdell, J. R. Smith, Watson, and others. Few of these prints fail in the artist-like qualities of breadth and transparency. Some (the 'Guardian Angels,' 'Virgin and Child,' and 'Collina,' are delightful examples) possess a charm and tenderness which will, one day, place them amongst the most treasured treasures of art."

Having thus given a general outline of the various methods of engraving, and some criticisms on such kind of art-productions, we proceed to detail many leading contributions to this Class in the Exhibition.

Amongst those of deceased engravers, were the following:—*Etchings*—By J. H. Mortimer, J. Barry, L. Schiavonetti, T. Stothard, Sir D. Wilkie, R. Hills, A. Geddes, W. Collins, J. M. W. Turner, and R. Brandard. *Line Engravings*—By W. Hogarth, including his own Portrait; "The Distressed Poet;" "The Enraged Musician;" "The Harlot's Progress;" "The Rake's Progress;" "Morning;" "Noon;" "Evening;" and "Night:" others by Sullivan, Vivares, Browne, Sir R. Strange, F. Bartolozzi, W. Woollett, J. Caldwall, Hall, Sherwin, Parker, Warren, Sharp, Holloway, J. Scott, A. Scott, J. Heath, Bromley, Raimbach, G. Cooke, W. B. Cooke, J. Landseer, J. Mitchell, J. Le Keux, C. Heath, F. Englehart, E. Smith, C. Fox, B. P. Gibbon, W. Finden, Radclyffe, Taylor, &c., &c. *Mezzotint*—By McArdell, Houston, Pether, Dixon, Doughty, Fisher, J. Watson, T. Watson, W. Dickinson, J. Jones, G. Marchi, J. B. Smith, V. Green, R. Earlom, Hodges, W. Ward, J. Ward, J. Bromley, S. W. Reynolds, J. M. W. Turner, C. Turner, Martin, Gibbon, &c. *Stipple*—By Bartolozzi, Haward, J. Strutt, Caroline Watson, L. and N. Schiavonetti, Collyer, Cardon, Scriven, Meyer, Lewis, &c. *Wood*—By Bewick, Branston, Clennell, C. Nesbit, Williams, and Landells.

Amongst the productions of living engravers, were some of the following:— *Etchings*—Several by George Cruikshank, our modern Hogarth; contributions of members of the Etching Club; T. W. Fairholt, Sir G. Hayter, Sir E. Landseer, E. Radclyffe, J. A. Whistler, &c. *Line*—By J. B. Allen, J. C. Armytage, J. Burnet, W. Chevalier, E. W. Cooke, J. Cousen, G. T. Doo, Golding, E. Goodall, R. Graves, W. Greatbach, W. Humphreys, T. Jeavons, F. Joubert, H. Lemon, T. A. Prior, J. Pye, E. Radclyffe, J. H. Robinson, C. Rolls, C. W. Sharpe, H. C. Shenton, J. Stephenson, L. Stocks, R. Wallis, J. H. Watt, J. T. Wilmore, &c. *Mezzotint*—By Atkinson, T. O. Barlow, S. Bellin, F. Bromley, S. Cousins, W. T. Davey, J. Faed, T. Landseer, C. G. Lewis, T. Lupton, G. Sanders, W. H. Simmons, F. Stackpoole, J. Stephenson, W. Walker, G. R. Ward, &c. *Stipple*—By F. Holl, W. Holl,

W. Walker. *Wood*—By the Brothers Dalziel, E. Evans, W. T. Green, W. Harvey, M. Jackson, J. and H. Leighton, W. J. Linton, W. Measom, J. Swain, W. L. Thomas, J. Thompson, J. L. Williams, &c. *Lithographs*—By T. S. Boys, J. D. Harding, R. J. Lane, J. H. Lynch, T. H. Maguire, &c.

With this list we conclude our notice of the production of British art in Architecture, Painting, Art Designs, Sculpture, and Engraving. Our remarks on the continental collections must necessarily be very brief.

FOREIGN DEPARTMENT.—The "schools" of art which were represented in the Exhibition of 1862, embraced those of France, Germany, Austria, Holland, Sweden, Norway, Denmark, Russia, Belgium, Spain, Switzerland, Italy, Rome, Greece; and contributions were also sent from Brazil, the United States, Venezuela, Portugal, and Turkey. We cannot give a detailed account of the works of the numerous artists, both living and dead, who were thus represented. Such would require a history of each school, and a critical analysis of those peculiarities by which they are distinguished. We have felt justified in entering into these subjects, and that but very briefly, in regard only to our own art-productions, with which, however, it has been frequently necessary to compare the paintings, &c., of foreign competitors. In respect to the latter, we must leave our readers to consult the numerous works, by eminent writers, directly bearing on such questions, and give here only an occasional glimpse at some of the rarities which were brought from abroad to grace our picture-gallery at the Exhibition.

France.—Architecture was but moderately represented, and the designs chiefly related to ecclesiastical matters. *Oil Paintings* were very numerous, and embraced every variety of the application of that branch of art. Amongst others, the works of Ary Scheffer, Ingres, Horace Vernet, Mdlle. Rosa Bonheur, Baudry, Boulanger, &c., found a place. *Sculpture* very amply represented the skill of the French artists. In Class XL., *Lithographs, Engravings*, &c., demonstrated the taste and artistic advancement which, as we have already remarked, characterise the productions of France.

Germany.—Architectural designs were exhibited in great variety. Amongst the works of oil painters we may specially name those of Hildebrant, Eichhorn, Krüger, Von Kloeber, Menzell, Richter, Wach: in water-colours, &c., those of Von Cornelius, Rethel: in sculpture, &c., Cauer, Schadow, Troschel, Wredow: in etchings and engravings, Keller, Eichens, Ernst, Gruner, Hoffman. *Austria.*—Architecture was but slightly represented. Oil and water-colour paintings were moderate in number; and the same remark also applies to sculpture and engravings. The Dutch school was largely shown in oil and water-colours, drawings, &c. The Swedish and Norwegian schools contributed in Classes XXXVIII. and XXXIX. In the Danish school we must especially notice the productions of the celebrated sculptor Thorvaldsen, whose reputation has become world-wide. They included " Mercury ;" " Jason ;" " Gonsalvi ;" a statue of himself; " The Three Graces," a relief; and " Alexander's Triumphal Entry into Babylon," a frieze. The Royal Gallery of Copenhagen, and private individuals, exhibited oil paintings, &c. Russian artists appeared in considerable numbers in paintings both of oil and water-colours; architecture, sculpture, and engravings being but moderately shown. Amongst the most notable productions of Belgian painters, were those of Bossuet, Clays, De Block, Gallait, Leys, Madou, Verboeckhoven, and Willems. The *Musée Royal* contributed several specimens of sculpture. Engravings and etchings were also shown. Numerous oil paintings were sent from Switzerland, nearly all of which were exhibited by the artists themselves, as were specimens of sculpture, engraving, &c.

The Italian and Roman schools occupied a conspicuous position, in respect to number and excellence, in most of the Fine Art Classes. Architectural designs, in the Italian department, were sent in large numbers from the Fine Arts Academy of Florence, and the Institute of Naples. The oil paintings were also numerous. Sculpture included works of Monti, Canova, and many other noted artists. Etchings and engravings were exhibited in considerable quantities; and the works of many eminent persons were thus afforded for study and comparison with those of other schools. In the Roman school, sculpture was the most prominent feature. The cameos and mosaics (some of the latter being sent from the Vatican) were beautiful specimens of art, and were constantly surrounded by admiring visitors. The modern Greek school was chiefly represented by sculpture; the works of L. and G. Phytalæ and J. Kossos (contributed by the artists) being in greatest numbers. The United States were represented in Class XXXVIII., by G. Harvey, J. W. Glass, D. Huntingdon, L. R. Mignot, J. F. Cropsey, W. J. Hays, M. K. Kellogg, and W. Page. In sculpture, by E. Kuntze; and, in engravings, by J. Smiley, the American Bank Note Company, and J. Sartain. The Turkish productions consisted of paintings by Musurus-Bey, a young artist, born in 1842.

THE END.

Printed in the United States
By Bookmasters